4th
EDITION

Organizational
Behavior

D0890287

Steven L. McShane
University of Victoria (Canada)

Mary Ann Von Glinow
Florida International University

Mc
Graw
Hill
Education

All credits appearing on page or at the end of the book are considered to be an extension of the copyright page.

The Internet addresses listed in the text were accurate at the time of publication. The inclusion of a website does not indicate an endorsement by the authors or McGraw-Hill Education, and McGraw-Hill Education does not guarantee the accuracy of the information presented at these sites.

mheducation.com/highered

about the
Authors

Steven L. McShane

Steven L. McShane is adjunct professor at the Peter B. Gustavson School of Business, University of Victoria (Canada). He previously held the positions of professor at Simon Fraser University Business School in Canada and professor of management at the University of Western Australia Business School. He currently teaches in the Shanghai Jiao Tong University IMBA program. Early in his career, Steve taught at Queen's University in Canada. Steve has received awards for his teaching quality and innovation, and receives high ratings from students in Perth, Shanghai, Singapore, Manila, and other cities where he has taught. He is also a popular visiting speaker, having given dozens of invited talks and seminars in recent years to faculty and students in the United States, China, Canada, Malaysia, India, and other countries.

Courtesy Steven McShane

Steve earned his PhD from Michigan State University, where he specialized in organizational behavior and labor relations. He also holds a Master's of Industrial Relations from the University of Toronto and an undergraduate degree from Queen's University in Canada. Steve is a past president of the Administrative Sciences Association of Canada (the Canadian equivalent of the Academy of Management) and served as director of graduate programs in Simon Fraser University's business faculty. He has conducted executive programs with Nokia, TÜV-SÜD, Wesfarmers Group, Main Roads WA, McGraw-Hill, ALCOA World Alumina Australia, and many other organizations.

Along with coauthoring *M:Organizational Behavior*, Fourth Edition, Steve is lead coauthor of *Organizational Behavior*, Eighth Edition (2018); *Canadian Organizational Behaviour*, Tenth Edition (2018); and *Organisational Behaviour: Asia Pacific*, Fifth Edition (2016). He is also coauthor of editions or translations of his organizational behavior books in China, India, Quebec, Taiwan, and Brazil. Steve has published several dozen articles and conference papers on workplace values, training transfer, organizational learning, exit–voice–loyalty, employee socialization, wrongful dismissal, media bias in business magazines, and other diverse topics.

Steve enjoys spending his leisure time hiking, swimming, body board surfing, canoeing, skiing, and traveling with his wife and two daughters.

Mary Ann Von Glinow

Dr. Von Glinow is a Knight Ridder Eminent Scholar Chair in International Management at Florida International University and is senior editor for the *Journal of International Business Studies (JIBS)*. She served as 2010 to 2012 president of the Academy of International Business (AIB) and the 1994–1995 president of the Academy of Management (AOM). Previously on the Marshall School faculty of the University of Southern California, she has an MBA and a PhD in management science from Ohio State University, and is a Fellow of the Academy of Management, the Academy of International Business, and the Pan-Pacific Business Association. She sits on 13 editorial review boards and numerous international panels and teaches in executive programs in Latin America, Asia, and the United States.

Courtesy Mary Ann Von Glinow

Dr. Von Glinow has authored over 100 journal articles and 13 books, most of which have been translated into Chinese, Hindi, and Spanish. Her book on organizational learning capability won a Gold Book Award from the Ministry of Economic Affairs in Taiwan in 2002. She is the 2005 recipient of the Academy of Management's Distinguished Service Award, one of the highest honors bestowed by the Academy.

Mary Ann has consulted widely and is on the board of directors of several organizations, including the advisory board to Volvo-Geely in China. She is actively involved in several animal welfare organizations and received the 1996 Humanitarian Award of the Year from Miami's Adopt-a-Pet.

Dedication

Dedicated with love and devotion to Donna, and to our wonderful daughters, Bryton and Madison

—S.L.M.

Dedicated to Zack, Emma, Googun, Blue, Chloe, Jackson, and Boomer

—M.A.V.G.

Brief Contents

Contents

©PeopleImages/Digital Vision/Getty Images

©Elnur/Shutterstock

©Moopixel/Shutterstock

©Hero Images/Getty Images

©EllisDon Corporation

©Jacob Lund/Shutterstock

What's New
in the Fourth Edition

M: Organizational Behavior, Fourth Edition, has been significantly revised, guided by useful feedback from reviewers and our active monitoring of evidence-based literature. All chapters have new examples and either new or revised factoids; most chapters have new conceptual content or literature foundation. The most substantial changes have occurred in Chapter 1 (introduction to OB), Chapter 4 (workplace emotions, attitudes, and stress), Chapter 6 (decision making and creativity), Chapter 8 (communication), and Chapter 10 (conflict and negotiation). The authors personally researched, selected, and wrote all of this content, thereby providing superior integration of knowledge and ensuring that the examples are relevant and recent. Here are the key changes we've made to this fourth edition, broken out by chapter:

Chapter 1: Introduction to the Field of Organizational Behavior

Technological change has been added in the section on contemporary developments facing organizations. The section on perspectives of organizational effectiveness has been streamlined. Most topics have updated content, particularly the text on the four contemporary developments, why study OB, and several aspects of organizational effectiveness.

Chapter 2: Individual Behavior, Personality, and Values

Several topics in this chapter have been updated, particularly coverage of the five-factor model of personality and work performance, values and individual behavior, and moral sensitivity.

Chapter 3: Perceiving Ourselves and Others in Organizations

This book pioneered the full model of self-concept and its relevance to organizational behavior. This edition further develops this important topic and provides new information on the opposing motives for distinctiveness and inclusion. The section on stereotyping also incorporates the concept of stereotype threat.

Chapter 4: Workplace Emotions, Attitudes, and Stress

This edition significantly revises and updates discussion on four key workplace stressors, with new writing about organizational constraints and interpersonal conflict as stressors. In addition, there is new content on attitude–behavior contingencies.

Chapter 5: Employee Motivation

New to this edition is the topic of intrinsic and extrinsic motivation, as well as the question of whether introducing extrinsic sources of motivation reduces intrinsic motivation. We also have reorganized and refined the writing on drives and needs, Maslow's needs hierarchy, and four-drive theory. The previous edition introduced the social and information processing characteristics of jobs. This edition further refines that emerging topic.

Chapter 6: Decision Making and Creativity

This chapter has been substantially revised and updated in several ways. Design thinking now receives more attention as a concept and practice to improve workplace creativity. The topic of problems with information processing when choosing alternatives also has been substantially updated. Additional updates have been made to solution-focused problems, problems with goals, implicit favorite bias, and satisficing (problems with maximization).

Chapter 7: Team Dynamics

This edition refines discussion introduced in the previous edition on the three characteristics that distinguish types of teams. It also offers more detail about social loafing, team mental models (as part of team development), and team development through team building.

Chapter 8: Communicating in Teams and Organizations

This edition substantially revises and updates the important topic of choosing the best communication medium. Specifically, this topic discusses four key factors (synchronicity, social presence, social acceptance, and media richness) as well as associated contingencies to consider when choosing a communication channel. This edition continues to shift the focus toward various forms of digital communication (less focus on email alone). Another noticeable change is the updated discussion on the characteristics and benefits of enterprise social media.

Chapter 9: Power and Influence in the Workplace

This chapter contains updates on topics including legitimate power, visibility, and organizational politics.

Chapter 10: Conflict and Negotiation in the Workplace

This edition substantially reorganizes and updates the entire section on resolving conflict through negotiation. The new or revised topics include distributive and integrative approaches to bargaining, understanding needs, bargaining zone dynamics, how BATNA increases bargaining power, the importance of listening, and strategies for making concessions. This edition also introduces recent evidence about gender differences in negotiation. Elsewhere in this chapter, we update the topics of task and relationship conflict and problems resulting from relationship conflict. We also revised portions on the topic of whether conflict is good or bad.

Chapter 11: Leadership in Organizational Settings

This chapter, substantially revised in the previous edition, includes updates on the topics of transformational leadership, comparing transformational with managerial leadership, and evaluating path–goal theory.

Chapter 12: Designing Organizational Structures

This chapter has been revised to include updates on span of control, problems with flatter structures, and types of divisional structure. It also includes numerous new in-text examples of companies that apply various forms of departmentalization.

Chapter 13: Organizational Culture

In addition to replacing most examples and updating references, this chapter has revised content on the topics of espoused versus enacted values, content of organizational culture, types of organizational culture artifacts, adaptive cultures, the integration strategy for merging cultures, and how founders and leaders shape and strengthen culture.

Chapter 14: Organizational Change

This edition includes updates on understanding resistance to change, social networks and viral change, and appreciative inquiry. As with other chapters, it also has several new real-world examples.

Organizational
Behavior

1 | Introduction to the Field of Organizational Behavior

Learning Objectives

After you read this chapter, you should be able to:

LO1-1 Define organizational behavior and organizations, and discuss the importance of this field of inquiry.

LO1-2 Debate the organizational opportunities and challenges of technological change, globalization, emerging employment relationships, and workforce diversity.

LO1-3 Discuss the anchors on which organizational behavior knowledge is based.

LO1-4 Compare and contrast the four perspectives of organizational effectiveness.

A pple and Amazon are the two most admired companies in the world, according to *Fortune* magazine's annual list. Yet neither of these firms was on anyone's radar screen two decades ago. Apple was on life support in the late 1990s, barely clinging to a few percentage points of market share in the computer industry. Amazon started selling books online in 1995, a few months after its founder, Jeff Bezos, took a course from the American Booksellers Association on how to start a bookstore![1]

The dramatic growth of Apple and Amazon illustrates the many workplace activities that contribute to success in today's turbulent economic environment. In every sector of the economy, organizations need skilled and motivated people who can realize their potential, work in teams, and maintain a healthy lifestyle. They need leaders with foresight and vision, who support innovative work practices and make decisions that consider the interests of multiple stakeholders. In other words, the best companies succeed through the concepts and practices that we discuss in this organizational behavior book.

Our purpose is to help you understand what goes on in organizations. We examine the factors that make companies effective, improve employee well-being, and drive successful collaboration among co-workers. We look at organizations from numerous and diverse perspectives, from the deepest foundations of employee thoughts and behavior (personality, self-concept, attitudes, etc.) to the complex interplay between the organization's structure and culture and its external environment. Along this journey, we emphasize why things happen and what you can do to predict and guide organizational events.

We begin this chapter by introducing you to the field of organizational behavior and why it is important to your career and to organizations. This is followed by an overview of four major societal developments facing organizations: technological change, globalization, emerging employment relationships, and increasing workforce diversity. We then describe four anchors that guide the development of organizational behavior knowledge. The latter part of this chapter describes the "ultimate dependent variable" in organizational behavior by presenting the four main perspectives of organizational effectiveness. The chapter closes with an integrative model of organizational behavior, which serves as a road map to guide you through the topics in this book.

> **LO1-1** Define organizational behavior and organizations, and discuss the importance of this field of inquiry.

THE FIELD OF ORGANIZATIONAL BEHAVIOR

Organizational behavior (OB) is the study of what people think, feel, and do in and around organizations. It looks at employee behavior, decisions, perceptions, and emotional responses. It examines how individuals and teams in organizations relate to each other and to their counterparts in other organizations. OB also encompasses the study of how organizations interact with their external environments, particularly in the context of employee behavior and decisions. OB researchers systematically study these topics at multiple levels of analysis, namely, the individual, team (including interpersonal), and organization.[3]

The definition of organizational behavior begs the question: What are organizations? **Organizations** are groups of people who work interdependently toward some purpose.[4] Notice that organizations are not buildings or government-registered entities. In fact, many organizations exist with neither physical walls nor government documentation to confer their legal status. Organizations have existed for as long as people have worked together. Massive temples dating back to 3500 BC were constructed through the

organizational behavior (OB) the study of what people think, feel, and do in and around organizations

organizations groups of people who work interdependently toward some purpose

The World's Most Admired Companies[2]

- 🏵 **1** Apple
- 🏵 **2** Amazon.com
- 🏵 **3** Starbucks
- 🏵 **4** Berkshire Hathaway
- 🏵 **5** Disney
- 🏵 **6** Alphabet (Google)
- 🏵 **7** General Electric
- 🏵 **8** Southwest Airlines
- 🏵 **9a** Facebook (tied)
- 🏵 **9b** Microsoft (tied)

BEST

organized actions of multitudes of people. Craftspeople and merchants in ancient Rome formed guilds, complete with elected managers. More than 1,000 years ago, Chinese factories were producing 125,000 tons of iron each year.[5]

One key feature of all organizations throughout history is that they are collective entities.[6] They consist of human beings—typically, but not necessarily, employees—who interact with each other in an *organized* way. This organized relationship requires communication, coordination, and collaboration to achieve organizational objectives. As such, all organizational members have degrees of interdependence; they accomplish goals by sharing materials, information, or expertise with coworkers.

A second key feature of organizations is that their members have a collective sense of purpose.

One key feature of all organizations is that they consist of human beings who interact with each other in an *organized* way.
©Image Source

This collective purpose isn't always well defined or agreed on. Most companies have vision and mission statements, but they are sometimes out of date or don't describe what employees actually try to achieve. Still, imagine an organization without a collective sense of purpose. It would be an assemblage of

had changed the name of its MBA human relations course to "Organizational Behavior."

Although the field of OB is recent, experts in other fields have been studying organizations for many centuries. The Greek philosopher Plato (400 BC) wrote about the essence of

> A company is one of humanity's most amazing inventions. . . . [It's] this abstract construct we've invented, and it's incredibly powerful.[7]
>
> —Steve Jobs, Apple and Pixar Animation cofounder

people without direction or unifying force. So, whether they are designing and marketing the latest communication technology at Apple or selling almost anything on the Internet at Amazon, people working in organizations do have some sense of collective purpose.

Historical Foundations of Organizational Behavior

Organizational behavior emerged as a distinct field sometime around the early 1940s.[8] During that decade, a few researchers began describing their research as organizational (rather than sociological or psychological). And by the late 1940s, Harvard

leadership, and the Chinese philosopher Confucius (500 BC) extolled the virtues of ethics and leadership. Economist Adam Smith (late 1700s) discussed the benefits of job specialization and division of labor. German sociologist Max Weber (early 1900s) wrote about rational organizations, the work ethic, and charismatic leadership. Around the same time, industrial engineer Frederick Winslow Taylor proposed systematic ways to organize work processes and motivate employees through goal setting and rewards.[9]

Political scientist Mary Parker Follett (1920s) offered new ways of thinking about constructive conflict, team dynamics, power, and leadership. Harvard professor Elton Mayo and his colleagues (1930s and 1940s) established the "human relations" school of management, which pioneered research on employee attitudes, formal team dynamics, informal groups, and supervisor leadership style. American executive and Harvard associate Chester Barnard (1930s) wrote insightful views regarding organizational communication, coordination, leadership and authority, organizations as open systems, and team dynamics.[10] This brief historical tour indicates that OB has been around for a long time; it just wasn't organized into a unified discipline until around World War II.

Why Study Organizational Behavior?

In all likelihood, you are reading this book as part of a required course in organizational behavior. Apart from degree or diploma requirements, why should you learn the ideas and practices discussed in this book? After all, who ever heard of a career path leading to a "vice president of OB" or a "chief OB officer"? Our answer to this question begins with survey findings that students who have been in the workforce for some time typically point to OB as one of their most valuable courses. Why? Because they have learned through experience that OB *does make a difference* to one's career success.[11] There are three main reasons why OB theories and practices are personally important to you (see Exhibit 1.1).

Frederick Winslow Taylor
©Paul Fearn/Alamy Stock Photo

Comprehend and Predict Workplace Events Everyone has an inherent drive to make sense of what is going on around him or her.[12] This need is particularly strong in organizations because they are highly complex and ambiguous contexts that have a profound effect on our lives. The field of organizational behavior uses scientific research to discover systematic relationships, which give us a valuable foundation for comprehending organizational life.[13] This knowledge satisfies our curiosity about why events occur and reduces our anxiety about circumstances that would otherwise be unexpected and unexplained. Furthermore, OB knowledge improves our ability to predict and anticipate future events so we can get along with others, achieve our goals, and minimize unnecessary career risks.

Adopt More Accurate Personal Theories A frequent misunderstanding is that OB is common sense. Of course, some OB knowledge is very similar to the theories you have developed through personal experience. But personal theories are usually not quite as precise as they need to be. Perhaps they explain and predict some situations, but not others. For example, one study found that when liberal arts students and chief executive officers were asked to choose the preferred organizational structure in various situations, their commonsense answers were typically wrong because they oversimplified well-known theory and evidence on that topic.[14] (We discuss organizational structures in Chapter 12.) Throughout this book you also will discover that OB research has debunked some ideas that people thought were "common sense." Overall, we believe the OB knowledge you will gain by reading this book will help you challenge and refine your personal theories, and give you more accurate and complete perspectives of organizational events.

Influence Organizational Events Probably the greatest value of OB knowledge is that it helps us get things done in the workplace by influencing organizational events.[15] By definition, organizations are people who work together to accomplish things, so we need a toolkit of knowledge and skills to work successfully with others. Studies consistently observe that the most important knowledge and skills that employers desire in employees relate to the topics we discuss in this book, such as building teams, motivating coworkers, handling workplace conflicts, making decisions, and changing employee behavior. No matter what career path you choose, you'll find that

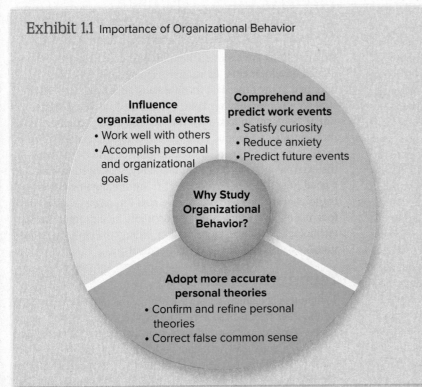

Exhibit 1.1 Importance of Organizational Behavior

Influence organizational events
- Work well with others
- Accomplish personal and organizational goals

Comprehend and predict work events
- Satisfy curiosity
- Reduce anxiety
- Predict future events

Why Study Organizational Behavior?

Adopt more accurate personal theories
- Confirm and refine personal theories
- Correct false common sense

OB concepts play an important role in performing your job and working more effectively within organizations.

Organizational Behavior Is for Everyone Organizational behavior is discussed by some writers as a topic for managers. Effective management does depend on OB concepts and practices, but this book pioneered the broader view that OB is valuable for everyone who works in and around organizations. Whether you are a software engineer, customer service representative, foreign exchange analyst, or chief executive officer, you need to understand and apply the many organizational behavior topics that are discussed in this book. In fact, OB knowledge is probably more valuable than ever before because employees increasingly need to be proactive, self-motivated, and able to work effectively with coworkers without management intervention. In the words of one forward-thinking OB writer more than four decades ago: Everyone is a manager.[16]

Probably the greatest value of OB knowledge is that it helps us get things done in the workplace by influencing organizational events.
©ColorBlind Images/Blend Images LLC

OB and the Bottom Line Up to this point, our answer to the question "Why study OB?" has focused on how organizational behavior knowledge benefits you as an individual. However, OB is also vital to the organization's survival and success.[17] For instance, the best 100 companies to work for in America (i.e., companies with the highest levels of employee satisfaction) enjoy significantly higher financial performance than other businesses within the same industry. Companies with higher levels of employee engagement have higher sales and profitability (see Chapter 5). OB practices also are associated with various indicators of hospital performance, such as lower patient mortality rates and higher patient satisfaction. Other studies have consistently found a positive relationship between the quality of leadership and the company's financial performance.

The bottom-line value of organizational behavior is supported by research into the best predictors of investment portfolio performance. These investigations suggest that leadership, performance-based rewards, employee development, employee attitudes, and other specific OB characteristics are important "positive screens" for selecting companies with the highest and most consistent long-term investment gains.[18] Overall, the organizational behavior concepts, theories, and practices presented throughout this book make a positive difference to you personally, to the organization, and ultimately to society.

CONTEMPORARY DEVELOPMENTS FACING ORGANIZATIONS

Organizations are experiencing unprecedented change. Technological developments, consumer expectations, global competition, and many other factors have substantially altered business strategy and everyday workplace activities. The field of organizational behavior plays a vital role in guiding organizations through this continuous turbulence. As we will explain in more detail later in this chapter, organizations are deeply affected by the external environment. Consequently, they need to maintain a good organization–environment fit by anticipating and adjusting to changes in society. Over the next few pages, we introduce four major environmental developments facing organizations: technological change, globalization, emerging employment relationships, and increasing workforce diversity.

Technological Change

Technological change has always been a disruptive force in organizations, as well as in society.[19] Waterwheels, cotton gins, steam engines, microprocessors (such as in automated systems and artificial intelligence), and many other innovations dramatically boost productivity, but also usually displace employees and render obsolete entire occupational groups. Other technologies, such as the telegraph, smartphone, and the Internet, have increased productivity but also altered work relationships and patterns of behavior with coworkers, clients, and suppliers. Still other technologies aim to improve health and well-being, such as the development of better medicines and medical equipment, new leisure apparatus, and environmentally safer materials.

Information technology is one of the most significant forms of technological change in recent times.[20] As we discuss in Chapter 8, communication patterns and power dynamics have substantially changed due to the introduction of email and other forms of digital messaging. Social media and other collaboration technologies are slowly replacing email, and will further reshape how people associate and coordinate with each other. Some OB experts argue that information technology gives employees a stronger voice through direct communication with executives and broader distribution of their opinions to coworkers and beyond.

Information technology also has created challenges, such as tethering people to their jobs for longer hours, reducing their attention spans at work, and increasing techno-stress. We discuss these concerns below and in Chapter 4 (workplace stress). At a macro-level, information technology has reconfigured entire organizations by integrating suppliers and other external entities into the transformation process. Eventually, technology may render organizations less of a place where people work and more of a process or network where people collaborate across space and time (see Chapter 12).

Globalization

Globalization refers to economic, social, and cultural connectivity with people in other parts of the world. Organizations globalize when they actively participate in other countries and cultures. Although businesses have traded goods across borders for centuries, the degree of globalization today is unprecedented because information technology and transportation systems allow a much more intense level of connectivity and interdependence around the planet.[22]

Globalization offers numerous benefits to organizations in terms of larger markets, lower costs, and greater access to knowledge and innovation. At the same time, there is considerable debate about whether globalization benefits developing nations and the extent to which it is responsible for increasing work intensification, reduced job security, and poor work–life balance in developed countries.[23]

The field of organizational behavior focuses on the effects of globalization on organizations and how to lead and work effectively in this emerging reality. Throughout this book, we will refer to the effects of globalization on teamwork, diversity, cultural values, organizational structure, leadership, and other themes. Globalization has brought more complexity and new ways of working to the workplace. It also requires additional knowledge and skills that we will discuss in this book, such as emotional intelligence, a global mindset, nonverbal communication, and conflict handling.

globalization economic, social, and cultural connectivity with people in other parts of the world

work–life balance the degree to which a person minimizes conflict between work and nonwork demands

Emerging Employment Relationships

Technology, globalization, and several other developments have substantially altered the employment relationship in most countries. Before the digital age, most employees would finish work after eight or nine hours and could separate their personal time from their employment. Today, they are more likely to be connected to work on a 24/7 schedule. Globalization increases competitive pressure to work longer and creates a 24-hour schedule because coworkers, suppliers, and clients work in different time zones. Information technology enables employers and others to easily and quickly communicate with employees beyond their traditional workday.

Little wonder that one of the most important employment issues over the past decade has been **work–life balance**. Work–life balance occurs when people are able to minimize conflict between their work and nonwork demands.[24] Most employees lack this balance because they spend too many hours each week performing or thinking about their job, whether at the workplace, at home,

Social Media Technology Reshapes the Workplace[21]

21% of 2,027 employed American adults say they spend between 1 and 6 hours using social media tools or mobile applications to help get their job done.

58% of 1,000 American employees polled say they would prefer to work at a company that uses internal (enterprise) social media.

46% of 9,908 information workers polled across 32 countries say that social media tools have somewhat or greatly increased their productivity.

42% of 9,908 information workers polled across 32 countries say that social media tools have resulted in more workplace collaboration.

60% of 2,186 American hiring and human resource managers say they use social media sites to research job candidates (up from 52% the previous year and 11% in 2006).

(photo): ©pictafolio/E+/Getty Images

telecommuting an arrangement whereby, supported by information technology, employees work from home one or more work days per month rather than commute to the office

or on vacation. This focus on work leaves too little time to fulfill nonwork needs and obligations. Our discussion of work-related stress (Chapter 4) will examine work–life balance issues in more detail.

Another employment relationship trend is for employees to work away from the organization's traditional common work site.[25] One form of this *remote work* arrangement involves performing most job duties at client sites throughout the day. Repair technicians and management consultants regularly work at client sites, for example. Longer-term remote work occurs where employees are assigned to partner organizations. For instance, biotechnology firm Anteo Diagnostics dispatches its scientists for several weeks or months to partner companies around the world, where they jointly investigate the effectiveness of Anteo's patented nano glue products on the partner firm's point-of-care technology.

Telecommuting The best-known form of remote work is **telecommuting** (also called *teleworking*) whereby information technology enables employees to work from home one or more workdays per month rather than commute to the office. An estimated 37 percent of U.S. workers telecommute, with almost one-third of them working from home at least six days each month. The U.S. government reports that 23 percent of employees perform some or all of their work at home (but that includes taking work home after attending the office, not just telecommuting).[26]

Is telecommuting good for employees and organizations? This question continues to be debated because it produces

Most employees lack work–life balance because they spend too many hours each week performing or thinking about their job, whether at the workplace, at home, or on vacation.
©ALMAGAMI/Shutterstock

Exhibit 1.2 Potential Benefits and Risks of Telecommuting

Potential Benefits	Potential Risks
• Better employee work–life balance	• More social isolation
• Attractive benefit for job applicants	• Lower team cohesion
• Low employee turnover	• Weaker organizational culture
• Higher employee productivity	• More stressful due to home space and roles
• Reduced greenhouse gas emissions	
• Reduced corporate real estate and office costs	

several potential benefits and risks (see Exhibit 1.2).[27] One advantage is that telecommuters usually experience better work–life balance because they have more time and somewhat more control to juggle work with family obligations. For example, a study of 25,000 IBM employees found that female telecommuters with children were able to work 40 hours per week, whereas female employees with children who work solely at the office could manage only 30 hours before feeling work–life balance tension. Work–life balance is less likely to improve when telecommuters lack sufficient workspace and privacy at home and have increased family responsibilities on telecommuting days.

Job applicants—particularly millennials—identify telecommuting as an attractive job feature, and turnover is usually lower among telecommuting employees. Research also indicates that telecommuters have higher productivity than nontelecommuters, likely because they experience less stress and tend to transfer some former commuting time to work time. Telecommuting also improves productivity by enabling employees to work at times when the weather or natural disasters block access to the office.

Several companies report that telecommuting has reduced greenhouse gas emissions and office expenses. For instance, health insurer Aetna estimates that its telecommuting employees (31 percent of the workforce) annually avoid using two million gallons of gas, thereby reducing carbon dioxide emissions by more than 23,000 metric tons. With many employees working from home, Aetna also has been able to reduce its real estate and related costs by between 15 and 25 percent.[28]

Telecommuting also has several disadvantages.[29] Telecommuters frequently report more social isolation. They also receive less word-of-mouth information, which may have implications for promotional opportunities and workplace relations. Telecommuting also tends to weaken relationships among coworkers, resulting in lower team cohesion. Organizational culture is also potentially weaker when most employees work from home for a significant part of their workweek.

surface-level diversity
the observable demographic or physiological differences in people, such as their race, ethnicity, gender, age, and physical disabilities

deep-level diversity
differences in the psychological characteristics of employees, including personalities, beliefs, values, and attitudes

Telecommuting success depends on several characteristics of the employee, job, and organization.[30] Employees who work effectively from home typically have higher self-motivation, self-organization, need for autonomy, and information technology skills. Those who telecommute most of the time also fulfill their social needs more from sources outside the workplace. Jobs are better suited to telecommuting when the tasks do not require resources at the workplace, the work is performed independently from coworkers, and task performance is measurable.

Organizations improve telecommuting success by rewarding and promoting employees based on their performance rather than their presence in the office (face time). Effective companies also help telecommuters maintain sufficient cohesion with their team and psychological connectedness with the organization. This occurs by limiting the number of telecommuting days, having special meetings or events where all employees assemble at the workplace, and regularly using video communication and other technology that improves personal relatedness.

(currently 18 percent), 14 percent will be of Asian descent (currently 6 percent), and 13 percent will be African American (currently 14 percent).[32]

Diversity also includes differences in personalities, beliefs, values, and attitudes.[33] We can't directly see this **deep-level diversity**, but it is evident in a person's choices, words, and actions. Deep-level diversity is revealed when employees have different perceptions and attitudes about the same situation (see Chapter 10) and when they form like-minded informal social groups (see Chapter 7). Some deep-level diversity is associated with surface-level attributes. For example, studies report significant differences between men and women regarding their preference of

> **Employees who work effectively from home typically have higher self-motivation, self-organization, need for autonomy, and information technology skills.**

connect

SELF-ASSESSMENT 1.1: Are You a Good Telecommuter?
Telecommuting is an increasingly popular workplace relationship, and it potentially offers benefits for both companies and telecommuters. However, some people are better suited than others to telecommuting and other forms of remote work. You can discover how well you adjust to telecommuting and remote work by locating this self-assessment in Connect if it is assigned by your instructor.

conflict-handling styles, ethical principles, and approaches to communicating with other people in various situations.[34]

An example of deep-level diversity is the variations in beliefs and expectations across generations.[35] Exhibit 1.3 illustrates the distribution of the American workforce by major generational cohorts: *Baby Boomers* (born from 1946 to 1964), *Generation Xers* (born from 1965 to 1980), and *Millennials* (also called *Generation Yers*, born between 1981 and 1997).

Generational deep-level diversity does exist to some extent, but it tends to be subtler than the popular press would suggest. Also, some generational differences are actually due to age, not cohort.[37] For instance, Millennials have a stronger motivation for personal development, advancement, and recognition, whereas Baby Boomers are more motivated by interesting and meaningful work. Research indicates that as Millennials age, their motivation for learning and advancement will wane and their motivation for interesting and meaningful work will increase.

Increasing Workforce Diversity

Immigrants to the United States and many other countries have much more multicultural origins than a few decades ago, resulting in a much more diverse workforce in most organizations. In addition, globalization has increased the diversity of people employees interact with in partner organizations (suppliers, clients, etc.) located elsewhere in the world.

When discussing workforce diversity, we usually think about **surface-level diversity**—the observable demographic and other overt differences among members of a group, such as their race, ethnicity, gender, age, and physical capabilities.[31] Surface-level diversity in the United States and many other countries has increased substantially over the past few decades. For instance, people with non-Caucasian or Hispanic origin currently represent almost 40 percent of the American population. Within the next 50 years, an estimated one-quarter of Americans will be Hispanic

Consequences of Diversity

Workforce diversity offers numerous advantages to organizations.[38] Teams with high informational diversity—members have different knowledge and skills—tend to be more creative and

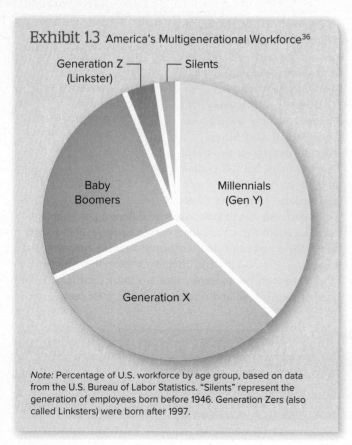

Exhibit 1.3 America's Multigenerational Workforce[36]

Note: Percentage of U.S. workforce by age group, based on data from the U.S. Bureau of Labor Statistics. "Silents" represent the generation of employees born before 1946. Generation Zers (also called Linksters) were born after 1997.

Diversity as Competitive Advantage at MasterCard

©Pau Barrena/Bloomberg/Getty Images

Supporting workforce diversity is the right thing to do as well as a source of competitive advantage at MasterCard Incorporated. "Our culture of inclusion has established us as a global company of empowered employees who use their diversity of thought, experience and background to advance innovation and MasterCard's contributions to society," says MasterCard president and CEO Ajay Banga (shown in this photo).

Banga personally chairs MasterCard's Global Diversity and Inclusion Council and meets several times each year with its eight Business Resource Groups. More than half of MasterCard's employees participate in these diversity-based groups, which serve as internal business consultants to guide the company on consumer preferences, cultural insights, and access to networks. "By valuing a culture of inclusion, we gain additional insights and perspectives that allow us to make the best decisions for our business and customers," explains Donna Johnson, MasterCard's chief diversity officer.[41]

make better decisions in complex situations compared to teams with less informational diversity. A workforce with surface- and deep-level diversity is also more representative of most communities, so companies are better able to recognize and address community needs. These and other benefits may explain why companies that win diversity awards have higher financial returns, at least in the short run.[39]

Diversity also poses challenges in the workplace.[40] One problem is that employees with diverse backgrounds usually take longer to perform effectively together because they experience numerous communication problems and create "faultlines" in informal group dynamics (see Chapter 7). Some forms of diversity also increase the risk of dysfunctional conflict, which reduces information sharing and satisfaction with coworkers (see Chapter 10). Research suggests that these problems can offset the advantages of diversity in some situations.

But even with these challenges, companies need to make diversity a priority because surface-level diversity and some forms of deep-level diversity are moral and legal imperatives. Companies that offer an inclusive workplace are, in essence, fulfilling the ethical standard of fairness in their decisions regarding employment and the allocation of rewards. Inclusive workplace practices improve the quality of hiring and promotion, and increase employee satisfaction and loyalty. Companies that create an inclusive workplace also nurture a culture of respect, which, in turn, improves cooperation and coordination among employees.

LO1-3 Discuss the anchors on which organizational behavior knowledge is based.

ANCHORS OF ORGANIZATIONAL BEHAVIOR KNOWLEDGE

Technological change, globalization, emerging employment relationships, and increasing workforce diversity are just a few of the societal changes that make organizational behavior knowledge more useful than ever before. To understand these and other topics, the field of organizational behavior relies on a set of basic beliefs or knowledge structures (see Exhibit 1.4). These conceptual anchors represent the principles on which OB knowledge is developed and refined.[42]

The Systematic Research Anchor

A key feature of OB knowledge is that it should be based on systematic research, which typically involves forming research questions, systematically collecting data, and testing hypotheses against those data.[43] Systematic research investigation is the basis for **evidence-based management**, which involves making decisions and taking actions guided by research evidence. It makes perfect sense that management practice should be founded on the best available systematic knowledge. Yet many of us who study organizations using systematic methods are amazed at how often corporate leaders and other staff embrace fads, untested consulting models, and their own pet beliefs without bothering to find out if they actually work![44]

Why don't decision makers consistently apply evidence-based management? One reason is that they are bombarded with ideas from consultant reports, popular business books, newspaper articles, and other sources, which makes it difficult to figure out which ones are based on good evidence. A second reason is that good OB research is necessarily generic; it is rarely described in the context of a specific problem in a specific organization. Decision makers therefore have the difficult task of figuring out which theories are relevant to their unique situation.

A third reason why organizational leaders follow popular management fads that lack research evidence is because the sources of these fads are rewarded for marketing their ideas, not for testing to see if they actually work. Indeed, some management concepts have become popular (some have even found their way into OB textbooks!) because of heavy marketing, not because of any evidence that they are valid. A fourth reason is that human beings are affected by several perceptual errors and decision-making biases, as we will learn in Chapter 3 and Chapter 6. For instance, decision makers have a natural tendency to look for evidence that supports their pet beliefs and ignore evidence that opposes those beliefs.

OB experts have identified several ways to create a more evidence-based organization.[45] First, be skeptical of hype, which is apparent when so-called experts say the idea is "new," "revolutionary," and "proven." In reality, most management ideas are adaptations, evolutionary, and never proven (science can disprove but never prove; it can only find evidence to support a practice). Second, the company should embrace collective expertise rather than rely on charismatic stars and management gurus. Third, stories provide useful illustrations and possibly preliminary evidence of a useful practice, but they should never become the main foundation to support management action. Instead, rely on more systematic investigation with a larger sample. Finally, take a neutral stance toward popular trends and ideologies. Executives tend to get caught up in what their counterparts at other companies are doing without determining the validity of those trendy practices or their relevance to their own organizations.

A key feature of OB knowledge is that it should be based on systematic research, which becomes the foundation for evidence-based management.
©Wavebreakmedia Ltd PH26L/Alamy Stock Photo

evidence-based management the practice of making decisions and taking actions based on research evidence

---

Exhibit 1.4 Anchors of Organizational Behavior Knowledge

Systematic research anchor	Study organizations using systematic research methods
Multidisciplinary anchor	Import knowledge from other disciplines, not just create its own knowledge
Contingency anchor	Recognize that the effectiveness of an action may depend on the situation
Multiple levels of analysis anchor	Understand OB events from three levels of analysis: individual, team, organization

The Multidisciplinary Anchor

Another organizational behavior anchor is that the field should welcome theories and knowledge from other disciplines, not just from its own isolated research base. For instance, psychological research has aided our understanding of individual and interpersonal behavior. Sociologists have contributed to our knowledge of team dynamics, organizational socialization, organizational power, and other aspects of the social system. OB knowledge also has benefited from knowledge in emerging fields such as communications, marketing, and information systems.

This practice of borrowing theory from other disciplines is inevitable. Organizations have central roles in society, so they are studied in many social sciences. Furthermore, organizations consist of people who interact with each other, so there is an inherent intersection between OB and most disciplines that study human beings. However, by relying too much on theories developed in other fields, OB faces the risk of lagging rather than leading in knowledge production. In contrast, OB-bred theories allow researchers to concentrate on the quality and usefulness of the theory, and be the first to understand and apply that knowledge.[46]

The Contingency Anchor

People and their work environments are complex, and the field of organizational behavior recognizes this by stating that the effect of one variable on another variable often depends on the characteristics of the situation or people involved. In practice, this means that we can't count on having the same result in every situation when we apply an intervention. Instead, a particular action may have different consequences under different conditions.[47] For example, earlier in this chapter we said that the success of telecommuting depends on specific characteristics of the employee, job, and organization. Contingencies are identified in many OB theories, such as the best leadership style, the best conflict-handling style, and the best organizational structure. Of course, it would be so much simpler if we could rely on "one best way" theories, in which a particular concept or practice has the same results in every situation. OB experts do try to keep theories as simple as possible, but the contingency anchor is always on their mind.[48]

The Multiple Levels of Analysis Anchor

Organizational behavior recognizes that what goes on in organizations can be placed into three levels of analysis: individual, team (including interpersonal), and organization. In fact, advanced empirical research currently being conducted carefully identifies the appropriate level of analysis for each variable in the study and then measures at that level of analysis. For example, team norms and cohesion are measured as team variables, not as characteristics of individuals within each team.

Although OB research and writing peg each variable within one of these levels of analysis, most variables are understood best by thinking of them from all three levels of analysis.[49] Communication is located in this book as a team (interpersonal) process, for instance, but it also includes individual and organizational processes. Therefore, you should try to think about each OB topic at the individual, team, and organizational levels, not just at one of these levels.

PERSPECTIVES OF ORGANIZATIONAL EFFECTIVENESS

Almost all organizational behavior theories have the implicit or explicit objective of making organizations more effective.[50] In fact, **organizational effectiveness** is considered the "ultimate dependent variable" in organizational behavior.[51] This means that organizational effectiveness is the outcome that most OB theories are ultimately trying to achieve. Many theories use different labels—organizational performance, success, goodness, health, competitiveness, excellence—but they are basically presenting models and recommendations that help organizations to be more effective.

Many years ago, OB experts thought the best indicator of a company's effectiveness was how well it achieved its stated objectives. According to this definition, Delta Air Lines would be an effective organization if it met or exceeded its annual sales and profit targets. Today, we know that this goal perspective might not indicate organizational effectiveness at all. Any leadership team could set corporate goals that are easy to achieve, yet the company would be left in the dust by competitors' more aggressive objectives. Worse still, some goals might ultimately put the company out of business. For example, they may focus employees on reducing costs whereas success may require more focus on product or service quality.

The best yardstick of organizational effectiveness is a composite of four perspectives: open systems, organizational learning, high-performance work practices, and stakeholders.[52] Organizations are effective when they have a good fit with their external environment, are learning organizations, have efficient and adaptive internal subsystems (i.e., high-performance work practices), and satisfy the needs of key stakeholders. Over the next few pages, we examine each of these perspectives in more detail.

Open Systems Perspective

The **open systems** perspective of organizational effectiveness is one of the earliest and most-entrenched ways of thinking about organizations.[53] Indeed, the other major organizational effectiveness perspectives mainly provide more detail to specific sections of the open systems model. This perspective views organizations as complex organisms that "live" within an external environment, as Exhibit 1.5 illustrates. The word *open* describes this permeable relationship, whereas *closed systems* operate without dependence on or interaction with an external environment.

As open systems, organizations depend on the external environment for resources, including raw materials, job applicants, financial resources, information, and equipment. The external environment also consists of rules and expectations, such as laws and cultural norms, that place demands on how organizations should operate. Some resources (e.g., raw materials) are imported from the external environment, are transformed into product or services, and then become outputs exported to the external environment. Other resources (e.g., job applicants, equipment) become subsystems in the transformation process.

Inside the organization are numerous subsystems, such as departments, teams, informal groups, information systems, work processes, and technological processes.[54] These subsystems are dependent on each other as they transform inputs into outputs. Some outputs (e.g., products and services) may be valued by the external environment, whereas other outputs (e.g., employee layoffs, pollution) are undesirable by-products that may have adverse effects on the environment and the organization's relationship with that environment. Throughout this process, organizations receive feedback from the external environment regarding the value of their outputs, the availability of future inputs, and the appropriateness of the transformation process.

Organization–Environment Fit

The open systems perspective states that organizations are effective when they maintain a good "fit" with their external environment.[55] Good fit exists when the organization's inputs, processes, and outputs are aligned with the external environment's needs, expectations, and resources. Organizations maintain a good environmental fit in three ways:

- **Adapt to the environment:** Effective organizations closely and continuously monitor the environment for emerging conditions that pose a threat or opportunity. Then they reconfigure their internal subsystems to align more closely with that shifting environment. There are many ways that companies are adaptive (called their *dynamic capability*), such as by changing the type or volume of products produced, shifting to different input resources that are more plentiful or reliable, and designing better production (transformation) processes.

- **Influence the environment:** Effective organizations don't merely respond to emerging conditions; they actively try to influence their

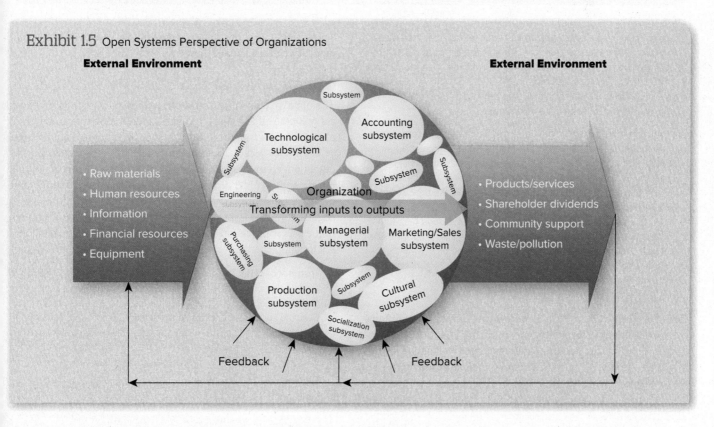

Exhibit 1.5 Open Systems Perspective of Organizations

The open systems perspective states that organizations are effective when they maintain a good "fit" with their external environment.
©Palto/Getty Images

energy. Another indicator is their *adaptability*. Organizations need to adapt to their external environment, and this usually includes a transformation process that adapts to new products and sometimes new ways of making those products. A third indicator of an effective transformation process is *innovativeness*. Innovation involves the discovery, design, and creation of products and work processes that are superior to what competitors can offer.

An important feature of an effective transformation process is how well the internal subsystems coordinate with each other.[58] Coordination is one of the most important OB concepts because organizations consist of people working together to achieve collective goals. As companies grow, they develop increasingly complex subsystems, which makes coordination more and more difficult. Complexity increases the risk that information gets lost, ideas and resources are hoarded, messages are misinterpreted, and rewards are distributed unfairly. Subsystems are interconnected, so small work practice changes in one subsystem may ripple through the organization and undermine the effectiveness of other subsystems. Consequently, organizations rely on

> An important feature of an effective transformation process is how well the internal subsystems coordinate with each other.

environment. For instance, businesses rely on marketing to increase demand for their products or services. Some firms gain exclusive rights to particular resources (e.g., sole provider of a popular brand) or restrict competitor access to valued resources. Still others lobby for legislation that strengthens their position in the marketplace or try to delay legislation that would disrupt their business activities.

- **Move to a more favorable environment:** Sometimes the current environment becomes so challenging that organizations cannot adapt or influence it enough to survive. For instance, the current environment might have extreme resource scarcity, too many competitors, too little demand for the firm's products, or onerous rules that make the transformation process too expensive. Under these circumstances, organizations often move to a more benevolent environment that can support their future. For example, Target closed its Canadian business after a few years because it underestimated the competition, stumbled on the transformation process (distribution and inventory challenges), and mismatched consumer expectations (location, pricing).[56]

Effective Transformation Process In addition to maintaining a good fit with the external environment, effective organizations have a transformation process that does well at converting inputs to outputs.[57] The most common indicator of effective internal subsystems is their *efficiency*. Efficient organizations produce more goods or services with less labor, materials, and

coordinating mechanisms to maintain an efficient, adaptive, and innovative transformation process (see Chapter 12).

Organizational Learning Perspective

The open systems perspective has traditionally focused on physical resources that enter the organization and are processed into physical goods (outputs). But whether their outputs are physical or cognitive, successful companies rely on knowledge as a key ingredient to success. This second perspective of organizational effectiveness, called **organizational learning**, states that the best organizations find ways to acquire, share, use, and store knowledge. Knowledge is a resource or asset, called **intellectual capital**, that exists in three forms: human capital, structural capital, and relationship capital.[59]

- **Human capital**: Human capital refers to the knowledge, skills, and abilities that employees carry around in their heads. It is a competitive advantage because employees are essential for the organization's survival and success, and their talents are difficult to find, to copy, and to replace with technology.[61] Human capital is also a huge risk for most organizations because it literally leaves the organization every day when employees go home![62]

- **Structural capital**: Even if every employee left the organization, some intellectual capital remains as structural capital. It includes the knowledge captured and retained in an organization's systems and structures, such as the documented work procedures, physical layout of production and office space, and the finished products (which can be reverse engineered to discover how they were made).[63]

- **Relationship capital**: Relationship capital is the value derived from an organization's relationships with customers, suppliers, and others who provide added mutual value for the organization. It includes the organization's goodwill, brand image, and combination of relationships that organizational members have with people outside the organization.[64]

An organization's intellectual capital develops and is maintained through the four organizational learning processes shown in Exhibit 1.6: acquiring, sharing, using, and storing knowledge.[65]

Acquiring Knowledge Acquiring knowledge refers to bringing in knowledge from the external environment as well as through discovery. It occurs daily when employees casually observe changes in the external environment as well as when they receive formal training from sources outside the organization. Knowledge acquisition also occurs through environmental

> ❝ An organization's ability to learn, and translate that learning into action rapidly, is the ultimate competitive advantage.[60]
>
> —Jack Welch, former CEO of General Electric ❞

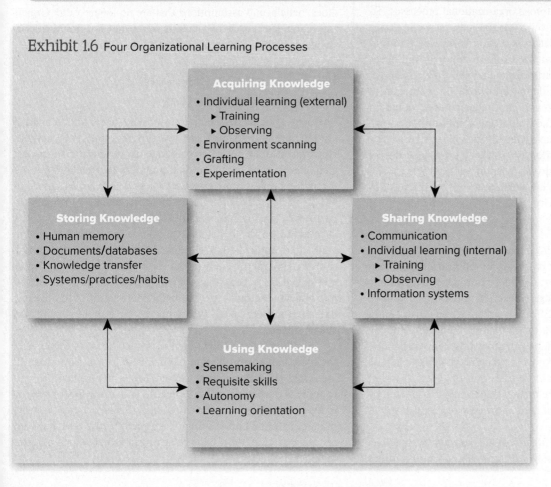

Exhibit 1.6 Four Organizational Learning Processes

Acquiring Knowledge
- Individual learning (external)
  ▸ Training
  ▸ Observing
- Environment scanning
- Grafting
- Experimentation

Storing Knowledge
- Human memory
- Documents/databases
- Knowledge transfer
- Systems/practices/habits

Sharing Knowledge
- Communication
- Individual learning (internal)
  ▸ Training
  ▸ Observing
- Information systems

Using Knowledge
- Sensemaking
- Requisite skills
- Autonomy
- Learning orientation

scanning, such as actively monitoring consumer trends, proposed government legislation, and competitor activities. A third method is to hire skilled staff and buy complementary businesses (called *grafting*). Finally, knowledge acquisition occurs through experimentation—generating new ideas and products through creative discovery and testing.

Sharing Knowledge Sharing knowledge refers to distributing knowledge throughout the organization. This mainly occurs through formal and informal communication with coworkers, as well as through various forms of in-house learning (training, observation, etc.). Companies encourage informal communication through

Having a Hoot with Organizational Learning

Hootsuite relies on organizational learning practices to retain its leadership in social media technology. The leading provider of social media management and analytics acquires knowledge by actively hiring new employees and buying entire companies (grafting). "Maybe the only person we can find is already within a startup. We want to get that person over, so we have to buy the company," says Hootsuite CEO Ryan Holmes.

Hootsuite encourages experimentation through Hoot-Hackathons, intensive two-day events during which employees work together to build new products. The company encourages knowledge sharing through open-space offices and a supportive culture. It also holds a monthly "parliament"—a social gathering hosted by two departments. "The real point [of parliament] is that team members from different departments collaborate in the creative process, building ties that carry over to more serious stuff," says Holmes.[67]

©Chaay Tee/Shutterstock

their organizational structure, workspace design, corporate culture, and social activities.[66] Company intranets and digital information repositories also support knowledge sharing.

Using Knowledge Knowledge is a competitive advantage only when it is applied to improve organizational processes. To use knowledge, employees need a mental map (sense making) so they are aware the knowledge exists and know where to find it in the organization. Knowledge use also requires employees with sufficient prerequisite knowledge and skills. For example, financial analysts need foundation knowledge in mathematics and financial products to use new knowledge on asset valuation methods. Autonomy is another important condition for knowledge use; employees must have enough freedom to try out new ideas. Knowledge use also flourishes where workplace norms strongly support organizational learning. These beliefs and norms represent a **learning orientation**, which we discuss further on the topics of creativity (Chapter 6) and organizational culture (Chapter 13).[68]

Storing Knowledge Storing knowledge is the process of retaining knowledge for later retrieval. Stored knowledge, often called *organizational memory*, includes knowledge that employees recall as well as knowledge embedded in the organization's systems and structures.[69] Effective organizations also retain knowledge in human capital by motivating employees to stay with the company. Furthermore, organizations encourage employees to share what they know so valuable knowledge is held by coworkers when an employee does quit or retire. Another strategy is to actively document knowledge when it is created by debriefing teams on details of their knowledge of clients or product development.

One last point about the organizational learning perspective: effective organizations not only learn; they also unlearn routines and patterns of behavior that are no longer appropriate.[70] Unlearning removes knowledge that no longer adds value and, in fact, may undermine the organization's effectiveness. Some forms of unlearning involve replacing dysfunctional policies, procedures, and routines. Other forms of unlearning erase attitudes, beliefs, and assumptions that are no longer valid. Organizational unlearning is particularly important for organizational change, which we discuss in Chapter 14.

High-Performance Work Practices Perspective

The open systems perspective states that successful companies are efficient and adaptive at transforming inputs into outputs. However, it does not offer guidance about specific subsystem characteristics or organizational practices that make the transformation process more effective. These details are addressed by another perspective of organizational effectiveness, called **high-performance work practices (HPWPs)**. The HPWP perspective is founded on the belief that human capital—the knowledge, skills, and abilities that employees possess—is an important source of competitive advantage for organizations.[71] Motivated and skilled employees offer competitive advantage by transforming inputs to outputs better, by being more sensitive to the external environment, and by having better relations with key stakeholders.

The HPWP perspective identifies specific ways to generate the most value from human capital. The four most frequently identified HPWP practices are employee involvement, job autonomy, competency development, and rewards for performance and competency development.[72] Each of these four work practices alone improves organizational effectiveness, but studies suggest that they have a stronger effect when bundled together.[73]

The four most frequently identified HPWP practices are employee involvement, job autonomy, competency development, and rewards for performance and competency development.
©OPOLJA/Shutterstock

The first two factors—involving employees in decision making and giving them more autonomy over their work activities—strengthen employee motivation as well as improve decisions, organizational responsiveness, and commitment to change. In high-performance workplaces, employee involvement and job autonomy often take the form of self-directed teams (see Chapter 7). The third factor, employee competency development, refers to recruiting, selecting, and training so employees are equipped with the relevant knowledge and skills. The fourth high-performance work practice is linking performance and skill development to various financial and nonfinancial rewards valued by employees.

High-performance work practices improve an organization's effectiveness in three ways.[75] First, as we mentioned earlier,

High Performance Work Practices in Selected OECD and Partner Countries[74]

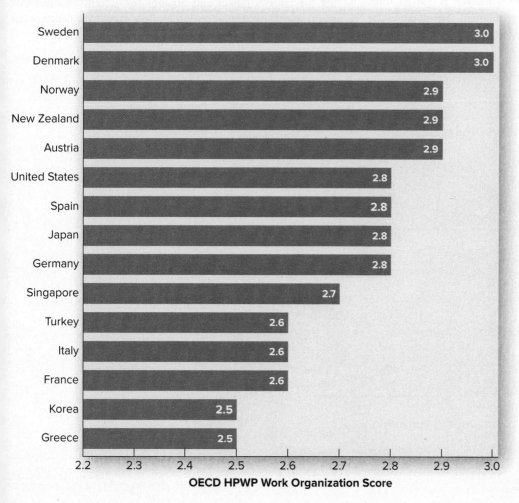

Country	OECD HPWP Work Organization Score
Sweden	3.0
Denmark	3.0
Norway	2.9
New Zealand	2.9
Austria	2.9
United States	2.8
Spain	2.8
Japan	2.8
Germany	2.8
Singapore	2.7
Turkey	2.6
Italy	2.6
France	2.6
Korea	2.5
Greece	2.5

OECD HPWP Work Organization Score

Average composite score on high-performance work practices reported by employees in selected countries. Higher scores indicate higher HPWP practices in that country. This scale represents "work organization" HPWP practices, which exclude rewards but include work flexibility/autonomy, planning one's own work, cooperating and sharing information with coworkers, and training others. Data were collected from more than 215,000 adults in OECD and partner countries with a minimum 4,000 respondents per country. This chart shows a selection of the 34 countries measured in the study.

these activities develop employee skills and knowledge (human capital), which directly improve individual behavior and performance. Second, companies with superior human capital tend to adapt better to rapidly changing environments. This adaptability occurs because employees are better at performing diverse tasks in unfamiliar situations when they are highly skilled and have more freedom to perform their work. A third explanation is that HPWP practices strengthen employee motivation and positive attitudes toward the employer. HPWPs represent the company's investment in its workforce, which motivates employees to reciprocate through greater effort in their jobs and assistance to coworkers.

The HPWP perspective is still developing, but it already reveals important information about specific organizational practices that improve an organization's effectiveness through its employees. Still, this perspective offers an incomplete picture of organizational effectiveness. The remaining gaps are filled by the stakeholder perspective of organizational effectiveness.

Stakeholder Perspective

The open systems perspective says that effective organizations adapt to the external environment. However, it doesn't offer much detail about the external environment. The stakeholder perspective offers more specific information and guidance by focusing on the organization's relationships with stakeholders. **Stakeholders** include organizations, groups, and other entities that affect, or are affected by, the company's objectives and actions.[76] The stakeholder perspective personalizes the open systems perspective; it identifies specific social entities in the external environment as well as employees and others within the organization (the internal environment). This perspective also recognizes that stakeholder relations are dynamic; they can be negotiated and influenced, not just taken as a fixed condition. In general, the stakeholder perspective states that organizations are more effective when they understand, manage, and satisfy stakeholder needs and expectations.[77]

There are many types of stakeholders, and they are continuously evolving. Consider the key stakeholders identified by CSL Limited in Exhibit 1.7. The global leader in blood-related products and vaccines pays attention to more than a dozen groups, and likely others that aren't included in this diagram. Understanding, managing, and satisfying the interests of stakeholders is challenging because they have conflicting interests and organizations lack sufficient resources to satisfy everyone. Therefore, organizational leaders need to decide how much priority to give to each group.[78] Research has identified several factors that influence the prioritization of stakeholders, including the entity's power and urgency for action, its legitimate claim to organizational resources, how executives perceive the

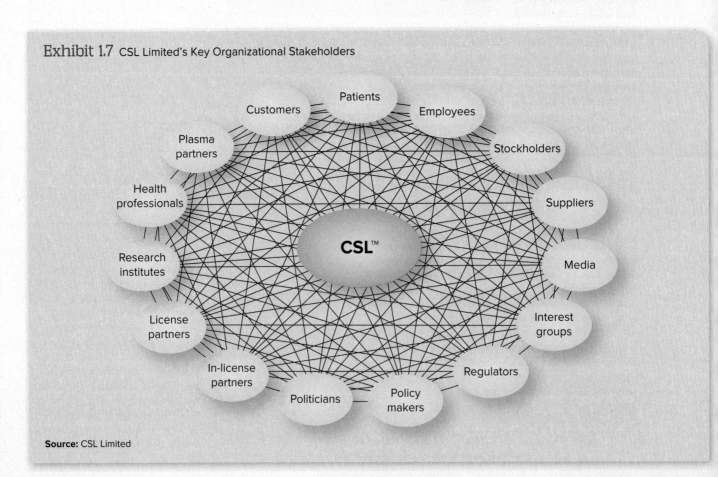

Exhibit 1.7 CSL Limited's Key Organizational Stakeholders

Source: CSL Limited

organization's environment, the organization's culture, and the personal values of the corporate board and CEO.

Values, Ethics, and Corporate Social Responsibility The stakeholder perspective provides valuable details about features of the external environment that are missing from the open systems perspective. Equally important, the stakeholder perspective incorporates values, ethics, and corporate social responsibility into the organizational effectiveness equation. As mentioned, personal values influence how corporate boards and CEOs allocate organizational resources to stakeholders.[79] **Values** are relatively stable, evaluative beliefs that guide our preferences for outcomes or courses of action in a variety of situations.[80] Values help us know what is right or wrong, or good or bad, in the world. Chapter 2 explains how values anchor our thoughts and to some extent motivate our actions.

Although values exist within individuals, groups of people often hold similar values, so we tend to ascribe these *shared values* to the team, department, organization, profession, or entire society. For example, Chapter 13 discusses the importance and dynamics of organizational culture, which includes shared values across the company. Many firms strive to become values-driven organizations, whereby employee decisions and behavior are guided mainly by the collective values identified as critical to the organization's success.[81]

By focusing on values, the stakeholder perspective also highlights the importance of ethics and corporate social responsibility. In fact, the stakeholder perspective emerged out of earlier writing on those two topics. **Ethics** refers to the study of moral principles or values that determine whether actions are right or wrong and outcomes are good or bad. We rely on our ethical values to determine "the right thing to do." Ethical behavior is driven by the moral principles we use to make decisions. These moral principles represent fundamental values. One recent survey of 7,700 employed Millennials in 29 countries reported that 87 percent believe "the success of a business should be measured in terms of more than just its financial performance." However, only 58 percent of them believe that businesses "behave in an ethical manner."[82] Chapter 2 discusses the main influences on ethical decisions and behavior in the workplace.

Corporate social responsibility (CSR) consists of organizational activities intended to benefit society and the environment beyond the firm's immediate financial interests or legal obligations.[83] It is the view that companies have a contract with society, in which they must serve stakeholders beyond stockholders and customers. In some situations, the interests of the firm's stockholders should be secondary to those of other stakeholders.[84] As part of CSR, many companies have adopted the triple-bottom-line philosophy: They try to support or "earn positive returns" in the economic, social, and environmental spheres of sustainability. Firms that adopt the triple bottom line aim to survive and be profitable in the marketplace (economic), but they also intend to maintain or improve conditions for society (social) as well as the physical environment.[85]

Not everyone agrees that organizations need to cater to a wide variety of stakeholders. Many years ago, economist Milton Friedman pronounced that "there is one and only one social responsibility of business—to use its resources and engage in activities designed to increase its profits."[87] Friedman is highly respected for developing economic

> Corporate social responsibility is the view that companies have a contract with society, in which they must serve stakeholders beyond stockholders and customers.

High Expectations for Corporate Social Responsibility[86]

89% of more than 2,000 executives surveyed say companies have a moral responsibility to address societal and environmental issues that go beyond legal requirements.

17% of 1,200 American consumers surveyed say they would not consider working for a company they believe is not socially responsible, even if they were well-qualified and the job pays well. (photo): ©CostinT/Getty Images

64% of 1,409 CEOs surveyed across 83 countries say that corporate social responsibility is core to their business (not just a stand-alone program).

80% of 18,150 adults surveyed globally say it is somewhat or very important for their own employer to be responsible to society and the environment.

theory, but few writers take this extreme view today. Almost all *Fortune* 500 companies publish sustainability reports, and the view among most executives is that corporate social responsibility is critically important to being competitive in today's marketplace. The emerging evidence is that companies with a positive CSR reputation tend to have better financial performance, more loyal employees (stronger organizational identification), and better relations with customers, job applicants, and other stakeholders.[88]

Connecting the Dots: An Integrative Model of Organizational Behavior

Open systems, organizational learning, high-performance work practices, and stakeholders represent the four perspectives of organizational effectiveness. Organizational effectiveness is the ultimate dependent variable in organizational behavior, so it is directly or indirectly predicted by all other OB variables. The

relationship between organizational effectiveness and other OB variables is shown in Exhibit 1.8. This diagram is an integrative road map for the field of organizational behavior, and for the structure of this book. It is a meta-model of the various OB topics and concepts, each of which has its own explanatory models. For instance, you will learn about employee motivation theories and practices in Chapter 5 and leadership theories and skills in Chapter 11. Exhibit 1.8 gives you a bird's-eye view of the book and its various topics, to see how they fit together.

As Exhibit 1.8 illustrates, individual inputs and processes influence individual outcomes, which in turn have a direct effect on the organization's effectiveness. For example, how well organizations transform inputs to outputs and satisfy key stakeholders is dependent on how well employees perform their jobs and make logical and creative decisions. Individual inputs, processes, and outcomes are identified in the two left-side boxes of our integrating OB model and are the center of attention in Part 2 of this book. After introducing a model of individual behavior and results, we will learn about personality and values—two of the most important individual characteristics—and later examine various individual processes, such as self-concept, perceptions, emotions, attitudes, motivation, and self-leadership.

Part 3 of this book directs our attention to team and interpersonal inputs, processes, and outcomes. These topics are found in the two boxes on the right side of Exhibit 1.8. The chapter on team dynamics (Chapter 7) offers an integrative model for that specific topic, which shows how team inputs (i.e., team composition, size, and other team characteristics) influence team processes (team development, cohesion, and others), which then affect team performance and other outcomes. Later chapters in Part 3 examine specific interpersonal and team processes listed in Exhibit 1.8, including communication, power and influence, conflict, and leadership.

Exhibit 1.8 illustrates that team processes and outcomes affect individual processes and outcomes. As an example, employee personal well-being is partly affected by the mutual support received from team members and other coworkers. The opposite is also true; individual processes affect team and interpersonal dynamics in organizations.

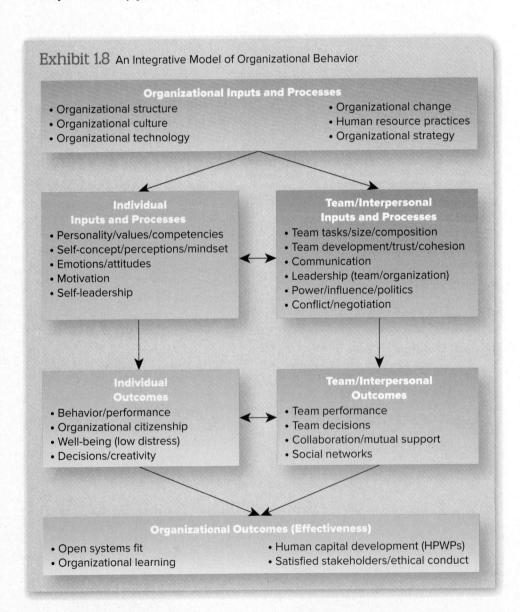

Exhibit 1.8 An Integrative Model of Organizational Behavior

Organizational Inputs and Processes
- Organizational structure
- Organizational culture
- Organizational technology
- Organizational change
- Human resource practices
- Organizational strategy

Individual Inputs and Processes
- Personality/values/competencies
- Self-concept/perceptions/mindset
- Emotions/attitudes
- Motivation
- Self-leadership

Team/Interpersonal Inputs and Processes
- Team tasks/size/composition
- Team development/trust/cohesion
- Communication
- Leadership (team/organization)
- Power/influence/politics
- Conflict/negotiation

Individual Outcomes
- Behavior/performance
- Organizational citizenship
- Well-being (low distress)
- Decisions/creativity

Team/Interpersonal Outcomes
- Team performance
- Team decisions
- Collaboration/mutual support
- Social networks

Organizational Outcomes (Effectiveness)
- Open systems fit
- Organizational learning
- Human capital development (HPWPs)
- Satisfied stakeholders/ethical conduct

For instance, we will learn that self-concept among individual team members influences the team's cohesion.

The top area of Exhibit 1.8 highlights the macro-level influence of organizational inputs and processes on both teams and individuals. These organizational-level variables are mainly discussed in Part 4, including organizational structure, organizational culture, and organizational change. However, we also will refer to human resource practices, information systems, and additional organizational-level variables throughout this book where they have a known effect on individual, interpersonal, and team dynamics.

THE JOURNEY BEGINS

This chapter gives you some background about the field of organizational behavior. But it's only the beginning of our journey. Throughout this book, we will challenge you to learn new ways of thinking about how people work in and around organizations. We begin this process in Chapter 2 by presenting a basic model of individual behavior, then introducing over the next few chapters various stable and mercurial characteristics of individuals that relate to elements of the individual behavior model. Next, this book moves to the team level of analysis. We examine a model of team effectiveness and specific features of high-performance teams. We also look at decision making and creativity, communication, power and influence, conflict, and leadership. Finally, we shift our focus to the organizational level of analysis, where the topics of organizational structure, organizational culture, and organizational change are examined in detail.

Study Checklist

Connect® Management is available for *M Organizational Behavior.* Additional resources include:

✓ Interactive Applications:
- **Case Analysis:** Apply concepts within the context of a real-world situation.
- **Drag and Drop:** Work through an interactive example to test your knowledge of the concepts.
- **Video Case:** See management in action through interactive videos.

✓ **SmartBook™**—SmartBook is the first and only adaptive reading experience available today. Distinguishing what you know from what you don't, and honing in on concepts you are most likely to forget, SmartBook personalizes content for you in a continuously adapting reading experience. Reading is no longer a passive and linear experience, but an engaging and dynamic one where you are more likely to master and retain important concepts and go to class better prepared.

©Natthawat Jamnapa/123RF

Notes

1. F. Manjoo and J. Caplan, "Apple Nation," *Fast Company*, no. 147 (2010): 69–76; R. L. Brandt, *One Click: Jeff Bezos and the Rise of Amazon.com* (New York: Portfolio/Penguin, 2011); "World's Most Admired Companies," *Fortune* (Time, Inc., February 16, 2017), http://beta.fortune.com/worlds-most-admired-companies/ (accessed February 27, 2017).

2. "World's Most Admired Companies," *Fortune* (Time, Inc., February 16, 2017), http://fortune.com/worlds-most-admired-companies/ (accessed June 18, 2017).

3. M. Warner, "Organizational Behavior Revisited," *Human Relations* 47 (1994): 1151–66; R. Westwood and S. Clegg, "The Discourse of Organization Studies: Dissensus, Politics, and Paradigms," in *Debating Organization: Point-Counterpoint in Organization Studies*, ed. R. Westwood and S. Clegg (Malden, MA: Wiley-Blackwell, 2003), 1–42.

4. R. N. Stern and S. R. Barley, "Organizations as Social Systems: Organization Theory's Neglected Mandate," *Administrative Science Quarterly* 41 (1996): 146–62; D. Katz and R. L. Kahn, *The Social Psychology of Organizations* (New York: Wiley, 1966), chap. 2.

5. L. E. Greiner, "A Recent History of Organizational Behavior," in *Organizational Behavior*, ed. S. Kerr (Columbus, OH: Grid, 1979), 3–14; J. Micklethwait and A. Wooldridge, *The Company: A Short History of a Revolutionary Idea* (New York: Random House, 2003).

6. T. Lawson, "The Nature of the Firm and Peculiarities of the Corporation," *Cambridge Journal of Economics* 39, no. 1 (2015): 1–32.

7. B. Schlender, "The Three Faces of Steve," *Fortune* (November 9, 1998): 96–101.

8. "A Field Is Born," *Harvard Business Review* 86, no. 7/8 (2008): 164; P. R. Lawrence, "The Key Job Design Problem Is Still Taylorism," *Journal of Organizational Behavior* 31, no. 2/3 (2010): 412–21; L. W. Porter and B. Schneider, "What Was, What Is, and What May Be in OP/OB," *Annual Review of Organizational Psychology and Organizational Behavior* 1, no. 1 (2014): 1–21.

9. T. Takala, "Plato on Leadership," *Journal of Business Ethics* 17 (1998): 785-98; J. A. Fernandez, "The Gentleman's Code of Confucius: Leadership by Values," *Organizational Dynamics* 33, no. 1 (2004): 21-31; A. M. Blake and J. L. Moseley, "Frederick Winslow Taylor: One Hundred Years of Managerial Insight," *International Journal of Management* 28, no. 4 (2011): 346-53; J. W. Stutje, ed., *Charismatic Leadership and Social Movements: The Revolutionary Power of Ordinary Men and Women,* International Studies in Social History (New York: Berghahn Books, 2012).

10. C. D. Wrege, "Solving Mayo's Mystery: The First Complete Account of the Origin of the Hawthorne Studies—the Forgotten Contributions of C. E. Snow and H. Hibarger" (paper presented at the Academy of Management Proceedings, August 1976), 12-16; P. Graham, ed., *Mary Parker Follett: Prophet of Management* (Boston: Harvard Business School Press, 1995); J. H. Smith, "The Enduring Legacy of Elton Mayo," *Human Relations* 51, no. 3 (1998): 221-49; E. O'Connor, "Minding the Workers: The Meaning of 'Human' and 'Human Relations' in Elton Mayo," *Organization* 6, no. 2 (1999): 223-46.

11. The extent to which OB influences career success depends on course pedagogy as well as the practical value of the OB concepts covered in the course. In fact, OB scholars have an ongoing debate about the practical relevance of OB research. See, for example: J. P. Walsh et al., "On the Relationship between Research and Practice: Debate and Reflections," *Journal of Management Inquiry* 16, no. 2 (2007): 128-54; R. Gulati, "Tent Poles, Tribalism, and Boundary Spanning: The Rigor-Relevance Debate in Management Research," *Academy of Management Journal* 50, no. 4 (2007): 775-82; J. Pearce and L. Huang, "The Decreasing Value of Our Research to Management Education," *Academy of Management Learning & Education* 11, no. 2 (2012): 247-62; J. M. Bartunek and S. L. Rynes, "Academics and Practitioners Are Alike and Unlike: The Paradoxes of Academic–Practitioner Relationships," *Journal of Management* 40, no. 5 (2014): 1181-201; N. Butler, H. Delaney, and S. Spoelstra, "Problematizing 'Relevance' in the Business School: The Case of Leadership Studies," *British Journal of Management* 26, no. 4 (2015): 731-44.

12. P. R. Lawrence and N. Nohria, *Driven: How Human Nature Shapes Our Choices* (San Francisco: Jossey-Bass, 2002).

13. S. L. Rynes et al., "Behavioral Coursework in Business Education: Growing Evidence of a Legitimacy Crisis," *Academy of Management Learning & Education* 2, no. 3 (2003): 269-83; R. P. Singh and A. G. Schick, "Organizational Behavior: Where Does It Fit in Today's Management Curriculum?," *Journal of Education for Business* 82, no. 6 (2007): 349.

14. R. L. Priem and J. Rosenstein, "Is Organization Theory Obvious to Practitioners? A Test of One Established Theory," *Organization Science* 11, no. 5 (2000): 509-24. MBA students in the study performed much better than the other two groups.

15. R. S. Rubin and E. C. Dierdorff, "How Relevant Is the MBA? Assessing the Alignment of Required Curricula and Required Managerial Competencies," *Academy of Management Learning & Education* 8, no. 2 (2009): 208-24; Y. Baruch and O. Lavi-Steiner, "The Career Impact of Management Education from an Average-Ranked University: Human Capital Perspective," *Career Development International* 20, no. 3 (2015): 218-37.

16. M. S. Myers, *Every Employee a Manager* (New York: McGraw-Hill, 1970).

17. M. A. West et al., "Reducing Patient Mortality in Hospitals: The Role of Human Resource Management," *Journal of Organizational Behavior* 27, no. 7 (2006): 983-1002; A. Edmans, "The Link between Job Satisfaction and Firm Value, with Implications for Corporate Social Responsibility," *Academy of Management Perspectives* 26, no. 4 (2012): 1-19; A. M. Baluch, T. O. Salge, and E. P. Piening, "Untangling the Relationship between HRM and Hospital Performance: The Mediating Role of Attitudinal and Behavioural HR Outcomes," *The International Journal of Human Resource Management* 24, no. 16 (2013): 3038-61; I. S. Fulmer and R. E. Ployhart, "'Our Most Important Asset': A Multidisciplinary/Multilevel Review of Human Capital Valuation for Research and Practice," *Journal of Management* 40, no. 1 (2014): 161-92; D. C. Hambrick and T. J. Quigley, "Toward More Accurate Contextualization of the CEO Effect on Firm Performance," *Strategic Management Journal* 35, no. 4 (2014): 473-91.

18. J. T. Comeault and D. Wheeler, "Human Capital-Based Investment Criteria for Total Shareholder Returns," in *Pensions at Work: Socially Responsible Investment of Union-Based Pension Funds*, ed. J. Quarter, I. Carmichael, and S. Ryan (Toronto: University of Toronto Press, 2008); R. Barker et al., "Can Company-Fund Manager Meetings Convey Informational Benefits? Exploring the Rationalisation of Equity Investment Decision Making by UK Fund Managers," *Accounting, Organizations and Society* 37, no. 4 (2012): 207-22; S. Abhayawansa, M. Aleksanyan, and J. Bahtsevanoglou, "The Use of Intellectual Capital Information by Sell-Side Analysts in Company Valuation," *Accounting and Business Research* 45, no. 3 (2015): 279-306.

19. M. L. Tushman and P. Anderson, "Technological Discontinuities and Organizational Environments," *Administrative Science Quarterly* 31, no. 3 (1986): 439-65; I. McNeil, ed., *An Encyclopedia of the History of Technology* (New York: Routledge, 1990); H. C. Lucas, *The Search for Survival: Lessons from Disruptive Technologies* (Westport, CT: Praeger, 2012); E. Brynjolfsson and A. McAfee, *The Second Machine Age: Work, Progress, and Prosperity in a Time of Brilliant Technologies* (New York: Norton, 2014); M. A. Schilling, "Technology Shocks, Technological Collaboration, and Innovation Outcomes," *Organization Science* 26, no. 3 (2015): 668-86.

20. W. R. Scott, "Comparing Organizations: Empirical and Theoretical Issues," in *Studying Differences between Organizations: Comparative Approaches to Organizational Research, Research in the Sociology of Organizations*, vol. 26, ed. B. G. King et al. (Bingley, UK: Emerald Group Publishing Limited, 2009), 45-62; S. J. Miles and W. G. Mangold, "Employee Voice: Untapped Resource or Social Media Time Bomb?," *Business Horizons* 57, no. 3 (2014): 401-11; S. Brooks, "Does Personal Social Media Usage Affect Efficiency and Well-Being?," *Computers in Human Behavior* 46 (2015): 26-37; J. C. Pillet and K. D. A. Carillo, "Email-Free Collaboration: An Exploratory Study on the Formation of New Work Habits among Knowledge Workers," *International Journal of Information Management* 36, no. 1 (2016): 113-25.

21. Gagen MacDonald, *Internal Social Media—A Business Driver* (Chicago: Gagen MacDonald, 2012); Microsoft, *Microsoft Survey on Enterprise Social Use and Perceptions* (Seattle, WA: Microsoft, 2013); Spherion, *Emerging Workforce Study* (Atlanta: Spherion, 2015); CareerBuilder, "Number of Employers Using Social Media to Screen Candidates Has Increased 500 Percent over the Last Decade," news release (Chicago: CareerBuilder, April 28, 2016).

22. Y. H. Ferguson and R. W. Mansbach, *Globalization: The Return of Borders to a Borderless World* (Abingdon, UK: Routledge, 2012). The early history of globalization is discussed in K. Moore and D. C. Lewis, *The Origins of Globalization* (Hoboken, NJ: Taylor and Francis, 2009). Five views of globalization and the effects of technology on globalization are discussed in R. Kwon, "What Factors Matter for Trade at the Global Level? Testing Five Approaches to Globalization, 1820-2007," *International Journal of Comparative Sociology* 54, no. 5/6 (2013): 391-419.

23. The ongoing debate regarding the advantages and disadvantages of globalization is discussed in M. F. Guillén, "Is Globalization Civilizing, Destructive or Feeble? A Critique of Five Key Debates in the Social Science Literature," *Annual Review of Sociology* 27 (2001): 235–60; J. Bhagwati, *In Defense of Globalization* (New York: Oxford University Press, 2004); M. Wolf, *Why Globalization Works* (New Haven, CT: Yale University Press, 2004).

24. E. Greenblatt, "Work/Life Balance: Wisdom or Whining," *Organizational Dynamics* 31, no. 2 (2002): 177–93; W. G. Bennis and R. J. Thomas, *Geeks and Geezers* (Boston: Harvard Business School Press, 2002), 74–79.

25. T. L. Johns, "The Third Wave of Virtual Work," *Harvard Business Review* 91, no. 1 (2013): 66–73.

26. J. M. Jones, "In U.S., Telecommuting for Work Climbs to 37%," news release (Washington, DC: Gallup, August 19, 2015); U.S. Bureau of Labor Statistics, "American Time Use Survey—2014 Results," news release (Washington, DC: U.S. Department of Labor, June 24, 2015).

27. E. J. Hill et al., "Workplace Flexibility, Work Hours, and Work–Life Conflict: Finding an Extra Day or Two," *Journal of Family Psychology* 24, no. 3 (2010): 349–58; M. C. Noonan and J. L. Glass, "The Hard Truth about Telecommuting," *Monthly Labor Review* 135, no. 6 (2012): 38–45; B. H. Martin and R. MacDonnell, "Is Telework Effective for Organizations?," *Management Research Review* 35, no. 7 (2012): 602–16; T. D. Allen, T. D. Golden, and K. M. Shockley, "How Effective Is Telecommuting? Assessing the Status of Our Scientific Findings," *Psychological Science in the Public Interest* 16, no. 2 (2015): 40–68; N. Bloom et al., "Does Working from Home Work? Evidence from a Chinese Experiment," *The Quarterly Journal of Economics* 130, no. 1 (2015): 165–218; R. S. Gajendran, D. A. Harrison, and K. Delaney-Klinger, "Are Telecommuters Remotely Good Citizens? Unpacking Telecommuting's Effects on Performance Via I-Deals and Job Resources," *Personnel Psychology* 68, no. 2 (2015): 353–93.

28. D. Meinert, "Make Telecommuting Pay Off," *HR Magazine*, June 2011, 33; M. McQuigge, "A Panacea for Some, Working from Home Still a Tough Sell for Some Employers," *Canadian Press* (Toronto), June 26, 2013; Aetna, "Teleworking on the Rise, Saving Costs and the Environment," May 2015, https://news.aetna.com/2015/05/teleworking-rise-saving-costs-environment/ (accessed March 4, 2016).

29. C. A. Bartel, A. Wrzesniewski, and B. M. Wiesenfeld, "Knowing Where You Stand: Physical Isolation, Perceived Respect, and Organizational Identification among Virtual Employees," *Organization Science* 23, no. 3 (2011): 743–57; E. E. Kossek, R. J. Thompson, and B. A. Lautsch, "Balanced Workplace Flexibility: Avoiding the Traps," *California Management Review* 57, no. 4 (2015): 5–25.

30. T. A. O'Neill, L. A. Hambley, and G. S. Chatellier, "Cyberslacking, Engagement, and Personality in Distributed Work Environments," *Computers in Human Behavior* 40 (2014): 152–60; N. W. Van Yperen, E. F. Rietzschel, and K. M. M. De Jonge, "Blended Working: For Whom It May (Not) Work," *PLoS ONE* 9, no. 7 (2014): e102921; D. Karis, D. Wildman, and A. Mané, "Improving Remote Collaboration with Video Conferencing and Video Portals," *Human–Computer Interaction* 31, no. 1 (2016): 1–58.

31. D. A. Harrison et al., "Time, Teams, and Task Performance: Changing Effects of Surface- and Deep-Level Diversity on Group Functioning," *Academy of Management Journal* 45, no. 5 (2002): 1029–46; W. J. Casper, J. H. Wayne, and J. G. Manegold, "Who Will We Recruit? Targeting Deep- and Surface-Level Diversity with Human Resource Policy Advertising," *Human Resource Management* 52, no. 3 (2013): 311–32; J. E. Mathieu et al., "A Review and Integration of Team Composition Models: Moving toward a Dynamic and Temporal Framework," *Journal of Management* 40, no. 1 (2014): 130–60.

32. J. M. Ortman and C. E. Guarneri, *United States Population Projections: 2000 to 2050* (Washington, DC: U.S. Census Bureau, December 11, 2009); D'V. Cohn, *Future Immigration Will Change the Face of America by 2065*, (Washington, DC: Pew Research Center, October 5, 2015); U.S. Census Bureau, "Quickfacts" (Washington, DC: U.S. Census Bureau, 2016), https://www.census.gov/quickfacts (accessed June 18, 2017).

33. J. Qin, N. Muenjohn, and P. Chhetri, "A Review of Diversity Conceptualizations: Variety, Trends, and a Framework," *Human Resource Development Review* 13, no. 2 (2014): 133–57.

34. M. H. Davis, S. Capobianco, and L. A. Kraus, "Gender Differences in Responding to Conflict in the Workplace: Evidence from a Large Sample of Working Adults," *Sex Roles* 63, no. 7 (2010): 500–14; J. L. Locke, *Duels and Duets: Why Men and Women Talk So Differently* (New York: Cambridge University Press, 2011); R. Friesdorf, P. Conway, and B. Gawronski, "Gender Differences in Responses to Moral Dilemmas: A Process Dissociation Analysis," *Personality and Social Psychology Bulletin* 41, no. 5 (2015): 696–713.

35. E. Bolland and C. Lopes, *Generations and Work* (New York: Palgrave Macmillan, 2014); P. Taylor, *The Next America: Boomers, Millennials, and the Looming Generational Showdown* (New York: PublicAffairs, 2014); J. Bristow, *Baby Boomers and Generational Conflict* (London: Palgrave Macmillan, 2015).

36. U.S. Bureau of Labor Statistics, "Labor Force Statistics from the Current Population Survey," *Division of Labor Force Statistics* (Washington, D.C.: U.S. Bureau of Labor Statistics, February 8, 2016), https://www.bls.gov/cps/cpsaat03.htm (accessed June 18, 2017).

37. E. Parry and P. Urwin, "Generational Differences in Work Values: A Review of Theory and Evidence," *International Journal of Management Reviews* 13 (2011): 79–96; D. T. A. M. Kooij et al., "Age and Work-Related Motives: Results of a Meta-Analysis," *Journal of Organizational Behavior* 32, no. 2 (2011): 197–225.

38. M.-E. Roberge and R. van Dick, "Recognizing the Benefits of Diversity: When and How Does Diversity Increase Group Performance?," *Human Resource Management Review* 20, no. 4 (2010): 295–308; M. Singal, "The Business Case for Diversity Management in the Hospitality Industry," *International Journal of Hospitality Management* 40 (2014): 10–19; C.-M. Lu et al., "Effect of Diversity on Human Resource Management and Organizational Performance," *Journal of Business Research* 68, no. 4 (2015): 857–61; Y. Zhang and M.-Y. Huai, "Diverse Work Groups and Employee Performance: The Role of Communication Ties," *Small Group Research* 47, no. 1 (2016): 28–57.

39. D. Porras, D. Psihountas, and M. Griswold, "The Long-Term Performance of Diverse Firms," *International Journal of Diversity* 6, no. 1 (2006): 25–34; R. A. Weigand, "Organizational Diversity, Profits and Returns in U.S. Firms," *Problems & Perspectives in Management* 5, no. 3 (2007): 69–83.

40. T. Kochan et al., "The Effects of Diversity on Business Performance: Report of the Diversity Research Network," *Human Resource Management* 42 (2003): 3–21; S. T. Bell et al., "Getting Specific about Demographic Diversity Variable and Team Performance Relationships: A Meta-Analysis," *Journal of Management* 37, no. 3 (2011): 709–43; S. M. B. Thatcher and P. C. Patel, "Group Faultlines: A Review, Integration, and Guide to Future Research," *Journal of Management* 38, no. 4 (2012): 969–1009; C. Ozgen et al., "Does Cultural Diversity of Migrant Employees Affect Innovation?," *International Migration Review* 48 (2014): S377–S416.

41. *Mastercard Diversity and Inclusion* (Purchase, NY: MasterCard, July 24, 2014); "Top 10 Employers Have More Women, Minority Leaders," *Diversity Inc.*, April 19, 2016; "Diversity in the Workplace," *About MasterCard*, 2016, www.diversityinc.com/mastercard-worldwide-2015/ (accessed July 12, 2016).

42. Most of these anchors are mentioned in J. D. Thompson, "On Building an Administrative Science," *Administrative Science Quarterly* 1, no. 1 (1956): 102–11.

43. This anchor has a colorful history dating back to critiques of business schools in the 1950s. Soon after, systematic research became a mantra for many respected scholars. See, for example, J. D. Thompson, "On Building an Administrative Science," *Administrative Science Quarterly* 1, no. 1 (1956): 102–11.

44. J. Pfeffer and R. I. Sutton, *Hard Facts, Dangerous Half-Truths, and Total Nonsense* (Boston: Harvard Business School Press, 2006); D. M. Rousseau and S. McCarthy, "Educating Managers from an Evidence-Based Perspective," *Academy of Management Learning & Education* 6, no. 1 (2007): 84–101; R. B. Briner and D. M. Rousseau, "Evidence-Based I–O Psychology: Not There Yet," *Industrial and Organizational Psychology* 4, no. 1 (2011): 3–22.

45. J. Pfeffer and R. I. Sutton, *Hard Facts, Dangerous Half-Truths, and Total Nonsense* (Boston: Harvard Business School Press, 2006).

46. M. N. Zald, "More Fragmentation? Unfinished Business in Linking the Social Sciences and the Humanities," *Administrative Science Quarterly* 41 (1996): 251–61; C. Heath and S. B. Sitkin, "Big-B versus Big-O: What Is Organizational About Organizational Behavior?," *Journal of Organizational Behavior* 22 (2001): 43–58; C. Oswick, P. Fleming, and G. Hanlon, "From Borrowing to Blending: Rethinking the Processes of Organizational Theory Building," *Academy of Management Review* 36, no. 2 (2011): 318–37.

47. C. M. Christensen and M. E. Raynor, "Why Hard-Nosed Executives Should Care about Management Theory," *Harvard Business Review* (2003): 66–74; C. E. J. Härtel and J. M. O'Connor, "Contextualizing Research: Putting Context Back into Organizational Behavior Research," *Journal of Management & Organization* 20, no. 4 (2014): 417–22. For an excellent critique of the "one best way" approach in early management scholarship, see P. F. Drucker, "Management's New Paradigms," *Forbes* (1998): 152–77.

48. H. L. Tosi and J. W. Slocum Jr., "Contingency Theory: Some Suggested Directions," *Journal of Management* 10 (1984): 9–26.

49. D. M. Rousseau and R. J. House, "Meso Organizational Behavior: Avoiding Three Fundamental Biases," in *Trends in Organizational Behavior*, ed. C. L. Cooper and D. M. Rousseau (Chichester, UK: Wiley, 1994), 13–30.

50. S. A. Mohrman, C. B. Gibson, and A. M. Mohrman Jr., "Doing Research That Is Useful to Practice: A Model and Empirical Exploration," *Academy of Management Journal* 44 (2001): 357–75; J. P. Walsh et al., "On the Relationship between Research and Practice," *Journal of Management Inquiry* 16, no. 2 (June 2007): 128–54. Similarly, in 1961, Harvard business professor Fritz Roethlisberger proposed that the field of OB is concerned with human behavior "from the points of view of both (a) its determination . . . and (b) its improvement." See P. B. Vaill, "F. J. Roethlisberger and the Elusive Phenomena of Organizational Behavior," *Journal of Management Education* 31, no. 3 (2007): 321–38.

51. R. H. Hall, "Effectiveness Theory and Organizational Effectiveness," *Journal of Applied Behavioral Science* 16, no. 4 (1980): 536–45; K. Cameron, "Organizational Effectiveness: Its Demise and Re-Emergence through Positive Organizational Scholarship," in *Great Minds in Management*, ed. K. G. Smith and M. A. Hitt (New York: Oxford University Press, 2005), 304–30.

52. A. A. Amirkhanyan, H. J. Kim, and K. T. Lambright, "The Performance Puzzle: Understanding the Factors Influencing Alternative Dimensions and Views of Performance," *Journal of Public Administration Research and Theory* 24, no. 1 (2014): 1–34.

53. Chester Barnard gives one of the earliest descriptions of organizations as systems interacting with external environments and that are composed of subsystems. See C. Barnard, *The Functions of the Executive* (Cambridge, MA: Harvard University Press, 1938), esp. chap. 6. Also see F. E. Kast and J. E. Rosenzweig, "General Systems Theory: Applications for Organization and Management," *Academy of Management Journal* 15, no. 4 (1972): 447–65; P. M. Senge, *The Fifth Discipline: The Art and Practice of the Learning Organization* (New York: Doubleday Currency, 1990); G. Morgan, *Images of Organization*, 2nd ed. (Newbury Park, CA: Sage, 1996); A. de Geus, *The Living Company* (Boston: Harvard Business School Press, 1997).

54. D. P. Ashmos and G. P. Huber, "The Systems Paradigm in Organization Theory: Correcting the Record and Suggesting the Future," *Academy of Management Review* 12, no. 4 (1987): 607–21.

55. D. Katz and R. L. Kahn, *The Social Psychology of Organizations* (New York: Wiley, 1966), chap. 2; J. McCann, "Organizational Effectiveness: Changing Concepts for Changing Environments," *Human Resource Planning* 27, no. 1 (2004): 42–50; A. H. Van de Ven, M. Ganco, and C. R. Hinings, "Returning to the Frontier of Contingency Theory of Organizational and Institutional Designs," *Academy of Management Annals* 7, no. 1 (2013): 391–438.

56. D. Dahlhoff, "Why Target's Canadian Expansion Failed," *Harvard Business Review* (2015), https://hbr.org/2015/01/why-targets-canadian-expansion-failed; "Brian Cornell Addresses Questions About Exiting Canada," *A Bullseye View* (Minneapolis: Target, January 15, 2015), https://corporate.target.com/article/2015/01/qa-brian-cornell-target-exits-canada (accessed February 28, 2017).

57. C. Ostroff and N. Schmitt, "Configurations of Organizational Effectiveness and Efficiency," *Academy of Management Journal* 36, no. 6 (1993): 1345–61; R. Andrews and T. Entwistle, "Four Faces of Public Service Efficiency," *Public Management Review* 15, no. 2 (2013): 246–64; R. M. Walker, J. Chen, and D. Aravind, "Management Innovation and Firm Performance: An Integration of Research Findings," *European Management Journal* 33, no. 5 (2015): 407–22.

58. K. E. Weick, *The Social Psychology of Organizing* (Reading, MA: Addison-Wesley, 1979); S. Brusoni and A. Prencipe, "Managing Knowledge in Loosely Coupled Networks: Exploring the Links between Product and Knowledge Dynamics," *Journal of Management Studies* 38, no. 7 (2001): 1019–35.

59. T. A. Stewart, *Intellectual Capital: The New Wealth of Organizations* (New York: Currency/Doubleday, 1997); L.-C. Hsu and C.-H. Wang, "Clarifying the Effect of Intellectual Capital on Performance: The Mediating Role of Dynamic Capability," *British Journal of Management* (2011): 179–205; A. L. Mention and N. Bontis, "Intellectual Capital and Performance within the Banking Sector of Luxembourg and Belgium," *Journal of Intellectual Capital* 14, no. 2 (2013): 286–309; K. Asiaei and R. Jusoh, "A Multidimensional View of Intellectual Capital: The Impact on Organizational Performance," *Management Decision* 53, no. 3 (2015): 668–97.

60. R. Slater, *Jack Welch & the G.E. Way: Management Insights and Leadership Secrets of the Legendary CEO* (New York: McGraw-Hill, 1999).

61. J. Barney, "Firm Resources and Sustained Competitive Advantage," *Journal of Management* 17, no. 1 (1991): 99–120.

62. J. P. Hausknecht and J. A. Holwerda, "When Does Employee Turnover Matter? Dynamic Member Configurations, Productive Capacity, and Collective Performance," *Organization Science* 24, no. 1 (2013): 210-25.

63. P. Cleary, "An Empirical Investigation of the Impact of Management Accounting on Structural Capital and Business Performance," *Journal of Intellectual Capital* 16, no. 3 (2015): 566-86; L. M. Gogan, D. C. Duran, and A. Draghici, "Structural Capital—A Proposed Measurement Model," *Procedia Economics and Finance* 23 (2015): 1139-46.

64. Some organizational learning researchers use the label "social capital" instead of "relationship capital." Social capital is discussed later in this book as the goodwill and resulting resources shared among members in a social network. The two concepts may be identical (as those writers suggest). However, we continue to use "relationship capital" for intellectual capital because social capital typically refers to individual relationships whereas relationship capital also includes value not explicit in social capital, such as the organization's goodwill and brand value.

65. G. Huber, "Organizational Learning: The Contributing Processes and Literature," *Organizational Science* 2 (1991): 88-115; D. A. Garvin, *Learning in Action: A Guide to Putting the Learning Organization to Work* (Boston: Harvard Business School Press, 2000); H. Shipton, "Cohesion or Confusion? Towards a Typology for Organizational Learning Research," *International Journal of Management Reviews* 8, no. 4 (2006): 233-52; D. Jiménez-Jiménez and J. G. Cegarra-Navarro, "The Performance Effect of Organizational Learning and Market Orientation," *Industrial Marketing Management* 36, no. 6 (2007): 694-708. One recent study suggests that these organizational learning processes aren't always beneficial because they may be more costly or burdensome than the value they create. See S. S. Levine and M. J. Prietula, "How Knowledge Transfer Impacts Performance: A Multilevel Model of Benefits and Liabilities," *Organization Science* 23, no. 6 (2012): 1748-66.

66. B. van den Hooff and M. Huysman, "Managing Knowledge Sharing: Emergent and Engineering Approaches," *Information & Management* 46, no. 1 (2009): 1-8.

67. M. Rodgers, "Culture Club: Ambrosia Humphrey—Hootsuite," *Perch Communications Blog*, September 9, 2013, http://perch.co/blog/culture-club-ambrosia-humphrey-hootsuite/; R. Holmes, "Innovate or Die: 3 Ways to Stay Ahead of the Curve," *HootSuite Blog*, September 13, 2013, http://blog.hootsuite.com/innovate-or-die-hackathon/; Q. Casey, "Buying the Company to Acquire the Talent," *Vancouver Sun*, December 17, 2013.

68. Learning orientation differs somewhat from "learning goal orientation," as well from the educational psychology meaning of this phrase. See G. T. M. Hult, R. F. Hurley, and G. A. Knight, "Innovativeness: Its Antecedents and Impact on Business Performance," *Industrial Marketing Management* 33, no. 5 (2004): 429-38; J. C. Real, J. L. Roldán, and A. Leal, "From Entrepreneurial Orientation and Learning Orientation to Business Performance: Analysing the Mediating Role of Organizational Learning and the Moderating Effects of Organizational Size," *British Journal of Management* 25, no. 2 (2014): 186-208; K. Tajeddini, "Analyzing the Influence of Learning Orientation and Innovativeness on Performance of Public Organizations: The Case of Iran," *Journal of Management Development* 35, no. 2 (2016): 134-53.

69. M. N. Wexler, "Organizational Memory and Intellectual Capital," *Journal of Intellectual Capital* 3, no. 4 (2002): 393-414; M. Fiedler and I. Welpe, "How Do Organizations Remember? The Influence of Organizational Structure on Organizational Memory," *Organization Studies* 31, no. 4 (2010): 381-407.

70. M. E. McGill and J. W. Slocum Jr., "Unlearn the Organization," *Organizational Dynamics* 22, no. 2 (1993): 67-79; A. E. Akgün, G. S. Lynn, and J. C. Byrne, "Antecedents and Consequences of Unlearning in New Product Development Teams," *Journal of Product Innovation Management* 23 (2006): 73-88.

71. L. Sels et al., "Unravelling the HRM-Performance Link: Value-Creating and Cost-Increasing Effects of Small Business HRM," *Journal of Management Studies* 43, no. 2 (2006): 319-42; G. S. Benson, S. M. Young, and E. E. Lawler III, "High-Involvement Work Practices and Analysts' Forecasts of Corporate Earnings," *Human Resource Management* 45, no. 4 (2006): 519-37; J. Combs et al., "How Much Do High-Performance Work Practices Matter? A Meta-Analysis of Their Effects on Organizational Performance," *Personnel Psychology* 59, no. 3 (2006): 501-28; G. A. Fine and T. Hallett, "Group Cultures and the Everyday Life of Organizations: Interaction Orders and Meso-Analysis," *Organization Studies* (2014): 1-20.

72. E. E. Lawler III, S. A. Mohrman, and G. E. Ledford Jr., *Strategies for High Performance Organizations* (San Francisco: Jossey-Bass, 1998); P. Tharenou, A. M. Saks, and C. Moore, "A Review and Critique of Research on Training and Organizational-Level Outcomes," *Human Resource Management Review* 17, no. 3 (2007): 251-73; D. Y. Jeong and M. Choi, "The Impact of High-Performance Work Systems on Firm Performance: The Moderating Effects of the Human Resource Function's Influence," *Journal of Management & Organization* 22, no. 3 (May 2016).

73. M. Subramony, "A Meta-Analytic Investigation of the Relationship between HRM Bundles and Firm Performance," *Human Resource Management* 48, no. 5 (2009): 745-68.

74. OECD, *Skills Matter: Further Results from the Survey of Adult Skills*, OECD Skills Studies (Paris: OECD Publishing, June 2016). Also from Annex A, spreadsheet data file associated with tables in the OECD publication.

75. J. Camps and R. Luna-Arocas, "A Matter of Learning: How Human Resources Affect Organizational Performance," *British Journal of Management* 23, no. 1 (2012): 1-21; R. R. Kehoe and P. M. Wright, "The Impact of High-Performance Human Resource Practices on Employees' Attitudes and Behaviors," *Journal of Management* 39, no. 2 (2013): 366-91; B. Fabi, R. Lacoursière, and L. Raymond, "Impact of High-Performance Work Systems on Job Satisfaction, Organizational Commitment, and Intention to Quit in Canadian Organizations," *International Journal of Manpower* 36, no. 5 (2015): 772-90.

76. J. Tullberg, "Stakeholder Theory: Some Revisionist Suggestions," *The Journal of Socio-Economics* 42 (2013): 127-35.

77. R. E. Freeman, J. S. Harrison, and A. C. Wicks, *Managing for Stakeholders: Survival, Reputation, and Success* (New Haven, CT: Yale University Press, 2007); B. L. Parmar et al., "Stakeholder Theory: The State of the Art," *Academy of Management Annals* 4, no. 1 (2010): 403-45; S. Sachs and E. Rühli, *Stakeholders Matter: A New Paradigm for Strategy in Society* (Cambridge, UK: Cambridge University Press, 2011).

78. A. Santana, "Three Elements of Stakeholder Legitimacy," *Journal of Business Ethics* 105, no. 2 (2012): 257-65; D. Crilly and P. Sloan, "Autonomy or Control? Organizational Architecture and Corporate Attention to Stakeholders," *Organization Science* 25, no. 2 (2014): 339-55; M. Hall, Y. Millo, and E. Barman, "Who and What Really Counts? Stakeholder Prioritization and Accounting for Social Value," *Journal of Management Studies* 52, no. 7 (2015): 907-34; D. Weitzner and Y. Deutsch, "Understanding Motivation and Social Influence in Stakeholder Prioritization," *Organization Studies* 36, no. 10 (2015): 1337-60.

79. R. E. Freeman, A. C. Wicks, and B. Parmar, "Stakeholder Theory and 'the Corporate Objective Revisited,'" *Organization Science* 15, no. 3 (2004): 364–69; B. R. Agle et al., "Dialogue: Toward Superior Stakeholder Theory," *Business Ethics Quarterly* 18, no. 2 (2008): 153–90; R. B. Adams, A. N. Licht, and L. Sagiv, "Shareholders and Stakeholders: How Do Directors Decide?," *Strategic Management Journal* 32, no. 12 (2011): 1331–55.

80. B. M. Meglino and E. C. Ravlin, "Individual Values in Organizations: Concepts, Controversies, and Research," *Journal of Management* 24, no. 3 (1998): 351–89; A. Bardi and S. H. Schwartz, "Values and Behavior: Strength and Structure of Relations," *Personality and Social Psychology Bulletin* 29, no. 10 (2003): 1207–20; S. Hitlin and J. A. Pilavin, "Values: Reviving a Dormant Concept," *Annual Review of Sociology* 30 (2004): 359–93.

81. Some popular books that emphasize the importance of personal and organizational values include J. C. Collins and J. I. Porras, *Built to Last: Successful Habits of Visionary Companies* (London: Century, 1995); C. A. O'Reilly III and J. Pfeffer, *Hidden Value* (Cambridge, MA: Harvard Business School Press, 2000); J. Reiman, *The Story of Purpose: The Path to Creating a Brighter Brand, a Greater Company, and a Lasting Legacy* (Hoboken, NJ: Wiley, 2013); R. Barrett, *The Values-Driven Organization: Unleashing Human Potential for Performance and Profit* (New York: Routledge, 2014); R. E. Freeman and E. R. Auster, *Bridging the Values Gap: How Authentic Organizations Bring Values to Life* (Oakland, CA: Berrett-Koehler, 2015).

82. *The 2016 Deloitte Millennial Survey: Winning over the Next Generation of Leaders* (New York: Deloitte Touche Tohmatsu, January 2016).

83. M. van Marrewijk, "Concepts and Definitions of CSR and Corporate Sustainability: Between Agency and Communion," *Journal of Business Ethics* 44 (2003): 95–105; M. L. Barnett, "Stakeholder Influence Capacity and the Variability of Financial Returns to Corporate Social Responsibility," *Academy of Management Review* 32, no. 3 (2007): 794–816.

84. L. S. Paine, *Value Shift* (New York: McGraw-Hill, 2003); A. Mackey, T. B. Mackey, and J. B. Barney, "Corporate Social Responsibility and Firm Performance: Investor Preferences and Corporate Strategies," *Academy of Management Review* 32, no. 3 (2007): 817–35.

85. S. Zadek, *The Civil Corporation: The New Economy of Corporate Citizenship* (London: Earthscan, 2001); S. Hart and M. Milstein, "Creating Sustainable Value," *Academy of Management Executive* 17, no. 2 (2003): 56–69.

86. "Four in Ten (37%) Employees Rate Corporate Social Responsibility 'Very Important' When It Comes to Their Employer," news release (New York: Ipsos, June 25, 2013); J. Browne, R. Nuttall, and T. Stadlen, *Connect: How Companies Succeed by Engaging Radically with Society* (London: WH Allen, 2015); Aflac, *National Survey on Corporate Social Responsibility* (Columbus, GA: Aflac, November 12, 2016); PricewaterhouseCoopers, *19th Annual Global CEO Survey: Redefining Business Success in a Changing World* (New York: PwC, January 2016).

87. M. Friedman, *Capitalism and Freedom*, 40th Anniversary ed. (Chicago: University of Chicago Press, 2002), chap. 8; N. Vorster, "An Ethical Critique of Milton Friedman's Doctrine on Economics and Freedom," *Journal for the Study of Religions and Ideologies* 9, no. 26 (2010): 163–88.

88. A. B. Carroll and K. M. Shabana, "The Business Case for Corporate Social Responsibility: A Review of Concepts, Research and Practice," *International Journal of Management Reviews* 12, no. 1 (2010): 85–105; H. Aguinis and A. Glavas, "What We Know and Don't Know about Corporate Social Responsibility: A Review and Research Agenda," *Journal of Management* 38, no. 4 (2012): 932–68.

2 | Individual Behavior, Personality, and Values

Learning Objectives

After you read this chapter, you should be able to:

LO2-1 Describe the four factors that directly influence individual behavior and performance.

LO2-2 Summarize the five types of individual behavior in organizations.

LO2-3 Describe personality and discuss how the "Big Five" personality dimensions and four MBTI types relate to individual behavior in organizations.

LO2-4 Summarize Schwartz's model of individual values and discuss the conditions where values influence behavior.

LO2-5 Describe three ethical principles and discuss three factors that influence ethical behavior.

LO2-6 Describe five values commonly studied across cultures.

Getting hired at Bridgewater Associates—the world's largest hedge fund—is not a cakewalk. The process begins with applicants watching online videos depicting the culture and daily office life at the Westport, Connecticut, investment firm. Next, they spend two or three more hours completing four online assessments, including a popular measure of personality traits (MBTI). Applicants who pass the online selection process engage in a structured interview over the phone with consultants, who further assess the individual's character. Even after accepting Bridgewater's job offer, new recruits take a final two-hour personality test developed by the company. Bridgewater then uses the application data to produce the new hire's "baseball card"—a compact profile of his or her personality, abilities, culture fit, and performance. Bridgeport employees can view any coworker's profile on their phone or tablet using the firm's highly secure baseball card app.[1]

The hiring process at Bridgewater Associates is unusual. But what the hedge fund has in common with other organizations is its attempt to understand each job applicant's ability, motivation, personality, values, and other personal characteristics. These characteristics are central topics in this chapter. We begin by introducing the four direct drivers of individual behavior and performance that enable employees at Bridgewater Associates and other companies to provide peak performance. Next, we review the five types of individual behavior that represent the individual-level dependent variables found in most organizational behavior research. We then turn our attention to personality and values, which are the two relatively stable characteristics of individuals. Finally, this chapter presents the topics of ethical and cross-cultural values.

LO2-1 Describe the four factors that directly influence individual behavior and performance.

MARS MODEL OF INDIVIDUAL BEHAVIOR AND PERFORMANCE

For most of the past century, experts have investigated the direct predictors of individual behavior and performance.[2] One of the earliest formulas was *performance = person × situation*, where *person* includes individual characteristics and *situation* represents external influences on the individual's behavior. Another frequently mentioned formula is *performance = ability × motivation*.[3] Sometimes known as the "skill-and-will" model, this formula elaborates two specific characteristics within the person that influence individual performance. Some organizational studies use the *ability-motivation-opportunity (AMO)* model, which refers to the three variables but with a limited interpretation of the situation. Along with ability, motivation, and situation, researchers have more recently identified a fourth key direct predictor of individual behavior and performance: role perceptions (the individual's expected role obligations).[4]

Exhibit 2.1 illustrates these four variables—motivation, ability, role perceptions, and situational factors—which are represented by the acronym *MARS*.[5] All four factors are critical influences on an individual's voluntary behavior and performance; if any one of them is low in a given situation, the employee would perform the task poorly. For example, motivated salespeople with clear role perceptions and sufficient resources (situational factors) will not perform their jobs as well if they lack sales skills and related knowledge (ability). Motivation, ability, and role perceptions are clustered together in the model because they are located within the person. Situational factors are external to the individual but still affect his or her behavior and performance.[6] The four MARS variables are the direct predictors of employee performance, customer service, coworker collegiality, ethical behavior, and all other forms of voluntary behavior in the workplace. Let's look in more detail at each of the four factors in the MARS model.

Employee Motivation

Motivation represents the forces within a person that affect his or her direction, intensity, and persistence of voluntary behavior.[7] *Direction* refers to the path along which people steer their effort. In other words, motivation is goal-directed, not random. People have choices about what they are trying to achieve and at what level of quality, quantity, and so forth. They are motivated to arrive at work on time, finish a project a few hours early, or aim for many other targets.

The second element of motivation, called *intensity*, is the amount of effort allocated to the goal. Intensity is all about how much people push themselves to complete a task. Two employees might be motivated to finish their project a few hours earlier than expected (direction), but only one of them puts forth enough effort (intensity) to achieve this goal. The third element of motivation is *persistence*, which refers to the length of time that the individual continues to exert effort toward an objective. Employees sustain their effort until they reach their goal or give up beforehand.

To help remember these three elements of motivation, consider the metaphor of driving a car in which the thrust of the engine is your effort. Direction refers to where you steer the car, intensity is how much you put your foot down on the gas pedal, and persistence is for how long you drive toward your

motivation the forces within a person that affect his or her direction, intensity, and persistence of voluntary behavior

destination. Remember that motivation is a force that exists within individuals; it is not their actual behavior. Thus, direction, intensity, and persistence are cognitive (thoughts) and emotional conditions that directly cause us to move.

Ability

Employee abilities also make a difference in behavior and task performance. **Ability** includes both the natural aptitudes and the learned capabilities required to successfully complete a task. *Aptitudes* are the natural talents that help employees learn specific tasks more quickly and perform them better. For example, finger dexterity is an aptitude by which individuals learn more quickly and potentially achieve higher performance at picking up and handling small objects with their fingers. Employees with high finger dexterity are not necessarily better than others at first; rather, they usually learn the skill faster and eventually reach a higher level of performance. *Learned capabilities* are the physical and mental skills and knowledge you have acquired. They tend to wane over time when not in use. Aptitudes and

> I believe the real difference between success and failure in a corporation can be very often traced to the question of how well the organization brings out the great energies and talents of its people.[8]
>
> —Thomas J. Watson Jr., IBM's second CEO

learned capabilities (skills and knowledge) are the main elements of a broader concept called *competencies*, which are characteristics of a person that result in superior performance.[9]

The challenge is to match a person's abilities with the job's requirements because a good match tends to increase employee performance and well-being. One matching strategy is to select applicants who already demonstrate the required competencies. For example, companies ask applicants to perform work samples, provide references for checking their past performance, and complete various selection tests. A second strategy is to train employees who lack specific knowledge or skills needed for the job.[10] The third person–job matching strategy is to redesign the job so that employees are given tasks only within their current abilities. For example, a complex task might be simplified—some aspects of the work are transferred to others—so a new employee performs only tasks that he or she is currently able to perform. As the employee becomes more competent at these tasks, other tasks are added back into the job.

Role Perceptions

Along with motivation and ability, employees require accurate **role perceptions** to perform their jobs well. Role perceptions refer to how clearly people understand the job duties (roles) assigned to or expected of them. These perceptions range from

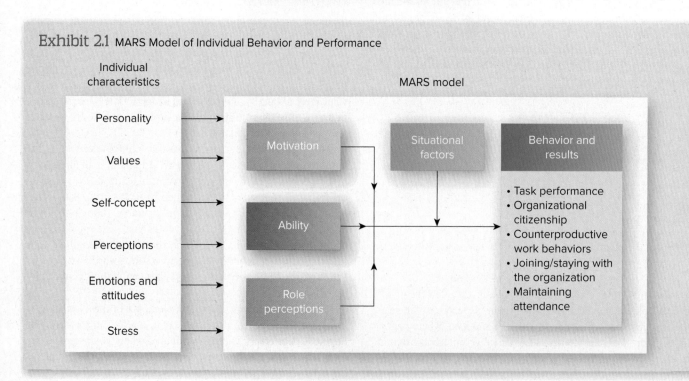

Exhibit 2.1 MARS Model of Individual Behavior and Performance

Mind the MARS Gap on Motivation, Ability, Role Perceptions, and Situational Factors[11]

60% of more than 13,000 employees surveyed across 34 countries say the skills gap is a real problem for their employer.

33% of 195,600 American employees surveyed are engaged at work (indicator of work motivation).

50% of 2.2 million employees surveyed worldwide strongly agree that they know what is expected of them at work.

25% of 2,061 UK adults surveyed say they receive insufficient training and development in their existing role.

24% of more than 400,000 employees surveyed across 500 organizations worldwide say that lack of tools is their top source of decreased productivity (second highest to unproductive coworkers).

(photo): ©Maren Wischnewski/Alamy Stock Photo

employees versus meeting with clients. The third form of role perceptions involves understanding the preferred behaviors or procedures for accomplishing tasks. Role ambiguity exists when an employee knows two or three ways to perform a task but misunderstands which of these the company prefers.

Role perceptions are important because they represent how well employees know where to direct their effort.[13] Employees with role clarity perform work more accurately and efficiently, whereas those with role ambiguity waste considerable time and energy by performing the wrong tasks or the right tasks in the wrong way. Furthermore, role clarity is essential for coordination with coworkers and other stakeholders. For instance, performers at Cirque du Soleil depend on one another to perform precise behaviors at exact times, such as catching each other in midair. Role clarity ensures that these expectations are met and the troupe's performances are executed safely. Finally, role clarity motivates employees because they have a higher belief that their effort will produce the expected outcomes. In other words, people are more confident when they know what is expected of them.

> **Lack of role clarity may be an increasing concern as organizations move away from precisely defined job descriptions to broader work responsibilities.**

role clarity to role ambiguity. Role ambiguity may be a serious problem in organizations. When 7,000 employees in a recent global survey were asked what would most improve their performance, "greater clarity about what the organization needs from me" was identified as the most important factor.[12]

Role clarity exists in three forms. First, employees have clear role perceptions when they understand the specific duties or consequences for which they are accountable. This may seem obvious, but people are occasionally evaluated on job duties they were never told were within their zone of responsibility. This lack of role clarity may be an increasing concern as organizations move away from precisely defined job descriptions to broader work responsibilities.

Second, role clarity exists when employees understand the priority of their various tasks and performance expectations. This is illustrated in the classic dilemma of quantity versus quality, such as how many customers to serve in an hour (quantity) versus how well each customer should be served (quality). Role clarity in the form of task priorities also exists in the dilemma of allocating personal time and resources, such as how much time managers should devote to coaching

Role clarity ensures that artists at Cirque du Soleil understand what is expected of them and of each other, thereby supporting the troupe's high quality and safe performance.
©Picture Perfect/REX/Shutterstock

Situational Factors

Individual behavior and performance also depend on the situation, which is any context beyond the employee's immediate control.[14] The situation has two main influences on individual behavior and performance.[15] One influence is that the work context constrains or facilitates behavior and performance. Employees who are motivated and skilled and know their role obligations will nevertheless perform poorly if they lack time, budget, physical work facilities, and other resources. The second influence is that the work environment provides cues to guide and motivate people. For example, companies install barriers and warning signs in dangerous areas. These workplace features are situational factors that cue employees to avoid the nearby hazards.

LO2-2 Summarize the five types of individual behavior in organizations.

TYPES OF INDIVIDUAL BEHAVIOR

The four elements of the MARS model—motivation, ability, role perceptions, and situational factors—affect all voluntary workplace behaviors and performance. There are many varieties of individual behavior, but most can be organized into the five categories described over the next few pages: task performance, organizational citizenship, counterproductive work behaviors, joining and staying with the organization, and maintaining work attendance (Exhibit 2.2).

Task Performance

Task performance refers to the individual's voluntary goal-directed behaviors that contribute to organizational objectives.[16] Most jobs require incumbents to complete several tasks. For example, foreign exchange traders at Morgan Stanley must be able to identify and execute profitable trades, work cooperatively with clients and coworkers, assist in training new staff, and work on special telecommunications equipment without error. All tasks involve various degrees of working with people, data, things, and ideas.[17] Foreign exchange traders mainly work with data (e.g., performing technical analysis of trends), people (e.g., sharing information with coworkers and clients), and ideas (interpreting charts and company reports).

There are three types of task performance: proficient, adaptive, and proactive.[18]

- *Proficient task performance* refers to performing the work efficiently and accurately. It involves accomplishing the assigned work at or above the expected standards of quality, quantity, and other indicators of effectiveness.

- *Adaptive task performance* refers to how well employees modify their thoughts and behavior to align with and support a new or changing environment. Essentially, adaptive task performance is about how well employees respond to change in the workplace and in their job duties.

- *Proactive task performance* refers to how well employees take the initiative to anticipate and introduce new work patterns that benefit the organization. Proactive behaviors bring about change in oneself, coworkers, and the workplace to achieve what is perceived to be a better future for the organization.

Employees are expected to perform their work proficiently. However, adaptive and proactive task performance are also important, particularly when the work is ambiguous or dynamic. These conditions exist when the client's expectations are unclear, resources to perform the work have uncertain availability, and the methods used to perform the work are rapidly evolving due to emerging technology.

Organizational Citizenship

Employee behavior extends beyond performing specific tasks. It also includes **organizational citizenship behaviors (OCBs)**, which are various forms of cooperation and helpfulness to others that support the organization's social and psychological context.[19] Some OCBs are directed toward individuals, such as assisting coworkers with their work problems, adjusting your work schedules to accommodate coworkers, showing

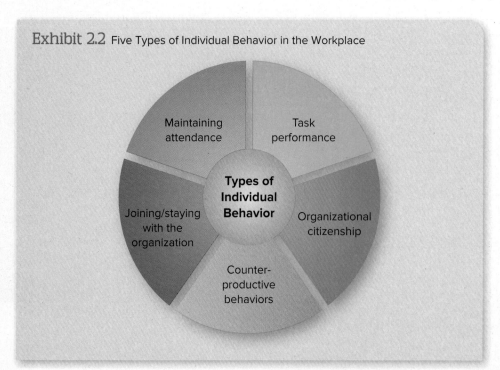

Exhibit 2.2 Five Types of Individual Behavior in the Workplace

Maintaining attendance

Task performance

Joining/staying with the organization

Types of Individual Behavior

Organizational citizenship

Counter-productive behaviors

Organizational citizenship behaviors are various forms of cooperation and helpfulness to others that support the organization's social and psychological context.
©baranq/Shutterstock

task performance the individual's voluntary goal-directed behaviors that contribute to organizational objectives

organizational citizenship behaviors (OCBs) various forms of cooperation and helpfulness to others that support the organization's social and psychological context

counterproductive work behaviors (CWBs) voluntary behaviors that have the potential to directly or indirectly harm the organization

genuine courtesy toward coworkers, and sharing your work resources (supplies, technology, staff) with coworkers. Other OCBs represent cooperation and helpfulness toward the organization, such as supporting the company's public image, offering ideas beyond those required for your own job, attending voluntary functions that support the organization, and keeping up with new developments in the organization. Some OCBs are discretionary behaviors (employees don't have to perform them), but employees are expected to engage in some forms of organizational citizenship even if they aren't explicitly stated in job descriptions.[20]

counterproductive work behaviors (CWBs). CWBs are voluntary behaviors that have the potential to directly or indirectly harm the organization or its stakeholders.[23] This concept includes a wide array of behaviors, both intentional and unintentional, such as harassing coworkers, creating unnecessary conflict, deviating from preferred work methods (e.g., shortcuts that undermine work quality), being untruthful, stealing, sabotaging work, and wasting resources. CWBs are not minor concerns; research suggests that they can substantially undermine the organization's effectiveness.

Joining and Staying with the Organization

Organizations are people working together toward common goals, so another critical set of behaviors is joining and staying with the company. Employers face skill shortages when the economy is booming, but employing qualified people can be a problem even during recessions.

Equally important is ensuring that employees stay with the company.[24] Employee turnover removes valuable knowledge,

> Employee turnover removes valuable knowledge, skills, and relationships with coworkers and external stakeholders, all of which take time for new staff to acquire.

OCBs can have a significant effect on individual, team, and organizational effectiveness.[21] Employees who help others have higher task performance because they receive more support from coworkers. OCBs also increase team performance where members depend on one another. However, OCBs take time and energy away from performing tasks, which can undermine career success in companies that reward task performance. Also, employees with high organizational citizenship tend to have higher work–family conflict because of the amount of time required for these activities.[22]

Counterproductive Work Behaviors

Organizational behavior is interested in all workplace behaviors, including dysfunctional activities collectively known as

skills, and relationships with coworkers and external stakeholders, all of which take time for new staff to acquire. In later chapters, we identify other problems with employee turnover, such as its adverse effect on customer service, team development, and corporate culture strength. Employee turnover does offer some benefits, such as removing people with counterproductive work behaviors and opening up positions to new employees with fresh ideas. But overall, turnover tends to have a negative effect on organizational effectiveness.

Maintaining Work Attendance

Along with attracting and retaining employees, organizations need everyone to show up for work at scheduled times, whether in-person or through remote work arrangements. American

personality the relatively enduring pattern of thoughts, emotions, and behaviors that characterize a person, along with the psychological processes behind those characteristics

employees are absent from scheduled work an average of only five days per year. Yet, even low absenteeism can lead to increased workloads or overtime among coworkers, lower performance by temporary staff filling the vacant position, poorer coordination in the work process, poorer customer service, and potentially more workplace accidents.[25]

What are the main causes of absenteeism and lateness?[26] Employees often point to situational factors, such as bad weather, transit strike, personal illness, and family demands (e.g., sick children). Some absenteeism occurs because employees need to get away from workplace bullying, difficult customers, boring work, and other stressful conditions. Absenteeism is also higher in organizations with generous sick leave because this benefit minimizes the financial loss of taking time away from work.

Another factor in absenteeism is the person's values and personality. Finally, studies report that absenteeism is higher in teams with strong absence norms, meaning that team members tolerate and even expect coworkers to take time off.

Although most companies focus on minimizing absenteeism, a more serious behavior may be *presenteeism*—showing up for work when unwell, injured, preoccupied by personal problems, or faced with dangerous conditions getting to work.[27] These employees tend to be less productive and may reduce the productivity of coworkers. In addition, they may worsen their own health and increase health and safety risks for coworkers. Presenteeism is more common among employees with low job security, with no sick leave benefits, and whose absence would immediately affect many people. Personality traits also motivate some people to show up for work when others would gladly recover at home.[28] Personality is a widely cited predictor of most forms of individual behavior. It is also the most stable personal characteristic, so we introduce this topic next.

LO2-3 Describe personality and discuss how the "Big Five" personality dimensions and four MBTI types relate to individual behavior in organizations.

PERSONALITY IN ORGANIZATIONS

Personality is the relatively enduring pattern of thoughts, emotions, and behaviors that characterize a person, along with the psychological processes behind those characteristics.[30] In essence, personality is the bundle of characteristics that make us similar to or different from other people. We estimate an individual's personality by what he or she says and does, and we infer the person's internal states—including thoughts and emotions—from these observable behaviors.

People engage in a wide range of behaviors in their daily lives, yet close inspection of those actions reveals discernible patterns called *personality traits*.[31] Traits are broad concepts that allow us to label and understand individual differences. For example, some of your friends are probably quite talkative, whereas others tend to be quieter. Some people like to take risks, whereas others are risk-averse. Each trait implies that there is something within the person, rather than environmental influences alone, that predicts this behavioral tendency. In fact, studies report that an individual's personality traits measured in childhood predict many behaviors and outcomes in adulthood, including educational attainment, employment success, marital relationships, illegal activities, and health-risk behaviors.[32]

Although people have behavioral tendencies, they do not act the same way in all situations. Such consistency would be considered abnormal because it indicates a person's insensitivity to social norms, reward systems, and other external conditions.[33] People vary their behavior to suit the situation, even if the

OB THEORY TO PRACTICE

The Doctor is Ill ... but Will See You Now

©pathdoc/Shutterstock

Most physicians urge sick patients to stay home, yet few take their own advice. Three-quarters of New Zealand doctors working in hospitals say they went to work while unwell over the previous year. Approximately the same percentage of Swedish doctors recently surveyed admitted that over the previous year, they had gone to work one or more times with an illness for which they would have advised patients to stay at home. "There is an unspoken understanding that you probably should be on your deathbed if you are calling in sick," says an attending physician at a Philadelphia hospital where 83 percent of doctors admitted working while sick within the previous year. "It inconveniences my colleagues, is complicated to pay back shifts, and makes me look bad to do so."[29]

Studies of identical twins reveal that heredity has a very large effect on personality.
©SuperStock

behavior is at odds with their personality. For example, talkative people remain relatively quiet in a library where "no talking" rules are explicit and strictly enforced. Even there, personality differences are apparent because talkative people tend to do more talking in libraries relative to other people talking in that setting.

Personality Determinants: Nature versus Nurture

Personality is shaped by both nature and nurture, although the relative importance of each continues to be debated and studied.[35] *Nature* refers to our genetic or hereditary origins—the genes that we inherit from our parents. Studies of identical twins reveal that heredity has a very large effect on personality; up to 50 percent of variation in behavior and 30 percent of temperament preferences can be attributed to a person's genetic characteristics. In other words, genetic code not only determines our eye color, skin tone, and physical shape; it also significantly affects our attitudes, decisions, and behavior.

Personality is also shaped by *nurture*—our socialization, life experiences, and other forms of interaction with the environment. Personality develops and changes mainly from childhood to young adulthood, typically stabilizing by around age 30. However, some personality changes continue to occur later in life. A few traits increase through to young adulthood, then decline in later years, whereas other traits tend to increase throughout most of our lifetime. Over a very long time, the type of work we perform also can influence our personality.[36]

The main explanation of why personality becomes more stable by adulthood is that we form a clearer and more rigid self-concept. This increasing clarity of "who we are" anchors our behavior with the help of our *executive function*. This is the part of the brain that monitors and regulates goal-directed behavior to keep it consistent with our self-concept. Our self-view becomes clearer and more stable with age, which increases the stability and consistency of our personality and behavior.[37] We discuss self-concept in more detail in Chapter 3. The main point here is that personality is not completely determined by heredity; life experiences, particularly early in life, also shape each individual's personality traits.

Five-Factor Model of Personality

Sociable, anxious, curious, dependable, suspicious, talkative, adventurous, and hundreds of other personality traits have been described over the years, so experts have tried to organize them into smaller clusters. The most researched and respected clustering of personality traits is the **five-factor (Big Five) model (FFM)**.[38] Several decades ago, personality experts identified more than 17,000 words that describe an individual's personality. These words were distilled down to five broad personality dimensions, each with a cluster of specific traits. Similar results were found in studies of different languages, suggesting that the five-factor model is fairly robust across cultures. These "Big Five" dimensions, represented by the handy acronym *CANOE*, are outlined in Exhibit 2.3 and described as follows:

- **Conscientiousness**. Characterizes people who are organized, dependable, goal-focused, thorough, disciplined, methodical, and industrious. People with low conscientiousness tend to be careless, disorganized, and less thorough.

- **Agreeableness**. Describes people who are trusting, helpful, good-natured, considerate, tolerant, selfless, generous, and flexible. People with low agreeableness tend to be uncooperative and intolerant of others' needs as well as more suspicious and self-focused.

five-factor (Big Five) model (FFM) the five broad dimensions representing most personality traits: conscientiousness, emotional stability, openness to experience, agreeableness, and extraversion

conscientiousness a personality dimension describing people who are organized, dependable, goal-focused, thorough, disciplined, methodical, and industrious

agreeableness a personality dimension describing people who are trusting, helpful, good-natured, considerate, tolerant, selfless, generous, and flexible

> One regrets the loss even of one's worst habits. . . . They are such an essential part of one's personality.[34]
>
> —Oscar Wilde, author (from *The Picture of Dorian Gray*)

- **Neuroticism.** Refers to people who tend to be anxious, insecure, self-conscious, depressed, and temperamental. In contrast, people with low neuroticism (high emotional stability) are poised, secure, and calm.

- **Openness to experience.** Characterizes people who are imaginative, creative, unconventional, curious, nonconforming, autonomous, and aesthetically perceptive. Those with low scores on this dimension tend to be more resistant to change, less open to new ideas, and more conventional and fixed in their ways.

- **Extraversion.** Describes people who are outgoing, talkative, energetic, sociable, and assertive. The opposite is *introversion*, which applies to those who are quiet, cautious, and less interactive with others. Extraverts get their energy from people and things around them, whereas introverts get their energy more from personal reflection on concepts and ideas. Introverts do not necessarily lack social skills. Instead, they are more inclined to direct their interests to ideas than to social events. Introverts feel more comfortable being alone than do extraverts.

connect
Mc Graw Hill Education

SELF-ASSESSMENT 2.1: What is Your Big Five Personality?

Personality experts have organized the dozens of personality traits into five main dimensions, known as the five-factor or "Big Five" model. Each dimension consists of several specific personality traits that cluster together. Most scholarly research on personality relies on this model, but it is also useful in everyday life as a relatively easy categorization of personalities. You can discover your Big Five personality by locating this self-assessment in Connect if it is assigned by your instructor.

connect
Mc Graw Hill Education

SELF-ASSESSMENT 2.2: Are You Introverted or Extraverted?

One of the most widely studied and discussed personality dimensions in the five-factor (Big Five) model of personality is introversion–extraversion. Introversion characterizes people who tend to be quiet, shy, and cautious. Extraversion characterizes people who tend to be outgoing, talkative, sociable, and assertive. You can discover your level of introversion or extraversion by locating this self-assessment in Connect if it is assigned by your instructor.

Exhibit 2.3 Five-Factor Model of Personality Dimensions

Personality dimension	People with higher scores on this dimension tend to be more:
Conscientiousness	Organized, dependable, goal-focused, thorough, disciplined, methodical, industrious
Agreeableness	Trusting, helpful, good-natured, considerate, tolerant, selfless, generous, flexible
Neuroticism	Anxious, insecure, self-conscious, depressed, temperamental
Openness to experience	Imaginative, creative, unconventional, curious, nonconforming, autonomous, perceptive
Extraversion	Outgoing, talkative, energetic, sociable, assertive

Five-Factor Model and Work Performance Personality mainly affects behavior and performance through motivation, specifically by influencing employees' direction and intensity of effort. Consequently, all of the five-factor model dimensions predict one or more types of employee behavior and performance to some extent. However, specific personality traits often predict employee performance better than the broad Big Five dimensions, which cluster several traits together. Also, the relationship between a personality dimension or trait and performance may be nonlinear. People with moderate extraversion perform better in sales jobs than those with high or low extraversion, for example.[39]

Exhibit 2.4 highlights which Big Five personality dimensions best predict five types of work behavior and performance.[40] Conscientiousness stands out as the best overall personality predictor of proficient task performance for most jobs. Conscientious employees set higher personal goals for themselves and are more persistent. People with higher conscientiousness also engage in more organizational citizenship and in less counterproductive work behavior.

Extraversion is the second best overall personality predictor of proficient task performance. It is also one of the better personality predictors of adaptive and proactive performance.

Assertiveness, a specific personality trait within the extraversion cluster, is a particularly strong predictor of adaptive and proactive performance. Assertive employees tend to have a "take charge" approach to situations, which is consistent with adapting to change and proactively initiating change. Extraversion is associated with influencing others and being comfortable in social settings, which (along with being assertive) explains why effective leaders and salespeople tend to be somewhat more extraverted than the general population.

Agreeableness is positively associated with organizational citizenship and negatively associated with counterproductive work behaviors.[41] The reason is that employees with high agreeableness are more cooperative, sensitive, flexible, and supportive. Agreeableness does not predict proficient or proactive task performance very well, mainly because it is associated with lower motivation to set goals and achieve results. However, agreeableness does predict one's performance as a team member as well as in customer service jobs.

Openness to experience is a weak predictor of proficient task performance, but it is one of the best personality predictors of adaptive and proactive performance. The main reason is that employees with higher openness scores have more curiosity,

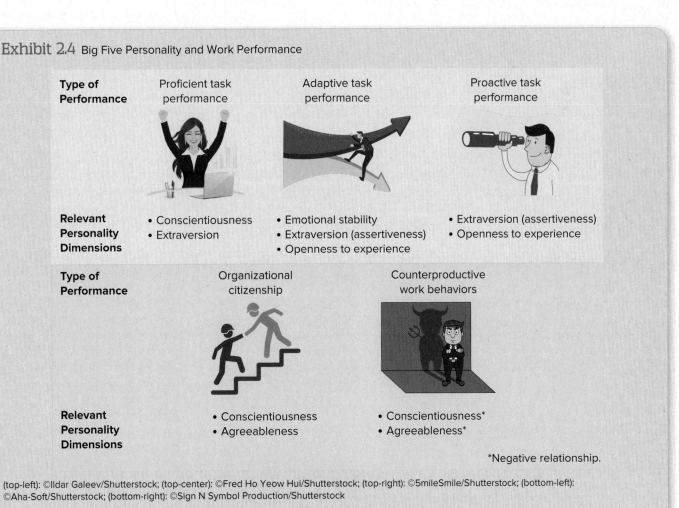

Exhibit 2.4 Big Five Personality and Work Performance

Type of Performance	Proficient task performance	Adaptive task performance	Proactive task performance
Relevant Personality Dimensions	• Conscientiousness • Extraversion	• Emotional stability • Extraversion (assertiveness) • Openness to experience	• Extraversion (assertiveness) • Openness to experience

Type of Performance	Organizational citizenship	Counterproductive work behaviors
Relevant Personality Dimensions	• Conscientiousness • Agreeableness	• Conscientiousness* • Agreeableness*

*Negative relationship.

imagination, and tolerance of change.[42] These traits also explain why openness to change is associated with successful performance in creative work.

Emotional stability (low neuroticism) is one of the best personality predictors of adaptive performance.[43] The central explanation is that employees with higher emotional stability cope better with the ambiguity and uncertainty of change. In contrast, those with higher neuroticism view change as a threat, so they tend to avoid change and experience more stress when faced with workplace adjustments. These characteristics would suggest that emotional stability also predicts proactive performance, but the limited research has reported mixed results.

Jungian Personality Theory and the Myers-Briggs Type Indicator

The five-factor model of personality has the most research support, but it is not the most popular personality test in practice. That distinction goes to Jungian personality theory, which is measured through the **Myers-Briggs Type Indicator (MBTI)** (see Exhibit 2.5). Nearly a century ago, Swiss psychiatrist Carl Jung suggested that personality is mainly represented by the individual's preferences regarding perceiving and judging information.[44] Jung explained that the perceiving function—how people prefer to gather information—occurs through two competing orientations: *sensing (S)* and *intuition (N)*. Sensing involves perceiving information directly through the five senses; it relies on an organized structure to acquire factual and preferably quantitative details. In contrast, intuition relies more on insight and subjective experience to see relationships among variables. Sensing types focus on the here and now, whereas intuitive types focus more on future possibilities.

Jung also proposed that the judging function—how people prefer making decisions based on what they have perceived—should consist of two competing processes: *thinking (T)* and *feeling (F)*. People with a thinking orientation rely on rational cause–effect logic and systematic data collection to make decisions. Those with a strong feeling orientation give more weight to their emotional responses to the options presented, as well as to how those choices affect others. Jung noted that in addition to the four core processes of sensing, intuition, thinking, and feeling, people differ in their level of extraversion–introversion, which was introduced earlier as one of the Big Five personality traits.

The MBTI extends Jung's list of personality traits described above by also measuring Jung's broader

Exhibit 2.5 Jungian and Myers-Briggs Type Indicator Types[45]

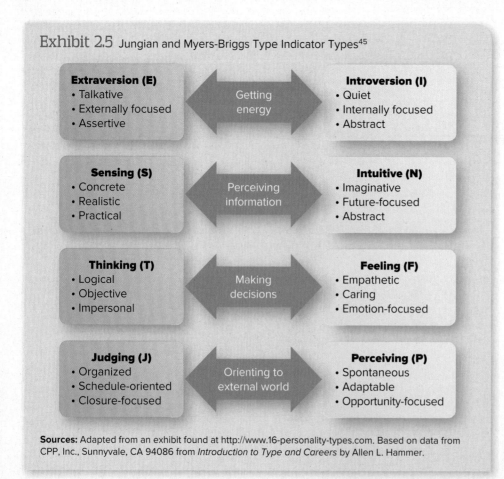

Extraversion (E)
- Talkative
- Externally focused
- Assertive

Getting energy

Introversion (I)
- Quiet
- Internally focused
- Abstract

Sensing (S)
- Concrete
- Realistic
- Practical

Perceiving information

Intuitive (N)
- Imaginative
- Future-focused
- Abstract

Thinking (T)
- Logical
- Objective
- Impersonal

Making decisions

Feeling (F)
- Empathetic
- Caring
- Emotion-focused

Judging (J)
- Organized
- Schedule-oriented
- Closure-focused

Orienting to external world

Perceiving (P)
- Spontaneous
- Adaptable
- Opportunity-focused

Sources: Adapted from an exhibit found at http://www.16-personality-types.com. Based on data from CPP, Inc., Sunnyvale, CA 94086 from *Introduction to Type and Careers* by Allen L. Hammer.

SELF-ASSESSMENT 2.4: Are You a Sensing or Intuitive Type?
Nearly a century ago, Swiss psychiatrist Carl Jung proposed that personality is primarily represented by the individual's preferences regarding perceiving and judging information. Jung explained that perceiving, which involves how people prefer to gather information or perceive the world around them, occurs through two competing orientations: sensing (S) and intuition (N). You can discover the extent to which you are a sensing or intuitive type by locating this self-assessment in Connect if it is assigned by your instructor.

categories of *perceiving* and *judging*, which represent a person's attitude toward the external world. People with a perceiving orientation are open, curious, and flexible. They prefer to keep their options open and to adapt spontaneously to events as they unfold. Judging types prefer order and structure and want to resolve problems quickly.

There are several reasons why the MBTI is popular, but it has a number of limitations. It is usually a poor predictor of job performance and should not be used for employment selection or promotion decisions.[46] There are also concerns about its measurement. MBTI can potentially identify employees who prefer face-to-face versus virtual teamwork, but the evidence so far suggests that it does not predict team development or leadership effectiveness.

ESTJ

The MBTI should not be used for employment selection or promotion decisions, but it can help in career counseling and executive coaching.
©Trinette Reed/Blend Images LLC; ©kyoshino/Getty Images

In spite of these limitations, the MBTI is the most widely studied measure of cognitive style in management research and is the most popular personality test for career counseling and executive coaching.[47] It is even being used by artificial intelligence engineers to adapt the behavior of robots to user preferences. MBTI takes a neutral or balanced approach by recognizing both the strengths and limitations of each personality type in different situations. In contrast, the five-factor model views people with higher scores as better than those with lower scores on each dimension. This may be a restrictive view of personality and makes the Big Five model more difficult to apply in coaching and development settings.[48]

> **LO2-4** Summarize Schwartz's model of individual values and discuss the conditions where values influence behavior.

VALUES IN THE WORKPLACE

Liam (not his real name) felt uncomfortable working in his previous project team at a consumer goods company. His coworkers were friendly and knowledgeable, but their views about customers and getting ahead in the company were irritating. Most of the other team members discussed new products as money makers without much thought to whether they actually satisfied customer needs. Conversations about getting ahead in the company focused on networking rather than achieving objectives. At one point, Liam felt so uncomfortable with the views of other team members that he began looking for a job at another company. Fortunately, he was transferred to a new project where most colleagues held values that were similar to his own.

Most of us have experienced situations similar to what Liam went through, where the values expressed by others clash with our own personal values. *Values*, a concept that we introduced in Chapter 1, are stable, evaluative beliefs that guide our preferences for outcomes or courses of action in a variety of situations.[49] They are the foundation of evaluations that something is right or wrong, good or bad, important or trivial. Values serve as a moral compass, advising and motivating what we ought to do in various situations. They also provide justification for past decisions and behavior.

People arrange values into a hierarchy of preferences, called a *value system*. Some individuals value new challenges more than they value conformity. Others value generosity more than frugality. Each person's unique value system is developed and

Values serve as a moral compass, advising and motivating what we ought to do in various situations.
©wavebreakmedia/Shutterstock

Values and personality traits are related to each other, but the two concepts differ in a few ways.[51] The most noticeable distinction is that values are evaluative; they tell us what we *ought* to do. Personality traits are descriptive; they are labels referring to what we naturally *tend* to do. A second distinction is that personality traits have minimal conflict with each other—you can have high agreeableness and high introversion, for example—whereas some values are opposed to other values. Someone who values excitement and challenge would have difficulty also valuing stability and moderation, for instance. Third, personality is somewhat more stable than values. The reason is that personality is influenced about equally by heredity and socialization, whereas values are influenced more by socialization than heredity.

Types of Values

Values come in many forms, and experts on this topic have devoted considerable attention to organizing them into clusters. By far, the most widely accepted model of personal values is the values circumplex developed and tested by social psychologist Shalom Schwartz and his colleagues.[52] This model clusters 57 values into 10 broad values categories that are organized into the circular model (circumplex) shown in Exhibit 2.6. The 10 categories include universalism, benevolence, tradition, conformity,

> ## Values and personality traits are related to each other, but the two concepts differ in a few ways.

reinforced through socialization from parents, religious institutions, friends, personal experiences, and the society in which he or she lives. As such, a person's hierarchy of values is stable and long-lasting. For example, one study found that value systems of a sample of adolescents were remarkably similar 20 years later when they were adults.[50]

Values exist only within individuals—we call them *personal values*. However, groups of people might hold the same or similar values, so we tend to ascribe these *shared values* to the team, department, organization, profession, or entire society. The values shared by people throughout an organization (*organizational values*) receive fuller discussion in Chapter 13 because they are a key part of corporate culture. The values shared across a society (*cultural values*) receive attention in the last section of this chapter.

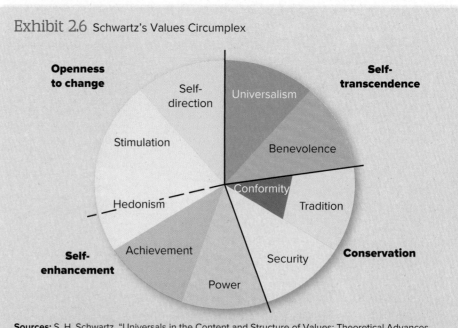

Exhibit 2.6 Schwartz's Values Circumplex

Sources: S. H. Schwartz, "Universals in the Content and Structure of Values: Theoretical Advances and Empirical Tests in 20 Countries," *Advances in Experimental Social Psychology* 25 (1992): 1–65; S. H. Schwartz and K. Boehnke, "Evaluating the Structure of Human Values with Confirmatory Factor Analysis," *Journal of Research in Personality* 38, no. 3 (2004): 230–55.

security, power, achievement, hedonism, stimulation, and self-direction. Each category is a cluster of more specific values (not shown). For example, conformity includes the specific values of politeness, honoring parents, self-discipline, and obedience.

These 10 broad values categories are further clustered into four quadrants. One quadrant, called *openness to change*, refers to the extent to which a person is motivated to pursue innovative ways. This quadrant includes the value categories of self-direction (creativity, independent thought), stimulation (excitement and challenge), and hedonism

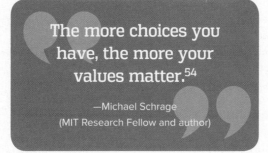

our values hierarchy, then a job opportunity offering new experiences will appeal to us more than a job opportunity with more predictable and stable work.

Second, values indirectly motivate behavior by framing our perceptions of reality. Specifically, values influence whether we notice something as well as how we interpret it. Our decisions and actions are affected by how we perceive those situations. Third, we are motivated to act consistently with how we define ourselves and want to be viewed by others. If achievement is a key feature of our self-view and public image, then we try to ensure that our behavior is consistent with that value. The more clearly a behavior is aligned with a specific value that identifies us, the more motivated we are to engage in that behavior.

Personal values guide our decisions and behavior to some extent, but this connection isn't as strong as we might like to believe.[55] One reason for this "disconnect" between personal values and individual behavior is the situation. Personal values motivate us to engage in specific

connect

SELF-ASSESSMENT 2.5: What Are Your Dominant Values?

Values are stable, evaluative beliefs that guide our preferences for outcomes or courses of action in a variety of situations. They are perceptions about what is good or bad, right or wrong. We arrange our personal values into a hierarchy of preferences, called a value system. Schwartz's values circumplex organizes the dozens of personal values into 10 categories placed in a circle (circumplex). You can discover your value system hierarchy in Schwartz's model by locating this self-assessment in Connect if it is assigned by your instructor.

(pursuit of pleasure, enjoyment, gratification of desires). The opposing quadrant is *conservation*, which is the extent to which a person is motivated to preserve the status quo. The conservation quadrant includes the value categories of conformity (adherence to social norms and expectations), security (safety and stability), and tradition (moderation and preservation of the status quo).

The third quadrant in Schwartz's circumplex model, called *self-enhancement*, refers to how much a person is motivated by self-interest. This quadrant includes the values categories of achievement (pursuit of personal success), power (dominance over others), and hedonism (a values category shared with openness to change). The opposite of self-enhancement is *self-transcendence*, which refers to motivation to promote the welfare of others and nature. Self-transcendence includes the value categories of benevolence (concern for others in one's life) and universalism (concern for the welfare of all people and nature).

Values and Individual Behavior

Personal values influence decisions and behavior in various ways.[53] First, values directly motivate our actions by shaping the relative attractiveness (*valence*) of the choices available. In other words, we experience more positive feelings toward alternatives that are aligned with our most important values. If stimulation is at the top of

behavior, but the MARS model points out that the situation can prevent us from engaging in values-consistent behavior. For example, individuals with strong self-transcendent values are

Personal values guide our decisions and behavior to some extent, but this connection isn't as strong as we might like to believe.
©Borya Galperin/Shutterstock

motivated to engage in recycling and other environmentally friendly behaviors, but lack of recycling facilities prevents or severely limits this behavior. People also deviate from their personal values due to strong counter-motivational forces. For instance, employees caught in illegal business dealings sometimes attribute their unethical activities to pressure from management to achieve their performance at any cost.

Another reason why decisions and behavior are inconsistent with our personal values is that we don't actively think about them much of the time.[56] Values are abstract concepts, so their relevance is not obvious in many situations. Furthermore, many daily decisions and actions occur routinely, so we don't actively evaluate their consistency with our values. We do consciously consider our values in some situations, of course, such as realizing how much we value security when deciding whether to perform a risky task. However, many daily events do not trigger values awareness, so we act without the guidance of our personal values. We literally need to be reminded of our values so they guide our decisions and actions.

The effect of values awareness on behavior was apparent in a study in which students were given a math test and received a payment for each correct answer.[57] One group submitted their results to the experimenter for scoring, so they couldn't lie about their results. A second group could lie because they scored the test themselves and told the experimenter their test score. A third group was similar to the second (they scored their own test), but that test included the following statement, and students were required to sign their name to that statement: "I understand that this short survey falls under (the university's) honor system." The researchers estimated that some students cheated when they scored their own test without the "honor system" statement, whereas no one given the "honor system" form lied about the results. The university didn't actually have an official honor statement, but the message made students pay attention to their honesty. In short, people are more likely to apply their values (honesty, in this case) when they are explicitly reminded of those values and recognize their relevance to the situation.

Values Congruence

Values tell us what is right or wrong and what we ought to do. This evaluative characteristic affects how comfortable we are with specific organizations and individuals. The key concept here is *values congruence*, which refers to how similar a person's values hierarchy is to the values hierarchy of another entity, such as the employee's team or organization. This section of the chapter began by describing Liam's values incongruence with his project team, which affected his satisfaction, cohesion, and potentially performance in that team. Congruence with the organization's values tends to increase the employee's job satisfaction, loyalty, and organizational citizenship. It also tends to reduce stress and turnover. Furthermore, employees are more likely to make decisions that are compatible with organizational expectations when their personal values are congruent with the organization's shared value.[59]

Are organizations the most successful when every employee's personal values align with the company's values? Not at all! While a large degree of values congruence is necessary for the reasons just noted, organizations also benefit from some level of incongruence. Employees with diverse values offer different perspectives, which potentially lead to better decision making. Also, too much congruence can create a "corporate cult" that potentially undermines creativity, organizational flexibility, and business ethics.

LO2-5 Describe three ethical principles and discuss three factors that influence ethical behavior.

ETHICAL VALUES AND BEHAVIOR

When 195 business leaders across 15 countries were asked to identify the most important leader competencies, "high ethics and moral standards" was the top-rated item from the list of

moral intensity the degree to which an issue demands the application of ethical principles

74 characteristics. Similarly, when 1,000 CEOs and other top-level executives around the world were asked to list the most important attributes of effective leaders, the most frequently mentioned characteristic was *integrity*—the leader's ethical standards.[60] These surveys reveal the importance of ethics in the workplace. *Ethics* refers to the study of moral principles or values that determine whether actions are right or wrong and outcomes are good or bad (see Chapter 1). People rely on their ethical values to determine "the right thing to do."

Three Ethical Principles

To better understand business ethics, we need to consider three distinct types of ethical principles: utilitarianism, individual rights, and distributive justice.[61] Your personal values might sway you more toward one principle than the others, but all three should be actively considered when making decisions.

- *Utilitarianism.* This principle says the only moral obligation is to seek the greatest good for the greatest number of people. In other words, we should choose the option that provides the highest degree of satisfaction to those affected. One problem is that utilitarianism requires a cost–benefit analysis, yet many outcomes aren't measurable. Another problem is that utilitarianism could justify actions that other principles would consider immoral because those means produce the greatest good overall.

- *Individual rights.* This principle says that everyone has the same set of natural rights, such as freedom of speech, freedom of movement, right to physical security, and right to fair trial. The individual rights principle extends beyond legal rights to human rights that everyone is granted as a moral norm of society. One problem with this principle is that some individual rights may conflict with others. The shareholders' right to be informed about corporate activities may ultimately conflict with an executive's right to privacy, for example.

- *Distributive justice.* This principle says that the benefits and burdens of similar individuals should be the same; otherwise they should be proportional. For example, employees who contribute equally in their work should receive similar rewards, whereas those who make a lesser contribution should receive less. A variation of this principle says that

> ## It takes many good deeds to build a good reputation and only one bad one to lose it.
>
> —Attributed to Benjamin Franklin

Utilitarianism, individual rights, and distributive justice are three ethical principles that should be considered when making decisions.
©alphaspirit/Shutterstock

inequalities are acceptable when they benefit the least well off in society. The main problem with the distributive justice principle is that it is difficult to agree on who is "similar" and what factors are "relevant." We discuss distributive justice further in Chapter 5.

Moral Intensity, Moral Sensitivity, and Situational Influences

Along with ethical principles and their underlying values, three other factors influence ethical conduct in the workplace: the moral intensity of the issue, the individual's moral sensitivity, and situational factors.[62]

Moral Intensity **Moral intensity** is the degree to which an issue demands the application of ethical principles. Decisions with high moral intensity have strong ethical implications that usually affect many people, so the decision maker needs to carefully apply ethical principles to make the best choice. The moral intensity of a situation is higher when (a) the consequences of the decision could be very good or bad, (b) there is high agreement by others that the decision outcomes are good or bad, (c) there is a high probability that the good or bad outcomes will occur, and (d) many people will experience the consequences of the decision.[63]

Moral Sensitivity Moral sensitivity (also called *ethical sensitivity*) is a characteristic of the person, namely his or her ability to detect a moral dilemma and estimate its relative importance.[64] People with high moral sensitivity can more quickly and accurately estimate the moral intensity of the issue. This awareness does not necessarily translate into more ethical behavior; it just means that people with higher moral sensitivity are more likely to know when unethical behavior occurs.

Several factors are associated with a person's moral sensitivity:[65]

- Expertise or knowledge of prescriptive norms and rules. For example, accountants are more morally sensitive regarding specific accounting procedures than are people who lack experience in this profession.

- Previous experience with specific moral dilemmas. Past incidents likely generate internal cues that trigger awareness of future ethical dilemmas with similar characteristics.

- Ability to empathize with those affected by the decision. On average, women have higher moral sensitivity compared to men, partly because women tend to have higher empathy.

- A strong self-view of being a morally sensitive person.[66] Employees who strongly define themselves by their moral character (called their *moral identity*) tend to have higher moral sensitivity because they put more energy into maintaining ethical conduct.

People with high moral sensitivity can more quickly and accurately estimate the moral intensity of the issue.
©DNY59/Getty Images

- A high degree of situational mindfulness.[67] **Mindfulness** refers to a person's receptive and impartial attention to and awareness of the present situation as well as to one's own thoughts and emotions in that moment. Mindfulness increases moral sensitivity because it involves actively monitoring the environment as well as being sensitive to our responses to that environment. This vigilance requires effort as well as skill to receptively evaluate our thoughts and emotions.

Situational Factors Along with moral intensity and moral sensitivity, ethical conduct is influenced by the situation in which the conduct occurs.[68] Some employees say they regularly experience pressure from top management that motivates them to lie to customers, breach regulations, or otherwise act unethically. Situational factors do not justify unethical conduct. Rather, we need to be aware of these factors so organizations can reduce their influence.

Supporting Ethical Behavior

Most large and medium-sized organizations in the United States and other developed countries maintain or improve ethical conduct through systematic practices. One of the most basic steps in this direction is a code of ethical conduct—a statement about desired activities, rules of conduct, and philosophy about the organization's relationship to its stakeholders and the environment.[70] These codes are supposed to motivate and guide employee behavior, signal the importance of ethical conduct, and build the firm's trustworthiness to stakeholders. However, critics suggest that they do little to reduce unethical conduct.

Another strategy to improve ethical conduct is to train and regularly evaluate employees about their knowledge of proper ethical conduct. Many large firms have annual quizzes to test employee awareness of company rules and practices on important ethical issues such as giving gifts and receiving sensitive information about competitors or governments. In some firms, employees participate in elaborate games that present increasingly challenging and complex moral dilemmas. An increasingly popular practice to improve ethical conduct is an ethics telephone hotline and website, typically operated by an independent organization, where employees can anonymously report suspicious behavior. A few very large businesses also employ ombudspersons who receive information confidentially from employees and proactively investigate possible wrongdoing. Ethics audits also are conducted in some organizations but are more common for evaluation of corporate social responsibility practices.[71]

Training, hotlines, audits, and related activities improve ethical conduct to some extent, but the most powerful foundation is a set of shared values that reinforces ethical conduct. As we describe in Chapter 13 (organizational culture), an ethical culture is supported by the conduct and vigilance of corporate leaders. By acting with the highest moral standards, leaders not only gain support and trust from followers; they role-model the ethical standards that employees are more likely to follow.[72]

Corporate Misconduct Reported in Selected Countries[69]

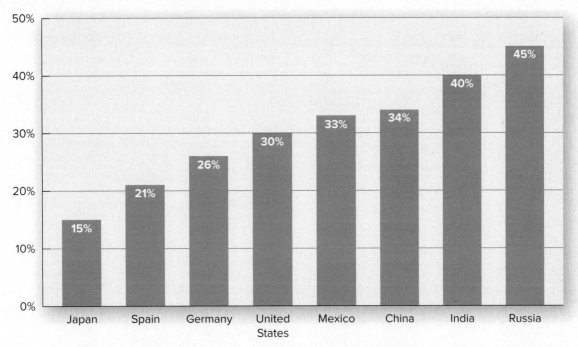

Percentage of employees surveyed in selected countries (1,000 respondents per country) who personally observed misconduct in their workplace within the previous 12 months.

LO2-6 Describe five values commonly studied across cultures.

VALUES ACROSS CULTURES

Globalization may be an emerging reality, but values still differ to some extent across geographic regions. Some cultures value group decisions, whereas others think that the leader should take charge. Meetings in Germany usually start on time, whereas they might be half an hour late in Brazil without much concern. We need to understand differences in cultural values to avoid unnecessary conflicts and misunderstandings between people from different countries. Over the next few pages, we introduce five values that have cross-cultural significance: individualism, collectivism, power distance, uncertainty avoidance, and achievement-nurturing orientation. Exhibit 2.7 summarizes these values and lists countries that have high, medium, or low emphasis on these values.

Individualism and Collectivism

Two seemingly inseparable cross-cultural values are individualism and collectivism. **Individualism** is the extent to which we value independence and personal uniqueness. Highly individualist people value personal freedom, self-sufficiency, control over their own lives, and appreciation of the unique qualities that distinguish them from others. Americans, Chileans, Canadians,

Exhibit 2.7 Five Cross-Cultural Values

Value	Sample Countries	Representative Beliefs/Behaviors in "High" Cultures
Individualism	High: United States, Chile, Canada, South Africa Medium: Japan, Denmark Low: Taiwan, Venezuela	Defines self more by one's uniqueness; personal goals have priority; decisions have low consideration of effect on others; relationships are viewed as more instrumental and fluid.
Collectivism	High: Israel, Taiwan Medium: India, Denmark Low: United States, Germany, Japan	Defines self more by one's in-group membership; goals of self-sacrifice and harmony have priority; behavior regulated by in-group norms; in-group memberships are viewed as stable with a strong differentiation with out-groups.
Power distance	High: India, Malaysia Medium: United States, Japan Low: Denmark, Israel	Reluctant to disagree with or contradict the boss; managers are expected and preferred decision makers; perception of dependence on (versus interdependence with) the boss.
Uncertainty avoidance	High: Belgium, Greece Medium: United States, Norway Low: Denmark, Singapore	Prefer predictable situations; value stable employment, strict laws, and low conflict; dislike deviations from normal behavior.
Achievement orientation	High: Austria, Japan Medium: United States, Brazil Low: Sweden, Netherlands	Focus on outcomes (versus relationships); decisions based on contribution (equity versus equality); low empathy or showing emotions (versus strong empathy and caring).

Sources: Individualism and collectivism descriptions and results are from the meta-analysis reported in D. Oyserman, H. M. Coon, and M. Kemmelmeier, "Rethinking Individualism and Collectivism: Evaluation of Theoretical Assumptions and Meta-Analyses," *Psychological Bulletin* 128, no. 1 (2002): 3–72. The other information is from G. Hofstede, *Culture's Consequences*, 2nd ed. (Thousand Oaks, CA: Sage, 2001).

and South Africans generally exhibit high individualism, whereas Taiwan and Venezuela are countries with low individualism.[74] **Collectivism** is the extent to which we value our duty to groups to which we belong and to group harmony. Highly

Globalization may be an emerging reality, but values still differ to some extent across geographic regions.
©Rawpixel.com/Shutterstock

collectivist people define themselves by their group memberships, emphasize their personal connection to others in their in-groups, and value the goals and well-being of people within those groups.[75] Low collectivism countries include the United States, Japan, and Germany, whereas Israel and Taiwan have relatively high collectivism.

Contrary to popular belief, individualism is not the opposite of collectivism. In fact, the two concepts are typically uncorrelated.[76] For example, cultures that highly value duty to one's group do not necessarily give a low priority to personal freedom and uniqueness. Generally, people across all cultures define themselves by both their uniqueness and their relationship to others. It is an inherent characteristic of everyone's self-concept, which we discuss in the next chapter. Some cultures clearly emphasize either personal uniqueness or group obligations, but both have a place in a person's values and self-concept.

Also note that people in Japan have relatively low collectivism. This is contrary to many cross-cultural books, a few of which claim that Japan is one of the most collectivist countries on the planet! There are several explanations for the historical misinterpretation, ranging from problems defining and measuring collectivism to erroneous reporting of early cross-cultural research. Whatever the reasons, studies consistently report that people in Japan tend to have relatively low collectivism and moderate individualism (as indicated in Exhibit 2.7).[77]

Power Distance

Power distance refers to the extent to which people accept unequal distribution of power in a society.[78] Those with high power distance value unequal power. Those in higher positions expect obedience to authority; those in lower positions are comfortable receiving commands from their superiors without consultation or debate. People with high power distance also prefer to resolve differences through formal procedures rather than direct informal discussion. In contrast, people with low power distance expect relatively equal power sharing. They view the relationship with their boss as one of interdependence, not dependence; that is, they believe their boss is also dependent on them, so they expect power sharing and consultation before decisions affecting them are made. People in India and Malaysia tend to have high power distance, whereas people in Denmark and Israel generally have low power distance. Americans collectively have medium-low power distance.

Uncertainty Avoidance

Uncertainty avoidance is the degree to which people tolerate ambiguity (low uncertainty avoidance) or feel threatened by ambiguity and uncertainty (high uncertainty avoidance). Employees with high uncertainty avoidance value structured situations in which rules of conduct and decision making are clearly documented. They usually prefer direct rather than indirect or ambiguous communications. Uncertainty avoidance tends to be high in Belgium and Greece and very high in Japan. It is generally low in Denmark and Singapore. Americans collectively have medium-low uncertainty avoidance.

Achievement-Nurturing Orientation

Achievement-nurturing orientation reflects a competitive versus cooperative view of relations with other people.[79] People with a high achievement orientation value assertiveness, competitiveness, and materialism. They appreciate people who are tough, and they favor the acquisition of money and material goods. In contrast, people in nurturing-oriented cultures emphasize relationships and the well-being of others. They focus on human interaction and caring rather than competition and personal success. People in Sweden, Norway, and the Netherlands have very low achievement orientation (i.e., they have a high nurturing orientation). In contrast, very high achievement orientation scores have been reported in Japan and Austria. The United States is located a little above the middle of the range on achievement-nurturing orientation.

Caveats about Cross-Cultural Knowledge

Cross-cultural organizational research has gained considerable attention over the past two decades, but we need to raise a few warning flags about cross-cultural knowledge. One problem is that too many studies have relied on small, convenient samples (such as students attending one university) to represent an entire culture.[81] The result is that many cross-cultural studies draw conclusions that might not generalize to the cultures they intended to represent. A second problem is that cross-cultural research and writing continue to rely on a major

collectivism a cross-cultural value describing the degree to which people in a culture emphasize duty to groups to which they belong and to group harmony

power distance a cross-cultural value describing the degree to which people in a culture accept unequal distribution of power in a society

uncertainty avoidance a cross-cultural value describing the degree to which people in a culture tolerate ambiguity (low uncertainty avoidance) or feel threatened by ambiguity and uncertainty (high uncertainty avoidance)

achievement-nurturing orientation cross-cultural value describing the degree to which people in a culture emphasize competitive versus cooperative relations with other people

study conducted almost four decades ago of 116,000 IBM employees across dozens of countries. That study helped ignite subsequent cross-cultural research, but its findings are becoming out-of-date as values in some cultures have shifted over the years.[82]

A third concern is that cross-cultural studies often assume that each country has one culture.[83] In reality, the United States and many other countries have become culturally diverse. For example, a major review of past studies reported that, on average, African Americans have significantly higher individualism than European and Hispanic Americans, whereas Asian Americans have the lowest individualism among these demographic groups.[84]

Several studies also report cultural variations across geographic regions within the United States.[85] Collectivism is highest among Americans living in the southern states, California, and Hawaii; it is lowest in the Mountain, Northwest, and Great Plains states. Openness to experience is highest in the New England, Middle Atlantic, and Pacific regions; it is lowest in the Great Plains and midwestern and southeastern states.[86] Cultural differences within the United States are partly due to regional institutions, such as local governments, educational systems, and dominant religious groups.[87] For instance, research suggests that the number of rules and social controls (called *cultural tightness*) within each state explains differences in personality and values across the country.[88] Another reason for regional differences is that people with specific personality traits and personal values tend to migrate to places with particular geographic characteristics (mountains, ocean).[89] In summary, we need to recognize that cultural diversity often exists within countries, such as within the United States.

Study Checklist

Connect® Management is available for *M Organizational Behavior.* Additional resources include:

✓ Interactive Applications:
- **Decision Generator**
- **Drag and Drop:** Work through an interactive example to test your knowledge of the concepts.
- **Video Case:** See management in action through interactive videos.

✓ **SmartBook™**—SmartBook is the first and only adaptive reading experience available today. Distinguishing what you know from what you don't, and honing in on concepts you are most likely to forget, SmartBook personalizes content for you in a continuously adapting reading experience. Reading is no longer a passive and linear experience, but an engaging and dynamic one where you are more likely to master and retain important concepts and go to class better prepared.

©Natthawat Jamnapa/123RF

Notes

1. K. Roose, "Ray Dalio Is Building a Baseball Card Collection," *New York Magazine*, June 14, 2012; R. Feloni, "Here's Why the World's Largest Hedge Fund Makes Applicants Take 5 Personality Tests before Sitting through Hours of Intensive Interviews," *Business Insider*, August 16, 2016; R. Feloni, "These Are the Personality Tests You Take to Get a Job at the World's Largest Hedge Fund," *Business Insider*, August 27, 2016.

2. L. L. Thurstone, "Ability, Motivation, and Speed," *Psychometrika* 2, no. 4 (1937): 249–54; N. R. F. Maier, *Psychology in Industry*, 2nd ed. (Boston: Houghton Mifflin, 1955); V. H. Vroom, *Work and Motivation* (New York: Wiley, 1964); J. P. Campbell et al., *Managerial Behavior, Performance, and Effectiveness* (New York: McGraw-Hill, 1970).

3. R. S. Dalal, D. P. Bhave, and J. Fiset, "Within-Person Variability in Job Performance: A Theoretical Review and Research Agenda," *Journal of Management* 40, no. 5 (2014): 1396–436; S. Aryee et al., "Developing and Leveraging Human Capital Resource to Promote Service Quality: Testing a Theory of Performance," *Journal of Management* 42, no. 2 (2016): 480–99.

4. E. E. Lawler III and L. W. Porter, "Antecedent Attitudes of Effective Managerial Performance," *Organizational Behavior and Human Performance* 2 (1967): 122–42; O.-P. Kauppila, "So, What Am I Supposed to Do? A Multilevel Examination of Role Clarity," *Journal of Management Studies* 51, no. 5 (2014): 737–63.

5. Only a few sources have included all four factors. These include J. P. Campbell and R. D. Pritchard, "Motivation Theory in Industrial and Organizational Psychology," in *Handbook of Industrial and Organizational Psychology*, ed. M. D. Dunnette (Chicago: Rand McNally, 1976), 62–130; T. R. Mitchell, "Motivation: New Directions for Theory, Research, and Practice," *Academy of Management Review* 7, no. 1 (1982): 80–88; G. A. J. Churchill et al., "The Determinants of Salesperson Performance: A Meta-Analysis," *Journal of Marketing Research* 22, no. 2 (1985): 103–18; R. E. Plank and D. A. Reid, "The Mediating Role of Sales Behaviors: An Alternative Perspective of Sales Performance and Effectiveness," *Journal of Personal Selling & Sales Management* 14, no. 3 (1994): 43–56. The "MARS" acronym was coined by senior officers in the Singapore Armed Forces during a senior officer program taught by Steve McShane.

6. Technically, the model proposes that situational factors moderate the effects of the three within-person factors. For instance, the effect of employee motivation on behavior and performance depends on (is moderated by) the situation.

7. G. P. Latham and C. C. Pinder, "Work Motivation Theory and Research at the Dawn of the Twenty-First Century," *Annual Review of Psychology* 56 (2005): 485–516; G. P. Latham, *Work Motivation: History, Theory, Research, and Practice*, rev. ed. (Thousand Oaks, CA: Sage, 2012), 7.

8. T. J. Watson Jr., *A Business and Its Beliefs* (New York: McGraw- Hill, 2003), 4.

9. L. M. Spencer and S. M. Spencer, *Competence at Work: Models for Superior Performance* (New York: Wiley, 1993); D. Bartram, "The Great Eight Competencies: A Criterion-Centric Approach to Validation," *Journal of Applied Psychology* 90, no. 6 (2005): 1185–203; R. A. Roe, "Using Competences in Employee Development," in *Wiley Blackwell Handbook of the Psychology of Training, Development, and Performance Improvement*, ed. K. Kraiger et al. (Chichester: Wiley, 2014), 303–35.

10. P. Tharenou, A. M. Saks, and C. Moore, "A Review and Critique of Research on Training and Organizational-Level Outcomes," *Human Resource Management Review* 17, no. 3 (2007): 251–73; Y. Kim and R. E. Ployhart, "The Effects of Staffing and Training on Firm Productivity and Profit Growth before, during, and after the Great Recession," *Journal of Applied Psychology* 99, no. 3 (2014): 361–89; M. Choi and H. J. Yoon, "Training Investment and Organizational Outcomes: A Moderated Mediation Model of Employee Outcomes and Strategic Orientation of the HR Function," *The International Journal of Human Resource Management* 26, no. 20 (2015): 2632–51.

11. *The Interserve Society Report* (Reading, UK: Interserve, January 30, 2015); J. Harter, "Obsolete Annual Review: Gallup's Advice" (Washington, DC: Gallup, Inc., September 28, 2015); Randstad, "Prospects for Older Workers Shrink While the Skills Gap Widens," *Randstad Workmonitor* (Amsterdam, The Netherlands: Randstad Holding nv, June 2016); TINYpulse, *The Tinypulse 2015 Employee Engagement & Organizational Culture Report: The Era of Personal and Peer Accountability* (Seattle: TINYpulse, February 2016); Gallup Inc., *State of the American Workplace* (Washington, DC: Gallup, February 23, 2017).

12. BlessingWhite, *Employee Engagement Research Update* (Princeton, NJ: BlessingWhite, January 2013).

13. E. C. Dierdorff, R. S. Rubin, and D. G. Bachrach, "Role Expectations as Antecedents of Citizenship and the Moderating Effects of Work Context," *Journal of Management* 38, no. 2 (2012): 573–98; A. Newman, B. Allen, and Q. Miao, "I Can See Clearly Now: The Moderating Effects of Role Clarity on Subordinate Responses to Ethical Leadership," *Personnel Review* 44, no. 4 (2015): 611–28.

14. W. H. Cooper and M. J. Withey, "The Strong Situation Hypothesis," *Personality and Social Psychology Review* 13, no. 1 (2009): 62–72; N. A. Bowling et al., "Situational Strength as a Moderator of the Relationship between Job Satisfaction and Job Performance: A Meta-Analytic Examination," *Journal of Business and Psychology* 30, no. 1 (2015): 89–104; T. A. Judge and C. P. Zapata, "The Person–Situation Debate Revisited: Effect of Situation Strength and Trait Activation on the Validity of the Big Five Personality Traits in Predicting Job Performance," *Academy of Management Journal* 58, no. 4 (2015): 1149–79; J. F. Rauthmann and R. A. Sherman, "Situation Change: Stability and Change of Situation Variables between and within Persons," *Frontiers in Psychology* 6 (2016).

15. L. H. Peters and E. J. O'Connor, "Situational Constraints and Work Outcomes: The Influences of a Frequently Overlooked Construct," *Academy of Management Review* 5, no. 3 (1980): 391–97; G. Johns, "Commentary: In Praise of Context," *Journal of Organizational Behavior* 22 (2001): 31–42; C. E. J. Härtel and J. M. O'Connor, "Contextualizing Research: Putting Context Back into Organizational Behavior Research," *Journal of Management & Organization* 20, no. 4 (2014): 417–22.

16. R. D. Hackett, "Understanding and Predicting Work Performance in the Canadian Military," *Canadian Journal of Behavioural Science* 34, no. 2 (2002): 131–40; J. P. Campbell and B. M. Wiernik, "The Modeling and Assessment of Work Performance," *Annual Review of Organizational Psychology and Organizational Behavior* 2, no. 1 (2015): 47–74.

17. L. Tay, R. Su, and J. Rounds, "People-Things and Data-Ideas: Bipolar Dimensions?," *Journal of Counseling Psychology* 58, no. 3 (2011): 424–40.

18. M. A. Griffin, A. Neal, and S. K. Parker, "A New Model of Work Role Performance: Positive Behavior in Uncertain and Interdependent Contexts," *Academy of Management Journal* 50, no. 2 (2007): 327–47; S. K. Baard, T. A. Rench, and S. W. J. Kozlowski, "Performance Adaptation: A Theoretical Integration and Review," *Journal of Management* 40, no. 1 (2014): 48–99; D. K. Jundt, M. K. Shoss, and J. L. Huang, "Individual Adaptive Performance in Organizations: A Review," *Journal of Organizational Behavior* 36, no. S1 (2015): S53–S71.

19. D. W. Organ, "Organizational Citizenship Behavior: It's Construct Clean-up Time," *Human Performance* 10 (1997): 85–97; J. A. LePine, A. Erez, and D. E. Johnson, "The Nature and Dimensionality of Organizational Citizenship Behavior: A Critical Review and Meta-Analysis," *Journal of Applied Psychology* 87 (2002): 52–65; N. P. Podsakoff et al., "Consequences of Unit-Level Organizational Citizenship Behaviors: A Review and Recommendations for Future Research," *Journal of Organizational Behavior* 35, no. S1 (2014): S87–S119.

20. E. W. Morrison, "Role Definitions and Organizational Citizenship Behavior: The Importance of the Employee's Perspective," *Academy of Management Journal* 37, no. 6 (1994): 1543–67; N. Podsakoff et al., "Individual- and Organizational-Level Consequences of Organizational Citizenship Behaviors: A Meta-Analysis," *Journal of Applied Psychology* 94, no. 1 (2009): 122–41; E. C. Dierdorff, R. S. Rubin, and D. G. Bachrach, "Role Expectations as Antecedents of Citizenship and the Moderating Effects of Work Context," *Journal of Management* 38, no. 2 (2012): 573–98.

21. M. Ozer, "A Moderated Mediation Model of the Relationship between Organizational Citizenship Behaviors and Job Performance," *Journal of Applied Psychology* 96, no. 6 (2011): 1328–36; T. M. Nielsen et al., "Utility of OCB: Organizational Citizenship Behavior and Group Performance in a Resource Allocation Framework," *Journal of Management* 38, no. 2 (2012): 668–94.

22. A. C. Klotz and M. C. Bolino, "Citizenship and Counterproductive Work Behavior: A Moral Licensing View," *Academy of Management Review* 38, no. 2 (2013): 292–306; M. C. Bolino et al., "Exploring the Dark Side of Organizational Citizenship Behavior," *Journal of Organizational Behavior* 34, no. 4 (2013): 542–59.

23. M. Rotundo and P. Sackett, "The Relative Importance of Task, Citizenship, and Counterproductive Performance to Global Ratings of Job Performance: A Policy-Capturing Approach," *Journal of Applied Psychology* 87 (2002): 66–80; N. A. Bowling and M. L. Gruys, "Overlooked Issues in the Conceptualization and Measurement of Counterproductive Work Behavior," *Human Resource Management Review* 20, no. 1 (2010): 54–61; B. Marcus et al., "The Structure of Counterproductive Work Behavior: A Review, a Structural Meta-Analysis, and a Primary Study," *Journal of Management* 42, no. 1 (2016): 203–33.

24. T.-Y. Park and J. Shaw, "Turnover Rates and Organizational Performance: A Meta-Analysis," *Journal of Applied Psychology* 98, no. 2 (2013): 268–309; J. I. Hancock et al., "Meta-Analytic Review of Employee Turnover as a Predictor of Firm Performance," *Journal of Management* 39, no. 3 (2013): 573–603; J. G. Messersmith et al., "Turnover at the Top: Executive Team Departures and Firm Performance," *Organization Science* 25, no. 3 (2014): 776–93; B. C. Holtom and T. C. Burch, "A Model of Turnover-Based Disruption in Customer Services," *Human Resource Management Review* 26, no. 1 (2016): 25–36.

25. P. S. Goodman and R. S. Atkin, "Effects of Absenteeism on Individuals and Organizations," in *Absenteeism: New Approaches to Understanding, Measuring and Managing Employee Attendance*, ed. P. S. Goodman and R. S. Atkin (San Francisco: Jossey-Bass, 1984), 276–321; D. A. Harrison and J. J. Martocchio, "Time for Absenteeism: A 20-Year Review of Origins, Offshoots, and Outcomes," *Journal of Management* 24, no. 3 (1998): 305–50.

26. A. Väänänen et al., "The Role of Work Group in Individual Sickness Absence Behavior," *Journal of Health and Social Behavior* 49, no. 4 (2008): 452–67; W. Beemsterboer et al., "A Literature Review on Sick Leave Determinants (1984–2004)," *International Journal of Occupational Medicine and Environmental Health* 22, no. 2 (2009): 169–79; C. M. Berry, A. M. Lelchook, and M. A. Clark, "A Meta-Analysis of the Interrelationships between Employee Lateness, Absenteeism, and Turnover: Implications for Models of Withdrawal Behavior,"*Journal of Organizational Behavior* 33, no. 5 (2012): 678–99; S. Störmer and R. Fahr, "Individual Determinants of Work Attendance: Evidence on the Role of Personality," *Applied Economics* 45, no. 19 (2012): 2863–75; M. Sliter, K. Sliter, and S. Jex, "The Employee as a Punching Bag: The Effect of Multiple Sources of Incivility on Employee Withdrawal Behavior and Sales Performance," *Journal of Organizational Behavior* 33, no. 1 (2012): 121–39; M. Biron and P. Bamberger, "Aversive Workplace Conditions and Absenteeism: Taking Referent Group Norms and Supervisor Support into Account," *Journal of Applied Psychology* 97, no. 4 (2012): 901–12.

27. G. Johns, "Presenteeism in the Workplace: A Review and Research Agenda," *Journal of Organizational Behavior* 31, no. 4 (2010): 519–42; R. K. Skagen and A. M. Collins, "The Consequences of Sickness Presenteeism on Health and Wellbeing over Time: A Systematic Review," *Social Science & Medicine* 161 (2016): 169–77.

28. G. Johns, "Attendance Dynamics at Work: The Antecedents and Correlates of Presenteeism, Absenteeism, and Productivity Loss," *Journal of Occupational Health Psychology* 16, no. 4 (2011): 483–500; D. Baker-McClearn et al., "Absence Management and Presenteeism: The Pressures on Employees to Attend Work and the Impact of Attendance on Performance," *Human Resource Management Journal* 20, no. 3 (2010): 311–28; R. Pohling et al., "Work-Related Factors of Presenteeism: The Mediating Role of Mental and Physical Health," *Journal of Occupational Health Psychology* 21, no. 2 (2016): 220–34.

29. M. B. Edmond, "How Sick Is Too Sick to Work? Presenteeism in Healthcare," *Medscape*, September 23, 2015; C. Chambers, *Superheroes Don't Take Sick Leave* (New Zealand: Association of Salaried Medical Specialists, November 2015); J. E. Szymczak et al., "Reasons Why Physicians and Advanced Practice Clinicians Work While Sick: A Mixed-Methods Analysis," *JAMA Pediatrics* 169, no. 9 (2015): 815–21; M. G. Sendén, K. Schenck-Gustafsson, and A. Fridner, "Gender Differences in Reasons for Sickness Presenteeism—A Study among GPs in a Swedish Health Care Organization," *Annals of Occupational and Environmental Medicine* 28, no. 50 (2016): 50.

30. Personality researchers agree on one point about the definition of personality: It is difficult to pin down. A definition necessarily captures one perspective of the topic more than others, and the concept of personality is itself very broad. The definition presented here is based on C. S. Carver and M. F. Scheier, *Perspectives on Personality*, 6th ed. (Boston: Allyn & Bacon, 2007); D. C. Funder, *The Personality Puzzle*, 4th ed. (New York: Norton, 2007).

31. D. P. McAdams and J. L. Pals, "A New Big Five: Fundamental Principles for an Integrative Science of Personality," *American Psychologist* 61, no. 3 (2006): 204–17.

32. B. W. Roberts and A. Caspi, "Personality Development and the Person-Situation Debate: It's Déjà Vu All over Again," *Psychological Inquiry* 12, no. 2 (2001): 104–109; N. A. Turiano et al., "Personality and Substance Use in Midlife: Conscientiousness as a Moderator and the Effects of Trait Change," *Journal of Research in Personality* 46, no. 3 (2012): 295–305; C. R. Gale et al., "Neuroticism and Extraversion in Youth Predict Mental Wellbeing and Life Satisfaction 40 Years Later," *Journal of Research in Personality* 47, no. 6 (2013): 687–97; M. Pluess and M. Bartley, "Childhood Conscientiousness Predicts the Social Gradient of Smoking in Adulthood: A Life Course Analysis," *Journal of Epidemiology and Community Health* 69, no. 4 (2015): 330–38; M. Blatný et al., "Personality Predictors of Successful Development: Toddler Temperament and Adolescent Personality Traits Predict Well-Being and Career Stability in Middle Adulthood," *PLoS ONE* 10, no. 4 (2015): e0126032.

33. W. Mischel, "Toward an Integrative Science of the Person," *Annual Review of Psychology* 55 (2004): 1–22; W. H. Cooper and M. J. Withey, "The Strong Situation Hypothesis," *Personality and Social Psychology Review* 13, no. 1 (2009): 62–72; T. A. Judge and C. P. Zapata, "The Person–Situation Debate Revisited," *Academy of Management Journal* 58, no. 4 (2015): 1149–79.

34. O. Wilde, *The Picture of Dorian Gray* (New York: Barnes & Noble, 2003), 340.

35. W. Bleidorn, "What Accounts for Personality Maturation in Early Adulthood?," *Current Directions in Psychological Science* 24, no. 3 (2015): 245–52; T. J. C. Polderman et al., "Meta-Analysis of the Heritability of Human Traits Based on Fifty Years of Twin Studies," *Nature Genetics* 47, no. 7 (2015): 702–709; L. Penke and M. Jokela, "The Evolutionary Genetics of Personality Revisited," *Current Opinion in Psychology* 7 (2016): 104–109.

36. B. W. Roberts, K. E. Walton, and W. Viechtbauer, "Patterns of Mean-Level Change in Personality Traits across the Life Course: A Meta-Analysis of Longitudinal Studies," *Psychological Bulletin* 132, no. 1 (2006): 1–25; A. Terracciano, P. T. Costa, and R. R. McCrae, "Personality Plasticity after Age 30," *Personality and Social Psychology Bulletin* 32, no. 8 (2006): 999–1009; R. Mıttus et al., "Within-Trait Heterogeneity in Age Group Differences in Personality Domains and Facets: Implications for the Development and Coherence of Personality Traits," *PLoS ONE* 10, no. 3 (2015): e0119667; C.-H. Wu, "Personality Change Via Work: A Job Demand-Control Model of Big-Five Personality Changes," *Journal of Vocational Behavior* 92 (2016): 157–66.

37. R. F. Baumeister, B. J. Schmeichel, and K. D. Vohs, "Self-Regulation and the Executive Function: The Self as Controlling Agent," in *Social Psychology: Handbook of Basic Principles*, ed. A. W. Kruglanski and E. T. Higgins (New York: Guilford, 2007), 516–39; K. Murdock, K. Oddi, and D. Bridgett, "Cognitive Correlates of Personality: Links between Executive Functioning and the Big Five Personality Traits," *Journal of Individual Differences* 34, no. 2 (2013): 97–104; P. Baggetta and P. A. Alexander, "Conceptualization and Operationalization of Executive Function," *Mind, Brain, and Education* 10, no. 1 (2016): 10–33.

38. J. M. Digman, "Personality Structure: Emergence of the Five-Factor Model," *Annual Review of Psychology* 41 (1990): 417–40; O. P. John and S. Srivastava, "The Big Five Trait Taxonomy: History, Measurement, and Theoretical Perspectives," in *Handbook of Personality: Theory and Research*, ed. L. A. Pervin and O. P. John (New York: Guilford Press, 1999), 102–38; R. R. McCrae, J. F. Gaines, and M. A. Wellington, "The Five-Factor Model in Fact and Fiction," in *Personality and Social Psychology*, 2nd ed., ed. H. A. Tennen and J. M. Suls, Handbook of Psychology, ed. I. B. Weiner, vol. 5 (New York: Wiley, 2012), 65–91.

39. H. Le et al., "Too Much of a Good Thing: Curvilinear Relationships between Personality Traits and Job Performance," *Journal of Applied Psychology* 96, no. 1 (2011): 113–33; A. M. Grant, "Rethinking the Extraverted Sales Ideal: The Ambivert Advantage," *Psychological Science* 24, no. 6 (2013): 1024–30; G. Blickle et al., "Extraversion and Job Performance: How Context Relevance and Bandwidth Specificity Create a Non-linear, Positive, and Asymptotic Relationship," *Journal of Vocational Behavior* 87 (2015): 80–88.

40. M. R. Barrick and M. K. Mount, "Yes, Personality Matters: Moving on to More Important Matters," *Human Performance* 18, no. 4 (2005): 359–72; P. R. Sackett and P. T. Walmsley, "Which Personality Attributes Are Most Important in the Workplace?," *Perspectives on Psychological Science* 9, no. 5 (2014): 538–51; L. M. Penney, E. David, and L. A. Witt, "A Review of Personality and Performance: Identifying Boundaries, Contingencies, and Future Research Directions," *Human Resource Management Review* 21, no. 4 (2011): 297–310; T. Judge et al., "Hierarchical Representations of the Five-Factor Model of Personality in Predicting Job Performance: Integrating Three Organizing Frameworks with Two Theoretical Perspectives," *Journal of Applied Psychology* 98, no. 6 (2013): 875–925; J. Huang et al., "Personality and Adaptive Performance at Work: A Meta-Analytic Investigation," *Journal of Applied Psychology* 99, no. 1 (2014): 162–79.

41. R. D. S. Chiaburu et al., "The Five-Factor Model of Personality Traits and Organizational Citizenship Behaviors: A Meta-Analysis," *Journal of Applied Psychology* 96, no. 6 (2011): 1140–66.

42. A. Neal et al., "Predicting the Form and Direction of Work Role Performance from the Big 5 Model of Personality Traits," *Journal of Organizational Behavior* 33, no. 2 (2012): 175–92.

43. J. L. Huang et al., "Personality and Adaptive Performance at Work," *Journal of Applied Psychology* 99, no. 1 (2014): 162–79.

44. C. G. Jung, *Psychological Types*, trans. H. G. Baynes (Princeton, NJ: Princeton University Press, 1971); I. B. Myers, *The Myers-Briggs Type Indicator* (Palo Alto, CA: Consulting Psychologists Press, 1987).

45. Adapted from an exhibit found at www.16-personality-types.com. Based on data from CPP, Inc., Sunnyvale, CA 94086 from *Introduction to Type and Careers* by Allen L. Hammer.

46. J. Michael, "Using the Myers-Briggs Type Indicator as a Tool for Leadership Development? Apply with Caution," *Journal of Leadership & Organizational Studies* 10 (2003): 68–81; R. M. Capraro and M. M. Capraro, "Myers-Briggs Type Indicator Score Reliability across Studies: A Meta-Analytic Reliability Generalization Study," *Educational and Psychological Measurement* 62 (2002): 590–602; B. S. Kuipers et al., "The Influence of Myers-Briggs Type Indicator Profiles on Team Development Processes," *Small Group Research* 40, no. 4 (2009): 436–64; F. W. Brown and M. D. Reilly, "The Myers-Briggs Type Indicator and Transformational Leadership," *Journal of Management Development* 28, no. 10 (2009): 916–32; A. Luse et al., "Personality and Cognitive Style as Predictors of Preference for Working in Virtual Teams," *Computers in Human Behavior* 29, no. 4 (2013): 1825–32.

47. R. B. Kennedy and D. A. Kennedy, "Using the Myers-Briggs Type Indicator in Career Counseling," *Journal of Employment Counseling* 41, no. 1 (2004): 38–44; K.-H. Lee, Y. Choi, and D. J. Stonier, "Evolutionary Algorithm for a Genetic Robot's Personality Based on the Myers-Briggs Type Indicator," *Robotics and Autonomous Systems* 60, no. 7 (2012): 941–61; S. J. Armstrong, E. Cools, and E. Sadler-Smith, "Role of Cognitive Styles in Business and Management: Reviewing 40 Years of Research," *International Journal of Management Reviews* 14, no. 3 (2012): 238–62.

48. J. B. Lloyd, "Unsubstantiated Beliefs and Values Flaw the Five-Factor Model of Personality," *Journal of Beliefs & Values* 36, no. 2 (2015): 156–64.

49. B. M. Meglino and E. C. Ravlin, "Individual Values in Organizations: Concepts, Controversies, and Research," *Journal of Management* 24, no. 3 (1998): 351–89; B. R. Agle and C. B. Caldwell, "Understanding Research on Values in Business," *Business and Society* 38, no. 3 (1999): 326–87; S. Hitlin and J. A. Pilavin, "Values: Reviving a Dormant Concept," *Annual Review of Sociology* 30 (2004): 359–93.

50. D. Lubinski, D. B. Schmidt, and C. P. Benbow, "A 20-Year Stability Analysis of the Study of Values for Intellectually Gifted Individuals from Adolescence to Adulthood," *Journal of Applied Psychology* 81 (1996): 443–51.

51. L. Parks and R. P. Guay, "Personality, Values, and Motivation," *Personality and Individual Differences* 47, no. 7 (2009): 675–84; L. Parks-Leduc, G. Feldman, and A. Bardi, "Personality Traits and Personal Values: A Meta-Analysis," *Personality and Social Psychology Review* 19, no. 1 (2015): 3–29.

52. S. H. Schwartz, "Universals in the Content and Structure of Values: Theoretical Advances and Empirical Tests in 20 Countries," *Advances in Experimental Social Psychology* 25 (1992): 1–65; D. Spini, "Measurement Equivalence of 10 Value Types from the Schwartz Value Survey across 21 Countries," *Journal of Cross-Cultural Psychology* 34, no. 1 (2003): 3–23; S. H. Schwartz and K. Boehnke, "Evaluating the Structure of Human Values with Confirmatory Factor Analysis," *Journal of Research in Personality* 38, no. 3 (2004): 230–55; S. H. Schwartz, "Studying Values: Personal Adventure, Future Directions," *Journal of Cross-Cultural Psychology* 42, no. 2 (2011): 307–19. Schwartz's model is currently being revised, but the new model is similar in overall design and still requires refinement. See S. H. Schwartz et al., "Refining the Theory of Basic Individual Values," *Journal of Personality and Social Psychology* 103, no. 4 (2012): 663–88.

53. N. T. Feather, "Values, Valences, and Choice: The Influence of Values on the Perceived Attractiveness and Choice of Alternatives," *Journal of Personality and Social Psychology* 68, no. 6 (1995): 1135–51; L. Sagiv, N. Sverdlik, and N. Schwarz, "To Compete or to Cooperate? Values' Impact on Perception and Action in Social Dilemma Games," *European Journal of Social Psychology* 41, no. 1 (2011): 64–77; S. H. Schwartz and T. Butenko, "Values and Behavior: Validating the Refined Value Theory in Russia," *European Journal of Social Psychology* 44, no. 7 (2014): 799–813.

54. M. Schrage, *Serious Play: How the World's Best Companies Simulate to Innovate* (Cambridge, MA: Harvard Business School Press, 1999), 98

55. G. R. Maio et al., "Addressing Discrepancies between Values and Behavior: The Motivating Effect of Reasons," *Journal of Experimental Social Psychology* 37, no. 2 (2001): 104–17; A. Bardi and S. H. Schwartz, "Values and Behavior: Strength and Structure of Relations," *Personality and Social Psychology Bulletin* 29, no. 10 (2003): 1207–20; L. Sagiv, N. Sverdlik, and N. Schwarz, "To Compete or to Cooperate? Values' Impact on Perception and Action in Social Dilemma Games," *European Journal of Social Psychology* 41, no. 1 (2011): 64–77; K. M. Sheldon and L. S. Krieger, "Walking the Talk: Value Importance, Value Enactment, and Well-Being," *Motivation and Emotion* 38 (2014): 609–19.

56. E. Dreezens et al., "The Missing Link: On Strengthening the Relationship between Values and Attitudes," *Basic and Applied Social Psychology* 30, no. 2 (2008): 142–52; S. Arieli, A. M. Grant, and L. Sagiv, "Convincing Yourself to Care About Others: An Intervention for Enhancing Benevolence Values," *Journal of Personality* 82, no. 1 (2014): 15–24.

57. N. Mazar, O. Amir, and D. Ariely, "The Dishonesty of Honest People: A Theory of Self-Concept Maintenance," *Journal of Marketing Research* 45 (2008): 633–44.

58. L. Colan, "The Authentic Workplace: Aligning Work and Personal Values," *Inc.*, November 30, 2016.

59. M. L. Verquer, T. A. Beehr, and S. H. Wagner, "A Meta-Analysis of Relations between Person–Organization Fit and Work Attitudes," *Journal of Vocational Behavior* 63 (2003): 473–89; J. W. Westerman and L. A. Cyr, "An Integrative Analysis of Person–Organization Fit Theories," *International Journal of Selection and Assessment* 12, no. 3 (2004): 252–61; J. R. Edwards and D. M. Cable, "The Value of Value Congruence," *Journal of Applied Psychology* 94, no. 3 (2009): 654–77; A. L. Kristof-Brown et al., "Collective Fit Perceptions: A Multilevel Investigation of Person–Group Fit with Individual-Level and Team-Level Outcomes," *Journal of Organizational Behavior* 35, no. 7 (2014): 969–89.

60. The Conference Board, *CEO Challenge 2014* (New York: The Conference Board, January 2014); S. Giles, "The Most Important Leadership Competencies, According to Leaders around the World," *Harvard Business Review Digital Articles* (March 2016): 2–6.

61. P. L. Schumann, "A Moral Principles Framework for Human Resource Management Ethics," *Human Resource Management Review* 11 (2001): 93–111; J. A. Boss, *Analyzing Moral Issues*, 6th ed. (New York: McGraw-Hill, 2013), chap. 1; A. Gustafson, "In Defense of a Utilitarian Business Ethic," *Business and Society Review* 118, no. 3 (2013): 325–60.

62. For analysis of these predictors of ethical conduct, see J. J. Kish-Gephart, D. A. Harrison, and L. K. Treviño, "Bad Apples, Bad Cases, and Bad Barrels: Meta-Analytic Evidence about Sources of Unethical Decisions at Work," *Journal of Applied Psychology* 95, no. 1 (2010): 1–32.

63. T. M. Jones, "Ethical Decision Making by Individuals in Organizations: An Issue-Contingent Model," *Academy of Management Review* 16 (1991): 366–95; T. Barnett, "Dimensions of Moral Intensity and Ethical Decision Making: An Empirical Study," *Journal of Applied Social Psychology* 31, no. 5 (2001): 1038–57; J. Tsalikis, B. Seaton, and P. Shepherd, "Relative Importance Measurement of the Moral Intensity Dimensions," *Journal of Business Ethics* 80, no. 3 (2008): 613–26; S. Valentine and D. Hollingworth, "Moral Intensity, Issue Importance, and Ethical Reasoning in Operations Situations," *Journal of Business Ethics* 108, no. 4 (2012): 509–23.

64. K. Weaver, J. Morse, and C. Mitcham, "Ethical Sensitivity in Professional Practice: Concept Analysis," *Journal of Advanced Nursing* 62, no. 5 (2008): 607–18; L. J. T. Pedersen, "See No Evil: Moral Sensitivity in the Formulation of Business Problems," *Business Ethics: A European Review* 18, no. 4 (2009): 335–48. According to one recent neuroscience study, the emotional aspect of moral sensitivity declines and the cognitive aspect increases between early childhood and young adulthood. See J. Decety, K. J. Michalska, and K. D. Kinzler, "The Contribution of Emotion and Cognition to Moral Sensitivity: A Neurodevelopmental Study," *Cerebral Cortex* 22, no. 1 (2012): 209–20.

65. D. You, Y. Maeda, and M. J. Bebeau, "Gender Differences in Moral Sensitivity: A Meta-Analysis," *Ethics & Behavior* 21, no. 4 (2011): 263–82; A. H. Chan and H. Cheung, "Cultural Dimensions, Ethical Sensitivity, and Corporate Governance," *Journal of Business Ethics* 110, no. 1 (2012): 45–59; J. R. Sparks, "A Social Cognitive Explanation of Situational and Individual Effects on Moral Sensitivity," *Journal of Applied Social Psychology* 45, no. 1 (2015): 45–54; S. J. Reynolds and J. A. Miller, "The Recognition of Moral Issues: Moral Awareness, Moral Sensitivity and Moral Attentiveness," *Current Opinion in Psychology* 6 (2015): 114–17.

66. J. Boegershausen, K. Aquino, and A. Reed II, "Moral Identity," *Current Opinion in Psychology* 6 (2015): 162–66.

67. N. Ruedy and M. Schweitzer, "In the Moment: The Effect of Mindfulness on Ethical Decision Making," *Journal of Business Ethics* 95, no. 1 (2010): 73–87.

68. M. H. Bazerman and F. Gino, "Behavioral Ethics: Toward a Deeper Understanding of Moral Judgment and Dishonesty," *Annual Review of Law and Social Science* 8, no. 1 (2012): 85–104; M. Knoll et al., "Examining the Moral Grey Zone: The Role of Moral Disengagement, Authenticity, and Situational Strength in Predicting Unethical Managerial Behavior," *Journal of Applied Social Psychology* 46, no. 1 (2016): 65–78.

69. Ethics & Compliance Initiative, *Global Business Ethics Survey: Measuring Risk and Promoting Workplace Integrity* (Arlington, VA: Ethics & Compliance Initiative, June 2016), 9.

70. H. Donker, D. Poff, and S. Zahir, "Corporate Values, Codes of Ethics, and Firm Performance: A Look at the Canadian Context," *Journal of Business Ethics* 82, no. 3 (2008): 527–37; G. Svensson et al., "Ethical Structures and Processes of Corporations Operating in Australia, Canada, and Sweden: A Longitudinal and Cross-Cultural Study," *Journal of Business Ethics* 86, no. 4 (2009): 485–506; L. Preuss, "Codes of Conduct in Organisational Context: From Cascade to Lattice-Work of Codes," *Journal of Business Ethics* 94, no. 4 (2010): 471–87.

71. G. Svensson et al., "Ethical Structures and Processes of Corporations Operating in Australia, Canada, and Sweden: A Longitudinal and Cross-Cultural Study," *Journal of Business Ethics* 86, no. 4 (2009): 485–506.

72. S. L. Grover, T. Nadisic, and D. L. Patient, "Bringing Together Different Perspectives on Ethical Leadership," *Journal of Change Management* 12, no. 4 (2012): 377–81; J. Jordan et al., "Someone to Look Up To: Executive-Follower Ethical Reasoning and Perceptions of Ethical Leadership," *Journal of Management* 39, no. 3 (2013): 660–83; J. Jaeger, "Compliance Culture Depends on Middle Management," *Compliance Week* (February 2014): 47–61.

73. "The TI Ethics Quick Test," *Corporate Governance* (Dallas: Texas Instruments, 2017), http://www.ti.com/corp/docs/company/citizen/ethics/quicktest.shtml (accessed June 16, 2017).

74. Individualism and collectivism information is from the meta-analysis by Oyserman et al., not the earlier findings by Hofstede. See D. Oyserman, H. M. Coon, and M. Kemmelmeier, "Rethinking Individualism and Collectivism: Evaluation of Theoretical Assumptions and Meta-Analyses," *Psychological Bulletin* 128, no. 1 (2002): 3–72. Consistent with Oyserman et al., a recent study found high rather than low individualism among Chileans. See A. Kolstad and S. Horpestad, "Self-Construal in Chile and Norway," *Journal of Cross-Cultural Psychology* 40, no. 2 (2009): 275–81.

75. F. S. Niles, "Individualism–Collectivism Revisited," *Cross-Cultural Research* 32 (1998): 315–41; C. P. Earley and C. B. Gibson, "Taking Stock in Our Progress on Individualism–Collectivism: 100 Years of Solidarity and Community," *Journal of Management* 24 (1998): 265–304; C. L. Jackson et al., "Psychological Collectivism: A Measurement Validation and Linkage to Group Member Performance," *Journal of Applied Psychology* 91, no. 4 (2006): 884–99.

76. D. Oyserman, H. M. Coon, and M. Kemmelmeier, "Rethinking Individualism and Collectivism: Evaluation of Theoretical Assumptions and Meta-Analyses," *Psychological Bulletin* 128, no. 1 (2002): 3–72. Also see F. Li and L. Aksoy, "Dimensionality of Individualism–Collectivism and Measurement Equivalence of Triandis and Gelfand's Scale," *Journal of Business and Psychology* 21, no. 3 (2007): 313–29. The "vertical–horizontal" distinction does not account for the lack of correlation between individualism and collectivism. See J. H. Vargas and M. Kemmelmeier, "Ethnicity and Contemporary American Culture: A Meta-Analytic Investigation of Horizontal–Vertical Individualism–Collectivism," *Journal of Cross-Cultural Psychology* 44, no. 2 (2013): 195–222.

77. M. Voronov and J. A. Singer, "The Myth of Individualism–Collectivism: A Critical Review," *Journal of Social Psychology* 142 (2002): 461–80; Y. Takano and S. Sogon, "Are Japanese More Collectivistic Than Americans?," *Journal of Cross-Cultural Psychology* 39, no. 3 (2008): 237–50; D. Dalsky, "Individuality in Japan and the United States: A Cross-Cultural Priming Experiment," *International Journal of Intercultural Relations* 34, no. 5 (2010): 429–35. Japan scored 46 on individualism in Hofstede's original study, placing it a little below the middle of the range and around the 60th percentile among the countries studied. Recent studies suggest that Japan has become even more individualistic in recent years. See Y. Ogihara et al., "Are Common Names Becoming Less Common? The Rise in Uniqueness and Individualism in Japan," *Frontiers in Psychology* 6 (2015): 1490.

78. G. Hofstede, *Culture's Consequences: Comparing Values, Behaviors, Institutions, and Organizations across Nations*, 2nd ed. (Thousand Oaks, CA: Sage, 2001).

79. G. Hofstede, *Culture's Consequences: Comparing Values, Behaviors, Institutions, and Organizations across Nations*, 2nd ed. (Thousand Oaks, CA: Sage, 2001). Hofstede used the terms *masculinity* and *femininity* for *achievement* and *nurturing orientation*, respectively. We (along with other writers) have adopted the latter two terms to minimize the sexist perspective of these concepts. Also, readers need to be aware that achievement orientation is assumed to be opposite of nurturing orientation, but this opposing relationship might be questioned.

80. T. Mickle and E. Pfanner, "Jim Beam's New Owner Mixes Global Cocktail," *The Wall Street Journal*, May 4, 2015, A1; K. Moritsugu, "Merging US, Japan Work Cultures a Challenge for Beam Suntory," Associated Press, January 15, 2016.

81. V. Taras, J. Rowney, and P. Steel, "Half a Century of Measuring Culture: Review of Approaches, Challenges, and Limitations Based on the Analysis of 121 Instruments for Quantifying Culture," *Journal of International Management* 15, no. 4 (2009): 357–73.

82. N. Jacob, "Cross-Cultural Investigations: Emerging Concepts," *Journal of Organizational Change Management* 18, no. 5 (2005): 514–28; V. Taras, B. L. Kirkman, and P. Steel, "Examining the Impact of Culture's Consequences: A Three-Decade, Multilevel, Meta-Analytic Review of Hofstede's Cultural Value Dimensions," *Journal of Applied Psychology* 95, no. 3 (2010): 405–39.

83. R. L. Tung and A. Verbeke, "Beyond Hofstede and GLOBE: Improving the Quality of Cross-Cultural Research," *Journal of International Business Studies* 41, no. 8 (2010): 1259–74.

84. D. Oyserman, H. M. Coon, and M. Kemmelmeier, "Rethinking Individualism and Collectivism: Evaluation of Theoretical Assumptions and Meta-Analyses," *Psychological Bulletin* 128, no. 1 (2002): 3–72. However, a recent meta-analysis found only minor differences across ethnic groups. See J. H. Vargas and M. Kemmelmeier, "Ethnicity and Contemporary American Culture: A Meta-Analytic Investigation of Horizontal–Vertical Individualism–Collectivism," *Journal of Cross-Cultural Psychology* 44, no. 2 (2013): 195–222.

85. J. A. Vandello and D. Cohen, "Patterns of Individualism and Collectivism across the United States," *Journal of Personality and Social Psychology* 77, no. 2 (1999): 279–92; B. MacNab, R. Worthley, and S. Jenner, "Regional Cultural Differences and Ethical Perspectives within the United States: Avoiding Pseudo-Emic Ethics Research," *Business and Society Review* 115, no. 1 (2010): 27–55; J. Lun, B. Mesquita, and B. Smith, "Self- and Other-Presentational Styles in the Southern and Northern United States: An Analysis of Personal Ads," *European Journal of Social Psychology* 41, no. 4 (2011): 435–45; P. J. Rentfrow et al., "Divided We Stand: Three Psychological Regions of the United States and Their Political, Economic, Social, and Health Correlates," *Journal of Personality and Social Psychology* 105, no. 6 (2013): 996–1012.

86. V. C. Plaut, H. Rose Markus, and M. E. Lachman, "Place Matters: Consensual Features and Regional Variation in American Well-Being and Self," *Journal of Personality and Social Psychology* 83, no. 1 (2002): 160–84; P. J. Rentfrow, "Statewide Differences in Personality: Toward a Psychological Geography of the United States," *American Psychologist* 65, no. 6 (2010): 548–58; K. H. Rogers and D. Wood, "Accuracy of United States Regional Personality Stereotypes," *Journal of Research in Personality* 44, no. 6 (2010): 704–13; J. Lieske, "The Changing Regional Subcultures of the American States and the Utility of a New Cultural Measure," *Political Research Quarterly* 63, no. 3 (2010): 538–52.

87. P. J. Rentfrow, "Statewide Differences in Personality: Toward a Psychological Geography of the United States," *American Psychologist* 65, no. 6 (2010): 548–58; J. Lieske, "The Changing Regional Subcultures of the American States and the Utility of a New Cultural Measure," *Political Research Quarterly* 63, no. 3 (2010): 538–52.

88. J. R. Harrington and M. J. Gelfand, "Tightness–Looseness across the 50 United States," *Proceedings of the National Academy of Sciences* 111, no. 22 (2014): 7990–95.

89. M. Motyl et al., "How Ideological Migration Geographically Segregates Groups," *Journal of Experimental Social Psychology* 51 (2014): 1–14; S. Oishi, T. Talhelm, and M. Lee, "Personality and Geography: Introverts Prefer Mountains," *Journal of Research in Personality* 58 (2015): 55–68.

3 | Perceiving Ourselves and Others in Organizations

Learning Objectives

After you read this chapter, you should be able to:

LO3-1 Describe the elements of self-concept and explain how each affects an individual's behavior and well-being.

LO3-2 Outline the perceptual process and discuss the effects of categorical thinking and mental models in that process.

LO3-3 Discuss how stereotyping, attribution, self-fulfilling prophecy, and the halo, false-consensus, primacy, and recency effects influence the perceptual process.

LO3-4 Discuss three ways to improve perceptions, with specific application to organizational situations.

LO3-5 Outline the main features of a global mindset and justify its usefulness to employees and organizations.

self-concept an individual's self-beliefs and self-evaluations

Perceiving ourselves and others is a critical skill for organizational leaders, says Chris Van Gorder. The CEO of Scripps Health in San Diego warns: "Psychological distance is extremely dangerous for leaders. When you lose perspective and start to think you're something more than just another member of the team, you undercut any progress you might have been making in building trust and affection between yourself and your workforce."

Van Gorder devotes almost half of his time to interacting with the health care organization's 14,000 employees in Southern California through training future leaders, doing weekly rounds, and occasionally working alongside staff in frontline roles. "Roll up your sleeves and get your hands dirty," Van Gorder advises. He learned the value of this meaningful interaction many years ago as vice president of support services at another hospital. "I didn't know how [the cleaning staff] did their work so I went down and actually started running the floor buffers with them," Van Gorder recalls. He adds that the employees enjoyed watching him as the buffer machine was bucking all over the floor.

Van Gorder also emphasizes that "it's important to show your empathy, don't merely feel it. Sometimes leaders mistakenly project a stoic persona, but by not demonstrating empathy leaders come across as cold and uncaring. This creates distance in relationships and undermines connection."[1]

self-fulfilling prophecy. This is followed by discussion of potentially effective ways to improve perceptions. The final section of this chapter reviews the main elements of global mindset, a largely perceptual process valued in this increasingly globalized world.

> **LO3-1** Describe the elements of self-concept and explain how each affects an individual's behavior and well-being.

SELF-CONCEPT: HOW WE PERCEIVE OURSELVES

Self-concept refers to an individual's self-beliefs and self-evaluations.[2] It is the "Who am I?" and "How do I feel about myself?" that people ask themselves and that guide their decisions and actions. Whether contemplating a career as a health care executive or in any other occupation, we compare our perceptions of that job with our current (perceived self) and desired (ideal self) images of ourselves. We also evaluate our current and desired abilities to determine whether there is a good fit with that type of work. Our self-concept is defined at three levels: individual, relational, and collective. Specifically, we view ourselves in terms of our personal traits (individual self); connections to friends and coworkers (relational self); and membership in teams, organizations, social groups, and other entities (collective self).[3]

> Whenever two people meet there are really six people present. There are the two people as they see themselves, the two people as they see each other, and the two people as they really are.[4]
>
> —Restated from Oliver Wendell Holmes Sr., medical scholar and author
> (in *The Autocrat of the Breakfast-Table*, 1858)

Chris Van Gorder's advice to executives about perceiving others and self-perception represent the two central topics in this chapter. First, we examine how people perceive themselves—their self-concept—and how that self-perception affects their decisions and behavior. Next, we focus on perceptions in organizational settings, beginning with how we select, organize, and interpret information. We also review several specific perceptual processes such as stereotyping, attribution, and

Self-Concept Complexity, Consistency, and Clarity

An individual's self-concept can be described by three characteristics: complexity, consistency, and clarity (see Exhibit 3.1). *Complexity* refers to the number of distinct and important roles or identities that people perceive about themselves.[5] Everyone has multiple self-views because each person sees himself or

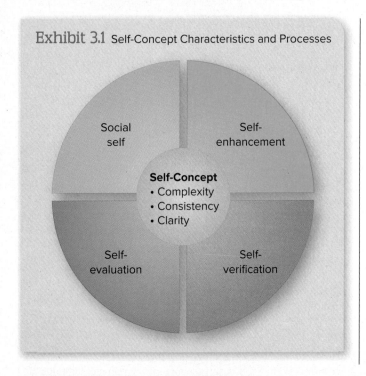

Exhibit 3.1 Self-Concept Characteristics and Processes

Social self

Self-enhancement

Self-Concept
- Complexity
- Consistency
- Clarity

Self-evaluation

Self-verification

multiple identities have a low correlation with each other, such as when they apply to fairly distinct spheres of life.

Although everyone has multiple selves, only some of those identities dominate their attention at one time.[6] A person's various selves are usually domain specific, meaning that a particular self-view (parent, manager, etc.) is more likely to be activated in some settings than in others. People shift their self-concept more easily when the activated self-view is important and compatible with the situation. For instance, as people travel from home to work, they can usually shift their self-view from being a parent to being an executive because each role is important and fits into the home and work contexts, respectively. In contrast, some employees struggle to focus on their occupational self-concept when working from home (telecommuting).

Consistency is the second characteristic of an individual's self-concept. High consistency exists when the individual's identities are compatible with each other and with the person's actual personality and values. Low consistency occurs when some self-views require personal characteristics that conflict with attributes required for other self-views, such as when a safety-conscious engineer also defines himself or herself as a risk-oriented acrobatic snowboarder. Self-concept consistency also

> ## High self-concept consistency exists when the individual's identities are compatible with each other and with the person's actual personality and values.

herself in different roles at various times (student, friend, daughter, sports fan, etc.). People are generally motivated to increase their complexity (called *self-expansion*) as they seek out new opportunities and social connections. A person's self-concept becomes more complex, for example, as he or she moves from being an accountant to a manager because the person has acquired additional roles.

Self-concept complexity isn't just how many identities a person has; it also is defined by the separation of those identities. An individual with several identities might still have low self-concept complexity when those identities are highly interconnected, such as when they are all work related (manager, engineer, family income earner). Complexity is higher when the

depends on how closely the person's identities align with his or her actual attributes. Low consistency exists when an individual's personality and values clash with the type of person he or she tries to become.

Clarity, the third characteristic of self-concept, refers to the degree to which a person's self-concept is clear, confidently defined, and stable.[7] Clarity occurs when we are confident about "who we are," can describe our important identities to others, and provide the same description of ourselves across time. Self-concept clarity increases with age because personality and values become relatively stable by adulthood and people develop better self-awareness through life experiences. Self-concept is also clearer when a person's multiple selves have higher consistency. This makes sense because low consistency produces ambiguity about a person's underlying characteristics. For example, someone whose self-view included both cautious engineer and risk-oriented snowboarder would have difficulty defining himself or herself clearly or with much confidence.[8]

People tend to have better psychological well-being when their multiple selves are compatible with each other and with the individual's actual personality and values (high consistency).
©alphaspirit/Shutterstock

Effects of Self-Concept Characteristics on Well-Being and Behavior Psychological well-being tends to be higher among people with fairly distinct multiple selves (complexity) that are well established (clarity) and require similar personal attributes that are compatible with the individual's character (consistency).[9] Self-concept complexity protects our self-esteem when some roles are threatened or damaged. A complex self is rather like a ship with several compartments that can be sealed off from one another. If one compartment is damaged, the other compartments (other identities) remain intact so the ship remains afloat. In contrast, people with low complexity, including those whose multiple selves are highly interconnected, suffer severe loss when they experience failure because these events affect a large part of themselves.

People also tend to have better psychological well-being when their multiple selves are compatible with each other and with the individual's actual personality and values (high consistency).[10] Self-concept complexity helps people adapt, but too much variation causes internal tension and conflict. Well-being also tends to increase with self-concept clarity. People who are unsure of their self-views are more easily influenced by others, experience more stress when making decisions, and feel more threatened by social forces that undermine their self-confidence and self-esteem.[11]

Self-concept complexity has both positive and negative influences on individual behavior and performance.[12] Employees with complex identities tend to have more adaptive decision making

People are inherently motivated to perceive themselves, and to be perceived by others, as above average in important ways.
©Spark Studio/Imagezoo/Getty Images

and performance. This likely occurs because multiple selves generate more diverse experiences and role patterns, so these employees can more easily alter their thinking and behavior to suit new tasks and work environments. A second benefit is that self-concept complexity often produces more diverse social networks, and this network diversity gives employees access to more resources and social support to perform their jobs.

Against these benefits is the problem that highly complex self-concepts require more effort to maintain and juggle, which can be stressful. In contrast, low complexity self-concepts have the advantage of requiring less effort and resources to develop. For example, people who define themselves mainly by their work (low complexity) often have better performance due to more investment in skill development, longer hours, and higher concentration on work. They also have lower absenteeism and turnover.

Self-concept clarity tends to improve performance and is considered vital for leadership roles.[13] Clarity also provides a clearer path forward, which enables people to direct their effort more efficiently toward career objectives. Another benefit is that people with high self-concept clarity feel less threatened by interpersonal conflict, so they use more constructive problem-solving behaviors to resolve the conflict. However, those with very high clarity may have role inflexibility, with the result that they cannot adapt to changing job duties or environmental conditions.

Along with the three self-concept characteristics, Exhibit 3.1 illustrates four processes that shape self-concept and motivate a person's decisions and behavior. Let's look at each of these four "selves": self-enhancement, self-verification, self-evaluation, and social self (social identity).

Self-Enhancement

People are inherently motivated to perceive themselves, and to be perceived by others, as above average in important ways, such as being competent, attractive, lucky, ethical, and valuable.[14] This phenomenon, called **self-enhancement**, occurs when individuals rate themselves above average, believe that they have a better-than-average probability of success, and attribute their successes to personal motivation or ability while blaming the situation for their mistakes. People don't believe they are above average in all circumstances, only for things that are important to them and are relatively common rather than rare.[15]

> **self-enhancement** a person's inherent motivation to have a positive self-concept (and to have others perceive him or her favorably), such as being competent, attractive, lucky, ethical, and important

Self-enhancement has both positive and negative consequences in organizational settings.[16] On the positive side, individuals tend to experience better mental and physical health when they amplify their self-concept. Overconfidence also generates a "can-do" attitude (which we discuss later) that motivates persistence in difficult or risky tasks. On the negative side, self-enhancement causes people to overestimate future returns in investment decisions and to engage in unsafe behavior (such as dangerous driving). It also accounts for executives repeating poor decisions (because they ignore negative feedback), launching misguided corporate diversification strategies, and acquiring excessive corporate debt.

Self-Verification

Individuals try to confirm and maintain their existing self-concept.[19] This process, called **self-verification**, stabilizes an individual's self-view, which in turn provides an important anchor that guides his or her thoughts and actions. Employees actively communicate their self-concept so coworkers understand it and provide verifying feedback when observed. For example, you might let coworkers know that you are a very organized person; later, they compliment you on occasions where you have indeed been very organized. Unlike self-enhancement, self-verification includes seeking feedback that is not necessarily flattering (e.g., "I'm a numbers person, not a people person"). Experts continue to debate whether and under what conditions people prefer information that supports self-enhancement or self-verification.[20] Do we prefer compliments rather than accurate critique about weaknesses that we readily acknowledge? The answer is likely complex; we enjoy compliments, but less so if they are significantly contrary to our self-view.

Self-verification is associated with several OB topics.[21] First, it affects the perceptual process that we describe later in this chapter. Specifically, employees are more likely to remember information that is consistent with their self-concept and nonconsciously screen out information (particularly negative information) that seems inconsistent with it. Second, people with high self-concept clarity will consciously dismiss feedback that contradicts their self-concept. Third, employees prefer interacting with others who affirm their self-views, which this affecting how well they get along with their boss and team members.

Self-Evaluation

Almost everyone strives to have a positive self-concept, but some people have a more positive evaluation of themselves than do others. This *self-evaluation* is mostly defined by three elements: self-esteem, self-efficacy, and locus of control.[22]

Self-Esteem Self-esteem—the extent to which people like, respect, and are satisfied with themselves—represents a comprehensive self-evaluation. People have degrees of self-esteem for each of their various roles, such as being a good student, a good driver, and a good parent. From these multiple self-appraisals, people form an overall evaluation of themselves, known as their global self-esteem. Those with high self-esteem are less influenced by others, tend to persist in spite of failure, and have a higher propensity to think logically.[24]

Self-Efficacy **Self-efficacy** refers to a person's belief about successfully completing a task.[25] Those with high

> ## The deepest urge in human nature is the desire to be important.[18]
>
> —John Dewey, educational philosopher

Self-Enhancement Makes Most of Us Above Average[17]

69% of U.S. federal government workers rated their performance as above average, compared with coworkers in their unit (only 1 percent rated their performance below average).

94% of university professors rated their teaching as above average compared with others at their university.

77% of Polish drivers rate themselves as more skillful than the average driver.

37% of Swedish student drivers overestimated their driving competence (13 percent underestimated their driving competence).

70% of college students recently said they have above-average academic ability (64% of college students in 1966 said they were above average).

74% of investment fund managers said they were above average at their jobs.

62% of recent college students said they have above-average leadership ability (only 41 percent of college students in 1966 claimed to be above average).

36.9% of consumers in a large U.S. survey panel overestimated their actual credit rating (only 4.6 percent underestimated their credit rating).

Excellent

Note: Some studies cited above are not representative of the entire population.
(photo): ©Aldo Murillo/E+/Getty Images

believe that life events are caused mainly by their personal characteristics (i.e., motivation and abilities). Those with an external locus of control believe events are due mainly to fate, luck, or conditions in the external environment. Locus of control is a generalized belief, but this belief varies to some extent with the situation. People with an external locus of control generally believe that life's outcomes are beyond their control, but they also believe they have control over the results of tasks they perform often. The individual's general locus of control would be most apparent in new situations, where his or her ability to control events is uncertain.

self-verification a person's inherent motivation to confirm and maintain his or her existing self-concept

self-efficacy a person's belief that he or she has the ability, motivation, correct role perceptions, and favorable situation to complete a task successfully

locus of control a person's general belief about the amount of control he or she has over personal life events

People with an internal locus of control have a more positive self-evaluation. They also tend to perform better in most employment situations, are more successful in their careers, earn more money, and are better suited for leadership positions. Internals also are more satisfied with their jobs, cope better in stressful situations, and are more motivated by performance-based reward systems.[28]

connect

SELF-ASSESSMENT 3.2: How Much General Self-Efficacy Do You Have?
Self-efficacy refers to a person's belief that he or she has the ability, motivation, and resources to complete a task successfully. Although self-efficacy is often situation-specific, people also develop a more general self-efficacy if they perform tasks in a variety of situations. You can discover your level of general self-efficacy by locating this self-assessment in Connect if it is assigned by your instructor.

self-efficacy have a "can-do" attitude. They believe they possess the energy (motivation), ability, clear expectations (role perceptions), and resources (situational factors) to perform the task. In other words, self-efficacy is an individual's perception regarding the MARS model in a specific situation. Self-efficacy is often task specific, but it also can be more generalized. People have a general self-efficacy when they believe they can be successful across a variety of situations.[26] Those with higher general self-efficacy have a more positive overall self-evaluation.

Locus of Control Locus of control is defined as a person's general beliefs about the amount of control he or she has over personal life events.[27] Individuals with an internal locus of control

The Social Self

We began this topic by stating that an individual's self-concept exists at three levels: individual, relational, and collective. These three levels recognize two opposing human motives that influence how people view themselves.[29] One motivation is to be distinctive and different from other people. The opposing need is for inclusion and assimilation with other people. The individual self, called *personal identity* or *internal self-concept*, fulfills the need for distinctiveness because it involves defining ourselves by our personality, values, abilities, qualifications, achievements and other personal attributes. Everyone has a unique combination of personal characteristics, and we embrace this uniqueness to some degree. For instance, an unusual skill or accomplishment that distinguishes you from coworkers is part of your personal identity.

The opposing need for inclusion and assimilation with other people is fulfilled through our relational and collective self-concepts.[30] Human beings are social animals; they have an inherent drive to be

connect

SELF-ASSESSMENT 3.3: What Is Your Locus of Control?
Locus of control is one component of self-evaluation, which is part of an individual's self-concept. It is a person's general belief about the amount of control he or she has over personal life events. You can discover your general locus-of-control orientation by locating this self-assessment in Connect if it is assigned by your instructor.

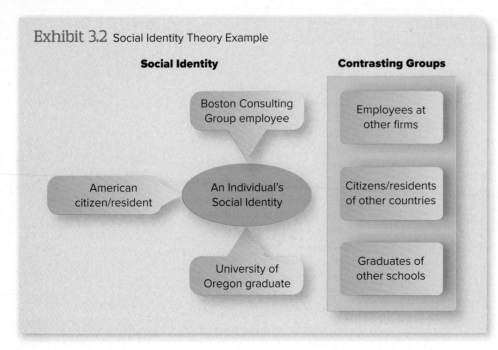

Exhibit 3.2 Social Identity Theory Example

Social Identity

Boston Consulting Group employee

American citizen/resident

An Individual's Social Identity

University of Oregon graduate

Contrasting Groups

Employees at other firms

Citizens/residents of other countries

Graduates of other schools

associated with others and to be recognized as part of social communities. Thus, everyone defines himself or herself to some degree by his or her interpersonal and collective relationships.[31] *Social identity* (also called *external self-concept*) is the central theme of **social identity theory**, which says that people define themselves by the groups to which they belong or have an emotional attachment. For instance, someone might have a social identity as an American citizen, a University of Oregon alumnus, and an employee at Boston Consulting Group (see Exhibit 3.2).

Social identity is a complex combination of many memberships arranged in a hierarchy of importance. One factor that determines importance is how easily you are identified as a member of the reference group, such as by your gender, age, and ethnicity. A second factor is your minority status in a group. It is difficult to ignore your gender in a class where most other students are the opposite gender, for example. In that context, gender tends to become a stronger defining feature of your social identity than it is in social settings where there are many people of your gender.

The group's status is another important social identity factor because association with the group makes us feel better about ourselves (i.e., self-enhancement). Medical doctors usually define themselves by their profession because of its high status. Some people describe themselves by where they work ("I work at Facebook") because their employer has a good reputation. Others never mention where they work because their employer is noted for poor relations with employees or has a poor reputation in the community.[32]

Everyone tries to balance personal and social identities to some degree, but the priority for uniqueness (personal identities) versus relatedness (social identities) differs from one person to the next. People whose self-concepts are heavily defined by social rather than personal identities are more motivated to abide by team norms and more easily influenced by peer pressure. Those who place more emphasis on personal identities, on the other hand, speak out more frequently against the majority and are less motivated to follow the team's wishes. Furthermore, expressing disagreement with others is a sign of distinctiveness and can help employees form a clearer self-concept, particularly when that disagreement is based on differences in personal values.[33]

Self-Concept and Organizational Behavior

Self-concept has become a hot topic in the social sciences and is starting to bloom in organizational behavior research.[34] Self-concept influences human perceptions, decision making, motivation, stress, team dynamics, leadership development, and several other OB topics. Therefore, you will read about self-concept throughout this book, including in later parts of this chapter.

People whose self-concepts are heavily defined by social rather than personal identities are more motivated to abide by team norms and more easily influenced by peer pressure.
©michaeljung/Shutterstock

PERCEIVING THE WORLD AROUND US

We spend considerable time perceiving ourselves, but most of our perceptual energy is directed toward the outer world. Whether as a forensic accountant, mechanical engineer, or senior executive, we need to make sense of our surroundings and to manage the conditions that challenge the accuracy of those perceptions. **Perception** is the process of receiving information about and making sense of the world around us. It includes determining which information to notice, as well as how to categorize and interpret it within the framework of our existing knowledge.

The perceptual process generally follows the steps shown in Exhibit 3.3. Perception begins when environmental stimuli are received through our senses. Most stimuli that bombard our senses are screened out; the rest are organized and interpreted. The process of attending to some information received by our senses and ignoring other information is called **selective attention**. Selective attention is influenced by characteristics of the person or object being perceived, particularly size, intensity, motion, repetition, and novelty. For example, a small, flashing red light on a nurses' workstation console is immediately noticed because it is bright (intensity), flashing (motion), and a rare event (novelty) and has symbolic meaning that a patient's vital signs are failing. Notice that selective attention also is influenced by the context in which the target is perceived. For instance, selective attention is triggered by things or people who might be out of context, such as someone with a foreign accent in a setting where most people have a local accent.

Characteristics of the perceiver also influence selective attention, usually without the perceiver's awareness.[35] When information is received through the senses, our brain quickly and nonconsciously assesses whether it is relevant or irrelevant to us and then attaches emotional markers (worry, happiness, boredom) to the retained information.[36] Emotional markers help us to store information in memory; those emotions are later reproduced when recalling the perceived information. The selective attention process is far from perfect, however. The Greek philosopher Plato acknowledged this imperfection long ago when he wrote that we see reality only as shadows reflecting against the rough wall of a cave.[37]

One selective attention bias is the effect of our assumptions and expectations about future events. You are more likely to notice a particular co-worker's email among the daily avalanche of messages when you expect to receive that email (even more so if it is important). Unfortunately, expectations and assumptions also cause us to screen out potentially important information. In one study, two groups of students were asked to watch a 30-second video clip in which several people passed around two basketballs. In one group, students were instructed simply to watch the video clip. Most of them readily noticed a person dressed in a gorilla suit walking among the players for nine seconds and stopping to thump his or her chest. In another group, students were asked to count the number of times one of the two basketballs was passed around. Only half of the people in this latter group noticed the intruding gorilla.[38]

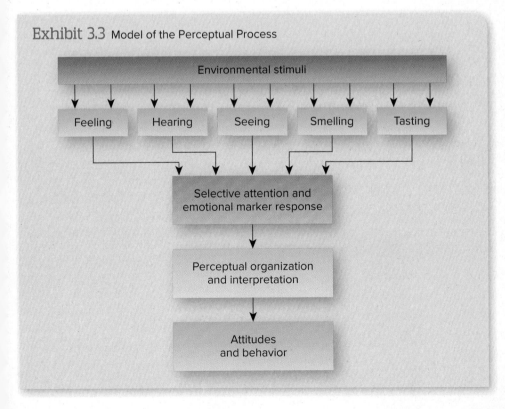

Exhibit 3.3 Model of the Perceptual Process

Environmental stimuli

Feeling | Hearing | Seeing | Smelling | Tasting

Selective attention and emotional marker response

Perceptual organization and interpretation

Attitudes and behavior

Another selective attention problem, called **confirmation bias**, is the nonconscious tendency for people to screen out information that is contrary to their decisions, beliefs, values, and assumptions, while more readily accepting information that confirms those elements.[39] When we make important decisions, such as investing in a costly project, we tend to pay attention to information that supports that decision, ignore information that questions the wisdom of the decision, and more easily recall the supportive than the opposing information. Confirmation bias occurred, for example, in an exercise where student pilots became unsure of their location. The study found that the pilots, in trying to determine their location, relied on less reliable information that was consistent with their assumptions rather than on more accurate information that was contrary to those assumptions. Confirmation bias is also a well-known perceptual problem when police detectives and other forensic experts form theories too early in the investigation.[40]

Perceptual Organization and Interpretation

We pay attention to a tiny fraction of the stimuli received by the senses. Even so, the human brain further reduces the huge volume and complexity of selected information through various perceptual grouping strategies. Perceptual grouping occurs mostly without our awareness, yet it is the foundation for making sense of things and fulfilling our need for cognitive closure. The most common and far-reaching perceptual grouping process is **categorical thinking**—the mostly nonconscious process of organizing people and objects into preconceived categories that are stored in our long-term memory.[42]

People are usually grouped together based on their observable similarity, such as gender, age, race, clothing style, and so forth. We discuss this categorization process in the next section on stereotyping. People also are grouped together based on their proximity to each other. If you notice a group of employees working in the same area and know that some of them are marketing staff, you will likely assume that the others in that group also are marketing staff.

Another form of perceptual grouping involves filling in missing information about people or places. When listening to others discuss what happened at a meeting you didn't attend, your mind fills in unstated details, such as who else was there and where it was held. Perceptual grouping also occurs when we think we see trends in otherwise ambiguous information. Several studies have found that people have a natural tendency to see patterns that, in fact, are random events. For example, people incorrectly believe that a sports player or gambler with a string of wins is more likely to win next time as well.[43]

The process of "making sense" of the world around us involves interpreting incoming information, not just organizing

One form of perceptual grouping involves filling in missing information about people or places.
©Romolo Tavani/Shutterstock

it. This happens as quickly as selecting and organizing because the previously mentioned emotional markers are tagged to incoming stimuli, which are essentially quick judgments about whether that information is good or bad for us. How much time does it take to make these quick judgments? Recent studies estimate that we make reliable judgments about another individual's trustworthiness after viewing a facial image for as little as 50 milliseconds (1/20th of a second). In fact, our opinion regarding whether we like or trust a stranger is about the same whether we see the person's face for a minute or a fraction of a second.[44] Collectively, these studies reveal that selective attention, perceptual organization, and interpretation operate very quickly and to a large extent without our awareness.

Mental Models To achieve our goals with some degree of predictability and sanity, we need road maps of the environments in which we live. These road maps, called **mental models**, are knowledge structures that we develop to describe, explain, and predict the world around us.[45] They consist of visual or relational images in our mind, such as what the classroom looks like or what happens when we submit an assignment late. Mental models partly rely on the process of perceptual grouping to make sense of things; they fill in the missing pieces, including the causal connection among events. For example, you have a mental model about attending a class

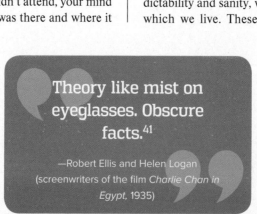

Theory like mist on eyeglasses. Obscure facts.[41]

—Robert Ellis and Helen Logan (screenwriters of the film *Charlie Chan in Egypt*, 1935)

SELF-ASSESSMENT 3.4: How Much Perceptual Structure Do You Need?
Some people have a greater need than do others to quickly or completely "make sense" of things around them. This personal need for perceptual structure relates to selective attention as well as perceptual organization and interpretation. You can discover your need for perceptual structure by locating this self-assessment in Connect if it is assigned by your instructor.

confirmation bias the process of screening out information that is contrary to our values and assumptions, and to more readily accept confirming information

categorical thinking organizing people and objects into preconceived categories that are stored in our long-term memory

mental models knowledge structures that we develop to describe, explain, and predict the world around us

stereotyping the process of assigning traits to people based on their membership in a social category

lecture or seminar, including assumptions or expectations about where the instructor and students arrange themselves in the room, how they ask and answer questions, and so forth. In other words, we create a mental image of a class in progress.

Mental models are important for sense making, yet they also make it difficult to see the world in different ways. For example, accounting professionals tend to see corporate problems from an accounting perspective, whereas marketing professionals see the same problems from a marketing perspective. Mental models also block our recognition of new opportunities. How do we change mental models? That's a tough challenge. After all, we developed these knowledge structures from several years of experience and reinforcement. The most important way to minimize the perceptual problems with mental models is to be aware of and frequently question them. We also need to be more aware of our assumptions, which are often based on mental models. Working with people from diverse backgrounds is another way to break out of existing mental models. Colleagues from different cultures and areas of expertise tend to have different mental models, so working with them makes our own assumptions more obvious.

LO3-3 Discuss how stereotyping, attribution, self-fulfilling prophecy, and the halo, false-consensus, primacy, and recency effects influence the perceptual process.

SPECIFIC PERCEPTUAL PROCESSES AND PROBLEMS

Within the general perceptual process are specific subprocesses and associated perceptual errors. In this section of the chapter, we examine several of these perceptual processes and biases as well as their implications for organizational behavior, beginning with the most widely known one: stereotyping.

Stereotyping in Organizations

Stereotyping is the perceptual process in which we assign characteristics to an identifiable group and then automatically transfer those features to anyone we believe is a member of that group.[46] The assigned characteristics tend to be difficult to observe, such as personality traits and abilities, but they also can include physical characteristics and a host of other qualities. If we learn that someone is a professor, for example, we implicitly assume the person is probably also intelligent, absent-minded, and socially challenged. Stereotypes are formed to some extent from personal experience, but they are mainly provided to us through media images (e.g., movie characters) and other cultural prototypes. Consequently, stereotypes are shared beliefs across an entire society and sometimes across several cultures, rather than beliefs that differ from one person to the next.

Historically, stereotypes were defined as exaggerations or falsehoods. This is often true, but some features of the stereotype are more likely to exist among its group members than in the general population.[47] Still, stereotypes embellish or distort the kernels of truth and include other features that are false.

Why People Stereotype Stereotyping occurs because, as a form of categorical thinking, it is a usually nonconscious "energy-saving" process that simplifies our understanding of the world. It is easier to remember features of a stereotype than the constellation of characteristics unique to everyone we meet. A second reason for stereotyping is that we have an innate need to understand and anticipate how others will behave. We don't have much information when first meeting someone, so we rely on stereotypes to fill in the missing pieces. The higher the perceiver's need for cognitive closure, the higher the reliance on stereotypes.[48]

One explanation for stereotyping is that it is motivated by the observer's need for social identity and self-enhancement.

stereotype threat an individual's concern about confirming a negative stereotype about his or her group

A third explanation for stereotyping is that it is motivated by the observer's need for social identity and self-enhancement. Earlier in this chapter we explained that people define themselves by the groups to which they belong or have an emotional attachment. They also are motivated to maintain a positive self-concept. This combination of social identity and self-enhancement leads to the process of categorization, homogenization, and differentiation:[49]

- *Categorization.* Social identity is a comparative process, and the comparison begins by categorizing people into distinct groups. By viewing someone (including yourself) as a Texan, for example, you remove that person's individuality and, instead, see him or her as a prototypical representative of the group called Texans. This categorization then allows you to distinguish Texans from people who live in, say, California or Maine.

- *Homogenization.* To simplify the comparison process, we tend to think that people within each group are very similar to each other. For instance, we think Texans collectively have similar attitudes and characteristics, whereas Californians collectively have their own set of characteristics. Of course, every individual is unique, but we often lose sight of this fact when thinking about our social identity and how we compare to people in other social groups.

- *Differentiation.* Along with categorizing and homogenizing people, we tend to assign more favorable characteristics to people in our groups than to people in other groups.[50] This differentiation is motivated by self-enhancement because being in a "better" group produces higher self-esteem. Differentiation is often subtle, but it can escalate into a "good guy–bad guy" contrast when groups engage in overt conflict with each other. In other words, when out-group members threaten our self-concept, we are particularly motivated (often without our awareness) to assign negative stereotypes to them. Some research suggests that men have stronger differentiation biases than do women, but we all differentiate to some extent.

Problems with Stereotyping Stereotyping information is necessarily inaccurate because these categories do not describe everyone (or even most people) assigned to the stereotyped group. For instance, the traditional stereotype of accountants (boring, cautious, calculating) perhaps describes a few people in this profession, but it is certainly not characteristic of all, or even most, accountants. Nevertheless, once we categorize someone as an accountant, the stereotypic nonobservable features of accountants are transferred to that person, even though we have no evidence that the person actually has those characteristics.

A second problem with stereotyping is **stereotype threat**, a phenomenon whereby members of a

Stereotyping distorts perceptions because these categories do not accurately describe every person, or even most people, assigned to the stereotyped group.
©wavebreakmedia/Shutterstock

stereotyped group are concerned that they might exhibit a negative feature of the stereotype. This concern and preoccupation adversely affect their behavior and performance, which often result in displaying the stereotype trait they are trying to avoid.[51] For example, women perform worse on math and science tests when sensitized to the generally false but widely held belief that women perform worse than men in these subjects. Test scores among women are lower even when they are a small minority with men in the class. Women achieve much higher scores when the gender stereotype or their minority status is not apparent, such as when taking the test with many women in the class.

Almost anyone can be affected by stereotype threat, but studies have particularly observed it in African Americans and other minority groups as well as older people. Stereotype threat occurs because members of a stereotyped group anxiously try to avoid confirming the undesirable trait and try to push the negative image from their mind. These two cognitive activities divert energy and attention, which makes it more difficult to perform the task well. The negative stereotype also can weaken self-efficacy; it is difficult to be confident in your ability when your group's stereotype suggests otherwise.

A third problem with stereotyping is that it lays the foundation for discriminatory attitudes and behavior. Most of this perceptual bias occurs as *unintentional (systemic) discrimination*, whereby decision makers rely on stereotypes to establish notions of the "ideal" person in specific roles. A person who doesn't fit the ideal has to work harder to get the same evaluation as someone who is compatible with the occupational stereotype.

Unintentional systemic discrimination also affects employment opportunities and salaries. Consider the following example: Science faculty from several research-intensive universities were given the application materials of an undergraduate student who was purportedly applying for a science laboratory manager job. Half of the faculty reviewed materials from a male applicant; the other half looked at materials from a female applicant. The male and female applicant materials were identical except for the name, yet the male applicant received significantly higher ratings than a female applicant on competence and hireability. Furthermore, faculty members recommended an average salary of $30,238 for the male applicant but only $26,507 for the female applicant. Female faculty exhibited as much gender bias as the male faculty.[52]

Worse than systemic discrimination is *intentional discrimination* or *prejudice*, in which people hold unfounded negative attitudes toward people belonging to a particular stereotyped group.[53] Systemic discrimination is implicit, automatic, and unintentional, whereas intentional discrimination deliberately puts the target person at an unfair disadvantage.

If stereotyping is such a problem, shouldn't we try to avoid this process altogether? Unfortunately, it's not that simple. Most experts agree that categorical thinking (including stereotyping) is an automatic and nonconscious process. Specialized training programs can minimize stereotype activation to some extent, but for the most part the process is hardwired in our brain cells.[54] Also remember that stereotyping helps us in several valuable (although fallible) ways described earlier: minimizing mental effort, filling in missing information, and supporting our social identity. The good news is that while it is very difficult to prevent the *activation* of stereotypes, we can minimize the *application* of stereotypic information. In other words, although we automatically categorize people and assign stereotypic traits to them, we can consciously minimize the extent to which we rely on that stereotypic information. Later in this chapter, we identify ways to minimize stereotyping and other perceptual biases.

employee makes poor-quality products on other machines (low distinctiveness), and other employees make good-quality products on this machine (low consensus).

attribution process the perceptual process of deciding whether an observed behavior or event is caused largely by internal or external factors

In contrast, we would decide that there is something wrong with the machine (an external attribution) if the employee consistently makes poor-quality products on this machine (high consistency), the employee makes good-quality products on other machines (high distinctiveness), and other employees make poor-quality products on this machine (high consensus). Notice that consistency is high for both internal and external attributions. This occurs because low consistency (the person's output quality on this machine is sometimes good and sometimes poor) weakens our confidence about whether the source of the problem is the person or the machine.

The attribution process is important because understanding cause–effect relationships enables us to work more effectively

> ## The good news is that while it is very difficult to prevent the *activation* of stereotypes, we can minimize the *application* of stereotypic information.

Attribution Theory

Another widely discussed perceptual phenomenon in organizational settings is the **attribution process**.[55] Attribution involves forming beliefs about the causes of behavior or events. Generally, we perceive whether an observed behavior or event is caused mainly by characteristics of the person (internal factors) or by the environment (external factors). Internal factors include the person's ability or motivation, whereas external factors include resources, coworker support, or luck. If someone doesn't show up for an important meeting, for instance, we infer either internal attributions (the coworker is forgetful, lacks motivation, etc.) or external attributions (traffic, a family emergency, etc.) to make sense of the person's absence.

People rely on the three attribution rules—consistency, distinctiveness, and consensus—to decide whether someone's behavior and performance are mainly caused by their personal characteristics or environmental influences (see Exhibit 3.4).[56] To illustrate how these three attribution rules operate, imagine a situation where an employee is making poor-quality products on a particular machine. We would probably conclude that the employee lacks skill or motivation (an internal attribution) if the employee consistently makes poor-quality products on this machine (high consistency), the

The attribution process is important because understanding cause–effect relationships enables us to work more effectively with others and to assign praise or blame to them.
©PhotoAlto sas/Alamy Stock Photo

self-serving bias the tendency to attribute our favorable outcomes to internal factors and our failures to external factors

fundamental attribution error the tendency to see the person rather than the situation as the main cause of that person's behavior

with others and to assign praise or blame to them.[57] Suppose a coworker didn't complete his or her task on a team project. You would approach this situation differently if you believed the coworker was lazy or lacked sufficient skill (an internal attribution) than if you believed the poor performance was due to lack of time or resources available to the coworker (an external attribution). Similarly, our respect for a leader depends on whether we believe his or her actions are due to personal characteristics or the situation. We also react differently to attributions of our own behavior and performance. Students who make internal attributions about their poor grades, for instance, are more likely to drop out of their programs than if they make external attributions about those grades.[58]

Attribution Errors The attribution process is susceptible to errors. One such error is **self-serving bias**—the tendency to attribute our failures to external causes more than internal causes,

while successes are due more to internal than external factors.[59] Simply put, we take credit for our successes and blame others or the situation for our mistakes. In annual reports, for example, executives mainly refer to their personal qualities as reasons for the company's successes and to competitors, unexpected legislation, and other external factors as reasons for the company's failures.[60] Self-serving bias occurs mainly because of the self-enhancement process described earlier in this chapter. By pointing to external causes of their own failures, and internal causes of their successes, people generate a more positive self-concept.

Another attribution error, **fundamental attribution error** (also called *correspondence bias*), is the tendency to overemphasize internal causes of another person's behavior and to discount or ignore external causes of his or her behavior.[61] We are more likely to attribute a coworker's late arrival for work to lack of motivation rather than to situational constraints (such as traffic congestion). This occurs because observers can't easily see the external factors that constrain another person's behavior. Also, people like to think that human beings (not the situation) are the prime sources of their behavior. Although fundamental attribution error does occur, recent reviews suggest it may be less common than previously thought.[62]

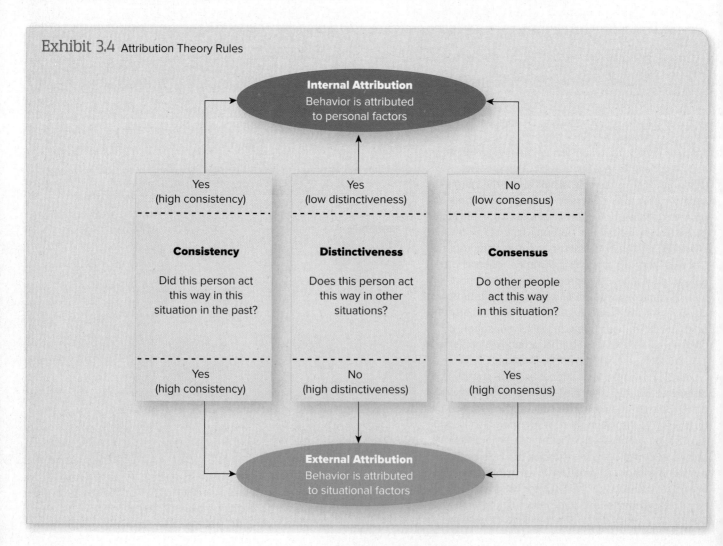

Exhibit 3.4 Attribution Theory Rules

Internal Attribution
Behavior is attributed to personal factors

| Yes (high consistency) | Yes (low distinctiveness) | No (low consensus) |

Consistency
Did this person act this way in this situation in the past?

Distinctiveness
Does this person act this way in other situations?

Consensus
Do other people act this way in this situation?

| Yes (high consistency) | No (high distinctiveness) | Yes (high consensus) |

External Attribution
Behavior is attributed to situational factors

Self-Fulfilling Prophecy

Self-fulfilling prophecy occurs when our expectations about another person cause that person to act in a way that is consistent with those expectations. In other words, our perceptions can influence reality. Exhibit 3.5 illustrates the four steps in the self-fulfilling prophecy process using the example of a supervisor and a subordinate.[63] The process begins when the supervisor forms expectations about the employee's future behavior and performance. These expectations are sometimes inaccurate because first impressions are usually formed from limited information. The supervisor's expectations influence his or her behavior toward employees. In particular, high-expectancy employees (those expected to do well) receive more emotional support through nonverbal cues (e.g., more smiling and eye contact), more frequent and valuable feedback and reinforcement, more challenging goals, better training, and more opportunities to demonstrate good performance.[64]

The third step in self-fulfilling prophecy includes two effects of the supervisor's behavior on the employee. First, through better training and more practice opportunities, a high-expectancy employee learns more skills and knowledge than a low-expectancy employee. Second, the high-expectancy employee becomes more self-confident, which results in higher motivation and willingness to set more challenging goals.[65] In the final step, high-expectancy employees have higher motivation and better skills, resulting in better performance, while the opposite is true of low-expectancy employees.

Self-fulfilling prophecy has been observed in many contexts. In one study, four Israeli Defense Force combat command course instructors were told that one-third of the incoming trainees had high command potential, one-third had normal potential, and the rest had unknown potential. The trainees had been randomly placed into these categories by the researchers, but the instructors were led to believe that the information they received was accurate. Consistent with self-fulfilling prophecy, high-expectancy soldiers performed significantly better by the end of the course than did trainees in the other groups. They also had more favorable attitudes toward the course and the instructor's leadership effectiveness. An analysis of dozens of leader intervention studies over the years found that self-fulfilling prophecy is one of the most powerful leadership effects on follower behavior and performance.[66]

Contingencies of Self-Fulfilling Prophecy The self-fulfilling prophecy effect is stronger in some situations than in others. It has a stronger effect at the beginning of a relationship, such as when employees are first hired. It is also stronger when several people (rather than just one person) hold the same expectations of the individual. In other words, we might be able to ignore one person's doubts about our potential but not the collective doubts of several people. The self-fulfilling prophecy effect is also stronger among people with a history of low achievement. These people tend to have lower self-esteem, so they are more easily influenced by others' opinions of them.[67]

The main lesson from the self-fulfilling prophecy literature is that leaders need to develop and maintain a positive, yet realistic, expectation toward all employees. This recommendation is consistent with the emerging philosophy of **positive organizational behavior**, which suggests that focusing on the positive rather than negative aspects of life will improve organizational success and individual well-being. Communicating hope and optimism is so important that it is identified as one of the critical success factors for physicians and surgeons. Training programs that make leaders aware of the power of positive expectations seem to have minimal effect, however. Instead, generating positive expectations and hope depends on a corporate culture of support and learning. Hiring

> **self-fulfilling prophecy** the perceptual process in which our expectations about another person cause that person to act more consistently with those expectations
>
> **positive organizational behavior** a perspective of organizational behavior that focuses on building positive qualities and traits within individuals or institutions as opposed to focusing on what is wrong with them

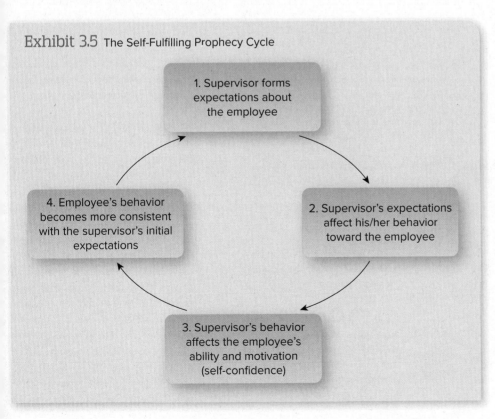

Exhibit 3.5 The Self-Fulfilling Prophecy Cycle

1. Supervisor forms expectations about the employee

2. Supervisor's expectations affect his/her behavior toward the employee

3. Supervisor's behavior affects the employee's ability and motivation (self-confidence)

4. Employee's behavior becomes more consistent with the supervisor's initial expectations

supervisors who are inherently optimistic toward their staff is another way of increasing the incidence of positive self-fulfilling prophecies.

Other Perceptual Effects

Self-fulfilling prophecy, attribution, and stereotyping are among the most common perceptual processes and biases in organizational settings, but there are many others. Four additional biases that have received attention in organizational settings are briefly described below.

Halo Effect The **halo effect** occurs when our general impression of a person, usually based on one prominent characteristic, distorts our perception of other characteristics of that person.[68] If a supervisor who values punctuality notices that an employee is sometimes late for work, the supervisor might form a negative overall opinion of the employee and evaluate that person's other traits unfavorably as well. The halo effect occurs most often when the manager lacks solid information—or isn't motivated to seek out the information—about the employee's performance on specific tasks. Instead, the manager relies on a general impression of the employee to fill in the missing information.

The halo effect occurs when our general impression of a person, usually based on one prominent characteristic, distorts our perception of other characteristics of that person.
(photo): ©YAY Media AS/Alamy

False-Consensus Effect The **false-consensus effect** (also called *similar-to-me effect*) occurs when people overestimate the extent to which others have similar beliefs or behaviors to our own.[69] Employees who are thinking of quitting their jobs overestimate the percentage of coworkers who also are thinking about quitting, for example. There are several explanations for false-consensus effect. One is that we are comforted believing that others are similar to us, particularly regarding less acceptable or divisive behavior. Put differently, we perceive "everyone does it" to create a more favorable view of behaviors that do not have a positive image (quitting our job, parking illegally, etc.).

A second explanation for false-consensus effect is that we interact more with people who have similar views and behaviors. This frequent interaction causes us to overestimate how common those views/behaviors are in the entire organization or society. Third, as noted earlier in this chapter, we are more likely to remember information that is consistent with our own views and selectively screen out information that is contrary to our beliefs. Fourth, our social identity process homogenizes people within groups, so we tend to think that everyone in that group has similar opinions and behavior, including the false-consensus attitude or behavior.

Primacy Effect The **primacy effect** is our tendency to rely on the first information we receive about people to quickly form an opinion of them.[70] It is the notion that first impressions are lasting impressions. This rapid perceptual organization and interpretation occurs because we need to make sense of the situation and, in particular, to trust others. The problem is that first impressions—particularly negative first impressions—are difficult to change. After categorizing someone, we tend to select subsequent information that supports our first impression and screen out information that opposes that impression.

First Impressions Count in Job Applications[71]

29% of chief financial officers say job applicants make the most mistakes in their résumé or cover letter (43% say most mistakes are made during the interview).

Some Résumé Gaffes

"Dear Sir or **Madman**."
"Assisted company executives with travel **arraignments**."
"I would like to work for a company that is **very lax** when it comes to **tardiness**."
"Instrumental for **ruining** entire operation for a Midwest chain store."
"My last employer **fried** me for no reason."
"Earned a diploma from a very **repudiated** college."
"Hope to hear from you, **shorty**."

36% of employers say they automatically dismiss a job applicant whose résumé is generic and doesn't seem personalized for the position.

43% of employers say they spend less than a minute looking at a résumé.

58% of employers identified typos as the most common problems with résumés that led them to automatically dismiss a job applicant.

(photo): ©pathdoc/Shutterstock

32% of employers say they automatically dismiss a job applicant whose résumé includes a large amount of wording from the job posting.

Recency Effect The **recency effect** occurs when the most recent information dominates our perceptions.[72] This perceptual bias is most common when people (especially those with limited experience) make a decision involving complex information. For instance, auditors must digest large volumes of information in their judgments about financial documents, and the most recent information received prior to the decision tends to get weighted more heavily than information received at the beginning of the audit. Similarly, when supervisors evaluate the performance of employees over the previous year, the most recent performance information dominates the evaluation because it is the most easily recalled.

LO3-4 Discuss three ways to improve perceptions, with specific application to organizational situations.

IMPROVING PERCEPTIONS

We can't bypass the perceptual process, but we should try to minimize perceptual biases and distortions. Three potentially effective ways to improve perceptions include awareness of perceptual biases, self-awareness, and meaningful interaction.

Awareness of Perceptual Biases

One of the most obvious and widely practiced ways to reduce perceptual biases is by knowing that they exist. For example, diversity awareness training tries to minimize discrimination by making people aware of systemic discrimination as well as prejudices that occur through stereotyping. This training also attempts to dispel myths about people from various cultural and demographic groups. Awareness of perceptual biases can reduce these biases to some extent by making people more mindful of their thoughts and actions. However, awareness training has only a limited effect.[73] One problem is that teaching people to reject incorrect stereotypes has the unintended effect of reinforcing rather than reducing reliance on those stereotypes. Another problem is that diversity training is ineffective for people with deeply held prejudices against those groups.

Improving Self-Awareness

A more successful way to minimize perceptual biases is by increasing self-awareness.[74] We need to become more aware of our beliefs, values, and attitudes and, from that insight, gain a better understanding of biases in our own decisions and behavior.

This self-awareness tends to reduce perceptual biases by making people more open-minded and nonjudgmental toward others. Self-awareness is equally important in other ways. The emerging concept of authentic leadership emphasizes self-awareness as the first step in a person's ability to effectively lead others (see Chapter 11). Essentially, we need to understand our own values, strengths, and biases as a foundation for building a vision and leading others toward that vision.[75]

But how do we become more self-aware? One approach is to complete formal tests that indicate any implicit biases we might have toward others. The Implicit Association Test (IAT) is one such instrument. Although the accuracy of the IAT is being hotly debated by scholars, it attempts to detect subtle racial, age, gender, disability, and other forms of bias by associating positive and negative words with specific groups of people.[76] Many people are much more cautious about their stereotypes and prejudices after discovering that their test results show a personal bias against older people or individuals from different ethnic backgrounds.[77]

Another way to reduce perceptual biases through increased self-awareness is by applying the **Johari Window**.[78] Developed by Joseph Luft and Harry Ingram (hence the name "Johari"), this model of self-awareness and mutual understanding divides information about you into four "windows"—open, blind, hidden, and unknown—based on whether your own values, beliefs, and experiences are known to you and to others (see Exhibit 3.6). The *open area* includes information about you that is known both to you and to others. The *blind area* refers to information that is known to others but not to you. For example, your colleagues might notice that you are self-conscious and awkward when meeting the company's chief executive officer, but you are unaware of this fact. Information known to you but unknown to others is found in the *hidden area*. Finally, the *unknown area* includes your values, beliefs, and experiences that are buried so deeply that neither you nor others are aware of them.

The main objective of the Johari Window is to increase the size of the open area so that both you and your colleagues are aware of your perceptual limitations. This objective is partly accomplished by reducing the hidden area through *disclosure*—informing others of your beliefs, feelings, and experiences that may influence the work relationship. The open area also increases through *feedback* from others about your behavior. Feedback reduces your blind area because, according to recent studies, people near you are good sources of information about many (but not all) of your traits and behaviors.[79] Finally, the combination of disclosure and feedback occasionally produces revelations about you in the unknown area.

contact hypothesis
a theory stating that the more we interact with someone, the less prejudiced or perceptually biased we will be against that person

empathy a person's understanding of and sensitivity to the feelings, thoughts, and situations of others

Meaningful Interaction

The Johari Window relies on direct conversations about ourselves and others, whereas *meaningful interaction* is a more indirect, yet potentially powerful, approach to improving self-awareness and mutual understanding.[80] Meaningful interaction is any activity in which people engage in valued (meaningful, not trivial) activities. The activities might be work related, such as when senior executives work alongside frontline staff. Or the activities might occur outside the workplace, such as when sales staff from several countries participate in outdoor challenges.

Meaningful interaction is founded on the **contact hypothesis**, which states that, under certain conditions, people who interact with each other will be less perceptually biased because they have a more personal understanding of the other person and their group.[81] Simply spending time with members of other groups can improve this understanding to some extent. However, meaningful interaction is strongest when people work closely and frequently with each other on a shared goal that requires mutual cooperation and reliance. Furthermore, everyone should have equal status in that context, should be engaged in a meaningful task, and should have positive experiences with each other in those interactions.

Meaningful interaction reduces dependence on stereotypes because we gain better knowledge about individuals and experience their unique attributes in action. Meaningful interaction also potentially improves empathy toward others. **Empathy** refers to understanding and being sensitive to the feelings, thoughts, and situations of others.[83] People empathize when they visualize themselves in the other person's place as if they are the other person. This perceptual experience is cognitive, emotional, and experiential. In other words, empathy occurs when we understand the other person's situation, feel his or her emotions in that context, and to some degree react to those thoughts and feelings as the other person does. Empathizing reduces attribution errors by improving our sensitivity to the external causes of another person's performance and behavior. However, trying to empathize with others without spending time with them might actually increase rather than reduce stereotyping and other perceptual biases.[84]

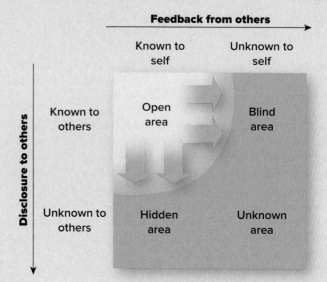

Exhibit 3.6 Johari Window Model of Self-Awareness and Mutual Understanding

Source: Based on J. Luft, *Of Human Interaction* (Palo Alto, CA: National Press Books, 1969).

OB THEORY TO PRACTICE

Improving Executive Empathy on the Frontlines

Rick Forman developed a newfound appreciation for the work and personal lives of his employees when he recently worked in disguise as a checkout cashier, washroom cleaner, and distribution center forklift operator. The founder and CEO of Forman Mills, a New Jersey–based discount clothing chain, had several frustrating experiences with outdated equipment and misguided work processes, which he later changed. Heartfelt conversations with coworkers (who didn't know he was the CEO) also gave Forman a reality check about how his 2,900 employees live and work. "It made me realize what people are going through," says Forman. "You are actually talking to real people and you can empathize with their lives."[82]

©Andrey Burkov/Shutterstock

SELF-ASSESSMENT 3.5: How Strong is Your Perspective Taking (Cognitive Empathy)?

Empathy refers to a person's understanding of and sensitivity to the feelings, thoughts, and situation of others. The "understanding" part of empathy is called perspective taking or cognitive empathy. It refers to a rational understanding of another person's circumstances. You can discover your level of cognitive empathy by locating this self-assessment in Connect if it is assigned by your instructor.

SELF-ASSESSMENT 3.6: How Strong is Your Emotional Empathy?

Empathy refers to a person's understanding of and sensitivity to the feelings, thoughts, and situation of others. The "sensitivity" part of empathy is called emotional empathy. It refers to experiencing the feelings of the other person. You can discover your level of emotional empathy by locating this self-assessment in Connect if it is assigned by your instructor.

LO3-5 Outline the main features of a global mindset and justify its usefulness to employees and organizations.

GLOBAL MINDSET: DEVELOPING PERCEPTIONS ACROSS BORDERS

Global mindset has become an important characteristic of job applicants at companies with international operations. A **global mindset** refers to an individual's ability to perceive, know about, and process information across cultures. It includes (a) an awareness of, openness to, and respect for other views and practices in the world; (b) the capacity to empathize and act effectively across cultures; (c) the ability to process complex information about novel environments; and (d) the ability to comprehend and reconcile intercultural matters with multiple levels of thinking.[85]

Let's look at each of these features. First, global mindset occurs as people develop more of a global than local/parochial frame of reference about their business and its environment. They also have more knowledge and appreciation of many cultures and do not judge the competence of others by their national or ethnic origins. Second, global mindset includes understanding the mental models held by colleagues from other cultures as well as their emotional experiences in a given

global mindset an individual's ability to perceive, appreciate, and empathize with people from other cultures, and to process complex cross-cultural information

situation. Furthermore, this empathy translates into effective use of words and behaviors that are compatible with the local culture. Third, people with a strong global mindset are able to process and analyze large volumes of information in new and diverse situations. Finally, global mindset involves the capacity to quickly develop useful mental models of situations, particularly at both the local and global levels of analysis.

A global mindset offers tremendous value to organizations as well as to the employee's career opportunities.[86] People who develop a global mindset form better relationships across cultures by understanding and showing respect to distant colleagues and partners. They can sift through huge volumes of ambiguous and novel information transmitted in multinational relationships. They have a capacity to form networks and exchange resources more rapidly across borders. They also develop greater sensitivity and respond more quickly to emerging global opportunities.

People who develop a global mindset form better relationships across cultures by understanding and showing respect to distant colleagues and partners.
©Rawpixel.com/Shutterstock

Developing a Global Mindset

Developing a global mindset involves improving one's perceptions, so the practices described earlier on awareness, self-awareness, and meaningful interaction are relevant. As with most perceptual capabilities, a global mindset begins with self-awareness—understanding one's own beliefs, values, and attitudes. Through self-awareness, people are more open-minded and nonjudgmental when receiving and processing complex information for decision making. In addition, companies develop a global mindset by giving employees opportunities to compare their own mental models with those of coworkers or partners from other regions of the world. For example, employees might participate in online forums about how well the product's design or marketing strategy is received in the United States versus India or Chile. When companies engage in regular discussions about global competitors, suppliers, and other stakeholders, they eventually move the employee's sphere of awareness more toward that global level.

A global mindset develops through better knowledge of people and cultures. Some of that knowledge is acquired through formal programs, such as expatriate and diversity training, but deeper absorption results from immersion in those cultures. Just as executives need to experience frontline jobs to better understand their customers and employees, employees also need to have meaningful interaction with colleagues from other cultures in those settings. The more people immerse themselves in the local environment (such as following local practices, eating local food, and using the local language), the more they tend to understand the perspectives and attitudes of their colleagues in those cultures.

OB THEORY TO PRACTICE

EY Employees Develop a Global Mindset through Immersion[87]

Jessica Grogan usually audits financial statements for clients in Buffalo, New York. But the EY (formerly called Ernst & Young) employee recently spent one week in Serra do Itajai National Park in Brazil with nine other EY colleagues from North and South America. Their tasks included providing strategic planning to a local eco-friendly hotel and an environmental consultancy company and helping scientists measure the diversity of birds in the park.

Grogan participated in one of EY's Corporate Responsibility Sabbaticals, which provide immersive volunteer experiences such as providing pro bono assistance for small businesses in developing countries. "The program helps our professionals grow into better leaders and teammates as they expand their global mindset by immersing themselves in a new culture alongside their colleagues," explains Deborah K. Holmes, EY's Americas director of corporate responsibility.

Jessica Grogan agrees that her experiences in Brazil were transformational. "I think the best thing I brought back was the global mindset I developed," she says. Of particular value was the opportunity to work with EY colleagues and clients from different backgrounds. "Just to get that diversity of thought, diversity of ideas and being able to bring it back, was the most rewarding part."

Study Checklist

Connect® Management is available for *M Organizational Behavior.* Additional resources include:

✓ Interactive Applications:
- **Decision Generator**
- **Sequencing**
- **Video Case:** See management in action through interactive videos.

✓ **SmartBook™**—SmartBook is the first and only adaptive reading experience available today. Distinguishing what you know from what you don't, and honing in on concepts you are most likely to forget, SmartBook personalizes content for you in a continuously adapting reading experience. Reading is no longer a passive and linear experience, but an engaging and dynamic one where you are more likely to master and retain important concepts and go to class better prepared.

©Natthawat Jamnapa/123RF

Notes

1. W. Danielson, "A Preview of the Front-Line Leader with Chris Van Gorder," podcast in *The Entrepreneur's Library* (November 3, 2014), 23:44:00; I. MacDonald, "Leading the Way: Scripps Health CEO Takes Hands-on Approach to Frontline Staff Engagement," *FierceHealthcare*, April 9, 2015; C. Van Gorder, *The Front-Line Leader: Building a High-Performance Organization from the Ground Up* (San Francisco: Jossey-Bass, 2015); C. Van Gorder, "Seven Simple Strategies for Frontline Leaders," *USCPrice* (Los Angeles: University of Southern California, February 3, 2015), http://exechealthadmin.usc.edu/blog/seven-simple-strategies-for-frontline-leaders (accessed January 14, 2017).

2. D. Cooper and S. M. B. Thatcher, "Identification in Organizations: The Role of Self-Concept Orientations and Identification Motives," *Academy of Management Review* 35, no. 4 (2010): 516-38; J. Schaubroeck, Y. J. Kim, and A. C. Peng, "The Self-Concept in Organizational Psychology: Clarifying and Differentiating the Constructs," in *International Review of Industrial and Organizational Psychology*, vol. 12, ed. G. P. Hodgkinson and J. K. Ford (New York: Wiley, 2012): 1-38.

3. V. L. Vignoles, S. J. Schwartz, and K. Luyckx, "Introduction: Toward an Integrative View of Identity," in *Handbook of Identity Theory and Research*, ed. J. S. Schwartz, K. Luyckx, and L. V. Vignoles (New York: Springer New York, 2011), 1-27; L. Gaertner et al., "A Motivational Hierarchy within: Primacy of the Individual Self, Relational Self, or Collective Self?," *Journal of Experimental Social Psychology* 48, no. 5 (2012).

4. O. W. Holmes, *The Autocrat of the Breakfast-Table* (Boston: Phillips, Sampson, 1858), 58-59. This quotation, which Steve McShane slightly rewrote to remove sexist language, has a long and convoluted history. Pioneering psychology professor William James is almost always cited as the source, yet there is no evidence that he wrote this statement or anything similar. The first attribution of this quotation to William James may have been a 1958 *RAND Memoranda* publication (p. 925), and later in *Reader's Digest* (1962). Even if James did publish something similar, it is a highly condensed version of the humorous discussion of "six persons" that Oliver Wendell Holmes Sr. published decades before James began his career. Most likely, a RAND Corporation editor crafted this quotation from vague memory of Holmes's story and misattributed William James as the author because one of Holmes's characters in the story was "James." We cite Holmes as the source because he wrote the story from which this quotation is derived.

5. E. J. Koch and J. A. Shepperd, "Is Self-Complexity Linked to Better Coping? A Review of the Literature," *Journal of Personality* 72, no. 4 (2004): 727-60; A. R. McConnell, "The Multiple Self-Aspects Framework: Self-Concept Representation and Its Implications," *Personality and Social Psychology Review* 15, no. 1 (2011): 3-27; L. F. Emery, C. Walsh, and E. B. Slotter, "Knowing Who You Are and Adding to It: Reduced Self-Concept Clarity Predicts Reduced Self-Expansion," *Social Psychological and Personality Science* 6, no. 3 (2015): 259-66.

6. C. M. Brown et al., "Between Two Selves: Comparing Global and Local Predictors of Speed of Switching between Self-Aspects," *Self and Identity* 15, no. 1 (2016): 72-89.

7. J. D. Campbell et al., "Self-Concept Clarity: Measurement, Personality Correlates, and Cultural Boundaries," *Journal of Personality and Social Psychology* 70, no. 1 (1996): 141-56.

8. J. Lodi-Smith and B. W. Roberts, "Getting to Know Me: Social Role Experiences and Age Differences in Self-Concept Clarity during Adulthood," *Journal of Personality* 78, no. 5 (2010): 1383-410.

9. E. J. Koch and J. A. Shepperd, "Is Self-Complexity Linked to Better Coping? A Review of the Literature," *Journal of Personality* 72, no. 4 (2004): 727-60; T. D. Ritchie et al., "Self-Concept Clarity Mediates the Relation between Stress and Subjective Well-Being," *Self and Identity* 10, no. 4 (2010): 493-508.

10. A. T. Brook, J. Garcia, and M. A. Fleming, "The Effects of Multiple Identities on Psychological Well-Being," *Personality and Social Psychology Bulletin* 34, no. 12 (2008): 1588-600; A. T. Church et al., "Relating Self-Concept Consistency to Hedonic and Eudaimonic Well-Being in Eight Cultures," *Journal of Cross-Cultural Psychology* 45, no. 5 (2014): 695-712.

11. J. D. Campbell, "Self-Esteem and Clarity of the Self-Concept," *Journal of Personality and Social Psychology* 59, no. 3 (1990).

12. S. Hannah et al., "The Psychological and Neurological Bases of Leader Self-Complexity and Effects on Adaptive Decision-Making," *Journal of Applied Psychology* 98, no. 3 (2013): 393-411; S. J. Creary, B. B. Caza, and L. M. Roberts, "Out of the Box? How Managing a Subordinate's Multiple Identities Affects the Quality of a Manager-Subordinate Relationship," *Academy of Management Review* 40, no. 4 (2015): 538-62.

13. C. Peus et al., "Authentic Leadership: An Empirical Test of Its Antecedents, Consequences, and Mediating Mechanisms," *Journal of Business Ethics* 107, no. 3 (2012): 331-48; F. O. Walumbwa, M. A. Maidique, and C. Atamanik, "Decision-Making in a Crisis: What Every Leader Needs to Know," *Organizational Dynamics* 43, no. 4 (2014): 284-93; B. Mittal, "Self-Concept Clarity: Exploring Its Role in Consumer Behavior," *Journal of Economic Psychology* 46 (2015): 98-110.

14. C. L. Guenther and M. D. Alicke, "Deconstructing the Better-Than-Average Effect," *Journal of Personality and Social Psychology* 99, no. 5 (2010): 755-70; S. Loughnan et al., "Universal Biases in Self-Perception: Better and More Human Than Average," *British Journal of Social Psychology* 49 (2010): 627-36; H. C. Boucher, "Understanding Western-East Asian Differences and Similarities in Self-Enhancement," *Social and Personality Psychology Compass* 4, no. 5 (2010): 304-17; A. Gregg, C. Sedikides, and J. Gebauer, "Dynamics of Identity: Between Self-Enhancement and Self-Assessment," in *Handbook of Identity Theory and Research*, ed. S. J. Schwartz, K. Luyckx, and V. L. Vignoles (New York: Springer, 2011), 305-27.

15. D. Dunning, C. Heath, and J. M. Suls, "Flawed Self-Assessment: Implications for Health, Education, and the Workplace," *Psychological Science in the Public Interest* 5, no. 3 (2004): 69-106; D. A. Moore, "Not So above Average after All: When People Believe They Are Worse Than Average and Its Implications for Theories of Bias in Social Comparison," *Organizational Behavior and Human Decision Processes* 102, no. 1 (2007): 42-58.

16. D. Gosselin et al., "Comparative Optimism among Drivers: An Intergenerational Portrait," *Accident Analysis & Prevention* 42, no. 2 (2010): 734-40; P. M. Picone, G. Battista Dagnino, and A. Minà, "The Origin of Failure: A Multidisciplinary Appraisal of the Hubris Hypothesis and Proposed Research Agenda," *Academy of Management Perspectives* 28, no. 4 (2014): 447-68; G. Chen, C. Crossland, and S. Luo, "Making the Same Mistake All over Again: CEO Overconfidence and Corporate Resistance to Corrective Feedback," *Strategic Management Journal* 36, no. 10 (2015): 1513-35.

17. K. P. Cross, "Not Can, but *Will* College Teaching Be Improved?," *New Directions for Higher Education*, no. 17 (1977): 1-15; U.S. Merit Systems Protection Board, *Accomplishing Our Mission: Results of the 2005 Merit Principles Survey* (Washington, DC: U.S. Merit Systems Protection Board, December 6, 2007); J. Montier, *Behavioral Investing* (Chicester, UK: Wiley, 2007), 82-83; V. G. Perry, "Is Ignorance Bliss? Consumer Accuracy in Judgments about Credit Ratings," *Journal of Consumer Affairs* 42, no. 2 (2008): 189-205; J. M. Twenge, W. K. Campbell, and B. Gentile, "Generational Increases in Agentic Self-Evaluations among American College Students, 1966-2009," *Self and Identity* 11, no. 4 (2011): 409-27; A. Sundström, "The Validity of Self-Reported Driver Competence: Relations between Measures of Perceived Driver Competence and Actual Driving Skill," *Transportation Research Part F: Traffic Psychology and Behaviour* 14, no. 2 (2011): 155-63.

18. This quotation has been cited since the 1930s, yet we were unable to find it in any of Dewey's writing. The earliest known reference to this quotation is Dale Carnegie's famous self-help book, where the statement is attributed to Dewey. See D. Carnegie, *How to Win Friends and Influence People*, 1st ed. (New York: Simon & Schuster, 1936), 43-44 (p. 19 in later editions).

19. W. B. Swann Jr., P. J. Rentfrow, and J. S. Guinn, "Self-Verification: The Search for Coherence," in *Handbook of Self and Identity*, ed. M. R. Leary and J. Tagney (New York: Guilford, 2002), 367–83; D. M. Cable and V. S. Kay, "Striving for Self-Verification during Organizational Entry," *Academy of Management Journal* 55, no. 2 (2012): 360–80.

20. F. Anseel and F. Lievens, "Certainty as a Moderator of Feedback Reactions? A Test of the Strength of the Self-Verification Motive," *Journal of Occupational & Organizational Psychology* 79, no. 4 (2006): 533–51; T. Kwang and W. B. Swann, "Do People Embrace Praise Even When They Feel Unworthy? A Review of Critical Tests of Self-Enhancement versus Self-Verification," *Personality and Social Psychology Review* 14, no. 3 (2010): 263–80.

21. M. R. Leary, "Motivational and Emotional Aspects of the Self," *Annual Review of Psychology* 58, no. 1 (2007): 317–44; A. Meister, K. A. Jehn, and S. M. B. Thatcher, "Feeling Misidentified: The Consequences of Internal Identity Asymmetries for Individuals at Work," *Academy of Management Review* 39, no. 4 (2014): 488–512.

22. We have described three components of core self-evaluation. The remaining component is the personality trait emotional stability, which was described in Chapter 2. However, personality is a behavior tendency, whereas core self-evaluation includes only "evaluation focused" variables. There is also recent concern about whether locus of control is part of self-evaluation. See R. E. Johnson, C. C. Rosen, and P. E. Levy, "Getting to the Core of Core Self-Evaluation: A Review and Recommendations," *Journal of Organizational Behavior* 29 (2008): 391–413; C.-H. Chang et al., "Core Self-Evaluations: A Review and Evaluation of the Literature," *Journal of Management* 38, no. 1 (2012): 81–128; R. E. Johnson et al., "Getting to the Core of Locus of Control: Is It an Evaluation of the Self or the Environment?," *Journal of Applied Psychology* 100, no. 5 (2015): 1568–78.

23. E. Dockterman, "Google Invests $50 Million to Close the Tech Gender Gap," *Time*, June 21, 2014, 16; M. della Cava, "Google, Pixar Team Up to Teach Kids Joy of Coding," *USA Today*, December 7, 2015, B4; C. Preece, "Is a Lack of Self-Belief Pushing Girls Away from STEM?," *IT Pro*, February 9, 2016; A.T. Kearney and Your Life, *Tough Choices: The Real Reasons A-Level Students Are Steering Clear of Science and Maths* (London: A.T. Kearney, February 2016).

24. W. B. Swann Jr., C. Chang-Schneider, and K. L. McClarty, "Do People's Self-Views Matter?: Self-Concept and Self-Esteem in Everyday Life," *American Psychologist* 62, no. 2 (2007): 84–94; J. L. Pierce, D. G. Gardner, and C. Crowley, "Organization-Based Self-Esteem and Well-Being: Empirical Examination of a Spillover Effect," *European Journal of Work and Organizational Psychology* 25, no. 2 (2016): 181–99.

25. A. Bandura, *Self-Efficacy: The Exercise of Control* (New York: W. H. Freeman, 1997). Evidence suggests that self-efficacy predicts performance. However, one recent study suggests that past performance predicts self-efficacy and that self-efficacy has a modest effect on future performance. See T. Sitzmann and G. Yeo, "A Meta-Analytic Investigation of the Within-Person Self-Efficacy Domain: Is Self-Efficacy a Product of Past Performance or a Driver of Future Performance?," *Personnel Psychology* 66, no. 3 (2013): 531–68.

26. G. Chen, S. M. Gully, and D. Eden, "Validation of a New General Self-Efficacy Scale," *Organizational Research Methods* 4, no. 1 (2001): 62–83.

27. J. B. Rotter, "Generalized Expectancies for Internal versus External Control of Reinforcement," *Psychological Monographs* 80, no. 1 (1966): 1–28.

28. T. W. H. Ng, K. L. Sorensen, and L. T. Eby, "Locus of Control at Work: A Meta-Analysis," *Journal of Organizational Behavior* 27 (2006): 1057–87; Q. Wang, N. A. Bowling, and K. J. Eschleman, "A Meta-Analytic Examination of Work and General Locus of Control," *Journal of Applied Psychology* 95, no. 4 (2010): 761–68.

29. G. J. Leonardelli, C. L. Pickett, and M. B. Brewer, "Optimal Distinctiveness Theory: A Framework for Social Identity, Social Cognition, and Intergroup Relations," in *Advances in Experimental Social Psychology*, ed. M. P. Zanna and J. M. Olson (San Diego, CA: Academic Press, 2010), 63–113; M. Ormiston, "Explaining the Link between Objective and Perceived Differences in Groups: The Role of the Belonging and Distinctiveness Motives," *Journal of Applied Psychology* 101, no. 2 (2016): 222–36.

30. We describe relational self-concept as a form of social identity because such connections are inherently social and the dyads are typically members of a collective entity. For example, an employee has a relationship identity with his/her boss, but this is connected to a social identity with the team or department. However, recent discussion suggests that relational self-concept also may be part of personal identity or a separate form of self-concept. See B. E. Ashforth, B. S. Schinoff, and K. M. Rogers, "'I Identify with Her,' 'I Identify with Him': Unpacking the Dynamics of Personal Identification in Organizations," *Academy of Management Review* 41, no. 1 (2016): 28–60.

31. M. A. Hogg and D. J. Terry, "Social Identity and Self-Categorization Processes in Organizational Contexts," *Academy of Management Review* 25 (2000): 121–40; C. Sedikides and A. P. Gregg, "Portraits of the Self," in *The Sage Handbook of Social Psychology*, ed. M. A. Hogg and J. Cooper (London: Sage, 2003), 110–38; S. A. Haslam and N. Ellemers, "Identity Processes in Organizations," in *Handbook of Identity Theory and Research*, ed. J. S. Schwartz, K. Luyckx, and L. V. Vignoles (New York: Springer New York, 2011), 715–44.

32. M. R. Edwards, "Organizational Identification: A Conceptual and Operational Review," *International Journal of Management Reviews* 7, no. 4 (2005): 207–30; E. S. Lee, T. Y. Park, and B. Koo, "Identifying Organizational Identification as a Basis for Attitudes and Behaviors: A Meta-Analytic Review," *Psychological Bulletin* 141, no. 5 (2015): 1049–80.

33. M. B. Brewer, "The Social Self: On Being the Same and Different at the Same Time," *Personality and Social Psychology Bulletin* 17, no. 5 (1991): 475–82; R. Imhoff and H.-P. Erb, "What Motivates Nonconformity? Uniqueness Seeking Blocks Majority Influence," *Personality and Social Psychology Bulletin* 35, no. 3 (2009): 309–20; K. R. Morrison and S. C. Wheeler, "Nonconformity Defines the Self: The Role of Minority Opinion Status in Self-Concept Clarity," *Personality and Social Psychology Bulletin* 36, no. 3 (2010): 297–308; M. G. Mayhew, J. Gardner, and N. M. Ashkanasy, "Measuring Individuals' Need for Identification: Scale Development and Validation," *Personality and Individual Differences* 49, no. 5 (2010): 356–61.

34. See, for example, W. B. Swann Jr., R. E. Johnson, and J. K. Bosson, "Identity Negotiation at Work," *Research in Organizational Behavior* 29 (2009): 81–109; J. L. Herman and S. J. Zaccaro, "The Complex Self-Concept of the Global Leader," in *Advances in Global Leadership*, vol. 8, ed. J. S. Oslanld, M. Li, and Y. Wang (Bingley, UK: Emerald Group Publishing Limited, 2014), 93–111; A. M. Grant, J. M. Berg, and D. M. Cable, "Job Titles as Identity Badges: How Self-Reflective Titles Can Reduce Emotional Exhaustion," *Academy of Management Journal* 57, no. 4 (2014): 1201–25; L. Ramarajan, "Past, Present and Future Research on Multiple Identities: Toward an Intrapersonal Network Approach," *The Academy of Management Annals* 8, no. 1 (2014): 589–659.

35. E. I. Knudsen, "Fundamental Components of Attention," *Annual Review of Neuroscience* 30, no. 1 (2007): 57–78. For an evolutionary psychology perspective of selective attention and organization, see L. Cosmides and J. Tooby, "Evolutionary Psychology: New Perspectives on Cognition and Motivation," *Annual Review of Psychology* 64, no. 1 (2013): 201–29.

36. A. Bechara and A. R. Damasio, "The Somatic Marker Hypothesis: A Neural Theory of Economic Decision," *Games and Economic Behavior* 52, no. 2 (2005): 336-72; T. S. Saunders and M. J. Buehner, "The Gut Chooses Faster Than the Mind: A Latency Advantage of Affective over Cognitive Decisions," *Quarterly Journal of Experimental Psychology* 66, no. 2 (2012): 381-88; A. Aite et al., "Impact of Emotional Context Congruency on Decision Making under Ambiguity," *Emotion* 13, no. 2 (2013): 177-82.

37. Plato, *The Republic*, trans. D. Lee (Harmondsworth, UK: Penguin, 1955).

38. D. J. Simons and C. F. Chabris, "Gorillas in Our Midst: Sustained Inattentional Blindness for Dynamic Events," *Perception* 28 (1999): 1059-74.

39. R. S. Nickerson, "Confirmation Bias: A Ubiquitous Phenomenon in Many Guises," *Review of General Psychology* 2, no. 2 (1998): 175-220; A. Gilbey and S. Hill, "Confirmation Bias in General Aviation Lost Procedures," *Applied Cognitive Psychology* 26, no. 5 (2012): 785-95; A. M. Scherer, P. D. Windschitl, and A. R. Smith, "Hope to Be Right: Biased Information Seeking Following Arbitrary and Informed Predictions," *Journal of Experimental Social Psychology* 49, no. 1 (2013): 106-12.

40. C. Wastell et al., "Identifying Hypothesis Confirmation Behaviors in a Simulated Murder Investigation: Implications for Practice," *Journal of Investigative Psychology and Offender Profiling* 9, no. 2 (2012): 184-98; D. K. Rossmo, "Case Rethinking: A Protocol for Reviewing Criminal Investigations," *Police Practice and Research* 17, no. 3 (2016): 212-28.

41. Earl Derr Biggars, the author of the Charlie Chan novels, is sometimes cited as the source of this quotation. However, this statement is found only in the 1935 film *Charlie Chan in Egypt*, which is based on Biggars' character. It does not appear in any Charlie Chan novels.

42. C. N. Macrae and G. V. Bodenhausen, "Social Cognition: Thinking Categorically about Others," *Annual Review of Psychology* 51 (2000): 93-120; K. A. Quinn and H. E. S. Rosenthal, "Categorizing Others and the Self: How Social Memory Structures Guide Social Perception and Behavior," *Learning and Motivation* 43, no. 4 (2012): 247-58; L. T. Phillips, M. Weisbuch, and N. Ambady, "People Perception: Social Vision of Groups and Consequences for Organizing and Interacting," *Research in Organizational Behavior* 34 (2014): 101-27.

43. S. Avugos et al., "The 'Hot Hand' Reconsidered: A Meta-Analytic Approach," *Psychology of Sport and Exercise* 14, no. 1 (2013): 21-27. For a discussion of cognitive closure and perception, see A. Roets et al., "The Motivated Gatekeeper of Our Minds: New Directions in Need for Closure Theory and Research," in *Advances in Experimental Social Psychology*, ed. M. O. James and P. Z. Mark (San Diego, CA: Academic Press, 2015), 221-83.

44. J. Willis and A. Todorov, "First Impressions: Making Up Your Mind after a 100-ms Exposure to a Face," *Psychological Science* 17, no. 7 (2006): 592-98; A. Todorov, M. Pakrashi, and N. N. Oosterhof, "Evaluating Faces on Trustworthiness after Minimal Time Exposure," *Social Cognition* 27, no. 6 (2009): 813-33. For related research on thin slices, see D. Kahneman, *Thinking Fast and Slow* (New York: Farrar, Strauss and Giroux, 2011); M. L. Slepian, K. R. Bogart, and N. Ambady, "Thin-Slice Judgments in the Clinical Context," *Annual Review of Clinical Psychology* 10, no. 1 (2014): 131-53.

45. P. M. Senge, *The Fifth Discipline: The Art and Practice of the Learning Organization* (New York: Doubleday Currency, 1990), chap. 10; T. J. Chermack, "Mental Models in Decision Making and Implications for Human Resource Development," *Advances in Developing Human Resources* 5, no. 4 (2003): 408-22; P. N. Johnson-Laird, "Mental Models and Deductive Reasoning," in *Reasoning: Studies of Human Inference and Its Foundations*, ed. J. E. Adler and L. J. Rips (Cambridge: Cambridge University Press, 2008); S. Ross and N. Allen, "Examining the Convergent Validity of Shared Mental Model Measures," *Behavior Research Methods* 44, no. 4 (2012): 1052-62.

46. G. W. Allport, *The Nature of Prejudice* (Reading, MA: Addison-Wesley, 1954); J. C. Brigham, "Ethnic Stereotypes," *Psychological Bulletin* 76, no. 1 (1971): 15-38; D. J. Schneider, *The Psychology of Stereotyping* (New York: Guilford, 2004); S. Kanahara, "A Review of the Definitions of Stereotype and a Proposal for a Progressional Model," *Individual Differences Research* 4, no. 5 (2006): 306-21.

47. L. Jussim, J. T. Crawford, and R. S. Rubinstein, "Stereotype (in)Accuracy in Perceptions of Groups and Individuals," *Current Directions in Psychological Science* 24, no. 6 (2015): 490-97.

48. C. N. Macrae, A. B. Milne, and G. V. Bodenhausen, "Stereotypes as Energy-Saving Devices: A Peek inside the Cognitive Toolbox," *Journal of Personality and Social Psychology* 66 (1994): 37-47; J. W. Sherman et al., "Stereotype Efficiency Reconsidered: Encoding Flexibility under Cognitive Load," *Journal of Personality and Social Psychology* 75 (1998): 589-606; C. N. Macrae and G. V. Bodenhausen, "Social Cognition: Thinking Categorically About Others," *Annual Review of Psychology* 51 (2000): 93-120; A.-K. Newheiser and J. F. Dovidio, "Individual Differences and Intergroup Bias: Divergent Dynamics Associated with Prejudice and Stereotyping," *Personality and Individual Differences* 53, no. 1 (2012): 70-74.

49. J. C. Turner and S. A. Haslam, "Social Identity, Organizations, and Leadership," in *Groups at Work: Theory and Research*, ed. M. E. Turner (Mahwah, NJ: Erlbaum, 2001), 25-65; J. Jetten, R. Spears, and T. Postmes, "Intergroup Distinctiveness and Differentiation: A Meta-Analytic Integration," *Journal of Personality and Social Psychology* 86, no. 6 (2004): 862-79; M. A. Hogg et al., "The Social Identity Perspective: Intergroup Relations, Self-Conception, and Small Groups," *Small Group Research* 35, no. 3 (2004): 246-76; K. Hugenberg and D. F. Sacco, "Social Categorization and Stereotyping: How Social Categorization Biases Person Perception and Face Memory," *Social and Personality Psychology Compass* 2, no. 2 (2008): 1052-72.

50. N. Halevy, G. Bornstein, and L. Sagiv, "'In-Group Love' and 'Out-Group Hate' as Motives for Individual Participation in Intergroup Conflict: A New Game Paradigm," *Psychological Science* 19, no. 4 (2008): 405-11; T. Yamagishi and N. Mifune, "Social Exchange and Solidarity: In-Group Love or Out-Group Hate?," *Evolution and Human Behavior* 30, no. 4 (2009): 229-37; N. Halevy, O. Weisel, and G. Bornstein, "'In-Group Love' and 'Out-Group Hate' in Repeated Interaction between Groups," *Journal of Behavioral Decision Making* 25, no. 2 (2012): 188-95; M. Parker and R. Janoff-Bulman, "Lessons from Morality-Based Social Identity: The Power of Outgroup 'Hate,' Not Just Ingroup 'Love,'" *Social Justice Research* 26, no. 1 (2013): 81-96.

51. T. Schmader and W. M. Hall, "Stereotype Threat in School and at Work: Putting Science into Practice," *Policy Insights from the Behavioral and Brain Sciences* 1, no. 1 (2014): 30-37; C. R. Pennington et al., "Twenty Years of Stereotype Threat Research: A Review of Psychological Mediators," *PLoS ONE* 11, no. 1 (2016): e0146487.

52. C. A. Moss-Racusin et al., "Science Faculty's Subtle Gender Biases Favor Male Students," *Proceedings of the National Academy of Sciences* 109, no. 41 (2012): 16474-79.

53. S. T. Fiske, "Stereotyping, Prejudice, and Discrimination," in *Handbook of Social Psychology*, ed. D. T. Gilbert, S. T. Fiske, and G. Lindzey (New York: McGraw-Hill, 1998): 357-411; M. Hewstone, M. Rubin, and H. Willis, "Intergroup Bias," *Annual Review of Psychology* 53 (2002): 575-604; C. Stangor, "The Study of

Stereotyping, Prejudice, and Discrimination within Social Psychology: A Quick History of Theory and Research," in *Handbook of Prejudice, Stereotyping, and Discrimination*, ed. T. D. Nelson (New York: Psychology Press, 2016), 1–22.

54. J. A. Bargh and T. L. Chartrand, "The Unbearable Automaticity of Being," *American Psychologist* 54, no. 7 (1999): 462–79; S. T. Fiske, "What We Know Now about Bias and Intergroup Conflict, the Problem of the Century," *Current Directions in Psychological Science* 11, no. 4 (2002): 123–28; R. Krieglmeyer and J. W. Sherman, "Disentangling Stereotype Activation and Stereotype Application in the Stereotype Misperception Task," *Journal of Personality and Social Psychology* 103, no. 2 (2012): 205–24. On the limitations of some stereotype training, see B. Gawronski et al., "When 'Just Say No' Is Not Enough: Affirmation versus Negation Training and the Reduction of Automatic Stereotype Activation," *Journal of Experimental Social Psychology* 44 (2008): 370–77.

55. H. H. Kelley, *Attribution in Social Interaction* (Morristown, NJ: General Learning Press, 1971); B. F. Malle, "Attribution Theories: How People Make Sense of Behavior," in *Theories of Social Psychology*, ed. D. Chadee (Chichester, UK: Blackwell, 2011), 72–95. This "internal–external" or "person–situation" perspective of the attribution process differs somewhat from the original "intentional–unintentional" perspective, which says that we try to understand the deliberate or accidental/involuntary reasons why people engage in behaviors, as well as the reasons for behavior. Some writers suggest the original perspective is more useful. See B. F. Malle, "Time to Give Up the Dogmas of Attribution: An Alternative Theory of Behavior Explanation," in *Advances in Experimental Social Psychology*, vol. 44, ed. K. M. Olson and M. P. Zanna (San Diego: Elsevier Academic, 2011), 297–352.

56. H. H. Kelley, "The Processes of Causal Attribution," *American Psychologist* 28 (1973): 107–28.

57. D. Lange and N. T. Washburn, "Understanding Attributions of Corporate Social Irresponsibility," *Academy of Management Review* 37, no. 2 (2012): 300–26. Recent reviews explain that attribution is an incomplete theory for understanding how people determine causation and assign blame. See S. A. Sloman and D. Lagnado, "Causality in Thought," *Annual Review of Psychology* 66, no. 1 (2015): 223–47; M. D. Alicke et al., "Causal Conceptions in Social Explanation and Moral Evaluation: A Historical Tour," *Perspectives on Psychological Science* 10, no. 6 (2015): 790–812.

58. J. M. Crant and T. S. Bateman, "Assignment of Credit and Blame for Performance Outcomes," *Academy of Management Journal* 36 (1993): 7–27; B. Weiner, "Intrapersonal and Interpersonal Theories of Motivation from an Attributional Perspective," *Educational Psychology Review* 12 (2000): 1–14; N. Bacon and P. Blyton, "Worker Responses to Teamworking: Exploring Employee Attributions of Managerial Motives," *International Journal of Human Resource Management* 16, no. 2 (2005): 238–55.

59. D. T. Miller and M. Ross, "Self-Serving Biases in the Attribution of Causality: Fact or Fiction?," *Psychological Bulletin* 82, no. 2 (1975): 213–25; J. Shepperd, W. Malone, and K. Sweeny, "Exploring Causes of the Self-Serving Bias," *Social and Personality Psychology Compass* 2, no. 2 (2008): 895–908.

60. E. W. K. Tsang, "Self-Serving Attributions in Corporate Annual Reports: A Replicated Study," *Journal of Management Studies* 39, no. 1 (2002): 51–65; N. J. Roese and J. M. Olson, "Better, Stronger, Faster: Self-Serving Judgment, Affect Regulation, and the Optimal Vigilance Hypothesis," *Perspectives on Psychological Science* 2, no. 2 (2007): 124–41; R. Hooghiemstra, "East–West Differences in Attributions for Company Performance: A Content Analysis of Japanese and U.S. Corporate Annual Reports," *Journal of Cross-Cultural Psychology* 39, no. 5 (2008): 618–29.

61. D. T. Gilbert and P. S. Malone, "The Correspondence Bias," *Psychological Bulletin* 117, no. 1 (1995): 21–38.

62. B. F. Malle, "The Actor–Observer Asymmetry in Attribution: A (Surprising) Meta-Analysis," *Psychological Bulletin* 132, no. 6 (2006): 895–919; C. W. Bauman and L. J. Skitka, "Making Attributions for Behaviors: The Prevalence of Correspondence Bias in the General Population," *Basic and Applied Social Psychology* 32, no. 3 (2010): 269–77.

63. Similar models are presented in D. Eden, "Self-Fulfilling Prophecy as a Management Tool: Harnessing Pygmalion," *Academy of Management Review* 9 (1984): 64–73; R. H. G. Field and D. A. Van Seters, "Management by Expectations (MBE): The Power of Positive Prophecy," *Journal of General Management* 14 (1988): 19–33; D. O. Trouilloud et al., "The Influence of Teacher Expectations on Student Achievement in Physical Education Classes: Pygmalion Revisited," *European Journal of Social Psychology* 32 (2002): 591–607.

64. P. Whiteley, T. Sy, and S. K. Johnson, "Leaders' Conceptions of Followers: Implications for Naturally Occurring Pygmalion Effects," *Leadership Quarterly* 23, no. 5 (2012): 822–34; J. Weaver, J. F. Moses, and M. Snyder, "Self-Fulfilling Prophecies in Ability Settings," *Journal of Social Psychology* 156, no. 2 (2016): 179–89.

65. D. Eden, "Interpersonal Expectations in Organizations," in *Interpersonal Expectations: Theory, Research, and Applications*, ed. P. D. Blanck (Cambridge: Cambridge University Press, 1993), 154–78.

66. D. Eden, "Pygmalion Goes to Boot Camp: Expectancy, Leadership, and Trainee Performance," *Journal of Applied Psychology* 67 (1982): 194–99; B. J. Avolio et al., "A Meta-Analytic Review of Leadership Impact Research: Experimental and Quasi-Experimental Studies," *The Leadership Quarterly* 20, no. 5 (2009): 764–84; P. Whiteley, T. Sy, and S. K. Johnson, "Leaders' Conceptions of Followers: Implications for Naturally Occurring Pygmalion Effects," *Leadership Quarterly* 23, no. 5 (2012): 822–34.

67. S. Madon, L. Jussim, and J. Eccles, "In Search of the Powerful Self-Fulfilling Prophecy," *Journal of Personality and Social Psychology* 72, no. 4 (1997): 791–809; A. E. Smith, L. Jussim, and J. Eccles, "Do Self-Fulfilling Prophecies Accumulate, Dissipate, or Remain Stable over Time?," *Journal of Personality and Social Psychology* 77, no. 3 (1999): 548–65; S. Madon et al., "Self-Fulfilling Prophecies: The Synergistic Accumulative Effect of Parents' Beliefs on Children's Drinking Behavior," *Psychological Science* 15, no. 12 (2005): 837–45.

68. W. H. Cooper, "Ubiquitous Halo," *Psychological Bulletin* 90 (1981): 218–44; P. Rosenzweig, *The Halo Effect . . . and the Eight Other Business Delusions That Deceive Managers* (New York: Free Press, 2007); J. W. Keeley et al., "Investigating Halo and Ceiling Effects in Student Evaluations of Instruction," *Educational and Psychological Measurement* 73, no. 3 (2013): 440–57.

69. B. Mullen et al., "The False Consensus Effect: A Meta-Analysis of 115 Hypothesis Tests," *Journal of Experimental Social Psychology* 21, no. 3 (1985): 262–83; F. J. Flynn and S. S. Wiltermuth, "Who's with Me? False Consensus, Brokerage, and Ethical Decision Making in Organizations," *Academy of Management Journal* 53, no. 5 (2010): 1074–89; B. Roth and A. Voskort, "Stereotypes and False Consensus: How Financial Professionals Predict Risk Preferences," *Journal of Economic Behavior & Organization* 107, Part B (2014): 553–65.

70. E. A. Lind, L. Kray, and L. Thompson, "Primacy Effects in Justice Judgments: Testing Predictions from Fairness Heuristic Theory," *Organizational Behavior and Human Decision Processes* 85 (2001): 189–210; T. Mann and M. Ferguson, "Can We Undo Our First Impressions? The Role of Reinterpretation in Reversing

Implicit Evaluations," *Journal of Personality & Social Psychology* 108, no. 6 (2015): 823–49; B. C. Holtz, "From First Impression to Fairness Perception: Investigating the Impact of Initial Trustworthiness Beliefs," *Personnel Psychology* 68, no. 3 (2015): 499–546.

71. Careerbuilder, "Careerbuilder Releases Study of Common and Not-So-Common Resume Mistakes That Can Cost You the Job," news release (Chicago: Careerbuilder, September 11, 2013); Accountemps, "Survey: Job Interview Trips up More Candidates Than Any Other Step in Hiring Process," news release (Menlo Park, CA: Accountemps, April 2, 2014); Careerbuilder, "Careerbuilder's Annual Survey Reveals the Most Outrageous Resume Mistakes Employers Have Found," news release (Chicago: Careerbuilder, September 22, 2016); "Top 25 Worst Resume Objective Statements," *Robert Half Blog*, May 17, 2017, https://www.roberthalf.com/blog/top-25-worst-resume-objective-statements.

72. D. D. Steiner and J. S. Rain, "Immediate and Delayed Primacy and Recency Effects in Performance Evaluation," *Journal of Applied Psychology* 74 (1989): 136–42; K. T. Trotman, "Order Effects and Recency: Where Do We Go from Here?," *Accounting & Finance* 40 (2000): 169–82; W. Green, "Impact of the Timing of an Inherited Explanation on Auditors' Analytical Procedures Judgements," *Accounting and Finance* 44 (2004): 369–92.

73. D. E. Hogan and M. Mallott, "Changing Racial Prejudice through Diversity Education," *Journal of College Student Development* 46, no. 2 (2005): 115–25; B. Gawronski et al., "When 'Just Say No' Is Not Enough: Affirmation versus Negation Training and the Reduction of Automatic Stereotype Activation," *Journal of Experimental Social Psychology* 44 (2008): 370–77; M. M. Duguid and M. C. Thomas-Hunt, "Condoning Stereotyping? How Awareness of Stereotyping Prevalence Impacts Expression of Stereotypes," *Journal of Applied Psychology* 100, no. 2 (2015): 343–59; F. Dobbin and A. Kalev, "Why Diversity Programs Fail," *Harvard Business Review* 94, no. 7/8 (2016): 52–60.

74. T. W. Costello and S. S. Zalkind, *Psychology in Administration: A Research Orientation* (Englewood Cliffs, NJ: Prentice Hall, 1963), 45–46; J. M. Kouzes and B. Z. Posner, *The Leadership Challenge*, 4th ed. (San Francisco: Jossey-Bass, 2007), chap. 3.

75. W. L. Gardner et al., "'Can You See the Real Me?' A Self-Based Model of Authentic Leader and Follower Development," *Leadership Quarterly* 16 (2005): 343–72; C. Peus et al., "Authentic Leadership: An Empirical Test of Its Antecedents, Consequences, and Mediating Mechanisms," *Journal of Business Ethics* 107, no. 3 (2012): 331–48.

76. A. G. Greenwald et al., "Understanding and Using the Implicit Association Test: III. Meta-Analysis of Predictive Validity," *Journal of Personality and Social Psychology* 97, no. 1 (2009): 17–41; M. C. Wilson and K. Scior, "Attitudes Towards Individuals with Disabilities as Measured by the Implicit Association Test: A Literature Review," *Research in Developmental Disabilities* 35, no. 2 (2014): 294–321; B. A. Nosek et al., "Understanding and Using the Brief Implicit Association Test: Recommended Scoring Procedures," *PLoS ONE* 9, no. 12 (2014): e110938; B. Schiller et al., "Clocking the Social Mind by Identifying Mental Processes in the IAT with Electrical Neuroimaging," *Proceedings of the National Academy of Sciences* 113, no. 10 (2016): 2786–91.

77. J. T. Jost et al., "The Existence of Implicit Bias Is Beyond Reasonable Doubt: A Refutation of Ideological and Methodological Objections and Executive Summary of Ten Studies That No Manager Should Ignore," *Research in Organizational Behavior* 29 (2009): 39–69. The science-as-male implicit stereotype is discussed in F. L. Smyth and B. A. Nosek, "On the Gender-Science Stereotypes Held by Scientists: Explicit Accord with Gender-Ratios, Implicit Accord with Scientific Identity," *Frontiers in Psychology* 6 (2015).

78. J. Luft, *Of Human Interaction* (Palo Alto, CA: National Press, 1969). For a variation of this model, see J. Hall, "Communication Revisited," *California Management Review* 15 (1973): 56–67. For recent discussion of the Johari blind spot, see A.-M. B. Gallrein et al., "You Spy with Your Little Eye: People Are 'Blind' to Some of the Ways in Which They Are Consensually Seen by Others," *Journal of Research in Personality* 47, no. 5 (2013): 464–71; A.-M. B. Gallrein et al., "I Still Cannot See It–A Replication of Blind Spots in Self-Perception," *Journal of Research in Personality* 60 (2016): 1–7.

79. S. Vazire and M. R. Mehl, "Knowing Me, Knowing You: The Accuracy and Unique Predictive Validity of Self-Ratings and Other-Ratings of Daily Behavior," *Journal of Personality and Social Psychology* 95, no. 5 (2008): 1202–16; D. Leising, A.-M. B. Gallrein, and M. Dufner, "Judging the Behavior of People We Know: Objective Assessment, Confirmation of Preexisting Views, or Both?," *Personality and Social Psychology Bulletin* 40, no. 2 (2014): 153–63.

80. T. F. Pettigrew and L. R. Tropp, "A Meta-Analytic Test of Intergroup Contact Theory," *Journal of Personality and Social Psychology* 90, no. 5 (2006): 751–83; Y. Amichai-Hamburger, B. S. Hasler, and T. Shani-Sherman, "Structured and Unstructured Intergroup Contact in the Digital Age," *Computers in Human Behavior* 52 (2015): 515–22.

81. The contact hypothesis was first introduced in G. W. Allport, *The Nature of Prejudice* (Reading, MA: Addison-Wesley, 1954), chap. 16.

82. J. M. Von Bergen, "'Undercover' Opens Forman Mills Boss' Eyes," *Philadelphia Inquirer*, January 20, 2015, C01; J. M. Von Bergen, "Forman Mills CEO Rick Forman Capitalized on 'Undercover Boss': TV Makeover Was the Real Thing," *Philadelphia Inquirer*, May 22, 2015, A19.

83. R. Elliott et al., "Empathy," *Psychotherapy* 48, no. 1 (2011): 43–49; J. Zaki, "Empathy: A Motivated Account," *Psychological Bulletin* 140, no. 6 (2014): 1608–47; E. Teding van Berkhout and J. Malouff, "The Efficacy of Empathy Training: A Meta-Analysis of Randomized Controlled Trials," *Journal of Counseling Psychology* 63, no. 1 (2016): 32–41.

84. M. Tarrant, R. Calitri, and D. Weston, "Social Identification Structures the Effects of Perspective Taking," *Psychological Science* 23, no. 9 (2012): 973–78; J. L. Skorinko and S. A. Sinclair, "Perspective Taking Can Increase Stereotyping: The Role of Apparent Stereotype Confirmation," *Journal of Experimental Social Psychology* 49, no. 1 (2013): 10–18.

85. There is no consensus on the meaning of global mindset. The elements identified in this book are common among most of the recent writing on this subject. See, for example, S. J. Black, "The Mindset of Global Leaders: Inquisitiveness and Duality," in *Advances in Global Leadership*, vol. 4, ed. W. H. Mobley and E. Weldon (Bingley, UK: Emerald Group Publishing Limited, 2005), 181–200; O. Levy et al., "What We Talk about When We Talk about 'Global Mindset': Managerial Cognition in Multinational Corporations," *Journal of International Business Studies* 38, no. 2 (2007): 231–58; S. Beechler and D. Baltzley, "Creating a Global Mindset," *Chief Learning Officer* 7, no. 6 (2008): 40–45; M. Javidan and D. Bowen, "The 'Global Mindset' of Managers: What It Is, Why It Matters, and How to Develop It," *Organizational Dynamics* 42, no. 2 (2013): 145–55.

86. A. K. Gupta and V. Govindarajan, "Cultivating a Global Mindset," *Academy of Management Executive* 16, no. 1 (2002): 116–26.

87. M. Glynn, "Putting Business Skills to Work–in a Brazilian Rainforest," *Buffalo News*, August 9, 2015; S. McCabe, "2016 EY-Earthwatch Ambassadors Program Donates 3,000 Hours of Research to Brazil, Mexico," *Accounting Today*, July 8, 2016.

4 | Workplace Emotions, Attitudes, and Stress

Learning Objectives

After you read this chapter, you should be able to:

LO4-1 Explain how emotions and cognition (conscious reasoning) influence attitudes and behavior.

LO4-2 Discuss the dynamics of emotional labor and the role of emotional intelligence in the workplace.

LO4-3 Summarize the consequences of job dissatisfaction, as well as strategies to increase organizational (affective) commitment.

LO4-4 Describe the stress experience and review four major stressors.

LO4-5 Identify five ways to manage workplace stress.

Google (and its parent company, Alphabet) may be known mainly for developing popular and groundbreaking technologies, but it is also a leader in generating employee happiness. The technology giant is rated as the best place to work in America and is at or near the top of similar lists in other countries. Most Google employees (86 percent in one survey) say they have high job satisfaction. Google pioneered the college campus model of workplace design, complete with rock-climbing walls, slides, unusual work spaces, free haircuts, foosball and other games, volleyball sandpits, free gourmet meals, laundry facilities, medical facilities, and massages. Employees also enjoy special events and outings, including parties at classy venues, overnight ski trips, and nature walks. They also get unlimited sick leave days and generous paid parental leave. Salaries at Google are among the highest in any business.

Beyond pay and perks, Google also generates positive vibes through much deeper sources. Most employees (73 percent) say their job is meaningful, mainly because the company makes products and services that are either widely used or innovations for the future. Another feel-good feature of working at Google is continuous learning through training programs, tech talks, and daily interaction with knowledgeable coworkers. The company applies effective strategies to minimize backstabbing and maximize positive team work experiences. Not surprisingly, almost all Google employees have high commitment to the company; in one recent survey, 96 percent said they are proud to work at Google.[1]

By any measure, Google sets the standard of excellence in employee emotions, attitudes, and well-being. This chapter presents current knowledge and practices about these three concepts. We begin by describing emotions and explaining how they influence attitudes and behavior. Next, we consider the dynamics of emotional labor, followed by the popular topic of emotional intelligence. The specific work attitudes of job satisfaction and organizational commitment are then discussed, including their association with various employee behaviors and work performance. The final section looks at work-related stress, including the stress experience, four prominent stressors, individual differences in stress, and ways to combat excessive stress.

LO4-1 Explain how emotions and cognition (conscious reasoning) influence attitudes and behavior.

EMOTIONS IN THE WORKPLACE

Emotions influence almost everything we do in the workplace. This is a strong statement, and one that you would rarely have found a dozen years ago among organizational behavior experts. Most OB theories still assume that a person's thoughts and actions are governed primarily or exclusively by logical thinking (called *cognition*).[2] Yet groundbreaking neuroscience discoveries have revealed that our perceptions, attitudes, decisions, and behavior are influenced by emotions as well as cognitions.[3] In fact, emotions may have a greater influence because they often occur before cognitive processes and, consequently, influence the latter. By ignoring emotionality, many theories have overlooked a large piece of the puzzle about human behavior in the workplace.

Emotions are physiological, behavioral, and psychological episodes experienced toward an object, person, or event that create a state of readiness.[4] These "episodes" are very brief events that

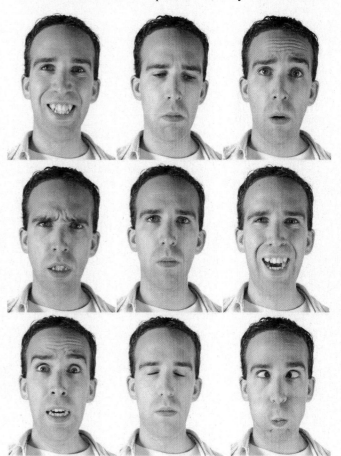

Emotions are physiological, behavioral, and psychological episodes experienced toward an object, person, or event that create a state of readiness.
©Richard Nelson/Cutcaster

typically subside or occur in waves lasting from milliseconds to a few minutes. Emotions are directed toward someone or something. For example, we experience joy, fear, anger, and other emotional episodes toward tasks, customers, or a software program we are using. This differs from *moods*, which are not directed toward anything in particular and tend to be longer-term emotional states.

Emotions are experiences. They represent changes in our physiological state (e.g., blood pressure, heart rate), psychological state (e.g., thought process), and behavior (e.g., facial expression).[5] Most of these emotional reactions are subtle; they occur without our awareness. This is an important point because

the topic of emotions often conjures up images of people "getting emotional." In reality, most emotions are fleeting, low-intensity events that influence our behavior without conscious awareness.[6] Finally, emotions put us in a state of readiness. When we get worried, for example, our heart rate and blood pressure increase to make our body better prepared to engage in fight or flight. Strong emotions trigger our conscious awareness of a threat or opportunity in the external environment.

Types of Emotions

People experience many emotions and various combinations of emotions, but all of them have two common features, illustrated in Exhibit 4.1.[8] One feature is that emotions vary in their level of activation. By definition, emotions put us in a state of readiness

> "Don't let us forget that the small emotions are the great captains of our lives, and that we obey them without knowing it."[7]
>
> —Vincent Van Gogh (late 1800s Dutch painter)

Exhibit 4.1 Circumplex Model of Emotions

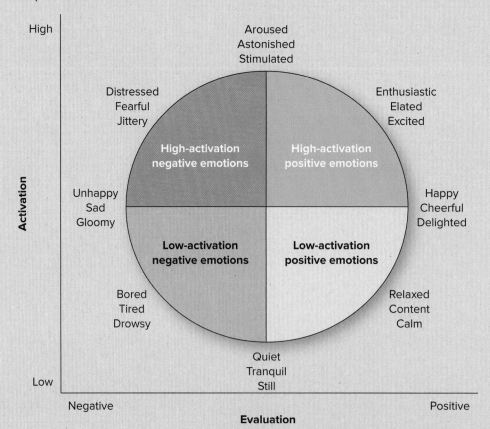

Sources: Adapted from J. A. Russell, "Core Affect and the Psychological Construction of Emotion," *Psychological Review* 110, no. 1 (2003): 145–72; M. Yik, J. A. Russell, and J. H. Steiger, "A 12-Point Circumplex Structure of Core Affect," *Emotion* 11, no. 4 (2011): 705–31.

attitudes the cluster of beliefs, assessed feelings, and behavioral intentions toward a person, object, or event (called an attitude object)

and, as we discuss in the next chapter, are the primary source of a person's motivation. Some emotional experiences, such as when we are suddenly surprised, are strong enough to consciously motivate us to act without careful thought. Most emotional experiences are more subtle, but even they activate enough to make us more aware of our environment.

A second feature is that all emotions have an associated valence (called *core affect*) signaling that the perceived object or event should be approached or avoided. In other words, all emotions evaluate environmental conditions as good or bad, helpful or harmful, positive or negative, and so forth. Furthermore, negative emotions tend to generate stronger levels of activation than do positive emotions.[9] Fear and anger, for instance, are more intense experiences than are joy and delight, so they have a stronger effect on our actions. This valence asymmetry likely occurs because negative emotions protect us from harm and are therefore more critical for our survival.

Emotions, Attitudes, and Behavior

To understand how emotions influence our thoughts and behavior in the workplace, we first need to know about attitudes. **Attitudes** represent the cluster of beliefs, assessed feelings, and behavioral intentions toward a person, object, or event (called an *attitude object*).[10] Attitudes are *judgments*, whereas emotions are *experiences*. In other words, attitudes involve evaluations of an attitude object, whereas emotions operate as events, usually without our awareness. Attitudes also might operate nonconsciously, but we are usually aware of and consciously think about those evaluations. Another distinction is that we experience most emotions very briefly, whereas our attitude toward someone or something is more stable over time.[11]

Until recently, experts believed that attitudes could be understood just by the three cognitive components illustrated on the left side of Exhibit 4.2: beliefs, feelings, and behavioral intentions. Now evidence suggests that a parallel emotional process is also at work, shown on the right side of the exhibit.[12] Using attitude toward mergers as an example, let's look more closely at this model, beginning with the traditional cognitive perspective of attitudes.

- *Beliefs.* These are your established perceptions about the attitude object—what you believe to be true. For example, you might believe that mergers reduce job security for employees in the merged firms or that mergers increase the company's competitiveness in this era of globalization. These beliefs are perceived facts that you acquire from experience and other forms of learning. Each of these beliefs also has a valence; that is, you have a positive or negative feeling about each belief (e.g., better job security is good).
- *Feelings.* This element represents your conscious positive or negative evaluations of the attitude object. Some people think mergers are good; others think they are bad. Your like or dislike of mergers represents your assessed feelings. According to the traditional cognitive perspective of attitudes (left side of the model), feelings are calculated from your beliefs about mergers and the associated feelings about those beliefs. Consider the example of your attitude toward mergers. If you believe that mergers typically have negative consequences such as layoffs and organizational politics, then you will form negative feelings toward mergers in general or about a specific planned merger in your organization.
- *Behavioral intentions.* This third element represents your motivation to engage in a particular behavior regarding the attitude object.[13] Upon hearing that the company will merge with another organization, you might become motivated to look for a job elsewhere or possibly to complain to management about the merger decision. Your feelings toward mergers motivate your behavioral intentions, and which actions you choose depends on your past experience, personality, and social norms of appropriate behavior.

Exhibit 4.2 Model of Emotions, Attitudes, and Behavior

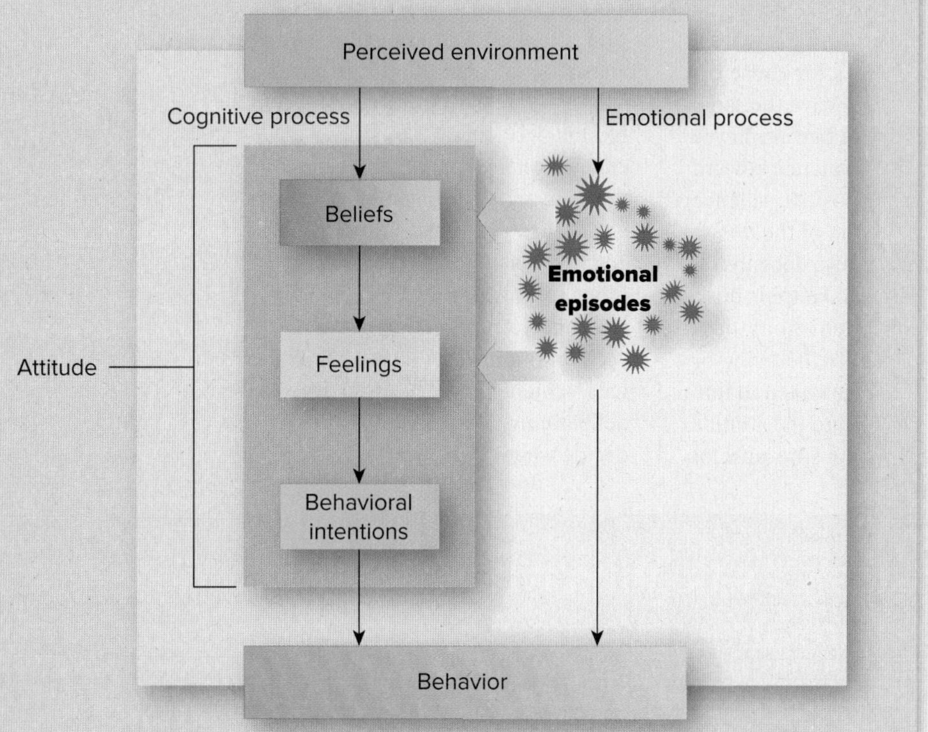

Attitude–Behavior Contingencies

The cognitive model of attitudes (beliefs-feelings-intentions) gives the impression that we can predict behavior from each element of the

Several contingencies at each stage in the cognitive model of attitudes weaken the ability to predict behavior from beliefs, feelings, and behavioral intentions.
©Peshkova/Shutterstock

individual's attitude. This is potentially true, but several contingencies at each stage in the model usually weaken that relationship. Let's begin with the beliefs–feelings link. People with the same beliefs might form quite different feelings toward the attitude object because they have different valences for those beliefs. Two employees who report to the same boss have the same belief that their boss makes them work hard. Yet one employee dislikes the boss because s/he has a negative valence toward hard work whereas the other employee has a positive valence toward hard work, and so has a positive evaluation of the boss.

The effect of feelings on behavioral intentions also depends on contingencies. Two employees might equally dislike their boss, but it isn't easy to predict their behavioral intentions from those feelings. One employee is motivated to complain to the union or upper management while the other employee is motivated to find a job elsewhere. People with the same feelings toward the attitude object often develop different behavioral intentions because of

their unique experiences, personal values, self-concept, and other individual differences. Later in this chapter we describe the four main responses to dissatisfaction and other negative attitudes.

Finally, the model indicates that behavioral intentions are the best predictors of a person's behavior. However, the strength of this link also depends on other factors, such as the person's ability, situational factors, and possibly role ambiguity (see the MARS model in Chapter 2). For example, two people might intend to quit because they dislike their boss, but only one does so because the other employee can't find another job.

How Emotions Influence Attitudes and Behavior

The cognitive model describes to some extent how employees form and change their attitudes, but emotions also have a central role in this process.[14] As the right side of Exhibit 4.2 illustrates, emotions are usually initiated by perceptions of the world around us. Our brain tags incoming sensory information with emotional markers based on a quick and imprecise evaluation of whether that information supports or threatens our innate drives. These markers are not calculated feelings; they are automatic and nonconscious emotional responses based on very thin slices of sensory information.[15] The experienced emotions then influence our feelings about the attitude object. For example, Google employees experience positive emotions from the high-quality free meals, fun-oriented and friendly work spaces, ongoing learning opportunities, and supportive coworkers, all of which generate positive attitudes toward the company.

To explain this process in more detail, consider once again your attitude toward mergers. You might experience worry, nervousness, or relief upon learning that your company intends to merge with a competitor. The fuzzy dots on the right side of Exhibit 4.2 depict the numerous emotional episodes you experience upon hearing the merger announcement, subsequently thinking about the merger, discussing the merger with coworkers, and so on. These emotions are transmitted to your brain's cognitive centers, where they are logically analyzed along with other information about the attitude object.[16] Thus, while you are consciously evaluating whether the merger is good or bad, your emotions are already sending core affect (good–bad) signals, which sway your conscious evaluation. In fact, we often deliberately "listen in" on our emotions to help us consciously decide whether to support or oppose something.[17]

> While you are consciously evaluating whether something is good or bad, your emotions are already sending core affect (good–bad) signals, which sway your conscious evaluation.

The influence of both cognitive reasoning and emotions on attitudes is most apparent when they disagree with each other. People occasionally experience this mental tug-of-war, sensing that something isn't right even though they can't think of any logical reason to be concerned. This conflicting experience indicates that the person's logical analysis of the situation (left side of Exhibit 4.2) generates feelings that differ from the emotional reaction (right side of Exhibit 4.2).[18] Should we pay attention to our emotional response or our logical analysis? This question is not easy to answer, but some studies indicate that while executives tend to make quick decisions based on their gut feelings (emotional response), the best decisions tend to occur when executives spend time logically evaluating the situation.[19] Therefore, we should pay attention to both the cognitive and emotional sides of the attitude model and hope they agree with each other most of the time!

Generating Positive Emotions at Work Google and many other companies seem to be well aware of the dual cognitive-emotional attitude process because they try to inject more positive experiences in the workplace.[20] Some critics might argue that the organization's main focus should be to create positive emotions through the job itself as well as natural everyday occurrences such as polite customers and supportive coworkers. Still, many people perform work that is difficult to enjoy

much of the time. Employees perform tasks that are repetitive or they necessarily interact with unfriendly customers. Research has found that humor and fun at work—whether natural or contrived—can potentially counteract some of the negative emotions from the work itself.[21] Overall, corporate leaders need to keep in mind that emotions shape employee attitudes and, as we will discuss later, attitudes influence various forms of work-related behavior.

One last comment about Exhibit 4.2: Notice the arrow from the emotional episodes to behavior. It indicates that emotions directly influence a person's behavior without conscious thought. This occurs when we jump suddenly if someone sneaks up on us. It also occurs in everyday situations because even low-intensity emotions automatically change our facial expressions. These actions are not carefully thought out. They are automatic emotional responses that are learned or hardwired by heredity for particular situations.[23]

Cognitive Dissonance

Imagine that you have just signed a contract for new electronic whiteboards to be installed throughout the company's meeting rooms. The deal was expensive but, after consulting several staff, you felt that the technology would be valuable in this electronic age. Yet, you felt a twinge of regret soon after signing the contract.

OB THEORY TO PRACTICE

A Short List of Fun Events for the Workplace[22]

Interesting work, supportive coworkers, a healthy work environment, and good pay are some of the well-established ways to make employees happier at work. But companies also try to introduce specific events to inject more positive emotions. Here are some of the more interesting (and apparently effective) fun strategies.

▶ Office races—individual and team races down hallways with tricycles, wheeled chairs, or scooters. At some fun-oriented businesses, employees start these races without formal planning.

▶ Peer learning classes on nonwork skills—from music lessons to printmaking, employees enjoy learning something different during lunch, after hours, or on special learning days.

▶ Treasure hunts—whether in the office or around the town, most employees enjoy the team camaraderie of figuring out clues to the prize while competing with other teams. At least one European company even rented a castle as the venue for this type of activity.

▶ Nature hikes—a half-day hike in the woods with coworkers through terrain that most can handle is a healthy break from office stress and builds positive relations with coworkers.

▶ Attending sports games—baseball, hockey, and many other sporting events are great to watch and share the enthusiasm with coworkers.

▶ Board games—from Monopoly to Settlers of Catan, board games have surprised many (initially skeptical) employees about how much

©g-stockstudio/Shutterstock

fun they are as office events. Some companies schedule board game events over an extended lunch break (with company-provided food, of course) or on special games days.

▶ Go-kart and bumper car races—these competitive activities rev up excitement for most employees without being dangerous (the vehicles are designed for anyone over 12 years old). For those with a more aggressive bent, there are also paintball and smurf battles.

This emotional experience is **cognitive dissonance**, which occurs when people perceive that their beliefs, feelings, and behavior are incongruent with each other.[24] This inconsistency generates emotions (such as feeling hypocritical) that motivate the person to create more consistency by changing one or more of these elements.

Why did you experience cognitive dissonance after purchasing the electronic whiteboards? Perhaps you remembered that some staff wanted flexibility, whereas the whiteboards require special markers and computer software. Or maybe you had a fleeting realization that buying electronic whiteboards costing several times more than traditional whiteboards is inconsistent with your personal values and company culture of thriftiness. Whatever the reason, the dissonance occurs because your attitude (it's good to be cost conscious) is inconsistent with your behavior (buying expensive whiteboards). Most people like to think of themselves—and be viewed by others—as rational and logical. Cognitive dissonance occurs when our behavior and beliefs conflict, which is not so rational.

How do we reduce cognitive dissonance?[25] Reversing the behavior might work, but few behaviors can be undone. In any event, dissonance still exists because others know about the behavior and that you performed it voluntarily. It would be too expensive to remove the electronic whiteboards after they have been installed and, in any event, coworkers already know that you made this purchase and did so willingly.

More often, people reduce cognitive dissonance by changing their beliefs and feelings. One dissonance-reducing strategy is to develop more favorable attitudes toward specific features of the decision, such as forming a more positive opinion about the whiteboards' capacity to store whatever is written on them. People also are motivated to discover positive features of the

Cognitive dissonance is an emotional experience that occurs when people perceive that their beliefs, feelings, and behavior are incongruent with each other.
©Sirtravelalot/Shutterstock

decision they didn't notice earlier (e.g., the boards can change handwriting into typed text) and to discover subsequent problems with the alternatives they didn't choose (e.g., few traditional boards can be used as projection screens). A third strategy is more indirect; rather than try to overlook the high price of the electronic whiteboards, you reduce dissonance by emphasizing how your other decisions have been frugal. This framing compensates for your expensive whiteboard fling and thereby maintains your self-concept as a thrifty decision maker. Each of these mental acrobatics maintains some degree of consistency between the person's behavior (buying expensive whiteboards) and attitudes (being thrifty).

Emotions and Personality

Throughout this section, we have implied that emotional experiences are triggered by workplace experiences. This is mostly true, but emotions are also partly determined by an individual's personality.[26] Some people experience positive emotions as a natural trait. People with higher emotional stability and extraverted personalities (see Chapter 2) tend to experience more positive emotions. Those with higher neuroticism (lower emotional stability) and introverted personalities tend to experience more negative emotions. Positive and negative emotional traits affect a

---

connect

SELF-ASSESSMENT 4.1: What is Your Emotional Personality?
Emotions are influenced by the situation, but also by the individual's own personality. In particular, people tend to have a dispositional mood, that is, the level and valence of emotion that they naturally experience due to their personality. You can discover your perceived dispositional mood by locating this self-assessment in Connect if it is assigned by your instructor.

person's attendance, turnover, and long-term work attitudes. Although positive and negative personality traits have some effect, other research concludes that the actual situation in which people work has a noticeably stronger influence on their attitudes and behavior.[27]

LO4-2 Discuss the dynamics of emotional labor and the role of emotional intelligence in the workplace.

MANAGING EMOTIONS AT WORK

People are expected to manage their emotions in the workplace. They must conceal their frustration when serving an irritating customer, display compassion to an ill patient, and hide their boredom in a long meeting with other executives. These are all forms of **emotional labor**—the effort, planning, and control needed to express organizationally desired emotions during interpersonal transactions.[28] Almost everyone is expected to abide by *display rules*—norms or explicit rules requiring us within our role to display specific emotions and to hide other emotions. Emotional labor demands are higher in jobs requiring a variety of emotions (e.g., anger as well as joy) and more intense emotions (e.g., showing delight rather than smiling weakly), as well as in jobs where interaction with clients is frequent and longer. Emotional labor also increases when employees must precisely rather than casually abide by the display rules.[29] This work requirement is most common in service industries, where employees have frequent face-to-face interaction with clients.

Emotional Display Norms across Cultures

Norms about displaying or hiding your true emotions vary considerably across cultures.[30] One major study points to Ethiopia, Japan, and Austria (among others) as cultures that discourage emotional expression. Instead, people are expected to be subdued, have relatively monotonic voice intonation, and avoid physical movement and touching that display emotions. In contrast, cultures such as Kuwait, Egypt, Spain, and Russia allow or encourage more vivid display of emotions and expect people to act more consistently with their true emotions. In these cultures, people are expected to more honestly reveal their thoughts and feelings, be dramatic in their conversational tones, and be animated in their use of nonverbal behaviors. For

example, 81 percent of Ethiopians and 74 percent of Japanese agreed that it is considered unprofessional to express emotions overtly in their culture, whereas 43 percent of Americans, 33 percent of Italians, and only 19 percent of Spaniards, Cubans, and Egyptians agreed with this statement.[31]

Employees experience the tension of emotional dissonance when they need to display emotions that are quite different from the emotions they are actually experiencing at that moment.
©RapidEye/E+/Getty Images

emotional labor the effort, planning, and control needed to express organizationally desired emotions during interpersonal transactions

emotional dissonance the psychological tension experienced when the emotions people are required to display are quite different from the emotions they actually experience at that moment

Emotional Dissonance

Most jobs expect employees to engage in some level of emotional labor, such as displaying courtesy to unruly passengers or maintaining civility to coworkers. Employees often need to display emotions that are quite different from the emotions they are actually experiencing at that moment. This incongruence produces an emotional tension called **emotional dissonance**. Most of us usually handle these discrepancies by engaging in *surface acting*; we pretend that we feel the expected emotion even though we actually experience a different emotion.

One problem with surface acting is that it can lead to higher stress and burnout.[32] By definition, emotional labor requires effort and attention, both of which consume personal energy. Emotional labor also may require employees to act contrary to their self-view, which can lead to psychological separation from self. These problems are greater when employees need to frequently display emotions that oppose their genuine emotions. A second problem with surface acting is that pretending to feel particular emotions can be challenging. A genuine emotion automatically activates a complex set of facial muscles and body positions, all of which are difficult to replicate when pretending to have these emotions. Meanwhile, our true emotions tend to reveal themselves as subtle gestures, usually without our awareness. More often than not, observers see when we are faking and sense that we are feeling a different emotion to the one we are displaying.[33]

Emotional dissonance can be reduced to some extent when employees view their surface acting as a natural part of their role. Flight attendants can remain pleasant to unruly passengers more easily when they define themselves by their customer service skill. By adopting this view, their faking is not deprivation of personal self-worth. Instead, it is demonstration of their skill and professionalism. The dissonant interactions are accomplishments rather than dreaded chores.[34]

Emotional intelligence includes a set of *abilities* that enable us to recognize and regulate our own emotions as well as the emotions of other people.
©Blend Images/Alamy Stock Photo

Another strategy is to engage in *deep acting* rather than surface acting.[35] Deep acting involves visualizing reality differently, which then produces emotions more consistent with the required emotions. Faced with an angry passenger, a flight attendant might replace hostile emotions with compassion by viewing the passenger's behavior as a sign of his or her discomfort or anxiety. Deep acting requires considerable emotional intelligence, which we discuss next.

EMOTIONAL INTELLIGENCE

Emotional intelligence (EI) is a set of *abilities* that enable us to recognize and regulate our own emotions as well as the emotions of other people. This definition refers to the four main dimensions shown in Exhibit 4.3.[36]

- *Awareness of our own emotions.* This is the ability to perceive and understand the meaning of our own emotions. People with higher EI have better awareness of their emotions and are better able to make sense of them. They can eavesdrop on their emotional responses to specific situations and use this awareness as conscious information.[37]

- *Management of our own emotions.* Emotional intelligence includes the ability to manage our own emotions, something that we all do to some extent. We keep disruptive impulses in check. We try not to feel angry or frustrated when events go against us. We try to feel and express joy and happiness toward others when the occasion calls for these emotional displays. We reenergize ourselves later in the workday. Notice that management of our own emotions goes beyond enacting desired emotions in a particular situation. It also includes generating or suppressing emotions. In other words, the deep acting described earlier requires high levels of the self-regulation component of emotional intelligence.

- *Awareness of others' emotions.* This is the ability to perceive and understand the emotions of other people.[38] It relates to *empathy*—having an understanding of and sensitivity to the feelings, thoughts, and situations of others (see Chapter 3). This ability includes understanding the other person's situation, experiencing his or her emotions, and knowing his or her needs, even when unstated. Awareness of others' emotions also includes being organizationally aware, such as sensing office politics and the presence of informal social networks.

- *Management of others' emotions.* This dimension of EI refers to managing other people's emotions. It includes consoling people who feel sad, emotionally inspiring team members to complete a class project on time, getting strangers to feel comfortable working with you, and dissipating coworker stress and other dysfunctional emotions that they experience.

The four dimensions of emotional intelligence form a hierarchy.[39] Awareness of your own emotions is lowest in that hierarchy because you need that awareness to engage in the higher levels of EI. You can't manage your own emotions if you don't know what they are (i.e., low self-awareness). Managing other people's emotions is the highest level of EI because this ability requires awareness of your own and others' emotions. To diffuse an angry conflict between two employees, for example, you need to understand the emotions they are experiencing and manage your emotions (and display of emotions).

Exhibit 4.3 Dimensions of Emotional Intelligence

		Yourself	Others
Abilities	Recognition of emotions	**Awareness of own emotions**	**Awareness of others' emotions**
	Regulation of emotions	**Management of own emotions**	**Management of others' emotions**

Sources: D. Goleman, "An EI-Based Theory of Performance," in *The Emotionally Intelligent Workplace,* ed. C. Cherniss and D. Goleman (San Francisco: Jossey-Bass, 2001), 28; P. J. Jordan and S. A. Lawrence, "Emotional Intelligence in Teams: Development and Initial Validation of the Short Version of the Workgroup Emotional Intelligence Profile (WEIP-S)," *Journal of Management & Organization* 15 (2009): 452–69.

SELF-ASSESSMENT 4.2: How Well Do You Recognize and Regulate Emotions?

Emotional intelligence is an important concept that potentially enables us to be more effective with others in the workplace and other social settings. Emotional intelligence is best measured as an ability test. However, you can estimate your level of emotional intelligence to some extent by reflecting on events that required your awareness and management of emotions. You can discover your perceived level of emotional intelligence by locating this self-assessment in Connect if it is assigned by your instructor.

Increasing Priority of Emotional Intelligence at Work[42]

73% of 2,317 Canadian managers polled indicate that they have no significant strengths in any of the key skill areas of emotional intelligence.

34% of 2,600 American hiring managers and HR professionals polled say they are placing greater emphasis on emotional intelligence when hiring and promoting employees.

95% of 600 human resource managers surveyed in the U.S. and Canada say it's important for employees to have a high emotional intelligence.

61% of 800 office workers surveyed in the U.S. and Canada admit they have let emotions get the better of them in the office.

59% of 2,600 hiring managers surveyed say they would not hire someone who has a high cognitive intelligence but low emotional intelligence.

(photo): ©Jack Hollingsworth/Blend Images LLC

Emotional Intelligence Outcomes and Development

Most jobs involve social interaction with coworkers or external stakeholders, so employees need emotional intelligence to work effectively.[40] Studies suggest that people with high EI are more effective team members, perform better in jobs requiring emotional labor, make better decisions involving other people, and maintain a more positive mindset for creative work. EI also is associated with effective leadership because leaders engage in emotional labor (e.g., showing patience to employees even when they might feel frustrated) as well as regulating the emotions of others (e.g., helping staff members feel optimism for the future even though they just lost an important contract). However, emotional intelligence does not improve some forms of performance, such as tasks that require minimal social interaction.[41]

Given the potential value of emotional intelligence, it's not surprising that some organizations try to measure this ability in job applicants. Several organizations also have training programs to improve employees' emotional intelligence.[43] These programs usually teach participants about the concept, test their EI when the program begins, and provide ongoing feedback about how well they understand and manage others' emotions. For instance, San Diego police introduced a course in which officers develop emotional intelligence and effective communication. "If you describe how a good officer anywhere does their job, you're describing what we've come to recognize as emotional intelligence," explains San Diego police psychologist Dan Blumberg. "It's someone who understands himself or herself and can understand emotions evoked during the job and manage their emotions effectively. They understand the emotions of others and are able to use emotions to create positive encounters."[44]

So far, this chapter has introduced the model of emotions and attitudes, as well as emotional intelligence, as the means by which we manage emotions in the workplace. The next two sections look at two specific attitudes: job satisfaction and organizational commitment. These two attitudes are so important in our understanding of workplace behavior that some experts suggest the two combined should be called "overall job attitude."[45]

OB THEORY TO PRACTICE

Improving Emotional Intelligence

1. Training programs—learn about emotional intelligence, then receive ongoing feedback in realistic situations.

2. Self-reflection—after an event, employees write a journal report on their experience in which they reflect on what happened and how it could be improved in the future.

3. Coaching—a professional coach observes the individual in work situations and listens to his or her nonobserved experiences, then provides debriefing feedback about how to improve his or her emotions-based behavior in those situations.

4. Maturity—people tend to improve their emotional intelligence with age due to improved self-awareness, reinforcement of emotions management, and numerous opportunities to develop their emotional intelligence skills.

JOB SATISFACTION

Probably the most studied attitude in organizational behavior is **job satisfaction**, a person's evaluation of his or her job and work context.[46] It is an *appraisal* of the perceived job characteristics, work environment, and emotional experiences at work. Satisfied employees have a favorable evaluation of their jobs, based on their observations and emotional experiences. Job satisfaction is best viewed as a collection of attitudes about different aspects of the job and work context. You might like your coworkers but be less satisfied with your workload, for instance.

How satisfied are employees at work? The answer depends on the person, the workplace, and the country. Global surveys, such as the one shown in Exhibit 4.4, indicate with some consistency that job satisfaction tends to be highest the United States, India, and some Nordic countries (such as Norway and Denmark). The lowest levels of overall job satisfaction are usually recorded in Hungary and some Asian countries (such as Japan and Hong Kong).[47]

Can we conclude from these surveys that most employees in the United States, India, and Norway are happy at work?

Possibly, but their overall job satisfaction probably isn't as high as these statistics suggest. One problem is that surveys often use a single direct question, such as "How satisfied are you with your job?" Many dissatisfied employees are reluctant to reveal their feelings in a direct question because this is tantamount to admitting that they made a poor job choice and are not enjoying a large part of their life. The inflated results are evident in the fact that employees tend to report less satisfaction when asked about specific aspects of their work. Furthermore, studies report that many employees plan to look for work within the next year or would leave their current employer if the right opportunity came along.[49]

A second problem is that cultural values make it difficult to compare job satisfaction across countries. People in China and Japan tend to subdue their emotions in public, and there is evidence that they also avoid extreme survey ratings such as "very satisfied." A third problem is that job satisfaction changes with economic conditions. Employees with the highest job satisfaction in current surveys tend to be in countries where the economies are chugging along quite well.[50]

Job Satisfaction and Work Behavior

Does job satisfaction influence workplace behavior? In general, yes! Job satisfaction affects many of the individual behaviors introduced in Chapter 2 (task performance, organizational citizenship, quitting, absenteeism, etc.).[51] However, a more precise answer is that the effect of job satisfaction and dissatisfaction on

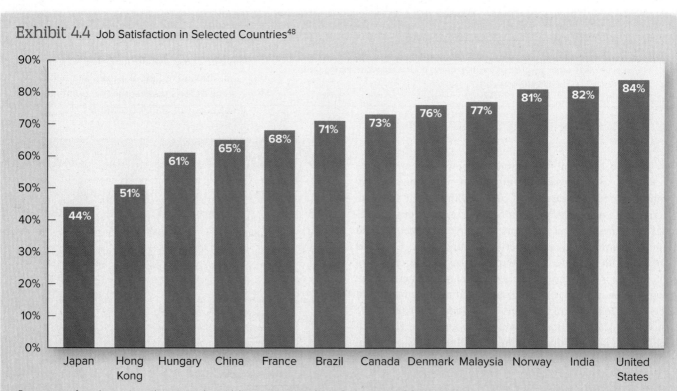

Exhibit 4.4 Job Satisfaction in Selected Countries[48]

Percentage of employees in each country who said they are, in general, satisfied or very satisfied working for their current employer. Survey data were collected in 2016 for Randstad Holdings nv, with a minimum of 400 employees in each country.

individual behavior depends on the person and the situation. A useful template for organizing and understanding the consequences of job dissatisfaction is the **exit–voice–loyalty–neglect (EVLN) model**. As the name suggests, the EVLN model identifies four ways that employees respond to dissatisfaction:[52]

- *Exit.* Exit includes leaving the organization, transferring to another work unit, or at least trying to get away from the dissatisfying situation. The traditional theory is that job dissatisfaction builds over time and eventually becomes strong enough that the employee is motivated to search for better work opportunities elsewhere. This is likely true to some extent, but the more recent view is that specific "shock events" quickly energize employees to think about and engage in exit behavior. For example, the emotional reaction you experience to an unfair management decision or a conflict episode with a coworker motivates you to look at job ads and speak to friends about job opportunities where they work. This begins the process of visualizing yourself working at another company and psychologically withdrawing from your current employer.[53]

- *Voice.* Voice is any attempt to change, rather than escape from, the dissatisfying situation. Voice can be a constructive response, such as recommending ways for management to improve the situation, or it can be more confrontational, such as filing formal grievances or forming a coalition to oppose a decision.[54] In the extreme, some employees might engage in counterproductive behaviors to get attention and force changes in the organization.

- *Loyalty.* In the original version of this model, loyalty was not an outcome of dissatisfaction. Rather, it predicted whether people chose exit or voice (i.e., high loyalty resulted in voice; low loyalty produced exit).[55] More recent writers describe loyalty as an outcome, but in various and somewhat unclear ways. Generally, they suggest that "loyalists" are employees who respond to dissatisfaction by patiently waiting—some say they "suffer in silence"—for the problem to work itself out or be resolved by others.[56]

- *Neglect.* Neglect includes reducing work effort, paying less attention to quality, and increasing absenteeism and lateness. It is generally considered a passive activity that has negative consequences for the organization.

Which of the four EVLN alternatives do employees use? It depends on the person and situation.[57] The individual's personality, values, and self-concept are important factors. For example, people with a high-conscientiousness personality are less likely to engage in neglect and more likely to engage in voice. Past experience also influences which EVLN action is applied. Employees who were unsuccessful with voice in the past are more likely to engage in exit or neglect when experiencing job dissatisfaction in the future. Another factor is loyalty, as it was originally intended in the EVLN model. Specifically, employees are more likely to quit when they have low loyalty to the company, and they are more likely to engage in voice when they have high loyalty. Finally, the response to dissatisfaction depends on the situation. Employees are less likely to use the exit option when there are few alternative job prospects, for example. Dissatisfied employees are more likely to use voice than the other options when they are aware that other employees are dependent on them.[58]

Job Satisfaction and Performance

Is a happy worker a more productive worker? Clive Schlee thinks so. The CEO of the British deli chain Pret a Manger believes that happy employees result in happier customers and higher sales. "The first thing I look at is whether staff are touching each other—are they smiling, reacting to each other, happy, engaged? I can almost predict sales on body language alone," he says. Secret shoppers scout Pret a Manger outlets each week. If the secret shopper is served by a positive and happy employee behind the counter, all staff members at that location receive a bonus.[59]

The "happy worker" hypothesis is generally true, according to major reviews of the research on this subject. In other words, there is a moderately positive relationship between job satisfaction and performance. Workers tend to be more productive to some extent when they have more positive attitudes toward their job and workplace.[60]

Voice is any attempt to change, rather than escape from, the dissatisfying situation, such as providing recommendations, complaining about the problem, mounting opposition through a coalition, or filing a formal grievance.
©John Lund/Nevada Wier/Getty Images

Job satisfaction has less effect on performance where employees' work effort is paced by technology or interdependence with coworkers in the production process.
©DreamPictures/Shannon Faulk/Getty Images

coworkers in the production process. An assembly-line worker, for instance, installs a fixed number of windshields each hour with about the same quality of installation whether he or she has high or low job satisfaction.

A third consideration is that job performance might cause job satisfaction, rather than vice versa.[61] Higher performers tend to have higher satisfaction because they receive more rewards and recognition than do low-performing employees. The connection between job satisfaction and performance isn't stronger because many organizations do not reward good performance very well.

Job Satisfaction and Customer Satisfaction

Wegmans Food Markets in Rochester, New York, has an unusual motto: *Employees first, customers second*. Why doesn't Wegmans have customers at the top of the stakeholder list? Their rationale is that customer satisfaction is a natural outcome of employee satisfaction. Put differently, it is difficult to keep customers happy if employee morale is low. Virgin founder Sir Richard Branson made this point many years ago: "It just seems common sense to me that if you start with a happy, well-motivated workforce, you're much more likely to have happy customers."[62]

Why does job satisfaction affect employee performance only to some extent? One reason is that general attitudes (such as job satisfaction) don't predict specific behaviors very well. As the EVLN model explained, reduced performance (a form of neglect) is only one of four possible responses to dissatisfaction. A second reason is that some employees have little control over their performance because their work effort is paced by technology or interdependence with

"We really believe that if you put the employees first, they really and truly will take better care of the customer than anybody else."[63]

—Kip Tindell, chair and cofounder of The Container Store

Research supports these beliefs. In fact, evidence suggests that job satisfaction has a stronger effect on customer service than on overall performance. The effect of job satisfaction on customer service and company profits is detailed in the **service profit chain model**, diagrammed in Exhibit 4.5. This model shows that

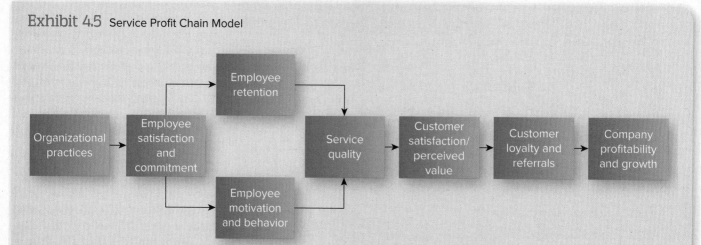

Exhibit 4.5 Service Profit Chain Model

Sources: This model is based on J. I. Heskett, W. E. Sasser, and L. A. Schlesinger, *The Service Profit Chain* (New York: Free Press, 1997); A. J. Rucci, S. P. Kirn, and R. T. Quinn, "The Employee-Customer-Profit Chain at Sears," *Harvard Business Review* 76 (1998): 83–97; S. P. Brown and S. K. Lam, "A Meta-Analysis of Relationships Linking Employee Satisfaction to Customer Responses," *Journal of Retailing* 84, no. 3 (2008): 243–55.

job satisfaction has a positive effect on customer service, which eventually benefits shareholder financial returns.

The service profit chain model process begins with workplace practices that increase or decrease job satisfaction. The resulting level of satisfaction then influences whether employees stay (employee retention) as well as their motivation and behavior on the job. Retention, motivation, and behavior affect service quality, which influences the customer's satisfaction, perceived value of the service, and tendency to recommend the service to others (referrals). These customer activities influence the company's profitability and growth. The service profit chain model has considerable research support. However, the benefits of job satisfaction take considerable time to flow through to the organization's bottom line.[64]

There are two key explanations why satisfied employees tend to produce happier and more loyal customers.[65] One explanation is that job satisfaction tends to put employees in a more positive mood, and people in a good mood more naturally and frequently display friendliness and positive emotions. When employees have good feelings, their behavior "rubs off" on most (but not all) customers, so customers feel happier and consequently form a positive evaluation of the service experience (i.e., higher service quality). The effect is also mutual—happy customers make employees happier—which can lead to a virtuous cycle of positive emotions in the service experience.

The second explanation is that satisfied employees are less likely to quit their jobs, so they have more work experience (i.e., better knowledge and skills) to serve clients. Lower turnover also enables customers to have the same employees serve them, so there is more consistent service. Some evidence indicates that customers build their loyalty to specific employees, not to the organization, so keeping employee turnover low tends to build customer loyalty.

Job Satisfaction and Business Ethics

Job satisfaction is important not only because of its effect on employee behavior. Job satisfaction is also an ethical issue that influences the organization's reputation in the community. People spend a large portion of their time working in organizations, and many societies now expect companies to provide work environments that are safe and enjoyable. Indeed, employees in several countries closely monitor ratings of the best companies to work for, an indication that employee satisfaction is a virtue worth considerable goodwill to employers. The importance of this is apparent when an organization has low job satisfaction. The company typically tries to hide this fact, and when morale problems become public, corporate leaders are usually quick to take steps to improve the situation.

ORGANIZATIONAL COMMITMENT

Organizational commitment represents the other half (with job satisfaction) of what some experts call "overall job attitude." **Affective organizational commitment** is the employee's emotional attachment to, involvement in, and identification with an organization. Affective commitment is a psychological bond whereby one chooses to be dedicated to and responsible for the organization.[66]

Affective commitment differs from **continuance commitment**, which is a calculative attachment to the organization. This calculation takes two forms.[67] One form occurs where an employee has no alternative employment opportunities (e.g., "I dislike working here, but there are no other jobs available."). This condition exists where unemployment is high, employees lack the skills sought by other employers, or the employee's skills are so specialized that there is limited demand for them nearby. The other form of continuance commitment occurs where leaving the company would be a significant financial sacrifice (e.g., "I hate this place but can't afford to quit!"). This perceived sacrifice condition occurs when the company offers high pay, benefits, and other forms of economic exchange in the employment relationship, or where quitting forfeits a large deferred financial bonus.

Consequences of Affective and Continuance Commitment

Affective commitment can be a significant competitive advantage.[68] Employees with a strong psychological connection with the organization are less likely to quit their jobs and be absent from work. They also have higher work motivation and organizational citizenship, as well as somewhat higher job performance. Organizational commitment also improves customer satisfaction because long-tenure employees have better knowledge of work practices and because clients like to do business with the same employees. One problem is that employees with very high affective commitment tend to have high conformity, which results in lower creativity. Another problem is that these employees are motivated to defend the organization, even if it involves illegal activity. However, most companies suffer from too little rather than too much affective commitment.

In contrast to the benefits of affective commitment, employees with high levels of continuance commitment tend to have *lower* performance and are *less* likely to engage in organizational citizenship behaviors. Furthermore, unionized employees with high continuance commitment are more likely to use formal grievances, whereas employees with high affective commitment engage in more cooperative problem solving when employee–employer relations sour.[69] Although some level of financial connection may be necessary, employers should not rely on

service profit chain model a theory explaining how employees' job satisfaction influences company profitability indirectly through service quality, customer loyalty, and related factors

affective organizational commitment an individual's emotional attachment to, involvement in, and identification with an organization

continuance commitment an individual's calculative attachment to an organization

SELF-ASSESSMENT 4.3: How Committed Are You to Your School?

Organizational (affective) commitment refers to an individual's emotional attachment to, involvement in, and identification with an organization. It is mostly discussed in this book as an employee's attitude toward the company where he or she works. But affective commitment is also relevant to a student's attitude toward the college or university where he or she is taking courses. You can discover your affective commitment as a student to the school where you are attending this program by locating this self-assessment in Connect if it is assigned by your instructor.

continuance commitment instead of affective commitment. Employers still need to win employees' hearts (affective commitment) beyond tying them financially to the organization (continuance commitment).

Building Organizational Commitment

There are almost as many ways to build and maintain affective commitment as there are topics in this book, but the most frequently mentioned strategies are

- *Justice and support.* Affective commitment is higher in organizations that fulfill their obligations to employees and abide by humanitarian values such as fairness, courtesy, forgiveness, and moral integrity. These values relate to the concept of organizational justice, which we discuss in the next chapter. Similarly, organizations that support employee well-being tend to cultivate higher levels of loyalty in return.[71]

- *Shared values.* The definition of affective commitment refers to a person's identification with the organization, and that identification is highest when employees believe their values are congruent with the organization's dominant values. Employees also experience more positive emotions when their personal values are aligned with corporate values and actions, which increases their motivation to stay with the organization.[72]

- *Trust.* **Trust** refers to positive expectations one person has toward another person in situations involving risk.[73] Trust means putting faith in the other person or group. It is also a reciprocal activity: To receive trust, you must demonstrate trust. Employees identify with and feel obliged to work for an organization only when they trust its leaders. This explains why layoffs are one of the greatest blows to affective commitment. By reducing job security, companies reduce the trust employees have in their employer and the employment relationship.[74]

- *Organizational comprehension.* Organizational comprehension refers to how well employees understand the organization, including its strategic direction, social dynamics, and physical layout.[75] This awareness is a necessary prerequisite to affective commitment because it is difficult to identify with or feel loyal to something that you don't know very well. Furthermore, lack of information produces uncertainty, and the resulting stress can distance employees from that source of uncertainty (i.e., the organization). The practical implication here is to ensure that employees

Affective Commitment around the Planet[70]

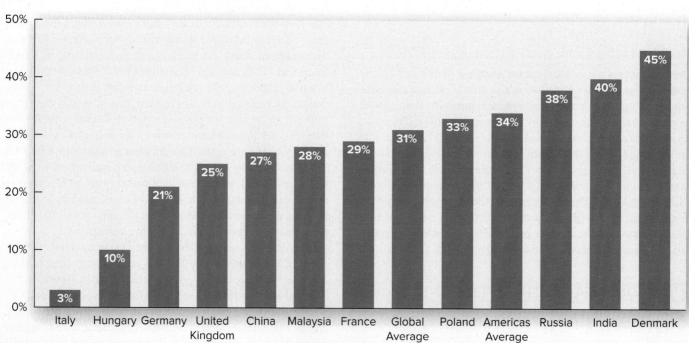

Percentage of employees surveyed in selected countries who say they feel "totally committed" to their employer. Almost 230,000 people in 31 countries across all regions were surveyed for Kelly Services.
©Image Credit

develop a reasonably clear and complete mental model of the organization. This occurs by giving staff information and opportunities to keep up to date about organizational events, interact with coworkers, discover what goes on in different parts of the organization, and learn about the organization's history and future plans.[76]

- *Employee involvement.* Employee involvement increases affective commitment by strengthening the employee's psychological ownership and social identity with the organization.[77] Employees feel part of the organization when they participate in decisions that guide the organization's future (see Chapter 6). Employee involvement also builds loyalty because it demonstrates the company's trust in its employees.

Organizational commitment and job satisfaction represent two of the most often studied and discussed attitudes in the workplace. Each is linked to emotional episodes and cognitive judgments about the workplace and relationship with the company. Emotions also play an important role in another concept that is on everyone's mind these days: stress. The final section of this chapter provides an overview of work-related stress and how it can be managed.

> **LO4-4** Describe the stress experience and review four major stressors.

WORK-RELATED STRESS AND ITS MANAGEMENT

When asked if they often feel stressed, most employees these days say, "Yes!" Not only do most people understand the concept; they claim to have plenty of personal experience with it. **Stress** is most often described as an adaptive response to a situation that is perceived as challenging or threatening to the person's well-being.[78] It is a physiological and psychological condition that prepares us to adapt to hostile or noxious environmental conditions. Our heart rate increases, muscles tighten, breathing speeds up, and perspiration increases. Our body also moves more blood to the brain, releases adrenaline and other hormones, fuels the system by releasing more glucose and fatty acids, activates systems that sharpen our senses, and conserves

> Organizational comprehension is a necessary prerequisite to affective commitment because it is difficult to identify with or feel loyal to something that you don't know very well.

> **trust** positive expectations one person has toward another person in situations involving risk

> **stress** an adaptive response to a situation that is perceived as challenging or threatening to the person's well-being

resources by shutting down our immune system. One school of thought suggests that stress is a negative evaluation of the external environment. However, critics of this *cognitive appraisal* perspective point out that stress is more accurately described as an emotional experience, which may occur before or after a conscious evaluation of the situation.[79]

Whether stress is a complex emotion or a cognitive evaluation of the environment, it has become a pervasive experience in the daily lives of most people. Stress is typically described as a negative experience. This is known as *distress*—the degree of physiological, psychological, and behavioral deviation from healthy functioning. However, some level and form of stress—called *eustress*—is a necessary part of life because it activates and motivates people to achieve goals, change their environments, and succeed in life's challenges.[80] Our focus is on the causes and management of distress because it has become a chronic problem in many societies.

General Adaptation Syndrome

The word *stress* was first used more than 500 years ago to describe the human response to harsh environmental conditions. However, it wasn't until the 1930s that researcher Hans Selye (often described as the "father" of stress research) first

Stressed Out, Burnt Out[81]

52% of more than 1,000 American workers surveyed say they are stressed at work on a day-to-day basis.

31% of 1,000 German workers surveyed report that they felt stressed at work the previous day.

58% of 400 Canadian workers surveyed say they are stressed at work on a day-to-day basis.

42% of 6,700 Americans surveyed say they have purposely changed jobs due to a stressful work environment.

66% of more than 900 Americans surveyed say their company/office does "nothing" to help alleviate stress in the workplace.

(source): ©donskarpo/Getty Images

general adaptation syndrome a model of the stress experience, consisting of three stages: alarm reaction, resistance, and exhaustion

stressors any environmental conditions that place a physical or emotional demand on the person

documented the stress experience, called the **general adaptation syndrome**. Selye determined that people have a fairly consistent and automatic physiological response to stressful situations, which helps them cope with environmental demands.[82]

The general adaptation syndrome consists of the three stages shown in Exhibit 4.6. The *alarm reaction* stage occurs when a threat or challenge activates the physiological stress responses that were noted above. The individual's energy level and coping effectiveness decrease in response to the initial shock. The second

stage, *resistance*, activates various biochemical, psychological, and behavioral mechanisms that give the individual more energy and engage coping mechanisms to overcome or remove the source of stress. To focus energy on the source of the stress, the body reduces resources to the immune system during this stage. This explains why people are more likely to catch a cold or some other illness when they experience prolonged stress. People have a limited resistance capacity, and if the source of stress persists, the

individual will eventually move into the third stage, *exhaustion*. Most of us are able to remove the source of stress or remove ourselves from that source before becoming too exhausted. However, people who frequently reach exhaustion have increased risk of long-term physiological and psychological damage.[83]

Consequences of Distress

Stress takes its toll on the human body.[84] Many people experience tension headaches, muscle pain, and related problems mainly due to muscle contractions from the stress response. High stress levels also contribute to cardiovascular disease, including heart attacks and strokes, and may be associated with some forms of cancer. One major review estimated that more than 100,000 deaths annually and as much as 8 percent of health care costs in the United States are due to the consequences of work-related stress. Stress also produces various psychological consequences such as job dissatisfaction, moodiness, depression, and lower organizational commitment. Furthermore, various behavioral outcomes have been linked to high or persistent stress, including lower job performance, poor decision making, and increased workplace accidents and aggressive behavior. Most people react to stress through "fight or flight," so, as a form of flight, increased absenteeism is another outcome of stress.[85]

Stressors: The Causes of Stress

Before identifying ways to manage work-related stress, we must first understand its causes, known as stressors. **Stressors** include any environmental conditions that place a physical or emotional demand on a person.[86] There are numerous stressors in the workplace and in life in general. Four of the most common work-related stressors are organizational constraints, interpersonal conflict, work overload, and low task control.[87]

Organizational Constraints Stress research has identified organizational constraints as one of the most pervasive causes of workplace stress.[88] This stressor includes lack of equipment, supplies, budget funding, coworker support, information, and other resources necessary to complete the required work. Most employees experience stress because these constraints interfere with task performance, which indirectly

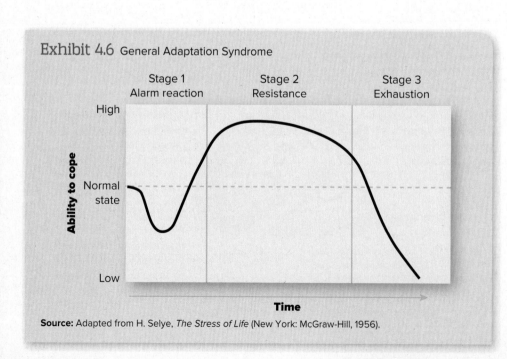

Exhibit 4.6 General Adaptation Syndrome

Stage 1 — Alarm reaction   Stage 2 — Resistance   Stage 3 — Exhaustion

Ability to cope: High — Normal state — Low

Time

Source: Adapted from H. Selye, *The Stress of Life* (New York: McGraw-Hill, 1956).

threatens their rewards, status, and job security. Organizational constraints refer to situational factors, which is one of the four direct predictors of individual behavior and performance (see the MARS model in Chapter 2). It is the only direct influence on individual performance that is beyond the employee's immediate control. This lack of control is a powerful stressor because it threatens the individual's fundamental drive to influence his or her external environment.

Interpersonal Conflict Employees usually agree on the organization's overall objectives, but they frequently disagree with each other regarding how to achieve those goals as well as how the work and resources should be distributed along that journey. Therefore, conflict is a way of life in organizations. As we will learn in Chapter 10, dysfunctional conflict can easily flair up and, left unchecked, escalate to a level that produces considerable stress and counterproductive work behaviors. Most interpersonal conflict is caused by structural sources such as ambiguous rules, lack of resources, and conflicting goals between employees or departments. However, a fast-growing form of interpersonal conflict is *psychological harassment*, which ranges from threats and bullying to subtle yet persistent forms of incivility.[89] *Sexual harassment* is also a major stressor that falls within the interpersonal conflict category. This occurs when a person's employment or job performance is conditional on unwanted sexual relations and/or the person experiences sexual conduct from others (such as posting pornographic material) that unreasonably interferes with work performance or creates an intimidating, hostile, or offensive working environment.[90]

Work Overload Work overload is one of the most common workplace stressors. Employees are under pressure to complete more work with more effort than they can provide within the allotted time.[91] Work overload is evident when employees consume more of their personal time to get the job done. Technology and globalization also contribute to work overload because they tether employees to work for more hours of the day. People increasingly work with coworkers in distant time zones, and their communication habits of being constantly "on" make it difficult to separate work from personal life. Some employees amplify their work overload by adopting an "ideal worker norm" in which they expect themselves and others to work longer hours. For many, toiling away far beyond the normal workweek is a badge of honor, a symbol of their superhuman capacity to perform above others. For example, 39 percent of millennial employees in one recent large-scale survey admitted that they work long hours and have a 24/7 schedule so they look like a "work martyr" to their boss.[92]

Low Task Control Workplace stress is higher when employees lack control over how and when they perform their tasks as well as lack control over the pace of work activity. Work is potentially more stressful when it is paced by a machine, it involves monitoring equipment, or the work schedule is controlled by someone else. Low task control is a stressor because employees face high workloads without the ability to adjust the pace of the load to their own energy, attention

Work overload is a common workplace stressor because employees are under pressure to complete more work with more effort than they can provide within the allotted time.
©Antonio Guillem/Shutterstock

span, and other resources. Furthermore, the degree to which low task control is a stressor increases with the burden of responsibility the employee must carry.[93] Assembly-line workers have low task control, but their stress can be fairly low if their level of responsibility is also low. In contrast, sports coaches are under immense pressure to win games (high responsibility), yet they have little control over what happens on the playing field (low task control).

Individual Differences in Stress

People exposed to the same stressor experience different levels of stress. One contributing factor is the employee's physical health. Regular exercise and a healthy lifestyle produce a larger store of energy to cope with stress. A second individual difference is the coping strategy employees use to ward off a particular stressor.[94] People sometimes figure out ways to remove the stressor or to minimize its presence. Seeking support from others, reframing the stressor in a more positive light, blaming others for the stressor, and denying the stressor's existence are some other coping mechanisms. Specific coping strategies work better for specific stressors, and some are better across all stressors.[95] Thus, someone who uses a less effective coping mechanism in a particular situation would experience more stress in response to that situation. People have a tendency to rely on one or two coping strategies, and those who rely on generally poor coping strategies (such as denying the stressor exists) are going to experience more stress.

Personality is the third and possibly the most important reason why people experience different levels of stress when faced with the same stressor.[96] Individuals with low neuroticism (high emotional stability) usually experience lower stress levels because, by definition, they are less prone to anxiety, depression, and other negative emotions. Extraverts also tend to experience lower stress than do introverts, likely because extraversion includes a degree of positive thinking and extraverts interact with others, which helps buffer the effect of stressors. Those with a positive self-concept–high self-esteem, self-efficacy, and internal locus of control (see Chapter 3)–feel more confident and in control when faced with a stressor. In other words, they tend to have a stronger sense of optimism.[97] Stress also tends to be higher among those who suffer from *workaholism*. Workaholics have an uncontrollable work motivation, constantly think about work, and have low work enjoyment.[98]

LO4-5 Identify five ways to manage workplace stress.

Managing Work-Related Stress

Many people deny the existence of their stress until it has more serious outcomes. This avoidance strategy creates a vicious cycle because the failure to cope with stress becomes another stressor on top of the one that created the stress in the first place. To prevent this vicious cycle, employers and employees need to apply one or more of the stress management strategies described next: remove the stressor, withdraw from the stressor, change stress perceptions, control stress consequences, and receive social support.[99]

Remove the Stressor There are many ways to remove the stressor, but some of the more common actions involve assigning employees to jobs that match their skills and preferences, reducing excessive workplace noise, having a complaint system that takes corrective action against harassment, and giving employees more control over the work process. Another important way that companies can remove stressors is through work–life balance initiatives. For example, personal leave benefits, such as maternity and paternity leave, temporarily offer employees paid nonwork time to manage special circumstances. Telecommuting potentially improves work–life balance by reducing or eliminating commuting time and increasing flexibility to perform nonwork obligations (such as picking up the kids from school).[101] Flexible work arrangements also enable employees to rearrange their time allocated to work and nonwork demands.

Withdraw from the Stressor Removing the stressor may be the ideal solution, but it is often not feasible. An alternative strategy is to permanently or temporarily remove employees from the stressor. Permanent withdrawal occurs when employees are transferred to jobs that are more compatible with their abilities and values. Temporarily withdrawing from stressors is the most frequent way that employees manage stress. Vacations and holidays are important opportunities for employees to recover from stress and reenergize for future challenges.[102] Many firms also provide innovative ways for employees to withdraw from stressful work throughout the day such as game rooms, ice cream cart breaks, nap rooms, and cafeterias that include live piano recitals.

Change Stress Perceptions How much stress employees experience depends on how they perceive the stressor.[104] Consequently, another way to manage stress is to help employees improve their self-concept so job challenges are

How Americans Cope with Work-Related Stress[100]

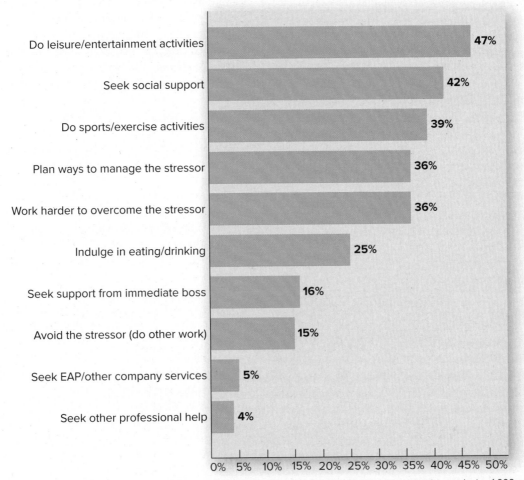

Activity	Percentage
Do leisure/entertainment activities	47%
Seek social support	42%
Do sports/exercise activities	39%
Plan ways to manage the stressor	36%
Work harder to overcome the stressor	36%
Indulge in eating/drinking	25%
Seek support from immediate boss	16%
Avoid the stressor (do other work)	15%
Seek EAP/other company services	5%
Seek other professional help	4%

This survey was conducted by Willis Towers Watson in 2013 from 5,070 Americans working at companies employing 1,000 or more people. Leisure/entertainment examples include shopping, reading, listening to music, watching movies/TV, and playing games. Social support sources include friends, family, and coworkers. Indulgence activities include eating less healthy food and drinking more alcohol. An "EAP" is an employee assistance program. Other professional help includes family doctor and psychologist. ©Image Credit

OB THEORY TO PRACTICE

Stress-Busting Power Naps at HubSpot

HubSpot has all the features that attract Millennial employees: games room, fully stocked kitchen, camping-themed meditation room, and a hammock-equipped nap room in a beach-like setting. A nap room? Yes, the Boston-based marketing-software company encourages employees not just to take a break from their busy workday, but to recharge the brain cells by nodding off for half an hour. "Getting 20 or 30 minutes to pay back some of the sleep I lost the night before can make me so much more effective," says a HubSpot executive. One recent survey estimated that 5 percent of large American firms have private spaces or pods designed for employees to take a nap.[103]

©David L. Ryan/The Boston Globe via Getty Images

not perceived as threatening. Personal goal setting and self-reinforcement also can reduce the stress that people experience when they enter new work settings. In addition, research suggests that some (but not all) forms of humor can improve optimism and create positive emotions by taking some psychological weight off a stressful situation.[105]

Control Stress Consequences Keeping physically fit and maintaining a healthy lifestyle are effective stress management strategies because they control stress consequences. Good physical fitness reduces the adverse physiological consequences of stress by helping employees moderate their breathing and heart rate, muscle tension, and stomach acidity. The key variable here is physical fitness, not exercise. Exercise leads to physical fitness, but research suggests that exercise does not reduce stress symptoms among people who are not yet physically fit.[106] Various forms of meditation reduce anxiety and other symptoms of stress, but their effect on blood pressure and other physiological symptoms is minimal.[107] Wellness programs also can assist in controlling the consequences of stress. These programs inform employees about better nutrition and fitness, regular sleep, and other good health habits. Many large companies offer *employee assistance programs (EAPs)*—counseling services that help employees resolve marital, financial, or work-related troubles.

Receive Social Support Social support occurs when coworkers, supervisors, family members, friends, and others provide emotional and/or informational support to buffer an individual's stress experience. For instance, employees whose managers are good at empathizing experienced fewer stress symptoms than do employees whose managers were less empathetic. Social support potentially (but not always) improves the person's optimism and self-confidence because support makes people feel valued and worthy. Social support also provides information to help the person interpret, comprehend, and possibly remove the stressor. For instance, to reduce a new employee's stress, coworkers could describe ways to handle difficult customers. Seeking social support is called a "tend and befriend" response to stress, and research suggests that women often take this route rather than the "fight-or-flight" response mentioned earlier.[108]

SELF-ASSESSMENT 4.6: How Do You Cope with Stressful Situations?
People cope with stress in several ways. The best coping strategy usually depends on the source of stress and other circumstances. However, people also have a natural preference for some types of coping strategies more than others. You can discover your preferences among four coping strategies by locating this self-assessment in Connect if it is assigned by your instructor.

Study Checklist

Connect® Management is available for *M Organizational Behavior.* Additional resources include:

✓ Interactive Applications:
- **Case Analysis:** Apply concepts within the context of a real-world situation.
- **Drag and Drop:** Work through an interactive example to test your knowledge of the concepts.
- **Video Case:** See management in action through interactive videos.

✓ **SmartBook™**—SmartBook is the first and only adaptive reading experience available today. Distinguishing what you know from what you don't, and honing in on concepts you are most likely to forget, SmartBook personalizes content for you in a continuously adapting reading experience. Reading is no longer a passive and linear experience, but an engaging and dynamic one where you are more likely to master and retain important concepts and go to class better prepared.

©Natthawat Jamnapa/123RF

Notes

1. J. D'Onfro, "An inside Look at Google's Best Employee Perks," *Inc.,* September 21, 2015; R. Gillett, "Why Google Is the Best Company to Work for in America," *Business Insider,* April 29, 2016; A. Hartmans, "What It's Really Like to Work at Google, the Best Company to Work for in the US," *Business Insider,* August 26, 2016; "Google Inc.," *Great Place to Work* (San Francisco: Great Place to Work® Institute, 2017), http://reviews.greatplacetowork.com/google-inc (accessed June 23, 2017).

2. Emotions are also cognitive processes. However, we use the narrow definition of *cognition* as a well-used label referring only to reasoning processes. Also, this and other chapters emphasize that emotional and cognitive processes are intertwined.

3. For discussion of emotions in marketing, economics, and sociology, see M. Hubert, "Does Neuroeconomics Give New Impetus to Economic and Consumer Research?," *Journal of Economic Psychology* 31, no. 5 (2010): 812-17; D. D. Franks, "Introduction," in *Neurosociology: The Nexus between Neuroscience and Social Psychology* (New York: Springer, 2010), 1-20; N. Martins, "Can Neuroscience Inform Economics? Rationality, Emotions and Preference Formation," *Cambridge Journal of Economics* 35, no. 2 (2011): 251-67; H. Plassmann, T. Z. Ramsøy, and M. Milosavljevic, "Branding the Brain: A Critical Review and Outlook," *Journal of Consumer Psychology* 22, no. 1 (2012): 18-36.

4. Although definitions of *emotion* vary, the definition stated here seems to be the most widely accepted. See, for example, N. H. Frijda, "Varieties of Affect: Emotions and Episodes, Moods, and Sentiments," in *The Nature of Emotion: Fundamental Questions*, ed. P. Ekman and R. J. Davidson (New York: Oxford University Press, 1994), 59-67; H. M. Weiss, "Conceptual and Empirical Foundations for the Study of Affect at Work," in *Emotions in the Workplace*, ed. R. G. Lord, R. J. Klimoski, and R. Kanfer (San Francisco: Jossey-Bass, 2002), 20-63; G. Van Kleef, H. van den Berg, and M. Heerdink, "The Persuasive Power of Emotions: Effects of Emotional Expressions on Attitude Formation and Change," *Journal of Applied Psychology* 100, no. 4 (2015): 1124-42.

5. R. Reisenzein, M. Studtmann, and G. Horstmann, "Coherence between Emotion and Facial Expression: Evidence from Laboratory Experiments," *Emotion Review* 5, no. 1 (2013): 16-23.

6. R. B. Zajonc, "Emotions," in *Handbook of Social Psychology*, ed. D. T. Gilbert, S. T. Fiske, and L. Gardner (New York: Oxford University Press, 1998), 591-634; P. Winkielman, "Bob Zajonc and the Unconscious Emotion," *Emotion Review* 2, no. 4 (2010): 353-62.

7. V. van Gogh, T. van Gogh, and I. Stone, *Dear Theo: The Autobiography* (New York: Doubleday, 1937; repr., 1995), 441. This quotation originally appeared in a letter sent by Vincent van Gogh to his brother Théo in 1889.

8. R. J. Larson, E. Diener, and R. E. Lucas, "Emotion: Models, Measures, and Differences," in *Emotions in the Workplace*, ed. R. G. Lord, R. J. Klimoski, and R. Kanfer (San Francisco: Jossey-Bass, 2002), 64-113; L. F. Barrett et al., "The Experience of Emotion," *Annual Review of Psychology* 58, no. 1 (2007): 373-403; M. Yik, J. A. Russell, and J. H. Steiger, "A 12-Point Circumplex Structure of Core Affect," *Emotion* 11, no. 4 (2011): 705-31.

9. R. F. Baumeister, E. Bratslavsky, and C. Finkenauer, "Bad Is Stronger Than Good," *Review of General Psychology* 5, no. 4 (2001): 323-70; A. Vaish, T. Grossmann, and A. Woodward, "Not All Emotions Are Created Equal: The Negativity Bias in Social-Emotional Development," *Psychological Bulletin* 134, no. 3 (2008): 383-403; R. H. Fazio et al., "Positive versus Negative Valence: Asymmetries in Attitude Formation and Generalization as Fundamental Individual Differences," in *Advances in Experimental Social Psychology*, vol. 51, ed. J. M. Olson and M. P. Zanna (Waltham, MA: Academic Press, 2015), 97-146; K. Bebbington et al., "The Sky Is Falling: Evidence of a Negativity Bias in the Social Transmission of Information," *Evolution and Human Behavior* 38, no. 1 (2017): 92-101.

10. A. P. Brief, *Attitudes in and around Organizations* (Thousand Oaks, CA: Sage, 1998); A. H. Eagly and S. Chaiken, "The Advantages of an Inclusive Definition of Attitude," *Social Cognition* 25, no. 5 (2007): 582-602; G. Bohner and N. Dickel, "Attitudes and Attitude Change," *Annual Review of Psychology* 62, no. 1 (2011): 391-417. The definition of *attitudes* is still being debated. This book adopts the three-component model (beliefs, feelings, behavioral intentions), whereas some writers describe attitude as relating only to the "feelings" component; however, they invariably include beliefs and intentions in their discussion of attitude. For definitions and various models of attitudes, see I. Ajzen, "Nature and Operation of Attitudes," *Annual Review of Psychology* 52 (2001): 27-58; D. Albarracin et al., "Attitudes: Introduction and Scope," in *The Handbook of Attitudes*, ed. D. Albarracin, B. T. Johnson, and M. P. Zanna (Mahwah, NJ: Erlbaum, 2005), 3-20; W. A. Cunningham and P. D. Zelazo, "Attitudes and Evaluations: A Social Cognitive Neuroscience Perspective," *TRENDS in Cognitive Sciences* 11, no. 3 (2007): 97-104; R. S. Dalal, "Job Attitudes: Cognition and Affect," in *Industrial and Organizational Psychology*, ed. I. B. Weiner, N. W. Schmitt, and S. Highhouse, Handbook of Psychology, *2nd ed., ed. I. B. Weiner, vol. 12 (New York: Wiley, 2012), 341-66.*

11. Neuroscience has a slightly more complicated distinction in that conscious awareness is "feeling a feeling," whereas "feeling" is a nonconscious sensing of the body state created by emotion, which itself is a nonconscious neural reaction to a stimulus. However, this distinction is not significant for scholars focused on human behavior rather than brain activity, and the labels collide with popular understanding of "feeling." See A. R. Damasio, *The Feeling of What Happens: Body and Emotion in the Making of Consciousness* (New York: Harcourt Brace, 1999); F. Hansen, "Distinguishing between Feelings and Emotions in Understanding Communication Effects," *Journal of Business Research* 58, no. 10 (2005): 1426-36; T. Bosse, C. M. Jonker, and J. Treur, "Formalisation of Damasio's Theory of Emotion, Feeling and Core Consciousness," *Consciousness and Cognition* 17, no. 1 (2008): 94-113.

12. W. A. Cunningham and P. D. Zelazo, "Attitudes and Evaluations: A Social Cognitive Neuroscience Perspective," *TRENDS in Cognitive Sciences* 11, no. 3 (2007): 97-104; M. D. Lieberman, "Social Cognitive Neuroscience: A Review of Core Processes," *Annual Review of Psychology* 58, no. 1 (2007): 259-89; M. Fenton-O'Creevy et al., "Thinking, Feeling and Deciding: The Influence of Emotions on the Decision Making and Performance of Traders," *Journal of Organizational Behavior* 32 (2011): 1044-61. The dual emotion-cognition processes are likely the same as the implicit-explicit attitude processes reported by several scholars, as well as tacit knowledge structures. See W. J. Becker and R. Cropanzano, "Organizational Neuroscience: The Promise and Prospects of an Emerging Discipline," *Journal of Organizational Behavior* 31, no. 7 (2010): 1055-59; D. Kahneman, *Thinking Fast and Slow* (New York: Farrar, Straus and Giroux, 2011).

13. S. Orbell, "Intention-Behavior Relations: A Self-Regulation Perspective," in *Contemporary Perspectives on the Psychology of Attitudes*, ed. G. Haddock and G. R. Maio (East Sussex, UK: Psychology Press, 2004), 145-68.

14. H. M. Weiss and R. Cropanzano, "Affective Events Theory: A Theoretical Discussion of the Structure, Causes and Consequences of Affective Experiences at Work," *Research in Organizational Behavior* 18 (1996): 1-74; A. Bechara et al., "Deciding Advantageously before Knowing the Advantageous Strategy," *Science* 275, no. 5304 (1997): 1293-95; B. Russell and J. Eisenberg, "The Role of Cognition and Attitude in Driving Behavior: Elaborating on Affective Events Theory," in *Experiencing and Managing Emotions in the Workplace*, ed. N. M. Ashkanasy, C. E. J. Hartel, and W. J. Zerbe (Bingley, UK: Emerald Group, 2012), 203-24.

15. J. A. Bargh and M. J. Ferguson, "Beyond Behaviorism: On the Automaticity of Higher Mental Processes," *Psychological Bulletin* 126, no. 6 (2000): 925-45; P. Winkielman and K. C. Berridge, "Unconscious Emotion," *Current Directions in Psychological Science* 13, no. 3 (2004): 120-23; A. Moors, "Automaticity: Componential, Causal, and Mechanistic Explanations," *Annual Review of Psychology* 67, no. 1 (2016): 263-87.

16. A. R. Damasio, *Descartes' Error: Emotion, Reason, and the Human Brain* (New York: Putnam Sons, 1994); P. Ekman, "Basic Emotions," in *Handbook of Cognition and Emotion*, ed. T. Dalgleish and M. Power (San Francisco: Jossey-Bass, 1999), 45-60; A. R. Damasio, *The Feeling of What Happens: Body and Emotion in the*

Making of Consciousness (New York: Harcourt Brace and Company, 1999); J. E. LeDoux, "Emotion Circuits in the Brain," *Annual Review of Neuroscience* 23 (2000): 155-84; R. Smith and R. D. Lane, "The Neural Basis of One's Own Conscious and Unconscious Emotional States," *Neuroscience & Biobehavioral Reviews* 57 (2015): 1-29.

17. M. T. Pham, "The Logic of Feeling," *Journal of Consumer Psychology* 14, no. 4 (2004): 360-69; N. Schwarz, "Feelings-as-Information Theory," in *Handbook of Theories of Social Psychology*, ed. P. Van Lange, A. Kruglanski, and E. T. Higgins (London: Sage, 2012), 289-308.

18. G. R. Maio, V. M. Esses, and D. W. Bell, "Examining Conflict between Components of Attitudes: Ambivalence and Inconsistency Are Distinct Constructs," *Canadian Journal of Behavioural Science* 32, no. 2 (2000): 71-83.

19. P. C. Nutt, *Why Decisions Fail* (San Francisco: Berrett-Koehler, 2002); S. Finkelstein, *Why Smart Executives Fail* (New York: Viking, 2003).

20. M. M. Jessica, J. G. David, and V. Chockalingam, "A Meta-Analysis of Positive Humor in the Workplace," *Journal of Managerial Psychology* 27, no. 2 (2012): 155-90; A. J. Elliot and M. A. Maier, "Color Psychology: Effects of Perceiving Color on Psychological Functioning in Humans," *Annual Review of Psychology* 65, no. 1 (2014): 95-120; F. Sobral and G. Islam, "He Who Laughs Best, Leaves Last: The Influence of Humor on the Attitudes and Behavior of Interns," *Academy of Management Learning & Education* 14, no. 4 (2015): 500-18.

21. N. Wijewardena, C. E. J. Hartel, and R. Samaratunge, "A Laugh a Day Is Sure to Keep the Blues Away: Managers' Use of Humor and the Construction and Destruction of Employees' Resilience," in *Emotions and Organizational Dynamism*, ed. W. J. Zerbe, C. E. J. Hartel, and N. M. Ashkanasy, Research on Emotion in Organizations, vol. 6 (Bradford, UK: Emerald Group, 2010), 259-78; C. Robert and J. E. Wilbanks, "The Wheel Model of Humor: Humor Events and Affect in Organizations," *Human Relations* 65, no. 9 (2012): 1071-99; J. Mesmer-Magnus, D. J. Glew, and C. Viswesvaran, "A Meta-Analysis of Positive Humor in the Workplace," *Journal of Managerial Psychology* 27, no. 2 (2012): 155-90.

22. M. Kohrman, "10 Ways to Make Your Office More Fun," *Fast Company*, July 23, 2013; J. Ball, "80 Unique & Quirky Corporate Event Ideas," *Friday Funnies* (Sutton Coldfield, UK: Coburg Banks, May 19, 2016), https://www.coburgbanks.co.uk/blog/friday-funnies/corporate-event-ideas/ (accessed June 23, 2017); "39 Insanely Fun Team Building Activities for Work ('Trust Falls' Not Included)," *SnackNation Blog* (Los Angeles: SnackNation, August 29, 2016), http://www.snacknation.com/blog/team-building-activities-for-work/ (accessed June 23, 2017).

23. H. M. Weiss and R. Cropanzano, "Affective Events Theory: A Theoretical Discussion of the Structure, Causes and Consequences of Affective Experiences at Work," *Research in Organizational Behavior* 18 (1996): 1-74.

24. L. Festinger, *A Theory of Cognitive Dissonance* (Evanston, IL: Row, Peterson, 1957); A. D. Galinsky, J. Stone, and J. Cooper, "The Reinstatement of Dissonance and Psychological Discomfort Following Failed Affirmation," *European Journal of Social Psychology* 30, no. 1 (2000): 123-47; J. Cooper, *Cognitive Dissonance: Fifty Years of a Classic Theory* (London: Sage, 2007).

25. G. R. Salancik, "Commitment and the Control of Organizational Behavior and Belief," in *New Directions in Organizational Behavior*, ed. B. M. Staw and G. R. Salancik (Chicago: St. Clair, 1977), 1-54; J. M. Jarcho, E. T. Berkman, and M. D. Lieberman, "The Neural Basis of Rationalization: Cognitive Dissonance Reduction during Decision-Making," *Social Cognitive and Affective Neuroscience* 6, no. 4 (2011): 460-67.

26. T. A. Judge, E. A. Locke, and C. C. Durham, "The Dispositional Causes of Job Satisfaction: A Core Evaluations Approach," *Research in Organizational Behavior* 19 (1997): 151-88; T. W. H. Ng and K. L. Sorensen, "Dispositional Affectivity and Work-Related Outcomes: A Meta-Analysis," *Journal of Applied Social Psychology* 39, no. 6 (2009): 1255-87.

27. J. Schaubroeck, D. C. Ganster, and B. Kemmerer, "Does Trait Affect Promote Job Attitude Stability?," *Journal of Organizational Behavior* 17 (1996): 191-96; C. Dormann and D. Zapf, "Job Satisfaction: A Meta-Analysis of Stabilities," *Journal of Organizational Behavior* 22 (2001): 483-504; A. C. Keller and N. K. Semmer, "Changes in Situational and Dispositional Factors as Predictors of Job Satisfaction," *Journal of Vocational Behavior* 83, no. 1 (2013): 88-98.

28. J. A. Morris and D. C. Feldman, "The Dimensions, Antecedents, and Consequences of Emotional Labor," *Academy of Management Review* 21 (1996): 986-1010. This is a person-centered definition, which is supplemented by other approaches to the topic. For recent reviews, see A. S. Wharton, "The Sociology of Emotional Labor," *Annual Review of Sociology* 35, no. 1 (2009): 147-65; F. M. Peart, A. M. Roan, and N. M. Ashkanasy, "Trading in Emotions: A Closer Examination of Emotional Labor," in *Experiencing and Managing Emotions in the Workplace*, ed. N. M. Ashkanasy, C. E. J. Hartel, and W. J. Zerbe, Research on Emotion in Organizations, vol. 8 (Bingley, UK: Emerald Group, 2012), 279-304; A. A. Grandey, J. M. Diefendorff, and D. E. Rupp, "Bringing Emotional Labor in Focus: A Review and Integration of Three Research Issues," in *Emotional Labor in the 21st Century: Diverse Perspectives on Emotion Regulation at Work*, ed. A. A. Grandey, J. M. Diefendorff, and D. E. Rupp, Series in Organization and Management (Hove, UK: Routledge, 2013), 3-28.

29. J. A. Morris and D. C. Feldman, "The Dimensions, Antecedents, and Consequences of Emotional Labor," *Academy of Management Review* 21 (1996): 986-1010; D. Zapf, "Emotion Work and Psychological Well-Being: A Review of the Literature and Some Conceptual Considerations," *Human Resource Management Review* 12 (2002): 237-68.

30. D. Matsumoto, S. H. Yoo, and J. Fontaine, "Mapping Expressive Differences around the World," *Journal of Cross-Cultural Psychology* 39, no. 1 (2008): 55-74; B. Q. Ford and I. B. Mauss, "Culture and Emotion Regulation," *Current Opinion in Psychology* 3 (2015): 1-5.

31. F. Trompenaars and C. Hampden-Turner, *Riding the Waves of Culture*, 2nd ed. (New York: McGraw-Hill, 1998), chap. 6. Also see S. Safdar et al., "Variations of Emotional Display Rules within and across Cultures: A Comparison between Canada, USA, and Japan," *Canadian Journal of Behavioural Science* 41, no. 1 (2009): 1-10.

32. W. J. Zerbe, "Emotional Dissonance and Employee Well-Being," in *Managing Emotions in the Workplace*, ed. N. M. Ashkanasy, W. J. Zerbe, and C. E. J. Hartel (Armonk, NY: M. E. Sharpe, 2002), 189-214; F. Cheung and C. Tang, "The Influence of Emotional Dissonance on Subjective Health and Job Satisfaction: Testing the Stress-Strain-Outcome Model," *Journal of Applied Social Psychology* 40, no. 12 (2010): 3192-217; A. A. Grandey, J. M. Diefendorff, and D. E. Rupp, "Bringing Emotional Labor in Focus: A Review and Integration of Three Research Issues," in *Emotional Labor in the 21st Century: Diverse Perspectives on Emotion Regulation at Work,* ed. A. A. Grandey, J. M. Diefendorff, and D. E. Rupp, Series in Organization and Management (Hove, UK: Routledge, 2013), 3-28.

33. N.-W. Chi et al., "Want a Tip? Service Performance as a Function of Emotion Regulation and Extraversion," *Journal of Applied Psychology* 96, no. 6 (2011): 1337-46; S. Côté, I. Hideg, and G. A. van Kleef, "The Consequences of Faking Anger in Negotiations," *Journal of Experimental Social Psychology* 49, no. 3 (2013): 453-63.

34. S. D. Pugh, M. Groth, and T. Hennig-Thurau, "Willing and Able to Fake Emotions: A Closer Examination of the Link between Emotional Dissonance and Employee Well-Being," *Journal of Applied Psychology* 96, no. 2 (2011): 377–90; R. S. Rubin et al., "A Reconceptualization of the Emotional Labor Construct: On the Development of an Integrated Theory of Perceived Emotional Dissonance and Emotional Labor," in *Emotions in Organizational Behavior*, ed. C. Hartel, N. M. Ashkanasy, and W. Zerbe (Hoboken, NJ: Taylor and Francis, 2012), 189–211.

35. J. D. Kammeyer-Mueller et al., "A Meta-Analytic Structural Model of Dispositonal Affectivity and Emotional Labor," *Personnel Psychology* 66, no. 1 (2013): 47–90; R. H. Humphrey, B. E. Ashforth, and J. M. Diefendorff, "The Bright Side of Emotional Labor," *Journal of Organizational Behavior* 36, no. 6 (2015): 749–69. Deep acting is considered an adaptation of method acting used by professional actors.

36. This model is very similar to Goleman's revised emotional intelligence model. See D. Goleman, R. Boyatzis, and A. McKee, *Primal Leadership* (Boston: Harvard Business School Press, 2002), chap. 3. Recent scholarly research has been converging toward this model (when framed as abilities), and a meta-analysis suggests this model provides the best fit to the data. See R. P. Tett and K. E. Fox, "Confirmatory Factor Structure of Trait Emotional Intelligence in Student and Worker Samples," *Personality and Individual Differences* 41 (2006): 1155–68; D. L. Joseph and D. A. Newman, "Emotional Intelligence: An Integrative Meta-Analysis and Cascading Model," *Journal of Applied Psychology* 95, no. 1 (2010): 54–78; X. Wei, Y. Liu, and N. Allen, "Measuring Team Emotional Intelligence: A Multimethod Comparison," *Group Dynamics: Theory, Research, & Practice* 20, no. 1 (2016): 34–50.

37. H. A. Elfenbein and N. Ambady, "Predicting Workplace Outcomes from the Ability to Eavesdrop on Feelings," *Journal of Applied Psychology* 87, no. 5 (2002): 963–71; T. Quarto et al., "Association between Ability Emotional Intelligence and Left Insula during Social Judgment of Facial Emotions," *PLoS ONE* 11, no. 2 (2016): e0148621.

38. For neurological evidence that people with higher EI have higher sensitivity to others' emotions, see W. D. S. Killgore et al., "Emotional Intelligence Correlates with Functional Responses to Dynamic Changes in Facial Trustworthiness," *Social Neuroscience* 8, no. 4 (2013): 334–46.

39. The hierarchical nature of the four EI dimensions is discussed by Goleman, but it is more explicit in the Salovey and Mayer model. See D. R. Caruso and P. Salovey, *The Emotionally Intelligent Manager* (San Francisco: Jossey-Bass, 2004). This hierarchy is also identified (without the self–other distinction) as a sequence in D. L. Joseph and D. A. Newman, "Emotional Intelligence: An Integrative Meta-Analysis and Cascading Model," *Journal of Applied Psychology* 95, no. 1 (2010): 54–78.

40. F. Walter, M. S. Cole, and R. H. Humphrey, "Emotional Intelligence: Sine Qua Non of Leadership or Folderol?," *Academy of Management Perspectives* 25, no. 1 (2011): 45–59; C. Farh, M.-G. Seo, and P. Tesluk, "Emotional Intelligence, Teamwork Effectiveness, and Job Performance: The Moderating Role of Job Context," *Journal of Applied Psychology* 97, no. 4 (2012): 890–900; A. Schlaerth, N. Ensari, and J. Christian, "A Meta-Analytical Review of the Relationship between Emotional Intelligence and Leaders' Constructive Conflict Management," *Group Processes & Intergroup Relations* 16, no. 1 (2013): 126–36; P. Fernández-Berrocal et al., "When to Cooperate and When to Compete: Emotional Intelligence in Interpersonal Decision-Making," *Journal of Research in Personality* 49 (2014): 21–24; M. Parke, M.-G. Seo, and E. Sherf, "Regulating and Facilitating: The Role of Emotional Intelligence in Maintaining and Using Positive Affect for Creativity," *Journal of Applied Psychology* 100, no. 3 (2015): 917–34.

41. EI predicts performance in high emotional labor jobs but not low emotional labor jobs. EI has a significant but modest correlation with supervisor ratings of all forms of performance. See D. L. Joseph and D. A. Newman, "Emotional Intelligence: An Integrative Meta-Analysis and Cascading Model," *Journal of Applied Psychology* 95, no. 1 (2010): 54–78; D. Joseph et al., "Why Does Self-Reported Emotional Intelligence Predict Job Performance? A Meta-Analytic Investigation of Mixed EI," *Journal of Applied Psychology* 100, no. 2 (2015): 298–342.

42. CareerBuilder, "Seventy-One Percent of Employers Say They Value Emotional Intelligence over IQ, According to Careerbuilder Survey," news release (Chicago: CareerBuilder, August 18, 2011); Ipsos Reid, "Nine in Ten (91%) Managers and Supervisors Agree It's Important to Improve Their Emotional Intelligence in the Workplace," news release (Toronto: Ipsos Reid, October 18, 2012); OfficeTeam, "Why You Need Emotional Intelligence at Work," news release (Menlo Park, CA: PR Newswire, February 23, 2017).

43. D. Matsumoto and H. S. Hwang, "Evidence for Training the Ability to Read Microexpressions of Emotion," *Motivation and Emotion* 35, no. 2 (2011): 181–91; L. J. M. Zijlmans et al., "Training Emotional Intelligence Related to Treatment Skills of Staff Working with Clients with Intellectual Disabilities and Challenging Behaviour," *Journal of Intellectual Disability Research* 55, no. 2 (2011): 219–30; D. Blanch-Hartigan, S. A. Andrzejewski, and K. M. Hill, "The Effectiveness of Training to Improve Person Perception Accuracy: A Meta-Analysis," *Basic and Applied Social Psychology* 34, no. 6 (2012): 483–98; J. Shaw, S. Porter, and L. ten Brinke, "Catching Liars: Training Mental Health and Legal Professionals to Detect High-Stakes Lies," *Journal of Forensic Psychiatry & Psychology* 24, no. 2 (2013): 145–59.

44. L. Winkley, "Teaching Cops Empathy to Deter Use of Force," *San Diego Union-Tribune*, February 12, 2016.

45. D. A. Harrison, D. A. Newman, and P. L. Roth, "How Important Are Job Attitudes? Meta-Analytic Comparisons of Integrative Behavioral Outcomes and Time Sequences," *Academy of Management Journal* 49, no. 2 (2006): 305–25. Another recent study concluded that job satisfaction and organizational commitment are so highly correlated that they represent the same construct. See H. Le et al., "The Problem of Empirical Redundancy of Constructs in Organizational Research: An Empirical Investigation," *Organizational Behavior and Human Decision Processes* 112, no. 2 (2010): 112–25. They also are considered the two central work-related variables in the broader concept of happiness at work. See C. D. Fisher, "Happiness at Work," *International Journal of Management Reviews* 12, no. 4 (2010): 384–412.

46. E. A. Locke, "The Nature and Causes of Job Satisfaction," in *Handbook of Industrial and Organizational Psychology*, ed. M. Dunnette (Chicago: Rand McNally, 1976), 1297–350; H. M. Weiss, "Deconstructing Job Satisfaction: Separating Evaluations, Beliefs and Affective Experiences," *Human Resource Management Review*, no. 12 (2002): 173–94. Some definitions still include emotion as an element of job satisfaction, whereas the definition presented in this book views emotion as a cause of job satisfaction. Also, this definition views job satisfaction as a "collection of attitudes," not several "facets" of job satisfaction.

47. International Survey Research, *Employee Satisfaction in the World's 10 Largest Economies: Globalization or Diversity?* (Chicago: International Survey Research, 2002); Kelly Services, Kelly Global Workforce Index, *American Workers Are Happy with Their Jobs and Their Bosses* (Troy, MI: Kelly Services, November 2006); European Commission, *Standard Eurobarometer 79/Spring 2013* (Brussels, Belgium: European Commission, May 2013).

48. Randstad, *Randstad Workmonitor 4th Quarter 2016* (Amsterdam: Randstad Holding nv, December 2016). Survey data were collected from 33 countries with a minimum of 400 interviews per country of adults working 24 hours or more per week. Respondents were asked: "How satisfied are you in general about working with your current employer?" This exhibit shows results from selected countries across the full range of results.

49. L. Saad, *Job Security Slips in U.S. Worker Satisfaction Rankings* (Princeton, NJ: Gallup, Inc., August 27, 2009); *Employee Engagement Report 2011* (Princeton, NJ: BlessingWhite, 2011). A recent Kelly Services Workforce Index survey reported that 66 percent of the 170,000 respondents in 30 countries plan to look for a job with another organization within the next year. See Kelly Global Workforce Index, *Acquisition and Retention in the War for Talent* (Troy, MI: Kelly Services, April 2012).

50. The problems with measuring attitudes and values across cultures are discussed in L. Saari and T. A. Judge, "Employee Attitudes and Job Satisfaction," *Human Resource Management* 43, no. 4 (2004): 395–407; A. K. Uskul et al., "How Successful You Have Been in Life Depends on the Response Scale Used: The Role of Cultural Mindsets in Pragmatic Inferences Drawn from Question Format," *Social Cognition* 31, no. 2 (2013): 222–36.

51. For a review of the various job satisfaction outcome theories, see R. S. Dalal, "Job Attitudes: Cognition and Affect," in *Industrial and Organizational Psychology*, ed. I. B. Weiner, N. W. Schmitt, and S. Highhouse, Handbook of Psychology, 2nd ed., ed. I. B. Weiner, vol. 12 (New York: John Wiley & Sons, 2012), 341–66.

52. D. Farrell, "Exit, Voice, Loyalty, and Neglect as Responses to Job Dissatisfaction: A Multidimensional Scaling Study," *Academy of Management Journal* 26, no. 4 (1983): 596–607; M. J. Withey and W. H. Cooper, "Predicting Exit, Voice, Loyalty, and Neglect," *Administrative Science Quarterly*, no. 34 (1989): 521–39; A. B. Whitford and S.-Y. Lee, "Exit, Voice, and Loyalty with Multiple Exit Options: Evidence from the US Federal Workforce," *Journal of Public Administration Research and Theory* 25, no. 2 (2015): 373–98. For a critique and explanation of historical errors in the EVLN model, see S. L. McShane, "Reconstructing the Meaning and Dimensionality of Voice in the Exit-Voice-Loyalty-Neglect Model," paper presented at the Voice and Loyalty Symposium, Annual Conference of the Administrative Sciences Association of Canada, Organizational Behaviour Division, Halifax, 2008.

53. T. R. Mitchell, B. C. Holtom, and T. W. Lee, "How to Keep Your Best Employees: Developing an Effective Retention Policy," *Academy of Management Executive* 15 (2001): 96–108; K. Morrell, J. Loan-Clarke, and A. Wilkinson, "The Role of Shocks in Employee Turnover," *British Journal of Management* 15 (2004): 335–49; M. Zhang, D. D. Fried, and R. W. Griffeth, "A Review of Job Embeddedness: Conceptual, Measurement Issues, and Directions for Future Research," *Human Resource Management Review* 22, no. 3 (2012): 220–31.

54. E. W. Morrison, "Employee Voice and Silence," *Annual Review of Organizational Psychology and Organizational Behavior* 1, no. 1 (2014): 173–97; M. R. Bashshur and B. Oc, "When Voice Matters: A Multilevel Review of the Impact of Voice in Organizations," *Journal of Management* 41, no. 5 (2015): 1530–54; P. K. Mowbray, A. Wilkinson, and H. H. M. Tse, "An Integrative Review of Employee Voice: Identifying a Common Conceptualization and Research Agenda," *International Journal of Management Reviews* 17, no. 3 (2015): 382–400.

55. A. O. Hirschman, *Exit, Voice, and Loyalty: Responses to Decline in Firms, Organizations, and States* (Cambridge, MA: Harvard University Press, 1970); E. A. Hoffmann, "Exit and Voice: Organizational Loyalty and Dispute Resolution Strategies," *Social Forces* 84, no. 4 (2006): 2313–30.

56. J. D. Hibbard, N. Kumar, and L. W. Stern, "Examining the Impact of Destructive Acts in Marketing Channel Relationships," *Journal of Marketing Research* 38 (2001): 45–61; J. Zhou and J. M. George, "When Job Dissatisfaction Leads to Creativity: Encouraging the Expression of Voice," *Academy of Management Journal* 44 (2001): 682–96.

57. M. J. Withey and I. R. Gellatly, "Situational and Dispositional Determinants of Exit, Voice, Loyalty and Neglect," *Proceedings of the Administrative Sciences Association of Canada, Organizational Behaviour Division*, 1998; D. C. Thomas and K. Au, "The Effect of Cultural Differences on Behavioral Responses to Low Job Satisfaction," *Journal of International Business Studies* 33, no. 2 (2002): 309–26; S. F. Premeaux and A. G. Bedeian, "Breaking the Silence: The Moderating Effects of Self-Monitoring in Predicting Speaking Up in the Workplace," *Journal of Management Studies* 40, no. 6 (2003): 1537–62; D. J. Travis, R. J. Gomez, and M. E. Mor Barak, "Speaking Up and Stepping Back: Examining the Link between Employee Voice and Job Neglect," *Children and Youth Services Review* 33, no. 10 (2011): 1831–41.

58. V. Venkataramani and S. Tangirala, "When and Why Do Central Employees Speak Up? An Examination of Mediating and Moderating Variables," *Journal of Applied Psychology* 95, no. 3 (2010): 582–91.

59. H. Wallop, "A Contented and Profitable Workforce?," *Daily Telegraph* (London), April 22, 2015, 15.

60. T. A. Judge et al., "The Job Satisfaction-Job Performance Relationship: A Qualitative and Quantitative Review," *Psychological Bulletin* 127, no. 3 (2001): 376–407; C. D. Fisher, "Why Do Lay People Believe That Satisfaction and Performance Are Correlated? Possible Sources of a Commonsense Theory," *Journal of Organizational Behavior* 24, no. 6 (2003): 753–77; L. Saari and T. A. Judge, "Employee Attitudes and Job Satisfaction," *Human Resource Management* 43, no. 4 (2004): 395–407. Other studies report stronger correlations with job performance when both the belief and feeling components of job satisfaction are consistent with each other and when overall job attitude (satisfaction and commitment combined) is being measured. See D. J. Schleicher, J. D. Watt, and G. J. Greguras, "Reexamining the Job Satisfaction-Performance Relationship: The Complexity of Attitudes," *Journal of Applied Psychology* 89, no. 1 (2004): 165–77; D. A. Harrison, D. A. Newman, and P. L. Roth, "How Important Are Job Attitudes? Meta-Analytic Comparisons of Integrative Behavioral Outcomes and Time Sequences," *Academy of Management Journal* 49, no. 2 (2006): 305–25. The positive relationship between job satisfaction and employee performance is also consistent with emerging research on the outcomes of positive organizational behavior. For example, see J. R. Sunil, "Enhancing Employee Performance through Positive Organizational Behavior," *Journal of Applied Social Psychology* 38, no. 6 (2008): 1580–600.

61. However, panel studies suggest that satisfaction has a stronger effect on performance than the other way around. For a summary, see C. D. Fisher, "Happiness at Work," *International Journal of Management Reviews* 12, no. 4 (2010): 384–412.

62. "The Greatest Briton in Management and Leadership," *Personnel Today* (2003): 20.

63. L. Wirthman, "Container Store Moves Ahead with Superb Communications among Employees," *Denver Post*, April 21, 2013.

64. J. I. Heskett, W. E. Sasser, and L. A. Schlesinger, *The Service Profit Chain* (New York: Free Press, 1997); S. P. Brown and S. K. Lam, "A Meta-Analysis of Relationships Linking Employee Satisfaction to Customer Responses," *Journal of Retailing* 84, no. 3 (2008): 243–55; T. J. Gerpott and M. Paukert, "The Relationship between Employee Satisfaction and Customer Satisfaction: A Meta-Analysis (*Der Zusammenhang Zwischen Mitarbeiter-Und Kundenzufriedenheit: Eine Metaanalyse*),"

Zeitschrift für Personalforschung 25, no. 1 (2011): 28–54; H. Evanschitzky, F. V. Wangenheim, and N. V. Wünderlich, "Perils of Managing the Service Profit Chain: The Role of Time Lags and Feedback Loops," *Journal of Retailing* 88, no. 3 (2012): 356–66; Y. Hong et al., "Missing Link in the Service Profit Chain: A Meta-Analytic Review of the Antecedents, Consequences, and Moderators of Service Climate," *Journal of Applied Psychology* 98, no. 2 (2013): 237–67.

65. W.-C. Tsai and Y.-M. Huang, "Mechanisms Linking Employee Affective Delivery and Customer Behavioral Intentions," *Journal of Applied Psychology* 87, no. 5 (2002): 1001–08; P. Guenzi and O. Pelloni, "The Impact of Interpersonal Relationships on Customer Satisfaction and Loyalty to the Service Provider," *International Journal of Service Industry Management* 15, no. 3/4 (2004): 365–84; S. J. Bell, S. Auh, and K. Smalley, "Customer Relationship Dynamics: Service Quality and Customer Loyalty in the Context of Varying Levels of Customer Expertise and Switching Costs," *Journal of the Academy of Marketing Science* 33, no. 2 (2005): 169–83; P. B. Barger and A. A. Grandey, "Service with a Smile and Encounter Satisfaction: Emotional Contagion and Appraisal Mechanisms," *Academy of Management Journal* 49, no. 6 (2006): 1229–38. On the reciprocal effect, see E. Kim and D. J. Yoon, "Why Does Service with a Smile Make Employees Happy? A Social Interaction Model," *Journal of Applied Psychology* 97, no. 5 (2012): 1059–67.

66. R. T. Mowday, L. W. Porter, and R. M. Steers, *Employee Organization Linkages: The Psychology of Commitment, Absenteeism, and Turnover* (New York: Academic Press, 1982); J. P. Meyer, "Organizational Commitment," *International Review of Industrial and Organizational Psychology* 12 (1997): 175–228. The definition and dimensions of organizational commitment continue to be debated. Some writers even propose that *affective commitment* refers only to one's psychological attachment to and involvement in the organization, whereas *identification* with the organization is a distinct concept further along a continuum of bonds. See O. N. Solinger, W. van Olffen, and R. A. Roe, "Beyond the Three-Component Model of Organizational Commitment," *Journal of Applied Psychology* 93, no. 1 (2008): 70–83; H. J. Klein, J. C. Molloy, and C. T. Brinsfield, "Reconceptualizing Workplace Commitment to Redress a Stretched Construct: Revisiting Assumptions and Removing Confounds," *Academy of Management Review* 37, no. 1 (2012): 130–51.

67. M. Taing et al., "The Multidimensional Nature of Continuance Commitment: Commitment Owing to Economic Exchanges versus Lack of Employment Alternatives," *Journal of Business and Psychology* 26, no. 3 (2011): 269–84; C. Vandenberghe and A. Panaccio, "Perceived Sacrifice and Few Alternatives Commitments: The Motivational Underpinnings of Continuance Commitment's Subdimensions," *Journal of Vocational Behavior* 81, no. 1 (2012): 59–72.

68. J. P. Meyer et al., "Affective, Continuance, and Normative Commitment to the Organization: A Meta-Analysis of Antecedents, Correlates, and Consequences," *Journal of Vocational Behavior* 61 (2002): 20–52; M. Riketta, "Attitudinal Organizational Commitment and Job Performance: A Meta-Analysis," *Journal of Organizational Behavior* 23 (2002): 257–66; J. P. Meyer and E. R. Maltin, "Employee Commitment and Well-Being: A Critical Review, Theoretical Framework and Research Agenda," *Journal of Vocational Behavior* 77, no. 2 (2010): 323–37.

69. J. P. Meyer et al., "Organizational Commitment and Job Performance: It's the Nature of the Commitment That Counts," *Journal of Applied Psychology* 74 (1989): 152–56; A. A. Luchak and I. R. Gellatly, "What Kind of Commitment Does a Final-Earnings Pension Plan Elicit?," *Relations Industrielles* 56 (2001): 394–417; Z. X. Chen and A. M. Francesco, "The Relationship between the Three Components of Commitment and Employee Performance in China," *Journal of Vocational Behavior* 62, no. 3 (2003): 490–510; H. Gill et al., "Affective and Continuance Commitment and Their Relations with Deviant Workplace Behaviors in Korea," *Asia Pacific Journal of Management* 28, no. 3 (2011): 595–607. The negative effect on performance might depend on the type of continuance commitment. See M. Taing et al., "The Multidimensional Nature of Continuance Commitment: Commitment Owing to Economic Exchanges versus Lack of Employment Alternatives," *Journal of Business and Psychology* 26, no. 3 (2011): 269–84.

70. Kelly Services, Kelly Global Workforce Index, *Engaging Active and Passive Job Seekers* (Troy, MI: Kelly Services, May 2014); Kelly Services, Kelly Global Workforce Index, *A World at Work* (Troy, MI: Kelly Services, September 2014).

71. J. E. Finegan, "The Impact of Person and Organizational Values on Organizational Commitment," *Journal of Occupational and Organizational Psychology* 73 (2000): 149–69; A. Panaccio and C. Vandenberghe, "Perceived Organizational Support, Organizational Commitment and Psychological Well-Being: A Longitudinal Study," *Journal of Vocational Behavior* 75, no. 2 (2009): 224–36.

72. A. L. Kristof-Brown, R. D. Zimmerman, and E. C. Johnson, "Consequences of Individuals' Fit at Work: A Meta-Analysis of Person-Job, Person-Organization, Person-Group, and Person-Supervisor Fit," *Personnel Psychology* 58, no. 2 (2005): 281–342; J. R. Edwards, "Chapter 4: Person-Environment Fit in Organizations: An Assessment of Theoretical Progress," *The Academy of Management Annals* 2 (2008): 167–230; M. E. Bergman et al., "An Event-Based Perspective on the Development of Commitment," *Human Resource Management Review* 23, no. 2 (2013): 148–60.

73. D. M. Rousseau et al., "Not So Different after All: A Cross-Discipline View of Trust," *Academy of Management Review* 23 (1998): 393–404.

74. D. K. Datta et al., "Causes and Effects of Employee Downsizing: A Review and Synthesis," *Journal of Management* 36, no. 1 (2010): 281–348.

75. Similar concepts on information acquisition are found in socialization and organizational change research. See, for example, P. Bordia et al., "Uncertainty during Organizational Change: Types, Consequences, and Management Strategies," *Journal of Business and Psychology* 18, no. 4 (2004): 507–32; H. D. Cooper-Thomas and N. Anderson, "Organizational Socialization: A Field Study into Socialization Success and Rate," *International Journal of Selection and Assessment* 13, no. 2 (2005): 116–28; T. N. Bauer, "Newcomer Adjustment during Organizational Socialization: A Meta-Analytic Review of Antecedents, Outcomes, and Methods," *Journal of Applied Psychology* 92, no. 3 (2007): 707–21.

76. T. S. Heffner and J. R. Rentsch, "Organizational Commitment and Social Interaction: A Multiple Constituencies Approach," *Journal of Vocational Behavior* 59 (2001): 471–90.

77. J. L. Pierce, T. Kostova, and K. T. Dirks, "Toward a Theory of Psychological Ownership in Organizations," *Academy of Management Review* 26, no. 2 (2001): 298–310; M. Mayhew et al., "A Study of the Antecedents and Consequences of Psychological Ownership in Organizational Settings," *The Journal of Social Psychology* 147, no. 5 (2007): 477–500; T.-S. Han, H.-H. Chiang, and A. Chang, "Employee Participation in Decision Making, Psychological Ownership and Knowledge Sharing: Mediating Role of Organizational Commitment in Taiwanese High-Tech Organizations," *The International Journal of Human Resource Management* 21, no. 12 (2010): 2218–33.

78. J. C. Quick et al., *Preventive Stress Management in Organizations* (Washington, DC: American Psychological Association, 1997), 3–4; R. S. DeFrank and J. M. Ivancevich, "Stress on the Job: An Executive Update," *Academy of Management Executive* 12 (1998): 55–66; A. L. Dougall and A. Baum, "Stress, Coping, and

Immune Function," in *Handbook of Psychology*, ed. M. Gallagher and R. J. Nelson (Hoboken, NJ: Wiley, 2003), 441-55. There are at least three schools of thought regarding the meaning of stress, and some reviews of the stress literature describe these schools without pointing to any one as the preferred definition. One reviewer concluded that the stress concept is so broad that it should be considered an umbrella concept, capturing a broad array of phenomena and providing a simple term for the public to use. See T. A. Day, "Defining Stress as a Prelude to Mapping Its Neurocircuitry: No Help from Allostasis," *Progress in Neuro-Psychopharmacology and Biological Psychiatry* 29, no. 8 (2005): 1195-200; R. Cropanzano and A. Li, "Organizational Politics and Workplace Stress," in *Handbook of Organizational Politics*, ed. E. Vigoda-Gadot and A. Drory (Cheltenham, UK: Edward Elgar, 2006), 139-60; R. L. Woolfolk, P. M. Lehrer, and L. A. Allen, "Conceptual Issues Underlying Stress Management," in *Principles and Practice of Stress Management*, ed. P. M. Lehrer, R. L. Woolfolk, and W. E. Sime (New York: Guilford Press, 2007), 3-15.

79. J. E. Finegan, "The Impact of Person and Organizational Values on Organizational Commitment," *Journal of Occupational and Organizational Psychology* 73 (2000): 149-69; A. L. Dougall and A. Baum, "Stress, Coping, and Immune Function," in *Handbook of Psychology,* ed. M. Gallagher and R. J. Nelson (Hoboken, NJ: Wiley, 2003), 441-55; R. S. Lazarus, *Stress and Emotion: A New Synthesis* (New York: Springer, 2006); L. W. Hunter and S. M. B. Thatcher, "Feeling the Heat: Effects of Stress, Commitment, and Job Experience on Job Performance," *Academy of Management Journal* 50, no. 4 (2007): 953-68.

80. M. G. González-Morales and P. Neves, "When Stressors Make You Work: Mechanisms Linking Challenge Stressors to Performance," *Work & Stress* 29, no. 3 (2015): 213-29; M. B. Hargrove, W. S. Becker, and D. F. Hargrove, "The HRD Eustress Model: Generating Positive Stress with Challenging Work," *Human Resource Development Review* 14, no. 3 (2015): 279-98.

81. Monster Worldwide, "Dangerously Stressful Work Environments Force Workers to Seek New Employment," news release (Weston, MA: Monster Worldwide, April 16, 2014); M. Nink, "The High Cost of Worker Burnout in Germany," *Gallup Business Journal*, March 17, 2016; Accountemps, "The Heat Is On: Six in 10 Employees Report Increased Work Stress," news release (Menlo Park, CA: PRNewswire, February 2, 2017); Accountemps, "The Heat Is On: Seven in 10 Canadian Employees Report Increased Work Stress," news release (Toronto: Robert Half, February 2, 2017).

82. H. Selye, "A Syndrome Produced by Diverse Nocuous Agents," *Nature* 138, no. 1 (1936): 32; H. Selye, *Stress without Distress* (Philadelphia: J. B. Lippincott, 1974). For the history of the word *stress*, see R. M. K. Keil, "Coping and Stress: A Conceptual Analysis," *Journal of Advanced Nursing* 45, no. 6 (2004): 659-65.

83. S. E. Taylor, R. L. Repetti, and T. Seeman, "Health Psychology: What Is an Unhealthy Environment and How Does It Get under the Skin?," *Annual Review of Psychology* 48 (1997): 411-47.

84. A. Rosengren et al., "Association of Psychosocial Risk Factors with Risk of Acute Myocardial Infarction in 11119 Cases and 13648 Controls from 52 Countries (the Interheart Study): Case-Control Study," *The Lancet* 364, no. 9438 (2004): 953-62; D. C. Ganster and C. C. Rosen, "Work Stress and Employee Health: A Multidisciplinary Review," *Journal of Management* 39, no. 5 (2013): 1085-122; J. Goh, J. Pfeffer, and S. A. Zenios, "The Relationship between Workplace Stressors and Mortality and Health Costs in the United States," *Management Science* 62, no. 2 (2016): 608-28.

85. R. C. Kessler, "The Effects of Stressful Life Events on Depression," *Annual Review of Psychology* 48 (1997): 191-214; M. S. Hershcovis et al., "Predicting Workplace Aggression: A Meta-Analysis," *Journal of Applied Psychology* 92, no. 1 (2007): 228-38.

86. K. Danna and R. W. Griffin, "Health and Well-Being in the Workplace: A Review and Synthesis of the Literature," *Journal of Management* 25, no. 3 (1999): 357-84.

87. C. C. Rosen et al., "Occupational Stressors and Job Performance: An Updated Review and Recommendations," in *New Developments in Theoretical and Conceptual Approaches to Job Stress*, ed. P. L. Perrewé and D. C. Ganster, Research in Occupational Stress and Well-Being, ed. P. Perrewé, J. Halbesleben, and C. Rose, vol. 8 (Bingley, UK: Emerald Group Publishing Limited, 2010), 1-60; A. E. Nixon et al., "Can Work Make You Sick? A Meta-Analysis of the Relationships between Job Stressors and Physical Symptoms," *Work & Stress* 25, no. 1 (2011): 1-22.

88. A. E. Nixon et al., "Can Work Make You Sick? A Meta-Analysis of the Relationships between Job Stressors and Physical Symptoms," *Work & Stress* 25, no. 1 (2011): 1-22; S. Pindek and P. E. Spector, "Organizational Constraints: A Meta-Analysis of a Major Stressor," *Work & Stress* 30, no. 1 (2016): 7-25.

89. C. M. Pearson and C. L. Porath, "On the Nature, Consequences and Remedies of Workplace Incivility: No Time for 'Nice'? Think Again," *Academy of Management Executive* 19, no. 1 (2005): 7-18; D. C. Yamada, "Workplace Bullying and American Employment Law: A Ten-Year Progress Report and Assessment," *Comparative Labor Law and Policy Journal* 32, no. 1 (2010): 251-84.

90. P. McDonald, "Workplace Sexual Harassment 30 Years On: A Review of the Literature," *International Journal of Management Reviews* 14, no. 1 (2012): 1-17.

91. N. A. Bowling et al., "A Meta-Analytic Examination of the Potential Correlates and Consequences of Workload," *Work & Stress* 29, no. 2 (2015): 95-113.

92. R. Drago, D. Black, and M. Wooden, *The Persistence of Long Work Hours*, Melbourne Institute Working Paper Series, Melbourne Institute of Applied Economic and Social Research, University of Melbourne, August 2005; L. Golden, "A Brief History of Long Work Time and the Contemporary Sources of Overwork," *Journal of Business Ethics* 84, no. S2 (2009): 217-27; M. Tarafdar, E. B. Pullins, and T. S. Ragu-Nathan, "Technostress: Negative Effect on Performance and Possible Mitigations," *Information Systems Journal* 25, no. 2 (2015): 103-32; E. Reid, "Embracing, Passing, Revealing, and the Ideal Worker Image: How People Navigate Expected and Experienced Professional Identities," *Organization Science* 26, no. 4 (2015): 997-1017; Project: Time Off, *The Work Martyr's Cautionary Tale: How the Millennial Experience Will Define America's Vacation Culture* (Washington, DC: Project: Time Off, August 17, 2016).

93. R. Karasek and T. Theorell, *Healthy Work: Stress, Productivity, and the Reconstruction of Working Life* (New York: Basic Books, 1990); N. Turner, N. Chmiel, and M. Walls, "Railing for Safety: Job Demands, Job Control, and Safety Citizenship Role Definition," *Journal of Occupational Health Psychology* 10, no. 4 (2005): 504-12.

94. R. S. Lazarus, *Stress and Emotion: A New Synthesis* (New York: Springer Publishing, 2006), chap. 5.

95. M. Zuckerman and M. Gagne, "The COPE Revised: Proposing a 5-Factor Model of Coping Strategies," *Journal of Research in Personality* 37 (2003): 169-204; S. Folkman and J. T. Moskowitz, "Coping: Pitfalls and Promise," *Annual Review of Psychology* 55 (2004): 745-74; C. A. Thompson et al., "On the Importance of Coping: A Model and New Directions for Research on Work and Family," *Research in Occupational Stress and Well-Being* 6 (2007): 73-113.

96. S. E. Taylor et al., "Psychological Resources, Positive Illusions, and Health," *American Psychologist* 55, no. 1 (2000): 99-109; F. Luthans and C. M. Youssef, "Emerging Positive Organizational Behavior," *Journal of Management* 33, no. 3 (2007): 321-49; P. Steel, J. Schmidt, and J. Shultz, "Refining the Relationship between Personality and Subjective Well-Being," *Psychological Bulletin* 134, no. 1 (2008): 138-61; G. Alarcon, K. J. Eschleman, and N. A. Bowling, "Relationships between Personality Variables and Burnout: A Meta-Analysis," *Work & Stress* 23, no. 3 (2009): 244-63; R. Kotov et al., "Linking 'Big' Personality Traits to Anxiety, Depressive, and Substance Use Disorders: A Meta-Analysis," *Psychological Bulletin* 136, no. 5 (2010): 768-821.

97. G. A. Bonanno, "Loss, Trauma, and Human Resilience: Have We Underestimated the Human Capacity to Thrive after Extremely Aversive Events?," *American Psychologist* 59, no. 1 (2004): 20-28; F. Luthans, C. M. Youssef, and B. J. Avolio, *Psychological Capital: Developing the Human Competitive Edge* (New York: Oxford University Press, 2007).

98. M. A. Clark et al., "All Work and No Play? A Meta-Analytic Examination of the Correlates and Outcomes of Workaholism," *Journal of Management* 42, no. 7 (2016): 1836-73; C. S. Andreassen et al., "The Relationships between Workaholism and Symptoms of Psychiatric Disorders: A Large-Scale Cross-Sectional Study," *PLoS ONE* 11, no. 5 (2016): e0152978.

99. This list is based on various reviews, but stress management interventions have been organized in several ways. See, for example, J. H. Ruotsalainen et al., "Preventing Occupational Stress in Healthcare Workers," *Cochrane Database of Systematic Reviews*, no. 4 (2015); L. E. Tetrick and C. J. Winslow, "Workplace Stress Management Interventions and Health Promotion," *Annual Review of Organizational Psychology and Organizational Behavior* 2, no. 1 (2015): 583-603.

100. Towers Watson, *The Business Value of a Healthy Workforce: United States, 2013/2014 Staying@Work Survey Report* (New York: Towers Watson, January 2014).

101. B. H. Martin and R. MacDonnell, "Is Telework Effective for Organizations?," *Management Research Review* 35, no. 7 (2012): 602-16; G. B. Cooke, J. Chowhan, and T. Cooper, "Dialing It In: A Missed Opportunity Regarding the Strategic Use of Telework?," *Relations Industrielles* 69, no. 3 (2014): 550-74; T. D. Allen, T. D. Golden, and K. M. Shockley, "How Effective Is Telecommuting? Assessing the Status of Our Scientific Findings," *Psychological Science in the Public Interest* 16, no. 2 (2015): 40-68.

102. C. Fritz et al., "Happy, Healthy, and Productive: The Role of Detachment from Work during Nonwork Time," *Journal of Applied Psychology* 95, no. 5 (2010): 977-83.

103. L. Evans, "Why You Should Let Your Employees Nap at Work," *Entrepreneur*, August 24, 2014; K. Martinez-Carter, "Asleep on the Job: Grabbing Forty Winks at Work," *BBC News*, January 9, 2014; S. Castellanos, "Five Top Nap Rooms at Boston-Area Tech Companies," *Boston Business Journal*, June 23, 2015; L. Moran, "Home Sweet Home, Hubspot Renews Lease for Global Headquarters in Cambridge," news release (Cambridge, MA: HubSpot, December 18, 2015).

104. M. Tuckey et al., "Hindrances Are Not Threats: Advancing the Multidimensionality of Work Stress," *Journal of Occupational Health Psychology* 20, no. 2 (2015): 131-47.

105. M. H. Abel, "Humor, Stress, and Coping Strategies," *Humor: International Journal of Humor Research* 15, no. 4 (2002): 365-81; N. A. Kuiper et al., "Humor Is Not Always the Best Medicine: Specific Components of Sense of Humor and Psychological Well-Being," *Humor: International Journal of Humor Research* 17, no. 1/2 (2004): 135-68; E. J. Romero and K. W. Cruthirds, "The Use of Humor in the Workplace," *Academy of Management Perspectives* 20, no. 2 (2006): 58-69; M. McCreaddie and S. Wiggins, "The Purpose and Function of Humor in Health, Health Care and Nursing: A Narrative Review," *Journal of Advanced Nursing* 61, no. 6 (2008): 584-95.

106. O. Kettunen et al., "Greater Levels of Cardiorespiratory and Muscular Fitness Are Associated with Low Stress and High Mental Resources in Normal but Not Overweight Men," *BMC Public Health* 16, no. 1 (2016): 788; M. Gerber et al., "Fitness Moderates the Relationship between Stress and Cardiovascular Risk Factors," *Medicine & Science in Sports & Exercise* 48, no. 11 (2016): 2075-81.

107. H. O. Dickinson et al., "Relaxation Therapies for the Management of Primary Hypertension in Adults," *Cochrane Database of Systematic Reviews*, no. 1 (2008).

108. C. Viswesvaran, J. I. Sanchez, and J. Fisher, "The Role of Social Support in the Process of Work Stress: A Meta-Analysis," *Journal of Vocational Behavior* 54, no. 2 (1999): 314-34; S. E. Taylor et al., "Biobehavioral Responses to Stress in Females: Tend-and-Befriend, Not Fight-or-Flight,"*Psychological Review* 107, no. 3 (2000): 411-29; T. A. Beehr, N. A. Bowling, and M. M. Bennett, "Occupational Stress and Failures of Social Support: When Helping Hurts," *Journal of Occupational Health Psychology* 15, no. 1 (2010): 45-59; B. A. Scott et al., "A Daily Investigation of the Role of Manager Empathy on Employee Well-Being," *Organizational Behavior and Human Decision Processes* 113, no. 2 (2010): 127-40; S. Y. Shin and S. G. Lee, "Effects of Hospital Workers? Friendship Networks on Job Stress," *PLoS ONE* 11, no. 2 (2016): e0149428.

5 | Employee Motivation

Learning Objectives

After you read this chapter, you should be able to:

LO5-1 Define employee engagement.

LO5-2 Explain how drives and emotions influence employee motivation, and discuss the employee motivation implications of four-drive theory, Maslow's needs hierarchy, intrinsic and extrinsic motivation, and learned needs theory.

LO5-3 Discuss the expectancy theory model, including its practical implications.

LO5-4 Outline organizational behavior modification (OB Mod) and social cognitive theory, and explain their relevance to employee motivation.

LO5-5 Describe the characteristics of effective goal setting and feedback.

LO5-6 Summarize equity theory and describe ways to improve procedural justice.

LO5-7 List the advantages and disadvantages of job specialization and explain how to improve employee motivation through job design.

For many years, the paychecks of almost all public transit bus drivers in Santiago, Chile, were determined by how many fare-paying passengers they served. This pay system motivated drivers to begin their route on time, take shorter breaks, drive efficiently, and ensure that passengers paid their fare. But it also motivated drivers to engage in less desirable behaviors.

To serve more passengers, bus drivers aggressively raced with competing buses to the next passenger waiting area, sometimes cutting off each other and risking the safety of people in nearby vehicles. Drivers skipped bus stops if there was only one person waiting and completely skipped stops with schoolchildren because those passengers paid only one-third of the regular fare. Drivers reduced time at each stop by speeding off before passengers were safely on board. Some also saved time by leaving the bus doors open, resulting in many passenger injuries and fatalities. Studies reported that Santiago's transit buses caused one fatal accident every three days. Drivers who were paid per passenger caused twice as many traffic accidents as drivers paid per hour.

Santiago later integrated its public transit system and drivers subsequently earned only hourly pay. Unfortunately, this arrangement no longer motivated drivers to ensure that passengers paid the fare. In fact, the number of freeloaders skyrocketed to about one-third of all passengers! Furthermore, drivers had to maintain their schedule, so some passenger stops were skipped altogether when drivers were behind schedule or at the end of their workday. Santiago recently changed driver pay once again, instituting a combination of fixed pay and bonuses determined by several performance indicators and reduced fare evasion. So far, drivers have been motivated to perform more of their expected duties (collecting fares, staying on schedule, driving safely, collecting waiting passengers, etc).[1]

Employee motivation can be complex, particularly when companies rely mainly on financial incentives and punishment as the main drivers of that effort. **Motivation** refers to the forces within a person that affect the direction, intensity, and persistence of voluntary behavior.[2] Motivated employees are willing to exert a particular level of effort (intensity), for a certain amount of time (persistence), toward a particular goal (direction). Motivation is one of the four essential drivers of individual behavior and performance (see Chapter 2).

We begin this chapter by discussing employee engagement, an increasingly popular concept associated with motivation. Next, we explain how drives and emotions are the prime movers of employee motivation and review associated needs-based theories. Our attention then turns to expectancy theory, a popular cognitive decision model of employee motivation. Organizational behavior modification and social cognitive theory are then introduced and linked to expectancy theory. Next, we consider theory and practice related to the important motivation topics of goal setting and feedback, and organizational justice. The final section of this chapter examines the effect of job design on employee motivation and performance.

motivation the forces within a person that affect his or her direction, intensity, and persistence of voluntary behavior

employee engagement individual emotional and cognitive motivation, particularly a focused, intense, persistent, and purposive effort toward work-related goals

LO5-1 Define employee engagement.

EMPLOYEE ENGAGEMENT

When executives discuss employee motivation these days, they are just as likely to use the phrase **employee engagement**. Although its definition is still being debated,[3] we define employee engagement as an individual's emotional and cognitive (logical) motivation, particularly a focused, intense, persistent, and purposive effort toward work-related goals. It is an emotional involvement in, commitment to, and satisfaction with the work. Employee engagement is associated with self-efficacy—the belief that you have the ability, role clarity, and resources to get the job done (see Chapter 3). Employee engagement also includes a high level of absorption in the work—the experience of focusing intensely on the task with limited awareness of events beyond that work.

Employee engagement is on the minds of many business leaders because of evidence that it predicts employee and work unit performance.[4] Unfortunately, surveys consistently report that few employees are fully engaged at work. In other words, their effort falls far short of its potential. The numbers vary across studies, but recent results from a widely recognized survey estimate that only 32 percent of employees in the United States are engaged, 51 percent are not engaged, and 17 percent are actively disengaged. Actively disengaged employees tend to be disruptive at work, not just disconnected from work.[5] These numbers are better than in most countries; only 13 percent of employees globally are engaged. Employees in several Asian countries (notably Japan, China, and South Korea) and a few European countries (notably Italy, Netherlands, and France) have the lowest levels of employee engagement, whereas the highest scores are usually found in the United States, Brazil, and India.

This leads to the question: What are the drivers of employee engagement? Goal setting, employee involvement, organizational

DHL Express Employees Get Engaged

Employee engagement is a key driver of business success at DHL Express, the global courier division of Germany's Deutsche Post. "We definitely see the value in having emotionally engaged and motivated employees," says Hennie Heymans, CEO of DHL Express Sub-Saharan Africa. "Engaged employees mean better revenue, profit, customer engagement, and safety."

As one of Africa's top-rated employers, DHL Express builds an engaged workforce through continuous development, such as online learning available to all staff and the Made in Africa initiative to train and mentor future leaders. "Employees should be encouraged to grow—both personally and professionally—and should be continuously motivated to broaden their horizons and fulfill their potential," says Lebo Tseladimitlwa, vice president of human resources at DHL Express Sub-Saharan Africa.

DHL Express also offers employee recognition awards, competitive pay, and a Certified International Specialist (CIS) program, in which all DHL employees learn how the company operates and the importance of everyone's role. "CIS is not a traditional training platform," says DHL Express Global CEO Ken Allen. "It was designed first and foremost as an engagement tool."[7]

©DHL Express Sub-Saharan Africa

justice, organizational comprehension (knowing what's going on in the company), employee development opportunities, sufficient resources, and an appealing company vision are some of the more commonly mentioned influences.[6] In other words, building an engaged workforce calls on most topics in this book, such as the MARS model (Chapter 2), building affective commitment (Chapter 4), motivation practices (Chapter 5), organizational-level communication (Chapter 8), and leadership (Chapter 11).

LO5-2 Explain how drives and emotions influence employee motivation, and discuss the employee motivation implications of four-drive theory, Maslow's needs hierarchy, intrinsic and extrinsic motivation, and learned needs theory.

EMPLOYEE DRIVES AND NEEDS

To build a more engaged and motivated workforce, we first need to understand where motivation begins, that is, the motivational "forces" or prime movers of employee behavior.[8] Our starting point is **drives** (also called *primary needs*), which we define as hardwired characteristics of the brain that attempt to keep us in balance by correcting deficiencies. Recent neuroscience (brain) research has highlighted the central role of emotions in this process. Specifically, drives produce emotions that energize us to act on our environment.[9] There is no agreed-upon list of human drives, but research has consistently identified several, such as the drive for social interaction, for competence, to comprehend our surroundings, and to defend ourselves against physiological and psychological harm.[10]

Drives are innate and universal, which means that everyone has them and they exist from birth. Drives are the starting point of motivation because they generate emotions, which put people in a state of readiness to act on their environment. Cognition (logical thinking) also plays an important role in motivation, but emotions are the real sources of energy in human behavior.[11] In fact, both words (*emotion* and *motivation*) originate from the same Latin word, *movere*, which means "to move."

Exhibit 5.1 illustrates how drives and emotions translate into felt needs and behavior. Drives, and the emotions generated by these drives, form human needs. We define **needs** as goal-directed

"The difference between a successful person and others is not a lack of strength, not a lack of knowledge, but rather in a lack of will."[12]

—Vince Lombardi, National Football League coach and executive

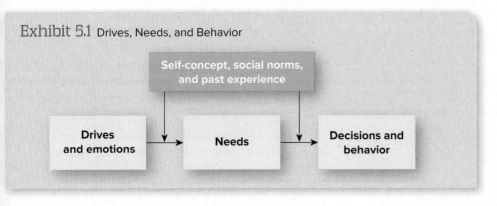

Exhibit 5.1 Drives, Needs, and Behavior

```
                    ┌──────────────────────────┐
                    │ Self-concept, social norms,│
                    │   and past experience     │
                    └──────────────────────────┘
                          │              │
                          ▼              ▼
┌─────────────┐     ┌──────────┐    ┌─────────────┐
│   Drives    │ ──▶ │  Needs   │ ─▶ │ Decisions and│
│ and emotions│     │          │    │   behavior   │
└─────────────┘     └──────────┘    └─────────────┘
```

drives hardwired characteristics of the brain that correct deficiencies or maintain an internal equilibrium by producing emotions to energize individuals

needs goal-directed forces that people experience

forces that people experience. They are the motivational forces of emotions channeled toward particular goals to correct deficiencies or imbalances. As one leading neuroscientist explains: "drives express themselves directly in background emotions and we eventually become aware of their existence by means of background feelings."[13] In other words, needs are the emotions we eventually become consciously aware of.

Consider the following example: You arrive at work to discover a stranger sitting at your desk. Seeing this situation produces emotions (worry, curiosity) that motivate you to act. These emotions are generated from drives, such as the drive to defend and drive to comprehend. When strong enough, these emotions motivate you to do something about this situation, such as finding out who that person is and possibly seeking reassurance from coworkers that your job is still safe. In this case, you have a need to make sense of what is going on (comprehend), to feel secure, and possibly to correct a sense of personal violation (defend). Notice that your emotional reactions to seeing the stranger sitting at your desk represent the forces that move you, and that your logical thinking plays an active role in channeling those emotions toward specific goals.

Individual Differences in Needs

Everyone has the same drives; they are hardwired in us through evolution. However, the intensity of needs in a particular situation varies from one person to the next. Exhibit 5.1 explains why this difference occurs. The left side of the model shows that the individual's self-concept (as well as personality and values), social norms, and past experience amplify or suppress emotions, thereby resulting in stronger or weaker needs.[14] For example, people who define themselves as very sociable typically experience a stronger need for social interaction if alone for a while, whereas people who view themselves as less sociable would experience a less intense need to be with others over that time. These individual differences also explain why needs can be "learned" to some extent. Socialization and reinforcement may increase or decrease a person's need for social interaction, achievement, and so on. We will discuss learned needs later in the chapter.

Individual differences—including self-concept, social norms, and past experience—influence the motivation process in a

second way. They regulate a person's motivated decisions and behavior, as the right side of Exhibit 5.1 illustrates. Consider the earlier example of the stranger sitting at your desk. You probably wouldn't walk up to the person and demand that he or she leave; such blunt behavior is contrary to social norms in most cultures. Employees who view themselves as forthright might approach the stranger directly, whereas those who have a different personality and self-view are more likely to first gather information from coworkers before approaching the intruder. In short, your drives (to comprehend, to defend, to socialize with

Everyone has the same drives, but the intensity of needs in a particular situation varies from one person to the next.
©K-PHOTOS/Alamy Stock Photo

four-drive theory a motivation theory based on the innate drives to acquire, bond, learn, and defend that incorporates both emotions and rationality

Maslow's needs hierarchy theory a motivation theory of needs arranged in a hierarchy, whereby people are motivated to fulfill a higher need as a lower one becomes gratified

others, etc.) and resulting emotions energize you to act, and your self-concept, social norms, and past experience direct that energy toward goal-directed behavior.

Exhibit 5.1 provides a useful template for understanding how drives and emotions are the prime sources of employee motivation and how individual characteristics (self-concept, experience, values) influence goal-directed behavior. You will see pieces of this theory when we discuss four-drive theory, expectancy theory, equity theory, and other concepts in this chapter. The remainder of this section describes theories that try to explain the dynamics of drives and needs.

Four-Drive Theory

How drives, needs, and emotions influence motivation is most effectively explained in **four-drive theory**. This theory states that emotions are the source of human motivation and that these emotions are generated through four drives identified from earlier psychological, sociological, and anthropological research. These drives are[15]

- *Drive to acquire.* This is the drive to seek out, take, control, and retain objects and personal experiences. It produces the need for achievement, competence, status, and self-esteem.[16] The drive to acquire also motivates competition.

- *Drive to bond.* This drive produces the need for belonging and affiliation. It explains why our self-concept is partly defined by associations with social groups (see Chapter 3). The drive to bond motivates people to co-operate and, consequently, is essential for organizations and societies.

- *Drive to comprehend.* People are inherently curious and need to make sense of their environment and themselves.[17] They are motivated to discover answers to unknown as well as conflicting ideas.

- *Drive to defend.* This is the drive to protect ourselves physically, psychologically, and socially. Probably the first drive to develop, it creates a fight-or-flight response when we are confronted with threats to our physical safety, our possessions, our self-concept, our values, and the well-being of others.

All drives are hardwired in our brains (innate) and exist in all human beings (universal). They are also independent of one another; there is no hierarchy of drives. Four-drive theory states that only the drive to defend is reactive—it is triggered by threat. The other three drives are proactive—they are regularly activated by our perceptions to seek fulfillment.

How Drives Influence Motivation and Behavior Recall from Chapter 3 that the stimuli received through our senses are quickly and nonconsciously tagged with emotional markers.[18] Four-drive theory proposes that the four drives determine which emotions are tagged to incoming stimuli. Most of the time, we aren't aware of our emotional experiences because they are subtle and fleeting. However, emotions do become conscious experiences when they are sufficiently strong or when they significantly conflict with one another.

We began this chapter's discussion about drives by explaining how our self-concept, social norms, and past experience direct the motivational force of our emotions to decisions and behavior. Four-drive theory specifically recognizes this process, except that self-concept is replaced with personal values (see Exhibit 5.2). In other words, the theory states that a person's "mental skill set" develops behavioral intentions that are acceptable to society, consistent with their own moral compass, and have a high probability of achieving the goal of fulfilling those felt needs.[19]

Practical Implications of Four-Drive Theory The main recommendation from four-drive theory is that jobs and workplaces should provide a balanced opportunity to fulfill the four drives.[20] There are really two recommendations here. The first is that the best workplaces help employees fulfill all four drives. Employees continually seek fulfillment of their innate drives, so successful companies provide sufficient rewards, learning opportunities, social interaction, and so forth for all employees.

The second recommendation is that fulfillment of the four drives must be kept in balance; that is, organizations should avoid too much or too little opportunity to fulfill each drive. The reason for this advice is that the four drives counterbalance each other. The drive to bond, which motivates mutual support and cohesion, counterbalances the drive to acquire, which motivates competitiveness. Therefore, an organization that fuels the drive to acquire without the drive to bond may eventually suffer from organizational politics and dysfunctional conflict. The drive to comprehend, which motivates investigation of the unknown, counterbalances the drive to defend, which motivates people to avoid the unknown. Change and novelty in the workplace will feed the drive to comprehend, but too much of it will trigger the drive to defend as employees become territorial and resistant to change.

Four-drive theory states that emotions are the source of human motivation and that these emotions are generated through the drive to acquire, bond, comprehend, and defend.
©Don Hammond/DesignPics

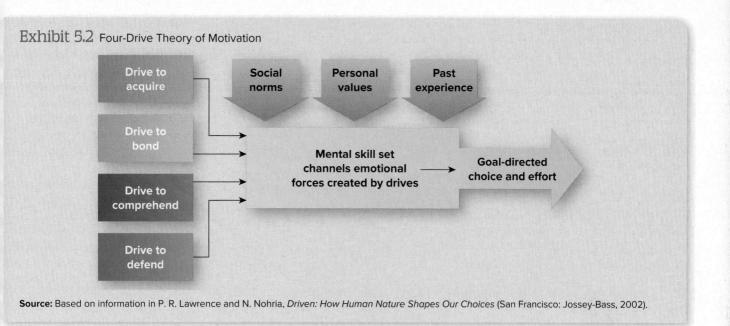

Exhibit 5.2 Four-Drive Theory of Motivation

Drive to acquire

Drive to bond

Drive to comprehend

Drive to defend

Social norms

Personal values

Past experience

Mental skill set channels emotional forces created by drives → Goal-directed choice and effort

Source: Based on information in P. R. Lawrence and N. Nohria, *Driven: How Human Nature Shapes Our Choices* (San Francisco: Jossey-Bass, 2002).

Maslow's Needs Hierarchy Theory

Four-drive theory is one of the few theories to incorporate recent neuroscience discoveries about the role of drives and emotions in human motivation. Mention needs and drives to most people, however, and they will probably refer to **Maslow's needs hierarchy theory**, which was developed by psychologist Abraham Maslow in the 1940s. Maslow condensed and organized the dozens of previously studied drives (which he called primary needs) into five basic categories, organized in a hierarchy from lowest to highest (see Exhibit 5.3): *physiological* (need for food, air, water, shelter, etc.), *safety* (need for security and stability), *belongingness/love* (need for interaction with and affection from others), *esteem* (need for self-esteem and social esteem/status), and *self-actualization* (need for self-fulfillment, realization of one's potential). Along with these five categories, Maslow identified the need to know and the need for aesthetic beauty as two innate drives that do not fit within the hierarchy.[21]

Maslow proposed that human beings are motivated by several of these primary needs (drives) at the same time, but the strongest source of motivation is the lowest unsatisfied need. As the person satisfies a lower-level need, the next higher need in the hierarchy becomes the strongest motivator and remains so even if never satisfied. The exception to this need fulfillment process is self-actualization. People have an ongoing need for self-actualization; it is never really fulfilled. Thus, while the bottom four groups are *deficiency needs* because they become activated when unfulfilled, self-actualization is known as a *growth need* because it continues to develop even when temporarily satiated.

In spite of its popularity, Maslow's needs hierarchy theory has been dismissed by most motivation experts.[22] Maslow assumed that everyone has the needs hierarchy that he depicted, whereas evidence suggests that each of us has a unique needs hierarchy. Some people place social status at the top of their personal hierarchy; others view personal development and growth above social relations or status. The reason why needs hierarchies differ from one person to the next is that employee needs are strongly influenced by self-concept, personal values, and personality.[23] People have different hierarchies of values (see Chapter 2), so they also have parallel differences in their needs hierarchies. If your most important values lean toward stimulation and self-direction, you probably pay more attention to self-actualization needs.[24]

Maslow's theory has become a historical footnote on employee motivation, but Maslow transformed how we think about human motivation.[25] First, Maslow emphasized that needs should be studied together (holistically) because human behavior is typically initiated by more than

Exhibit 5.3 Maslow's Needs Hierarchy

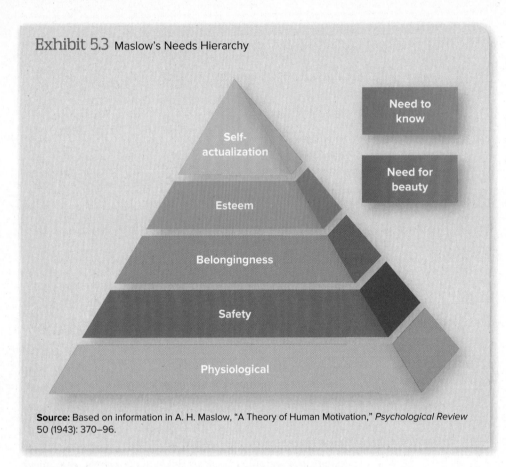

Self-actualization

Esteem

Belongingness

Safety

Physiological

Need to know

Need for beauty

Source: Based on information in A. H. Maslow, "A Theory of Human Motivation," *Psychological Review* 50 (1943): 370–96.

one need at the same time. Previously, motivation experts had studied separately each of the dozens of needs and their underlying drives.[26] Second, Maslow recognized that motivation can be shaped by human thoughts (including self-concept, social norms, past experience), whereas earlier motivation experts focused mainly on how instincts motivated behavior.[27] Third, Maslow popularized the concept of *self-actualization*, suggesting that people are naturally motivated to reach their potential.[28] This positive view of motivation contrasted with previous motivation theories, which focused on need deficiencies such as hunger. By emphasizing motivation through growth and personal development rather than deficiencies, Maslow is considered a pioneer in *positive organizational behavior* (see Chapter 3).

Intrinsic and Extrinsic Motivation

By extolling the importance of self-actualization, Maslow launched an entirely new way of thinking about human motivation. People experience self-actualization by applying their skills and knowledge, observing how their talents achieve meaningful results, and experiencing personal growth through learning. These are the conditions for *intrinsic motivation*,

> Intrinsic motivation occurs when people seek need fulfillment from doing the activity itself, not as a means to some other outcome.

which refers to motivation controlled by the individual and experienced from the activity itself.[29] Intrinsic motivation occurs when people seek need fulfillment from doing the activity itself, not as a means to some other outcome. They enjoy applying their talents toward a meaningful task and experiencing progress or success in that task.

Behavior is intrinsically motivated when it is anchored in the innate drives for competence and autonomy.[30] People feel competent when applying their skills and observing positive, meaningful outcomes from those talents. People feel autonomous when their motivation is self-initiated rather than controlled from an external source. Intrinsic motivation contrasts with *extrinsic motivation*, which occurs when people are motivated to receive something that is beyond their personal control for instrumental reasons. In other words, they direct their effort toward a reward controlled by others that indirectly fulfills a need.

Extrinsic sources of motivation exist throughout organizations, such as pay incentives, recognition awards, and frequent reminders from the boss about work deadlines. These are extrinsic motivators because the outcomes (bonus, award, happy boss) are controlled by others and are not need fulfillment in themselves. The recognition award is a means to satisfy status needs, for example. However, extrinsic motivation also occurs when employees create their own internal pressure to act in association with external factors. For instance, we often experience an extrinsic motivation to complete our part of a team project because we worry how team members will react if we complete the work poorly or behind schedule.

Does Extrinsic Motivation Undermine Intrinsic Motivation? There are two contrasting hypotheses about how extrinsic and intrinsic motivation work together.[31] The additive view suggests that someone performing an intrinsically motivating job becomes even more motivated by also receiving an extrinsic source of motivation for that work. The extrinsic motivator energizes the employee more than the intrinsic motivator alone. The contrasting hypothesis is that introducing extrinsic sources of motivation will reduce intrinsic motivation. For example, employees who were energized

Pay incentives, recognition awards, and frequent reminders from the boss about work deadlines are extrinsic motivators because the outcomes are controlled by others and are not need fulfillment in themselves.
©Peshkova/Shutterstock

from the work itself will experience less of that intrinsic motivation when they receive extrinsic rewards such as a performance bonus. The explanation is that introducing extrinsic motivators diminishes the employee's feeling of autonomy, which is a key source of intrinsic motivation.

Which hypothesis is correct? So far, the research evidence is mixed.[32] Extrinsic motivators may reduce existing intrinsic motivation to some extent and under some conditions, but the effect is often minimal. Extrinsic rewards do not undermine intrinsic motivation when they are unexpected, such as a surprise bonus; when they have low value relative to the intrinsic motivator; and when they are not contingent on specific behavior (such as receiving a fixed salary). But when employees are engaged in intrinsically motivating work, employers should be careful about the potential unintended effect of undermining that motivation with performance bonuses and other sources of extrinsic motivation.[33]

Learned Needs Theory

Earlier in this chapter, we explained that needs are shaped, amplified, or suppressed through self-concept, social norms, and past experience. Maslow observed that individual differences influence need strength. Psychologist David McClelland further investigated the idea that need strength can be altered through social influences. McClelland examined three "learned" needs: achievement, affiliation, and power.[34]

- *Need for Achievement.* People with a high **need for achievement (nAch)** choose moderately challenging tasks, desire unambiguous feedback and recognition for their success, and prefer working alone rather than in teams. Except as a source of feedback, money is a weak motivator for people with high nAch, whereas it can be a strong motivator for those with low nAch.[35] Successful entrepreneurs tend to have high nAch, possibly because they establish challenging goals for themselves and thrive on competition.[36]

- *Need for Affiliation.* People with a high **need for affiliation (nAff)** seek approval from others, want to conform to others' wishes and expectations, and avoid conflict and confrontation. High-nAff employees generally work well in jobs where the main task is cultivating long-term relations. However, they tend to be less effective at allocating scarce resources and making other decisions that potentially generate conflict. Leaders and others in decision-making positions require a relatively low need for affiliation so their choices and actions are not biased by a personal need for approval.[37]

- *Need for Power.* People with a high **need for power (nPow)** want to exercise control over others, are highly involved in team decisions, rely on persuasion, and are concerned about maintaining their leadership position. Individuals who enjoy their power for its own sake, use it to advance personal interests, and wear their power as a status symbol have *personalized power*. Others mainly have a high need for *socialized power* because they desire power as a means to help others.[38] McClelland argues that effective leaders should have a high need for socialized rather than personalized power. They must have a high degree of altruism and social responsibility and be concerned about the consequences of their own actions on others.

McClelland developed training programs to test the idea that needs can be learned (amplified or suppressed) through reinforcement, learning, and social conditions. For example, one program increased achievement motivation by having participants write achievement-oriented stories, practice achievement-oriented behaviors in business games, and meet frequently with a reference group with other trainees to maintain their new-found achievement motivation.[39] Essentially, McClelland's program changed how people

need for achievement (nAch) a learned need in which people want to accomplish reasonably challenging goals and desire unambiguous feedback and recognition for their success

need for affiliation (nAff) a learned need in which people seek approval from others, conform to their wishes and expectations, and avoid conflict and confrontation

need for power (nPow) a learned need in which people want to control their environment, including people and material resources, to benefit either themselves (personalized power) or others (socialized power)

viewed themselves (their self-concept), which amplified their need for achievement, affiliation, or power.

EXPECTANCY THEORY OF MOTIVATION

The theories described so far mainly explain what motivates us—the prime movers of employee motivation—but they don't tell us what we are motivated to do. Four-drive theory recognizes that social norms, personal values, and past experience direct our effort, but it doesn't offer any detail about what goals we choose or where our effort is directed under various circumstances.

Expectancy theory offers more detail by predicting the goal-directed behavior where employees are most likely to direct their effort. Essentially, the theory states that work effort is aimed toward behaviors that people believe will produce the most favorable outcomes. It assumes that people are rational decision makers who choose where to direct their effort based on the probability of outcomes occurring and the positive or negative valences (expected satisfaction) of those outcomes (see Chapter 6).[40] This calculation, illustrated in Exhibit 5.4, states that an individual's effort level depends on three factors: effort-to-performance

(E-to-P) expectancy, performance-to-outcome (P-to-O) expectancy, and outcome valences. Employee motivation is influenced by all three components of the expectancy theory model. If any component weakens, motivation weakens.

- *E-to-P expectancy.* This is the individual's perception that his or her effort will result in a particular level of performance. In some situations, employees may believe that they can unquestionably accomplish the task (a probability of 1.0). In other situations, they expect that even their highest level of effort will not result in the desired performance level (a probability of 0.0). In most cases, the E-to-P expectancy falls somewhere between these two extremes.

- *P-to-O expectancy.* This is the perceived probability that a specific behavior or performance level will lead to a particular outcome. In extreme cases, employees may believe that accomplishing a particular task (performance) will definitely result in a particular outcome (a probability of 1.0), or they may believe that successful performance will have no effect on this outcome (a probability of 0.0). More often, the P-to-O expectancy falls somewhere between these two extremes.

- *Outcome valences.* A *valence* is the anticipated satisfaction or dissatisfaction that an individual feels toward an outcome.[41] It ranges from negative to positive. (The actual range doesn't matter; it may be from -1 to $+1$ or from -100 to $+100$.) Outcomes have a positive valence when they are consistent with our values and satisfy our needs; they have a negative valence when they oppose our values and inhibit need fulfillment.

Applying Expectancy Theory

One of the appealing characteristics of expectancy theory is that it provides clear guidelines for increasing employee motivation, at least extrinsic motivation.[42] Several practical applications of expectancy theory are described below.

Increasing E-to-P Expectancies

E-to-P expectancies are influenced by the individual's belief that he or she can successfully complete the task. Some companies increase this can-do attitude by assuring employees that they have the necessary skills and knowledge, clear role perceptions, and necessary resources to reach the desired levels of performance. An important part of this process involves matching employee abilities to job requirements and clearly communicating the tasks required for the job. Similarly, E-to-P expectancies are learned, so behavior modeling and supportive feedback typically strengthen the individual's belief that he or she is able to perform the task.

Increasing P-to-O Expectancies

The most obvious ways to improve P-to-O expectancies are to measure

Exhibit 5.4 Expectancy Theory of Motivation

E-to-P expectancy	P-to-O expectancy	Valence
Probability that a specific effort level will result in a specific performance level	Probability that a specific performance level will result in specific outcomes	Anticipated satisfaction from the outcome

Effort → Performance → Outcome 1 +/−, Outcome 2 +/−, Outcome 3 +/−

Performance-to-Outcome Expectancy: The Missing Link[43]

56% of 8,254 employees surveyed in the United States, Canada, and five European countries say that they have a good understanding of how people are compensated at all levels of their company (36% say they don't have a good understanding).

44% of 31,000 employees surveyed in 29 countries say they see a clear link between performance and pay in their organization.

44% of more than 4,000 employees in the United States and Canada say their manager differentiates between high and low performers.

37% of American employees surveyed see NO link at all between their performance and their pay.

34% of U.S. federal government employees surveyed say that differences in performance are recognized in a meaningful way in their work unit.

©alxpin/Getty Images

employee performance accurately and distribute more valued rewards to those with higher job performance. P-to-O expectancies are perceptions, so employees also need to believe that higher performance will result in higher rewards. Furthermore, they need to know how that connection occurs, so leaders should use examples, anecdotes, and public ceremonies to illustrate when behavior has been rewarded.

Increasing Outcome Valences One size does not fit all when motivating and rewarding people. The valence of a reward varies from one person to the next because they have different needs. One solution is to individualize rewards by allowing employees to choose the rewards of greatest value to them. When this isn't possible, companies should ensure that everyone values the reward (i.e., positive valence). Finally, we need to watch out for countervalent outcomes. For example, if a company offers individual performance bonuses, it should beware of team norms that discourage employees from working above a minimum standard. These norms and associated peer pressure are countervalent outcomes to the bonus.

Overall, expectancy theory is a useful model that explains how people rationally figure out the best direction, intensity, and persistence of effort. It has been tested in a variety of situations and predicts employee motivation in different cultures.[44] One limitation with expectancy theory, however, is that it mainly explains extrinsic motivation; the model's features do not fit easily with intrinsic motivation. Another concern is that the theory ignores emotions as a source of motivation. The valence element of expectancy theory captures some of this emotional process, but only peripherally.[45] A third issue is that expectancy theory outlines how expectancies (probability of outcomes) affect motivation, but it doesn't explain how employees develop these expectancies.

Two theories that provide this explanation are organizational behavior modification and social cognitive theory, which we describe next.

OB THEORY TO PRACTICE

Putting Expectancy Theory into Practice

Increasing E → P expectancies

▶ Select people with the required skills and knowledge.

▶ Provide required training and clarify job requirements.

▶ Provide sufficient time and resources.

▶ Assign simpler or fewer tasks until employees can master them.

▶ Provide examples of similar employees who have successfully performed the task.

▶ Provide coaching to employees who lack self-confidence.

Increasing P → O expectancies

▶ Measure job performance accurately.

▶ Clearly explain the outcomes that will result from successful performance.

▶ Describe how the employee's rewards were based on past performance.

▶ Provide examples of other employees whose good performance has resulted in higher rewards.

Increasing outcome valences

▶ Distribute rewards that employees value.

▶ Individualize rewards.

▶ Minimize the presence of countervalent outcomes.

ORGANIZATIONAL BEHAVIOR MODIFICATION AND SOCIAL COGNITIVE THEORY

Expectancy theory states that motivation is determined by employee beliefs about expected performance and outcomes. But how do employees learn these expectancy beliefs? For example, how do they form the impression that a particular work activity is more likely to produce a promotion whereas other activities have little effect on promotions? Two theories—organizational behavior modification (OB Mod) and social cognitive theory—answer this question by explaining how people *learn* what to expect from their actions. As such, OB Mod and social cognitive theory supplement expectancy theory by explaining how people learn the expectancies that affect motivation.

Organizational Behavior Modification

For most of the first half of the 1900s, the dominant paradigm about managing individual behavior was *behaviorism*, which argues that a good theory should rely exclusively on behavior and the environment and ignore nonobservable cognitions and emotions.[46] Although behaviorists don't deny the existence of human thoughts and attitudes, they are unobservable and, therefore, irrelevant to scientific study. A variation of this paradigm, called **organizational behavior modification (OB Mod)**, eventually entered organizational studies of motivation and learning.[47]

A-B-Cs of OB Mod The core elements of OB Mod are depicted in the A-B-C model shown in Exhibit 5.5. Essentially, OB Mod attempts to change behavior (B) by managing its antecedents (A) and consequences (C).[48] *Consequences* are events following a particular behavior that influence its future occurrence. Consequences include receiving words of thanks from coworkers after assisting them, receiving preferred work schedules after being with the company longer than the average employee, and finding useful information on your smartphone after checking for new messages. Consequences also include no outcome at all, such as when no one says anything to you about how well you have been serving customers.

Antecedents are events preceding the behavior, informing employees that a particular action will produce specific consequences. An antecedent could be a sound from your smartphone signaling that a text message has arrived. Or it could be your supervisor's request to complete a specific task by tomorrow. Notice that antecedents do not cause behavior. The sound from your smartphone doesn't cause you to open the text message. Rather, the sound (antecedent) is a cue signaling that if you look at your phone messages (behavior), you will find a new message with potentially useful information (consequence).

Contingencies and Schedules of Reinforcement OB Mod identifies four types of consequences, called the *contingencies of reinforcement*.[49] *Positive reinforcement* occurs when the introduction of a consequence increases or maintains the frequency or future probability of a specific behavior. Receiving praise from coworkers is an example of positive reinforcement because the praise usually maintains or increases your likelihood of helping them in future. *Punishment* occurs when a consequence decreases the frequency or future probability of a specific behavior occurring. Most of us would consider being demoted or criticized by our coworkers as forms of punishment. A third type of consequence is *extinction*. The extinction consequence occurs when the target behavior decreases because no consequence follows it. For instance, research suggests that performance tends

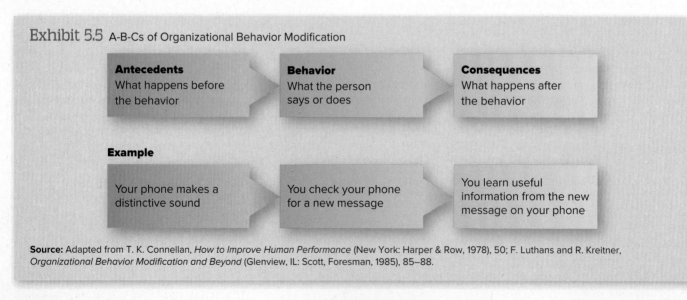

Exhibit 5.5 A-B-Cs of Organizational Behavior Modification

Antecedents What happens before the behavior	**Behavior** What the person says or does	**Consequences** What happens after the behavior

Example

Your phone makes a distinctive sound	You check your phone for a new message	You learn useful information from the new message on your phone

Source: Adapted from T. K. Connellan, *How to Improve Human Performance* (New York: Harper & Row, 1978), 50; F. Luthans and R. Kreitner, *Organizational Behavior Modification and Beyond* (Glenview, IL: Scott, Foresman, 1985), 85–88.

The extinction consequence occurs when the target behavior decreases because no consequence follows it.
©Kjetil Kolbjornsrud/Shutterstock

for learning new tasks is *continuous reinforcement*—providing positive reinforcement after every occurrence of the desired behavior. Aside from learning, the best schedule for motivating people is a *variable ratio schedule* in which employee behavior is reinforced after a variable number of times. Salespeople experience variable ratio reinforcement because they make a successful sale (the reinforcer) after a varying number of client calls. The variable ratio schedule makes behavior highly resistant to extinction because the reinforcer is never expected at a particular time or after a fixed number of accomplishments.

> ## Aside from learning, the best schedule for motivating people is a *variable ratio schedule* in which employee behavior is reinforced after a variable number of times.

to decline when managers stop congratulating employees for their good work.[50]

The fourth consequence in OB Mod, called *negative reinforcement*, is often confused with punishment. It's actually the opposite; negative reinforcement occurs when the removal or avoidance of a consequence increases or maintains the frequency or future probability of a specific behavior. It is usually the removal of punishment. For example, managers apply negative reinforcement when they *stop* criticizing employees whose substandard performance has improved.

Which of these four consequences works best? In most situations, positive reinforcement should follow desired behaviors and extinction (do nothing) should follow undesirable behaviors. Positive reinforcement is preferred because it leverages the power of *positive organizational behavior*; focusing on the positive rather than negative aspects of life will improve organizational success and individual well-being (see Chapter 3). In contrast, punishment and negative reinforcement generate negative emotions and attitudes toward the punisher (e.g., supervisor) and organization. However, punishment (dismissal, suspension, demotion, etc.) may be necessary for extreme behaviors, such as deliberately hurting a coworker or stealing inventory. Indeed, research suggests that, under some conditions, punishment maintains a sense of fairness among those who are affected by or aware of the employee's indiscretion.[51]

Along with the four consequences, OB Mod considers the frequency and timing of these reinforcers (called the *schedules of reinforcement*).[52] The most effective reinforcement schedule

Social Cognitive Theory

Organizational behavior modification states that behavior is learned only through personal interaction with the environment.[53] This view is no longer accepted; instead, experts recognize that people also learn and are motivated by observing others and inferring possible consequences of their actions. This contemporary view is explained by **social cognitive theory**, which states that much learning occurs by observing and modeling others as well as by anticipating the consequences of our behavior.[54] There are several pieces to social cognitive theory, but the three most relevant to employee motivation are learning behavior consequences, behavior modeling, and self-regulation.

Learning Behavior Consequences People learn the consequences of behavior by observing or hearing about what happened to other people, not just by directly experiencing the consequences.[55] Hearing that a coworker was fired for being rude to a client increases your belief that rude behavior will result in being fired. In the language of expectancy theory, learning behavior consequences changes a person's perceived P-to-O probability. Furthermore, people logically anticipate consequences in related situations. For instance, the story about the fired employee might also strengthen your P-to-O expectancy that being rude toward coworkers and suppliers (not just clients) will get you fired.

Behavior Modeling Along with observing others, people learn by imitating and practicing their behaviors.[56] Direct sensory experience helps us acquire tacit knowledge and skills, such as the subtle person–machine interaction while driving a vehicle. Behavior modeling also increases self-efficacy (see Chapter 3) because people gain more self-confidence after observing others and performing the task successfully themselves. Self-efficacy particularly improves when observers are similar to the model in age, experience, gender, and related features.

Self-Regulation An important feature of social cognitive theory is that human beings set goals and engage in other forms of intentional, purposive action. They establish their own short- and long-term objectives, choose their own standards of achievement, work out a plan of action, consider backup alternatives, and have the forethought to anticipate the consequences of their goal-directed behavior. Furthermore, people self-regulate by engaging in **self-reinforcement**; they reward and punish themselves for exceeding or falling short of their self-set goals.[57] For example, you might have a goal of completing the rest of this chapter, after which you reward yourself by having a snack. Raiding the refrigerator is a form of self-induced positive reinforcement for completing this reading assignment.

OB Mod and social cognitive theory explain how people learn probabilities of successful performance (E-to-P

Social cognitive theory states that people self-regulate through self-reinforcement; they reward and punish themselves for exceeding or falling short of their self-set goals.
©Tim Teebken/Photodisc/Getty Images

expectancies) as well as probabilities of various outcomes from that performance (P-to-O expectancies). As such, these theories explain motivation through their relationship with expectancy theory of motivation, described earlier. Elements of these theories also help us understand other motivation processes. For instance, self-regulation is the cornerstone of motivation through goal setting and feedback, which we discuss next.

LO5-5 Describe the characteristics of effective goal setting and feedback.

GOAL SETTING AND FEEDBACK

The City of Toronto's call center—311 Toronto—is a busy place. The center operates 24 hours per day, 7 days per week, and answers 1.5 million nonemergency calls in 180 languages each year. One of the center's objectives is to answer 80 percent of those calls within 75 seconds. It currently exceeds that goal (82 percent of calls are answered within 75 seconds) with an average talk time of 279 seconds. The 311 center also has a target of resolving 70 percent of calls at the first point of contact (i.e., not forwarding the caller elsewhere or calling back later), and exceeds this goal by addressing 73.7 percent of calls during the first contact.[58] Contact centers often have large digital displays that give employees visual feedback in the form of statistics associated with these key performance indicators.

The 311 Toronto operations and most other customer contact centers rely on goal setting to motivate employees and clarify their role perceptions. **Goal setting** potentially improves employee performance in two ways: (1) by amplifying the intensity and persistence of effort and (2) by giving employees clearer role perceptions so their effort is channeled toward behaviors that will improve work performance. Goal setting is more complex than simply telling someone to "do your best." It requires

Most customer contact centers rely on goal setting to motivate employees and clarify their role perceptions.
©MBI/Alamy Stock Photo

The SMARTER Approach to Goal Setting

S *pecific.* Goals lead to better performance when they are specific. Specific goals state what needs to be accomplished; how it should be accomplished; and where, when, and with whom it should be accomplished. Specific goals clarify performance expectations, so employees can direct their effort more efficiently and reliably.

M *easurable.* Goals need to be measurable because motivation occurs when people have some indication of their progress and achievement of those goals. This measurement ideally includes how much (quantity), how well (quality), and at what cost the goal was achieved. Be aware, however, that some types of employee performance are difficult to measure, and they risk being neglected in companies preoccupied with quantifiable outcomes.[61]

A *chievable.* One of the trickiest aspects of goal setting is developing goals that are sufficiently but not overly challenging.[62] Easy goals result in performance that is well below the employee's potential. Yet, goals that are too challenging also may lead to reduced effort if employees believe there is a low probability of accomplishing them (i.e., low E-to-P expectancy). Recent studies also have found that very difficult goals increase the probability that employees will engage in unethical behavior to achieve them.[63]

R *elevant.* Goals need to be relevant to the individual's job and within his or her control. For example, a goal to reduce waste materials would have little value if employees don't have much control over waste in the production process.

T *ime-framed.* Goals need a due date. They should specify when the objective should be completed or when it will be assessed for comparison against a standard.

E *xciting.* Goals tend to be more effective when employees are committed to them, not just compliant. Challenging goals tend to be more exciting for most (but not all) employees because they are more likely to fulfill a person's growth needs when the goal is achieved. Goal commitment also increases when employees are involved in goal setting.[64]

R *eviewed.* The motivational value of goal setting depends on employees receiving feedback about reaching those goals.[65] Effective feedback requires measurement, which we discussed earlier in this list, but it also includes reflecting or discussing with others your goal progress and accomplishment. Reviewing goal progress and achievement helps employees redirect their effort. It is also a potential source of recognition that fulfills growth needs.

several specific characteristics.[59] One popular acronym—SMARTER—captures these characteristics fairly well:[60] Effective goals are specific, measurable, achievable, relevant to the employee's job, set within a time frame, exciting to create employee commitment, and reviewed both during and after the goal has been accomplished.

Characteristics of Effective Feedback

Feedback—information that lets us know whether we have achieved the goal or are properly directing our effort toward it—is a critical partner with goal setting. Feedback contributes to motivation and performance by clarifying role perceptions, improving employee skills and knowledge, and strengthening self-efficacy.[66] Effective feedback has many of the same characteristics as effective goal setting. It should be *specific* and *relevant*, that is, the information should refer to specific metrics (e.g., sales increased by 5 percent last month) and to the individual's behavior or outcomes within his or her control. Feedback also should be *timely*; the information should be available soon after the behavior or results occur so that employees see a clear association between their actions and the consequences. Feedback also should be *credible*. Employees are more likely to accept this information from trustworthy and believable sources.

One other important characteristic of effective feedback is that it should be *sufficiently frequent.* How frequent is "sufficiently"? The answer depends on at least two things. One consideration is the employee's knowledge and experience with the task. Employees working on new tasks should receive more frequent feedback because they require more behavior guidance and reinforcement. Employees who perform familiar tasks can receive less frequent feedback. The second factor is how long it takes to complete the task (i.e., its cycle time). Less frequent feedback usually occurs in jobs with a long cycle time (e.g., executives and scientists) because indicators of goal progress and accomplishment in these jobs are less frequent than in jobs with a short cycle time (e.g., grocery store cashiers).

Feedback through Strengths-Based Coaching Forty years ago, Peter Drucker observed that leaders are more effective when they focus on strengths rather than weaknesses. "The effective executive builds on strengths—their own strengths, the strengths of superiors, colleagues, subordinates; and on the strength of the situation," wrote the late management guru.[68] Maximizing employees' potential by focusing on their strengths rather than weaknesses is the essence of **strengths-based coaching** (also

strengths-based coaching a positive organizational behavior approach to coaching and feedback that focuses on building and leveraging the employee's strengths rather than trying to correct his or her weaknesses

SELF-ASSESSMENT 5.3: What Is Your Goal Orientation?
Everyone sets goals for themselves, but people differ in the nature of those goals. Some view goals as challenges that assist learning. Others see goals as demonstrations of one's competence. Still others view goals as threatening one's image if they are not achieved. You can discover your dominant goal orientation by locating this self-assessment in Connect if it is assigned by your instructor.

many callers are waiting and the average time they have been waiting.

Some companies set up *multisource (360-degree) feedback*, which, as the name implies, is information about an employee's performance collected from a full circle of people, including subordinates, peers, supervisors, and customers. Multisource feedback tends to provide more complete and accurate information than feedback from a supervisor alone.[73] However, the process can be expensive and time-consuming, and the feedback tends to be ambiguous, conflicting, and inflated rather than accurate because coworkers try to minimize interpersonal conflict.

The preferred feedback source depends on the purpose of the information. Feedback from nonsocial sources, such as computer printouts or feedback directly from the job, is better when employees need to learn about goal progress and accomplishment. This is because information from nonsocial sources is considered more accurate than information from social sources. Negative feedback from nonsocial sources is also less damaging to self-esteem. In contrast, social sources tend to delay negative

> ## "Success is achieved by developing our strengths, not by eliminating our weaknesses."[72]
> — Marilyn vos Savant, author and magazine columnist

known as *appreciative coaching*).[69] In strengths-based coaching, employees describe areas of work where they excel or demonstrate potential. The coach guides this discussion by asking exploratory questions that help employees discover ways to build on these strengths. Situational barriers, as well as strategies to overcome those barriers, are identified to further support the employee's potential.

Strengths-based coaching is more motivating than traditional performance reviews because employees seek out feedback about their strengths, whereas they either become defensive about negative feedback or allow that information to weaken their self-efficacy.[70] Strengths-based coaching also recognizes that poor performance on some tasks is due more to motivation than ability. People can learn new skills throughout their working lives, but their weaker performance on some tasks is often due to lower motivation associated with their personality, interests, and preferences. These individual differences become quite stable fairly early in a person's career.[71]

Sources of Feedback

Feedback can originate from nonsocial or social sources. Nonsocial sources provide feedback without someone communicating that information. Corporate intranets allow many executives to receive feedback instantaneously on their computer, usually in the form of graphic output on an executive dashboard. Employees at contact centers view electronic displays showing how

information, leave some of it out, and distort the bad news in a positive way.[74] Employees should receive some positive feedback from social sources. It feels better to have coworkers say that you are performing the job well than to discover this from data on an impersonal computer screen.

Feedback from nonsocial sources is considered more accurate than information from social sources, which is better when employees need to learn about goal progress and accomplishment.
©Dan Bannister/Blend Images LLC

Evaluating Goal Setting and Feedback

Goal setting (in partnership with feedback) is generally a highly effective practice for employee motivation and performance.[75] Putting goal setting into practice can be challenging, however.[76] It tends to focus employees on a narrow subset of measurable performance indicators while ignoring aspects of job performance that are difficult to measure. There is also evidence that very difficult goals motivate some people to engage in unethical behavior to achieve those goals. Difficult goals are also stressful, which can undermine overall job performance.

Yet another problem is that goal setting tends to interfere with the learning process in new, complex jobs. Therefore, setting performance goals is effective in established jobs but should be avoided where an intense learning process is occurring. A final issue is that when goal achievement is tied to financial rewards, many employees are motivated to set easy goals (while making the boss think they are difficult) so that they have a higher probability of receiving the bonus or pay increase. As a former Ford Motor Company CEO once quipped: "At Ford, we hire very smart people. They quickly learn how to make relatively easy goals look difficult!"[77]

> **LO5-6** Summarize equity theory and describe ways to improve procedural justice.

ORGANIZATIONAL JUSTICE

Treating employees fairly is both morally correct and good for employee motivation, loyalty, and well-being. Yet feelings of injustice are regular occurrences in the workplace. To minimize these incidents, we need to first understand that there are two forms of organizational justice: distributive justice and procedural justice.[78] **Distributive justice** refers to perceived fairness in the outcomes we receive compared to our contributions and the outcomes and contributions of others. **Procedural justice** refers to fairness of the procedures used to decide the distribution of resources.

At its most basic level, the employment relationship is about employees exchanging their time, skills, and behavior for pay, fulfilling work, skill development opportunities, and so forth. What is considered "fair" in this exchange relationship varies with each person and situation.[79] An *equality principle* operates when we believe that everyone in the group should receive the same outcomes, such as when everyone gets subsidized meals in the company cafeteria. The *need principle* is applied when we believe that those with the greatest need should receive more outcomes than others with less need. This occurs, for instance, when employees get paid time off to recover from illness. The *equity principle* infers that people should be paid in proportion to their contribution. The equity principle is the most common distributive justice rule in organizational settings, so let's look at it in more detail.

Equity Theory

Feelings of equity are explained by **equity theory**, which says that employees determine feelings of equity by comparing their own outcome/input ratio to the outcome/input ratio of some

Not Paid What (They Believe) They're Worth[80]

53% of 31,000 employees surveyed globally say they are being paid fairly compared with others who fill similar positions in other companies.

36% of 1,000 Australian advertising professionals surveyed say their bosses are NOT overpaid (26% say they ARE overpaid).

44% of 7,700 executives and managers surveyed in several countries (5,136 in the United States) say that employees at their companies are paid fairly.

26% of 14,000 New Zealand public servants surveyed agree that their pay is fair compared to similar jobs in the wider labor market (53% disagree; 21% neither agree nor disagree).

20% of 71,000 employees surveyed (most in the United States) say that they are paid fairly.

©Don Farrall/Getty Images

other person.[81] As Exhibit 5.6 illustrates, the outcome/input ratio is the value of the outcomes you receive divided by the value of the inputs you provide in the exchange relationship. Inputs include such things as skill, effort, reputation, performance, experience, and hours worked. Outcomes are what employees receive from the organization such as pay, promotions, recognition, interesting jobs, and opportunities to improve one's skills and knowledge.

Equity theory states that we compare our outcome/input ratio with that of a comparison other.[82] The comparison other might be another person or group of people in other jobs (e.g., comparing your pay with your boss's pay) or another organization. Some research suggests that employees frequently collect information on several referents to form a "generalized" comparison other.[83] For the most part, however, the comparison other varies from one person to the next and is not easily identifiable.

The comparison of our own outcome/input ratio with the ratio of someone else results in perceptions of equity, underreward inequity, or overreward inequity. In the equity condition, people believe that their outcome/input ratio is similar to the ratio of the comparison other. In the underreward inequity situation, people believe their outcome/input ratio is lower than the comparison other's ratio. In the overreward inequity condition, people believe their ratio of outcomes/inputs is higher than the comparison other's ratio.

Inequity and Employee Motivation How do perceptions of equity or inequity affect employee motivation? The answer is illustrated in Exhibit 5.7. When people believe they are under- or overrewarded, they experience negative emotions (called

inequity tension).[84] As we have pointed out throughout this chapter, emotions are the engines of motivation. In the case of inequity, people are motivated to reduce the emotional tension. Most people have a strong emotional response when they believe a situation is unfair, and this emotion nags at them until they take steps to correct the perceived inequity.

There are several ways to try to reduce the inequity tension.[85] Let's consider each of these in the context of underreward inequity. One action is to reduce our inputs so the outcome/input ratio is similar to that of the higher-paid coworker. Some employees do this by working more slowly, offering fewer suggestions, and engaging in less organizational citizenship behavior. A second action is to increase our outcomes. Some people who think they are underpaid ask for a pay raise. Others make unauthorized use of company resources. A third behavioral response is to increase the comparison other's inputs. We might subtly ask the better-paid coworker to do a larger share of the work, for instance. A fourth action is to reduce the comparison other's outcomes. This might occur by ensuring that the coworker gets less desirable jobs or working conditions. Another action, although uncommon, is to ask the company to reduce the coworker's pay so it is the same as yours.

A fifth action is perceptual rather than behavioral. It involves changing our beliefs about the situation. For example, we might believe that the coworker really is doing more (e.g., working longer hours) for that higher pay. Alternatively, we might change our perceptions of the value of some outcomes. We might initially believe it is unfair that a coworker gets more work-related travel than we do, but later we conclude that this travel is more inconvenient than desirable. A sixth action to reduce the inequity tension is to change the comparison other. Rather than

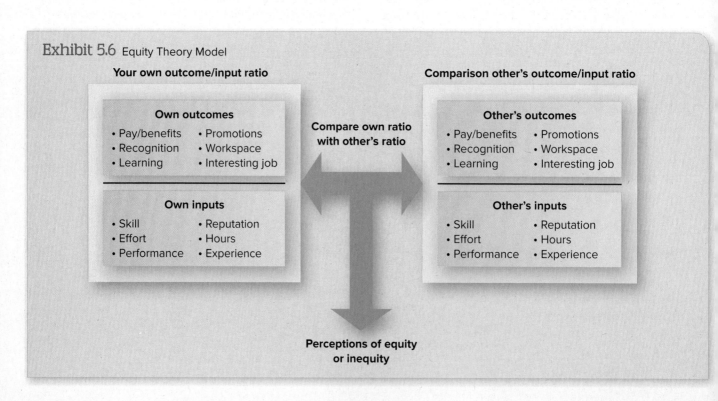

Exhibit 5.6 Equity Theory Model

Your own outcome/input ratio

Own outcomes
- Pay/benefits
- Recognition
- Learning
- Promotions
- Workspace
- Interesting job

Own inputs
- Skill
- Effort
- Performance
- Reputation
- Hours
- Experience

Compare own ratio with other's ratio

Comparison other's outcome/input ratio

Other's outcomes
- Pay/benefits
- Recognition
- Learning
- Promotions
- Workspace
- Interesting job

Other's inputs
- Skill
- Effort
- Performance
- Reputation
- Hours
- Experience

Perceptions of equity or inequity

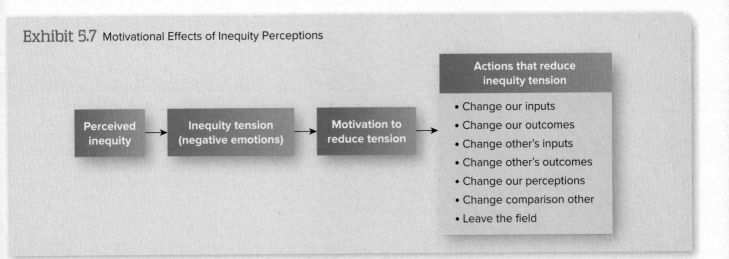

Exhibit 5.7 Motivational Effects of Inequity Perceptions

Perceived inequity → Inequity tension (negative emotions) → Motivation to reduce tension →

Actions that reduce inequity tension

- Change our inputs
- Change our outcomes
- Change other's inputs
- Change other's outcomes
- Change our perceptions
- Change comparison other
- Leave the field

> "I was underpaid for the first half of my life. I don't mind being overpaid for the second half."[86]
> —Pierre Burton, journalist and popular history author

compare ourself with the higher-paid coworker, we might increasingly compare ourself with a friend or neighbor who works in a similar job. Finally, if the inequity tension is strong enough and can't be reduced through other actions, we might leave the field. This occurs by moving to another department, joining another company, or keeping away from the work site where the overpaid coworker is located.

People who feel overreward inequity would reverse these actions. Some overrewarded employees reduce their feelings of inequity by working harder; others encourage the underrewarded coworker to work at a more leisurely pace. A common reaction, however, is that the overrewarded employee changes his or her perceptions to justify the more favorable outcomes, such as believing the assigned work is more difficult or his or her skills are more valuable than the lower-paid coworker's skills.

Evaluating Equity Theory Equity theory is widely studied and quite successful at predicting various situations involving feelings of workplace injustice.[87] However, it isn't so easy to put into practice because the equity theory model doesn't identify the comparison other and doesn't indicate which inputs or outcomes are most valuable to each employee. The best solution here is for leaders to know their employees well enough to minimize the risk of inequity feelings. Open communication is also key, enabling employees to let decision makers know when they believe decisions are unfair. A second problem is that equity theory accounts for only some of our feelings of fairness or justice in the workplace. Experts now say that procedural justice is at least as important as distributive justice.

Procedural Justice

At the beginning of this section we defined two main forms of organizational justice: distributive and procedural. *Procedural justice* refers to fairness of the procedures used to decide the distribution of resources.[88] In other words, people evaluate fairness of the distribution of resources (distributive justice) as well as fairness of the conditions determining that distribution and its possible alteration (procedural justice).

There are several ways to improve procedural justice.[89] A good way to start is by giving employees "voice" in the process; encourage them to present their facts and perspectives on the issue. Voice also provides a "value-expressive" function; employees tend to feel better after having an opportunity to speak their mind. Procedural justice is also higher when the decision

SELF-ASSESSMENT 5.4: How Sensitive Are You to Inequities?
Correcting feelings of inequity is one of the most powerful motivating forces in the workplace. But people react differently to equitable and inequitable situations based on their equity sensitivity. Equity sensitivity refers to a person's outcome/input preferences and reaction to various outcome/input ratios when compared to other people. You can discover your level of equity sensitivity by locating this self-assessment in Connect if it is assigned by your instructor.

A key element of procedural justice is to give employees "voice" in the process so they can present their facts and perspectives on the issue.
©Tetra Images/Corbis

maker is perceived as unbiased, relies on complete and accurate information, applies existing policies consistently, and has listened to all sides of the dispute. If employees still feel unfairness in the allocation of resources, these feelings may dissipate if the company has an appeal process in which the decision is reviewed by a higher level of management.

Finally, people usually feel less injustice when they are given a full explanation of the decision and they are treated with respect throughout the complaint process. If employees believe a decision is unfair, refusing to explain how the decision was made could fuel their feelings of inequity. For instance, one study found that nonwhite nurses who experienced racism tended to file grievances only after experiencing disrespectful treatment in their attempt to resolve the racist situation. Another study reported that employees with repetitive strain injuries were more likely to file workers' compensation claims after experiencing disrespectful behavior from management. A third study noted that employees have stronger feelings of injustice

when the manager has a reputation of treating people unfairly most of the time.[90]

Consequences of Procedural Injustice Procedural justice has a strong influence on a person's emotions and motivation. Employees tend to experience anger toward the source of the injustice, which generates various response behaviors that scholars categorize as either withdrawal or aggression.[91] Notice how these actions are similar to the fight-or-flight responses described earlier in the chapter regarding situations that activate our drive to defend. Research suggests that being treated unfairly threatens our self-esteem and social status, particularly when others see that we have been unjustly treated. Employees retaliate to restore their self-esteem and reinstate their status and power in the relationship with the perpetrator of the injustice. Employees also engage in these counterproductive behaviors to educate the decision maker, thereby trying to minimize the likelihood of future injustices.[92]

> **LO5-7** List the advantages and disadvantages of job specialization and explain how to improve employee motivation through job design.

JOB DESIGN

How do you build a better job? That question has challenged organizational behavior experts, psychologists, engineers, and economists for a few centuries. Some jobs have very few tasks and usually require very little skill. Other jobs are immensely complex and require years of experience and learning to master them. From one extreme to the other, jobs have different effects on work efficiency and employee motivation. The ideal, at least from the organization's perspective, is to find the right combination so that work is performed efficiently but employees are engaged and satisfied.[93] This objective requires careful **job design**—the process of assigning tasks to a job, including the interdependency of those tasks with other jobs. A *job* is a set of tasks performed by one person. To understand this issue more fully, let's begin by describing early job design efforts aimed at increasing work efficiency through job specialization.

Job Design and Work Efficiency

By any measure, supermarket cashiers have highly repetitive work. One consulting firm estimated that cashiers should be able to scan each item in an average of 4.6 seconds. A British tabloid recently reported that cashiers at five supermarket chains in that country actually took between 1.75 and 3.25 seconds to scan each item from a standardized list of 20 products. Along with scanning, cashiers process the payment, move the divider stick, and (in some stores) bag the checked groceries.[94]

Supermarket cashiers perform jobs with a high degree of **job specialization**. Job specialization occurs when the work required to serve a customer—or provide any other product or

Supermarket cashier jobs have high job specialization; the cycle time is about 4 seconds to scan each grocery item before they repeat the activity with the next item.
©Antenna/Getty Images

changing over to a different type of activity. Even when people can change tasks quickly, their mental attention lingers on the previous type of work, which slows down performance on the new task.[95] A second reason for increased work efficiency is that employees can become proficient more quickly in specialized jobs. There are fewer physical and mental skills to learn and therefore less time required to train and develop people for high performance. Third, shorter work cycles give employees more frequent practice with the task, so jobs are mastered more quickly. Fourth, specialization tends to increase work efficiency by allowing employees with specific aptitudes or skills to be matched more precisely to the jobs for which they are best suited.[96]

The benefits of job specialization were noted more than 2,300 years ago by the Chinese philosopher Mencius and the Greek philosopher Plato. Scottish economist Adam Smith wrote 250 years ago about the advantages of job specialization. Smith described a small factory where 10 pin makers collectively produced as many as 48,000 pins per day because they performed specialized tasks. One person straightened the metal, another cut it, another sharpened one end of the cut piece, yet another added a white tip to the other end, and so forth. In contrast, Smith explained that if these 10 people worked alone producing complete pins, they would collectively manufacture no more than 200 pins per day.[97]

Scientific Management

One of the strongest advocates of job specialization was Frederick Winslow Taylor, an American industrial engineer who introduced the principles of scientific management in the early 1900s.[98] Scientific management consists of a toolkit of activities. Some of these interventions—employee selection, training, goal setting, and work incentives—are common today but were rare until Taylor popularized them. However, scientific management is mainly associated with high levels of job specialization and standardization of tasks to achieve maximum efficiency.

According to Taylor, the most effective companies have detailed procedures and work practices developed by engineers, enforced by supervisors, and executed by employees. Even the supervisor's tasks should be divided: One person manages operational efficiency, another manages inspection, and another is the disciplinarian. Taylor and other industrial engineers demonstrated that scientific management significantly improves work efficiency. No doubt, some of the increased productivity can be credited to training, goal setting, and work incentives, but job specialization quickly became popular in its own right.

service—is subdivided into separate jobs assigned to different people. For instance, supermarkets have separate jobs for checking out customers, stocking shelves, preparing fresh foods, and so forth. Except in the smallest family grocery stores, one person would not perform all of these tasks as part of one job. Each resulting job includes a narrow subset of tasks, usually completed in a short cycle time. *Cycle time* is the time required to complete the task before starting over with another item or client. Supermarket cashiers have a cycle time of about 4 seconds to scan each item before they repeat the activity with the next item. They also have a cycle time for serving each customer, which works out to somewhere between 20 and 40 times per hour in busy stores.

Why would companies divide work into such tiny bits? The simple answer is that job specialization potentially improves work efficiency. One reason for this higher efficiency is that employees have less variety of tasks to juggle (such as checking out customers versus stocking shelves), so there is less time lost

Problems with Job Specialization

Frederick Winslow Taylor and his contemporaries focused on how job specialization reduces labor "waste" by improving the mechanical efficiency of work (i.e., skills matching, faster learning, less switchover time). Yet they didn't seem to notice how this extreme job specialization adversely affects employee attitudes and motivation. Some jobs—such as scanning grocery items—can be so specialized that they soon become tedious, trivial, and socially isolating. Specialized jobs with very short cycle times often produce higher levels of employee turnover and absenteeism. Companies sometimes have to pay higher wages to attract job applicants to this dissatisfying, narrowly defined work.[99]

Job specialization affects output quality, but in two opposing ways. Job incumbents of specialized jobs potentially produce higher-quality results because, as we mentioned earlier, they master their work faster than do employees in jobs with many and varied tasks. This higher proficiency explains why specialist lawyers tend to provide better quality service than do generalist lawyers.[100] But many jobs (such as supermarket cashiers) are specialized to the point that they are highly repetitive and tedious. In these repetitive jobs, the positive effect of higher proficiency is easily offset by the negative effect of lower attentiveness and motivation caused by the tedious work patterns.

Job specialization also undermines work quality. By performing a small part of the overall work, employees have difficulty striving for better quality or even noticing flaws with that overall output. As one observer of an automobile assembly line reports: "Often [employees] did not know how their jobs related to the total picture. Not knowing, there was no incentive to strive for quality—what did quality even mean as it related to a bracket whose function you did not understand?"[101]

Job Design and Work Motivation

Frederick Winslow Taylor may have overlooked the motivational effect of job characteristics, but it is now the central focus of many job design initiatives. The motivational potential of the job itself is the focus of the **job characteristics model**, shown in Exhibit 5.8. The job characteristics model identifies five core job dimensions that produce three psychological states.

Exhibit 5.8 The Job Characteristics Model

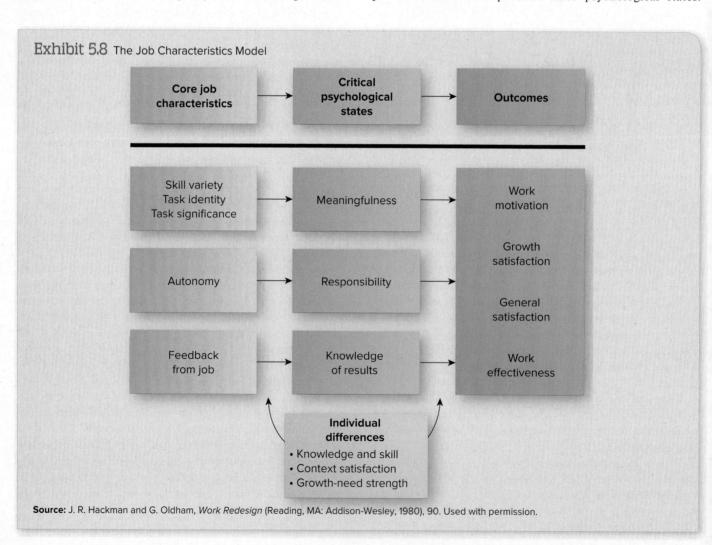

Source: J. R. Hackman and G. Oldham, *Work Redesign* (Reading, MA: Addison-Wesley, 1980), 90. Used with permission.

Employees who experience these psychological states tend to have higher levels of internal work motivation (motivation from the work itself), job satisfaction (particularly satisfaction with the work itself), and work effectiveness.[102]

Core Job Characteristics The job characteristics model identifies five core job characteristics. Under the right conditions, employees are more motivated and satisfied when jobs have higher levels of these characteristics:

- *Skill variety.* **Skill variety** refers to the use of different skills and talents to complete a variety of work activities. For example, sales clerks who normally only serve customers might be assigned the additional duties of stocking inventory and changing storefront displays.

- *Task identity.* **Task identity** is the degree to which a job requires completion of a whole or identifiable piece of work, such as assembling an entire broadband modem rather than just soldering in the circuitry.

- *Task significance.* **Task significance** is the degree to which the job affects the organization and/or larger society. It is an observable characteristic of the job (you can see how it benefits others) as well as a perceptual awareness. For example, some companies ask customers to speak to employees about the importance of the products or services to them.

- *Autonomy.* Jobs with high levels of autonomy provide freedom, independence, and discretion in scheduling the work and determining the procedures to be used to complete the work. In autonomous jobs, employees make their own decisions rather than rely on detailed instructions from supervisors or procedure manuals. Autonomy is considered the core motivational element of job design.[103] As we learned in Chapter 4, autonomy is also an important mechanism to reduce stress in some situations.

- *Job feedback.* Job feedback is the degree to which employees can tell how well they are doing from direct sensory information from the job itself. Airline pilots can tell how well they land their aircraft, and road crews can see how well they have prepared the roadbed and laid the asphalt.

skill variety the extent to which employees must use different skills and talents to perform tasks within their jobs

task identity the degree to which a job requires completion of a whole or an identifiable piece of work

task significance the degree to which a job has a substantial impact on the organization and/or larger society

Critical Psychological States The five core job characteristics affect employee motivation and satisfaction through three critical psychological states, shown in Exhibit 5.8. Skill variety, task identity, and task significance directly contribute to the job's *experienced meaningfulness*—the belief that one's work is worthwhile or important. Autonomy directly contributes to feelings of *experienced responsibility*—a sense of being personally accountable for the work outcomes. The third critical psychological state is *knowledge of results*—an awareness of the work outcomes based on information from the job itself.

Individual Differences Job design doesn't increase work motivation for everyone in every situation. Employees must have the required skills and knowledge to master the more challenging work. Otherwise, job design tends to increase stress and reduce job performance. The original model also states that employees will be motivated by the five core job characteristics only when they are satisfied with their work context (e.g., working conditions, job security) and have a high *growth need strength*. Growth need strength refers to an individual's need for personal growth and development, such as work that offers challenges, cognitive stimulation, learning, and independent thought and action.[105] However, research findings have been mixed, suggesting that employees might be motivated by job design no

matter how they feel about their job context or how high or low they score on growth needs.[106]

Social and Information Processing Job Characteristics

The job characteristics model overlooks two clusters of job features: social characteristics and information processing demands.[107] One social characteristic is the extent to which the job requires employees to interact with other people (coworkers, clients, government representatives, etc.). This required social interaction is associated with emotional labor, discussed in Chapter 4, as well as with **task interdependence**, which is the extent to which employees need to share materials, information, or expertise with each other (see Chapter 7). A second social characteristic of the job is feedback from others. The job characteristics model identifies feedback from the job itself as a source of motivation. Feedback from clients, co-workers, and other social sources is also important, particularly for rapid learning and when the feedback is favorable.

The other cluster of job characteristics missing from the job characteristics model relates to the information processing demands of the job.[108] One information processing demand is how predictable the job duties are from one day to the next (called *task variability*). Employees in jobs with high task variability have nonroutine work patterns; they perform different types of tasks from one day to the next and don't know which tasks are required until that time. The second information processing demand, called *task analyzability*, refers to how much the job can be performed using known procedures and rules. Jobs with high task analyzability have a ready-made "cookbook" to guide people in those jobs through most decisions and actions, whereas jobs with low task analyzability require employee creativity and judgment to determine the best course of action. Task variability and task analyzability are important job characteristics to consider when designing organizational structures, so we discuss both of them in Chapter 12.

Job Design Practices That Motivate

Three main strategies can increase the motivational potential of jobs: job rotation, job enlargement, and job enrichment.

Job Rotation Many grocery stores reduce the tedium of checkout work by moving cashiers to other jobs during the work shift. This job rotation adds some skill variety into the workday, and many companies have found that it improves employee motivation and satisfaction to some extent. A second benefit of job rotation is that it minimizes health risks from repetitive strain and heavy lifting because employees use different muscles and physical positions in the various jobs. A third benefit is that job rotation supports multiskilling; employees learn several jobs, which makes it easier for the company to fill temporary vacancies.

Job Enlargement **Job enlargement** adds tasks to an existing job. This might involve combining two or more complete jobs into one or just adding one or two more tasks to an existing job. Either way, skill variety increases because there are more tasks to perform.

Job Enrichment **Job enrichment** occurs when employees are given more responsibility for scheduling, coordinating, and planning their own work.[109] For example, employees have more enriched jobs when they are responsible for a variety of tasks and have enough autonomy to plan their work and choose when to perform each task. Job enrichment potentially increases job satisfaction and work motivation, and reduces absenteeism and turnover. Productivity is also higher when task identity and job feedback are improved. Product and service quality tend to improve because job enrichment increases the jobholder's felt responsibility and sense of ownership over the product or service.[110]

One way to increase job enrichment is by combining highly interdependent tasks into one job. This *natural grouping* approach occurs in the video journalist job because it naturally groups tasks together to complete an entire product (i.e., a news story). By forming natural work units, jobholders have stronger feelings of responsibility for an identifiable body of work. They feel a sense of ownership and, therefore, tend to increase job quality. Forming natural work units increases task identity and task significance because employees perform a complete product or service and can more readily see how their work affects others.

A second job enrichment strategy, called *establishing client relationships*, involves putting employees in direct contact with their clients rather than using another job group or the supervisor as the liaison between the employee and the customer. Establishing client relationships increases task significance because employees see a line-of-sight connection between their work and consequences for customers. By being directly responsible for specific clients, employees also have more information and can make better decisions affecting those clients.[111]

> Forming natural work units increases task identity and task significance because employees perform a complete product or service and can more readily see how their work affects others.

Study Checklist

©Natthawat Jamnapa/123RF

Notes

1. I. Tiznado et al., "Incentive Schemes for Bus Drivers: The Case of the Public Transit System in Santiago, Chile," *Research in Transportation Economics* 48 (2014): 77–83; R. M. Johnson, D. H. Reiley, and J. C. Muñoz, "'The War for the Fare': How Driver Compensation Affects Bus System Performance," *Economic Inquiry* 53, no. 3 (2015): 1401–19.

2. C. C. Pinder, *Work Motivation in Organizational Behavior* (Upper Saddle River, NJ: Prentice Hall, 1998); R. M. Steers, R. T. Mowday, and D. L. Shapiro, "The Future of Work Motivation Theory," *Academy of Management Review* 29 (2004): 379–87.

3. W. H. Macey and B. Schneider, "The Meaning of Employee Engagement," *Industrial and Organizational Psychology* 1 (2008): 3–30; A. M. Saks and J. A. Gruman, "What Do We Really Know about Employee Engagement?," *Human Resource Development Quarterly* 25, no. 2 (2014): 155–82.

4. D. Macleod and N. Clarke, *Engaging for Success: Enhancing Performance through Employee Engagement* (London: UK Government, Department for Business Innovation and Skills, July 2009); P. M. Bal and A. H. De Lange, "From Flexibility Human Resource Management to Employee Engagement and Perceived Job Performance across the Lifespan: A Multisample Study," *Journal of Occupational and Organizational Psychology* 88 (2015): 126–54.

5. S. Crabtree, "Worldwide, 13% of Employees Are Engaged at Work," news release (Washington, DC: Gallup, Inc., October 8, 2013); A. Adkins, "Employee Engagement in U.S. Stagnant in 2015," news release (Washington, DC: Gallup, Inc., January 13, 2016); Aon Hewitt, *2017 Trends in Global Employee Engagement* (Chicago: Aon Hewitt, April 10, 2017).

6. Several sources attempt to identify and organize the drivers of employee engagement. See, for example, D. Robinson, S. Perryman, and S. Hayday, *The Drivers of Employee Engagement* (Brighton, UK: Institute for Employment Studies, 2004); W. H. Macey et al., *Employee Engagement: Tools for Analysis, Practice, and Competitive Advantage* (Malden, MA: Wiley-Blackwell, 2009); D. Macleod and N. Clarke, *Engaging for Success: Enhancing Performance through Employee Engagement* (London: UK Government, Department for Business Innovation and Skills, July 2009); M. Stairs and M. Galpin, "Positive Engagement: From Employee Engagement to Workplace Happiness," in *Oxford Handbook of Positive Psychology of Work,* ed. P. A. Linley, S. Harrington, and N. Garcea (New York: Oxford University Press, 2010), 155–72.

7. C. Shaw, "DHL Express Recognises Excelling Employees," *Times of Swaziland,* June 28, 2013; K. Allen, "The Art of Engagement" (Bonn, Germany: Deutsche Post DHL, August 12, 2013), http://www.dpdhl.com/en/logistics_around_us/from_our_divisions/ken_allen_the_art_of_engagement.html (accessed August 21, 2013); "Employee Engagement Crucial for Business Success," *How We Made It in Africa,* February 20, 2015; "Engaged Employees Are Better Performers," *The Citizen* (Gauteng, South Africa), February 24, 2015.

8. The confusing array of definitions about drives and needs has been the subject of criticism for a half century. See, for example, R. S. Peters, "Motives and Motivation," *Philosophy* 31 (1956): 117–30; H. Cantril, "Sentio, Ergo Sum: 'Motivation' Reconsidered," *Journal of Psychology* 65, no. 1 (1967): 91–107; G. R. Salancik and J. Pfeffer, "An Examination of Need-Satisfaction Models of Job Attitudes," *Administrative Science Quarterly* 22, no. 3 (1977): 427–56.

9. D. W. Pfaff, *Drive: Neurobiological and Molecular Mechanisms of Sexual Motivation* (Cambridge, MA: MIT Press, 1999); A. Blasi, "Emotions and Moral Motivation," *Journal for the Theory of Social Behaviour* 29, no. 1 (1999): 1–19; T. V. Sewards and M. A. Sewards, "Fear and Power-Dominance Drive Motivation: Neural Representations and Pathways Mediating Sensory and Mnemonic Inputs, and Outputs to Premotor Structures," *Neuroscience and Biobehavioral Reviews* 26 (2002): 553–79; K. C. Berridge, "Motivation Concepts in Behavioral Neuroscience," *Physiology & Behavior* 81, no. 2 (2004): 179–209. We distinguish drives from emotions, but future research may find that the two concepts are not so different as is stated here. Woodworth is credited with either coining or popularizing the term *drives* in the context of human motivation. His classic book is certainly the first source to discuss the concept in detail. See R. S. Woodworth, *Dynamic Psychology* (New York: Columbia University Press, 1918).

10. G. Loewenstein, "The Psychology of Curiosity: A Review and Reinterpretation," *Psychological Bulletin* 116, no. 1 (1994): 75–98; A. E. Kelley, "Neurochemical Networks Encoding Emotion and Motivation: An Evolutionary Perspective," in *Who Needs Emotions? The Brain Meets the Robot,* ed. J. M. Fellous and M. A. Arbib (New York: Oxford University Press, 2005), 29–78; M. R. Leary, "Motivational and Emotional Aspects of the Self," *Annual Review of Psychology* 58, no. 1 (2007): 317–44; L. A. Leotti, S. S. Iyengar, and K. N. Ochsner, "Born to Choose: The Origins and Value of the Need for Control," *Trends in Cognitive Sciences* 14, no. 10 (2010): 457–63.

11. K. Passyn and M. Sujan, "Self-Accountability Emotions and Fear Appeals: Motivating Behavior," *Journal of Consumer Research* 32, no. 4 (2006): 583–89; S. G. Barsade and D. E. Gibson, "Why Does Affect Matter in Organizations?," *Academy of Management Perspectives* 21, no. 2 (2007): 36–59.

12. V. Lombardi Jr., What *It Takes to Be #1: Vince Lombardi on Leadership* (New York: McGraw-Hill, 2001), 39.

13. A. R. Damasio, *The Feeling of What Happens: Body and Emotion in the Making of Consciousness* (New York: Harcourt Brace, 1999), 286.

14. S. Hitlin, "Values as the Core of Personal Identity: Drawing Links between Two Theories of Self," *Social Psychology Quarterly* 66, no. 2 (2003): 118–37; B. Monin, D. A. Pizarro, and J. S. Beer, "Deciding versus Reacting: Conceptions of Moral Judgment and the Reason-Affect Debate," *Review of General Psychology* 11, no. 2 (2007): 99–111; D. D. Knoch and E. E. Fehr, "Resisting the Power of Temptations. The Right Prefrontal Cortex and Self-Control," *Annals of the New York Academy of Sciences* 1104, no. 1 (2007): 123.

15. P. R. Lawrence and N. Nohria, *Driven: How Human Nature Shapes Our Choices* (San Francisco: Jossey-Bass, 2002); N. Nohria, B. Groysberg, and L. E. Lee, "Employee Motivation: A Powerful New Model," *Harvard Business Review* (2008): 78–84. On the application of four-drive theory to leadership, see P. R. Lawrence, *Driven to Lead* (San Francisco: Jossey-Bass, 2010).

16. The drive to acquire is likely associated with research on getting ahead, desire for competence, the selfish gene, and desire for social distinction. See R. H. Frank, *Choosing the Right Pond: Human Behavior and the Quest for Status* (New York: Oxford University Press, 1985); L. Gaertner et al., "The 'I,' the 'We,' and the 'When': A Meta-Analysis of Motivational Primacy in Self-Definition," *Journal of Personality and Social Psychology* 83, no. 3 (2002): 574–91; J. Hogan and B. Holland, "Using Theory to Evaluate Personality and Job-Performance Relations: A Socioanalytic Perspective," *Journal of Applied Psychology* 88, no. 1 (2003): 100–12; R. Dawkins, *The Selfish Gene,* 30th anniversary ed. (Oxford, UK: Oxford University Press, 2006); M. R. Leary, "Motivational and Emotional Aspects of the Self," *Annual Review of Psychology* 58, no. 1 (2007): 317–44; B. S. Frey, "Awards as Compensation," *European Management Journal* 4 (2007): 6–14.

17. J. Litman, "Curiosity and the Pleasures of Learning: Wanting and Liking New Information," *Cognition and Emotion* 19, no. 6 (2005): 793–814; T. G. Reio Jr. et al., "The Measurement and Conceptualization of Curiosity," *Journal of Genetic Psychology* 167, no. 2 (2006): 117–35.

18. A. R. Damasio, *Descartes' Error: Emotion, Reason, and the Human Brain* (New York: Putnam Sons, 1994); A. Bechara et al., "Deciding Advantageously before Knowing the Advantageous Strategy," *Science* 275, no. 5304 (1997): 1293–95; J. E. LeDoux, "Emotion Circuits in the Brain," *Annual Review of Neuroscience* 23 (2000): 155–84; P. Winkielman and K. C. Berridge, "Unconscious Emotion," *Current Directions in Psychological Science* 13, no. 3 (2004): 120–23; M. Reimann and A. Bechara, "The Somatic Marker Framework as a Neurological Theory of Decision-Making: Review, Conceptual Comparisons, and Future Neuroeconomics Research," *Journal of Economic Psychology* 31, no. 5 (2010): 767–76.

19. P. R. Lawrence and N. Nohria, *Driven: How Human Nature Shapes Our Choices* (San Francisco: Jossey-Bass, 2002), 145–47; R. F. Baumeister, E. J. Masicampo, and K. D. Vohs, "Do Conscious Thoughts Cause Behavior?," *Annual Review of Psychology* 62, no. 1 (2011): 331–61.

20. P. R. Lawrence and N. Nohria, *Driven: How Human Nature Shapes Our Choices* (San Francisco: Jossey-Bass, 2002), chap. 11.

21. A. H. Maslow, "A Theory of Human Motivation," *Psychological Review* 50 (1943): 370–96; A. H. Maslow, *Motivation and Personality* (New York: Harper & Row, 1954).

22. D. T. Hall and K. E. Nougaim, "An Examination of Maslow's Need Hierarchy in an Organizational Setting," *Organizational Behavior and Human Performance* 3, no. 1 (1968): 12; M. A. Wahba and L. G. Bridwell, "Maslow Reconsidered: A Review of Research on the Need Hierarchy Theory," *Organizational Behavior and Human Performance* 15 (1976): 212–40; E. L. Betz, "Two Tests of Maslow's Theory of Need Fulfillment," *Journal of Vocational Behavior* 24, no. 2 (1984): 204–20; P. A. Corning, "Biological Adaptation in Human Societies: A 'Basic Needs' Approach," *Journal of Bioeconomics* 2, no. 1 (2000): 41–86. For a recent proposed revision of the model, see D. T. Kenrick et al., "Renovating the Pyramid of Needs: Contemporary Extensions Built upon Ancient Foundations," *Perspectives on Psychological Science* 5, no. 3 (2010): 292–314.

23. L. Parks and R. P. Guay, "Personality, Values, and Motivation," *Personality and Individual Differences* 47, no. 7 (2009): 675–84.

24. B. A. Agle and C. B. Caldwell, "Understanding Research on Values in Business," *Business and Society* 38 (1999): 326–87; B. Verplanken and R. W. Holland, "Motivated Decision Making: Effects of Activation and Self-Centrality of Values on Choices and Behavior," *Journal of Personality and Social Psychology* 82, no. 3 (2002): 434–47; S. Hitlin and J. A. Pilavin, "Values: Reviving a Dormant Concept," *Annual Review of Sociology* 30 (2004): 359–93.

25. K. Dye, A. J. Mills, and T. G. Weatherbee, "Maslow: Man Interrupted—Reading Management Theory in Context," *Management Decision* 43, no. 10 (2005): 1375–95.

26. A. H. Maslow, "A Preface to Motivation Theory," *Psychosomatic Medicine* 5 (1943): 85–92.

27. S. Kesebir, J. Graham, and S. Oishi, "A Theory of Human Needs Should Be Human-Centered, Not Animal-Centered," *Perspectives on Psychological Science* 5, no. 3 (2010): 315–19.

28. A. H. Maslow, *Maslow on Management* (New York: Wiley, 1998).

29. M. Gagné and E. L. Deci, "Self-Determination Theory and Work Motivation," *Journal of Organizational Behavior* 26, no. 4 (2005): 331–62; C. P. Cerasoli, J. M. Nicklin, and M. T. Ford, "Intrinsic Motivation and Extrinsic Incentives Jointly Predict Performance: A 40-Year Meta-Analysis," *Psychological Bulletin* 140, no. 4 (2014): 980–1008.

30. M. Gagné and D. Bhave, "Autonomy in the Workplace: An Essential Ingredient to Employee Engagement and Well-Being in Every Culture," in *Human Autonomy in Cross-Cultural Context,* ed. V. I. Chirkov, R. M. Ryan, and K. M. Sheldon, Cross-Cultural Advancements in Positive Psychology (Dordrecht, Netherlands: Springer Netherlands, 2011), 163–87; E. L. Deci and M. R. Ryan, "The Importance of Universal Psychological Needs for Understanding Motivation in the Workplace," in *The Oxford Handbook of Work Engagement, Motivation, and Self-Determination Theory,* ed. M. Gagne (New York: Oxford University Press, 2014), 13–32.

31. A. Kohn, *Punished by Rewards* (Boston: Houghton Mifflin, 1993); C. C. Pinder, *Work Motivation in Organizational Behavior,* 2nd ed. (New York: Psychology Press, 2008), chap. 3.

32. C. P. Cerasoli, J. M. Nicklin, and M. T. Ford, "Intrinsic Motivation and Extrinsic Incentives Jointly Predict Performance: A 40-Year Meta-Analysis," *Psychological Bulletin* 140, no. 4 (2014): 980-1008; Y. Garbers and U. Konradt, "The Effect of Financial Incentives on Performance: A Quantitative Review of Individual and Team-Based Financial Incentives," *Journal of Occupational and Organizational Psychology* 87, no. 1 (2014): 102-37. Earlier meta-analyses are discussed in C. C. Pinder, *Work Motivation in Organizational Behavior* (Upper Saddle River, NJ: Prentice Hall, 1998), 86-91.

33. J. Schroeder and A. Fishbach, "How to Motivate Yourself and Others? Intended and Unintended Consequences," *Research in Organizational Behavior* 35 (2015): 123-41.

34. D. C. McClelland, *The Achieving Society* (New York: Van Nostrand Reinhold, 1961); D. C. McClelland and D. H. Burnham, "Power Is the Great Motivator," *Harvard Business Review* 73 (1995): 126-39; D. Vredenburgh and Y. Brender, "The Hierarchical Abuse of Power in Work Organizations," *Journal of Business Ethics* 17 (1998): 1337-47; S. Shane, E. A. Locke, and C. J. Collins, "Entrepreneurial Motivation," *Human Resource Management Review* 13, no. 2 (2003): 257-79.

35. D. C. McClelland, *The Achieving Society* (New York: Van Nostrand Reinhold, 1961).

36. M. Frese and M. M. Gielnik, "The Psychology of Entrepreneurship," *Annual Review of Organizational Psychology and Organizational Behavior* 1, no. 1 (2014): 413-38.

37. W. H. Decker, T. J. Calo, and C. H. Weer, "Affiliation Motivation and Interest in Entrepreneurial Careers," *Journal of Managerial Psychology* 27, no. 3 (2012): 302-20; G. A. Yukl, *Leadership in Organizations*, 8th ed. (Upper Saddle River, NJ: Pearson Education, 2013), chap. 6; S. Leroy et al., "Synchrony Preference: Why Some People Go with the Flow and Some Don't," *Personnel Psychology* 68, no. 4 (2015): 759-809.

38. J. C. Magee and C. A. Langner, "How Personalized and Socialized Power Motivation Facilitate Antisocial and Prosocial Decision-Making," *Journal of Research in Personality* 42, no. 6 (2008): 1547-59; D. Rus, D. van Knippenberg, and B. Wisse, "Leader Self-Definition and Leader Self-Serving Behavior," *Leadership Quarterly* 21, no. 3 (2010): 509-29; C. Case and J. Maner, "Divide and Conquer: When and Why Leaders Undermine the Cohesive Fabric of Their Group," *Journal of Personality and Social Psychology* 107, no. 6 (2014): 1033-50.

39. D. Miron and D. C. McClelland, "The Impact of Achievement Motivation Training on Small Business," *California Management Review* 21 (1979): 13-28.

40. Expectancy theory of motivation in work settings originated in V. H. Vroom, *Work and Motivation* (New York: Wiley, 1964). The version of expectancy theory presented here was developed by Edward Lawler. Lawler's model provides a clearer presentation of the model's three components. P-to-O expectancy is similar to "instrumentality" in Vroom's original expectancy theory model. The difference is that instrumentality is a correlation whereas P-to-O expectancy is a probability. See J. P. Campbell et al., *Managerial Behavior, Performance, and Effectiveness* (New York: McGraw-Hill, 1970); E. E. Lawler III, *Motivation in Work Organizations* (Monterey, CA: Brooks-Cole, 1973); D. A. Nadler and E. E. Lawler, "Motivation: A Diagnostic Approach," in *Perspectives on Behavior in Organizations*, ed. J. R. Hackman, E. E. Lawler III, and L. W. Porter (New York: McGraw-Hill, 1983), 67-78.

41. M. Zeelenberg et al., "Emotional Reactions to the Outcomes of Decisions: The Role of Counterfactual Thought in the Experience of Regret and Disappointment," *Organizational Behavior and Human Decision Processes* 75, no. 2 (1998): 117-41; B. A. Mellers, "Choice and the Relative Pleasure of Consequences," *Psychological Bulletin* 126, no. 6 (2000): 910-24; R. P. Bagozzi, U. M. Dholakia, and S. Basuroy, "How Effortful Decisions Get Enacted: The Motivating Role of Decision Processes, Desires, and Anticipated Emotions," *Journal of Behavioral Decision Making* 16, no. 4 (2003): 273-95. The neuropsychology of valences and its associated "expected utility" is discussed in A. Bechara and A. R. Damasio, "The Somatic Marker Hypothesis: A Neural Theory of Economic Decision," *Games and Economic Behavior* 52, no. 2 (2005): 336-72.

42. D. A. Nadler and E. E. Lawler, "Motivation: A Diagnostic Approach," in *Perspectives on Behavior in Organizations,* ed. J. R. Hackman, E. E. Lawler III, and L. W. Porter (New York: McGraw-Hill, 1983), 70-73.

43. A. Fisher, "Expecting a Fat Year-End Bonus? Don't Get Your Hopes Up," *Fortune*, December 5, 2012; U.S. Office of Personnel Management, *Federal Employee Viewpoint Survey* (Washington, DC: Office of Personnel Management, September 2016); Willis Towers Watson, *Under Pressure to Remain Relevant, Employers Look to Modernize the Employee Value Proposition* (London: Willis Towers Watson, September 9, 2016); Willis Towers Watson, "U.S. Employees Give Performance Management Programs Mediocre Grades," news release (Arlington, VA: Willis Towers Watson, December 6, 2016); Glassdoor, *Global Salary Transparency Survey: Employee Perceptions of Talking Pay* (Mill Valley, CA: Glassdoor, April 2016).

44. For recent applications of expectancy in diverse settings, see R. L. Purvis, T. J. Zagenczyk, and G. E. McCray, "What's in It for Me? Using Expectancy Theory and Climate to Explain Stakeholder Participation, Its Direction and Intensity," *International Journal of Project Management* 33, no. 1 (2015): 3-14; E. Shweiki et al., "Applying Expectancy Theory to Residency Training: Proposing Opportunities to Understand Resident Motivation and Enhance Residency Training," *Advances in Medical Education and Practice* 6 (2015): 339-46; K. N. Bauer et al., "Re-Examination of Motivation in Learning Contexts: Meta-Analytically Investigating the Role Type of Motivation Plays in the Prediction of Key Training Outcomes," *Journal of Business and Psychology* 31, no. 1 (2016): 33-50.

45. This limitation was recently acknowledged by Victor Vroom, who had introduced expectancy theory in his 1964 book. See G. P. Latham, *Work Motivation: History, Theory, Research, and Practice* (Thousand Oaks, CA: Sage, 2007), 47-48.

46. J. B. Watson, *Behavior: An Introduction to Comparative Psychology* (New York: Henry Holt, 1914).

47. B. F. Skinner, *About Behaviorism* (New York: Knopf, 1974); J. Komaki, T. Coombs, and S. Schepman, "Motivational Implications of Reinforcement Theory," in *Motivation and Leadership at Work*, ed. R. M. Steers, L. W. Porter, and G. A. Bigley (New York: McGraw-Hill, 1996), 34-52; R. G. Miltenberger, *Behavior Modification: Principles and Procedures* (Pacific Grove, CA: Brooks/Cole, 1997).

48. T. K. Connellan, *How to Improve Human Performance* (New York: Harper & Row, 1978), 48-57; F. Luthans and R. Kreitner, *Organizational Behavior Modification and Beyond* (Glenview, IL: Scott, Foresman, 1985), 85-88.

49. B. F. Skinner, *Science and Human Behavior* (New York: Free Press, 1965); R. G. Miltenberger, *Behavior Modification: Principles and Procedures* (Pacific Grove, CA: Brooks/Cole, 1997), chaps. 4-6.

50. T. R. Hinkin and C. A. Schriesheim, "'If You Don't Hear from Me You Know You Are Doing Fine,'" *Cornell Hotel & Restaurant Administration Quarterly* 45, no. 4 (2004): 362-72.

51. L. K. Trevino, "The Social Effects of Punishment in Organizations: A Justice Perspective," *Academy of Management Review* 17 (1992): 647–76; L. E. Atwater et al., "Recipient and Observer Reactions to Discipline: Are Managers Experiencing Wishful Thinking?," *Journal of Organizational Behavior* 22, no. 3 (2001): 249–70.

52. G. P. Latham and V. L. Huber, "Schedules of Reinforcement: Lessons from the Past and Issues for the Future," *Journal of Organizational Behavior Management* 13 (1992): 125–49; B. A. Williams, "Challenges to Timing-Based Theories of Operant Behavior," *Behavioural Processes* 62 (2003): 115–23.

53. J. A. Bargh and M. J. Ferguson, "Beyond Behaviorism: On the Automaticity of Higher Mental Processes," *Psychological Bulletin* 126, no. 6 (2000): 925–45. Some writers argue that behaviorists long ago accepted the relevance of cognitive processes in behavior modification. See I. Kirsch et al., "The Role of Cognition in Classical and Operant Conditioning," *Journal of Clinical Psychology* 60, no. 4 (2004): 369–92.

54. A. Bandura, *Social Foundations of Thought and Action: A Social Cognitive Theory* (Englewood Cliffs, NJ: Prentice Hall, 1986); A. Bandura, "Social Cognitive Theory of Self-Regulation," *Organizational Behavior and Human Decision Processes* 50, no. 2 (1991): 248–87; A. Bandura, "Social Cognitive Theory: An Agentic Perspective," *Annual Review of Psychology* 52, no. 1 (2001): 1–26.

55. M. E. Schnake, "Vicarious Punishment in a Work Setting," *Journal of Applied Psychology* 71 (1986): 343–45; L. K. Trevino, "The Social Effects of Punishment in Organizations: A Justice Perspective," *Academy of Management Review* 17 (1992): 647–76; J. Malouff et al., "Effects of Vicarious Punishment: A Meta-Analysis," *Journal of General Psychology* 136, no. 3 (2009): 271–86.

56. A. Pescuric and W. C. Byham, "The New Look of Behavior Modeling," *Training & Development* 50 (1996): 24–30.

57. A. Bandura, "Self-Reinforcement: Theoretical and Methodological Considerations," *Behaviorism* 4 (1976): 135–55; C. A. Frayne and J. M. Geringer, "Self-Management Training for Improving Job Performance: A Field Experiment Involving Salespeople," *Journal of Applied Psychology* 85, no. 3 (2000): 361–72; J. B. Vancouver and D. V. Day, "Industrial and Organisation Research on Self-Regulation: From Constructs to Applications," *Applied Psychology: An International Journal* 54, no. 2 (2005): 155–85.

58. City of Toronto, *Budget 2016: Internal and Financial Services: 311 Toronto* (Toronto: City of Toronto, 2016); City of Toronto, "Performance Reports: 311 Toronto" (Toronto: City of Toronto, 2017), http://www1.toronto.ca (accessed March 15, 2017).

59. E. A. Locke and G. P. Latham, *A Theory of Goal Setting and Task Performance* (Englewood Cliffs, NJ: Prentice Hall, 1990); G. P. Latham, "Goal Setting: A Five-Step Approach to Behavior Change," *Organizational Dynamics* 32, no. 3 (2003): 309–18.

60. There are several variations of the SMARTER goal-setting model; "achievable" is sometimes "acceptable," "reviewed" is sometimes "recorded," and "exciting" is sometimes "ethical." Based on the earlier SMART model, the SMARTER goal-setting model seems to originate in British sports psychology writing around the mid-1990s. For early examples, see P. Butler, *Performance Profiling* (Leeds, UK: The National Coaching Foundation, 1996), 36; R. C. Thelwell and I. A. Greenlees, "The Effects of a Mental Skills Training Program Package on Gymnasium Triathlon Performance," *The Sports Psychologist* 15, no. 2 (2001): 127–41.

61. The value and limitations of measurement are discussed in J. M. Henshaw, *Does Measurement Measure Up? How Numbers Reveal and Conceal the Truth* (Baltimore, MD: Johns Hopkins Press, 2006).

62. A. C. Crossley, C. Cooper, and T. Wernsing, "Making Things Happen through Challenging Goals: Leader Proactivity, Trust, and Business-Unit Performance," *Journal of Applied Psychology* 98, no. 3 (2013): 540–49; A. Kruglanski et al., "The Rocky Road from Attitudes to Behaviors: Charting the Goal Systemic Course of Actions," *Psychological Review* 122, no. 4 (2015): 598–620.

63. Z. Zhang and M. Jia, "How Can Companies Decrease the Disruptive Effects of Stretch Goals? The Moderating Role of Interpersonal—and Informational—Justice Climates," *Human Relations* 66, no. 7 (2013): 993–1020; L. D. Ordóñez and D. T. Welsh, "Immoral Goals: How Goal Setting May Lead to Unethical Behavior," *Current Opinion in Psychology* 6 (2015): 93–96.

64. E. A. Locke and G. P. Latham, *A Theory of Goal Setting and Task Performance* (Englewood Cliffs, NJ: Prentice Hall, 1990), chaps. 6 and 7; H. Klein, J. T. Cooper, and C. A. Monahan, "Goal Commitment," in *New Developments in Goal Setting and Task Performance*, ed. E. A. Locke and G. P. Latham (London: Taylor and Francis, 2012), 65–89.

65. M. London, E. M. Mone, and J. C. Scott, "Performance Management and Assessment: Methods for Improved Rater Accuracy and Employee Goal Setting," *Human Resource Management* 43, no. 4 (2004): 319–36; G. P. Latham and C. C. Pinder, "Work Motivation Theory and Research at the Dawn of the Twenty-First Century," *Annual Review of Psychology* 56 (2005): 485–516.

66. G. P. Latham, *Work Motivation: History, Theory, Research, and Practice* (Thousand Oaks, CA: Sage, 2007), 198–203; A. Baker et al., "Feedback and Organizations: Feedback Is Good, Feedback-Friendly Culture Is Better," *Canadian Psychology* 54, no. 4 (2013): 260–68.

67. Adobe Systems, *Adobe Check-In: Career Grows When Feedback Flows* (San Jose, CA: Adobe Systems, 2014), YouTube video; A. Fisher, "How Adobe Keeps Key Employees from Quitting," *Fortune*, June 16, 2015; P. Cappelli and A. Tavis, "The Performance Management Revolution," *Harvard Business Review* 94 (2016): 58–67; D. Morris, "2017: The Year Performance Reviews Get the Axe," *Conversations*, Adobe Systems, January 11, 2017, https://blogs.adobe.com/conversations; D. Morris, "Yes, You Can Reward Employees without Ratings and Rankings," *Conversations*, Adobe Systems, February 16, 2017, https://blogs.adobe.com/conversations.

68. P. Drucker, *The Effective Executive* (Oxford, UK: Butterworth-Heinemann, 2007), 22. Drucker's emphasis on strengths also was noted in D. K. Whitney and A. Trosten-Bloom, *The Power of Appreciative Inquiry: A Practical Guide to Positive Change*, 2nd ed. (San Francisco: Berrett-Koehler, 2010), xii.

69. M. Buckingham, *Go Put Your Strengths to Work* (New York: Free Press, 2007); A. L. Clancy and J. Binkert, "Appreciative Coaching: Pathway to Flourishing," in *Excellence in Coaching: The Industry Guide*, ed. J. Passmore (London: Kogan Page, 2010), 147–56; H. Aguinis, R. K. Gottfredson, and H. Joo, "Delivering Effective Performance Feedback: The Strengths-Based Approach," *Business Horizons* 55, no. 2 (2012): 105–11.

70. A. N. Kluger and D. Nir, "The Feedforward Interview," *Human Resource Management Review* 20, no. 3 (2010): 235–46; H. Aguinis, R. K. Gottfredson, and H. Joo, "Delivering Effective Performance Feedback: The Strengths-Based Approach," *Business Horizons* 55, no. 2 (2012): 105–11.

71. A. Terracciano, P. T. Costa, and R. R. McCrae, "Personality Plasticity after Age 30," *Personality and Social Psychology Bulletin* 32, no. 8 (2006): 999–1009; M. R. Leary, "Motivational and Emotional Aspects of the Self," *Annual Review of Psychology* 58, no. 1 (2007): 317–44.

72. Cited in H. Aguinis, R. K. Gottfredson, and H. Joo, "Delivering Effective Performance Feedback: The Strengths-Based Approach," *Business Horizons* 55, no. 2 (2012): 105–11.

73. J. W. Smither, M. London, and R. R. Reilly, "Does Performance Improve Following Multisource Feedback? A Theoretical Model, Meta-Analysis, and Review of Empirical Findings," *Personnel Psychology* 58, no. 1 (2005): 33–66; L. E. Atwater, J. F. Brett, and A. C. Charles, "Multisource Feedback: Lessons Learned and Implications for Practice," *Human Resource Management* 46, no. 2 (2007): 285–307; M. C. Campion, E. D. Campion, and M. A. Campion, "Improvements in Performance Management through the Use of 360 Feedback," *Industrial and Organizational Psychology* 8, no. 1 (2015): 85–93.

74. S. J. Ashford and G. B. Northcraft, "Conveying More (or Less) Than We Realize: The Role of Impression Management in Feedback Seeking," *Organizational Behavior and Human Decision Processes* 53 (1992): 310–34; J. R. Williams et al., "Increasing Feedback Seeking in Public Contexts: It Takes Two (or More) to Tango," *Journal of Applied Psychology* 84 (1999): 969–76.

75. J. B. Miner, "The Rated Importance, Scientific Validity, and Practical Usefulness of Organizational Behavior Theories: A Quantitative Review," *Academy of Management Learning and Education* 2, no. 3 (2003): 250–68. Also see C. C. Pinder, *Work Motivation in Organizational Behavior* (Upper Saddle River, NJ: Prentice Hall, 1998), 384.

76. P. M. Wright, "Goal Setting and Monetary Incentives: Motivational Tools That Can Work Too Well," *Compensation and Benefits Review* 26 (1994): 41–49; S. Kerr and D. LePelley, "Stretch Goals: Risks, Possibilities, and Best Practices," in *New Developments in Goal Setting and Task Performance*, ed. E. A. Locke and G. P. Latham (London: Taylor and Francis, 2012), 21–32; L. D. Ordóñez and D. T. Welsh, "Immoral Goals: How Goal Setting May Lead to Unethical Behavior," *Current Opinion in Psychology* 6 (2015): 93–96.

77. G. P. Latham, *Work Motivation: History, Theory, Research, and Practice* (Thousand Oaks, CA: Sage, 2007), 188.

78. J. A. Colquitt et al., "Justice at the Millennium, a Decade Later: A Meta-Analytic Test of Social Exchange and Affect-Based Perspectives," *Journal of Applied Psychology* 98, no. 2 (2013): 199–236; J. Brockner et al., "Riding the Fifth Wave: Organizational Justice as Dependent Variable," *Research in Organizational Behavior* 35 (2015): 103–21. The literature identifies up to six types of justice. However, we focus on the two main types and subsume interpersonal justice within procedural justice based on the idea that interpersonal justice is a procedural characteristic.

79. M. Deutsch, "Equity, Equality, and Need: What Determines Which Value Will Be Used as the Basis of Distributive Justice?," *Journal of Social Issues* 31, no. 3 (1975): 137–49; D.A. Morand and K.K. Merriman, "Equality Theory" as a Counterbalance to Equity Theory in Human Resource Management," *Journal of Business Ethics* 111, no. 1 (2012): 133–44; T. Reeskens and W. van Oorschot, "Equity, Equality, or Need? A Study of Popular Preferences for Welfare Redistribution Principles across 24 European Countries," *Journal of European Public Policy* 20, no. 8 (2013): 1174–95.

80. "B&T Salary Survey," *B&T Magazine* 64, no. 2812 (2015): 56–63; G. Plimmer and C. Cantal, *Workplace Dynamics in New Zealand Public Services*, Centre for Labour, Employment and Work (Wellington, NZ: Victoria University of Wellington, November 2016); Willis Towers Watson, "Only Half of U.S. Employees Think They Are Paid Fairly Compared to Counterparts," news release (Arlington, VA: Willis Towers Watson, November 10, 2016); *Comp Is Culture: 2017 Compensation Best Practices Report* (Seattle: PayScale, February 14, 2017).

81. J. S. Adams, "Toward an Understanding of Inequity," *Journal of Abnormal and Social Psychology* 67 (1963): 422–36; P. H. Siegel, M. Schraeder, and R. Morrison, "A Taxonomy of Equity Factors," *Journal of Applied Social Psychology* 38, no. 1 (2008): 61–75; R. Cropanzano, D. E. Bowen, and S. W. Gilliland, "The Management of Organizational Justice," *Academy of Management Perspectives* 21, no. 4 (2007): 34–48.

82. C. T. Kulik and M. L. Ambrose, "Personal and Situational Determinants of Referent Choice," *Academy of Management Review* 17 (1992): 212–37; J. Shin and Y. W. Sohn, "Effects of Employees' Social Comparison Behaviors on Distributive Justice Perception and Job Satisfaction," *Social Behavior and Personality* 43, no. 7 (2015): 1071–83; C. M. Sterling and G. Labianca, "Costly Comparisons: Managing Envy in the Workplace," *Organizational Dynamics* 44, no. 4 (2015): 296–305.

83. T. P. Summers and A. S. DeNisi, "In Search of Adams' Other: Reexamination of Referents Used in the Evaluation of Pay," *Human Relations* 43 (1990): 497–511.

84. The emotive dynamics of feelings of inequity are studied in A. W. Cappelen et al., "Equity Theory and Fair Inequality: A Neuroeconomic Study," *Proceedings of the National Academy of Sciences* 111, no. 43 (2014): 15368–72.

85. Y. Cohen-Charash and P. E. Spector, "The Role of Justice in Organizations: A Meta-Analysis," *Organizational Behavior and Human Decision Processes* 86 (2001): 278–321; B. Walker and R. T. Hamilton, "Employee–Employer Grievances: A Review," *International Journal of Management Reviews* 13, no. 1 (2011): 40–58; R. Cropanzano and C. Moliner, "Hazards of Justice: Egocentric Bias, Moral Judgments, and Revenge-Seeking," in *Deviant and Criminal Behavior in the Workplace*, ed. S. M. Elias (New York: New York University Press, 2013), 155–77; B. C. Holtz and C. M. Harold, "Interpersonal Justice and Deviance: The Moderating Effects of Interpersonal Justice Values and Justice Orientation," *Journal of Management* 39, no. 2 (2013): 339–65; C. L. Wilkin and C. E. Connelly, "Green with Envy and Nerves of Steel: Moderated Mediation between Distributive Justice and Theft," *Personality and Individual Differences* 72 (2015): 160–64.

86. Canadian Press, "Pierre Berton, Canadian Cultural Icon, Enjoyed Long and Colourful Career," *Times Colonist* (Victoria, BC), November 30, 2004.

87. J. Fizel, A. C. Krautman, and L. Hadley, "Equity and Arbitration in Major League Baseball," *Managerial and Decision Economics* 23, no. 7 (2002): 427–35; M. Ezzamel and R. Watson, "Pay Comparability across and within UK Boards: An Empirical Analysis of the Cash Pay Awards to CEOs and Other Board Members," *Journal of Management Studies* 39, no. 2 (2002): 207–32.

88. D. R. Bobocel and L. Gosse, "Procedural Justice: A Historical Review and Critical Analysis," in *Oxford Handbook of Justice in the Workplace*, ed. R. S. Cropanzano and M. L. Ambrose (New York: Oxford University Press, 2015), 51–88.

89. J. Greenberg and E. A. Lind, "The Pursuit of Organizational Justice: From Conceptualization to Implication to Application," in *Industrial and Organizational Psychology: Linking Theory with Practice*, ed. C. L. Cooper and E. A. Locke (London: Blackwell, 2000), 72–108 ; C. B. Goldberg, M. A. Clark, and A. B. Henley, "Speaking Up: A Conceptual Model of Voice Responses Following the Unfair Treatment of Others in Non-Union Settings," *Human Resource Management* 50, no. 1 (2011): 75–94; M. R. Bashshur, "When Voice Matters: A Multilevel Review of the Impact of Voice in Organizations," *Journal of Management* 41, no. 5 (2015): 1530–54.

90. R. Hagey et al., "Immigrant Nurses' Experience of Racism," *Journal of Nursing Scholarship* 33 (2001): 389-95; K. Roberts and K. S. Markel, "Claiming in the Name of Fairness: Organizational Justice and the Decision to File for Workplace Injury Compensation," *Journal of Occupational Health Psychology* 6 (2001): 332-47; D. A. Jones and D. P. Skarlicki, "The Effects of Overhearing Peers Discuss an Authority's Fairness Reputation on Reactions to Subsequent Treatment," *Journal of Applied Psychology* 90, no. 2 (2005): 363-72.

91. D. T. Miller, "Disrespect and the Experience of Injustice," *Annual Review of Psychology* 52 (2001): 527-53.

92. M. L. Ambrose, M. A. Seabright, and M. Schminke, "Sabotage in the Workplace: The Role of Organizational Injustice," *Organizational Behavior and Human Decision Processes* 89, no. 1 (2002): 947-65.

93. M. A. Campion et al., "Work Redesign: Eight Obstacles and Opportunities," *Human Resource Management* 44, no. 4 (2005): 367-90; S.-J. Cullinane et al., "Job Design under Lean Manufacturing and Its Impact on Employee Outcomes," *Organizational Psychology Review* 3, no. 1 (2013): 41-61.

94. A. Shinnar et al., "Survey of Ergonomic Features of Supermarket Cash Registers," *International Journal of Industrial Ergonomics* 34, no. 6 (2004): 535-41; V. O'Connell, "Stores Count Seconds to Trim Labor Costs," *The Wall Street Journal*, November 13, 2008; A. Kihlstedt and G. M. Hägg, "Checkout Cashier Work and Counter Design—Video Movement Analysis, Musculoskeletal Disorders and Customer Interaction," *International Journal of Industrial Ergonomics* 41, no. 3 (2011): 201-07; "One Checkout Item Every Three Seconds," *Mail Online* (London), July 8, 2012. Average scanning times vary considerably with the scanning technology, product standardization, and ergonomic design of the cashier station.

95. S. Leroy, "Why Is It So Hard to Do My Work? The Challenge of Attention Residue When Switching between Work Tasks," *Organizational Behavior and Human Decision Processes* 109, no. 2 (2009): 168-81.

96. H. Fayol, *General and Industrial Management*, trans. C. Storrs (London: Pitman, 1949); E. E. Lawler III, *Motivation in Work Organizations* (Monterey, CA: Brooks/Cole, 1973), chap. 7; M. A. Campion, "Ability Requirement Implications of Job Design: An Interdisciplinary Perspective," *Personnel Psychology* 42 (1989): 1-24.

97. A. Smith, *An Inquiry into the Nature and Causes of the Wealth of Nations*, ed. E. Cannan, 5th ed. (London: Methuen and Co., 1904), 8-9.

98. F. W. Taylor, *The Principles of Scientific Management* (New York: Harper & Row, 1911); R. Kanigel, *The One Best Way: Frederick Winslow Taylor and the Enigma of Efficiency* (New York: Viking, 1997); M. Derksen, "Turning Men into Machines? Scientific Management, Industrial Psychology, and the 'Human Factor,'" *Journal of the History of the Behavioral Sciences* 50, no. 2 (2014): 148-65.

99. C. R. Walker and R. H. Guest, *The Man on the Assembly Line* (Cambridge, MA: Harvard University Press, 1952); W. F. Dowling, "Job Redesign on the Assembly Line: Farewell to Blue-Collar Blues?," *Organizational Dynamics* (1973): 51-67; E. E. Lawler III, *High-Involvement Management* (San Francisco: Jossey-Bass, 1986).

100. R. Moorhead, "Lawyer Specialization—Managing the Professional Paradox," *Law & Policy* 32, no. 2 (2010): 226-59.

101. M. Keller, *Rude Awakening* (New York: Harper Perennial, 1989), 128.

102. J. R. Hackman and G. Oldham, *Work Redesign* (Reading, MA: Addison-Wesley, 1980).

103. M. Gagné and D. Bhave, "Autonomy in the Workplace: An Essential Ingredient to Employee Engagement and Well-Being in Every Culture," in *Human Autonomy in Cross-Cultural Context,* ed. V. I. Chirkov, R. M. Ryan, and K. M. Sheldon, Cross-Cultural Advancements in Positive Psychology (Springer: Netherlands, 2011), 163-87.

104. R. Feintzeig, "I Don't Have a Job—I Have a Higher Calling," *The Wall Street Journal*, February 25, 2015, B1; B. N. Pfau, "How an Accounting Firm Convinced Its Employees They Could Change the World," *Harvard Business Review Blog*, October 6, 2015.

105. C. E. Shalley, L. L. Gilson, and T. C. Blum, "Interactive Effects of Growth Need Strength, Work Context, and Job Complexity on Self-Reported Creative Performance," *Academy of Management Journal* 52, no. 3 (2009): 489-505.

106. R. B. Tiegs, L. E. Tetrick, and Y. Fried, "Growth Need Strength and Context Satisfactions as Moderators of the Relations of the Job Characteristics Model," *Journal of Management* 18, no. 3 (1992): 575-93; J. E. Champoux, "A Multivariate Test of the Job Characteristics Theory of Work Motivation," *Journal of Organizational Behavior* 12, no. 5 (1991): 431-46.

107. G. R. Oldham and J. R. Hackman, "Not What It Was and Not What It Will Be: The Future of Job Design Research," *Journal of Organizational Behavior* 31, no. 2-3 (2010): 463-79; A. M. Grant, Y. Fried, and T. Juillerat, "Work Matters: Job Design in Classic and Contemporary Perspectives," in *APA Handbook of Industrial and Organizational Psychology,* ed. S. Zedeck (Washington, DC: American Psychological Association, 2011), 417-53.

108. C. Perrow, "A Framework for the Comparative Analysis of Organizations," *American Sociological Review* 32, no. 2 (1967): 194-208; R. L. Daft and N. B. Macintosh, "A Tentative Exploration into the Amount and Equivocality of Information Processing in Organizational Work Units," *Administrative Science Quarterly* 26, no. 2 (1981): 207-24. This job characteristics category is part of "job complexity," the latter of which has too many dimensions and interpretations. See P. Liu and Z. Li, "Task Complexity: A Review and Conceptualization Framework," *International Journal of Industrial Ergonomics* 42, no. 6 (2012): 553-68.

109. J. R. Hackman et al., "A New Strategy for Job Enrichment," *California Management Review* 17, no. 4 (1975): 57-71; R. W. Griffin, *Task Design: An Integrative Approach* (Glenview, IL: Scott Foresman, 1982).

110. P. E. Spector and S. M. Jex, "Relations of Job Characteristics from Multiple Data Sources with Employee Affect, Absence, Turnover Intentions, and Health," *Journal of Applied Psychology* 76 (1991): 46-53; P. Osterman, "How Common Is Workplace Transformation and Who Adopts It?," *Industrial and Labor Relations Review* 47 (1994): 173-88; R. Saavedra and S. K. Kwun, "Affective States in Job Characteristics Theory," *Journal of Organizational Behavior* 21 (2000): 131-46.

111. J. R. Hackman and G. Oldham, *Work Redesign* (Reading, MA: Addison-Wesley, 1980), 137-38.

6 | Decision Making and Creativity

Learning Objectives

After you read this chapter, you should be able to:

LO6-1 Describe the elements of rational choice decision making.

LO6-2 Explain why people differ from rational choice decision making when identifying problems/opportunities, evaluating/choosing alternatives, and evaluating decision outcomes.

LO6-3 Discuss the roles of emotions and intuition in decision making.

LO6-4 Describe employee characteristics, workplace conditions, and specific activities that support creativity.

LO6-5 Describe the benefits of employee involvement and identify four contingencies that affect the optimal level of employee involvement.

decision making the conscious process of making choices among alternatives with the intention of moving toward some desired state of affairs

Target Corporation saw a unique opportunity to realize its dream of international expansion when a Canadian discount retail chain (Zellers) was put up for sale. Target executives believed that acquiring an existing business would give it a solid start against Walmart, which was already well-established in Canada and may have otherwise bought parts or all of Zellers. Canada also was appealing because of its geographic and cultural proximity and because it experienced a less severe recession a few years earlier compared to the United States. At the time of the Zellers acquisition, Target was enjoying solid growth, which made the executive team more confident that the Canadian expansion also would succeed.

Target moved quickly—too quickly, according to some critics. It launched three test stores a few months after the takeover, then 21 more a few months later. In spite of logistical and store refitting problems, another 100 Target stores opened across Canada within the first year. But even before the first store, executives discovered problems with the distribution, sales checkout, and technology systems. The distribution system failure alone led to severe inventory shortages and empty shelves. Some critics also claimed that Zellers stores were in poor locations, making it difficult for Target Canada to attract customers.

But perhaps the greatest misstep was that Target underestimated the level of competition in the Canadian discount retail market. "We were not as sharp on pricing as we should have been, which led to pricing perception issues," admitted Target chairman and CEO Brian Cornell. "Unfortunately, the negative guest (customer) sentiment became too much to overcome." Cornell, who joined Target a year after the company expanded into Canada, shut down the Canadian business. Target took a $5.4 billion write down of the Canadian operations, a business that was open for business for just two years.[1]

Target Corporation and every other organization depend on effective decision making to effectively allocate resources, improve products and services, and more generally maintain a good fit with the external environment. Decision making is not only a critical management skill; it is also a core activity for all staff members directly in their jobs and through employee involvement. This chapter examines each of these themes. We begin by discussing the rational choice view of decision making. Next, the human limitations of rational choice are discussed. We also examine the emerging view that decisions consist of a complex interaction of logic and emotion. The latter part of this chapter focuses on two topics that intertwine with decision making: creativity and employee involvement.

> **LO6-1** Describe the elements of rational choice decision making.

RATIONAL CHOICE DECISION MAKING

Decision making is the process of making choices among alternatives with the intention of moving toward some desired state of affairs.[2] This is vital to an organization's health, rather like breathing is to a human being. Indeed, leaders increasingly view themselves as physicians who resuscitate organizations by encouraging and teaching employees at all levels to make decisions more effectively and creatively. All businesses, governments, and not-for-profit agencies depend on employees to foresee and correctly identify problems, to survey alternatives, to pick the best alternative based on several relevant factors, and to execute those decisions effectively.

Rational choice decision making selects the best alternative by calculating the probability that various outcomes will occur from the choices and the expected satisfaction from each of those outcomes.
©ESB Professional/Shutterstock

How should people make decisions in organizations? Most business leaders would likely answer this question by saying that effective decision making involves identifying, selecting, and applying the best possible alternative. In other words, the best decisions use pure logic and all available information to choose the alternative with the highest value—such as highest expected profitability, customer satisfaction, employee well-being, or some combination of these outcomes. These decisions sometimes involve complex calculations of data to produce a formula that points to the best choice.

In its extreme form, rational choice decision making has dominated in Western societies for most of written history.[4] It was established 2,500 years ago when Plato and his contemporaries in ancient Greece raised logical debate and reasoning to a fine art. About 400 years ago, Descartes and other European philosophers emphasized that the ability to make logical decisions is one of the most important accomplishments of human beings. In the 1700s, Scottish philosophers refined the notion that the best choice is the one that offers the greatest satisfaction.

Rational choice decision making selects the best alternative by calculating the probability that various outcomes will occur from the choices and the expected satisfaction from each of those outcomes.[5] We have already seen how similar calculations of probability and valences are used in two earlier organizational behavior theories, namely the attitude model in Chapter 4 and expectancy theory of motivation in Chapter 5.

To understand the rational choice calculation, consider the example in Exhibit 6.1.[6] Your company wants to choose a new supplier of a particular raw material, and the preferred supplier should be the best based on three outcomes (called selection criteria): Does the supplier provide a high-quality product (+9) with low prices (+6) and on-time delivery (+4)?[7] The numbers, which are on a plus or minus 10-point scale, indicate each outcome's importance or expected satisfaction (valence). You discover that supplier A has excellent on-time delivery (about 90 percent probability of exceeding the company's expectations) whereas it has a 70 percent probability of reliably providing a product with exceptional quality. Supplier B has a 90 percent chance of providing very high product quality but a lower likelihood (40 percent) of offering the best prices.

Which of these two suppliers should be selected? A rational choice decision maker would choose Supplier A because that company offers the greatest satisfaction (expected positive emotions). This satisfaction is calculated by multiplying the

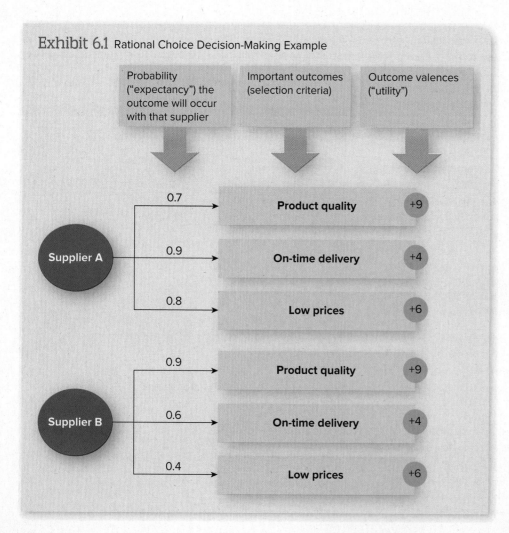

Exhibit 6.1 Rational Choice Decision-Making Example

valence of each outcome with the probability of that outcome occurring, then adding those results across all three outcomes. The supplier with the higher score is the better choice, given available information. The key point from this example is that all rational decisions rely primarily on two pieces of information: (a) the probability that each outcome will occur and (b) the valence or expected satisfaction of each outcome.

Rational Choice Decision-Making Process

Calculating the best alternative is at the heart of rational choice decision making, but it goes hand-in-hand with the systematic decision process illustrated in Exhibit 6.2.[8] The first step is to identify the problem or recognize an opportunity. A *problem* is a deviation between the current and the desired situation—the gap between "what is" and "what ought to be." This deviation is a symptom of more fundamental causes that need to be corrected.[9] The "ought to be" refers to goals, and these goals later help evaluate the selected choice. For instance, if a customer contact center's goal is to answer incoming client calls within 30 seconds, the problem is the gap between that goal and the actual time the contact center takes to answer most client calls. An *opportunity* is a deviation between current expectations and a potentially better situation that was not previously expected. In other words, an opportunity exists when decision makers discover that some choices may produce better results than current goals or expectations.

The second step involves choosing the best decision process. This step is really a meta-decision—deciding how to decide—because it refers to choosing among the different approaches and processes to make the decision.[10] One meta-decision is whether to solve the problem alone or involve others in the process.

Later in this chapter, we'll examine the contingencies of employee involvement in decision making. Another meta-decision is whether to assume the decision is programmed or nonprogrammed. *Programmed decisions* follow standard operating procedures; they have been resolved in the past, so the optimal solution has already been identified and documented. In contrast, *nonprogrammed decisions* require all steps in the decision model because the problems are new, complex, or ill-defined.

The third step in the rational choice decision process is to identify and/or develop a list of possible choices. This usually begins by searching for ready-made solutions, such as practices that have worked well on similar problems. If an acceptable solution cannot be found, then decision makers need to design a custom-made solution or modify an existing one. The fourth step is to select the best choice by applying the rational choice calculation we described in Exhibit 6.1. Choosing the alternative that offers the greatest satisfaction or value requires the decision maker to have information about all possible alternatives and their outcomes. That condition is usually impossible, but the rational choice view of decision making assumes this can be accomplished with ease.

The fifth step is to implement the selected alternative. Rational choice decision making assumes that implementation occurs without any problems. The final step is to evaluate whether the gap has narrowed between "what is" and "what ought to be." Ideally, this information should come from systematic benchmarks so that relevant feedback is objective and easily observed.

Problems with Rational Choice Decision Making

The rational choice view of decision making seems so logical, yet there are several reasons why it is impossible to apply in reality.[11] Therefore, we need to understand why people have imperfect rationality. Over the next several pages we reexamine each step in the rational choice decision-making process, but with more detail about what really happens through the lens of "imperfect rationality."

LO6-2 Explain why people differ from rational choice decision making when identifying problems/opportunities, evaluating/choosing alternatives, and evaluating decision outcomes.

IDENTIFYING PROBLEMS AND OPPORTUNITIES

When Albert Einstein was asked how he would save the world in one hour, he replied that the first 55 minutes should be spent defining the problem and the last 5 minutes solving it.[12] Einstein's point is that problem identification is not just the first step in decision making; it is arguably the most important step. But problems and opportunities are not clearly labeled objects

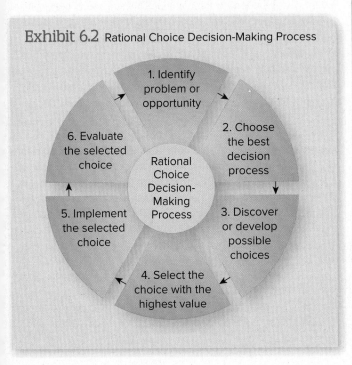

Exhibit 6.2 Rational Choice Decision-Making Process

Rational Choice Decision-Making Process

1. Identify problem or opportunity
2. Choose the best decision process
3. Discover or develop possible choices
4. Select the choice with the highest value
5. Implement the selected choice
6. Evaluate the selected choice

that appear on our desks. Instead, they are conclusions that we form from ambiguous and conflicting information.[13]

Problems with Problem Identification

The problem identification stage is, itself, filled with problems. Here are five of the most widely recognized concerns.[14]

Mental Models Decision makers are victims of their own problem framing due to existing mental models. **Mental models** are knowledge structures that we develop to describe, explain, and predict the world around us. They fill in information that we don't immediately see, which helps us understand and navigate in our surrounding environment (see Chapter 3). Many mental images are also prototypes—they represent models of how things should be. Unfortunately, these mental models can blind us from seeing unique problems or opportunities because they produce a negative evaluation of things that deviate from the mental model. If an idea doesn't fit the existing mental model of how things should work, then it is quickly dismissed as unworkable or undesirable.

Decisive Leadership Various studies have found that executives are valued for their decisiveness, including how quickly they determine that the situation is a problem, opportunity, or nothing worth their attention.[16] Consequently, many leaders announce problems or opportunities before having a chance to logically assess the situation. The result is often a misguided effort to solve an ill-defined problem or resources wasted on a poorly identified opportunity.

Stakeholder Framing Employees, suppliers, customers, and other stakeholders provide (or hide) information in ways that make the decision maker see the situation as a problem, opportunity, or steady sailing. Employees point to external factors rather than their own faults as the cause of production delays. Suppliers market their new products as unique opportunities and competitor products as problems to be avoided. Many other stakeholders also offer concise evaluations of the situation in the hope the decision maker will accept their verdict without further analysis. Decision makers fall prey to these constructed realities because they have a need to simplify the daily bombardment of complex and often ambiguous information.

Perceptual Defense People sometimes fail to become aware of problems because they block out bad news as a coping mechanism. Their brain refuses to see information that threatens their self-concept. The tendency to engage in perceptual defense varies from one decision maker to the next. Studies also report that perceptual defense is more common when decision makers have limited options to solve the problem.[17]

Solution-Focused Problems Some decision makers describe the problem as a veiled solution.[18] For instance, someone might say: "The problem is that we need more control over our suppliers." This isn't a description of the problem; it is a rephrased statement of a solution to a problem that has not been adequately diagnosed. One reason why people fall into the solution-focused

I suppose it is tempting, if the only tool you have is a hammer, to treat everything as if it were a nail.[19]

—Abraham Maslow, psychologist and scholar

problem trap is that they have been reinforced by past successes, so those solutions quickly come to mind when new problems arise. Solution-focused problem identification also occurs because decision makers are comforted by closure to problems, so they seek out solutions while still defining the problem. Unfortunately, they fail to fully diagnose the underlying causes that need to be addressed.

Identifying Problems and Opportunities More Effectively

Recognizing problems and opportunities will always be a challenge, but one way to improve the process is by becoming aware of the five problem identification biases just described. For example, by recognizing that mental models restrict a person's perspective of the world, decision makers are more motivated to consider other perspectives of reality. Along with increasing their awareness of problem identification flaws, leaders require considerable willpower to resist the temptation of looking decisive when a more thoughtful examination of the situation should occur.

A third way to improve problem identification is to create a norm of "divine discontent." Decision makers with this mindset are never satisfied with current conditions, so they more actively search for problems and opportunities.[20] Fourth, employees can minimize problem identification errors by discussing the situation with colleagues and clients. It is much easier to discover blind spots in problem identification when listening to how others perceive the situation. Opportunities also become apparent when outsiders explore this information from their different mental models.

SEARCHING FOR, EVALUATING, AND CHOOSING ALTERNATIVES

According to rational choice decision making, people rely on logic to evaluate and choose alternatives. This view assumes that decision makers have well-articulated and agreed-on organizational goals, that they efficiently and simultaneously process facts about all alternatives and the consequences of those alternatives, and that they choose the alternative with the highest payoff.

Nobel Prize–winning organizational scholar Herbert Simon questioned these assumptions a half century ago. He argued that people engage in **bounded rationality**. Specifically, they process limited and imperfect information and rarely try to select the best choice.[21] Bounded rationality is the dominant theory explaining why it is impossible to apply rational choice decision making. However, other theories point to additional flaws overlooked by bounded rationality. Collectively, these imperfect rationality theories identify several ways that human decision making differs from rational choice decision making, as illustrated in Exhibit 6.3. These differences are so significant that many economists are now moving away from rational choice assumptions in their theories. Let's look at these differences in terms of goals, information processing, and maximization.

Problems with Goals

The rational choice view assumes that organizational goals are clear and agreed on. Goals are necessary to identify "what ought to be" and, therefore, provide a standard against which each alternative is evaluated. Unfortunately, organizational goals are often ambiguous or in conflict with each other.[22] Ambiguous goals make it difficult to know if a particular choice has greater value to the organization. For example, "satisfy customer needs" may refer to providing efficient service, a variety of services, more personalized service, and other possibilities. When goals conflict, decision makers rarely have a guide map to determine which ones should take priority.

Problems with Information Processing

Rational choice decision making also makes several questionable assumptions about the human capacity to process information. It assumes that decision makers can process information about all alternatives and their consequences. In reality, people evaluate only a few alternatives and only some of the main outcomes of those alternatives.[23] For example, there are more than a dozen tablet brands to choose from and dozens of features to consider, yet people typically evaluate only a few brands and a few features.

A related problem is that decision makers typically evaluate alternatives sequentially rather than all at the same time. This sequential evaluation occurs partly because all alternatives are not usually available to the decision maker at the same time.[25] Consequently, as a new alternative comes along, it is compared to an **implicit favorite**—an alternative that the decision maker prefers

mental models knowledge structures that we develop to describe, explain, and predict the world around us

bounded rationality the view that people are bounded in their decision-making capabilities, including access to limited information, limited information processing, and tendency toward satisficing rather than maximizing when making choices

implicit favorite a preferred alternative that the decision maker uses repeatedly as a comparison with other choices

confirmation bias the process of screening out information that is contrary to our values and assumptions, and to more readily accept confirming information

and that is used as a comparison with other choices. When choosing a new tablet, for example, people typically have an implicit favorite brand or model against which they compare the other brands. Sometimes, decision makers aren't even aware of this favoritism![26]

Why do decision makers rely on an implicit favorite? One reason is that human beings like to compare two choices rather than systematically evaluate many alternatives at the same time.[27] An implicit favorite becomes a common anchor point against which to compare all other choices one at a time. A second reason is because people are cognitive misers. They minimize mental effort by forming preferences quickly, and then looking mainly for evidence that supports the preference. In other words, they engage in **confirmation bias**, which we discussed in Chapter 3.[28]

Decision makers have an implicit favorite because of their need to form preferences quickly, compare options, and maintain consistency between their decision and attitudes.
©Mirexon/Shutterstock

> ❝ Some problems are so complex that you have to be highly intelligent and well-informed just to be undecided about them.[24] ❞
>
> —Laurence J. Peter, educational scholar and author

Exhibit 6.3 Rational Choice Assumptions versus Organizational Behavior Findings about Choosing Alternatives

Rational choice paradigm assumptions	Observations from organizational behavior
Goals are clear, compatible, and agreed upon.	Goals are ambiguous, are in conflict, and lack full support.
Decision makers can calculate all alternatives and their outcomes.	Decision makers have limited information-processing abilities.
Decision makers evaluate all alternatives simultaneously.	Decision makers evaluate alternatives sequentially.
Decision makers use absolute standards to evaluate alternatives.	Decision makers evaluate alternatives against an implicit favorite.
Decision makers use factual information to choose alternatives.	Decision makers process perceptually distorted information.
Decision makers choose the alternative with the highest payoff.	Decision makers choose the alternative that is good enough (satisficing).

But likely the main reason why decision makers compare alternatives against an implicit favorite is the hard-wired human need to minimize **cognitive dissonance** (see Chapter 4).[29] Just as people want their behavior to be consistent with their attitudes, decision makers want their choices to be consistent with their beliefs and feelings about which alternative offers the highest satisfaction. Therefore, they distort information (usually nonconsciously) to ensure it supports an implicit favorite. This information distortion during the decision-making process includes ignoring or underweighting problems with the implicit favorite, overweighting attributes in which the implicit favorite is better, underweighting features in which the alternative is superior, and overweighting problems with the alternative.

Biased Decision Heuristics The cornerstone of rational choice decision making is to calculate the alternative with the highest satisfaction. However, psychologists Amos Tversky and Daniel Kahneman discovered that human beings have built-in *decision heuristics* that automatically distort those calculations. Three of the most widely studied heuristic biases are anchoring and adjustment, availability, and representativeness:[30]

- **Anchoring and adjustment heuristic.** This heuristic states that we are influenced by an initial anchor point and do not sufficiently move away from that point as new information is provided.[31] The anchor point might be an initial offer price, initial opinion of someone, or initial estimated probability that something will occur. One explanation for this effect is that human beings tend to compare alternatives rather than evaluate them purely against objective criteria. Therefore, if someone requests a high initial price for a car we want to buy, we naturally compare—and thereby anchor—our alternative offer against that high initial price.

- **Availability heuristic.** The availability heuristic is the tendency to estimate the probability of something occurring by how easily we can recall those events. Unfortunately, how easily we recall something is due to more than just its frequency (probability).[32] For instance, we easily remember emotional events (such as earthquakes and shark attacks), so we overestimate how often these traumatic events occur. We also have an easier time recalling recent events. If the media report several incidents of air pollution, we likely give more pessimistic estimates of air quality generally than if there have been no recent reports.

- **Representativeness heuristic.** This heuristic states that we pay more attention to whether something resembles (is representative of) something else than to more precise statistics about its probability.[33] Suppose that one-fifth of the students in your class are in engineering and the others are business majors. There is only a 20 percent chance that any classmate is from engineering, yet we don't hesitate to assume a student is from engineering if he or she looks and acts like (is representative of) our stereotype of an engineering student.

Problems with Maximization

One of the main assumptions of the rational choice decision making is that people want to—and are able to—choose the alternative with the highest payoff. Yet rather than aiming for maximization, people tend to engage in **satisficing**—they choose an alternative that is satisfactory or "good enough."[34] People satisfice when they select the first alternative that exceeds a standard of acceptance for their needs and preferences.

Satisficing—or at least choosing a standard below maximization—is usually necessary because decision makers lack enough information, time, and information processing capacity to figure out the best choice. Studies report that people like to have choices, but making decisions when there are many alternatives can be cognitively and emotionally draining. Consequently, decision makers satisfice as a way to minimize cognitive effort.[35] They also respond to a large number of choices by discarding many of them using easily identifiable factors (e.g., color, size) and by evaluating alternatives using only a handful of criteria.

Satisficing also occurs because alternatives present themselves over time, not all at once. Consider the process of hiring new employees. It is impossible to choose the best possible job candidate because people apply over a period of time and the best candidate might not apply until next month, after earlier

Decision makers minimize cognitive effort by satisficing, which includes setting "good enough" standards and evaluating alternatives using a few easily observable criteria.
©Racorn/Shutterstock

candidates have found other jobs. Consequently, decision makers rely on sequential evaluation of new alternatives against an implicit favorite. This necessarily calls for a satisficing decision rule—choose the first alternative that is "good enough."

Maximization—or at least human attempts to choose the best alternative—can result in better decisions when some alternatives are clearly better than others. But maximizing decision makers run into trouble where there are many alternatives, those alternatives have many features, and the quality of those features for each alternative is ambiguous. For example, it is difficult to choose the best possible car because of the large number of choices, the many features to consider for each choice, and the unclear qualities of some of those features. Under those conditions, maximization leads to a spiral of endless trade-offs among features across the various choices, which can actually result in worse decisions and less satisfied decision makers.[36]

When presented with a large number of choices, people often choose a decision strategy

Moods and specific emotions influence the process of evaluating alternatives.
©Ned Frisk/Blend Images LLC

that is even less cognitively challenging than satisficing; they don't make any decision at all! In one study, grocery store customers saw one of two jam-tasting booths. Thirty percent of consumers who visited the booth displaying 6 types of jam purchased one of those products. In contrast, only 3 percent of customers who saw the booth displaying 24 types of jam made a purchase. The larger number of choices discouraged them from making any decision. Other studies revealed similar results in decisions about chocolates, term essays, and pension plan investment options.[37]

Selecting Opportunities

Opportunities are just as important as problems, but what happens when an opportunity is "discovered" and selected is quite different from the process of problem solving. Decision makers seldom choose from among several opportunities; after all, the opportunity *is* the solution, so why look for others! An opportunity is usually experienced as an exciting and rare revelation, so decision makers tend to have an emotional attachment to the opportunity. Unfortunately, this emotional preference motivates decision makers to implement the opportunity and short-circuit any detailed assessment of it.[38]

LO6-3 Discuss the roles of emotions and intuition in decision making.

Emotions and Making Choices

Over the previous pages, we described the findings by Herbert Simon and other experts about how people are far from perfect at rational decision making. However, these scholars neglected

to mention another problem: The rational choice view completely ignores the effect of emotions in human decision making. Just as both the rational and emotional brain centers alert us to problems, they also influence our choice of alternatives.[39] Emotions affect the evaluation of alternatives in three ways.

Emotions Form Early Preferences The emotional marker process described in previous chapters (Chapters 3, 4, and 5) shapes our preference for each alternative before we consciously evaluate those alternatives. Our brain very quickly attaches specific emotions to information about each alternative, and our preferred alternative is strongly influenced by those initial emotional markers.[40] Of course, logical analysis also influences which alternative we choose, but it requires strong logical evidence to change our initial preferences (initial emotional markers). Yet even logical analysis depends on emotions to sway our decision. Specifically, neuroscientific evidence says that information produced from logical analysis is tagged with emotional markers that then motivate us to choose or avoid a particular alternative. Ultimately, emotions, not rational logic, energize us to make the preferred choice. In fact, people with damaged emotional brain centers have difficulty making choices.

Emotions Change the Decision Evaluation Process Moods and specific emotions influence the *process* of evaluating alternatives.[41] For instance, we pay more attention to details when in a negative mood, possibly because a negative mood signals that there is something wrong that requires attention. When in a positive mood, on the other hand, we pay less attention to details and rely on a more programmed decision routine. This phenomenon explains why executive teams in successful companies are often less vigilant about competitors and other environmental threats.[42] Research also suggests that decision makers rely on stereotypes and other shortcuts to speed up the choice process when they experience anger. Anger also makes them more optimistic about the success of risky alternatives, whereas the emotion of fear tends to make them less optimistic. Overall, emotions shape *how* we evaluate information, not just which choice we select.

Emotions Serve as Information When We Evaluate Alternatives The third way that emotions influence the evaluation of alternatives is through a process called "emotions as information." Marketing experts have found that we listen in on our emotions to gain guidance when making choices.[43] This intuition the ability to know when a problem or opportunity exists and to select the best course of action without conscious reasoning

process is similar to having a temporary improvement in emotional intelligence. Most emotional experiences remain below the level of conscious awareness, but people actively try to be more sensitive to these subtle emotions when making a decision.

When buying a new car, for example, you not only logically evaluate each vehicle's features; you also try to gauge your emotions when visualizing what it would be like to own each of the cars on your list of choices. Even if you have solid information about the quality of each vehicle on key features (purchase price, fuel efficiency, maintenance costs, resale value, etc.), you are swayed by your emotional reaction and actively try to sense that emotional response when thinking about it. Everyone consciously pays attention to his or her emotions to some degree when choosing alternatives. This phenomenon ties directly into our next topic, intuition.

Intuition and Making Choices

Do you rely on your "gut instinct" to help make decisions? These emotional experiences potentially (but not necessarily) indicate your intuition—the ability to know when a problem or opportunity exists and to select the best course of action without conscious reasoning.[44] Some people rely more on intuition, whereas others rely more on logical analysis when making decisions (see Chapter 2 on the MBTI thinking versus feeling orientation). However, emotions are always present in human decision making, so intuition and logical analysis are not opposites and never completely replace each other.[45] Some people pay more attention to emotional signals, whereas others pay more attention to logic, but emotions are always involved.

Intuition is both an emotional experience and a rapid nonconscious analytic process. The gut feelings we experience are emotional signals that have enough intensity to make us consciously aware of them. These signals warn us of impending danger or motivate us to take advantage of an opportunity. Some intuition also directs us to preferred choices relative to other alternatives in the situation.

All gut feelings are emotional signals, but not all emotional signals are intuition. The main distinction is that intuition involves rapidly comparing our observations with deeply held patterns learned through experience.[46] These "templates of the mind" represent tacit knowledge that has been implicitly acquired over time. They are mental models that help us understand whether the current situation is good or bad, depending on how well that situation fits our mental model. When a template fits or doesn't fit the current situation, emotions are produced that motivate us to act. Studies have found that when chess masters quickly scan a chessboard, they experience emotional signals that the chess configuration poses an opportunity or threat. These emotional signals motivate closer observation to logically confirm the situation and to act on it. Thus, intuition signals that a problem or opportunity exists long before conscious rational analysis has occurred.

A key message here is that some emotional signals are not intuition, so gut feelings shouldn't always guide our decisions. The problem is that emotional responses are not always based on well-grounded mental models. Instead, we sometimes compare the current situation to more remote templates, which may or may not be relevant. A new employee might feel confident about relations with a supplier, whereas an experienced employee senses potential problems. The difference is that the new employee relies on templates from other experiences or industries that might not work well in this situation. Thus, the extent to which our gut feelings in a situation represent intuition depends on our level of experience in that situation.

So far, we have described intuition as an emotional experience (gut feeling) and a process in which we compare the current situation with well-established templates of the mind. Intuition also relies on *action scripts*—programmed decision routines that speed up our response to pattern matches or mismatches.[47] Action scripts effectively shorten the decision-making process by jumping from problem identification to selection of a solution. In other words, action scripting is a form of programmed decision making. Action scripts are generic, so we need to consciously adapt them to the specific situation.

> The extent to which our gut feelings in a situation represent intuition depends on our level of experience in that situation.

Making Choices More Effectively

It is very difficult to get around the human limitations of making choices, but a few strategies help minimize these concerns. One important

connect

SELF-ASSESSMENT 6.1: What is Your Preferred Decision-Making Style?
Effective decision making is a critical part of most jobs, particularly in professional and executive positions. But people have different decision-making styles, including how much they rely on facts and logical analysis or emotional responses and gut instinct. You can discover your preferred decision-making style by locating this self-assessment in Connect if it is assigned by your instructor.

scenario planning a systematic process of thinking about alternative futures and what the organization should do to anticipate and react to those environments

escalation of commitment the tendency to repeat an apparently bad decision or allocate more resources to a failing course of action

self-enhancement a person's inherent motivation to have a positive self-concept (and to have others perceive him or her favorably), such as being competent, attractive, lucky, ethical, and important

prospect theory effect a natural tendency to feel more dissatisfaction from losing a particular amount than satisfaction from gaining an equal amount

discovery is that decisions tend to have a higher failure rate when leaders are decisive rather than contemplative about the available options. Of course, decisions also can be ineffective when leaders take too long to make a choice, but research indicates that a lack of logical evaluation of alternatives is a greater concern. By systematically assessing alternatives against relevant factors, decision makers minimize the implicit favorite and satisficing problems that occur when they rely on general subjective judgments. This recommendation does not suggest that we ignore intuition; rather, it suggests that we use it in combination with careful analysis of relevant information.[48]

A second piece of advice is to remember that decisions are influenced by both rational and emotional processes. Therefore, some decision makers deliberately revisit important issues later when their initial emotions have subsided and they can look at the information in a different mood. For example, if you sense that your team is feeling somewhat too self-confident when making an important competitive decision, you might decide to have the team members revisit the decision a few days later when they are thinking more critically.

Another strategy is **scenario planning**, which is a disciplined method for imagining possible futures.[50] It typically involves thinking about what would happen if a significant environmental condition changed and what the organization should do to anticipate and react to such an outcome. Scenario planning is a useful vehicle for choosing the best solutions under possible scenarios long before they occur because alternative courses of action are evaluated without the pressure and emotions that occur during real emergencies.

IMPLEMENTING DECISIONS

Implementing decisions is often skipped over in most writing about decision making. Yet leading business writers emphasize that execution—translating decisions into action—is one of the most important and challenging tasks in the decision-making process.[51] Implementing decisions is mainly about organizational change, which we discuss in Chapter 14, but also relates to leadership (Chapter 11) and several other topics throughout this book.

Intuition versus Data Analysis: Crunch Your Hunch[49]

84% of 300 UK recruitment professionals surveyed identify intuition as the most cost-efficient recruitment tool (but only the third most effective tool).

61% of 2,037 professionals surveyed globally somewhat or strongly agree that there is pressure from senior management for the organization to become more data driven and analytical.

68% of 600 American and UK executives surveyed say senior management in their organization is highly or totally committed to analytics and fact-based decision making.

70% of 1,018 Australian small to medium enterprise owners surveyed say they trusted their gut instinct over any professional advice.

©Jonathan Evans/Photographer's Choice RF/Getty Images

EVALUATING DECISIONS

Contrary to the rational choice view, decision makers aren't completely honest with themselves when evaluating the effectiveness of their decisions. Earlier in this chapter, we explained that decision makers engage in confirmation bias to support their implicit favorite during the decision-making process. This bias continues long after the decision has been made (which is why it is also called *postdecisional justification*). Decision makers ignore or underemphasize negative outcomes of the choice they made and overemphasize new information about its positive features. Confirmation bias gives people an excessively optimistic evaluation of their decisions, but only until they receive very clear and undeniable information to the contrary.

> When presented with evidence that a project is in trouble, the self-enhancement process biases our interpretation of the information as a temporary aberration from an otherwise positive trend line. "

Escalation of Commitment

Another reason why decision makers don't evaluate their decisions very well is due to **escalation of commitment**—the tendency to repeat an apparently bad decision or allocate more resources to a failing course of action.[52] Why are decision makers led deeper and deeper into failing projects? Several explanations have been identified and discussed over the years, but the four main influences are self-justification effect, self-enhancement effect, prospect theory effect, and sunk costs effect.

Self-Justification Effect People try to convey a positive public image of themselves. In decision making, this self-justification typically involves appearing to be rational and competent. Decision makers are therefore motivated to demonstrate that their choices will be successful, which includes continuing to support a decision even when it is not having the desired outcomes. In contrast, pulling the plug symbolizes the project's failure and the decision maker's incompetence. This self-justification effect is particularly evident when decision makers are personally identified with the project, have staked their reputations to some extent on the project's success, and have low self-esteem.[53]

Self-Enhancement Effect People have a natural tendency to feel good about themselves—to feel luckier, more competent, and more successful than average—regarding things that are important to them (see Chapter 3).[54] This **self-enhancement** supports a positive self-concept, but it also increases the risk of escalation of commitment. When presented with evidence that a project is in trouble, the self-enhancement process biases our interpretation of the information as a temporary aberration from an otherwise positive

trend line. And when we eventually realize that the project isn't going as well as planned, we continue to invest in the project because our probability of rescuing the project is above average.

Self-justification and self-enhancement often occur together, but they are different mechanisms. Self-justification is a deliberate attempt to maintain a favorable public image, whereas self-enhancement operates mostly nonconsciously, distorting information so we do not recognize the problem sooner and biasing our probabilities of success so we continue to invest in the losing project.[55]

Prospect Theory Effect **Prospect theory effect** is the tendency to experience stronger negative emotions when losing something of value than the positive emotions when gaining something of equal value. This prospect theory effect motivates us to avoid losses, which typically occurs by taking the risk of investing more in that losing project. Stopping a project is a certain loss, which evokes more negative emotions to most people than the uncertainty of success associated with continuing to fund the project. Given the choice, decision makers choose escalation of commitment, which is the less painful option at the time.[56]

Sunk Costs Effect Another disincentive to axing a failing project is sunk costs—the value of resources already invested in the decision.[57] The rational choice view states that investing resources should be determined by expected future gains and risk, not the size of earlier resources invested in the project. Yet people inherently feel motivated to invest more resources in projects that have high sunk costs. A variation of sunk costs is time investment. Time is a resource, so the more time decision makers have devoted to a project, the more motivated they are to continue investing in that project. Finally, sunk costs can take the form of closing costs, that is, the financial or nonfinancial penalties associated with shutting down a project. As with other forms of sunk costs, the higher the closing costs, the more motivated decision makers are to engage in escalation of commitment.

Escalation of commitment occurs partly because people are motivated to invest resources in projects with high sunk costs (large amounts already spent), whereas they should consider only the expected future gains.
©pogonici/Shutterstock

creativity the development of original ideas that make a socially recognized contribution

divergent thinking reframing a problem in a unique way and generating different approaches to the issue

Escalation of commitment is usually framed as poor decision making, but persistence may be the better choice under some circumstances.[58] Indeed, many breakthroughs have occurred because of the decision makers' persistence and optimism. Continuing with a losing project may be prudent when the cost overruns are small relative to the project cost, the benefits of success are high, and the rewards of a successful project are received quickly. Some experts also suggest that throwing more money into a failing project is sometimes a logical attempt to further understand an ambiguous situation. By adding more resources, the decision maker gains new information about the project's development, which provides more feedback about the project's future success. This strategy is particularly common where the project has high closing costs.

Evaluating Decision Outcomes More Effectively

One of the most effective ways to minimize escalation of commitment and confirmation bias is to ensure that the people who made the original decision are not the same people who later evaluate that decision. Target Corporation was able to withdraw early from the ill-fated Canadian expansion probably because Target's CEO did not make the original decision. This separation of roles minimizes the self-justification effect. A second strategy is to publicly establish a preset level at which the decision is abandoned or reevaluated. This is similar to a stop-loss order in the stock market, whereby the stock is sold if it falls below a certain price. The problem with this solution is that conditions are often so complex that it is difficult to identify an appropriate point to abandon a project.[59]

A third strategy is to find a source of systematic and clear feedback.[60] At some point, even the strongest escalation and confirmation bias effects deflate when the evidence highlights the project's failings. A fourth strategy to improve the decision evaluation process is to involve several people in the evaluation. Coworkers continuously monitor each other and might notice problems sooner than someone working alone on the project.

LO6-4 Describe employee characteristics, workplace conditions, and specific activities that support creativity.

CREATIVITY

The entire decision-making process described over the preceding pages depends on **creativity** —the development of original ideas that make a socially recognized contribution.[61] Creativity operates when imagining opportunities such as how Infosys's expertise can improve value for its clients. It is also applied when developing and selecting alternatives because we need to visualize the future in different ways and to figure out how each choice might be useful or a liability in those scenarios.

The Creative Process

How does creativity occur? That question has puzzled experts for hundreds of years and has been the fascination of many scientists who saw how creative thinking led to their own important discoveries. The four-stage model shown in Exhibit 6.4 was introduced nearly a century ago, yet is still considered the most elegant representation of the creative process.[62]

The first stage, *preparation,* involves developing a clear understanding of what you are trying to achieve through a novel solution and then actively studying information seemingly related to the topic. The second stage, called *incubation*, is the period of reflective thought. We put the problem aside, but our mind is still working on it in the background.[63] The important condition here is to maintain a low-level awareness by frequently revisiting the problem. Incubation does not mean that you forget about the problem or issue.

Incubation assists **divergent thinking**—reframing the problem

Exhibit 6.4 The Creative Process Model

Preparation	Incubation	Illumination	Verification
• Understand the problem or opportunity • Investigate information that seems relevant to the issue	• Period of reflective thought • Nonconscious or low-level awareness, not direct attention to the issue • Active divergent thinking process	• Sudden awareness of a novel, although vague and incomplete, idea entering one's consciousness • May include an initial period of "fringe" awareness	• Detailed logical and experimental evaluation of the illuminated idea • Further creative thinking

Source: Based on G. Wallas, *The Art of Thought* (London: Jonathan Cape, 1926), chap. 4.

in a unique way and generating different approaches to the issue. This contrasts with *convergent thinking*—calculating the conventionally accepted "right answer" to a logical problem. Divergent thinking breaks us away from existing mental models so that we can apply concepts or processes from completely different areas of life.

The third stage of creativity, called *illumination* (or *insight*), refers to the experience of suddenly becoming aware of a unique idea.[64] Illumination is often visually depicted as a lightbulb, but a better image would be a flash of light or perhaps a briefly flickering candle because this stage begins with a "fringe" awareness before the idea fully enters our consciousness. These bits of inspiration are fleeting and can be quickly lost if not documented. For this reason, many creative people keep a journal or notebook nearby so they can jot down their ideas before they disappear. Also, flickering ideas don't keep a particular schedule; they might come to you at any time of day or night.

Illumination presents ideas that are usually vague, roughly drawn, and untested. *Verification* therefore provides the essential final stage of creativity, whereby we flesh out the illuminated ideas and subject them to detailed logical evaluation and experimentation. This stage often calls for further creativity as the ideas evolve into finished products or services. Thus, although verification is labeled the final stage of creativity, it is really the beginning of a long process of creative decision making toward development of an innovative product or service.

Characteristics of Creative People

Everyone is creative, but some people have a higher potential for creativity. Four of the main characteristics that give individuals more creative potential are intelligence, persistence, knowledge and experience, and a cluster of personality traits and values representing independent imagination (see Exhibit 6.5).

- *Cognitive and practical intelligence.* Creative people have above-average intelligence to synthesize information, analyze ideas, and apply

The Creativity Advantage[65]

85% of 1,068 hiring managers believe that creativity is valuable to society.

80% of 2,606 U.S. workers polled believe there is increasing pressure to be productive rather than creative at work.

27% of 2,606 U.S. workers polled say their organization does nothing to encourage employee creativity (support employee curiosity).

73% of 175 public sector creative professionals polled in the U.S. and Canada believe that creativity is undervalued in government.

28% of 7,800 Millennials surveyed across 26 countries say their organization does NOT (not at all or not very much) reward its people for innovative ideas.

51% of 1,068 hiring managers believe businesses grasp the importance of creativity.

©ansonsaw/Getty Images

Exhibit 6.5 Characteristics of Creative People

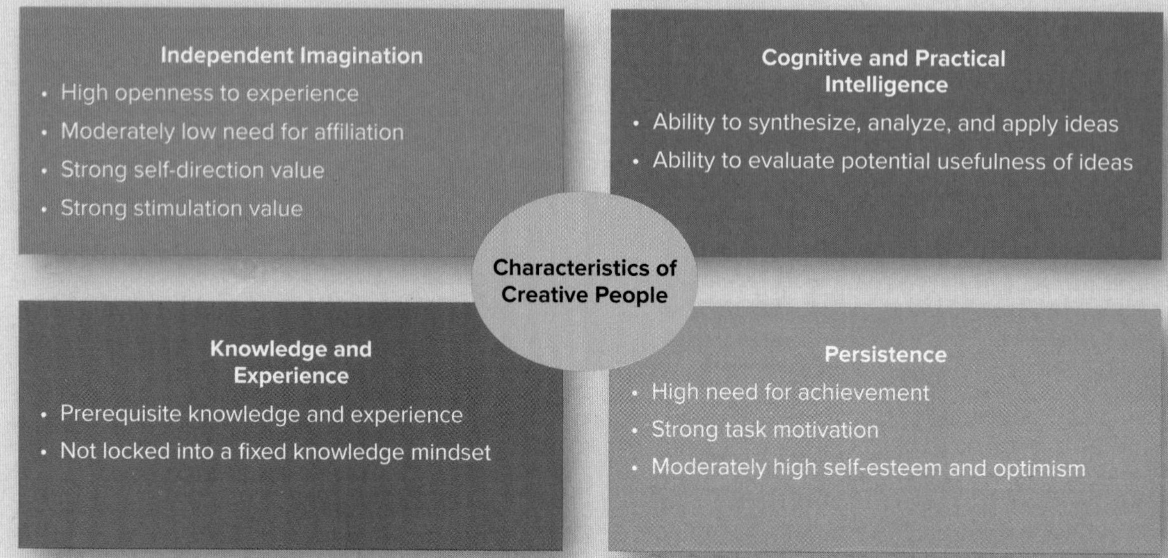

Independent Imagination
- High openness to experience
- Moderately low need for affiliation
- Strong self-direction value
- Strong stimulation value

Cognitive and Practical Intelligence
- Ability to synthesize, analyze, and apply ideas
- Ability to evaluate potential usefulness of ideas

Characteristics of Creative People

Knowledge and Experience
- Prerequisite knowledge and experience
- Not locked into a fixed knowledge mindset

Persistence
- High need for achievement
- Strong task motivation
- Moderately high self-esteem and optimism

> ## People have a general tendency to dismiss or criticize creative ideas, so creative people need persistence to withstand these negative social forces.

their ideas.[66] They recognize the significance of small bits of information and are able to connect them in ways that few others can imagine. They also have *practical intelligence*—the capacity to evaluate the potential usefulness of their ideas.

- *Persistence.* Creative people have persistence, which is based on a higher need for achievement, a strong motivation from the task itself, and a moderate or high degree of self-esteem. Persistence is vital because people need this motivation to continue working on and investing in a project in spite of failures and advice from others to quit. In fact, people have a general tendency to dismiss or criticize creative ideas, so creative people need persistence to withstand these negative social forces.[67]

- *Knowledge and experience.* Creative people require a foundation of knowledge and experience to discover or acquire new knowledge.[68] However, this expertise is a double-edged sword. As people acquire knowledge and experience about a specific topic, their mental models tend to become more rigid. They are less adaptable to new information or rules about that knowledge domain. Some writers suggest that expertise also increases "mindless behavior" because expertise reduces the tendency to question why things happen.[69] To overcome the limitations of expertise, some corporate leaders like to hire people from other industries and areas of expertise.

- *Independent imagination.* Creative people possess a cluster of personality traits and values that support an independent imagination: high openness to experience, moderately low need for affiliation, and strong values around self-direction and stimulation.[70] Openness to experience is a Big Five personality dimension representing the extent to which a person is imaginative, curious, sensitive, open-minded, and original (see Chapter 2). Creative people have a moderately low need for affiliation so they are less embarrassed when making mistakes. Self-direction includes the values of creativity and independent thought; stimulation includes the values of excitement and challenge. Together, these values form openness to change—representing the motivation to pursue innovative ways (see Chapter 2).

connect

SELF-ASSESSMENT 6.3: Do You Have a Creative Personality?
Everyone is creative to some extent, but some people have personality traits and personal values that give them higher creative potential. You can discover the extent to which you have a creative personality by locating this self-assessment in Connect if it is assigned by your instructor.

Organizational Conditions Supporting Creativity

Intelligence, persistence, expertise, and independent imagination represent a person's creative potential, but the extent to which these characteristics produce more creative output depends on how well the work environment supports the creative process.[71] Several job and workplace characteristics have been identified in the literature, and different combinations of situations can equally support creativity; there isn't one best work environment.[73]

One of the most important conditions for creativity is a **learning orientation**. The workplace supports a learning orientation when reasonable mistakes are tolerated and expected as part of the discovery process. A second condition for creativity is motivation from the job itself.[74] Employees tend to be more creative when they believe their work benefits the organization and/or larger society (i.e., task significance) and when they have the freedom to pursue novel ideas without bureaucratic delays (i.e., autonomy). Creativity is about changing things, and change is possible only when employees have the authority to experiment. More generally, jobs encourage creativity when they are challenging and aligned with the employee's knowledge and skills.

Along with a learning orientation and intrinsically motivating jobs, creativity blossoms through open communication and

learning orientation
beliefs and norms that support the acquisition, sharing, and use of knowledge as well as work conditions that nurture these learning processes

sufficient resources. Creative organizations also provide a comfortable degree of job security, which explains why creativity suffers during times of downsizing and corporate restructuring.[75] Some companies also support creativity by designing nontraditional workspaces, such as unique building design or unconventional office areas.[76] Google is one example. The Internet innovator has funky offices in several countries that include hammocks, gondola- and hive-shaped privacy spaces, slides, and brightly painted walls.

To some degree, creativity also improves with support from leaders and coworkers. One study reported that effective product champions provide enthusiastic support for new ideas. Other studies suggest that coworker support can improve creativity in some situations whereas competition among coworkers improves creativity in other situations.[77] Similarly, it isn't clear how much pressure should be exerted on employees to produce creative ideas. Extreme time pressures are well-known creativity inhibitors, but lack of pressure doesn't seem to produce the highest creativity either.

Activities That Encourage Creativity

We have described two cornerstones of creativity in organizations: hiring people with strong creative potential and providing a work environment that supports creativity. The third cornerstone is activities that help employees think more creatively. Four types of creativity-building activities are redefining the problem, associative play, cross-pollination, and design thinking.

- *Redefining the problem.* Revisit projects that have been set aside. After a period of neglect, these projects might be seen in new ways.[78] You also can see the problem from different perspectives by asking coworkers

OB THEORY TO PRACTICE

Striving for the Creativity of a Fintech

BNY Mellon is America's oldest bank, yet it is striving for the creativity of a financial technology start-up company (fintech). BNY Mellon already has innovation centers in Silicon Valley, Jersey City, London, India, and, most recently, Pittsburgh (see photo). These centers generate ideas and prototypes of emerging client services and business processes through design thinking. The bank also sparks creativity through innovation jams, hackathons, and open innovation forums. "Our ambition is to combine the creativity and energy of Silicon Valley with the banking acumen of the financial capitals of the world," says a BNY Mellon senior executive.[72]

©BNY Mellon

Along with hiring people with strong creative potential and providing a work environment that supports creativity, companies rely on activities that stimulate creative thinking.
©Olena Yakobchuk/Shutterstock

design thinking a human-centered, solution-focused creative process that applies both intuition and analytical thinking to clarify problems and generate innovative solutions

employee involvement the degree to which employees influence how their work is organized and carried out

unfamiliar with the issue to explore the problem. By verbalizing the problem, listening to questions, and hearing what others think, you are more likely to view the problem in a new light.[79]

- *Associative play.* Associative play is literally playing games, particularly with unusual twists to the traditional equipment or rules. Creative thinking emerges naturally from playful activities, and then carries over to work-related problem solving.[80] Challenge employees to create something new with a specific purpose (cleaning cutlery) using existing unrelated products (e.g., blow dryer and electric toothbrush). Apply morphological analysis, which involves systematically investigating all combinations of characteristics of a product, event, or other target.[81] For instance, employees at a food manufacturer might investigate all combinations of yogurt-based products by considering the contents (fruit, low-fat, etc.), occasion (breakfast, dessert, etc.), target group (children, older adults, etc.), size, and packaging. A novel, yet commercially successful, innovation may emerge from the resulting list

- *Cross-pollination.* Creativity is sparked when people from different areas of the organization exchange ideas or when new people are brought into an existing team.[82] This may occur through social gathering or, as a few firms do, asking employees to move their desks every few months to another location with employees who are only acquaintances.

- *Design thinking.* **Design thinking** is an emerging set of practices that are human-centered, are solution-focused, and apply both intuition and analytical thinking.[83] It recognizes that creativity depends on collaboration among people with diverse knowledge and experiences who can empathize with the end user.[84] Design thinkers also preserve ambiguity; they question and refine the problem statement and continually question emerging solutions. They review and learn from past solutions, then use

tools to imagine better solutions for the future. Design thinkers spend more time trying out ideas with low-cost prototypes, rather than analyzing those ideas at a purely conceptual level.[85] They live by the mantra "fail fast, fail often," meaning that prototypes are made quickly and frequently, and that failures are a natural part of the creative process (i.e., a learning orientation).

LO6-5 Describe the benefits of employee involvement and identify four contingencies that affect the optimal level of employee involvement.

EMPLOYEE INVOLVEMENT IN DECISION MAKING

Employee involvement (also called *participative management*) refers to the degree to which employees influence how their work is organized and carried out.[86] Employee involvement has become a natural process in every organization, but the optimal level of involvement depends on the situation.[87] A low level of involvement occurs where employees are individually asked for specific information but the problem is not described to them. Somewhat higher involvement occurs where the problem is described and employees are asked individually or collectively for information relating to that problem.

Moving further up the involvement scale, the problem is described to employees, who are collectively given responsibility for developing recommendations. However, the decision maker is not bound to accept those recommendations. At the highest level of involvement, the entire decision-making process is handed over to employees. They identify the problem, discover alternative solutions, choose the best alternative, and implement that choice. The original decision maker serves only as a facilitator to guide the team's decision process and keep everyone on track.

Employee involvement has become a natural process in every organization, but the optimal level of involvement depends on the situation.
©Rawpixel.com/Shutterstock

OB THEORY TO PRACTICE

Design Thinking Practices

▷ Involve several people so the issue and possible solutions are viewed from several angles.

▷ Include clients and end users to enable an iterative process of problem identification and solution development.

▷ Preserve ambiguity rather than seek clarity too quickly.

▷ Question and refine the stated problem.

▷ Develop more than one solution to the problem.

▷ Review past solutions to understand how those inventions tried to satisfy human needs.

▷ Use foresight tools to imagine better solutions for the future.

▷ Build several low-cost prototypes to test ideas.

▷ Don't analyze alternatives at a purely conceptual level.

▷ Tolerate failure; embrace a learning orientation.

Benefits of Employee Involvement

For the past half century, organizational behavior experts have advised that employee involvement potentially improves decision-making quality and commitment.[88] To begin with, it improves the identification of problems and opportunities. Employees are, in many respects, the sensors of the organization's environment. When the organization's activities misalign with customer expectations, employees are usually the first to know. Employee involvement provides a conduit for organizational leaders to be alerted to such problems.[89] Employee involvement also can potentially improve the number and quality of solutions generated. In a well-managed meeting, team members create synergy by pooling their knowledge to form new alternatives. In other words, several people working together can potentially generate better solutions than the same people working alone.

A third benefit of employee involvement is that, under specific conditions, it improves the evaluation of alternatives. Numerous studies on participative decision making, task conflict, and team dynamics have found that involvement brings out more diverse perspectives, tests ideas, and provides more valuable knowledge, all of which help the decision maker select the best alternative.[90] A mathematical theorem introduced in 1785 by the Marquis de Condorcet states that the alternative selected by the team's majority is more likely to be correct than is the alternative selected by any team member individually.[91]

Along with improving decision quality, involvement tends to strengthen employee commitment to the decision. Rather than viewing themselves as agents of someone else's decision, those who participate in a decision feel personally responsible for its success. Involvement also has positive effects on employee motivation, satisfaction, and turnover. It also increases skill variety, feelings of autonomy, and task identity, all of which increase job enrichment and potentially employee motivation. Participation is also a critical practice in organizational change because employees are more motivated to implement the decision and less likely to resist changes resulting from the decision.[93]

Contingencies of Employee Involvement

If employee involvement is so wonderful, why don't leaders leave all decisions to employees? The answer is that there is an optimal level of employee involvement, and that ideal level depends on the situation. The employee involvement model shown in Exhibit 6.6 lists four contingencies—decision structure, source of decision knowledge, decision commitment, and risk of conflict—in the decision process.[94]

- *Decision structure.* At the beginning of this chapter, we learned that some decisions are programmed whereas others are nonprogrammed. Programmed decisions are less likely to need employee involvement because the solutions are already worked out from past incidents. In other words, the benefits of employee involvement increase with the novelty and complexity of the problem or opportunity.

- *Source of decision knowledge.* Subordinates should be involved in some level of decision making when the leader lacks sufficient knowledge and subordinates have additional information to improve decision quality. In many cases, employees are closer to customers and production activities, so they often know where the company can save money, improve product or service quality, and realize opportunities. This is particularly true for complex decisions where employees are more likely to possess relevant information.

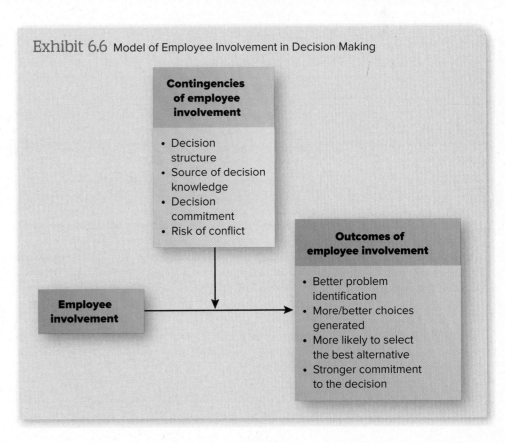

Exhibit 6.6 Model of Employee Involvement in Decision Making

Contingencies of employee involvement
- Decision structure
- Source of decision knowledge
- Decision commitment
- Risk of conflict

Employee involvement

Outcomes of employee involvement
- Better problem identification
- More/better choices generated
- More likely to select the best alternative
- Stronger commitment to the decision

- *Decision commitment.* Participation tends to improve employee commitment to the decision. If employees are unlikely to accept a decision made without their involvement, some level of participation is usually necessary.

- *Risk of conflict.* Two types of conflict undermine the benefits of employee involvement. First, if employee goals and norms conflict with the organization's goals, only a low level of employee involvement is advisable. Second, the degree of involvement depends on whether employees will agree with each other on the preferred solution. If conflict is likely to occur, high involvement (i.e., employees make the decision) would be difficult to achieve.

Employee involvement is an important component of the decision-making process. To make the best decisions, we need to involve people who have valuable information and who will be more motivated to implement the decision. Employee involvement is a formative stage of team dynamics, so it carries many of the benefits and challenges of working in teams. The next chapter provides a closer look at team dynamics, including processes for making decisions in teams.

Study Checklist

Connect® Management is available for *M Organizational Behavior.* Additional resources include:

✓ Interactive Applications:
- **Drag and Drop:** Work through an interactive example to test your knowledge of the concepts.
- **Sequencing**
- **Video Case:** See management in action through interactive videos.

✓ **SmartBook™**—SmartBook is the first and only adaptive reading experience available today. Distinguishing what you know from what you don't, and honing in on concepts you are most likely to forget, SmartBook personalizes content for you in a continuously adapting reading experience. Reading is no longer a passive and linear experience, but an engaging and dynamic one where you are more likely to master and retain important concepts and go to class better prepared.

©Natthawat Jamnapa/123RF

Notes

1. P. Wahba, "Why Target Failed in Canada," *Fortune*, January 15, 2015; D. Dahlhoff, "Why Target's Canadian Expansion Failed," *Harvard Business Review* (2015), https://hbr.org/2015/01/why-targets-canadian-expansion-failed; "Brian Cornell Addresses Questions About Exiting Canada," *A Bullseye View* (Minneapolis: Target, January 15, 2015), https://corporate.target.com/article/2015/01/qa-brian-cornell-target-exits-canada (accessed February 28, 2017).

2. F. A. Shull Jr., A. L. Delbecq, and L. L. Cummings, *Organizational Decision Making* (New York: McGraw-Hill, 1970), 31.

3. S. R. Covey, *The Wisdom and Teachings of Stephen R. Covey* (New York: Free Press, 2012).

4. Harvard Business School, *Decision Making: 5 Steps to Better Results* (Cambridge, MA: Harvard Business School Press, 2006), chap. 1; D. Baltzly, "Stoicism", *Stanford Encyclopedia of Philosophy* (2008), http://plato.stanford.edu/entries/stoicism/ (accessed March 30, 2008); I. Pownall, *Effective Management Decision Making* (Holstebro, DK: Ventus Publishing, 2012), chap. 1; C. P. Webel, *The Politics of Rationality: Reason through Occidental History* (New York: Routledge, 2014), chaps. 1 and 3.

5. J. G. March and H. A. Simon, *Organizations* (New York: Wiley, 1958); K. Manktelow, *Thinking and Reasoning: An Introduction to the Psychology of Reason, Judgment and Decision Making* (Hoboken, NJ: Taylor & Francis, 2012), chap. 8.

6. This example differs from the game theory model in classic economic theory. In classic economic theory, the "outcomes" are alternatives, so the probabilities must add up to 1.0. For example, if there is a 30 percent probability that your company will choose supplier A, then there is necessarily a 70 percent chance that the company will choose supplier B (if those are the only choices). The current example, which is much more relevant to business decisions, differs because rational choice decision making calculates each alternative's composite valence from a set of criteria (outcomes) associated with all alternatives. These probabilities do not add up to 1.0 because they refer to entities that are not perfectly correlated (e.g., a supplier might have a high probability of offering quality products, reliable delivery, and low prices). The current application of rational choice decision making may be more consistent with the founding theories of utilitarianism.

7. These criteria are commonly used in supplier selection modeling. See, for example, H. Karimi and A. Rezaeinia, "Supplier Selection Using Revised Multi-Segment Goal Programming Model," *International Journal of Advanced Manufacturing Technology* 70, no. 5/8 (2014): 1227–34.

8. This model is adapted from several sources, including H. A. Simon, *The New Science of Management Decision* (New York: Harper & Row, 1960); H. Mintzberg, D. Raisinghani, and A. Théorét, "The Structure of 'Unstructured' Decision Processes," *Administrative Science Quarterly* 21 (1976): 246–75; W. C. Wedley and R. H. G. Field, "A Predecision Support System," *Academy of Management Review* 9 (1984): 696–703.

9. P. F. Drucker, *The Practice of Management* (New York: Harper & Brothers, 1954), 353–57; B. M. Bass, *Organizational Decision Making* (Homewood, IL: Irwin, 1983), chap. 3.

10. L. R. Beach and T. R. Mitchell, "A Contingency Model for the Selection of Decision Strategies," *Academy of Management Review* 3 (1978): 439–49; I. L. Janis, *Crucial Decisions* (New York: Free Press, 1989), 35–37; W. Zhongtuo, "Meta-Decision Making: Concepts and Paradigm," *Systematic Practice and Action Research* 13, no. 1 (2000): 111–15.

11. J. de Jonge, *Rethinking Rational Choice Theory: A Companion on Rational and Moral Action* (Basingstoke, UK: Palgrave Macmillan, 2011).

12. A. Howard, "Opinion," *Computing* (1999): 18.

13. For a recent discussion on problem finding in organizations, see M. A. Roberto, *Know What You Don't Know: How Great Leaders Prevent Problems before They Happen* (Saddle River, NJ: Wharton School Publishing, 2009).

14. T. K. Das and B. S. Teng, "Cognitive Biases and Strategic Decision Processes: An Integrative Perspective," *Journal of Management Studies* 36, no. 6 (1999): 757–78; P. Bijttebier, H. Vertommen, and G. V. Steene, "Assessment of Cognitive Coping Styles: A Closer Look at Situation-Response Inventories," *Clinical Psychology Review* 21, no. 1 (2001): 85–104; P. C. Nutt, "Expanding the Search for Alternatives during Strategic Decision-Making," *Academy of Management Executive* 18, no. 4 (2004): 13–28.

15. J. Portman, "Harry Potter Was Almost a Yankee," *Vancouver Sun*, July 5, 2007.

16. P. C. Nutt, *Why Decisions Fail* (San Francisco: Berrett-Koehler, 2002); S. Finkelstein, *Why Smart Executives Fail* (New York: Viking, 2003).

17. M. Hock and H. W. Krohne, "Coping with Threat and Memory for Ambiguous Information: Testing the Repressive Discontinuity Hypothesis," *Emotion* 4, no. 1 (2004): 65–86; J. Brandtstadter, A. Voss, and K. Rothermund, "Perception of Danger Signals: The Role of Control," *Experimental Psychology* 51, no. 1 (2004): 24–32.

18. E. Witte, "Field Research on Complex Decision-Making Processes—The Phase Theorum," *International Studies of Management and Organization*, no. 56 (1972): 156–82; J. A. Bargh and T. L. Chartrand, "The Unbearable Automaticity of Being," *American Psychologist* 54, no. 7 (1999): 462–79.

19. A. H. Maslow, *The Psychology of Science: A Reconnaissance* (Chapel Hill, NC: Maurice Bassett Publishing, 2002).

20. R. Rothenberg, "Ram Charan: The Thought Leader Interview," *strategy + business*, Fall 2004.

21. H. A. Simon, *Administrative Behavior*, 2nd ed. (New York: Free Press, 1957); H. A. Simon, "Rational Decision Making in Business Organizations," *American Economic Review* 69, no. 4 (1979): 493–513.

22. M. D. Cohen, J. G. March, and J. P. Olsen, "A Garbage Can Model of Organizational Choice," *Administrative Science Quarterly* 17, no. 1 (1972): 1–25.

23. H. A. Simon, *Administrative Behavior*, 2nd ed. (New York: Free Press, 1957), xxv, 80–84.

24. L. J. Peter, *Peter's Almanac* (New York: Morrow, 1982).

25. S. Sacchi and M. Burigo, "Strategies in the Information Search Process: Interaction among Task Structure, Knowledge, and Source," *Journal of General Psychology* 135, no. 3 (2008): 252–70.

26. Current researchers refer to implicit favorite as "predecision information distortion" and the "coherence effect," but these theories are essentially implicit favorite bias. P. O. Soelberg, "Unprogrammed Decision Making," *Industrial Management Review* 8 (1967): 19–29; K. H. Ehrhart and J. C. Ziegert, "Why Are Individuals Attracted to Organizations?," *Journal of Management* 31, no. 6 (2005): 901–19; J. E. Russo, "The Predecisional Distortion of Information," in *Neuroeconomics, Judgment, and Decision Making*, ed. E. A. Wilhelms and V. F. Reyna, *Frontiers of Cognitive Psychology* (New York: Psychology Press, 2015), 91–110.

27. Milton Rokeach famously stated, "Life is ipsative, because decisions in everyday life are inherently and phenomenologically ipsative decisions." M. Rokeach, "Inducing Changes and Stability in Belief Systems and Personality Structures," *Journal of Social Issues* 41, no. 1 (1985): 153–71.

28. R. S. Nickerson, "Confirmation Bias: A Ubiquitous Phenomenon in Many Guises," *Review of General Psychology* 2, no. 2 (1998): 175–220; O. Svenson, I. Salo, and T. Lindholm, "Post-Decision Consolidation and Distortion of Facts," *Judgment and Decision Making* 4, no. 5 (2009): 397–407; A. M. Scherer, P. D. Windschitl, and A. R. Smith, "Hope to Be Right: Biased Information Seeking Following Arbitrary and Informed Predictions," *Journal of Experimental Social Psychology* 49, no. 1 (2013): 106–12.

29. A. L. Brownstein, "Biased Predecision Processing," *Psychological Bulletin* 129, no. 4 (2003): 545–68; M. Nurek, O. Kostopoulou, and Y. Hagmayer, "Predecisional Information Distortion in Physicians' Diagnostic Judgments: Strengthening a Leading Hypothesis or Weakening Its Competitor?," *Judgment and Decision Making* 9, no. 6 (2014): 572–85; D. Simon, D. Stenstrom, and S. Read, "The Coherence Effect: Blending Cold and Hot Cognitions," *Journal of Personality & Social Psychology* 109, no. 3 (2015): 369–94; M. L. DeKay, "Predecisional Information Distortion and the Self-Fulfilling Prophecy of Early Preferences in Choice," *Current Directions in Psychological Science* 24, no. 5 (2015): 405–11.

30. T. Gilovich, D. Griffin, and D. Kahneman, *Heuristics and Biases: The Psychology of Intuitive Judgment* (Cambridge: Cambridge University Press, 2002); D. Kahneman, "Maps of Bounded Rationality: Psychology for Behavioral Economics," *American Economic Review* 93, no. 5 (2003): 1449–75; F. L. Smith et al., "Decision-Making Biases and Affective States: Their Potential Impact on Best Practice Innovations," *Canadian Journal of Administrative Sciences* 27, no. 4 (2010): 277–91.

31. A. Tversky and D. Kahneman, "Judgment under Uncertainty: Heuristics and Biases," *Science* 185, no. 4157 (1974): 1124–31; I. Ritov, "Anchoring in Simulated Competitive Market Negotiation," *Organizational Behavior and Human Decision Processes* 67, no. 1 (1996): 16; D. Ariely, G. Loewenstein, and A. Prelec, "'Coherent Arbitrariness': Stable Demand Curves without Stable Preferences," *Quarterly Journal of Economics* 118 (2003): 73; N. Epley and T. Gilovich, "Are Adjustments Insufficient?," *Personality and Social Psychology Bulletin* 30, no. 4 (2004): 447–60; J. D. Jasper and S. D. Christman, "A Neuropsychological Dimension for Anchoring Effects," *Journal of Behavioral Decision Making* 18 (2005): 343–69; S. D. Bond et al., "Information Distortion in the Evaluation of a Single Option," *Organizational Behavior & Human Decision Processes* 102 (2007): 240–54.

32. A. Tversky and D. Kahneman, "Availability: A Heuristic for Judging Frequency and Probability," *Cognitive Psychology* 5 (1973): 207–32.

33. D. Kahneman and A. Tversky, "Subjective Probability: A Judgment of Representativeness," *Cognitive Psychology* 3, no. 3 (1972): 430; T. Gilovich, *How We Know What Isn't So: The Fallibility of Human Reason in Everyday Life* (New York: Free Press, 1991); B. D. Burns, "Heuristics as Beliefs and as Behaviors: The Adaptiveness of the 'Hot Hand,'" *Cognitive Psychology* 48 (2004): 295–331; E. M. Altmann and B. D. Burns, "Streak Biases in Decision Making: Data and a Memory Model," *Cognitive Systems Research* 6, no. 1 (2005): 5–16.

34. H. A. Simon, "Rational Choice and the Structure of Environments," *Psychological Review* 63 (1956): 129–38.

35. S. Botti and S. S. Iyengar, "The Dark Side of Choice: When Choice Impairs Social Welfare," *Journal of Public Policy and Marketing* 25, no. 1 (2006): 24–38; K. D. Vohs et al., "Making Choices Impairs Subsequent Self-Control: A Limited-Resource Account of Decision Making, Self-Regulation, and Active Initiative," *Journal of Personality and Social Psychology* 94, no. 5 (2008): 883–98.

36. K. Jain, J. N. Bearden, and A. Filipowicz, "Do Maximizers Predict Better Than Satisficers?," *Journal of Behavioral Decision Making* 26, no. 1 (2013): 41–50; W. Mao, "When One Desires Too Much of a Good Thing: The Compromise Effect under Maximizing Tendencies," *Journal of Consumer Psychology* 26, no. 1 (2016): 66–80.

37. S. Botti and S. S. Iyengar, "The Dark Side of Choice: When Choice Impairs Social Welfare," *Journal of Public Policy & Marketing* 25, no. 1 (2006): 24–38; S. Iyengar, *The Art of Choosing* (New York: Hachette, 2010), 177–95.

38. P. C. Nutt, "Search during Decision Making," *European Journal of Operational Research* 160 (2005): 851–76.

39. P. Winkielman et al., "Affective Influence on Judgments and Decisions: Moving towards Core Mechanisms," *Review of General Psychology* 11, no. 2 (2007): 179–92.

40. P. Winkielman and K. C. Berridge, "Unconscious Emotion," *Current Directions in Psychological Science* 13, no. 3 (2004): 120–23; A. Bechara and A. R. Damasio, "The Somatic Marker Hypothesis: A Neural Theory of Economic Decision," *Games and Economic Behavior* 52, no. 2 (2005): 336–72; T. S. Saunders and M. J. Buehner, "The Gut Chooses Faster Than the Mind: A Latency Advantage of Affective over Cognitive Decisions," *Quarterly Journal of Experimental Psychology* 66, no. 2 (2013): 381–88; A. Moors, "Automaticity: Componential, Causal, and Mechanistic Explanations," *Annual Review of Psychology* 67, no. 1 (2016): 263–87.

41. J. P. Forgas and J. M. George, "Affective Influences on Judgments and Behavior in Organizations: An Information Processing Perspective," *Organizational Behavior and Human Decision Processes* 86 (2001): 3–34; G. Loewenstein and J. S. Lerner, "The Role of Affect in Decision Making," in *Handbook of Affective Sciences*, ed. R. J. Davidson, K. R. Scherer, and H. H. Goldsmith (New York: Oxford University Press, 2003), 619–42; M. T. Pham, "Emotion and Rationality: A Critical Review and Interpretation of Empirical Evidence," *Review of General Psychology* 11, no. 2 (2007): 155–78; J. P. Forgas and A. S. Koch, "Mood Effects on Cognition," in *Handbook of Cognition and Emotion*, ed. M. D. Robinson, E. R. Watkins, and E. Harmon-Jones (New York: Guilford, 2013), 231–51.

42. D. Miller, *The Icarus Paradox* (New York: HarperBusiness, 1990); D. Miller, "What Happens after Success: The Perils of Excellence," *Journal of Management Studies* 31, no. 3 (1994): 325–68; A. C. Amason and A. C. Mooney, "The Icarus Paradox Revisited: How Strong Performance Sows the Seeds of Dysfunction in Future Strategic Decision-Making," *Strategic Organization* 6, no. 4 (2008): 407–34.

43. M. T. Pham, "The Logic of Feeling," *Journal of Consumer Psychology* 14 (2004): 360–69; N. Schwarz, "Feelings-as-Information Theory," in *Handbook of Theories of Social Psychology*, ed. P. Van Lange, A. Kruglanski, and E. T. Higgins (London: Sage, 2012), 289–308.

44. O. Behling and N. L. Eckel, "Making Sense out of Intuition," *Academy of Management Executive* 5 (1991): 46–54; R. M. Hogarth, "Intuition: A Challenge for Psychological Research on Decision Making," *Psychological Inquiry* 21, no. 4 (2010): 338–53; S. Epstein, "Demystifying Intuition: What It Is, What It Does, and How It Does It," *Psychological Inquiry* 21, no. 4 (2010): 295–312.

45. Y. Wang et al., "Meta-Analytic Investigations of the Relation between Intuition and Analysis," *Journal of Behavioral Decision Making* 30, no. 1 (2017): 15–25; K. Hamilton, S.-I. Shih, and S. Mohammed, "The Development and Validation of the Rational and Intuitive Decision Styles Scale," *Journal of Personality Assessment* (2016): 1–13.

46. W. G. Chase and H. A. Simon, "Perception in Chess," *Cognitive Psychology* 4, no. 1 (1973): 55–81; G. Klein, *Intuition at Work* (New York: Currency/Doubleday, 2003); E. Dane, K. W. Rockmann, and M. G. Pratt, "When Should I Trust My Gut? Linking Domain Expertise to Intuitive Decision-Making Effectiveness," *Organizational Behavior and Human Decision Processes* 119, no. 2 (2012): 187–94; A. Linhares and D. M. Chada, "What Is the Nature of the Mind's Pattern-Recognition Process?," *New Ideas in Psychology* 31, no. 2 (2013): 108–21.

47. G. Klein, *Intuition at Work* (New York: Currency/Doubleday, 2003), 12–13, 16–17.

48. Y. Ganzach, A. H. Kluger, and N. Klayman, "Making Decisions from an Interview: Expert Measurement and Mechanical Combination," *Personnel Psychology* 53 (2000): 1–20; A. M. Hayashi, "When to Trust Your Gut," *Harvard Business Review* 79 (2001): 59–65. Evidence of high failure rates from quick decisions is reported in P. C. Nutt, *Why Decisions Fail* (San Francisco, CA: Berrett-Koehler, 2002); P. C. Nutt, "Search during Decision Making," *European Journal of Operational Research* 160 (2005): 851–76; P. C. Nutt, "Investigating the Success of Decision Making Processes," *Journal of Management Studies* 45, no. 2 (2008): 425–55.

49. Accenture, "Organizations Make Strides in Adoption of Analytics, but Struggle to Capitalize on Investments, Accenture Research Finds," news release (New York: Accenture, March 5, 2013); Wolters Kluwer, "Survey Finds Most SMEs Shun Professional Advice, Possibly at Their Peril," news release (Sydney: Wolters Kluwer, April 11, 2013); *The Recruitment Reality Check* (London: Monster UK and University College London, March 17, 2014); D. Kiron, K. Prentice, and R. B. Ferguson, *The Analytics Mandate* (Cambridge, MA: MIT Sloan Management Review and SAS Institute, May 12, 2014).

50. R. Bradfield et al., "The Origins and Evolution of Scenario Techniques in Long Range Business Planning," *Futures* 37, no. 8 (2005): 795–812; G. Wright, G. Cairns, and P. Goodwin, "Teaching Scenario Planning: Lessons from Practice in Academe and Business," *European Journal of Operational Research* 194, no. 1 (2009): 323–35; T. J. Chermack, *Scenario Planning in Organizations* (San Francisco: Berrett-Koehler, 2011).

51. J. Pfeffer and R. I. Sutton, "Knowing 'What' to Do Is Not Enough: Turning Knowledge into Action," *California Management Review* 42, no. 1 (1999): 83–108; R. Charan, C. Burke, and L. Bossidy, *Execution: The Discipline of Getting Things Done* (New York: Crown Business, 2002).

52. B. M. Staw and J. Ross, "Behavior in Escalation Situations: Antecedents, Prototypes, and Solutions," in *Research in Organizational Behavior*, ed. L. L. Cummings and B. M. Staw (Greenwich, CT: JAI, 1987), 39–78; J. Brockner, "The Escalation of Commitment to a Failing Course of Action: Toward Theoretical Progress," *Academy of Management Review* 17, no. 1 (1992): 39–61; D. J. Sleesman et al., "Cleaning up the Big Muddy: A Meta-Analytic Review of the Determinants of Escalation of Commitment," *Academy of Management Journal* 55, no. 3 (2012): 541–62.

53. F. D. Schoorman and P. J. Holahan, "Psychological Antecedents of Escalation Behavior: Effects of Choice, Responsibility, and Decision Consequences," *Journal of Applied Psychology* 81 (1996): 786–93; D. Steinkühler, M. D. Mahlendorf, and M. Brettel, "How Self-Justification Indirectly Drives Escalation of Commitment—A Motivational Perspective," *Schmalenbach Business Review: ZFBF* 66, no. 2 (2014): 191–222.

54. C. L. Guenther and M. D. Alicke, "Deconstructing the Better-Than-Average Effect," *Journal of Personality and Social Psychology* 99, no. 5 (2010): 755–70; S. Loughnan et al., "Universal Biases in Self-Perception: Better and More Human Than Average," *British Journal of Social Psychology* 49 (2010): 627–36.

55. M. Keil, G. Depledge, and A. Rai, "Escalation: The Role of Problem Recognition and Cognitive Bias," *Decision Sciences* 38, no. 3 (2007): 391–421.

56. G. Whyte, "Escalating Commitment in Individual and Group Decision Making: A Prospect Theory Approach," *Organizational Behavior and Human Decision Processes* 54 (1993): 430–55; D. Kahneman and J. Renshon, "Hawkish Biases," in *American Foreign Policy and the Politics of Fear: Threat Inflation Since 9/11*, ed. T. Thrall and J. Cramer (New York: Routledge, 2009), 79–96.

57. D. J. Sleesman et al., "Cleaning up the Big Muddy: A Meta-Analytic Review of the Determinants of Escalation of Commitment," *Academy of Management Journal* 55, no. 3 (2012): 541–62.

58. J. D. Bragger et al., "When Success Breeds Failure: History, Hysteresis, and Delayed Exit Decisions," *Journal of Applied Psychology* 88, no. 1 (2003): 6–14; H. Drummond, "Escalation of Commitment: When to Stay the Course?," *The Academy of Management Perspectives* 28, no. 4 (2014): 430–46.

59. I. Simonson and B. M. Staw, "De-Escalation Strategies: A Comparison of Techniques for Reducing Commitment to Losing Courses of Action," *Journal of Applied Psychology* 77 (1992): 419–26; W. Boulding, R. Morgan, and R. Staelin, "Pulling the Plug to Stop the New Product Drain," *Journal of Marketing Research*, no. 34 (1997): 164–76; B. M. Staw, K. W. Koput, and S. G. Barsade, "Escalation at the Credit Window: A Longitudinal Study of Bank Executives' Recognition and Write-Off of Problem Loans," *Journal of Applied Psychology* 82, no. 1 (1997): 130–42; M. Keil and D. Robey, "Turning around Troubled Software Projects: An Exploratory Study of the Deescalation of Commitment to Failing Courses of Action," *Journal of Management Information Systems* 15 (1999): 63–87; B. C. Gunia, N. Sivanathan, and A. D. Galinsky, "Vicarious Entrapment: Your Sunk Costs, My Escalation of Commitment," *Journal of Experimental Social Psychology* 45, no. 6 (2009): 1238–44.

60. D. Ghosh, "De-Escalation Strategies: Some Experimental Evidence," *Behavioral Research in Accounting* 9 (1997): 88–112.

61. M. I. Stein, "Creativity and Culture," *Journal of Psychology* 36 (1953): 311–22; M. A. Runco and G. J. Jaeger, "The Standard Definition of Creativity," *Creativity Research Journal* 24, no. 1 (2012): 92–96.

62. G. Wallas, *The Art of Thought* (London: Jonathan Cape, 1926). For recent applications of Wallas's classic model, see T. Kristensen, "The Physical Context of Creativity," *Creativity and Innovation Management* 13, no. 2 (2004): 89–96; U. E. Haner, "Spaces for Creativity and Innovation in Two Established Organizations," *Creativity and Innovation Management* 14, no. 3 (2005): 288–98.

63. R. S. Nickerson, "Enhancing Creativity," in *Handbook of Creativity,* ed. R. J. Sternberg (New York: Cambridge University Press, 1999), 392–430.

64. For a thorough discussion of illumination or insight, see R. J. Sternberg and J. E. Davidson, *The Nature of Insight* (Cambridge, MA: MIT Press, 1995).

65. *Big Demands and High Expectations*, The Deliotte Millennial Survey (New York: Deloitte Touche Tohmatsu, January 2014); *Seeking Creative Candidates: Hiring for the Future* (San Jose, CA: Adobe, September 2014); Adobe, "New Adobe Study Uncovers Creativity Gap in Government," news release (San Jose, CA: Adobe, March 30, 2016); M. Hvisdos, "How to Foster Curiosity and Creativity in the Workplace," *Training*, June 8, 2016.

66. R. J. Sternberg and L. A. O'Hara, "Creativity and Intelligence," in *Handbook of Creativity,* ed. R. J. Sternberg (New York: Cambridge University Press, 1999), 251–72; S. Taggar, "Individual Creativity and Group Ability to Utilize Individual Creative Resources: A Multilevel Model," *Academy of Management Journal* 45 (2002): 315–30.

67. G. J. Feist, "The Influence of Personality on Artistic and Scientific Creativity," in *Handbook of Creativity*, ed. R. J. Sternberg (New York: Cambridge University Press, 1999), 273–96; T. Åsterbro, S. A. Jeffrey, and G. K. Adomdza, "Inventor Perseverance after Being Told to Quit: The Role of Cognitive Biases," *Journal of Behavioral Decision Making* 20 (2007): 253–72; J. S. Mueller, S. Melwani, and J. A. Goncalo, "The Bias against Creativity: Why People Desire but Reject Creative Ideas," *Psychological Science* 23, no. 1 (2012): 13–17.

68. R. W. Weisberg, "Creativity and Knowledge: A Challenge to Theories," in *Handbook of Creativity*, ed. R. J. Sternberg (New York: Cambridge University Press, 1999), 226–50.

69. E. Dane, "Reconsidering the Trade-Off between Expertise and Flexibility: A Cognitive Entrenchment Perspective," *Academy of Management Review* 35, no. 4 (2010): 579–603; R. I. Sutton, *Weird Ideas That Work* (New York: Free Press, 2002), 53–54, 121.

70. G. J. Feist, "The Influence of Personality on Artistic and Scientific Creativity," in *Handbook of Creativity*, ed. R. J. Sternberg (New York: Cambridge University Press, 1999), 273–96; C. E. Shalley, J. Zhou, and G. R. Oldham, "The Effects of Personal and Contextual Characteristics on Creativity: Where Should We Go from Here?," *Journal of Management* 30, no. 6 (2004): 933–58; S. J. Dollinger, K. K. Urban, and T. A. James, "Creativity and Openness to Experience: Validation of Two Creative Product Measures," *Creativity Research Journal* 16, no. 1 (2004): 35–47; T. S. Schweizer, "The Psychology of Novelty-Seeking, Creativity and Innovation: Neurocognitive Aspects within a Work-Psychological Perspective," *Creativity and Innovation Management* 15, no. 2 (2006): 164–72; S. Acar and M. A. Runco, "Creative Abilities: Divergent Thinking," in *Handbook of Organizational Creativity*, ed. M. Mumford (Waltham, MA: Academic Press, 2012), 115–39.

71. C. E. Shalley, J. Zhou, and G. R. Oldham, "The Effects of Personal and Contextual Characteristics on Creativity: Where Should We Go from Here?," *Journal of Management* 30, no. 6 (2004): 933–58; S. J. Dollinger, K. K. Urban, and T. A. James, "Creativity and Openness to Experience: Validation of Two Creative Product Measures," *Creativity Research Journal* 16, no. 1 (2004): 35–47; T. M. Amabile et al., "Leader Behaviors and the Work Environment for Creativity: Perceived Leader Support," *The Leadership Quarterly* 15, no. 1 (2004): 5–32; S. T. Hunter, K. E. Bedell, and M. D. Mumford, "Climate for Creativity: A Quantitative Review," *Creativity Research Journal* 19, no. 1 (2007): 69–90; T. C. DiLiello and J. D. Houghton, "Creative Potential and Practised Creativity: Identifying Untapped Creativity in Organizations," *Creativity and Innovation Management* 17, no. 1 (2008): 37–46.

72. "BNY Mellon Looks to Tap in to UK Startup Culture with New EMEA Innovation Centre," *Finextra*, November 11, 2015; S. Kumar, "Relaunching Innovation: Lessons from Silicon Valley," *Banking Perspective*, March 2016, 18–23; BNY Mellon, "Rewarding 'Intrapreneurship,'" BNY Mellon, 2016, http://www.bnymellon.com/us/en/who-we-are/people-report/lead/rewarding-intrapreneurship.jsp (accessed April 26, 2016).

73. R. Westwood and D.R. Low, "The Multicultural Muse: Culture, Creativity and Innovation," *International Journal of Cross Cultural Management* 3, no. 2 (2003): 235–59.

74. T. M. Amabile, "Motivating Creativity in Organizations: On Doing What You Love and Loving What You Do," *California Management Review* 40 (1997): 39–58; A. Cummings and G. R. Oldham, "Enhancing Creativity: Managing Work Contexts for the High Potential Employee," *California Management Review*, no. 40 (1997): 22–38; F. Coelho and M. Augusto, "Job Characteristics and the Creativity of Frontline Service Employees," *Journal of Service Research* 13, no. 4 (2010): 426–38.

75. T. M. Amabile, "Changes in the Work Environment for Creativity during Downsizing," *Academy of Management Journal* 42 (1999): 630–40.

76. J. Moultrie et al., "Innovation Spaces: Towards a Framework for Understanding the Role of the Physical Environment in Innovation," *Creativity & Innovation Management* 16, no. 1 (2007): 53–65.

77. J. M. Howell and K. Boies, "Champions of Technological Innovation: The Influence of Contextual Knowledge, Role Orientation, Idea Generation, and Idea Promotion on Champion Emergence," *The Leadership Quarterly* 15, no. 1 (2004): 123–43; C. E. Shalley, J. Zhou, and G. R. Oldham, "The Effects of Personal and Contextual Characteristics on Creativity: Where Should We Go from Here?," *Journal of Management* 30, no. 6 (2004): 933–58; S. J. Dollinger, K. K. Urban, and T. A. James, "Creativity and Openness to Experience: Validation of Two Creative Product Measures," *Creativity Research Journal* 16, no. 1 (2004): 35–47; S. Powell, "The Management and Consumption of Organisational Creativity," *Journal of Consumer Marketing* 25, no. 3 (2008): 158–66.

78. A. Hiam, "Obstacles to Creativity—and How You Can Remove Them," *Futurist* 32 (1998): 30–34.

79. M. A. West, *Developing Creativity in Organizations* (Leicester, UK: BPS Books, 1997), 33–35.

80. For discussion of how play affects creativity, see S. Brown, *Play: How It Shapes the Brain, Opens the Imagination, and Invigorates the Soul* (New York: Avery, 2009); C. Mainemelis and D. D. Dionysiou, "Play, Flow, and Timelessness," in *The Oxford Handbook of Creativity, Innovation, and Entrepreneurship*, ed. C. Shalley, M. Hitt, and J. Zhou (New York: Oxford University Press, 2015), 121–40.

81. T. Ritchey, *Wicked Problems—Social Messes: Decision Support Modelling with Morphological Analysis*, Risk, Governance and Society (Berlin: Springer-Verlag, 2011); S. Seidenstricker and C. Linder, "A Morphological Analysis-Based Creativity Approach to Identify and Develop Ideas for BMI: A Case Study of a High-Tech Manufacturing Company," *International Journal of Entrepreneurship and Innovation Management* 18, no. 5–6 (2014): 409–24.

82. A. Hargadon and R. I. Sutton, "Building an Innovation Factory," *Harvard Business Review* 78 (2000): 157–66; T. Kelley, *The Art of Innovation* (New York: Currency Doubleday, 2001), 158–62; P. F. Skilton and K. J. Dooley, "The Effects of Repeat Collaboration on Creative Abrasion," *Academy of Management Review* 35, no. 1 (2010): 118–34.

83. C. Meinel and L. Leifer, "Introduction—Design Thinking Is Mainly about Building Innovators," in *Design Thinking Research: Building Innovators*, ed. H. Plattner, C. Meinel, and L. Leifer (Cham, Switzerland: Springer International, 2015), 1–11.

84. E. Köppen and C. Meinel, "Empathy Via Design Thinking: Creation of Sense and Knowledge," in *Design Thinking Research: Building Innovators*, ed. H. Plattner, C. Meinel, and L. Leifer (Cham, Switzerland: Springer International, 2015), 15–28.

85. J. Kolko, "Design Thinking Comes of Age," *Harvard Business Review* 93, no. 9 (2015): 66–71; C. Vetterli et al., "How Deutsche Bank's IT Division Used Design Thinking to Achieve Customer Proximity," *MIS Quarterly Executive* 15, no. 1 (2016): 37–53.

86. M. Fenton-O'Creevy, "Employee Involvement and the Middle Manager: Saboteur or Scapegoat?," *Human Resource Management Journal*, no. 11 (2001): 24–40. Also see V. H. Vroom and A. G. Jago, *The New Leadership: Managing Participation in Organizations* (Englewood Cliffs, NJ: Prentice Hall, 1988).

87. V. H. Vroom and A. G. Jago, *The New Leadership: Managing Participation in Organizations* (Englewood Cliffs, NJ: Prentice Hall, 1988).

88. Some of the early OB writing on employee involvement includes C. Argyris, *Personality and Organization* (New York: Harper & Row, 1957); D. McGregor, *The Human Side of Enterprise* (New York: McGraw-Hill, 1960); R. Likert, *New Patterns of Management* (New York: McGraw-Hill, 1961).

89. A. G. Robinson and D. M. Schroeder, *Ideas Are Free* (San Francisco: Berrett-Koehler, 2004).

90. R. J. Ely and D. A. Thomas, "Cultural Diversity at Work: The Effects of Diversity Perspectives on Work Group Processes and Outcomes," *Administrative Science Quarterly* 46 (2001): 229–73; E. Mannix and M. A. Neale, "What Differences Make a Difference?: The Promise and Reality of Diverse Teams in Organizations," *Psychological Science in the Public Interest* 6, no. 2 (2005): 31–55.

91. D. Berend and J. Paroush, "When Is Condorcet's Jury Theorem Valid?," *Social Choice and Welfare* 15, no. 4 (1998): 481–88.

92. This quotation has a long and convoluted history. It has been attributed (incorrectly) to Benjamin Franklin and to Native Americans. The quotation stated here was popular in education during the 1960s and is cited in the 1975 source below. However, this quotation is almost certainly an adaptation of writing by Chinese Confucian philosopher Xun Kuang (circa 250 BC). A simplified version of his original statement is: "I hear and I forget; I see and I remember; I do and I understand." R. E. Keeton, "Tell Me, Show Me, Involve Me," *Learning and the Law* 2 (1975): 16–21, 64–65.

93. K. T. Dirks, L. L. Cummings, and J. L. Pierce, "Psychological Ownership in Organizations: Conditions under Which Individuals Promote and Resist Change," *Research in Organizational Change and Development*, no. 9 (1996): 1–23; J. P. Walsh and S. F. Tseng, "The Effects of Job Characteristics on Active Effort at Work," *Work & Occupations* 25, no. 1 (1998): 74–96; B. Scott-Ladd and V. Marshall, "Participation in Decision Making: A Matter of Context?," *Leadership & Organization Development Journal* 25, no. 8 (2004): 646–62.

94. V. H. Vroom and A. G. Jago, *The New Leadership: Managing Participation in Organizations* (Englewood Cliffs, NJ: Prentice Hall, 1988).

PART 3

7 | Team Dynamics

Learning Objectives

After you read this chapter, you should be able to:

LO7-1 Explain why employees join informal groups, and discuss the benefits and limitations of teams.

LO7-2 Outline the team effectiveness model and discuss how task characteristics, team size, and team composition influence team effectiveness.

LO7-3 Discuss how the four team processes—team development, norms, cohesion, and trust—influence team effectiveness.

LO7-4 Discuss the characteristics and factors required for the success of self-directed teams and virtual (remote) teams.

LO7-5 Identify four constraints on team decision making and discuss the advantages and disadvantages of four structures aimed at improving team decision making.

B uurtzorg Nederland employs approximately 8,000 professionals (mostly registered nurses) in more than 700 self-directed teams across the Netherlands. "There are no managers to call for help or to take responsibility; teams resolve issues for themselves," observes a British nurse who recently studied the nonprofit community health care organization's team structure. In fact, the company's motto is (translated): "How do you manage professionals? You don't!" The head office has only 45 people in administration and another 15 coaches to help teams improve their work relationships.

Each team consists of up to 12 nurses responsible for between 50 and 60 home care patients, most of whom are elderly, disabled, or terminally ill. Patients are usually served by a subteam of employees rather than by one team member alone. Team members have considerable autonomy to care for patients. Issues are discussed and creatively resolved by team members at weekly meetings.

Team members also use the company's secure social network system to share information and solutions with other Buurtzorg teams.

Buurtzorg measures performance at the team level, including patient satisfaction, work efficiency, and cost savings. Every employee can view a dashboard that provides feedback on the team's performance compared with other teams across the organization. Independent studies have reported that the company's self-directed teams are significantly more cost-efficient than traditional (mostly nonteam) services, even though Buurtzorg employees have higher education and more training. Buurtzorg's employees also enjoy the team structure. The company has been the top employer in the Netherlands for several consecutive years.[1]

Teamwork is woven into the organizational structure at Buurtzorg Nederland. Why are teams so important at this company and many others, and how can organizations strengthen their potential for organizational effectiveness? We find the answers to these and other questions in this chapter on team dynamics. This chapter begins by defining *teams*, examining the reasons why organizations rely on teams, and explaining why people join informal groups in organizational settings. A large segment of this chapter examines a model of team effectiveness, which includes team and organizational environment; team design; and the team processes of development, norms, cohesion, and trust. We then turn our attention to two specific types of teams: self-directed teams and virtual (also called remote) teams. The final section of this chapter looks at the challenges and strategies for making better decisions in teams.

LO7-1 Explain why employees join informal groups, and discuss the benefits and limitations of teams.

TEAMS AND INFORMAL GROUPS

Teams are groups of two or more people who interact with and influence each other, are mutually accountable for achieving common goals associated with organizational objectives, and perceive themselves as a social entity within an organization.[2]

This definition has a few important components worth repeating. First, all teams exist to fulfill some purpose, such as creating an industrial mold, assembling a product, designing a new social welfare program, or making an important decision. Second, team members are held together by their interdependence and need for collaboration to achieve common goals. All teams require some form of communication so that members can coordinate and share common objectives. Third, team members influence each other, although some members may be more influential than others regarding the team's goals and activities. Finally, a team exists when its members perceive themselves to be a team. They feel connected to each other through a common interest or purpose.

There are many types of teams in organizations, and each type can be distinguished by three characteristics: team permanence, skill diversity, and authority dispersion (see Exhibit 7.1).[3] Team permanence refers to how long that type of team usually exists. Accounting, marketing, and other departments are usually long-lasting structures, so these teams have high permanence. In contrast, task forces usually have low permanence because most are formed temporarily to solve a problem, realize an opportunity, or design a product or service. An emerging trend is the formation of teams that exist even more briefly, sometimes only for one eight-hour shift.[4]

A second distinguishing characteristic is the team's skill diversity. A team has high skill diversity when its members possess different skills and knowledge, whereas low diversity exists when team members have similar abilities and, therefore, are interchangeable. Most functional departments have low skill diversity because they organize employees around their common

Exhibit 7.1 Team Permanence, Skill Diversity, and Authority Dispersion for Selected Team Types

Team Type	Description	Typical Characteristics
Departmental teams	Teams that consist of employees who have similar or complementary skills and are located in the same unit of a functional structure; usually minimal task interdependence because each person works with clients or with employees in other departments.	*Team permanence:* High—departments continue indefinitely. *Skill diversity:* Low to medium—departments are often organized around common skills (e.g., accounting staff located in the accounting department). *Authority dispersion:* Low—departmental power is usually concentrated in the departmental manager.
Self-directed teams	Teams whose members are organized around work processes that complete an entire piece of work requiring several interdependent tasks and have substantial autonomy over the execution of those tasks (i.e., they usually control inputs, flow, and outputs with little or no supervision).	*Team permanence:* High—teams are usually assigned indefinitely to a specific cluster of production or service activities. *Skill diversity:* Medium to high—members typically perform different tasks requiring diverse skill sets, but cross-training can somewhat reduce skill diversity. *Authority dispersion:* High—team members share power, usually with limited hierarchical authority.
Task force (project) teams	Cross-functional teams whose members are usually drawn from several disciplines to solve a specific problem, realize an opportunity, or design a product or service.	*Team permanence:* Low—teams typically disband on completion of a specific project. *Skill diversity:* Medium to high—members are typically drawn from several functional specializations associated with the complexity of the problem or opportunity. *Authority dispersion:* Medium—teams often have someone with formal authority (project leader), but members also have moderate power due to their expertise and functional representation.

skill sets (e.g., people with accounting expertise are located in the accounting department). In contrast, self-directed teams, which we discuss later in this chapter, are responsible for producing an entire product or service, which usually requires members with dissimilar skills and knowledge to perform the diverse tasks in that work. Cross-training increases interchangeability of team members to some extent, but moderately high skill diversity is still likely where the team's work is complex.

Authority dispersion, the third distinguishing characteristic of teams, refers to the degree to which decision-making responsibility is distributed throughout the team (high dispersion) or is vested in one or a few members of the team (low dispersion). Departmental teams tend to have low authority dispersion because power is somewhat concentrated in a formal manager. Self-directed teams usually have high authority dispersion because the entire team makes key decisions and hierarchical authority is limited.

Informal Groups

This chapter mainly focuses on formal teams, but employees also belong to informal groups. All teams are groups; however, many groups do not satisfy our definition of teams. Groups include people assembled together, whether or not they have any interdependence or organizationally focused objective. The friends you meet for lunch are an *informal group*, but they wouldn't be called a team because they have little or no interdependence (each

person could just as easily eat lunch alone) and no organizationally mandated purpose. Instead, they exist primarily for the benefit of their members.

Why do informal groups exist? One reason is that human beings are social animals. Our drive to bond is hardwired through

Informal groups exist in organizations because people have a drive to bond, define themselves partly by their social identity, need others to help accomplish nontask goals, and rely on social interaction to minimize stress.
©Jetta Productions/Blend Images/Getty Images

evolutionary development, creating a need to belong to informal groups.[5] This is evident by the fact that people invest considerable time and effort forming and maintaining social relationships without any special circumstances or ulterior motives. A second reason why people join informal groups is provided by social identity theory, which states that individuals define themselves by their group affiliations (see Chapter 3). Thus, we join groups—particularly those that are viewed favorably by others and that have values similar to our own—because they shape and reinforce our self-concept.[6]

A third reason why informal groups exist is that they accomplish personal objectives that cannot be achieved by individuals working alone. For example, employees will sometimes congregate to oppose organizational changes because this collective effort has more power than individuals who try to bring about change alone. These informal groups, called *coalitions*, are discussed in Chapter 9. A fourth explanation for informal groups is that we are comforted by the mere presence of other people and are therefore motivated to be near them in stressful situations. When in danger, people congregate near each other even though doing so serves no protective purpose. Similarly, employees tend to mingle more often after hearing rumors that the company

ADVANTAGES AND DISADVANTAGES OF TEAMS

Why are teams becoming so important in so many other companies around the world? The answer to this question has a long history.[9] Early research on British coal mining in the 1940s, the Japanese economic miracle of the 1970s, and a huge number of investigations since then have revealed that *under the right conditions*, teams make better decisions, develop better products and services, and create a more engaged workforce than do employees working alone.[10] Similarly, team members can quickly share information and coordinate tasks, whereas these processes are slower and prone to more errors in traditional departments led by supervisors. Teams typically provide superior customer service because they offer clients more knowledge and expertise than individuals working alone can offer.

Research on the changing nature of scientific research provides further evidence that teams outperform individuals, at least in complex work. A study of almost 20 million research

> Talent wins games, but teamwork and intelligence win championships.[11]
>
> —Michael Jordan, professional basketball player and sports executive

might be acquired by a competitor. As Chapter 4 explained, this social support minimizes stress by providing emotional and/or informational resources to buffer the stress experience.[7]

Informal Groups and Organizational Outcomes Informal groups are not created to serve corporate objectives, yet they have a profound influence on the organization and its employees. Informal groups potentially minimize employee stress because, as mentioned, group members provide emotional and informational social support. This stress-reducing capability of informal groups improves employee well-being, which potentially increases organizational effectiveness. Informal groups are also the backbone of *social networks*, which are important sources of trust building, information sharing, power, influence, and employee well-being in the workplace.[8] Chapter 8 describes the increasing popularity of enterprise social networking sites similar to Facebook and LinkedIn that encourage employees to form informal groups. Chapter 9 explains how social networks are a source of influence in organizational settings. Employees with strong informal networks tend to have more power and influence because they receive better information and preferential treatment from others and their talent is more visible to key decision makers.

publications reported that the percentage of journal articles written by teams rather than individuals has increased substantially over the past five decades. Team-based articles also had a much higher number of subsequent citations, suggesting that journal articles written by teams are superior to articles written by individuals.[12]

Teams are potentially more productive because, in many situations, their members are more motivated than when working alone.[13] There are three motivating forces at work. First, employees have a drive to bond and are motivated to fulfill the goals of groups to which they belong. This felt obligation is particularly strong when the employee's social identity is connected to the team. Second, members have high accountability to fellow team members, who monitor performance more closely than a traditional supervisor. This accountability is particularly strong when the team's performance depends on the worst performer, such as on an assembly line. Third, each team member creates a moving performance standard for the others. When a few employees complete tasks faster, other team members recognize that they could work faster. This benchmark effect also motivates because employees are often apprehensive that their performance will be compared to others' performance.

OB THEORY TO PRACTICE

What Organizations Say About Teamwork[14]

Company	What They Say About Teamwork
Audi Hungaria Motor (Hungarian division of the German automobile manufacturer)	"Employees in administration and production always work in teams. Personnel selection takes account not only of specialist qualifications and work experience, but also of team capabilities, language knowledge and social competence."
National Aeronautics and Space Administration	"NASA's most powerful tool for achieving mission success is a multi-disciplinary team of diverse competent people across all NASA Centers. Our approach to teamwork is based on a philosophy that each team member brings unique experience and important expertise to project issues."
Amgen	"Our teams work quickly to move scientific breakthroughs from the lab through the clinic to the marketplace and to support other aspects of our business. Diverse teams working together generate the best decisions for patients, staff and stockholders. Our team structure provides opportunities for Amgen staff to impact the direction of the organization, to gain broader perspective about other functions within Amgen and to reach their full potential."
General Dynamics Mission Systems–Canada	"At General Dynamics Mission Systems–Canada, teamwork is not a buzzword, it is the foundation of everything we do. Our collaborative, multi-function, dialogue-driven, teams create the innovations that enable us to succeed with our customers."

The Challenges of Teams

Teams are potentially very productive, but they are not always as effective as individuals working alone.[15] The main problem is that teams have additional costs called **process losses**—resources (including time and energy) expended on team development and maintenance rather than on performing the task.[16]

Team members need time and effort to resolve their disagreements, develop mutual understanding of their goals, determine the best strategy for accomplishing those goals, negotiate their specific roles, and agree on informal rules of conduct. An employee working alone on a project does not have these disagreements, misunderstandings, divergent viewpoints, or coordination problems within himself or herself (at least, not nearly as much as with other people). Teams may be necessary when the work is so complex that it requires knowledge and skills from several people. But when the work can be performed by one person, process losses can make a team less effective than an individual working alone.

Process losses are amplified when more people are added or replace others on the team.[17] The new team members consume time and effort figuring out how to work well with other team members. Performance also suffers among current team members while their attention is diverted from task performance to accommodating and integrating the newcomer. Process losses tend to increase as the team adds more members because a larger team requires more coordination, more time for conflict resolution, and so forth. The software industry even has a name for the problems of adding people to a team: **Brooks's law** says that adding more people to a late software project only makes it later! Although process losses are well known, research has found that managers consistently underestimate these costs when adding more people to an existing team.[18]

Social Loafing The process losses just described mainly refer to coordination challenges, but teams also suffer from motivational process losses. The best-known motivational process loss is **social loafing**, which occurs when people exert less effort (and usually perform at a lower level) in teams than working alone.[20]

Social loafing is more likely to occur when individual performance is hidden or difficult to distinguish from the performance of other team members.
©KeyStock/Shutterstock

Social loafing is more pervasive under several conditions.[21] Social loafing is more likely to occur when individual performance is hidden or difficult to distinguish from the performance of other team members. In team settings, individual performance is less visible in larger rather than smaller teams. It is also hidden when the team produces a single output (e.g., solving a client's problem) rather than separate outputs for each team member (e.g., each member reviews several accounting reports per day). Second, social loafing is more common when the work is boring or the team's overall task has low task significance (see Chapter 5). Third, individual characteristics explain why some people are more likely to engage in social loafing. For instance, social loafing is more prevalent among team members with low conscientiousness and low agreeableness personality traits as well as low collectivist values.

Fourth, social loafing is more prevalent when employees lack motivation to help the team achieve its goals. This lack of motivation occurs when individual members have low social identity with the team and the team has low cohesion. Lack of motivation also occurs when employees believe other team members aren't pulling their weight. In other words, social loafers provide only as much effort as they believe others will provide, which is

their way of maintaining fairness in work allocation. Employees also exert less effort when they believe they have little control over the team's success, such as when the team is large (their contribution has minimal effect on the team's performance) and when the team is dependent on other members with known performance problems.

Overall, teams can be very powerful forces for competitive advantage, or they can be much more trouble than they are worth. To understand when teams are better than individuals working alone, we need to more closely examine the conditions that make teams effective or ineffective. The next few sections of this chapter discuss the model of team effectiveness.

LO7-2 Outline the team effectiveness model and discuss how task characteristics, team size, and team composition influence team effectiveness.

A MODEL OF TEAM EFFECTIVENESS

Why are some teams effective while others fail? To answer this question, we first need to clarify the meaning of team effectiveness. A team is effective when it benefits the organization and its members, and survives long enough to accomplish its mandate.[22] First, teams exist to serve some organizational purpose, so effectiveness is partly measured by the achievement of that objective. Second, a team's effectiveness relies on the satisfaction and well-being of its members. People join groups to fulfill their personal needs, so effectiveness is partly measured by this need fulfillment. Finally, team effectiveness includes the team's ability to survive long enough to fulfill its purpose. Earlier, we pointed out that very short-lived teams are an emerging trend in organizations. Yet even these "flash teams" could fall apart literally (people refuse to join or stay with the team) or cognitively (members become emotionally disengaged from the team).

Researchers have developed several models over the years to identify the features or conditions that make some teams more effective than others.[23] Exhibit 7.2 integrates the main components of these team effectiveness models. We will closely examine each component over the next several pages. This exhibit is a meta-model because each component (team development, team cohesion, etc.) includes its own set of theories to explain how that component operates.

OB THEORY TO PRACTICE

Minimizing Social Loafing

▸ *Form smaller teams*—Splitting the team into several smaller groups reduces social loafing because each person's performance becomes more noticeable and important for team performance. A smaller group also potentially increases individual commitment to and identity with the team.

▸ *Specialize tasks*—Individual effort is easier to observe when each team member performs a different work activity. For example, rather than pooling their effort for all incoming customer inquiries, each customer service representative might be assigned a particular type of client.

▸ *Measure individual performance*—Individual effort is easier to observe when measured at the individual level. However, this recommendation is feasible only when output is distinct for each member and can be quantified to some extent. This action is difficult when the team produces a single output, such as solving a client's problem.

▸ *Increase job enrichment*—Team members are more motivated when their task has high motivation potential, such as requiring more skill variety or having direct contact with clients. Social loafing is less common when the team's overall objective has high task significance.

▸ *Select motivated, team-oriented employees*—Employees are less susceptible to social loafing when they are self-motivated, have moderately high conscientiousness and agreeableness personality traits, have a somewhat collectivist value orientation, and develop a strong social identity with the team.

Exhibit 7.2 Team Effectiveness Model

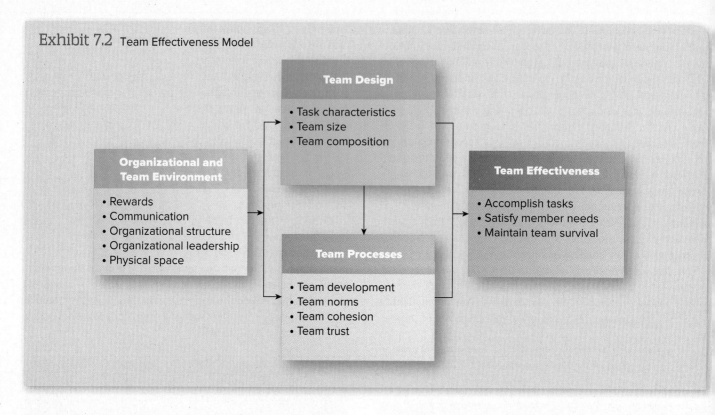

Team Design
- Task characteristics
- Team size
- Team composition

Organizational and Team Environment
- Rewards
- Communication
- Organizational structure
- Organizational leadership
- Physical space

Team Processes
- Team development
- Team norms
- Team cohesion
- Team trust

Team Effectiveness
- Accomplish tasks
- Satisfy member needs
- Maintain team survival

Organizational and Team Environment

The organizational and team environment represents all conditions beyond the team's boundaries that influence its effectiveness. The environment is typically viewed as a resource pool that either supports or inhibits the team's ability to function and achieve its objectives.[24] Team members tend to work together more effectively when they receive some team-based rewards, when the organization's structure assigns discrete clusters of work activity to teams, when information systems support team coordination, and when the physical layout of the team's workspace encourages frequent communication. For example, many companies have moved teams into open offices and special team spaces, resulting in better communication and stronger cohesion among team members. The team's leadership also plays an important role, such as by supporting teamwork rather than "star" individuals and by valuing the team's diversity.[25]

Along with being a resource, the environment generates drivers for change within teams. External competition is an environmental condition that affects team dynamics, such as increasing motivation of team members to work together. Another

OB THEORY TO PRACTICE

Obeya Room Strengthens Team Performance

Many years ago, Toyota Motor Company discovered that it could speed up new car design by forming a cross-functional team and having the team members meet regularly in an "obeya"—Japanese for "large room." Many companies have recently introduced obeya rooms to improve team performance on complex problems through face-to-face interaction. German engineering firm Siemens has introduced obeya rooms to support product development and production process decision making. Siemens quality systems manager Annemarie Kreyenberg noticed that the obeya room at her worksite in Germany has changed the company's culture. "The behavior of people in this [obeya] room was an excellent reflection of the progress of the cultural change," she observes. "Teams and managers experimented with new behaviors, creating role models and examples for the entire organization."[26]

©Sam Edwards/OJO Images/Getty Images

task interdependence
the extent to which team members must share materials, information, or expertise in order to perform their jobs

environmental driver would be changing societal expectations, such as higher safety standards, which require teams to alter their norms of behavior. These external forces for change not only motivate teams to redesign themselves, they also refocus the team's attention. For instance, teams develop better ways of working together so they provide better customer service.

TEAM DESIGN ELEMENTS

Even when it operates in a team-friendly environment, the team's effectiveness will fall short of its potential if the task characteristics, team size, and team composition are poorly designed.

Task Characteristics

Teams are more effective than individuals in specific types of tasks. They are better for work that is too complex for any individual to perform, such as launching the business in a new market, developing a computer operating system, or constructing a bridge. Complex work requires skills and knowledge beyond one person's abilities. Teams are particularly well suited for complex work that can be divided into more specialized roles, and where the people in those specialized roles are able to coordinate frequently with each other.

Task complexity demands teamwork, but teams work better when the work is well structured rather than ambiguous or novel. Team members on an automobile assembly line have well-structured tasks. They perform the same set of tasks each day—they have low *task variability* (see Chapter 5)—and the work is predictable enough for well-established procedures (high *task analyzability*). The main benefit of well-structured tasks is that it is easier to coordinate the work among several people. In contrast, ambiguous and unpredictable tasks are more difficult to coordinate among team members, which leads to higher process losses and errors. Teams can still perform these less-structured tasks reasonably well when their roles are well defined, however. During surgery, for example, medical team members know generally what to expect of each other even when unique problems arise.[27]

Another task-related influence on team effectiveness is **task interdependence**—the extent to which team members must share materials, information, or expertise to perform their jobs.[28] Apart from complete independence, there are three levels of task interdependence, as illustrated in Exhibit 7.3. The lowest level of interdependence, called *pooled interdependence*, occurs when an employee or work unit shares a common resource, such as machinery, administrative support, or a budget, with other employees or work units. This interdependence exists when each member works alone but shares raw materials or machinery to perform her or his otherwise independent tasks. Interdependence is higher under *sequential interdependence*, in which the output of one person becomes the direct input for another person or unit. Employees on an assembly line typically have sequential interdependence because each team member's output is forwarded to the next person on the line for further assembly of the product or service.

Reciprocal interdependence, in which work output is exchanged back and forth among individuals, produces the highest degree of interdependence. People who design a new product or service would typically have reciprocal interdependence because their design decisions affect others involved in the design process. Any decision made by the design engineers would influence the work of the manufacturing engineer and purchasing specialist, and vice versa. Employees with reciprocal interdependence should be organized into teams to facilitate coordination in their interwoven relationship.

As a rule, the higher the level of task interdependence, the greater the need to organize people into teams rather than have them work alone. A team structure improves interpersonal communication and thus results in better coordination. High task interdependence also motivates most people to be part of the team. However, the rule that a team should be formed when employees have high interdependence applies when team members have the same task goals, such as serving the same clients or collectively assembling the same product. When team members have different goals (such as serving different clients) but must depend on other team members to achieve those unique goals, teamwork might create excessive conflict. Under these circumstances, the company should try to reduce the level of interdependence or rely on supervision as a buffer or mediator among employees.

Team Size

Teams need to be large enough to provide the necessary abilities and viewpoints to perform the work, yet small enough to maintain efficient coordination and meaningful involvement of each member.[29] Small teams (say, less than a dozen members) operate effectively because they have less process loss. Members of

Task complexity demands teamwork, but teams work better when the work is well structured rather than ambiguous or novel.
©Kristy-Anne Glubish/Design Pics

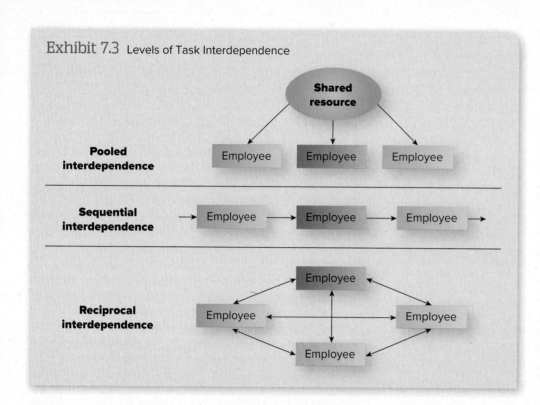

Exhibit 7.3   Levels of Task Interdependence

Pooled interdependence

Shared resource

Employee   Employee   Employee

Sequential interdependence

Employee → Employee → Employee →

Reciprocal interdependence

Employee

Employee   Employee

Employee

Team Composition

Team effectiveness depends on the qualities of the people who are members of those teams.[32] Of course, teams perform better when their members are highly motivated, possess the required abilities, and have clear role perceptions to perform the individual tasks assigned to them (see MARS model in Chapter 2). But effective teams also need these people to be motivated and able to work effectively in teams. The "Five Cs" model illustrated in Exhibit 7.4 identifies the five types of team member behaviors mentioned most often in the team dynamics literature: cooperating, coordinating, communicating, comforting, and conflict handling. The first three types of behavior

> You need to have a balance between having enough [team members] to do all the things that need to be done, while keeping the team small enough so that it is cohesive and can make decisions effectively and speedily.[31]
>
> —Jim Hassell, Group CEO of BAI Communications

smaller teams also tend to feel more engaged because they have more influence on the group's norms and goals and feel more responsible for the team's successes and failures. Also, members of smaller teams get to know each other better, which improves mutual trust as well as perceived support, help, and assistance from those team members.[30]

Should companies have 100-person teams if the task is highly complex? The answer is that a group this large probably isn't a team, even if management calls it one. A team exists when its members interact and influence each other, are mutually accountable for achieving common goals associated with organizational objectives, and perceive themselves as a social entity within an organization. It is very difficult for everyone in a 100-person work unit to influence each other and perceive themselves as members of the same team. However, such complex tasks can usually be divided into several teams.

are mainly (but not entirely) task-related, while the last two primarily assist team maintenance:[33]

- *Cooperating.* Effective team members are willing and able to work with others. This includes sharing resources and being sufficiently flexible to accommodate the needs of other team members.

- *Coordinating.* Effective team members actively manage the team's work so that it is performed efficiently and harmoniously. This includes keeping the team on track and helping integrate the work performed by different members. To effectively coordinate, team members must know the other team members' work to some extent, not just their own.

- *Communicating.* Effective team members transmit information freely (rather than hoarding), efficiently (using the best channel and language), and respectfully (minimizing arousal of negative emotions).[34] They also listen actively to coworkers.

- *Comforting.* Effective team members help coworkers maintain a positive and healthy psychological state. They show empathy, provide

Exhibit 7.4 Five Cs of Effective Team Member Behavior

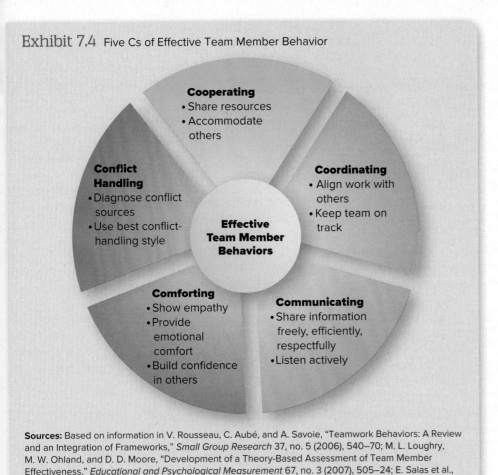

Cooperating
• Share resources
• Accommodate others

Coordinating
• Align work with others
• Keep team on track

Conflict Handling
• Diagnose conflict sources
• Use best conflict-handling style

Effective Team Member Behaviors

Comforting
• Show empathy
• Provide emotional comfort
• Build confidence in others

Communicating
• Share information freely, efficiently, respectfully
• Listen actively

Sources: Based on information in V. Rousseau, C. Aubé, and A. Savoie, "Teamwork Behaviors: A Review and an Integration of Frameworks," *Small Group Research* 37, no. 5 (2006), 540–70; M. L. Loughry, M. W. Ohland, and D. D. Moore, "Development of a Theory-Based Assessment of Team Member Effectiveness," *Educational and Psychological Measurement* 67, no. 3 (2007), 505–24; E. Salas et al., "Understanding and Improving Teamwork in Organizations: A Scientifically Based Practical Guide," *Human Resource Management* 54, no. 4 (2015): 599–622.

A second reason is that diverse team members have a broader pool of technical abilities. Financial services teams consist of people with expertise in diverse areas, such as stocks, bonds, derivatives, cash management, and other asset classes. Some teams also have diverse investment philosophies (fundamentals, technical, momentum, etc.) and expertise across regions of the world.

Another advantage of diverse teams is that they often provide better representation of the team's constituents, such as other departments or clients from similarly diverse backgrounds. This representation brings different viewpoints to the decision; it also gives stakeholders a belief that they have a voice in that decision process. As we learned in Chapter 5, voice is an important ingredient in procedural justice, so stakeholders are more likely to believe the team's decision is fair when the team mirrors the surface or deep-level diversity of its constituents.

Against these advantages are a number of challenges created by team diversity. Employees with diverse backgrounds take longer to become a

emotional comfort, and build coworker feelings of confidence and self-worth.

• *Conflict handling.* Conflict is inevitable in social settings, so effective team members have the skills and motivation to resolve disagreements among team members. This requires effective use of various conflict-handling styles as well as diagnostic skills to identify and resolve the structural sources of conflict.

Team Diversity Diversity, another important dimension of team composition, has both positive and negative effects on teams.[36] The main advantage of diverse teams is that they make better decisions than do homogeneous teams in some situations. One reason is that people from different backgrounds tend to see a problem or opportunity from different angles. Team members have different mental models, so they are more likely to identify viable solutions to difficult problems.

Rating Teamwork Skills in College Graduates and Coworkers[35]

86% of 5,601 senior (graduating) students at 394 American universities and colleges say they are very or extremely proficient in teamwork/collaboration.

60% of 2,138 American hiring managers and human resource professionals surveyed say that being team-oriented is an important characteristic they look for in job applicants.

44% of more than 40,000 employees surveyed in 300 global companies identify teamwork as the most important attribute when rating their co-workers.

©Ingram Publishing

83% of 400 American employees surveyed say it is very important that college graduates work effectively with others in teams (second highest competency, below oral communication).

37% of 400 American employers surveyed say that recent college graduates are well prepared at working with others in teams.

high-performing team. This occurs partly because bonding is slower among people who are different from each other, especially when teams have deep-level diversity (i.e., different beliefs and values). Diverse teams are susceptible to "faultlines"—hypothetical dividing lines that may split a team into subgroups along gender, ethnic, professional, or other dimensions.[37] These faultlines undermine team effectiveness by reducing the motivation to communicate and coordinate with teammates on the other side of the hypothetical divisions. In contrast, members of teams with minimal diversity experience higher satisfaction, less conflict, and better interpersonal relations. As a result, homogeneous teams tend to be more effective on tasks requiring a high degree of cooperation and coordination, such as emergency response teams.

> "Two sets of processes are the essence of team development: developing team identity and developing team mental models and coordinating routines."

development as new members join or other conditions disrupt the team's maturity. *Forming*, the first stage of team development, is a period of testing and orientation in which members learn about each other and evaluate the benefits and costs of continued membership. People tend to be polite, will defer to authority, and try to find out what is expected of them and how they will fit into the team. The *storming* stage is marked by interpersonal conflict as members become more proactive and compete for various team roles. Members try to establish norms of appropriate behavior and performance standards.

During the *norming* stage, the team develops its first real sense of cohesion as roles are established and a consensus forms around group objectives and a common or complementary team-based mental model. By the *performing* stage, team members have learned to efficiently coordinate and resolve conflicts. In high-performance teams, members are highly cooperative, have a high level of trust in each other, are committed to group objectives, and identify with the team. Finally, the *adjourning* stage occurs when the team is about to disband. Team members shift their attention away from task orientation to a relationship focus.

LO7-3 Discuss how the four team processes—team development, norms, cohesion, and trust—influence team effectiveness.

TEAM PROCESSES

The third set of elements in the team effectiveness model, collectively known as *team processes*, includes team development, norms, cohesion, and trust. These elements represent characteristics of the team that continuously evolve.

Team Development

Team members must resolve several issues and pass through several stages of development before emerging as an effective work unit. They need to get to know and trust each other, understand and agree on their respective roles, discover appropriate and inappropriate behaviors, and learn how to coordinate with each other. The longer team members work together, the better they develop common or complementary mental models, mutual understanding, and effective performance routines to complete the work.

A popular model that captures many team development activities is shown in Exhibit 7.5.[38] The diagram shows teams moving systematically from one stage to the next, while the dashed lines illustrate that teams might fall back to an earlier stage of

Developing Team Identities and Mental Models Although this model depicts team development fairly well, it is not a perfect representation of the process. For instance, it does not show that some teams remain in a particular stage longer than others and does not explain why teams sometimes regress back to earlier stages of development. The model also masks two sets of processes that are the essence of team development: developing team identity and developing team mental models and coordinating routines.[39]

- *Developing team identity.* Team development is apparent when its members shift from viewing the team as something "out there" to something that is part of themselves. In other words, team development occurs when employees make the team part of their social identity and take ownership of the team's success.[40]

- *Developing team mental models and coordinating routines.* Team development includes forming shared mental models of the work and team relationship.[41] Team mental models are knowledge structures mutually held by team members about expectations and ideals of the collective task and team dynamics. These mental models are shared or complementary. They include expectations and ideals about how the work should be accomplished as well as how team members should support each other. As team members form shared mental models, they also develop coordinating routines.[42] Each member develops habitual work practices that coordinate almost automatically with other members. They also develop action scripts to quickly adjust work behaviors in response to changes in activity by other team members.

Exhibit 7.5 Stages of Team Development

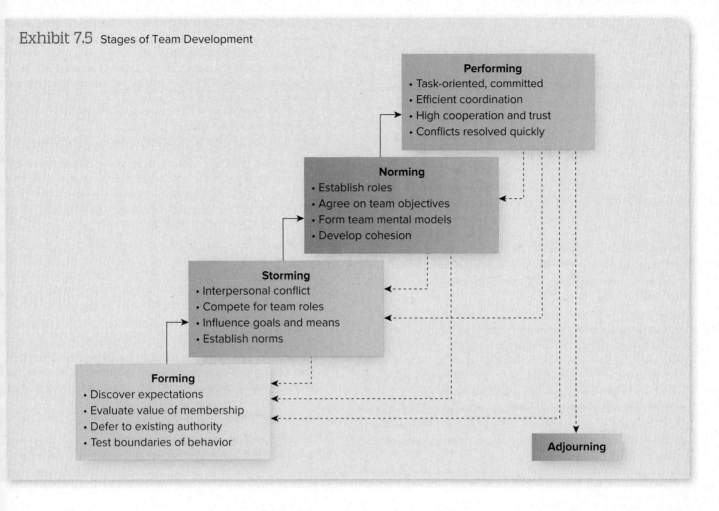

Performing
- Task-oriented, committed
- Efficient coordination
- High cooperation and trust
- Conflicts resolved quickly

Norming
- Establish roles
- Agree on team objectives
- Form team mental models
- Develop cohesion

Storming
- Interpersonal conflict
- Compete for team roles
- Influence goals and means
- Establish norms

Forming
- Discover expectations
- Evaluate value of membership
- Defer to existing authority
- Test boundaries of behavior

Adjourning

O B   T H E O R Y   T O   P R A C T I C E

Team Development Supports 36th CRG's Rapid Deployment

The 36th Contingency Response Group (CRG) is a rapid-deployment unit that establishes and maintains airfield operations before the main units arrive in humanitarian and disaster relief situations. The 44 team members achieve this efficiency through shared mental models and routines of coordination. They know their roles, each other's roles, and what an efficient operation should look like. Following Nepal's devastating earthquake, for example, the 36th CRG crew flew from Andersen Air Force Base, Guam, and within an hour of arrival was moving cargo off the Kathmandu airfield. Over the next month, they and the Nepalese army unloaded more than 200 aircraft.

"Our diverse team strives to keep aircraft ground times to a minimum which is what allows a larger throughput of aircraft and humanitarian aid," explains 36th CRG operations officer Capt. Brint Ingersoll. "We team up with other professionals to make this a very fluid, very efficient process." This photo shows 36th CRG crew members during their flight to the Nepal deployment.[43]

role a set of behaviors that people are expected to perform because they hold certain positions in a team and organization

team building a process that consists of formal activities intended to improve the development and functioning of a work team

norms the informal rules and shared expectations that groups establish to regulate the behavior of their members

Team Roles An important part of the team development process is forming and reinforcing team roles. A **role** is a set of behaviors that people are expected to perform because they hold formal or informal positions in a team and organization.[44] Some roles help the team achieve its goals; other roles maintain relationships within the team. Team members are assigned specific roles within their formal job responsibilities. For example, team leaders are usually expected to initiate discussion, ensure that everyone has an opportunity to present his or her views, and help the team reach agreement on the issues discussed.

Many team roles aren't formally embedded in job descriptions. Instead, they are informally assigned or claimed as part of the team development process. Team members are attracted to informal roles that suit their personality and values as well as the wishes of other team members. These informal roles are shared, but many are eventually associated with specific team members through subtle positioning and negotiation. Several experts have tried to categorize the various team roles. One recent model identifies six role categories: organizer, doer, challenger, innovator, team builder, and connector.[45]

- *Goal setting:* Some interventions help team members clarify the team's performance goals, increase the team's motivation to accomplish these goals, and establish a mechanism for systematic feedback on the team's goal performance. For example, a team-building program for a junior league ice hockey team in Finland included at the beginning of the season identifying distant goals (e.g., to be among the league's top three teams) and then specific goals to reach those distant goals. Each week throughout the season, subteams of three to six players reflected on these team goals and identified related individual goals and training.[48]

- *Problem solving:* This type of team building focuses on decision making, including how the team identifies problems and searches for alternatives. It also potentially develops critical thinking skills. Some team-building interventions are simulation games in which teams practice problem solving in hypothetical situations.

- *Role clarification:* This type of team building clarifies and reconstructs each member's perceptions of her or his role as well as the role expectations of other team members. Role-definition team building also helps the team develop the shared mental models that we discussed earlier, such as how to interact with clients, maintain machinery, and participate productively in meetings.

- *Interpersonal relations:* This is the oldest and still the most common type of team building. It tries to help team members learn more about each other, build trust in each other, manage conflict within the team, and strengthen team members' social identity with the team.[49] Some of the most popular team-building interventions today attempt to improve interpersonal relations within the team.

Do team-building interventions improve team development and effectiveness? The answer is that all four types of team building are potentially effective, but some interventions work better than others and in some situations more than others. One major review identified role clarification and goal setting as the most successful types of team building. One study found that team-building interventions are most effective when participants receive training on specific team skills, such as coordinating, conflict resolving, and communicating.[51]

Accelerating Team Development through Team Building
Team development takes time, but organizations often try to accelerate this process through **team building**, which consists of formal activities to improve the development and functioning of a work team.[46] Team building may be applied to new teams, but it is more commonly introduced for existing teams that have regressed to earlier stages of team development due to membership turnover or loss of focus. Team development is a complex process so, not surprisingly, there are several types of team building to serve different objectives. Team-building interventions often are organized into the following four categories; some team-building activities include two or more of these categories:[47]

However, many team-building activities are less successful.[52] One problem is that team-building interventions are used as general solutions to general team problems. A better approach is to begin with a sound diagnosis of the team's health and then select team-building interventions that address specific weaknesses.[53] Another problem is that team building is applied as a one-shot medical inoculation that every team should receive when it is formed. In truth, team building is an ongoing process, not a three-day jump start.[54] Finally, we must remember that team building occurs on the job, not just on an obstacle course or in a national park. Organizations should encourage team members to reflect on their work experiences and to experiment with just-in-time learning for team development.

Popular Team-Building Activities[50]

Team-Building Activity	Description	Example
Team volunteering events	Teams of employees spend a day providing a public service to the community.	Nicor Gas employees in Illinois volunteer their time in teams to help the community, such as building a house for Habitat for Humanity.
Team scavenger/treasure hunt events	Teams follow instructions to find clues or objects collected throughout the building or community.	Employees at Treatwell, Europe's largest hair salon booking website, engaged in a scavenger hunt around Barcelona, Spain, with teams comprising staff from the firm's 10 countries.
Team sports or exercise events	Wide variety of sports or health activities, such as sports tournaments across departments.	Ecommerce software developer Shopify holds an annual beach Volleyball Day, in which employee teams wear themed clothing (e.g., lumberjacks) and later enjoy a huge banquet picnic.
Team cooking events	Team members either learn how to cook a quality meal or several teams compete in teams to make the best dish with given ingredients.	Employee teams at software company Cobalt participated in an Iron Chef competition, where they had one hour to make the best dish that incorporated a themed ingredient.

Team Norms

Norms are the informal rules and shared expectations that groups establish to regulate the behavior of their members. Norms apply only to behavior, not to private thoughts or feelings. Furthermore, norms exist only for behaviors that are important to the team.[55] Norms are enforced in various ways. Coworkers display their displeasure if we are late for a meeting or if we don't have our part of a project completed on time. Norms also are directly reinforced through praise from high-status members, more access to valued resources, or other rewards available to the team. These forms of peer pressure and reinforcement can occur even when team members work remotely from each other. But team members often conform to prevailing norms without direct reinforcement or punishment because they identify with the group and want to align their behavior with the team's expectations. The more closely the person's social identity is connected to the group, the more the individual is motivated to avoid negative sanctions from that group.[56]

How Team Norms Develop Norms develop during team formation because people need to anticipate or predict how others will act. Even subtle events during the team's initial interactions, such as where team members sit in the first few meetings, can plant norms that are later difficult to change. Norms also form as team members discover behaviors that help them function more effectively, such as the need to respond quickly to text messages.[57] A critical event in the team's history, such as an injury or lost contract, is often a powerful foundation for a new norm. Third, norms are influenced by the experiences and values that members bring to the team. If members of a new team value work–life balance, they will likely develop norms that discourage long hours and work overload.[58]

Preventing and Changing Dysfunctional Team Norms
Two of the best ways to establish desired norms in new teams are to clearly state the norms up front and to select people whose values are compatible with those norms. As an example, if organizational leaders want their teams to have strong safety

Two of the best ways to establish desired norms in new teams are to clearly state the norms up front and to select people whose values are compatible with those norms.
©John Lund/Sam Diephuis/Blend Images LLC

norms, they should hire people who already value safety and who clearly identify the importance of safety when the team is formed.

The suggestions so far refer to new teams, but how can organizational leaders maintain desirable norms in older teams? Various studies suggest that team norms can be organizationally induced. That is, leaders can potentially introduce new norms and alter existing ones.[59] By speaking up or actively coaching the team, they may be able to subdue dysfunctional norms while developing useful norms. A second suggestion is to introduce team-based rewards that counter dysfunctional norms. However, studies report that employees might continue to abide by a dysfunctional team norm (such as restricting their work performance) even though this behavior reduces their paycheck. Finally, if dysfunctional norms are deeply ingrained and the previous solutions don't work, it may be necessary to disband the group and form a new team whose members have more favorable norms.

Team Cohesion

Team cohesion refers to the degree of attraction people feel toward the team and their motivation to remain members. It is a characteristic of the team, including the extent to which its members are attracted to the team, are committed to the team's goals or tasks, and feel a collective sense of team pride.[60] Thus, team cohesion is an emotional experience, not just a calculation of whether to stay or leave the team. It exists when team members make the team part of their social identity. Team development tends to improve cohesion because members strengthen their identity to the team during the development process.

Influences on Team Cohesion Six of the most important influences on team cohesion are described below. Some of these conditions strengthen the individual's social identity with the team; others strengthen the individual's belief that team membership will fulfill personal needs.

- *Member similarity.* A well-established research finding is that we are attracted more to coworkers who are similar to us.[61] This similarity-attraction effect occurs because we assume that people are more trustworthy and more likely to accept us if they look and act like us. We also believe that these similar others will create fewer conflicts and violations of our expectations. Thus, teams have higher cohesion or become cohesive more quickly when members are similar to each other. In contrast, high cohesion is more difficult and takes longer for teams with diverse members. This difficulty depends on the form of diversity, however. Teams consisting of people from different job groups seem to get together just as well as teams of people from the same job.[62]

- *Team size.* Smaller teams tend to have more cohesion than larger teams. One reason is that it is easier for a few people to agree on goals and coordinate work activities. Another reason is that members have more influence in smaller teams, so they feel a greater sense of involvement and ownership in the team. However, small teams have less cohesion when they lack enough qualified members to perform the required tasks.

- *Member interaction.* Teams tend to have more cohesion when their members interact with each other fairly regularly. More frequent interaction occurs when team members perform highly interdependent tasks and work in the same physical area.

- *Somewhat difficult entry.* Teams tend to have more cohesion when entry to the team is restricted. The more elite the team, the more prestige it confers on its members, and the more they tend to value their membership in the unit. At the same time, research suggests that severe initiations can weaken team cohesion because of the adverse effects of humiliation, even for those who successfully endure the initiation.[63]

- *Team success.* Team cohesion increases with the team's level of success because people are attracted to groups that fulfill their needs and goals.[64] Furthermore, individuals are more likely to attach their social identity to successful teams than to those with a string of failures.

- *External competition and challenges.* Teams tend to have more cohesion when they face external competition or a challenging objective that is important. Employees value their membership on the team because of its ability to overcome the threat or competition and as a form of social support. However, cohesion can dissipate when external threats are severe because these threats are stressful and cause teams to make less effective decisions.[65]

OB THEORY TO PRACTICE

Communal Meals Build Team Cohesion

When Patrick Mathieu became a firefighter at the Fire Rescue Department in Waterloo, Ontario, Canada, he soon learned that communal meals support the team's cohesion and trust. "In the fire service, we pride ourselves on teamwork and unity," says Mathieu (second from right in this photo). "Eating and cooking is part of our firefighter culture and I have seen the immense team-building benefits that result from a platoon cooking together."

A recent study supports Mathieu's observations. It found that fire stations in the United States where the team usually ate together performed better than stations where firefighters ate alone. The higher performance was attributed to better cooperation, trust, and other outcomes of high cohesion.

Mathieu has become a popular chef at his fire station in Waterloo and recently competed in a Canada-wide cooking contest. But the favorite dish among firefighters in his platoon is jalapeño kettle chip fish tacos, partly because everyone is involved in its creation. "With everyone in the kitchen, we talk, laugh, joke and create something special together," he says. "It brings us in for bonding, just like a family dinner." Mathieu notes that there is one risk of cooking great meals in a firehouse. "You make the call for everyone to come to dinner. Boom— the alarm goes off. Yep, the meal sits and waits until we come back."[66]

©Richard Hutchings/Science Source

Consequences of Team Cohesion

Teams with higher cohesion tend to perform better than those with low cohesion.[67] In fact, the team's existence depends on a minimal level of cohesion because it motivates team members to remain members and to help the team achieve its objectives. Members of high-cohesion teams spend more time together, share information more frequently, and are more satisfied with each other. They provide each other with better social support in stressful situations and work to minimize dysfunctional conflict.[68] When conflict does arise, high-cohesion team members tend to resolve their differences swiftly and effectively.

However, the relationship between team cohesion and team performance depends on two conditions. First, team cohesion has less effect on team performance when the team has low task interdependence.[69] High cohesion motivates employees to coordinate and cooperate with other team members. But people don't need to cooperate or coordinate as much when their work doesn't depend on other team members (low task interdependence), so the motivational effect of high cohesion is less relevant in teams with low interdependence.

Second, the effect of cohesion on team performance depends on whether the team's norms are compatible with or opposed to the organizational objectives.[70] As Exhibit 7.6 illustrates, teams with high cohesion perform better when their norms are aligned with the organization's objectives, whereas higher cohesion can potentially reduce team performance when norms are counterproductive. This effect occurs because cohesion motivates employees to perform at a level more consistent with team norms. If a team's norm tolerates or encourages absenteeism, employees will be more motivated to take unjustified sick leave. If the team's norm discourages absenteeism, employees are more motivated to avoid taking sick leave.

One last comment about team cohesion and performance: Earlier in this section we said that team success (performance) increases cohesion, whereas we are now saying that team cohesion causes team performance. Both statements are correct. Teams with higher cohesion perform better, and teams with better performance become more cohesive. A major review of past studies indicated that both effects are about the same. However, most teams in those studies likely had fairly low cohesion because they involved short-lived student teams, whereas cohesion takes considerable time to fully develop. When studying teams with a much longer life span, team cohesion has a much stronger effect on team performance than the effect of team performance on team cohesion.[71]

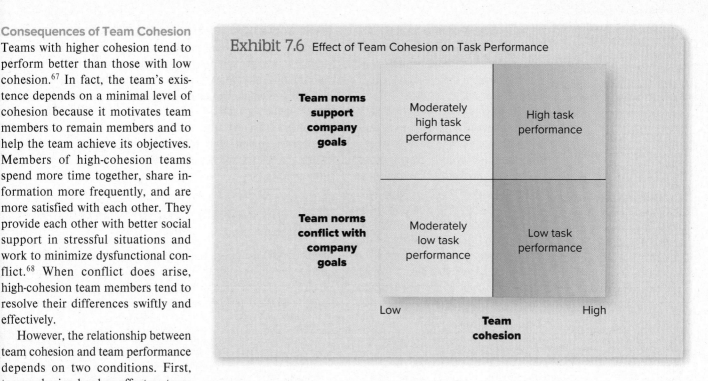

Exhibit 7.6 Effect of Team Cohesion on Task Performance

Team norms support company goals	Moderately high task performance	High task performance
Team norms conflict with company goals	Moderately low task performance	Low task performance
	Low	High

Team cohesion

Team Trust

Any relationship—including the relationship among team members—depends on a certain degree of trust. *Trust* refers to positive expectations one person has toward another person in situations involving risk (see Chapter 4).[72] Trust is ultimately perceptual; we trust others on the basis of our beliefs about their ability, integrity, and benevolence. Trust is also an emotional event; we experience positive feelings toward those we trust.[73]

Trust is built on three foundations in a hierarchy from lowest to highest: calculus, knowledge, and identification.[74] *Calculus-based trust* represents a logical calculation that other team members will act appropriately because they face sanctions if their actions violate reasonable expectations.[75] It offers the lowest potential trust and is easily broken by a violation of expectations. *Knowledge-based trust* is based on the predictability of another team member's behavior. This predictability refers only to "positive expectations," as the definition of trust states, because you would not trust someone who tends to engage in harmful or dysfunctional behavior. Knowledge-based trust includes our confidence in the other person's abilities, such as the confidence that exists when we trust a physician.[76] Knowledge-based trust offers a higher potential level of trust and is more stable because it develops over time.

Potentially the strongest and most robust of all three types of trust is *identification-based trust*, which is based on mutual understanding and an emotional bond among team members. It occurs when team members think, feel, and act like each other. High-performance teams exhibit this level of trust because they share the same values and mental models. The individual's self-concept is based partly on membership in the team, and he or she believes the members' values highly overlap, so any transgressions by other team members are quickly forgiven. People are more reluctant to acknowledge a violation of this high-level trust because it strikes at the heart of their self-concept.

Dynamics of Team Trust

Employees typically join a team with a moderate or high level—not a low level—of trust in their new coworkers.[77] The main explanation for the initially high trust (called *swift trust*) in organizational settings is that people usually believe fellow team members are reasonably competent (knowledge-based trust) and they tend to develop some degree of social identity with the team (identification-based trust). Even when working with strangers, most of us display some level of trust, if only because it supports our self-concept of being a good person. However, trust is fragile in new relationships because it is based on assumptions rather than well-established experience. Studies report that trust tends to decrease rather than increase over time.[78]

The team effectiveness model is a useful template for understanding how teams work—and don't work—in organizations. With this knowledge in hand, let's briefly investigate two types of teams that have emerged over the past couple of decades to become important forms of teamwork in organizations: self-directed teams and virtual (also called remote) teams.[79]

LO7-4 Discuss the characteristics and factors required for the success of self-directed teams and virtual (remote) teams.

SELF-DIRECTED TEAMS

Self-directed teams (SDTs) are cross-functional groups organized around work processes that complete an entire piece of work requiring several interdependent tasks and have substantial autonomy over the execution of those tasks.[80] This definition captures two distinct features. First, SDTs complete an entire piece of work requiring several interdependent tasks. This type of work arrangement clusters the team members together while minimizing interdependence and interaction with employees outside the team. The result is a close-knit group of employees who depend on each other to accomplish their individual tasks. Second, SDTs have substantial autonomy over the execution of their tasks. In particular, these teams plan, organize, and control work activities with little or no direct involvement of a higher-status supervisor.

Success Factors for Self-Directed Teams

Self-directed teams are found in several industries, ranging from petrochemical plants to aircraft parts manufacturing. Most of the top-rated manufacturing firms in North America apparently rely on SDTs.[81] Indeed, self-directed teams have become such a popular way to organize employees that many companies don't realize they have them.

The popularity of SDTs is consistent with research indicating that they potentially increase both productivity and job satisfaction.[82] However, the success of self-directed teams depends on several factors.[83] SDTs should be responsible for an entire work process, such as making an entire product or providing a service. This structure keeps each team sufficiently independent from other teams, yet it demands a relatively high degree of interdependence among employees within the team.[84] SDTs also should have sufficient autonomy to organize and coordinate their work. Autonomy allows them to respond more quickly and effectively to client and stakeholder demands. It also motivates team members through feelings of empowerment. Finally, SDTs are more successful when the work site and technology support coordination and communication among team members and increase job enrichment.[85] Too often, management calls a group of employees a "team," yet the work layout, assembly-line structure, and other technologies isolate the employees from each other.

VIRTUAL (REMOTE) TEAMS

Virtual (remote) teams are teams whose members operate across space, time, and organizational boundaries and are linked through information technologies to achieve organizational tasks.[86] Virtual teams differ from traditional teams in two ways: (1) one or more members work remotely some of the time

A team's virtuality or remoteness depends on the geographic dispersion of its members, percentage of members who work apart, and percentage of time that members work apart.
©Rawpixel.com/Shutterstock

necessary. In Chapter 1, we learned that organizational learning is one of four perspectives of organizational effectiveness. Virtual teams represent a natural part of the organizational learning process because they encourage employees to share and use knowledge where geography limits more direct forms of collaboration. Globalization makes virtual teams increasingly necessary because employees are spread around the planet rather than around one building or city. Thus, global businesses depend on virtual teamwork to leverage the potential of their employees.

Success Factors for Virtual Teams

Virtual teams face all the challenges of traditional teams, compounded by problems arising from time and distance. These challenges increase with the team's virtuality, particularly when the team exists for only a short time.[89] Fortunately, OB research has identified the following strategies to minimize most virtual team problems.[90] First, virtual team members need to apply the effective team behaviors described earlier in this chapter. They also require good communication technology skills, strong self-leadership skills to motivate and guide their behavior without

> Many of the principles for successful remote teams relate mostly to creating structures, such as clear operational objectives, documented work processes, and agreed-on roles and responsibilities.

rather than always co-located (they don't work in the same physical area) and (2) due to their lack of co-location, members of remote teams depend primarily on information technologies rather than face-to-face interaction to communicate and coordinate their work effort. A team's remoteness or virtuality depends on the geographic dispersion of its members, percentage of members who work apart, and percentage of time that members work apart.[87] For example, a team has low virtuality when all of its members live in the same city and only one or two members work from home each day. High virtuality exists when team members are spread around the world and only a couple of members have ever met in person.

Remote teams have become commonplace in most organizations. One reason is that most people perform knowledge work rarther than physical production work, so they can practice their trade almost anywhere. The second reason is that information technologies have made it easier than ever before to communicate and coordinate with other knowledge workers at a distance.[88]

Knowledge-based work and information technologies have made remote teams possible, whereas organizational learning and globalization are two reasons why they are increasingly

peers or bosses nearby, and higher emotional intelligence so that they can decipher the feelings of other team members from email and other limited communication media.

Second, virtual teams should have a toolkit of communication channels (texting, virtual whiteboards, videoconferencing, etc.) as well as the freedom to choose the channels that work best for them. This may sound obvious, but unfortunately senior management tends to impose technology on virtual teams, often based on advice from external consultants, and expects team members to use the same communication technology throughout their work. In contrast, research suggests that communication channels gain and lose importance over time, depending on the task and level of trust.

Third, remote teams need plenty of structure. In one review, many of the principles for successful virtual teams related mostly to creating these structures, such as clear operational objectives, documented work processes, and agreed-on roles and responsibilities.[91] The final recommendation is that remote team members should meet face-to-face fairly early in the team development process. This idea may seem contradictory to the entire notion of virtual teams, but so far, no technology has replaced face-to-face interaction for high-level bonding and mutual understanding.[92]

> ## Insanity in individuals is something rare—but in groups, parties, nations, and epochs, it is the rule.[96]
>
> —Friedrich Nietzsche

LO7-5 Identify four constraints on team decision making and discuss the advantages and disadvantages of four structures aimed at improving team decision making.

TEAM DECISION MAKING

Self-directed teams, virtual/remote teams, and practically all other groups are expected to make decisions. Teams are potentially more effective than individuals at identifying problems, choosing alternatives, and evaluating their decisions. To leverage these benefits, however, we first need to understand the constraints on effective team decision making. Then, we look at specific team structures that try to overcome these constraints.

Constraints on Team Decision Making

Anyone who has spent enough time in the workplace can recite several ways in which teams stumble in decision making. The four most common problems are time constraints, evaluation apprehension, pressure to conform, and overconfidence.

Time Constraints There's a saying that committees keep minutes and waste hours. This reflects the fact that teams take longer than individuals to make decisions.[93] Teams consume time organizing, coordinating, and maintaining relationships (i.e., process losses). Team members require time to build rapport, agree on rules and norms of behavior in the decision process, and understand each other's ideas.

Another time-related constraint in most team structures is that only one person can speak at a time.[94] This problem, known as **production blocking**, undermines idea generation in a few ways. First, team members need to listen in on the conversation to find an opportune time to speak up, but this monitoring makes it difficult for them to concentrate on their own ideas. Second, ideas are fleeting, so the longer they wait to speak up, the more likely their flickering ideas will die out. Third, team members might remember their fleeting thoughts by concentrating on them, but this causes them to pay less attention to the conversation. By ignoring what others are saying, team members miss other potentially good ideas.

Evaluation Apprehension Team members are often reluctant to mention ideas that seem silly because they believe (often correctly) that other team members are silently evaluating them.[95] This **evaluation apprehension** is based on the individual's desire to create a favorable self-presentation and need to protect self-esteem. It is most common when meetings are attended by people with different levels of status or expertise or when members formally evaluate each other's performance throughout the year (as in 360-degree feedback). Creative ideas often sound bizarre or illogical when first presented, so evaluation apprehension tends to discourage employees from mentioning them in front of coworkers.

Pressure to Conform Team cohesion leads employees to conform to the team's norms. This control keeps the group organized around common goals, but it also may cause team members to suppress their dissenting opinions, particularly when a strong team norm is related to the issue. When someone does state a point of view that violates the majority opinion, other members might punish the violator or try to persuade him or her that the opinion is incorrect. Conformity also can be subtle. To some extent, we depend on the opinions that others hold to validate our own views. If coworkers don't agree with us, we begin to question our own opinions even without overt peer pressure.

Overconfidence (Inflated Team Efficacy) Teams are more successful when their members have collective confidence in how well they work together and the likely success of their team effort.[97] This **team efficacy** is similar to the power of individual self-efficacy, which we discussed in Chapter 3. High-efficacy teams set more challenging goals and are more motivated to achieve them, both of which increase team performance. Unfortunately, teams make worse decisions when they become overconfident and develop a false sense of invulnerability.[98] In other words, the team's efficacy far exceeds reality regarding its abilities and the favorableness of the situation. Overconfident teams are less vigilant when making decisions, partly because they have more positive than negative emotions and moods during these events. They also engage in less-constructive debate and are less likely to seek out or accept information located outside the team, both of which undermine the quality of team decisions.

Why do teams become overconfident? The main reason is a team-level variation of self-enhancement (see Chapter 3), whereby team members have a natural motivation to believe the team's capabilities and situation are above average. Overconfidence is more common in highly cohesive teams

> Creative ideas often sound bizarre or illogical when first presented, so evaluation apprehension tends to discourage employees from mentioning them in front of coworkers.

because people engage in self-enhancement for things that are important to them (such as a cohesive team). It is also stronger when the team has external threats or competition because these adversaries generate "us–them" differentiation. Team efficacy is further inflated by the mutually reinforcing beliefs among team members. We develop a clearer and higher opinion of the team when others echo that opinion.

Improving Creative Decision Making in Teams

Team decision making is fraught with problems, but several solutions also emerge from these bad-news studies. Team members need to be confident in their decision making but not so confident that they collectively feel invulnerable. This calls for team norms that encourage critical thinking as well as team membership with sufficient diversity. Checks and balances need to be in place to prevent the leader or other individuals from dominating the discussion. The team also should be large enough to possess the collective knowledge to resolve the problem yet small enough that the team doesn't consume too much time or restrict individual input.

Along with these general recommendations, OB studies have identified four team structures that encourage creativity in a team setting: brainstorming, brainwriting, electronic brainstorming, and nominal group technique:

- *Brainstorming.* **Brainstorming** is a team event in which participants try to think up as many ideas as possible.[99] The process consists of four rules to maximize the number and quality of ideas presented: (1) Speak freely—describe even the craziest ideas; (2) don't criticize others or their ideas; (3) provide as many ideas as possible—the quality of ideas increases with the quantity of ideas; and (4) build on the ideas that others have presented. Brainstorming rules potentially increase divergent thinking and minimize evaluation apprehension, but field research indicates that these benefits require an experienced facilitator and participants who work together in a supportive culture.[100]

Brainstorming rules potentially increase divergent thinking and minimize evaluation apprehension, but field research indicates that these benefits require an experienced facilitator and participants who work together in a supportive culture.
©wavebreakmedia/Shutterstock

- *Brainwriting.* **Brainwriting** is a variation of brainstorming that minimizes the problem of production blocking by removing conversation during idea generation.[101] There are many forms of brainwriting, but they all have the common feature that individuals write down their ideas rather than verbally describe them. In one version, participants write their ideas on cards and place them in the center of the table. At any time, participants can pick up one or more cards in the center to spark their thinking or further build (piggyback) on those ideas. The limited research on brainwriting suggests that it produces more and better-quality ideas than brainstorming due to the lack of production blocking.

- *Electronic Brainstorming.* **Electronic brainstorming** is similar to brainwriting but uses computer technology rather than handwritten cards to document and share ideas. After receiving the question or issue, participants enter their ideas using special computer software. The ideas are distributed anonymously to other participants, who are encouraged to piggyback on those ideas. Team members eventually vote electronically on the ideas presented. Face-to-face discussion usually follows. Electronic brainstorming tends to minimize production blocking, evaluation apprehension, and conformity problems because participants' ideas are anonymous.[102] However, many executives consider electronic brainstorming too structured and technology-bound.

- *Nominal Group Technique.* Another variation of brainwriting, **nominal group technique**, adds a verbal element to the process.[103] The problem is described, team members silently and independently write down as many solutions as they can, then they describe their solutions to the other team members, usually in a round-robin format. As with brainstorming, there is no criticism or debate, just clarification. Finally, participants silently and independently rank-order or vote on each proposed solution. Nominal group technique has been used in real-world decisions and tends to improve the quality of ideas generated. However, production blocking and evaluation apprehension still occur to some extent. Training improves this structured approach to team decision making.[104]

production blocking a time constraint in team decision making due to the procedural requirement that only one person may speak at a time

evaluation apprehension a decision-making problem that occurs when individuals are reluctant to mention ideas that seem silly because they believe (often correctly) that other team members are silently evaluating them

team efficacy the collective belief among team members in the team's capability to successfully complete a task

brainstorming a freewheeling, face-to-face meeting where team members aren't allowed to criticize but are encouraged to speak freely, generate as many ideas as possible, and build on the ideas of others

brainwriting a variation of brainstorming whereby participants write (rather than speak about) and share their ideas

electronic brainstorming a form of brainstorming that relies on networked computers for submitting and sharing creative ideas

nominal group technique a variation of brainwriting consisting of three stages in which participants (1) silently and independently document their ideas, (2) collectively describe these ideas to the other team members without critique, and then (3) silently and independently evaluate the ideas presented

Study Checklist

Connect® Management is available for *M Organizational Behavior.* Additional resources include:

✓ Interactive Applications:

- **Case Analysis:** Apply concepts within the context of a real-world situation.
- **Drag and Drop:** Work through an interactive example to test your knowledge of the concepts.
- **Video Case:** See management in action through interactive videos.

✓ **SmartBook™**—SmartBook is the first and only adaptive reading experience available today. Distinguishing what you know from what you don't, and honing in on concepts you are most likely to forget, SmartBook personalizes content for you in a continuously adapting reading experience. Reading is no longer a passive and linear experience, but an engaging and dynamic one where you are more likely to master and retain important concepts and go to class better prepared.

©Natthawat Jamnapa/123RF

Notes

1. K. Monsen and J. deBlok, "Buurtzorg Nederland," *American Journal of Nursing* 113, no. 8 (2013): 55–59; A. Cooper, "Buurtzorg: What's It All About?," *Viewpoints* (London: The Queen's Nursing Institute, August 12, 2014), http://theqni.tumblr.com/post/94532689636/buurtzorg-whats-it-all-about (accessed May 9, 2016); J. D. Blok, "Neighbourhood Scheme Transforms Services," *Primary Health Care* 25, no. 2 (2015); B. Gray, D. O. Sarnak, and J. Burgers, *Home Care by Self-Governing Nursing Teams: The Netherlands' Buurtzorg Model* (New York: The Commonwealth Fund, May 29, 2015).

2. E. Sundstrom, "The Challenges of Supporting Work Team Effectiveness," in *Supporting Work Team Effectiveness*, ed. E. Sundstrom and Associates (San Francisco: Jossey-Bass, 1999), 6–9; S. A. Mohrman, S. G. Cohen, and A. M. Mohrman Jr., *Designing Team-Based Organizations: New Forms for Knowledge Work* (San Francisco: Jossey-Bass, 1995), 39–40; M. E. Shaw, *Group Dynamics*, 3rd ed. (New York: McGraw-Hill, 1981), 8.

3. J. R. Hollenbeck, B. Beersma, and M. E. Schouten, "Beyond Team Types and Taxonomies: A Dimensional Scaling Conceptualization for Team Description," *Academy of Management Review* 37, no. 1 (2012): 82–106. This article uses the term *skill differentiation*, whereas we use *skill diversity*, which is a more common label to describe variations among team members; skill differences represent a form of deep-level diversity. The original article also uses the label *authority differentiation*, whereas we believe that *authority dispersion* is more consistent with power variations, such as in decentralization of organizational structures.

4. S. I. Tannenbaum et al., "Teams Are Changing: Are Research and Practice Evolving Fast Enough?," *Industrial and Organizational Psychology* 5, no. 1 (2012): 2–24; R. Wageman, H. Gardner, and M. Mortensen, "The Changing Ecology of Teams: New Directions for Teams Research," *Journal of Organizational Behavior* 33, no. 3 (2012): 301–15.

5. P. R. Lawrence and N. Nohria, *Driven: How Human Nature Shapes Our Choices* (San Francisco: Jossey-Bass, 2002); J. R. Spoor and J. R. Kelly, "The Evolutionary Significance of Affect in Groups: Communication and Group Bonding," *Group Processes & Intergroup Relations* 7, no. 4 (2004): 398–412.

6. M. A. Hogg et al., "The Social Identity Perspective: Intergroup Relations, Self-Conception, and Small Groups," *Small Group Research* 35, no. 3 (2004): 246–76; S. A. Haslam and N. Ellemers, "Identity Processes in Organizations," in *Handbook of Identity Theory and Research*, ed. J. S. Schwartz, K. Luyckx, and L. V. Vignoles (New York: Springer New York, 2011), 715–44; R. Spears, "Group Identities: The Social Identity Perspective," in *Handbook of Identity Theory and Research*, ed. S. J. Schwartz, K. Luyckx, and V. L. Vignoles (New York: Springer New York, 2011), 201–24; S. K. Kang and G. V. Bodenhausen, "Multiple Identities in Social Perception and Interaction: Challenges and Opportunities," *Annual Review of Psychology* 66, no. 1 (2015): 547–74.

7. S. Cohen, "The Pittsburgh Common Cold Studies: Psychosocial Predictors of Susceptibility to Respiratory Infectious Illness," *International Journal of Behavioral Medicine* 12, no. 3 (2005): 123–31; S. Y. Shin and S. G. Lee, "Effects of Hospital Workers? Friendship Networks on Job Stress," *PLoS ONE* 11, no. 2 (2016): e0149428.

8. R. Cross and R. J. Thomas, *Driving Results through Social Networks: How Top Organizations Leverage Networks for Performance and Growth* (San Francisco: Jossey-Bass, 2009); R. McDermott and D. Archibald, "Harnessing Your Staff's Informal Networks," *Harvard Business Review* 88, no. 3 (2010): 82–89; J. Nieves and J. Osorio, "The Role of Social Networks in Knowledge Creation," *Knowledge Management Research & Practice* 11, no. 1 (2013): 62–77.

9. M. Moldaschl and W. Weber, "The 'Three Waves' of Industrial Group Work: Historical Reflections on Current Research on Group Work," *Human Relations* 51 (1998): 347–88. Several popular books in the 1980s encouraged teamwork, based on the Japanese economic miracle. These books include W. Ouchi, *Theory Z: How American Management Can Meet the Japanese Challenge* (Reading, MA: Addison-Wesley, 1981); R. T. Pascale and A. G. Athos, *Art of Japanese Management* (New York: Simon & Schuster, 1982).

10. C. R. Emery and L. D. Fredenhall, "The Effect of Teams on Firm Profitability and Customer Satisfaction," *Journal of Service Research* 4 (2002): 217–29; G. S. Van der Vegt and O. Janssen, "Joint Impact of Interdependence and Group Diversity on Innovation," *Journal of Management* 29 (2003): 729–51.

11. M. Jordan, *I Can't Accept Not Trying: Michael Jordan on the Pursuit of Excellence* (San Francisco: Harper, 1994), 24.

12. S. Wuchty, B. F. Jones, and B. Uzzi, "The Increasing Dominance of Teams in Production of Knowledge," *Science* 316 (2007): 1036–39. For a detailed analysis of teamwork in scientific research, see N. J. Cooke and M. L. Hilton, National Research Council, *Enhancing the Effectiveness of Team Science* (Washington, DC: National Academies Press, 2015).

13. R. E. Baumeister and M. R. Leary, "The Need to Belong: Desire for Interpersonal Attachments as a Fundamental Human Motivation," *Psychological Bulletin* 117 (1995): 497–529; J. M. Feinberg and J. R. Aiello, "Social Facilitation: A Test of Competing Theories," *Journal of Applied Social Psychology* 36, no. 5 (2006): 1087–109; A. M. Grant, "Relational Job Design and the Motivation to Make a Prosocial Difference," *Academy of Management Review* 32, no. 2 (2007): 393–417; N. L. Kerr and D. H. Seok, "'. . . with a Little Help from My Friends': Friendship, Effort Norms, and Group Motivation Gain," *Journal of Managerial Psychology* 26, no. 3 (2011): 205–18; D. Herbst and A. Mas, "Peer Effects on Worker Output in the Laboratory Generalize to the Field," *Science* 350, no. 6260 (2015): 545–49.

14. This information is from the websites of these companies, mostly on their "Careers" or "Our Values" pages.

15. E. A. Locke et al., "The Importance of the Individual in an Age of Groupism," in *Groups at Work: Theory and Research*, ed. M. E. Turner (Mahwah, NJ: Erlbaum, 2001), 501–28; N. J. Allen and T. D. Hecht, "The 'Romance of Teams': Toward an Understanding of Its Psychological Underpinnings and Implications," *Journal of Occupational and Organizational Psychology* 77 (2004): 439–61.

16. I. D. Steiner, *Group Process and Productivity* (New York: Academic Press, 1972); N. L. Kerr and S. R. Tindale, "Group Performance and Decision Making," *Annual Review of Psychology* 55 (2004): 623–55.

17. M. W. McCarter and R. M. Sheremeta, "You Can't Put Old Wine in New Bottles: The Effect of Newcomers on Coordination in Groups," *PLoS ONE* 8, no. 1 (2013): e55058.

18. B. R. Staats, K. L. Milkman, and C. R. Fox, "The Team Scaling Fallacy: Underestimating the Declining Efficiency of Larger Teams," *Organizational Behavior and Human Decision Processes* 118, no. 2 (2012): 132–42. Brooks's law is discussed in F. P. Brooks, ed., *The Mythical Man-Month: Essays on Software Engineering*, 2nd ed. (Reading, MA: Addison-Wesley, 1995).

19. The origin of this quotation remains unknown. The earliest publication of this quotation that we could find is in *Madison (WI) Magazine* 43 (2001): 62.

20. S. J. Karau and K. D. Williams, "Social Loafing: A Meta-Analytic Review and Theoretical Integration," *Journal of Personality and Social Psychology* 65 (1993): 681–706; R. C. Liden et al., "Social Loafing: A Field Investigation," *Journal of Management* 30 (2004): 285–304.

21. B. Latane, K. Williams, and S. Harkins, "Many Hands Make Light the Work: The Causes and Consequences of Social Loafing," *Journal of Personality & Social Psychology* 37, no. 6 (1979): 822–32; U.-C. Klehe and N. Anderson, "The Moderating Influence of Personality and Culture on Social Loafing in Typical versus Maximum Performance Situations," *International Journal of Selection and Assessment* 15, no. 2 (2007): 250–62; R. B. Lount and S. L. Wilk, "Working Harder or Hardly Working? Posting Performance Eliminates Social Loafing and Promotes Social Laboring in Workgroups," *Management Science* 60, no. 5 (2014): 1098–106; M. C. Schippers, "Social Loafing Tendencies and Team Performance: The Compensating Effect of Agreeableness and Conscientiousness," *Academy of Management Learning & Education* 13, no. 1 (2014): 62–81; B. Meyer, C. C. Schermuly, and S. Kauffeld, "That's Not My Place: The Interacting Effects of Faultlines, Subgroup Size, and Social Competence on Social Loafing Behaviour in Work Groups," *European Journal of Work and Organizational Psychology* 25, no. 1 (2016): 31–49.

22. G. P. Shea and R. A. Guzzo, "Group Effectiveness: What Really Matters?," *Sloan Management Review* 27 (1987): 33–46; J. R. Hackman et al., "Team Effectiveness in Theory and in Practice," in *Industrial and Organizational Psychology: Linking Theory with Practice*, ed. C. L. Cooper and E. A. Locke (Oxford, UK: Blackwell, 2000), 109–29.

23. M. A. West, C. S. Borrill, and K. L. Unsworth, "Team Effectiveness in Organizations," *International Review of Industrial and Organizational Psychology* 13 (1998): 1–48; M. A. Marks, J. E. Mathieu, and S. J. Zaccaro, "A Temporally Based Framework and Taxonomy of Team Processes," *Academy of Management Review* 26, no. 3 (2001): 356–76; J. E. McGrath, H. Arrow, and J. L. Berdahl, "The Study of Groups: Past, Present, and Future," *Personality & Social Psychology Review* 4, no. 1 (2000): 95–105.

24. M. Kouchaki et al., "The Treatment of the Relationship between Groups and Their Environments: A Review and Critical Examination of Common Assumptions in Research," *Group & Organization Management* 37, no. 2 (2012): 171–203.

25. E. Sundstrom, "The Challenges of Supporting Work Team Effectiveness," in *Supporting Work Team Effectiveness*, ed. E. Sundstrom and Associates (San Francisco, CA: Jossey-Bass, 1999), 6–9; G. L. Stewart, "A Meta-Analytic Review of Relationships between Team Design Features and Team Performance," *Journal of Management* 32, no. 1 (2006): 29–54; H. Huettermann, S. Doering, and S. Boerner, "Leadership and Team Identification: Exploring the Followers' Perspective," *Leadership Quarterly* 25, no. 3 (2014): 413–32; J. E. Mathieu, L. D'Innocenzo, and M. R. Kukenberge, "Contextual Issues in Project Performance: A Multilevel Perspective," in *The Psychology and Management of Project Teams: An Interdisciplinary Perspective*, ed. B. Hobbs, E. K. Kelloway, and F. Chiocchio (New York: Oxford University Press, 2015), 101–36; F. Schölmerich, C. C. Schermuly, and J. Deller, "How Leaders' Diversity Beliefs Alter the Impact of Faultlines on Team Functioning," *Small Group Research* 47, no. 2 (2016): 177–206; S. A. Conroy and N. Gupta, "Team Pay-for-Performance: The Devil Is in the Details," *Group & Organization Management* 41, no. 1 (2016): 32–65.

26. "Siemens Industry Motion Control," *Works Management Factory Tours* (October 2, 2013), www.wmfactorytours.co.uk/article-details/siemens-industry-motion-control/ 56719/ (accessed May 9, 2016); F. Mathijssen, "The Story of Nike's Obeya," *Planet Lean*, December 11, 2014; A. Kreyenberg, "The Obeya Room—Tool and Mirror for Culture Change," in *agile42 Connect* (Berlin 2015); F. Parisot, "PSA Généralise Les Réunions Virtuelles (PSA Generalizes Virtual Meetings)," *L'usine Nouvelle*, January 15, 2015.

27. M. A. Campion, E. M. Papper, and G. J. Medsker, "Relations between Work Team Characteristics and Effectiveness: A Replication and Extension," *Personnel Psychology* 49 (1996): 429–52; N. Sivasubramaniam, S. J. Liebowitz, and C. L. Lackman, "Determinants of New Product Development Team Performance: A Meta-Analytic Review," *Journal of Product Innovation Management* 29, no. 5 (2012): 803–20; M. A. Valentine and A. C. Edmondson, "Team Scaffolds: How Mesolevel Structures Enable Role-Based Coordination in Temporary Groups," *Organization Science* 26, no. 2 (2015): 405–22.

28. G. Van der Vegt and E. Van de Vliert, "Intragroup Interdependence and Effectiveness: Review and Proposed Directions for Theory and Practice," *Journal of Managerial Psychology* 17, no. 1/2 (2002): 50–67; J. Lyubovnikova et al., "24-Karat or Fool's Gold? Consequences of Real Team and Co-Acting Group Membership in Healthcare Organizations," *European Journal of Work and Organizational Psychology* 24, no. 6 (2015): 929–50; S. H. Courtright et al., "Structural Interdependence in Teams: An Integrative Framework and Meta-Analysis," *Journal of Applied Psychology* 100, no. 6 (2015): 1825–46.

29. J. R. Katzenbach and D. K. Smith, *The Wisdom of Teams: Creating the High-Performance Organization* (Boston: Harvard University Press, 1993), 45–47; C. Aube, V. Rousseau, and S. Tremblay, "Team Size and Quality of Group Experience: The More the Merrier?," *Group Dynamics: Theory Research and Practice* 15, no. 4 (2011): 357–75; J. S. Mueller, "Why Individuals in Larger Teams Perform Worse," *Organizational Behavior and Human Decision Processes* 117, no. 1 (2012): 111–24; Y.-N. Lee, J. P. Walsh, and J. Wang, "Creativity in Scientific Teams: Unpacking Novelty and Impact," *Research Policy* 44, no. 3 (2015): 684–97.

30. J. S. Mueller, "Why Individuals in Larger Teams Perform Worse," *Organizational Behavior and Human Decision Processes* 117, no. 1 (2012): 111–24.

31. J. O'Toole, "The Power of Many: Building a High-Performance Management Team," 2003, http://ceoforum.com.au.

32. J. E. Mathieu et al., "A Review and Integration of Team Composition Models: Moving toward a Dynamic and Temporal Framework," *Journal of Management* 40, no. 1 (2014): 130–60; N. J. Allen and T. O'Neill, "Team Composition and Performance: Considering the Project-Team Challenge," in *The Psychology and Management of Project Teams: An Interdisciplinary Perspective*, ed. B. Hobbs, E. K. Kelloway, and F. Chiocchio (New York: Oxford University Press, 2015), 301–28.

33. F. P. Morgeson, M. H. Reider, and M. A. Campion, "Selecting Individuals in Team Settings: The Importance of Social Skills, Personality Characteristics, and Teamwork Knowledge," *Personnel Psychology* 58, no. 3 (2005): 583–611; V. Rousseau, C. Aubé, and A. Savoie, "Teamwork Behaviors: A Review and an Integration of Frameworks," *Small Group Research* 37, no. 5 (2006): 540–70; M. L. Loughry, M. W. Ohland, and D. D. Moore, "Development of a Theory-Based Assessment of Team Member Effectiveness," *Educational and Psychological Measurement* 67, no. 3 (2007): 505–24; E. Salas et al., "Understanding and Improving Teamwork in Organizations: A Scientifically Based Practical Guide," *Human Resource Management* 54, no. 4 (2015): 599–622.

34. S. McComb et al., "The Five Ws of Team Communication," *Industrial Management* 54, no. 5 (2012): 10–13.

35. TINYpulse, *7 Vital Trends Disrupting Today's Workplace*, 2013 TINYpulse Employee Engagement Survey (Seattle: TINYpulse, December 2013); CareerBuilder, "Overwhelming Majority of Companies Say Soft Skills Are Just as Important as Hard Skills, According to a New Careerbuilder Survey," news release (Chicago: CareerBuilder, April 10, 2014); Association of American Colleges & Universities, *Falling Short? College Learning and Career Success* (Washington, DC: Hart Research Associates, January 20, 2015); *The Class of 2016 Student Survey Report* (Bethlehem, PA: National Association of Colleges and Employers, October 2016).

36. D. van Knippenberg, C. K. W. De Dreu, and A. C. Homan, "Work Group Diversity and Group Performance: An Integrative Model and Research Agenda," *Journal of Applied Psychology* 89, no. 6 (2004): 1008–22; E. Mannix and M. A. Neale, "What Differences Make a Difference?: The Promise and Reality of Diverse Teams in Organizations," *Psychological Science in the Public Interest* 6, no. 2 (2005): 31–55; L. M. Shore et al., "Inclusion and Diversity in Work Groups: A Review and Model for Future Research," *Journal of Management* 37, no. 4 (2011): 1262–89; S. K. Horwitz, "Functional Diversity in Project Teams: Working across Boundaries," in *The Psychology and Management of Project Teams: An Interdisciplinary Perspective*, ed. B. Hobbs, E. K. Kelloway, and F. Chiocchio (New York: Oxford University Press, 2015), 329–63.

37. D. C. Lau and J. K. Murnighan, "Interactions within Groups and Subgroups: The Effects of Demographic Faultlines," *Academy of Management Journal* 48, no. 4 (2005): 645–59; S. M. B. Thatcher and P. C. Patel, "Group Faultlines: A Review, Integration, and Guide to Future Research," *Journal of Management* 38, no. 4 (2012): 969–1009; M. Shemla et al., "A Review of Perceived Diversity in Teams: Does How Members Perceive Their Team's Composition Affect Team Processes and Outcomes?," *Journal of Organizational Behavior* 37 (2016): S89–S106.

38. B. W. Tuckman and M. A. C. Jensen, "Stages of Small-Group Development Revisited," *Group and Organization Studies* 2 (1977): 419–42; B. W. Tuckman, "Developmental Sequence in Small Groups," *Group Facilitation* (2001): 66–81.

39. G. R. Bushe and G. H. Coetzer, "Group Development and Team Effectiveness: Using Cognitive Representations to Measure Group Development and Predict Task Performance and Group Viability," *Journal of Applied Behavioral Science* 43, no. 2 (2007): 184–212.

40. C. Lee, J. L. Farh, and Z. J. Chen, "Promoting Group Potency in Project Teams: The Importance of Group Identification," *Journal of Organizational Behavior* 32, no. 8 (2011): 1147–62.

41. L. A. DeChurch and J. R. Mesmer-Magnus, "The Cognitive Underpinnings of Effective Teamwork: A Meta-Analysis," *Journal of Applied Psychology* 95, no. 1 (2010): 32–53; Y. Reuveni and D. R. Vashdi, "Innovation in Multidisciplinary Teams: The Moderating Role of Transformational Leadership in the Relationship between Professional Heterogeneity and Shared Mental Models," *European Journal of Work and Organizational Psychology* 24, no. 5 (2015): 678–92; C. Aubé, V. Rousseau, and S. Tremblay, "Perceived Shared Understanding in Teams: The Motivational Effect of Being 'on the Same Page,'" *British Journal of Psychology* 106, no. 3 (2015): 468–86.

42. R. Rico, M. Sánchez-Manzanares, and C. Gibson, "Team Implicit Coordination Processes: A Team Knowledge-Based Approach," *Academy of Management Review* 33, no. 1 (2008): 163–84; J. C. Gorman, "Team Coordination and Dynamics: Two Central Issues," *Current Directions in Psychological Science* 23, no. 5 (2014): 355–60; J. Schmutz et al., "Effective Coordination in Medical Emergency Teams: The Moderating Role of Task Type," *European Journal of Work and Organizational Psychology* 24, no. 5 (2015): 761–76.

43. A. Conner, Pacific Air Forces, "36th CRG Expands US Military Support to Nepal," news release (Guam: U.S. Air Force, May 7, 2015); "U.S. Airmen and Nepalese Soldiers Unload Aid for Nepal" (YouTube, May 13, 2015), www.youtube.com/watch?v=RuohLCF7eNc (accessed May 11, 2016); J. Hlad, "Airlift to Nepal," *Air Force Magazine*, January 2016, 48–52.

44. A. P. Hare, "Types of Roles in Small Groups: A Bit of History and a Current Perspective," *Small Group Research* 25 (1994): 443–48; A. Aritzeta, S. Swailes, and B. Senior, "Belbin's Team Role Model: Development, Validity and Applications for Team Building," *Journal of Management Studies* 44, no. 1 (2007): 96–118.

45. J. E. Mathieu et al., "Team Role Experience and Orientation: A Measure and Tests of Construct Validity," *Group & Organization Management* 40, no. 1 (2015): 6–34. Also see J. K. Summers, S. E. Humphrey, and G. R. Ferris, "Team Member Change, Flux in Coordination, and Performance: Effects of Strategic Core Roles, Information Transfer, and Cognitive Ability," *Academy of Management Journal* 55, no. 2 (2012): 314–38; N. Lehmann-Willenbrock, S. J. Beck, and S. Kauffeld, "Emergent Team Roles in Organizational Meetings: Identifying Communication Patterns Via Cluster Analysis," *Communication Studies* 67, no. 1 (2016): 37–57.

46. W. G. Dyer, *Team Building: Current Issues and New Alternatives*, 3rd ed. (Reading, MA: Addison-Wesley, 1995); C. A. Beatty and B. A. Barker, *Building Smart Teams: Roadmap to High Performance* (Thousand Oaks, CA: Sage, 2004).

47. E. Sundstrom, K. De Meuse, and D. Futrell, "Work Teams: Applications and Effectiveness," *American Psychologist* 45, no. 2 (1990): 120–33; C. Klein et al., "Does Team Building Work?," *Small Group Research* 40, no. 2 (2009): 181–222.

48. E. Rovio et al., "Using Team Building Methods with an Ice Hockey Team: An Action Research Case Study," *Sport Psychologist* 26, no. 4 (2012): 584–603.

49. D. R. Seibold and R. A. Meyers, "Interventions in Groups: Methods for Facilitating Team Development," in *Research Methods for Studying Groups and Teams: A Guide to Approaches, Tools, and Technologies*, ed. A. Hollingshead and M. S. Poole (New York: Routledge, 2012), 418–41; A. Hämmelmann and R. van Dick, "Building the Team: Effect on the Individual—An Evaluation of Team Building Interventions (Entwickeln Im Team—Effekte Für Den Einzelnen: Eine Evaluation Von Teamentwicklungsmaßnahmen)," *Gruppendynamik und Organisationsberatung* 44, no. 2 (2013): 221–38.

50. D. Hempstead, "Heatwave Hits Ottawa," *Ottawa Sun*, July 4, 2013; K. Scott, "Treatwell Flies Global Workforce to Barcelona for Team-Building Exercise," *Employee Benefits (London, UK)*, September 14, 2016; "Local Faith Communities Start Aurora Habitat for Humanity Home; Nicor Gas Employees Pitch In," *Daily Herald (Arlington Heights, IL)*, May 23, 2017; R. Inman, "Why We Used an Iron Chef Competition as a Team Building Exercise," *Cobalt Blog*, February 2, 2017, http://www.cobalt.net/used-iron-chef-competition-team-building-exercise.

51. C. Klein et al., "Does Team Building Work?," *Small Group Research* 40, no. 2 (2009): 181–222; I. Nadler, P. M. Sanderson, and H. G. Liley, "The Accuracy of Clinical Assessments as a Measure for Teamwork Effectiveness," *Simulation in Healthcare* 6, no. 5 (2011): 260–68.

52. R. W. Woodman and J. J. Sherwood, "The Role of Team Development in Organizational Effectiveness: A Critical Review," *Psychological Bulletin* 88 (1980): 166–86.

53. L. Mealiea and R. Baltazar, "A Strategic Guide for Building Effective Teams," *Personnel Management* 34, no. 2 (2005): 141–60.

54. G. E. Huszczo, "Training for Team Building," *Training and Development Journal* 44 (1990): 37–43; P. McGraw, "Back from the Mountain: Outdoor Management Development Programs and How to Ensure the Transfer of Skills to the Workplace," *Asia Pacific Journal of Human Resources* 31 (1993): 52–61.

55. D. C. Feldman, "The Development and Enforcement of Group Norms," *Academy of Management Review* 9 (1984): 47–53; E. Fehr and U. Fischbacher, "Social Norms and Human Cooperation," *Trends in Cognitive Sciences* 8, no. 4 (2004): 185–90.

56. N. Ellemers and F. Rink, "Identity in Work Groups: The Beneficial and Detrimental Consequences of Multiple Identities and Group Norms for Collaboration and Group Performance," *Advances in Group Processes* 22 (2005): 1–41. For research on norm development and reinforcement in virtual teams, see K. Moser and C. Axtell, "The Role of Norms in Virtual Work: A Review and Agenda for Future Research," *Journal of Personnel Psychology* 12, no. 1 (2013): 1–6.

57. K. D. Opp, "How Do Norms Emerge? An Outline of a Theory," *Mind & Society* 2, no. 1 (2001): 101–28.

58. J. J. Dose and R. J. Klimoski, "The Diversity of Diversity: Work Values Effects on Formative Team Processes," *Human Resource Management Review* 9, no. 1 (1999): 83–108.

59. S. Taggar and R. Ellis, "The Role of Leaders in Shaping Formal Team Norms," *Leadership Quarterly* 18, no. 2 (2007): 105–20; B. A. De Jong, K. M. Bijlsma-Frankema, and L. B. Cardinal, "Stronger Than the Sum of Its Parts? The Performance Implications of Peer Control Combinations in Teams," *Organization Science* 25, no. 6 (2014): 1703–21.

60. D. J. Beal et al., "Cohesion and Performance in Groups: A Meta-Analytic Clarification of Construct Relations," *Journal of Applied Psychology* 88, no. 6 (2003): 989–1004; S. W. J. Kozlowski and D. R. Ilgen, "Enhancing the Effectiveness of Work Groups and Teams," *Psychological Science in the Public Interest* 7, no. 3 (2006): 77–124.

61. R. M. Montoya, R. S. Horton, and J. Kirchner, "Is Actual Similarity Necessary for Attraction? A Meta-Analysis of Actual and Perceived Similarity," *Journal of Social and Personal Relationships* 25, no. 6 (2008): 889–922; M. T. Rivera, S. B. Soderstrom, and B. Uzzi, "Dynamics of Dyads in Social Networks: Assortative, Relational, and Proximity Mechanisms," *Annual Review of Sociology* 36 (2010): 91–115.

62. D. van Knippenberg, C. K. W. De Dreu, and A. C. Homan, "Work Group Diversity and Group Performance: An Integrative Model and Research Agenda," *Journal of Applied Psychology* 89, no. 6 (2004): 1008–22; K. A. Jehn, G. B. Northcraft, and M. A. Neale, "Why Differences Make a Difference: A Field Study of Diversity, Conflict, and Performance in Workgroups," *Administrative Science Quarterly* 44, no. 4 (1999): 741–63. For evidence that diversity/similarity does not always influence cohesion, see S. S. Webber and L. M. Donahue, "Impact of Highly and Less Job-Related Diversity on Work Group Cohesion and Performance: A Meta-Analysis," *Journal of Management* 27, no. 2 (2001): 141–62.

63. E. Aronson and J. Mills, "The Effects of Severity of Initiation on Liking for a Group," *Journal of Abnormal and Social Psychology* 59 (1959): 177–81; J. E. Hautaluoma and R. S. Enge, "Early Socialization into a Work Group: Severity of Initiations Revisited," *Journal of Social Behavior & Personality* 6 (1991): 725–48.

64. B. Mullen and C. Copper, "The Relation between Group Cohesiveness and Performance: An Integration," *Psychological Bulletin* 115 (1994): 210–27; C. J. Fullagar and D. O. Egleston, "Norming and Performing: Using Microworlds to Understand the Relationship between Team Cohesiveness and Performance," *Journal of Applied Social Psychology* 38, no. 10 (2008): 2574–93; R. Wageman et al., *Senior Leadership Teams* (Boston: Harvard Business School Press, 2008): 69–70.

65. M. Rempel and R. J. Fisher, "Perceived Threat, Cohesion, and Group Problem Solving in Intergroup Conflict," *International Journal of Conflict Management* 8 (1997): 216–34; M. E. Turner and T. Horvitz, "The Dilemma of Threat: Group Effectiveness and Ineffectiveness under Adversity," in *Groups at Work: Theory and Research*, ed. M. E. Turner (Mahwah, NJ: Erlbaum, 2001), 445–70.

66. K. M. Kniffin et al., "Eating Together at the Firehouse: How Workplace Commensality Relates to the Performance of Firefighters," *Human Performance* 28, no. 4 (2015): 281–306; J. Hicks, "Ready to Handle the Heat: Waterloo Firefighter a Culinary Contender on Chopped Canada," *Waterloo Regional Record* (Kitchener, Ontario, Canada), January 29, 2015, A1; P. Mathieu, "Recipe Rescue: Bond over Meal Prep," *Canadian Firefighter*, April 11, 2016.

67. A. V. Carron et al., "Cohesion and Performance in Sport: A Meta-Analysis," *Journal of Sport and Exercise Psychology* 24 (2002): 168–88; D. J. Beal et al., "Cohesion and Performance in Groups: A Meta-Analytic Clarification of Construct Relations," *Journal of Applied Psychology* 88, no. 6 (2003): 989–1004; L. A. DeChurch and J. R. Mesmer-Magnus, "The Cognitive Underpinnings of Effective Teamwork: A Meta-Analysis," *Journal of Applied Psychology* 95, no. 1 (2010): 32–53; S. M. Gully, D. J. Devine, and D. J. Whitney, "A Meta-Analysis of Cohesion and Performance: Effects of Level of Analysis and Task Interdependence," *Small Group Research* 43, no. 6 (2012): 702–25.

68. W. Piper et al., "Cohesion as a Basic Bond in Groups," *Human Relations* 36 (1983): 93–108; C. A. O'Reilly, D. E. Caldwell, and W. P. Barnett, "Work Group Demography, Social Integration, and Turnover," *Administrative Science Quarterly* 34 (1989): 21–37.

69. S. M. Gully, D. J. Devine, and D. J. Whitney, "A Meta-Analysis of Cohesion and Performance: Effects of Level of Analysis and Task Interdependence," *Small Group Research* 43, no. 6 (2012): 702–25.

70. K. L. Gammage, A. V. Carron, and P. A. Estabrooks, "Team Cohesion and Individual Productivity: The Influence of the Norm for Productivity and the Identifiability of Individual Effort," *Small Group Research* 32 (2001): 3–18; C. Langfred, "Is Group Cohesiveness a Double-Edged Sword? An Investigation of the Effects of Cohesiveness on Performance," *Small Group Research* 29 (1998): 124–43; N. L. Jimmieson, M. Peach, and K. M. White, "Utilizing the Theory of Planned Behavior to Inform Change Management," *Journal of Applied Behavioral Science* 44, no. 2 (2008): 237–62. Concerns about existing research on cohesion-performance are discussed in M. Casey-Campbell and M. L. Martens, "Sticking It All Together: A Critical Assessment of the Group Cohesion–Performance Literature," *International Journal of Management Reviews* 11, no. 2 (2009): 223–46.

71. J. Mathieu et al., "Modeling Reciprocal Team Cohesion-Performance Relationships, as Impacted by Shared Leadership and Members' Competence," *Journal of Applied Psychology* 100, no. 3 (2015): 713–34.

72. D. M. Rousseau et al., "Not So Different after All: A Cross-Discipline View of Trust," *Academy of Management Review* 23 (1998): 393–404; R. Searle, A. Weibel, and D. N. Den Hartog, "Employee Trust in Organizational Contexts," in *International Review of Industrial and Organizational Psychology 2011* (New York: Wiley, 2011), 143–91.

73. D. J. McAllister, "Affect- and Cognition-Based Trust as Foundations for Interpersonal Cooperation in Organizations," *Academy of Management Journal* 38, no. 1 (1995): 24–59; M. Williams, "In Whom We Trust: Group Membership as an Affective Context for Trust Development," *Academy of Management Review* 26, no. 3 (2001): 377–96; M. Pirson and D. Malhotra, "Foundations of Organizational Trust: What Matters to Different Stakeholders?," *Organization Science* 22, no. 4 (2011): 1087–104.

74. R. J. Lewicki, E. C. Tomlinson, and N. Gillespie, "Models of Interpersonal Trust Development: Theoretical Approaches, Empirical Evidence, and Future Directions," *Journal of Management* 32, no. 6 (2006): 991–1022.

75. R. J. Lewicki, E. C. Tomlinson, and N. Gillespie, "Models of Interpersonal Trust Development: Theoretical Approaches, Empirical Evidence, and Future Directions," *Journal of Management* 32, no. 6 (2006): 991–1022; F. Y. Kuo and C. P. Yu, "An Exploratory Study of Trust Dynamics in Work-Oriented Virtual Teams," *Journal of Computer-Mediated Communication* 14, no. 4 (2009): 823–54.

76. E. M. Whitener et al., "Managers as Initiators of Trust: An Exchange Relationship Framework for Understanding Managerial Trustworthy Behavior," *Academy of Management Review* 23 (1998): 513–30; J. M. Kouzes and B. Z. Posner, *The Leadership Challenge*, 3rd ed. (San Francisco: Jossey-Bass, 2002), chap. 2; T. Simons, "Behavioral Integrity: The Perceived Alignment between Managers' Words and Deeds as a Research Focus," *Organization Science* 13, no. 1 (2002): 18–35.

77. S. L. Jarvenpaa and D. E. Leidner, "Communication and Trust in Global Virtual Teams," *Organization Science* 10 (1999): 791–815; L. P. Robert, A. R. Dennis, and Y. T. C. Hung, "Individual Swift Trust and Knowledge-Based Trust in Face-to-Face and Virtual Team Members," *Journal of Management Information Systems* 26, no. 2 (2009): 241–79; C. B. Crisp and S. L. Jarvenpaa, "Swift Trust in Global Virtual Teams: Trusting Beliefs and Normative Actions," *Journal of Personnel Psychology* 12, no. 1 (2013): 45–56.

78. K. T. Dirks and D. L. Ferrin, "The Role of Trust in Organizations," *Organization Science* 12, no. 4 (2004): 450–67.

79. Two of the most important changes in teams are empowerment (evident in self-directed teams) and technology and distance (evident in virtual teams). See S. I. Tannenbaum et al., "Teams Are Changing: Are Research and Practice Evolving Fast Enough?," *Industrial and Organizational Psychology* 5, no. 1 (2012): 2–24.

80. S. A. Mohrman, S. G. Cohen, and A. M. Mohrman Jr., *Designing Team-Based Organizations: New Forms for Knowledge Work* (San Francisco: Jossey-Bass, 1995), 39–40; D. E. Yeatts and C. Hyten, *High-Performing Self-Managed Work Teams: A Comparison of Theory and Practice* (Thousand Oaks, CA: Sage, 1998); E. E. Lawler, *Organizing for High Performance* (San Francisco: Jossey-Bass, 2001); R. J. Torraco, "Work Design Theory: A Review and Critique with Implications for Human Resource Development," *Human Resource Development Quarterly* 16, no. 1 (2005): 85–109.

81. P. Panchak, "Production Workers Can Be Your Competitive Edge," *Industry Week*, October 2004, 11; S. K. Muthusamy, J. V. Wheeler, and B. L. Simmons, "Self-Managing Work Teams: Enhancing Organizational Innovativeness," *Organization Development Journal* 23, no. 3 (2005): 53–66.

82. C. R. Emery and L. D. Fredenhall, "The Effect of Teams on Firm Profitability and Customer Satisfaction," *Journal of Service Research* 4 (2002): 217–29; A. Krause and H. Dunckel, "Work Design and Customer Satisfaction: Effects of the Implementation of Semi-Autonomous Group Work on Customer Satisfaction Considering Employee Satisfaction and Group Performance (translated abstract)," *Zeitschrift für Arbeits-und Organisationspsychologie* 47, no. 4 (2003): 182–93; H. van Mierlo et al., "Self-Managing Teamwork and Psychological Well-Being: Review of a Multilevel Research Domain," *Group & Organization Management* 30, no. 2 (2005): 211–35; G. L. Stewart, S. H. Courtright, and M. R. Barrick, "Peer-Based Control in Self-Managing Teams: Linking Rational and Normative Influence with Individual and Group Performance," *Journal of Applied Psychology* 97, no. 2 (2012): 435–47.

83. M. Moldaschl and W. Weber, "The 'Three Waves' of Industrial Group Work: Historical Reflections on Current Research on Group Work," *Human Relations* 51 (1998): 347–88; W. Niepce and E. Molleman, "Work Design Issues in Lean Production from a Sociotechnical Systems Perspective: Neo-Taylorism or the Next Step in Sociotechnical Design?," *Human Relations* 51, no. 3 (1998): 259–87; J. L. Cordery et al., "The Impact of Autonomy and Task Uncertainty on Team Performance: A Longitudinal Field Study," *Journal of Organizational Behavior* 31 (2010): 240–58.

84. E. Ulich and W. G. Weber, "Dimensions, Criteria, and Evaluation of Work Group Autonomy," in *Handbook of Work Group Psychology*, ed. M. A. West (Chichester, UK: Wiley, 1996), 247–82.

85. K. P. Carson and G. L. Stewart, "Job Analysis and the Sociotechnical Approach to Quality: A Critical Examination," *Journal of Quality Management* 1 (1996): 49–65; C. C. Manz and G. L. Stewart, "Attaining Flexible Stability by Integrating Total Quality Management and Socio-Technical Systems Theory," *Organization Science* 8 (1997): 59–70.

86. J. Lipnack and J. Stamps, *Virtual Teams: People Working across Boundaries with Technology* (New York: Wiley, 2001); G. Hertel, S. Geister, and U. Konradt, "Managing Virtual Teams: A Review of Current Empirical Research," *Human Resource Management Review* 15 (2005): 69–95.

87. L. Schweitzer and L. Duxbury, "Conceptualizing and Measuring the Virtuality of Teams," *Information Systems Journal* 20, no. 3 (2010): 267–95; M. K. Foster et al., "Rethinking Virtuality and Its Impact on Teams," *Small Group Research* 46, no. 3 (2015): 267–99.

88. L. L. Gilson et al., "Virtual Teams Research: 10 Years, 10 Themes, and 10 Opportunities," *Journal of Management* 41, no. 5 (2015): 1313–37.

89. J. L. Cordery and C. Soo, "Overcoming Impediments to Virtual Team Effectiveness," *Human Factors and Ergonomics in Manufacturing & Service Industries* 18, no. 5 (2008): 487–500; A. Ortiz de Guinea, J. Webster, and D. S. Staples, "A Meta-Analysis of the Consequences of Virtualness on Team Functioning," *Information & Management* 49, no. 6 (2012): 301–08.

90. G. Hertel, U. Konradt, and K. Voss, "Competencies for Virtual Teamwork: Development and Validation of a Web-Based Selection Tool for Members of Distributed Teams," *European Journal of Work and Organizational Psychology* 15, no. 4 (2006): 477–504; J. M. Wilson et al., "Perceived Proximity in Virtual Work: Explaining the Paradox of Far-but-Close," *Organization Studies* 29, no. 7 (2008): 979–1002; L. L. Martins and M. C. Schilpzand, "Global Virtual Teams: Key Developments, Research Gaps, and Future Directions," *Research in Personnel and Human Resources Management* 30 (2011): 1–72.

91. G. G. Harwood, "Design Principles for Successful Virtual Teams," in *The Handbook of High-Performance Virtual Teams: A Toolkit for Collaborating across Boundaries*, ed. J. Nemiro and M. M. Beyerlein (San Francisco: Jossey-Bass, 2008), 59–84. Also see H. Duckworth, "How TRW Automotive Helps Global Virtual Teams Perform at the Top of Their Game," *Global Business and Organizational Excellence* 28, no. 1 (2008): 6–16; L. Dubé and D. Robey, "Surviving the Paradoxes of Virtual Teamwork," *Information Systems Journal* 19, no. 1 (2009): 3–30.

92. L. Dubé and D. Robey, "Surviving the Paradoxes of Virtual Teamwork," *Information Systems Journal* 19, no. 1 (2009): 3–30.

93. V. H. Vroom and A. G. Jago, *The New Leadership* (Englewood Cliffs, NJ: Prentice Hall, 1988), 28–29.

94. M. Diehl and W. Stroebe, "Productivity Loss in Idea-Generating Groups: Tracking Down the Blocking Effects," *Journal of Personality and Social Psychology* 61 (1991): 392–403; B. A. Nijstad, W. Stroebe, and H. F. M. Lodewijkx, "Production Blocking and Idea Generation: Does Blocking Interfere with Cognitive Processes?," *Journal of Experimental Social Psychology* 39, no. 6 (2003): 531–48; B. A. Nijstad and W. Stroebe, "How the Group Affects the Mind: A Cognitive Model of Idea Generation in Groups," *Personality & Social Psychology Review* 10, no. 3 (2006): 186–213; W. Stroebe, B. A. Nijstad, and E. F. Rietzschel, "Beyond Productivity Loss in Brainstorming Groups: The Evolution of a Question," in *Advances in Experimental Social Psychology*, ed. P. Z. Mark and M. O. James (Academic Press, 2010), 157–203.

95. B. E. Irmer, P. Bordia, and D. Abusah, "Evaluation Apprehension and Perceived Benefits in Interpersonal and Database Knowledge Sharing," *Academy of Management Proceedings* (2002): B1–B6.

96. F. W. Nietzsche, *Beyond Good and Evil: Prelude to a Philosophy of the Future*, trans. H. Zimmern (London: G. Allen & Unwin, 1906), chap. 4, statement 156.

97. A. D. Stajkovic, D. Lee, and A. J. Nyberg, "Collective Efficacy, Group Potency, and Group Performance: Meta-Analyses of Their Relationships, and Test of a Mediation Model," *Journal of Applied Psychology* 94, no. 3 (2009): 814–28; J. Schepers et al., "Fields of Gold: Perceived Efficacy in Virtual Teams of Field Service Employees," *Journal of Service Research* 14, no. 3 (2011): 372–89. OB experts describe team efficacy as efficacy toward a specific task, whereas team potency is the team's general efficacy.

98. D. Miller, *The Icarus Paradox: How Exceptional Companies Bring About Their Own Downfall* (New York: HarperBusiness, 1990); G. Whyte, "Recasting Janis's Groupthink Model: The Key Role of Collective Efficacy in Decision Fiascoes," *Organizational Behavior and Human Decision Processes* 73, no. 2–3 (1998): 185–209; K. Tasa and G. Whyte, "Collective Efficacy and Vigilant Problem Solving in Group Decision Making: A Non-Linear Model," *Organizational Behavior and Human Decision Processes* 96, no. 2 (2005): 119–29; H. J. M. Kooij-de Bode, D. Van Knippenberg, and W. P. Van Ginkel, "Good Effects of Bad Feelings: Negative Affectivity and Group Decision-Making," *British Journal of Management* 21, no. 2 (2010): 375–92; S. K. Lam and J. Schaubroeck, "Information Sharing and Group Efficacy Influences on Communication and Decision Quality," *Asia Pacific Journal of Management* 28, no. 3 (2011): 509–28; J. A. Minson and J. S. Mueller, "The Cost of Collaboration: Why Joint Decision Making Exacerbates Rejection of Outside Information," *Psychological Science* 23, no. 3 (2012): 219–24; K. D. Clark and P. G. Maggitti, "TMT Potency and Strategic Decision-Making in High Technology Firms," *Journal of Management Studies* 49, no. 7 (2012): 1168–93.

99. The term *brainstorm* dates back to a New York murder trial in February 1907, during which an alienist (psychiatrist) gave expert testimony that the accused had a "brain storm," which he described as a form of temporary insanity. But by the mid-1920s, a brainstorm was associated with creative thinking. For example, *Popular Science* magazine's lead article in April 1926 described innovative camera operators, one of whom received a film award for a brainstorm of filming while strapped to a windmill. Advertising executive Alex Osborn (the *O* in BBDO, the largest creative agency owned by Omnicom) first described the brainstorming process in the little-known 1942 booklet *How to Think Up* (p. 29). Osborn gave a fuller description of the brainstorming process in his popular 1948 (*Your Creative Power*) and 1953 (*Applied Imagination*) books. See A. F. Osborn, *How to Think Up* (New York: McGraw-Hill, 1942), chap. 4; A. F. Osborn, *Your Creative Power* (New York: Scribner's Sons, 1948); A. F. Osborn, *Applied Imagination* (New York: Scribner's Sons, 1953).

100. R. I. Sutton and A. Hargadon, "Brainstorming Groups in Context: Effectiveness in a Product Design Firm," *Administrative Science Quarterly* 41 (1996): 685–718; T. Kelley, *The Art of Innovation* (New York: Currency Doubleday, 2001); T. Kelley, *The Ten Faces of Innovation* (New York: Doubleday, 2005); K. Sawyer, *Group Genius: The Creative Power of Collaboration* (New York: Basic Books, 2007).

101. P. A. Heslin, "Better Than Brainstorming? Potential Contextual Boundary Conditions to Brainwriting for Idea Generation in Organizations," *Journal of Occupational and Organizational Psychology* 82, no. 1 (2009): 129–45; J. S. Linsey and B. Becker, "Effectiveness of Brainwriting Techniques: Comparing Nominal Groups to Real Teams," in *Design Creativity 2010*, ed. T. Taura and Y. Nagai (London: Springer London, 2011), 165–71; N. Michinov, "Is Electronic Brainstorming or Brainwriting the Best Way to Improve Creative Performance in Groups? An Overlooked Comparison of Two Idea-Generation Techniques," *Journal of Applied Social Psychology* 42 (2012): E222–E243.

102. R. B. Gallupe, L. M. Bastianutti, and W. H. Cooper, "Unblocking Brainstorms," *Journal of Applied Psychology* 76 (1991): 137–42; W. H. Cooper et al., "Some Liberating Effects of Anonymous Electronic Brainstorming," *Small Group Research* 29, no. 2 (1998): 147–78; A. R. Dennis, B. H. Wixom, and R. J. Vandenberg, "Understanding Fit and Appropriation Effects in Group Support Systems Via Meta-Analysis," *MIS Quarterly* 25, no. 2 (2001): 167–93; D. M. DeRosa, C. L. Smith, and D. A. Hantula, "The Medium Matters: Mining the Long-Promised Merit of Group Interaction in Creative Idea Generation Tasks in a Meta-Analysis of the Electronic Group Brainstorming Literature," *Computers in Human Behavior* 23, no. 3 (2007): 1549–81.

103. A. L. Delbecq, A. H. Van de Ven, and D. H. Gustafson, *Group Techniques for Program Planning: A Guide to Nominal Group and Delphi Processes* (Middleton, WI: Green Briar Press, 1986).

104. S. Frankel, "NGT + MDS: An Adaptation of the Nominal Group Technique for Ill-Structured Problems," *Journal of Applied Behavioral Science* 23 (1987): 543–51; H. Barki and A. Pinsonneault, "Small Group Brainstorming and Idea Quality: Is Electronic Brainstorming the Most Effective Approach?," *Small Group Research* 32, no. 2 (2001): 158–205; P. P. Lago et al., "Structuring Group Decision Making in a Web-Based Environment by Using the Nominal Group Technique," *Computers & Industrial Engineering* 52, no. 2 (2007): 277–95.

8 | Communicating in Teams and Organizations

Learning Objectives

After you read this chapter, you should be able to:

LO8-1 Explain why communication is important in organizations, and discuss four influences on effective communication encoding and decoding.

LO8-2 Compare and contrast the advantages of and problems with electronic mail, other verbal communication media, and nonverbal communication.

LO8-3 Discuss the relevance of synchronicity, social presence, social acceptance, and media richness when choosing the preferred communication channel.

LO8-4 Discuss various barriers (noise) to effective communication, including cross-cultural and gender-based differences in communication.

LO8-5 Explain how to get your message across more effectively, and summarize the elements of active listening.

LO8-6 Summarize effective communication strategies in organizational hierarchies, and review the role and relevance of the organizational grapevine.

Organizations are currently experiencing a turbulent change in how employees communicate with each other. High-quality videoconferences, channel-based text messaging systems, sophisticated corporate-strength social media, smartphone videos and messages, and other methods didn't exist a decade ago. Indeed, many organizations in the United States and other countries are still struggling with whether—let alone determining how—to incorporate these new ways of interacting in the workplace. Digital communication offers significant potential for information sharing and social bonding. Equally important, employees use these emerging communication channels in their private lives and expect to have them available at work.

Communication refers to the process by which information is transmitted and *understood* between two or more people. We emphasize the word *understood* because transmitting the sender's intended meaning is the essence of good communication. This chapter begins by discussing the importance of effective communication, outlining the communication process model, and discussing factors that improve communication coding and decoding. Next, we identify types of communication channels, including email and social media, followed by factors to consider when choosing a communication medium. The chapter then identifies barriers to effective communication. The latter part of the chapter looks at communication in organizational hierarchies and offers insight about the pervasive organizational grapevine.

> ## An organization comes into being when there are persons able to communicate with each other.[2]
> —Chester Barnard, pioneering OB scholar and telecommunications CEO

LO8-1 Explain why communication is important in organizations, and discuss four influences on effective communication encoding and decoding.

THE IMPORTANCE OF COMMUNICATION

Effective communication is vital to all organizations, so much so that no company could exist without it. The reason? Recall from Chapter 1 that organizations are defined as groups of people who work interdependently toward some purpose. People work interdependently only when they can communicate with each other. Although organizations rely on a variety of coordinating mechanisms (which we discuss in Chapter 12), frequent, timely, and accurate communication remains the primary means through which employees and work units effectively synchronize their work.[1]

In addition to coordination, communication is critical for organizational learning. It is the means through which knowledge enters the organization and is distributed to employees.[3] A third function of communication is decision making. Imagine the challenge of making a decision without any information about the decision context, the alternatives available, the likely outcomes of those options, or the extent to which the decision is achieving its objectives. All of these ingredients require communication from coworkers and stakeholders in the external environment. For example, airline cockpit crews make much better decisions—and thereby cause far fewer accidents—when the captain encourages the other pilots to openly share information.[4]

A fourth function of communication is to change behavior.[5] When conveying information to others, we are often trying to alter their beliefs, feelings, and ultimately their behavior. This influence process might be passive, such as merely describing the situation more clearly and fully. But communication is often a deliberate attempt to change someone's thoughts and actions. We will discuss the topic of persuasion later in this chapter.

A fifth function of communication is to support employee well-being.[6] One way communication minimizes stress is by conveying knowledge that helps employees better manage their work environment. For instance, research shows that new employees adjust much better to the organization when coworkers communicate subtle nuggets of wisdom, such as how to complete work procedures correctly, find useful resources, handle difficult customers, and avoid office politics.[7] The second way communication minimizes stress is emotionally; talking with others can be a soothing balm during difficult times. Indeed,

Effective communication is vital to all organizations because it is the primary means through which employees and work units synchronize their work.
©Alexey Y. Petrov/Shutterstock

people are less susceptible to colds, cardiovascular disease, and other physical and mental illnesses when they have regular social interaction.[8] In essence, people have an inherent drive to bond, to validate their self-worth, and to maintain their social identity. Communication is the means through which these drives and needs are fulfilled.

A MODEL OF COMMUNICATION

To understand the key features of effective interpersonal communication, let's examine the model presented in Exhibit 8.1, which provides a useful "conduit" metaphor for thinking about the communication process.[9] According to this model, communication flows through one or more channels (also called *media*) between the sender and receiver. The sender forms a message and encodes it into words, gestures, voice intonations, and other symbols or signs. Next, the encoded message is transmitted to the intended receiver through voice, text, nonverbal cues, or other channels. The receiver senses and decodes the incoming message into something meaningful. Ideally, the decoded meaning is what the sender had intended.

In most situations, the sender looks for evidence that the other person received and understood the transmitted message. This feedback may involve the receiver repeating the message back to the sender or demonstrating awareness of the message indirectly through the receiver's subsequent actions. Notice that feedback repeats the communication process. Intended feedback is encoded, transmitted, received, and decoded from the receiver to the sender of the original message.

This model recognizes that communication is not a free-flowing conduit. Rather, the transmission of meaning from one person to another is hampered by *noise*—the psychological, social, and structural barriers that distort and obscure the sender's intended message. If any part of the communication process is distorted or broken, the sender and receiver will not have a common understanding of the message.

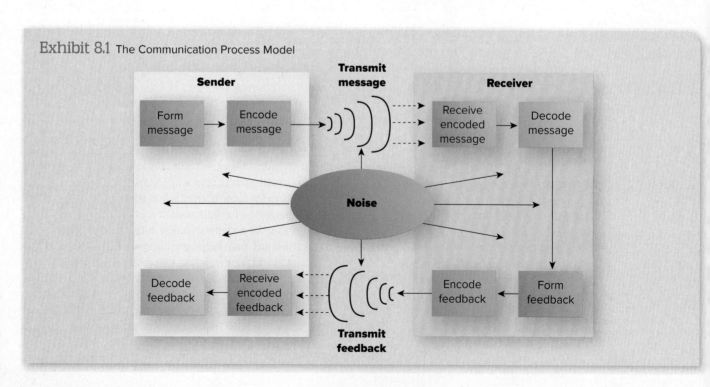

Exhibit 8.1 The Communication Process Model

Influences on Effective Encoding and Decoding

According to the communication process model, effective communication depends on the sender's and receiver's ability, motivation, role clarity, and situational support to efficiently and accurately encode and decode information. Four main factors influence the effectiveness of this encoding–decoding process.[10]

First, the sender and receiver encode and decode more effectively when they have similar "codebooks," which are dictionaries of symbols, language, gestures, idioms, and other tools used to convey information. With similar codebooks, the communication participants are able to encode and decode more accurately because they assign the same or similar meaning to the transmitted symbols and signs. Communication efficiency also improves because there is less need for redundancy (repeating the message in different ways) and less need for confirmation feedback ("So, you are saying that . . . ?").

Second, the encoding–decoding process improves with experience because the sender learns which words, symbols, voice intonations, and other features transmit the message more clearly and persuasively to others. Third, the encoding–decoding process is better when the sender and receiver are skilled and motivated to use the selected communication channel(s). Some people prefer face-to-face conversations, others prefer tweets and text messages, and still others prefer writing and receiving detailed reports. Even when the sender and receiver have the same codebooks, the message can get lost in translation when one or both parties use a channel that they dislike or don't know how to use very well.[11]

Fourth, the encoding–decoding process depends on the sender's and receiver's shared mental models of the communication context. Mental models are visual or relational images of the communication setting, whereas codebooks are symbols used to convey message content (see Chapter 3). For example, a Russian cosmonaut and American astronaut might have shared mental models about the layout and features of the international space station (communication context), yet they experience poor communication because of language differences (i.e., different codebooks). Shared mental models potentially enable more accurate transmission of the message content and reduce the need for communication about the message context.

People who communicate with similar codebooks are able to encode and decode more accurately because they assign the same or similar meaning to the transmitted symbols and signs.
©Jorg Greuel/Photodisc/Getty Images

OB THEORY TO PRACTICE

Encoding and Decoding More Effectively

The message is more likely to be received and understood when

▶ Both sender and receiver possess similar "codebooks" of symbols, language, gestures, etc.

▶ The sender has experience encoding that particular message.

▶ Both sender and receiver have the skill and motivation to use the selected communication channel(s).

▶ Both sender and receiver have shared mental models of the communication context.

LO8-2 Compare and contrast the advantages of and problems with electronic mail, other verbal communication media, and nonverbal communication.

COMMUNICATION CHANNELS

A central feature of the communication model is the channel (also called the *medium*) through which information is transmitted. There are two main types of channels: verbal and nonverbal. Verbal communication uses words, so it includes spoken or written channels. Nonverbal communication is any part of communication that does not use words. Spoken and written communication are both verbal (i.e., they both use words), but they are quite different from each other and have different strengths and weaknesses in communication effectiveness, which we discuss later in this section. Also, written communication has traditionally been much slower than spoken communication at transmitting messages, although electronic mail, Twitter tweets, and other online communication channels have significantly improved written communication efficiency.

Internet and Digital Communication

Instant messaging, social media, and other contemporary digital communication activities didn't exist in organizations a dozen years ago, whereas they are now gaining popularity. However, email is still the medium of choice in most workplaces.[12] Email messages can be written, edited, and transmitted quickly. Information can be effortlessly appended and conveyed to many people. Email is also asynchronous (messages are sent and received at different times), so there is no need to coordinate a communication session. With advances in computer search technology, email software also has become a somewhat efficient filing cabinet.[13]

Email is the preferred medium for sending well-defined information for decision making. It is also the first choice for coordinating work, although text messages may soon overtake email for this objective. The introduction of email has substantially altered the directional flow of information as well as increased the volume and speed of those messages throughout the organization.[14] In particular, email has reduced face-to-face and telephone communication but increased communication with people further up the hierarchy. Email potentially improves employee–manager relations, except where these messages are used by the manager to control employee behavior.

Several studies suggest that email reduces social and organizational status differences between sender and receiver, mainly because there are fewer cues to indicate these differences than in face-to-face interactions. However, status differences still exist to some extent in written digital communication.[15] For instance, one study found that managers signaled their status by replying to emails less quickly and with shorter messages. Even text messages can convey status differences. Emerging evidence suggests that people assign higher status to senders of messages that include an elite signature (e.g., "Sent from my iPhone").

Email and other forms of written digital communication potentially reduce stereotyping and prejudice because age, race, and other features of the participants are unknown or less noticeable.[16] Text messages and emails allow more time to craft diplomatic messages than in face-to-face interactions. However, diplomatic writing mainly occurs when there is potential conflict or perceived prejudice. In other situations, the lack of face-to-face contact may increase reliance on stereotypes and produce messages that reflect those biases.

Problems with Email and Other Digital Message Channels

Email, text messages, and other written digital message channels dominate organizational communication, but they have several limitations. Here are the top four complaints:

People consistently and significantly overestimate the degree to which they understand the emotional meaning of digital messages.
©ESB Professional/Shutterstock

Poor Communication of Emotions People rely on facial expressions and other nonverbal cues to interpret the emotional meaning of words; email and text messages lack this parallel communication channel. Indeed, people consistently and significantly overestimate the degree to which they understand the emotional tone of digital messages.[17] Senders try to clarify the emotional tone of their messages by using expressive language ("Wonderful to hear from you!"), highlighting phrases in boldface or quotation marks, and inserting graphic faces (called emojis or "smileys") representing the desired emotion. Studies suggest that writers are getting better at using these emotion symbols. Still, they do not replace the full complexity of real facial expressions, voice intonation, and hand movements.[18]

Less Politeness and Respectfulness Digital messages are often less diplomatic than written letters. Indeed, the term *flaming* has entered our language to describe messages that convey strong negative emotions. Receivers are partly to blame because they tend to infer more negative emotional meaning to the digital message than was intended by the sender.[19] Even so, flame wars occur mostly because senders tend to send disparaging messages digitally more often than by other communication channels. One reason is that individuals can post digital messages before their emotions subside, whereas the sender of a traditional memo or letter would have time for sober second thoughts. A second reason why employees are more likely to send disrespectful messages digitally than in face-to-face conversation is that digital messages have low social presence (they are impersonal), which reduces the sender's empathy and sensitivity. Fortunately, organizations are responding with explicit norms and rules that minimize flaming and cyberbullying.[20]

Cumbersome Medium for Ambiguous, Complex, and Novel Situations Digital messages are incredibly efficient for well-defined situations, such as confirming the location of a meeting or giving basic instructions for a routine activity. But this form of communication can be cumbersome and dysfunctional in ambiguous, complex, and novel situations. As we will describe later in this section, these circumstances require communication channels that transmit a larger volume of information with more rapid feedback. In other words, when the issue gets messy, stop emailing or texting and start talking, preferably face-to-face.

Contributes to Information Overload Digital messages contribute to information overload.[21] The phenomenal growth of email is one culprit. Approximately 72 trillion emails—more than half of which are in business settings—are now transmitted annually around the world, up from just 1.1 trillion in 1998. Almost two-thirds of all emails are spam![22] The email glut occurs because messages are created and copied to many people without much effort.

Workplace Communication through Social Media

Although email still dominates most workplace communication, it eventually may be overtaken by emerging forms of social media. Social media are Internet- or mobile-based channels that allow users to generate and interactively share information. They cover a wide range of categories, including social networks (Facebook, LinkedIn, Google+), microblogs (Twitter), blogs and blog communities (Typepad, BlogHer), site comments and forums (FlyerTalk, Whirlpool), multimedia sharing (YouTube, Pinterest), and shared publishing (Wikipedia).

Unlike traditional websites that merely "push" information from the creator to the audience, social media are more conversational and reciprocally interactive between sender and receiver, resulting in a sense of community.[23] Social media are "social" because they encourage formation of communities through links, interactive conversations, and (for some platforms) common space for collaborative content development. The audience can become participants in the conversation by contributing feedback and by linking someone else's content to their own social media spaces. Some social media platforms also enable users the right to develop a public identity.

Each type of social media serves a unique combination of functions, such as presenting the individual's identity, enabling conversations, sharing information, sensing the presence of others in the virtual space, maintaining relationships, revealing reputation or status, and supporting communities (see Exhibit 8.2).[24] For instance, Facebook has a strong emphasis on maintaining relationships but relatively low emphasis on sharing information or forming communities (groups). Wikis, on the other hand, focus on sharing information or forming communities but have a much lower emphasis on presenting the user's identity or reputation.

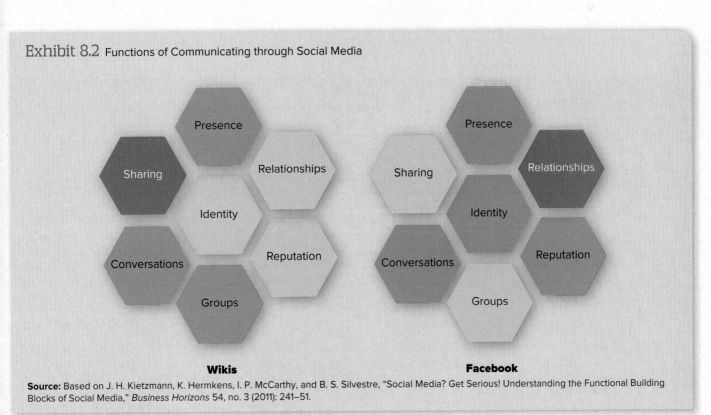

Exhibit 8.2 Functions of Communicating through Social Media

Wikis

Facebook

Source: Based on J. H. Kietzmann, K. Hermkens, I. P. McCarthy, and B. S. Silvestre, "Social Media? Get Serious! Understanding the Functional Building Blocks of Social Media," *Business Horizons* 54, no. 3 (2011): 241–51.

emotional contagion
the nonconscious process of "catching" or sharing another person's emotions by mimicking that person's facial expressions and other nonverbal behavior

There is increasing evidence that enterprise social media platforms such as Yammer, IBM Connections, Facebook at Work, and Slack can improve knowledge sharing and socializing among employees under some conditions.[25] When a major credit card company introduced one of these enterprise social media platforms, its employees were 31 percent better at finding information and 71 percent better at finding the person with the original information. A large-scale study of Twitter tweets reported that this form of communication aided employees in transmitting knowledge, maintaining collegiality among coworkers, and strengthening their professional network. Many social media platforms enable feedback, which potentially gives employees more voice. One study found evidence of this voice, but only where these feedback mechanisms received management support.

Millennials are the strongest advocates of social media in the workplace, whereas one recent study reported that older employees remain skeptical. Most corporate leaders are in the latter age cohort, which may explain why companies have been slow to adopt enterprise social media.[26] In fact, many organizations simply ban employee access to any social media (usually after discovering excessive employee activity on Facebook) without thinking through the longer-term potential of these communication channels.

Nonverbal Communication

Nonverbal communication includes facial gestures, voice intonation, physical distance, and even silence.[28] This communication channel is necessary where noise or physical distance prevents effective verbal exchanges and where the need for immediate feedback precludes written communication. But even in quiet face-to-face meetings, most information is communicated nonverbally. Rather like a parallel conversation, nonverbal cues signal subtle information to both parties, such as reinforcing their interest in the verbal conversation or demonstrating their relative status in the relationship.[29] Unfortunately, we often transmit messages nonverbally without being aware of this conversation.

Nonverbal communication differs from verbal (i.e., written and spoken) communication in a couple of ways. First, it is less rule-bound than verbal communication. We receive considerable formal training on how to understand spoken words, but very little on how to understand the nonverbal signals that accompany those words. Consequently, nonverbal cues are generally more ambiguous and susceptible to misinterpretation. At the same time, many facial expressions (such as smiling) are hardwired and universal, thereby providing the only reliable means of communicating across cultures.

The other difference between verbal and nonverbal communication is that the former is typically conscious, whereas most nonverbal communication is automatic and nonconscious. We normally plan the words we say or write, but we rarely plan every blink, smile, or other gesture during a conversation. Indeed, as we just mentioned, many of these facial expressions communicate the same meaning across cultures because they are hardwired, nonconscious responses to human emotions.[31] For example, pleasant emotions cause the brain center to widen the mouth, whereas negative emotions produce constricted facial expressions (squinting eyes, pursed lips, etc.).

Emotional Contagion One of the most fascinating aspects of nonverbal communication is **emotional contagion**, which is the

---

Bosch Employees Improve Collaboration through Social Media

A few years ago, Robert Bosch GmbH asked hundreds of its employees to describe their image of a future workplace that supports collaboration and idea generation. From this feedback, the German engineering and electronics company introduced Bosch Connect, an enterprise social media platform developed by IBM combined with Skype.

Bosch Connect includes several conditions to support digital collaboration. First, the online communities are self-organizing; employees set them

© Krisztian Bocsi/Bloomberg/Getty Images

up without seeking permission from management. Second, the communities are transparent, not hidden or restrictive. This means that any Bosch employee can join a community if it is public, or can ask to join if it is moderated. Third, employees are encouraged to ask questions and offer suggestions, even for communities outside their work specialization.

Bosch Connect has significantly boosted productivity and is now part of everyday work for most of the company's 300,000 employees. For example, one team completed a customer localization project in six days using Bosch Connect rather than email, compared to similar projects that took up to four weeks without Bosch Connect (i.e., mainly used email). Bosch's social media platform is particularly popular among younger employees. "I'm used to chatting electronically with friends and family and using various social media channels to communicate in my private life," says Ee Von Lim, a Bosch accounting manager in Singapore. "Now when I'm collaborating with colleagues, communication is just as intuitive. That makes me more productive—and my work more fun."[27]

Top 10 Body Language Mistakes in Job Interviews[30]

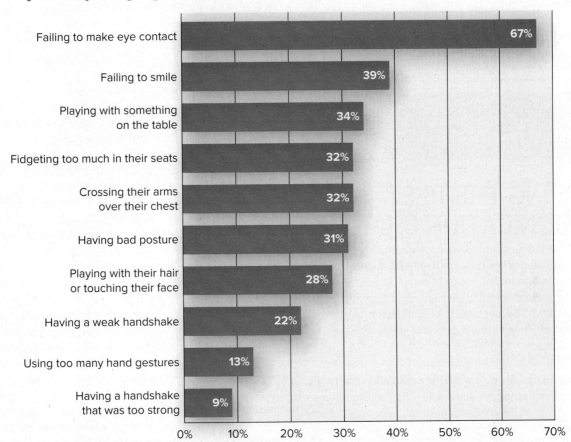

Failing to make eye contact	67%
Failing to smile	39%
Playing with something on the table	34%
Fidgeting too much in their seats	32%
Crossing their arms over their chest	32%
Having bad posture	31%
Playing with their hair or touching their face	28%
Having a weak handshake	22%
Using too many hand gestures	13%
Having a handshake that was too strong	9%

Percentage of 2,605 U.S. human resource and hiring managers surveyed who identified each of these behaviors as the biggest body language mistakes made by job candidates during hiring interviews.
© Image Credit

> ## The most important thing in communication is hearing what isn't said.[32]
>
> —Peter Drucker, scholar, consultant, and "father" of management theory

automatic process of "catching" or sharing another person's emotions by mimicking that person's facial expressions and other nonverbal behavior. Technically, human beings have brain receptors that cause them to mirror what they observe. In other words, to some degree our brain causes us to act as though we are the person we are watching.[33]

Consider what happens when you see a coworker accidentally bang his or her head against a filing cabinet. Chances are, you wince and put your hand on your own head as if you had hit the cabinet. Similarly, while listening to someone describe a positive event, you tend to smile and exhibit other emotional displays of happiness. While some of our nonverbal communication is planned, emotional contagion represents nonconscious behavior—we automatically mimic and synchronize our nonverbal behaviors with other people.[34]

Emotional contagion influences communication and social relationships in three ways.[35] First, mimicry provides continuous feedback, communicating that we understand and empathize with the sender. To consider the significance of this, imagine employees remaining expressionless after watching a coworker bang his or her head! The lack of parallel behavior conveys a lack of understanding or caring. A second function is that mimicking the nonverbal behaviors of other people seems to be a way of receiving emotional meaning from those people. If a coworker is angry with a client, your tendency to frown and show anger while listening helps you experience that emotion more fully. In other words, we receive meaning by expressing the sender's emotions as well as by listening to the sender's words.

The third function of emotional contagion is to fulfill the drive to bond that we mentioned earlier in this chapter and was introduced in Chapter 5. Bonding develops through each person's awareness of a collective sentiment. Through nonverbal expressions of emotional contagion, people see others share the same emotions that they feel. This strengthens relations among team members as well as between leaders and followers by providing evidence of their similarity.

LO8-3 Discuss the relevance of synchronicity, social presence, social acceptance, and media richness when choosing the preferred communication channel.

CHOOSING THE BEST COMMUNICATION CHANNEL

Employees have more communication channels to choose from than ever before, ranging from physical and technological forms of face-to-face interaction to a multitude of ways to transmit written messages. Which communication channel is most appropriate in a particular situation? The four most important factors to consider are summarized in Exhibit 8.3 and described in this section.

Synchronicity

Communication channels vary in their **synchronicity**, that is, the extent to which they require or allow both sender and receiver to be actively involved in the conversation at the same time.[36] Face-to-face conversations are almost always synchronous, whereas email communication exchanges allow each party to participate at different times (asynchronous). Online texting can be asynchronous, but it often occurs as a synchronous conversation. Synchronous communication is better when the information is required quickly (high immediacy) or where the issue is complex and therefore requires the parties to address several related decisions. Asynchronous communication is better when the issue is simple, the issue has low time urgency, getting both parties together at the same time is costly, and/or the receiver would benefit from time to reflect on the message before responding.

Social Presence

Social presence refers to how much the communication channel creates psychological closeness to others, awareness of their humanness, and appreciation of the interpersonal relationship.[37] Some communication channels make us more aware that there is another human being (or several others) in the conversation, and they produce a sense of mutual relationship. Face-to-face interactions almost always have the highest social presence, whereas low social presence would typically occur when sending an email to a large distribution list. Social presence is also stronger in synchronous communication because immediate responses by the other party to our messages increase the sense of connectedness with that person. Although social presence is mostly affected by specific channel characteristics, message content also plays a role. For example, social presence is affected by how casually or formally the message is conveyed and by how much personal information about the sender is included in the message.

A communication channel is valued for its social presence effect when the purpose of the dialogue is to understand and empathize with the other person or group. People are also more willing to listen and help others when there is a degree of interpersonal relationship or feeling of human connectedness. Therefore, channels with high social presence are better when the sender wants to influence the receiver.

Social Acceptance

Social acceptance refers to how well the communication medium is approved and supported by those involved in the exchange.[38] One social acceptance factor is the set of norms held

Exhibit 8.3 Factors in Choosing the Best Communication Channel

Channel Choice Factor	Description	Depends on . . .
Synchronicity	The channel requires or allows the sender and receiver to communicate with each other at the same time (synchronous) or at different times (asynchronous)	• Time urgency (immediacy) • Complexity of the topic • Cost of both parties communicating at the same time • Whether receiver should have time to reflect before responding
Social presence	The channel creates psychological closeness to others, awareness of their humanness, and appreciation of the interpersonal relationship	• Need to empathize with others • Need to influence others
Social acceptance	The channel is approved and supported by others (receiver, team, organization, or society)	• Organizational, team, and cultural norms • Each party's preferences and skills with the channel • Symbolic meaning of the channel
Media richness	The channel has high data-carrying capacity—the volume and variety of information that can be transmitted during a specific time	• Situation is nonroutine • Situation is ambiguous

A communication channel is valued for its social presence effect when the purpose of the dialogue is to understand and empathize with the other person or group.
©LWA/Larry Williams/Blend Images LLC

by the team, organization, and society. Norms explain why face-to-face meetings are daily events among staff in some firms, whereas computer-based videoconferencing (such as Skype) and Twitter tweets are the media of choice in other organizations. Studies report that national culture plays an important role in preferences for specific communication channels.[39] For instance, Koreans are much less likely than Americans to email corporate executives because in Korea email is considered insufficiently respectful of the superior's status. Other research has found that the preference for email depends on the culture's emphasis on context, time, and space in social relationships.

A second social acceptance factor is the sender's and receiver's preferences for specific communication channels.[40] You may have noticed that some coworkers ignore (or rarely check) voice mail, yet they quickly respond to text messages or Twitter tweets. These preferences are due to personality traits as well as previous experience and reinforcement with particular channels.

A third social acceptance factor is the symbolic meaning of a channel.[41] Some communication channels are viewed as impersonal whereas others are more personal; some are considered professional whereas others are casual; some are "cool" whereas others are old-fashioned. For instance, phone calls and other synchronous communication channels convey a greater sense of urgency than do text messages and other asynchronous channels. The importance of a channel's symbolic meaning is perhaps most apparent in stories about managers who use emails or text messages to inform employees that they are fired or laid off. These communication events make headlines because email and text messages have low social presence and therefore are considered inappropriate (too impersonal) for transmission of that particular information.[42]

Media Richness

Media richness refers to the communication channel's data-carrying capacity—the volume and variety of information that can

be transmitted during a specific time.[43] Exhibit 8.4 illustrates various communication channels arranged in a hierarchy of richness, with face-to-face interaction at the top and lean data-only reports at the bottom. A communication channel has high richness when it is able to convey multiple cues (such as both verbal and nonverbal information), allows timely feedback from receiver to sender, allows the sender to customize the message to the receiver, and makes use of complex symbols (such as words and phrases with multiple meanings).

Face-to-face communication has very high media richness because it allows us to communicate both verbally and nonverbally at the same time, to get feedback almost immediately from the receiver, to quickly adjust our message and style, and to use complex language such as metaphors and idioms

Face-to-face communication has very high media richness, so many hospital teams have brief stand-up daily huddles to share information and expectations about the day's work.
©pixdeluxe/Getty Images

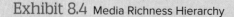

Exhibit 8.4 Media Richness Hierarchy

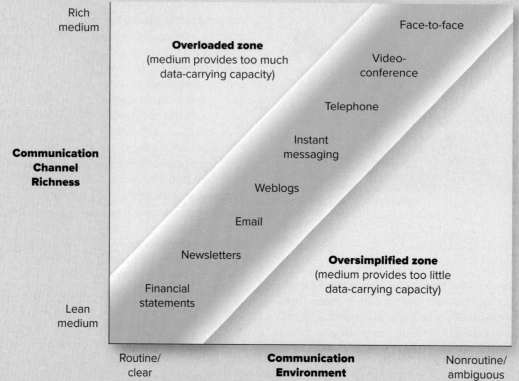

Sources: Based on R. H. Lengel and R. L. Daft, "The Selection of Communication Media as an Executive Skill," *Academy of Management Executive* 2, no. 3 (August 1988): 226; R. L. Daft and R. H. Lengel, "Information Richness: A New Approach to Managerial Behavior and Organization Design," *Research in Organizational Behavior* 6 (1984): 199.

(e.g., "spilling the beans"). For example, department and shift teams in many hospitals have brief stand-up daily huddles during which team members share information and expectations about the day's work.[44] Rich media tend to be synchronous and have high social presence, but not always.

According to media richness theory, rich media are better than lean media when the communication situation is nonroutine and ambiguous. In nonroutine situations (such as an unexpected and unusual emergency), the sender and receiver have little common experience, so they need to transmit a large volume of information with immediate feedback. Lean media work well in routine situations because the sender and receiver have common expectations through shared mental models. Ambiguous situations also require rich media because the parties must share large amounts of information with immediate feedback to resolve multiple and conflicting interpretations of their observations and experiences.[45]

Choosing the wrong medium reduces communication effectiveness. When the situation is routine or clear, using a rich medium—such as holding a special meeting—would be a waste of time.[46] On the other hand, if a unique and ambiguous issue is handled through email or another lean medium, then issues take longer to resolve and misunderstandings are more likely to occur.

Exceptions to the Media Richness Theory Research generally supports media richness theory for traditional channels (face-to-face, written memos, etc.). However, the model doesn't fit reality nearly as well when digital communication channels are studied.[47] Three factors seem to explain why digital channels may have more media richness than media richness theory predicts:

1. *Ability to multicommunicate.* It is usually difficult (as well as rude) to communicate face-to-face with someone while simultaneously transmitting messages to another person using another medium. Most digital communication channels, on the other hand, require less social etiquette and attention, so employees can easily engage in two or more communication events at the same time. In other words, they can multicommunicate.[48] For example, employees tap out text messages to a client while simultaneously listening to a discussion at a large meeting. Research consistently finds that people multitask less efficiently than they assume,[49] but the volume of information transmitted simultaneously through two digital communication channels is sometimes greater than through one high media richness channel.

2. *Communication proficiency.* Earlier in this chapter we explained that communication effectiveness is partially determined by the sender's ability and motivation to use the selected communication channel. People with higher proficiency can "push" more information through the channel, thereby increasing the channel's information flow. Experienced smartphone users, for instance, can whip through messages in a flash,

persuasion the use of facts, logical arguments, and emotional appeals to change another person's beliefs and attitudes, usually for the purpose of changing the person's behavior

Digital channels have more media richness than the theory predicts possibly because there is considerable variation in the proficiency with which people can "push" information through these types of channels.
©ra2studio/Shutterstock

whereas new users struggle to type notes and organize incoming messages. In contrast, there is less variation in the ability to communicate through casual conversation and other natural channels because most of us develop good levels of proficiency throughout life and possibly through hardwired evolutionary development.[50]

3. *Social presence effects*. Channels with high media richness tend to have more social presence.[51] This improves empathy, but it also sensitizes both parties to their relative status and self-presentation, which can distort or divert attention away from the message.[52] During a personal meeting with the company's CEO, for example, you might become more focused on the CEO's evaluation of you than on what the CEO is saying to you. In other words, the benefits of channels with high media richness may be offset by more social presence distractions, whereas lean media have much less social presence to distract or distort the transmitted information.

Communication Channels and Persuasion

Some communication channels are more effective than others for **persuasion**, that is, changing another person's beliefs and attitudes. Studies support the long-held view that spoken communication, particularly face-to-face interaction, is more persuasive than emails, websites, and other forms of written communication. There are three main reasons for this persuasive effect.[53] First, spoken communication is typically accompanied by nonverbal communication. People are persuaded more when they receive both emotional and logical messages, and the combination of spoken with nonverbal communication provides

this dual punch. A lengthy pause, raised voice tone, and (in face-to-face interaction) animated hand gestures can amplify the emotional tone of the message, thereby signaling the vitality of the issue.

A second reason why conversations are more persuasive is that spoken communication offers the sender high-quality, immediate feedback about whether the receiver understands and accepts the message (i.e., is being persuaded). This feedback allows the sender to adjust the content and emotional tone of the message more quickly than with written communication. A third reason is that people are persuaded more under conditions of high social presence than low social presence. Listeners have higher motivation to pay attention and consider the sender's ideas in face-to-face conversations (high social presence). In contrast, persuasive communication through a website, email, and other low social presence channels are less effective due to the higher degree of anonymity and psychological distance from the persuader.

Although spoken communication tends to be more persuasive, written communication also can persuade others to some extent. Written messages have the advantage of presenting more technical detail than can occur through conversation. This factual information is valuable when the issue is important to the receiver. Also, people experience a moderate degree of social presence in written communication with friends and coworkers, so written messages can be persuasive when sent and received with close associates.

> **LO8-4** Discuss various barriers (noise) to effective communication, including cross-cultural and gender-based differences in communication.

COMMUNICATION BARRIERS (NOISE)

In spite of the best intentions of sender and receiver to communicate, several barriers (called "noise" earlier in Exhibit 8.1) inhibit the effective exchange of information. One barrier is that both sender and receiver have imperfect perceptual processes. As receivers, we don't listen as well as senders assume, and our needs and expectations influence what signals get noticed and ignored.

> Spoken (particularly face-to-face) conversation is more persuasive than leaner communication channels because it offers the sender high-quality, immediate feedback about whether the receiver understands and accepts the message.

information overload
a condition in which the volume of information received exceeds the person's capacity to process it

We aren't any better as senders, either. Some studies suggest that we have difficulty stepping out of our own perspectives and stepping into the perspectives of others, so we overestimate how well other people understand the message we are communicating.[54]

Language issues can be huge sources of communication noise because sender and receiver might not have the same codebook. They might not speak the same language, or might have different meanings for particular words and phrases. The English language (among others) also has built-in ambiguities that cause misunderstandings. Consider the phrase "Can you close the door?" You might assume the sender is asking whether shutting the door is permitted. However, the question might be asking whether you are physically able to shut the door or whether the door is designed such that it can be shut. In fact, this question might not be a question at all; the person could be politely *telling* you to shut the door.[56]

The ambiguity of language isn't always dysfunctional noise.[57] Corporate leaders sometimes purposively use obscure language to reflect the ambiguity of the topic or to avoid unwanted emotional responses produced by more specific words. They might use metaphors to represent an abstract vision of the company's future, or use obtuse phrases such as "rightsizing" and

> ## The greatest barrier to communication is the illusion that it has been achieved.[55]
>
> —Joseph W. Coffman, president of Tecnifax Corporation, inventor, communication expert

"restructuring" to obscure the underlying message that people will be fired or laid off. Studies report that effective communicators also use more abstract words and symbols when addressing diverse or distant (not well known to the speaker) audiences because abstraction increases the likelihood that the message is understood across a broader range of listeners.

Jargon—specialized words and phrases for specific occupations or groups—is usually designed to improve communication efficiency. However, it is a source of communication noise when transmitted to people who do not possess the jargon codebook. Furthermore, people who use jargon excessively put themselves in an unflattering light.

Another source of noise in the communication process is the tendency to filter messages. Filtering may involve deleting or delaying negative information or using less harsh words so the message sounds more favorable.[58] Filtering is less likely to occur when corporate leaders create a "culture of candor." This culture develops when leaders themselves communicate truthfully, seek out diverse sources for information, and protect and reward those who speak openly and with honesty.[59]

Information Overload

Start with a daily avalanche of email, then add in cell phone calls, text messages, PDF file downloads, web pages, hard copy documents, some Twitter tweets, blogs, wikis, and other sources of incoming information. Altogether, you have created a perfect recipe for **information overload**.[60] Information overload occurs whenever the job's information load exceeds the individual's capacity to get through it. Employees have a certain *information-processing capacity*—the amount of information that they are able to process in a fixed unit of time. At the same time, jobs have a varying *information load*—the amount of information to be processed per unit of time. Information overload creates noise in the communication system because information gets overlooked or misinterpreted when people can't process it fast enough. The result is poorer-quality decisions as well as higher stress.[61]

Information overload problems can be minimized by increasing our information-processing capacity, by reducing the job's information load, or through a combination of both. Studies suggest that employees often increase their information-processing capacity by temporarily reading faster, scanning through documents more efficiently, and removing distractions that slow information-processing speed. Time management also increases information-processing capacity. When information overload is temporary, employees can increase their information-processing capacity by working longer hours.

Information load can be reduced by buffering, omitting, and summarizing. Buffering involves having incoming communication

Information overload occurs whenever the job's information load exceeds the individual's capacity to get through it.
©alphaspirit/Shutterstock

filtered, usually by an assistant. Omitting occurs when we decide to overlook messages, such as using software rules to redirect emails from distribution lists to folders that we rarely look at. Summarizing involves digesting a condensed version of the complete communication, such as reading an executive summary rather than the full report.

CROSS-CULTURAL AND GENDER COMMUNICATION

Globalization and increasing cultural diversity have created more cross-cultural communication issues.[62] Voice intonation is one form of cross-cultural communication barrier. How loudly, deeply, and quickly people speak vary across cultures, and these voice intonations send secondary messages that have different meanings in different societies.

Language is an obvious cross-cultural communication challenge. Words are easily misunderstood in verbal communication, because either the receiver has a limited vocabulary or the sender's accent distorts the usual sound of some words. For example, KPMG staff from the United Kingdom sometimes referred to another person's suggestions as "interesting." They had to clarify to their German colleagues that "interesting" might not be complimenting the idea.[63]

Another cross-cultural dimension of communication is how people interpret conversational gaps (silence) and overlaps. Silence is revered in Japan because it symbolizes respect, indicates that the listener is thoughtfully contemplating what has just been said, and is a way of avoiding overt conflict.[64] Consequently, the informal communication practice in Japan and a few other countries is to let the other person finish speaking and sometimes wait a second or two before saying anything. In contrast, most people in

the United States and similar cultures avoid silence and interpret those incidents as a sign of disagreement. Conversational overlaps are considered rude in Japan, but people in Brazil, France, and a few other countries tend to view them favorably as an indication of the other person's interest and involvement in the conversation. Meetings in countries that expect overlapping conversations can seem like a chaotic cacophony to those from other cultures.

Nonverbal Differences across Cultures

Nonverbal communication represents another potential area for misunderstanding across cultures. Many nonconscious or involuntary nonverbal cues (such as smiling) have the same meaning around the world, but deliberate gestures often have different interpretations. For example, most of us shake our head from side to side to say, "No," but a variation of head shaking means "I understand" to many people in India. Filipinos raise their eyebrows to give an affirmative answer, yet Arabs interpret this expression (along with clicking one's tongue) as a negative response. Most Americans are taught to maintain eye contact with the speaker to show interest and respect, whereas some North American native groups learn at an early age to show respect by looking down when an older or more senior person is talking to them.[66]

Gender Differences in Communication

Men and women have similar communication practices, but there are subtle distinctions that can occasionally lead to misunderstanding and conflict (see Exhibit 8.5).[67] One distinction is that men are more likely than women to view conversations as negotiations of relative status and power. They assert their power by directly giving advice to others (e.g., "You should do the following") and using combative language. There is also evidence that men dominate the talk time in conversations with women, as well as interrupt more and adjust their speaking style less than do women.

Men engage in more "report talk," in which the primary function of the conversation is impersonal and efficient information exchange. Women also do report talk, particularly when conversing with men, but conversations among women have a higher incidence of relationship building through "rapport talk."[68] Women use more tentative speech patterns, including modifiers ("It might be a good idea . . ."), disclaimers ("I'm not certain, but . . ."), and tag questions ("This works, doesn't it?"). They also make more use of indirect requests ("Do you think you should . . . ?"), apologize more often, and seek advice from others more quickly than do men. These gender differences are modest, however, mainly because men also use these speech patterns to some extent. Research does clearly indicate that women are more sensitive than men to nonverbal cues in face-to-face meetings. Together, these conditions can create communication conflicts. Women who describe problems get frustrated that men offer advice rather than rapport, whereas men become frustrated because they can't understand why women don't appreciate their advice.

LO8-5 Explain how to get your message across more effectively, and summarize the elements of active listening.

IMPROVING INTERPERSONAL COMMUNICATION

Effective interpersonal communication depends on the sender's ability to get the message across and the receiver's performance as an active listener. In this section, we outline these two essential features of effective interpersonal communication.

Exhibit 8.5 Gender Differences in Communication

When Men Communicate	When Women Communicate
• Report talk—give advice, assert power	• Rapport talk—relationship building
• Give advice directly	• Give advice indirectly
• Dominant conversation style	• Flexible conversation style
• Apologize less often	• Apologize more often
• Less sensitive to nonverbal cues	• More sensitive to nonverbal cues

Photos: ©McGraw-Hill Education

Getting Your Message Across

This chapter began with the statement that effective communication occurs when the other person receives and understands the message. This is more difficult to accomplish than most people believe. To get your message across to the other person, you first need to empathize with the receiver, such as being sensitive to words that may be ambiguous or trigger the wrong emotional response. Second, be sure that you repeat the message, such as by rephrasing the key points a couple of times. Third, your message competes with other messages and noise, so find a time when the receiver is less likely to be distracted by these other matters. Finally, if you are communicating bad news or criticism, focus on the problem, not the person.

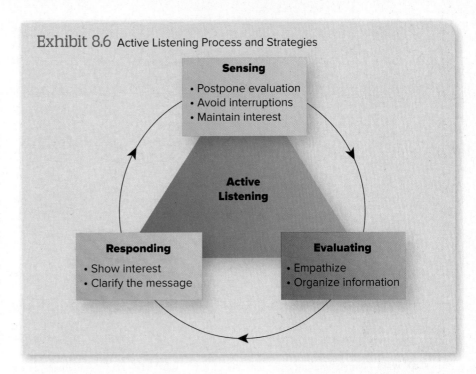

Exhibit 8.6 Active Listening Process and Strategies

Sensing
- Postpone evaluation
- Avoid interruptions
- Maintain interest

Active Listening

Responding
- Show interest
- Clarify the message

Evaluating
- Empathize
- Organize information

> ## Nature gave us one tongue, but two ears, so we may listen twice as much as we speak.[69]
>
> —Epictetus, Greek philosopher

Active Listening

Active listening is a process of mindfully sensing the sender's signals, evaluating them accurately, and responding appropriately. These three components of listening—sensing, evaluating, and responding—reflect the listener's side of the communication model described at the beginning of this chapter. Listeners receive the sender's signals, decode them as intended, and provide appropriate and timely feedback to the sender (see Exhibit 8.6). Active listeners constantly cycle through sensing, evaluating, and responding during the conversation and engage in various activities to improve these processes.[70]

- *Sensing*. Sensing is the process of receiving signals from the sender and paying attention to them. Active listeners improve sensing in three ways. First, they postpone evaluation by not forming an opinion until the speaker has finished. Second, they avoid interrupting the speaker's conversation. Third, they remain motivated to listen to the speaker.

- *Evaluating*. This component of listening includes understanding the message meaning, evaluating the message, and remembering the message. To improve their evaluation of the conversation, active listeners empathize with the speaker—they try to understand and be sensitive to the speaker's feelings, thoughts, and situation. Evaluation also improves by organizing the speaker's ideas during the communication episode.

- *Responding*. This third component of listening involves providing feedback to the sender, which motivates and directs the speaker's communication. Active listeners accomplish this by maintaining sufficient eye contact and sending back channel signals (e.g., "I see"), both of which show interest. They also respond by clarifying the message—rephrasing the speaker's ideas at appropriate breaks ("So you're saying that . . . ?").

IMPROVING COMMUNICATION THROUGHOUT THE HIERARCHY

So far, we have looked at micro-level issues in the communication process, namely, sending and receiving information between two employees or the informal exchanges of information across several people. But in this era where knowledge is competitive advantage, corporate leaders also need to maintain an open flow of communication up, down, and across the entire organization. In this section, we discuss three organizationwide communication strategies: workspace design, Internet-based communication, and direct communication with top management.

Workspace Design

To improve information sharing and create a more sociable work environment, many organizations have torn down the cubicle walls. In addition, they have incorporated informal spaces for small teams and happenstance gatherings.[71] The location and design of hallways, offices, cubicles, and communal areas (cafeterias, elevators) all shape to whom we speak as well as the frequency of that communication. Although these open-space arrangements increase the amount of face-to-face communication,

Communicating Up and Down the Hierarchy[75]

52% of 451 internal communications professionals surveyed across several countries say their biggest barrier to successful internal communication is the lack of line manager communication skills.

50% of 1,900 managers surveyed in Singapore, Hong Kong, and China say that lack of communication from their senior management is a key barrier to successful organizational change.

33% of more than 423,000 UK National Health System employees surveyed report good communication between senior managers and staff.

47% of 182,165 Canadian federal government employees surveyed say that essential information flows effectively from senior management to staff in their department.

60% of 407,789 U.S. federal government employees surveyed agree that their managers communicate the goals and priorities of their organization.

©Robert Churchill/Getty Images

they also potentially produce more noise, distractions, and loss of privacy.[72] Open workspaces can potentially have minimal noise problems because employees tend to speak more softly and white noise technology blocks out most voices. Still, the challenge is to increase social interaction without raising noise and distraction levels.

Another workspace strategy is to cloister employees into team spaces, but also encourage sufficient interaction with people from other teams. Pixar Animation Studios constructed its campus in Emeryville, California, with these principles in mind. The building encourages communication among team members. At the same time, the campus encourages happenstance interactions with people on other teams. Pixar executives call this the "bathroom effect" because team members must leave their isolated pods to fetch their mail, have lunch, or visit the restroom.[73]

Internet-Based Organizational Communication

For decades, employees received official company news through hard-copy newsletters and magazines. Some firms still use these communication devices, but most have supplemented or replaced them completely with web-based sources of information. The traditional company magazine is now typically published on web pages or distributed in PDF format. The advantage of these *e-zines* is that company news can be prepared and distributed quickly.

Employees are increasingly skeptical of information that has been screened and packaged by management, so a few companies such as IBM are encouraging employees to post their own news on internal blogs and wikis. Wikis are collaborative web spaces in which anyone in a group can write, edit, or remove material from the website. *Wikipedia*, the popular online encyclopedia, is a massive public example of a wiki. The accuracy of

wikis depends on the quality of participants, but IBM experts say that errors are quickly identified by IBM's online community. Another concern is that wikis have failed to gain employee support, likely because wiki involvement takes time and the company does not reward or recognize those who provide this time to wiki development.[74]

Direct Communication with Top Management

According to various surveys, effective organizational communication includes regular interaction directly between senior executives and employees further down the hierarchy. One form of direct communication is through town hall meetings, where executives brief a large gathering of staff on the company's current strategy and results. Although the communication is mostly from executives to employees, town hall meetings are more personal and credible than video or written channels. Also, these events usually provide some opportunity for employees to ask questions. Another strategy is for senior executives to hold roundtable forums with a small representation of employees, mainly to hear their opinions on various issues.

A less formal approach to direct communication is **management by walking around (MBWA)**. Coined by people at Hewlett-Packard four decades ago, this is essentially the practice in which senior executives get out of their offices and casually chat with employees on a daily or regular basis.[76] Some executives, such as Jet.com cofounder and CEO Marc Lore, don't even have an office or a desk; they move around to different workspaces, which makes MBWA a natural part of their daily activity. These direct communication strategies

OB THEORY TO PRACTICE

Google Keeps Employees Informed through Weekly All-Hands TGIF Meetings

Google has becomes one of the world's largest technology companies, yet its cofounders still hold town hall sessions every Friday (called TGIF all-hands meetings). Thousands of employees attend in person or by video link; many others watch the recorded broadcast later. Google executives update employees on strategic and operational developments. They also devote half an hour to answering questions that employees submit through an online system. There are more questions than time allows, but Google has a transparent way to choose the best questions. Before each session, Google employees vote on which submitted questions are most important. The executives answer the questions that receive the most votes.[77]

©Tzido/iStock/Getty Images Plus

potentially minimize filtering because executives listen directly to employees. They also help executives acquire a deeper meaning and quicker understanding of internal organizational problems. A third benefit of direct communication is that employees might have more empathy for decisions made further up the corporate hierarchy.

COMMUNICATING THROUGH THE GRAPEVINE

Organizational leaders may try their best to quickly communicate breaking news to employees through emails, Twitter tweets, and other direct formal channels, but employees still rely to some extent on the corporate grapevine. The grapevine is an unstructured and informal network founded on social relationships rather than organizational charts or job descriptions. What do employees think about the grapevine? Surveys have found that almost all employees use the grapevine, but very few of them prefer this source of information. In one survey, only one-third of employees believe grapevine information is credible. In other words, employees turn to the grapevine when they have few other options.[78]

Grapevine Characteristics

Research conducted several decades ago reported that the grapevine transmits information very rapidly in all directions throughout the organization. The typical pattern is a cluster chain, whereby a few people actively transmit information to many others. The grapevine works through informal social networks, so it is more active where employees have similar backgrounds and are able to communicate easily. Many rumors seem to have at least a kernel of truth, possibly because they are transmitted through media-rich communication channels (e.g., face-to-face) and employees are motivated to communicate effectively. Nevertheless, the grapevine distorts information by deleting fine details and exaggerating key points of the story.[79]

Some of these characteristics might still be true, but the grapevine almost certainly has changed as email, social networking sites, and Twitter tweets have replaced the traditional water cooler as sources of gossip. For example, several Facebook sites are unofficially themed around specific companies, allowing employees and customers to vent their complaints about the organization. Along with altering the speed and network of corporate grapevines, the Internet has expanded these networks around the globe, not just around the next cubicle.

Grapevine Benefits and Limitations

Should the grapevine be encouraged, tolerated, or quashed? The difficulty in answering this question is that the grapevine has both benefits and limitations.[80] One benefit, as was mentioned earlier, is that employees rely on the grapevine when information is not available through formal channels. It is also the main conduit through which organizational stories and other symbols of the organization's culture are communicated. A third benefit of the grapevine is that this social interaction relieves anxiety. This explains why rumor mills are most active during times of uncertainty.[81] Finally, the grapevine is associated with the drive to bond. Being a recipient of gossip is a sign of inclusion, according to evolutionary psychologists. Trying to quash the grapevine is, in some respects, an attempt to undermine the natural human drive for social interaction.[82]

While the grapevine offers these benefits, it is not a preferred communication medium. Grapevine information is sometimes so distorted that it escalates rather than reduces employee anxiety. Furthermore, employees develop more negative attitudes toward the organization when management is slower than the grapevine in communicating information. What should corporate leaders do with the grapevine? The best advice seems to be to listen to the grapevine as a signal of employee anxiety, then correct the cause of this anxiety. Some companies also listen to the grapevine and step in to correct blatant errors and fabrications. Most important, corporate leaders need to view the grapevine as a competitor and meet this challenge by directly informing employees of news before it spreads throughout the grapevine.

> The grapevine works through informal social networks, so it is more active where employees have similar backgrounds and are able to communicate easily.

Study Checklist

Connect® Management is available for *M Organizational Behavior.* Additional resources include:

✓ Interactive Applications:
- **Case Analysis:** Apply concepts within the context of a real-world situation.
- **Drag and Drop:** Work through an interactive example to test your knowledge of the concepts.
- **Video Case:** See management in action through interactive videos.

✓ **SmartBook**™—SmartBook is the first and only adaptive reading experience available today. Distinguishing what you know from what you don't, and honing in on concepts you are most likely to forget, SmartBook personalizes content for you in a continuously adapting reading experience. Reading is no longer a passive and linear experience, but an engaging and dynamic one where you are more likely to master and retain important concepts and go to class better prepared.

©Natthawat Jamnapa/123RF

Notes

1. A. H. Van de Ven, A. L. Delbecq, and R. Koenig Jr., "Determinants of Coordination Modes within Organizations," *American Sociological Review* 41, no. 2 (1976): 322-38; J. H. Gittell, R. Seidner, and J. Wimbush, "A Relational Model of How High-Performance Work Systems Work," *Organization Science* 21, no. 2 (2010): 490-506; R. Foy et al., "Meta-Analysis: Effect of Interactive Communication between Collaborating Primary Care Physicians and Specialists," *Annals of Internal Medicine* 152, no. 4 (2010): 247-58.

2. C. Barnard, *The Functions of the Executive* (Cambridge, MA: Harvard University Press, 1938), 82. Barnard's entire statement also refers to the other features of organizations that we describe in Chapter 1, namely that (a) people are willing to contribute their effort to the organization and (b) they have a common purpose.

3. M. T. Hansen, M. L. Mors, and B. Løvås, "Knowledge Sharing in Organizations: Multiple Networks, Multiple Phases," *Academy of Management Journal* 48, no. 5 (2005): 776-93; S. R. Murray and J. Peyrefitte, "Knowledge Type and Communication Media Choice in the Knowledge Transfer Process," *Journal of Managerial Issues* 19, no. 1 (2007): 111-33; S. L. Hoe and S. L. McShane, "Structural and Informal Knowledge Acquisition and Dissemination in Organizational Learning: An Exploratory Analysis," *Learning Organization* 17, no. 4 (2010): 364-86.

4. J. O'Toole and W. Bennis, "What's Needed Next: A Culture of Candor," *Harvard Business Review* 87, no. 6 (2009): 54-61.

5. W. J. L. Elving, "The Role of Communication in Organisational Change," *Corporate Communications* 10, no. 2 (2005): 129-38; P. M. Leonardi, T. B. Neeley, and E. M. Gerber, "How Managers Use Multiple Media: Discrepant Events, Power, and Timing in Redundant Communication," *Organization Science* 23, no. 1 (2012): 98-117; D. A. Tucker, P. Yeow, and G. T. Viki, "Communicating during Organizational Change Using Social Accounts: The Importance of Ideological Accounts," *Management Communication Quarterly* 27, no. 2 (2013): 184-209.

6. N. Ellemers, R. Spears, and B. Doosje, "Self and Social Identity," *Annual Review of Psychology* 53 (2002): 161-86; S. A. Haslam and S. Reicher, "Stressing the Group: Social Identity and the Unfolding Dynamics of Responses to Stress," *Journal of Applied Psychology* 91, no. 5 (2006): 1037-52; M. T. Gailliot and R. F. Baumeister, "Self-Esteem, Belongingness, and Worldview Validation: Does Belongingness Exert a Unique Influence Upon Self-Esteem?," *Journal of Research in Personality* 41, no. 2 (2007): 327-45.

7. A. M. Saks, K. L. Uggerslev, and N. E. Fassina, "Socialization Tactics and Newcomer Adjustment: A Meta-Analytic Review and Test of a Model," *Journal of Vocational Behavior* 70, no. 3 (2007): 413-46.

8. S. Cohen, "The Pittsburgh Common Cold Studies: Psychosocial Predictors of Susceptibility to Respiratory Infectious Illness," *International Journal of Behavioral Medicine* 12, no. 3 (2005): 123-31; B. N. Uchino, "Social Support and Health: A Review of Physiological Processes Potentially Underlying Links to Disease Outcomes," *Journal of Behavioral Medicine* 29, no. 4 (2006): 377-87.

9. C. E. Shannon and W. Weaver, *The Mathematical Theory of Communication* (Urbana: University of Illinois Press, 1949); R. M. Krauss and S. R. Fussell, "Social Psychological Models of Interpersonal Communication," in *Social Psychology: Handbook of Basic Principles,* ed. E. T. Higgins and A. Kruglanski (New York: Guilford Press, 1996), 655-701.

10. R. Cross and R. J. Thomas, *Driving Results through Social Networks: How Top Organizations Leverage Networks for Performance and Growth* (San Francisco: Jossey-Bass, 2009); R. McDermott and D. Archibald, "Harnessing Your Staff's Informal Networks," *Harvard Business Review* 88, no. 3 (2010): 82-89; J. Nieves and J. Osorio, "The Role of Social Networks in Knowledge Creation," *Knowledge Management Research & Practice* 11, no. 1 (2013): 62-77.

11. P. Shachaf and N. Hara, "Behavioral Complexity Theory of Media Selection: A Proposed Theory for Global Virtual Teams," *Journal of Information Science* 33 (2007): 63-75.

12. One study found that email was the first or second choice for almost every situation (urgency, confidentiality, accountability, integrity, and social interaction). See P. Palvia et al., "Contextual Constraints in Media Choice: Beyond Information Richness," *Decision Support Systems* 51, no. 3 (2011): 657-70.

13. N. B. Ducheneaut and L. A. Watts, "In Search of Coherence: A Review of E-Mail Research," *Human-Computer Interaction* 20, no. 1-2 (2005): 11-48; R. S. Mano and G. S. Mesch, "E-Mail Characteristics, Work Performance and Distress," *Computers in Human Behavior* 26, no. 1 (2010): 61-69.

14. W. Lucas, "Effects of E-mail on the Organization," *European Management Journal* 16, no. 1 (1998): 18-30; G. de La Rupelle, C. Guthrie, and M. Kalika, "La relation entre l'intensité perçue d'utilisation de la messagerie électronique et la qualité de la relation hiérarchique," *Relations Industrielles* 70, no. 1 (2015): 157-85; C. M. Brotheridge, D. J. Neufeld, and B. Dyck, "Communicating Virtually in a Global Organization," *Journal of Managerial Psychology* 30, no. 8 (2015): 909-24.

15. N. Panteli, "Richness, Power Cues and Email Text," *Information & Management* 40, no. 2 (2002): 75-86; C. T. Carr and C. Stefaniak, "Sent from My iPhone: The Medium and Message as Cues of Sender Professionalism in Mobile Telephony," *Journal of Applied Communication Research* 40, no. 4 (2012): 403-24; D. C. DeAndrea, "Advancing Warranting Theory," *Communication Theory* 24, no. 2 (2014): 186-204; C. M. Brotheridge, D. J. Neufeld, and B. Dyck, "Communicating Virtually in a Global Organization," *Journal of Managerial Psychology* 30, no. 8 (2015): 909-24.

16. J. B. Walther et al., "Computer-Mediated Communication and the Reduction of Prejudice: A Controlled Longitudinal Field Experiment among Jews and Arabs in Israel," *Computers in Human Behavior* 52 (2015): 550-58.

17. J. Kruger et al., "Egocentrism over E-Mail: Can We Communicate as Well as We Think?," *Journal of Personality and Social Psychology* 89, no. 6 (2005): 925-36.

18. J. B. Walther, "Language and Communication Technology: Introduction to the Special Issue," *Journal of Language and Social Psychology* 23, no. 4 (2004): 384-96; J. B. Walther, T. Loh, and L. Granka, "Let Me Count the Ways: The Interchange of Verbal and Nonverbal Cues in Computer-Mediated and Face-to-Face Affinity," *Journal of Language and Social Psychology* 24, no. 1 (2005): 36-65; K. Byron, "Carrying Too Heavy a Load? The Communication and Miscommunication of Emotion by Email," *Academy of Management Review* 33, no. 2 (2008): 309-27; J. M. Whalen, P. M. Pexman, and A. J. Gill, "'Should Be Fun—Not!': Incidence and Marking of Nonliteral Language in E-Mail," *Journal of Language and Social Psychology* 28, no. 3 (2009): 263-80.

19. K. Byron, "Carrying Too Heavy a Load? The Communication and Miscommunication of Emotion by Email," *Academy of Management Review* 33, no. 2 (2008): 309-27.

20. G. Hertel, S. Geister, and U. Konradt, "Managing Virtual Teams: A Review of Current Empirical Research," *Human Resource Management Review* 15 (2005): 69-95; H. Lee, "Behavioral Strategies for Dealing with Flaming in an Online Forum," *The Sociological Quarterly* 46, no. 2 (2005): 385-403.

21. S. R. Barley, D. E. Meyerson, and S. Grodal, "E-Mail as a Source and Symbol of Stress," *Organization Science* 22, no. 4 (2011): 887-906; N. Sobotta and M. Hummel, "A Capacity Perspective on E-Mail Overload: How E-Mail Use Contributes to Information Overload" (paper presented at the 2015 48th Hawaii International Conference on System Sciences, January 5-8, 2015), 692-701.

22. The Radicati Group, *Email Statistics Report, 2014-2018* (Palo Alto, CA: April 2014); Symantec, *Symantec Intelligence Report* (Mountain View, CA: January 2014).

23. R. D. Waters et al., "Engaging Stakeholders through Social Networking: How Nonprofit Organizations Are Using Facebook," *Public Relations Review* 35, no. 2 (2009): 102-106; J. Cunningham, "New Workers, New Workplace? Getting the Balance Right," *Strategic Direction* 26, no. 1 (2010): 5; A. M. Kaplan and M. Haenlein, "Users of the World, Unite! The Challenges and Opportunities of Social Media," *Business Horizons* 53, no. 1 (2010): 59-68.

24. J. H. Kietzmann et al., "Social Media? Get Serious! Understanding the Functional Building Blocks of Social Media," *Business Horizons* 54, no. 3 (2011): 241-51; J. W. Treem and P. M. Leonardi, "Social Media Use in Organizations: Exploring the Affordances of Visibility, Editability, Persistence, and Association," *Communication Yearbook* 36 (2012): 143-89.

25. "The Coworker Network," *Kellogg Insight,* June 3, 2013; W. van Zoonen, T. G. L. A. van der Meer, and J. W. M. Verhoeven, "Employees Work-Related Social-Media Use: His Master's Voice," *Public Relations Review* 40, no. 5 (2014): 850-52; G. Martin, E. Parry, and P. Flowers, "Do Social Media Enhance Constructive Employee Voice All of the Time or Just Some of the Time?," *Human Resource Management Journal* 25, no. 4 (2015): 541-62; W. van Zoonen, J. W. M. Verhoeven, and R. Vliegenthart, "How Employees Use Twitter to Talk about Work: A Typology of Work-Related Tweets," *Computers in Human Behavior* 55, pt. A (2016): 329-39.

26. P. W. Cardon and B. Marshall, "The Hype and Reality of Social Media Use for Work Collaboration and Team Communication," *International Journal of Business Communication* 52, no. 3 (2015): 273-93; C. Li, "Why No One Uses the Corporate Social Network," *Harvard Business Review Online,* April 7, 2015, https://hbr.org/2015/04/why-no-one-uses-the-corporate-socialnetwork.

27. M. Göhring and K. Perschke, "Internal Community Management @ Bosch," in *KnowTech 2014* (Hanau, Germany: BitKom KnowTech, 2014); R. Roewekamp, "Bosch Bricht Ins Vernetzte Arbeiten Auf (Bosch Launches into Connected Work)," *CIO* (German edition), November 19, 2015; Robert Bosch GmbH, "Boosting Agility on the Job: Bosch Invests in the Workplace of the Future," news release (Stuttgart, Germany: ENP Newswire, June 15, 2015); J. Heinz and A. Kumar, "Enterprise Social Networks—The Nerve-Center of Future Organizations," in *Connect2016* (Orlando, FL: IBM, 2016).

28. D. G. Leathers and M. H. Eaves, *Successful Nonverbal Communication: Principles and Applications,* 4th ed. (New York: Routledge, 2015).

29. L. Z. Tiedens and A. R. Fragale, "Power Moves: Complementarity in Dominant and Submissive Nonverbal Behavior," *Journal of Personality and Social Psychology* 84, no. 3 (2003): 558-68.

30. CareerBuilder, "Careerbuilder Releases Annual List of Strangest Interview and Body Language Mistakes," news release (Chicago: CareerBuilder, January 12, 2017).

31. P. Ekman and E. Rosenberg, *What the Face Reveals: Basic and Applied Studies of Spontaneous Expression Using the Facial Action Coding System* (Oxford, UK: Oxford University Press, 1997); P. Winkielman and K. C. Berridge, "Unconscious Emotion," *Current Directions in Psychological Science* 13, no. 3 (2004): 120-23.

32. J. Champy, *What I Learned from Peter Drucker* (Boston: New Word City, 2010), chap. 4.

33. W. J. Becker and R. Cropanzano, "Organizational Neuroscience: The Promise and Prospects of an Emerging Discipline," *Journal of Organizational Behavior* 31, no. 7 (2010): 1055-59.

34. M. Sonnby-Borgstrom, P. Jonsson, and O. Svensson, "Emotional Empathy as Related to Mimicry Reactions at Different Levels of Information Processing," *Journal of Nonverbal Behavior* 27 (2003): 3-23; S. K. Johnson, "I Second That Emotion: Effects of Emotional Contagion and Affect at Work on Leader and Follower

Outcomes," *Leadership Quarterly* 19, no. 1 (2008): 1–19; V. Vijayalakshmi and S. Bhattacharyya, "Emotional Contagion and Its Relevance to Individual Behavior and Organizational Processes: A Position Paper," *Journal of Business and Psychology* 27, no. 3 (2012): 363–74.

35. J. R. Kelly and S. G. Barsade, "Mood and Emotions in Small Groups and Work Teams," *Organizational Behavior and Human Decision Processes* 86 (2001): 99–130; T. L. Chartrand and J. L. Lakin, "The Antecedents and Consequences of Human Behavioral Mimicry," *Annual Review of Psychology* 64, no. 1 (2013): 285–308.

36. A. R. Dennis, R. M. Fuller, and J. S. Valacich, "Media, Tasks, and Communication Processes: A Theory of Media Synchronicity," *MIS Quarterly* 32, no. 3 (2008): 575–600; S. Taipale, "Synchronicity Matters: Defining the Characteristics of Digital Generations," *Information, Communication & Society* 19, no. 1 (2016): 80–94.

37. R. E. Rice, "Media Appropriateness: Using Social Presence Theory to Compare Traditional and New Organizational Media," *Human Communication Research* 19, no. 4 (1993): 451–84; D. Gooch and L. Watts, "The Impact of Social Presence on Feelings of Closeness in Personal Relationships," *Interacting with Computers* 27, no. 6 (2015): 661–74.

38. J. Fulk, "Social Construction of Communication Technology," *Academy of Management Journal* 36, no. 5 (1993): 921–50; L. K. Treviño, J. Webster, and E. W. Stein, "Making Connections: Complementary Influences on Communication Media Choices, Attitudes, and Use," *Organization Science* 11, no. 2 (2000): 163–82; B. van den Hooff, J. Groot, and S. de Jonge, "Situational Influences on the Use of Communication Technologies," *Journal of Business Communication* 42, no. 1 (2005): 4–27; J. W. Turner et al., "Exploring the Dominant Media: How Does Media Use Reflect Organizational Norms and Affect Performance?," *Journal of Business Communication* 43, no. 3 (2006): 220–50; M. B. Watson-Manheim and F. Bélanger, "Communication Media Repertoires: Dealing with the Multiplicity of Media Choices," *MIS Quarterly* 31, no. 2 (2007): 267–93.

39. Z. Lee and Y. Lee, "Emailing the Boss: Cultural Implications of Media Choice," *IEEE Transactions on Professional Communication* 52, no. 1 (2009): 61–74; D. Holtbrügge, A. Weldon, and H. Rogers, "Cultural Determinants of Email Communication Styles," *International Journal of Cross Cultural Management* 13, no. 1 (2013): 89–110.

40. R. C. King, "Media Appropriateness: Effects of Experience on Communication Media Choice," *Decision Sciences* 28, no. 4 (1997): 877–910.

41. A. K. C. Au and D. K. S. Chan, "Organizational Media Choice in Performance Feedback: A Multifaceted Approach," *Journal of Applied Social Psychology* 43, no. 2 (2013): 397–407; K. K. Stephens, A. K. Barrett, and M. J. Mahometa, "Organizational Communication in Emergencies: Using Multiple Channels and Sources to Combat Noise and Capture Attention," *Human Communication Research* 39, no. 2 (2013): 230–51.

42. K. Griffiths, "KPMG Sacks 670 Employees by E-Mail," *The Independent* (London), November 5, 2002, 19; "Shop Worker Sacked by Text Message," *The Post* (Claremont/Nedlands, Western Australia), July 28, 2007, 1, 78.

43. R. L. Daft and R. H. Lengel, "Information Richness: A New Approach to Managerial Behavior and Organization Design," *Research in Organizational Behavior* 6 (1984): 191–233; R. H. Lengel and R. L. Daft, "The Selection of Communication Media as an Executive Skill," *Academy of Management Executive* 2 (1988): 225–32.

44. H. Rodriguez et al., "Huddle Up!: The Adoption and Use of Structured Team Communication for VA Medical Home Implementation," *Health Care Management Review* 40, no. 4 (2015): 286–99; R. W. Quinn and J. S. Bunderson, "Could We Huddle on This Project? Participant Learning in Newsroom Conversations," *Journal of Management* 42, no. 2 (2016): 386–418.

45. R. E. Rice, "Task Analyzability, Use of New Media, and Effectiveness: A Multi-Site Exploration of Media Richness," *Organization Science* 3 (1992): 475–500.

46. V. W. Kupritz and E. Cowell, "Productive Management Communication: Online and Face-to-Face," *Journal of Business Communication* 48, no. 1 (2011): 54–82.

47. R. F. Otondo et al., "The Complexity of Richness: Media, Message, and Communication Outcomes," *Information & Management* 45, no. 1 (2008): 21–30.

48. N. L. Reinsch Jr., J. W. Turner, and C. H. Tinsley, "Multicommunicating: A Practice Whose Time Has Come?," *Academy of Management Review* 33, no. 2 (2008): 391–403; A. F. Cameron and J. Webster, "Multicommunicating: Juggling Multiple Conversations in the Workplace," *Information Systems Research* 24, no. 2 (2013): 352–71.

49. S. Xu, Z. Wang, and P. David, "Media Multitasking and Well-Being of University Students," *Computers in Human Behavior* 55, pt. A (2016): 242–50.

50. J. R. Carlson and R. W. Zmud, "Channel Expansion Theory and the Experiential Nature of Media Richness Perceptions," *Academy of Management Journal* 42 (1999): 153–70; N. Kock, "Media Richness or Media Naturalness? The Evolution of Our Biological Communication Apparatus and Its Influence on Our Behavior toward E-Communication Tools," *IEEE Transactions on Professional Communication* 48, no. 2 (2005): 117–30.

51. V. W. Kupritz and E. Cowell, "Productive Management Communication: Online and Face-to-Face," *Journal of Business Communication* 48, no. 1 (2011): 54–82.

52. D. Muller, T. Atzeni, and F. Butera, "Coaction and Upward Social Comparison Reduce the Illusory Conjunction Effect: Support for Distraction–Conflict Theory," *Journal of Experimental Social Psychology* 40, no. 5 (2004): 659–65; L. P. Robert and A. R. Dennis, "Paradox of Richness: A Cognitive Model of Media Choice," *IEEE Transactions on Professional Communication* 48, no. 1 (2005): 10–21.

53. E. V. Wilson, "Perceived Effectiveness of Interpersonal Persuasion Strategies in Computer-Mediated Communication," *Computers in Human Behavior* 19, no. 5 (2003): 537–52; K. Sassenberg, M. Boos, and S. Rabung, "Attitude Change in Face-to-Face and Computer-Mediated Communication: Private Self-Awareness as Mediator and Moderator," *European Journal of Social Psychology* 35 (2005): 361–74; P. Di Blasio and L. Milani, "Computer-Mediated Communication and Persuasion: Peripheral vs. Central Route to Opinion Shift," *Computers in Human Behavior* 24, no. 3 (2008): 798–815.

54. J. Kruger et al., "Egocentrism over E-Mail: Can We Communicate as Well as We Think?," *Journal of Personality and Social Psychology* 89, no. 6 (2005): 925–36.

55. Most sources incorrectly attribute this famous quotation (usually with "accomplished" rather than "achieved") to the Irish playwright and social critic George Bernard Shaw. To the best of our knowledge, it was first uttered in the late 1950s by Joe Coffman, president of Tecnifax Corporation (which made visual education technology). Coffman held patents for specialized slide transparencies and related apparatus on overhead projectors. Given the company's products,

Coffman was also an enthusiast of visual and interpersonal communication. Twice each year at its head office in Holyoke, Massachusetts, Tecnifax held international seminars on communication practices. This quotation was originally published in a 1960 article summarizing a public health conference, during which one of the speakers credited Coffman as the originator of this quotation. There is one more twist to the origins of this quotation. Coffman may have adapted it from the following passage in William H. Whyte's 1950 *Fortune* magazine article on communication, which became one of *Fortune*'s most-read articles: "The great enemy of communication, we find, is the illusion of it." See W. H. Whyte, "Is Anybody Listening," *Fortune,* September 1950, 77-83, 167-78; "Web of Mutual Anticipations: Conference Report," *Public Health Reports* 75, no. 10 (1960): 927-32; D. M. Davis, *A Biased Biography: Mine* (Lincoln, NE: iUniverse, 2004); "The Biggest Problem in Communication Is the Illusion That It Has Taken Place," *Quote Investigator,* August 31, 2014, http://quoteinvestigator.com/2014/08/31/illusion/.

56. R. M. Krauss, "The Psychology of Verbal Communication," in *International Encyclopedia of the Social and Behavioral Sciences,* ed. N. Smelser and P. Baltes (London: Elsevier, 2002), 16161-65.

57. A. M. Carton, C. Murphy, and J. R. Clark, "A (Blurry) Vision of the Future: How Leader Rhetoric about Ultimate Goals Influences Performance," *Academy of Management Journal* 57, no. 6 (2014): 1544-70; P. D. Joshi et al., "Communicating with Distant Others: The Functional Use of Abstraction," *Social Psychological and Personality Science* 7, no. 1 (2016): 37-44.

58. D. Goleman, R. Boyatzis, and A. McKee, *Primal Leaders* (Boston: Harvard Business School Press, 2002), 92-95.

59. J. O'Toole and W. Bennis, "What's Needed Next: A Culture of Candor," *Harvard Business Review* 87, no. 6 (2009): 54-61.

60. T. W. Jackson and P. Farzaneh, "Theory-Based Model of Factors Affecting Information Overload," *International Journal of Information Management* 32, no. 6 (2012): 523-32.

61. A. G. Schick, L. A. Gordon, and S. Haka, "Information Overload: A Temporal Approach," *Accounting, Organizations & Society* 15 (1990): 199-220; A. Edmunds and A. Morris, "The Problem of Information Overload in Business Organisations: A Review of the Literature," *International Journal of Information Management* 20 (2000): 17-28; R. Pennington, "The Effects of Information Overload on Software Project Risk Assessment," *Decision Sciences* 38, no. 3 (2007): 489-526.

62. D. C. Thomas and K. Inkson, *Cultural Intelligence: People Skills for Global Business* (San Francisco: Berrett-Koehler, 2004), chap. 6; D. Welch, L. Welch, and R. Piekkari, "Speaking in Tongues," *International Studies of Management & Organization* 35, no. 1 (2005): 10-27.

63. T. Craig, "Different Strokes," *Personnel Today,* November 25, 2008, 190.

64. D. C. Barnlund, *Communication Styles of Japanese and Americans: Images and Realities* (Belmont, CA: Wadsworth, 1988); H. Yamada, *American and Japanese Business Discourse: A Comparison of Interaction Styles* (Norwood, NJ: Ablex, 1992), chap. 2; T. Hasegawa and W. B. Gudykunst, "Silence in Japan and the United States," *Journal of Cross-Cultural Psychology* 29, no. 5 (1998): 668-84; M. Fujio, "Silence during Intercultural Communication: A Case Study," *Corporate Communications* 9, no. 4 (2004): 331-39.

65. Adapted from M. Nakamoto, "Cross-Cultural Conversations," *Financial Times* (London), January 12, 2012, 16.

66. P. Harris and R. Moran, *Managing Cultural Differences* (Houston, TX: Gulf, 1987); H. Blagg, "A Just Measure of Shame?," *British Journal of Criminology* 37 (1997): 481-501; R. E. Axtell, *Gestures: The Do's and Taboos of Body Language around the World,* rev. ed. (New York: Wiley, 1998).

67. D. Tannen, *You Just Don't Understand: Men and Women in Conversation* (New York: Ballantine Books, 1990); J. L. Locke, *Duels and Duets: Why Men and Women Talk So Differently* (Cambridge, UK: Cambridge University Press, 2011); M. R. Atai and F. Chahkandi, "Democracy in Computer-Mediated Communication: Gender, Communicative Style, and Amount of Participation in Professional Listservs," *Computers in Human Behavior* 28, no. 3 (2012): 881-88; A. B. Hancock and B. A. Rubin, "Influence of Communication Partner's Gender on Language," *Journal of Language and Social Psychology* 34, no. 1 (2015): 46-64.

68. A. Mulac et al., "'Uh-Huh. What's That All About?' Differing Interpretations of Conversational Backchannels and Questions as Sources of Miscommunication across Gender Boundaries," *Communication Research* 25 (1998): 641-68; N. M. Sussman and D. H. Tyson, "Sex and Power: Gender Differences in Computer-Mediated Interactions," *Computers in Human Behavior* 16 (2000): 381-94; C. Leaper and R. D. Robnett, "Women Are More Likely Than Men to Use Tentative Language, Aren't They? A Meta-Analysis Testing for Gender Differences and Moderators," *Psychology of Women Quarterly* 35, no. 1 (2011): 129-42.

69. This quotation is varied slightly from the original translations by E. Carter, *All the Works of Epictetus, Which Are Now Extant,* 3rd ed., vol. 2 (London: J. and F. Rivington, 1768), 333; T. W. Higginson, *The Works of Epictetus* (Boston: Little, Brown, and Company, 1866), 428.

70. L. B. Comer and T. Drollinger, "Active Empathetic Listening and Selling Success: A Conceptual Framework," *Journal of Personal Selling & Sales Management* 19 (1999): 15-29; T. Drollinger, L. B. Comer, and P. T. Warrington, "Development and Validation of the Active Empathetic Listening Scale," *Psychology and Marketing* 23, no. 2 (2006): 161-80; P. JungKun et al., "The Role of Listening in E-Contact Center Customer Relationship Management," *Journal of Services Marketing* 29, no. 1 (2015): 49-58.

71. T. J. Allen, "Architecture and Communication among Product Development Engineers," *California Management Review* 49, no. 2 (2007): 23-41; M. C. Davis, D. J. Leach, and C. W. Clegg, "The Physical Environment of the Office: Contemporary and Emerging Issues," in *International Review of Industrial and Organizational Psychology 2011* (Wiley, 2011), 193-237; J. Kim and R. de Dear, "Workspace Satisfaction: The Privacy-Communication Trade-Off in Open-Plan Offices," *Journal of Environmental Psychology* 36 (2013): 18-26.

72. G. Evans and D. Johnson, "Stress and Open-Office Noise," *Journal of Applied Psychology* 85 (2000): 779-83; A. Seddigh et al., "The Association between Office Design and Performance on Demanding Cognitive Tasks," *Journal of Environmental Psychology* 42 (2015): 172-81; M. Pierrette et al., "Noise Effect on Comfort in Open-Space Offices: Development of an Assessment Questionnaire," *Ergonomics* 58, no. 1 (2015): 96-106.

73. S. P. Means, "Playing at Pixar," *Salt Lake Tribune* (Utah), May 30, 2003, D1; G. Whipp, "Swimming against the Tide," *Los Angeles Daily News,* May 30, 2003, U6.

74. C. Wagner and A. Majchrzak, "Enabling Customer-Centricity Using Wikis and the Wiki Way," *Journal of Management Information Systems* 23, no. 3 (2006): 17-43; C. Karena, "Working the Wiki Way," *Sydney Morning Herald,* March 6, 2007; R. B. Ferguson, "Build a Web 2.0 Platform and Employees Will Use It," *eWeek,* June 20, 2007.

75. Treasury Board of Canada Secretariat, "2014 Public Service Employee Survey: Summary Report," *Public Service Employee Surveys* (Ottawa: Government of Canada, March 5, 2015) (accessed June 30, 2017); U.S. Office of Personnel Management, *Federal Employee Viewpoint Survey* (Washington, DC: Office of Personnel Management, September 2016); S. Gopal and D. Lucy, Profile Search and Selection and Roffey Park, *Working in Asia: Key HR and Leadership Priorities for 2016,* (Horsham, UK: Roffey Park Institute, May 2016); National Health Service, "Staff Survey 2016 Detailed Spreadsheets" (London: National Health Service, 2016); *State of the Sector 2017* (London: Gatehouse, February 2017).

76. The original term is "management by *wandering* around," but this has been replaced with "walking around" over the years. See W. Ouchi, *Theory Z* (New York: Avon Books, 1981), 176–77; T. Peters and R. Waterman, *In Search of Excellence* (New York: Harper and Row, 1982), 122.

77. L. Bock, *Work Rules! Insights from Google That Will Transform How You Live and Lead* (New York: Hachette, 2015), 42.

78. R. Rousos, "Trust in Leaders Lacking at Utility," *The Ledger* (Lakeland, FL), July 29, 2003, B1; B. Whitworth and B. Riccomini, "Management Communication: Unlocking Higher Employee Performance," *Communication World,* March/April 2005, 18–21.

79. K. Davis, "Management Communication and the Grapevine," *Harvard Business Review* 31 (1953): 43–49; W. L. Davis and J. R. O'Connor, "Serial Transmission of Information: A Study of the Grapevine," *Journal of Applied Communication Research* 5 (1977): 61–72.

80. S. R. Clegg and A. van Iterson, "Dishing the Dirt: Gossiping in Organizations," *Culture and Organization* 15, no. 3/4 (2009): 275–89; C. Mills, "Experiencing Gossip: The Foundations for a Theory of Embedded Organizational Gossip," *Group & Organization Management* 35, no. 2 (2010): 213–40.

81. R. L. Rosnow, "Inside Rumor: A Personal Journey," *American Psychologist* 46 (1991): 484–96; C. J. Walker and C. A. Beckerle, "The Effect of State Anxiety on Rumor Transmission," *Journal of Social Behavior & Personality* 2 (1987): 353–60; M. Noon and R. Delbridge, "News from Behind My Hand: Gossip in Organizations," *Organization Studies* 14 (1993): 23–36.

82. N. Nicholson, "Evolutionary Psychology: Toward a New View of Human Nature and Organizational Society," *Human Relations* 50 (1997): 1053–78; E. K. Foster, "Research on Gossip: Taxonomy, Methods, and Future Directions," *Review of General Psychology* 8, no. 2 (2004): 78–99; B. Beersma and G. A. Van Kleef, "Why People Gossip: An Empirical Analysis of Social Motives, Antecedents, and Consequences," *Journal of Applied Social Psychology* 42, no. 11 (2012): 2640–70.

9 | Power and Influence in the Workplace

Learning Objectives

After you read this chapter, you should be able to:

LO9-1 Describe the dependence model of power and the five sources of power in organizations.

LO9-2 Discuss the four contingencies of power.

LO9-3 Explain how people and work units gain power through social networks.

LO9-4 Describe eight types of influence tactics, three consequences of influencing others, and three contingencies to consider when choosing an influence tactic.

LO9-5 Identify the organizational conditions and personal characteristics associated with organizational politics, as well as ways to minimize organizational politics.

One of the most popular topics in organizational behavior classes is about managing your boss. The theme may sound manipulative, but managing your boss is actually a valuable process of gaining power and using influence for the benefit of the organization. Most executives say it is a key factor in everyone's career success.

"Managing up is about setting boundaries and rules on how you and your manager work together," explains Tomas Kucera, vice president of business operations at SolarWinds, the Austin, Texas, firm that develops enterprise information technology infrastructure management software. "It is about understanding the needs of the other person and helping them to achieve their goals."

There are many ways to manage your boss—or anyone else in and around organizations—such as aligning communication and work styles, becoming a valuable resource, being solution-oriented rather than problem-oriented, and supporting your manager's career success by performing your own job well. These and other practices develop power bases and apply influence tactics that ultimately change (or stabilize) the behavior of others. These activities are not unusual. On the contrary, OB experts point out that power and influence are inherent in all organizations. They exist in every business and in every decision and action.[1]

This chapter unfolds as follows: First, we define power and present a basic model depicting the dynamics of power in organizational settings. The chapter then discusses the five bases of power. Next, we look at the contingencies necessary to translate those sources into meaningful power. Our attention then turns to social networks and how they provide power to members through social capital. The latter part of this chapter examines the various types of influence in organizational settings as well as the contingencies of effective influence strategies. The final section of this chapter looks at situations in which influence becomes organizational politics, as well as ways of minimizing political behavior.

LO9-1 Describe the dependence model of power and the five sources of power in organizations.

THE MEANING OF POWER

Power is the capacity of a person, team, or organization to influence others.[2] There are a few important features of this definition. First, power is not the act of changing someone's attitudes or behavior; it is only the *potential* to do so. People frequently have power they do not use; they might not even know they have power. Second, power is based on the target's *perception* that the power holder controls (i.e., possesses, has access to, or regulates) a valuable resource that can help the target achieve his or her goals.[3] People might generate power by convincing others that they control something of value, whether or not they actually control that resource. This perception also is formed from the power holder's behavior, such as someone who is not swayed by authority or norms. For instance, people are perceived as more powerful just by engaging in behavior that deviates from norms, such as putting their feet on a table.[4] However, power is not your own perception or feeling of power; it exists only when others believe you have power.

Third, power involves asymmetric (unequal) *dependence* of one party on another party.[5] This dependent relationship is illustrated in Exhibit 9.1. The line from Person B to the goal shows that he or she believes Person A controls a resource that can help or hinder Person B in achieving that goal. Person A—the power holder in this illustration—might have power over Person B by controlling a desired job assignment, useful information, rewards, or even the privilege of being associated with Person A! For example, if you believe a coworker

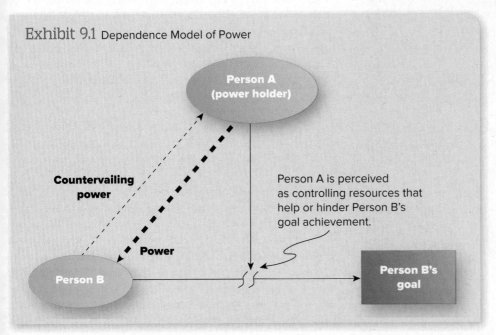

Exhibit 9.1 Dependence Model of Power

Person A (power holder)

Countervailing power

Power

Person B

Person A is perceived as controlling resources that help or hinder Person B's goal achievement.

Person B's goal

countervailing power the capacity of a person, team, or organization to keep a more powerful person or group in the exchange relationship

legitimate power an agreement among organizational members that people in certain roles can request certain behaviors of others

has expertise (the resource) that would substantially help you write a better report (your goal), then that coworker has some power over you because you value that expertise to achieve your goal. Whatever the resource is, Person B is *dependent* on Person A (the power holder) to provide the resource so Person B can reach his or her goal.

Although dependence is a key element of power relationships, we use the phrase *asymmetric dependence* because the less powerful party still has some degree of power—called **countervailing power**—over the stronger power holder. In Exhibit 9.1, Person A dominates the power relationship, but Person B has enough countervailing power to keep Person A in the exchange relationship and ensure that person uses his or

Power involves asymmetric dependence of one party on another party because the less powerful party has countervailing power over the stronger power holder.
©Image Source/Getty Images

her dominant power judiciously. For example, although managers have power over subordinates in many ways (e.g., control of job security and preferred work assignments), employees have countervailing power by possessing skills and knowledge to keep production humming and customers happy, something that management can't accomplish alone.

One other key feature is that all power relationships depend on some minimum level of trust. Trust indicates a level of expectation that the more powerful party will deliver the resource. For example, you trust your employer to give you a paycheck at the end of each pay period. Even those in extremely dependent situations will usually walk away from the relationship if they lack a minimum level of trust in the more powerful party.

Let's look at this power dependence model in the employee–manager relationship. You depend on your boss to support your continued employment, satisfactory work arrangements, and other valued resources. At the same time, the manager depends on you to complete required tasks and to work effectively with others in the completion of their work. Managers (and the companies they represent) typically have more power, whereas employees have weaker countervailing power. But sometimes employees do have more power than their bosses in the employment relationship. Notice that the strength of your power in the employee–manager relationship doesn't depend on your actual control over valued resources; it depends on the perceptions that your boss and others have about your control of these resources. Finally, trust is an essential ingredient in this relationship. Even with strong power, the employee–manager relationship comes apart when one party no longer sufficiently trusts the other.

The dependence model reveals only the core features of power dynamics between people and work units in organizations. We also need to learn about the specific sources of power and contingencies that effectively convert power into influence. As Exhibit 9.2 illustrates, power is derived from five sources: legitimate, reward, coercive, expert, and referent. The model also identifies four contingencies of power: the employee's or department's substitutability, centrality, visibility, and discretion. Over the next few pages, we will discuss each of these sources and contingencies of power in the context of organizations.

SOURCES OF POWER IN ORGANIZATIONS

There are five main sources of power in human interactions.[6] Three of these—legitimate, reward, and coercive—originate mostly (but not completely) from the power holder's formal position or informal role. In other words, the person is granted these sources of power formally by the organization or informally by coworkers. Two other sources of power—expert and referent—originate mainly from the power holder's own characteristics; in other words, people carry these power bases around with them. However, even personal sources of power are not

Exhibit 9.2 Sources and Contingencies of Power

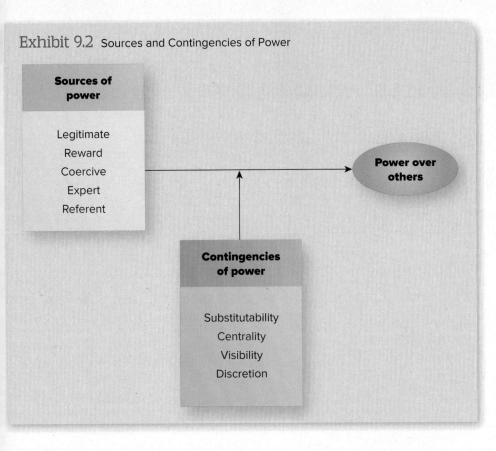

Sources of power

Legitimate
Reward
Coercive
Expert
Referent

Contingencies of power

Substitutability
Centrality
Visibility
Discretion

Power over others

completely within the person because they depend on how others perceive them.

Legitimate Power

Legitimate power is an agreement among organizational members that people in certain roles can request a set of behaviors from others. This perceived right or obligation originates from formal job descriptions as well as informal rules of conduct. It is usually the most important source of power in organizational settings, particularly between employees and managers.[7] For example, managers have a legitimate right to tell employees what tasks to perform, whom to work with, what company resources they can use, and so forth. Employees follow the boss's requests because they have agreed to follow a range of requests from people in positions of higher authority. Employee motivation to comply with these requests occurs separately from the manager's ability to reward or punish employees.

Notice that legitimate power has restrictions; it gives the power holder only the right to ask others to perform a limited domain of behaviors. This domain—known as the "zone of indifference"—is the set of behaviors that individuals are willing to engage in at the other person's request.[8] Although most employees accept the boss's right to deny them access to Facebook during company time, some might draw the line when the boss asks them to work several hours beyond the regular workday. They either overtly refuse to follow orders or engage in delaying and other evasive tactics.

The size of the zone of indifference (and, consequently, the magnitude of legitimate power) increases with the level of trust in the power holder. Some values and personality traits also make people more obedient to authority. Those who value conformity and tradition as well as have high power

---

OB THEORY TO PRACTICE

Deference to Authority Leads People to the Extreme

A French television program revealed how far people are willing to follow orders. As a variation of the 1960s experiments conducted by Stanley Milgram, 80 contestants administered electric shocks whenever a volunteer (an actor who didn't receive the shocks at all) answered a question incorrectly. Shocks increased in 20-volt increments, from 20 volts for the first mistake through to 460 volts. Contestants often hesitated after hearing the volunteer screaming for them to stop, yet continued the shocks after the television host reminded them that their job was to apply punishment for wrong answers. Only 16 of the 80 contestants refused to administer the strongest shocks.[10]

©Yami 2

distance (i.e., they accept an unequal distribution of power) tend to have higher deference to authority. The organization's culture represents another influence on the willingness of employees to follow orders. A 3M scientist might continue to work on a project after being told by superiors to stop working on it because the 3M culture supports an entrepreneurial spirit, which includes ignoring your boss's authority from time to time.[9]

Managers are not the only people with legitimate power in organizations. Employees also have legitimate power over their bosses and coworkers through legal and administrative rights as well as informal norms.[11] For example, an organization might give employees the right to request information that is required for their job. Laws give employees the right to refuse to work in unsafe conditions. Subtler forms of legitimate power also exist.[12] Human beings have a **norm of reciprocity**—a feeling of obligation to help someone who has helped you. If a coworker previously helped you handle a difficult client, that coworker has power because you feel an obligation to help the coworker on something of similar value in the future. The norm of reciprocity is a form of legitimate power because it is an informal rule of conduct that we are expected to follow.

Legitimate Power through Information Control A particularly potent form of legitimate power occurs when people have the right to control information that others receive.[14] These information gatekeepers have power in two ways. First, information is a resource, so those who need information are dependent on the gatekeeper to provide that resource. For example, the map department of a mining company has considerable power when other departments are dependent on the map department to deliver maps required for exploration projects.

Second, information gatekeepers gain power by selectively distributing information in a way that affects how those receiving the information perceive the situation compared to their perception if they received all of the information.[15] As we learned in the previous chapter on communication, information is often filtered as it flows up the hierarchy, which enables those transmitting the information to frame the situation in a more positive light. This framing allows the information gatekeeper to steer the executive team toward one decision rather than another.

Reward Power

Reward power is derived from the person's ability to control the allocation of rewards valued by others and to remove negative sanctions (i.e., negative reinforcement). Managers have formal authority that gives them power over the distribution of organizational rewards such as pay, promotions, time off, vacation schedules, and work assignments. Employees also have reward power over their bosses through their feedback and ratings in 360-degree feedback systems. These ratings affect supervisors' promotions and other rewards, so supervisors tend to pay more attention to employee needs after 360-degree feedback is introduced.

Coercive Power

Coercive power is the ability to apply punishment. This occurs when managers warn employees about the consequences of poor performance, yet employees also have coercive power. For example, employees might criticize coworkers when they disregard team norms.[16] Some firms rely on this coercive power from other team members to control coworker behavior in team settings.

Expert Power

Legitimate, reward, and coercive power originate mostly from the position.[17] Expert power, on the other hand, originates from within the power holder. It is an individual's or work unit's capacity to influence others by possessing knowledge or skills valued by others. An important form of expert power is the perceived ability to manage uncertainties in the business environment. Organizations are more effective when they operate in predictable environments, so they value people who can cope with turbulence in consumer trends, societal changes, unstable supply lines, and so forth. Expertise can help companies cope with uncertainty in three ways. These coping strategies are

An important form of expert power is the perceived ability to manage uncertainties in the business environment.
©Darren Greenwood/DesignPics

arranged in a hierarchy of importance, with prevention being the most powerful:[18]

- *Prevention*—The most effective strategy is to prevent environmental changes from occurring. For example, financial experts acquire power by preventing the organization from experiencing a cash shortage or breaching debt covenants.

- *Forecasting*—The next best strategy is to predict environmental changes or variations. In this respect, trendspotters and other marketing specialists gain power by predicting changes in consumer preferences.

- *Absorption*—People and work units also gain power by absorbing or neutralizing the impact of environmental shifts as they occur. An example is the ability of maintenance crews to come to the rescue when machines break down.

Many people respond to expertise just as they respond to authority—they mindlessly follow the guidance of these experts.[19] In one classic study, for example, a researcher posing as a hospital physician telephoned on-duty nurses to prescribe a specific dosage of medicine to a hospitalized patient. None of the nurses knew the person calling, and hospital policy forbade them from accepting treatment by telephone (i.e., the caller lacked legitimate power). Furthermore, the medication was unauthorized and the prescription was twice the maximum daily dose. Yet, almost all 22 nurses who received the telephone call followed the "doctor's" orders until stopped by researchers.[20]

This doctor–nurse study is a few decades old, but the power of expertise remains just as strong today, sometimes with tragic consequences. Not long ago, the Canadian justice system discovered that one of its "star" expert witnesses—the head of pediatric forensic pathology at a children's hospital in Toronto—had provided inaccurate cause of death evaluations in at least 20 cases, a dozen of which resulted in wrongful or highly questionable criminal convictions. The pathologist's reputation as a renowned authority was the main reason why his often-weak evidence was accepted without question. "Experts in a courtroom—we give great deference to experts," admits a Canadian defense lawyer familiar with this situation.[21]

Referent Power

People have **referent power** when others identify with them, like them, or otherwise respect them. As with expert power, referent power originates within the power holder. It is largely a function of the person's interpersonal skills. Referent power is also associated with **charisma**. Experts have difficulty agreeing on the meaning of charisma, but it is most often described as a form of

interpersonal attraction whereby followers ascribe almost magical powers to the charismatic individual.[22] Some writers describe charisma as a special "gift" or trait within the charismatic person, while others say it is mainly in the eyes of the beholder. However, all agree that charisma produces a high degree of trust, respect, and devotion toward the charismatic individual.

LO9-2 Discuss the four contingencies of power.

CONTINGENCIES OF POWER

Let's say that you have expert power because of your ability to forecast and possibly even prevent dramatic changes in the organization's environment. Does this expertise mean that you are influential? Not necessarily. As was illustrated earlier in Exhibit 9.2, sources of power generate power only under certain conditions. Four important contingencies of power are substitutability, centrality, visibility, and discretion.[23]

Substitutability

Power is strongest when the individual or work unit has a monopoly over a valued resource. In other words, they are nonsubstitutable. Conversely, power decreases as the number of alternative sources of the critical resource increases. If you—and no one else—have expertise across the organization on an important issue, you would be more powerful than if several people in your company possess this valued knowledge. Substitutability refers not only to other sources that offer the resource, but also to substitutions of the resource itself. For instance, the power of a labor union weakens when the company introduces technologies that replace the need for the union's members. Technology is a substitute for employees and, consequently, reduces union power.

Controlling access to the resource increases nonsubstitutability. Professions and labor unions gain power by controlling knowledge,

> Many people respond to expertise just as they respond to authority—they mindlessly follow the guidance of these experts.

tasks, or labor to perform important activities. For instance, the medical profession has considerable power in society partly because it controls who can perform specific medical procedures. Labor unions that dominate an industry effectively control access to labor needed to perform key jobs. Employees are less substitutable when they operate special equipment or possess other knowledge that isn't documented or widely held by others.

Nonsubstitutability also occurs when people differentiate their resource from the alternatives. We should all do this when developing our personal brand. Our public image and reputation should be authentic (who we really are and what we can deliver), but it also needs to be unique and valuable, which leverages the power of nonsubstitutability. "Be unique about something. Be a specialist in something. Be known for something. Drive something," advises Barry Salzberg, the former global CEO of Deloitte Touche Tohmatsu Limited who now teaches at Columbia Business School. "That's very, very important for success in leadership because there are so many highly talented people. What's different about you—that's your personal brand."[24]

Centrality

Centrality refers to the power holder's importance based on the degree and nature of interdependence with others.[25] Centrality increases with the number of people dependent on you as well as how quickly and severely they are affected by that dependence. Think about your own centrality for a moment: If you decided not to show up for work or school tomorrow, how many people would have difficulty performing their jobs

An employee's personal brand should be authentic, but also unique and valuable, which leverages the power of nonsubstitutability.
©CSP_szefei/Fotosearch/age fotostock

because of your absence? How soon after they arrive at work would these coworkers notice that you are missing and have to adjust their tasks and work schedule as a result? If you have high centrality, many people in the organization would be adversely affected by your absence, and they would be affected quickly.

Visibility

Power does not flow to unknown people in the organization. Instead, employees gain power when their talents remain in the forefront of the minds of their boss, coworkers, and others. In other words, power increases with visibility. This visibility can occur, for example, by taking on people-oriented jobs and projects that require frequent interaction with senior executives. Employees also gain visibility by being, quite literally, visible. Some people strategically locate themselves in more visible work areas, such as those closest to the boss or where other employees frequently pass by.

People often use public symbols as subtle (and not-so-subtle) cues to make their power sources known to others. Many professionals display their educational diplomas and awards on office walls to remind visitors of their expertise. Medical professionals wear white coats with stethoscopes around their necks to symbolize their legitimate and expert power in hospital settings. Other people play the game of "face time"—spending more time at work and showing that they are working productively.

Discretion

The freedom to exercise judgment—to make decisions without referring to a specific rule or receiving permission from someone else—is another important contingency of power in organizations.[26] Consider the *lack* of power of many first-line supervisors. They may have legitimate, reward, and coercive power over employees, but this power is often curtailed by specific rules that supervisors must follow to use their power bases.[27]

> **LO9-3** Explain how people and work units gain power through social networks.

THE POWER OF SOCIAL NETWORKS

"It's not what you know, but who you know that counts!" This often-heard statement reflects the idea that employees get ahead not just by developing their competencies, but by locating

People often use public symbols, such as displaying their credentials and awards, to make their power sources known to others.
©Don Klumpp/The Image Bank/Getty Images

centrality a contingency of power pertaining to the degree and nature of interdependence between the power holder and others

social networks social structures of individuals or social units that are connected to each other through one or more forms of interdependence

social capital the knowledge and other resources available to people or social units (teams, organizations) from a durable network that connects them to others

themselves within **social networks**—social structures of individuals or social units (e.g., departments, organizations) that are connected to each other through one or more forms of interdependence.[28] Some networks are held together due to common interests, such as when employees who have dogs or other pets spend more time together. Other networks form around common status, expertise, kinship, or physical proximity. For instance, employees are more likely to form networks with coworkers who have common educational backgrounds and occupational interests.[29]

Social networks exist everywhere because people have a drive to bond. However, there are cultural differences in the norms of active network involvement. Social networking may be more of a central life activity in Asian cultures that emphasize *guanxi*, a Chinese term referring to an individual's network of social connections. Guanxi is an expressive activity because interacting with family and friends reinforces one's self-concept. It is also an instrumental activity for receiving favors and opportunities from others. Guanxi is sometimes so pervasive, however, that several experts warn it can undermine the organization's effectiveness.[30]

Social Capital and Sources of Power

Social networks generate power through **social capital**—the goodwill and resulting resources shared among members in a social network.[31] This goodwill motivates and enables network members to share resources with each other because social networks produce trust, support, and empathy among network members.

Social networks potentially enhance and maintain the power of its members through three resources: information, visibility, and referent power. Probably the best-known resource is information from other network members, which improves the individual's expert power.[32] The goodwill of social capital opens communication pipelines among those within the network. Network members receive valuable knowledge more easily and more quickly from fellow network members than do people outside that network.[33] With better information access and timeliness, members have more power because their expertise is a

Social networks potentially enhance and maintain the power of its members through three resources: information, visibility, and referent power.
©Helder Almeida/Shutterstock

scarce resource; it is not widely available to people outside the network.

Increased visibility is a second contributor to a person's power through social networks. When asked to recommend someone for valued positions, other network members more readily think of you than of people outside the network. They are more likely to mention your name when asked to identify people with expertise in your areas of knowledge. A third resource from social networks is increased referent power. People tend to gain referent power through networking because members of the network identify with or at least have greater trust in each other. Referent power is also apparent by the fact that reciprocity increases among network members as they become more embedded in the network.[34]

A common misperception is that social networks are free spirits that cannot be orchestrated by corporate leaders. In reality, company structures and practices can shape these networks to some extent.[35] But even if organizational leaders don't try to manage social networks, they need to be aware of them. Indeed, people gain power in organizations by knowing what the social networks around them look like.[36]

SELF-ASSESSMENT 9.1: Do You Have a Guanxi Orientation?
Connections and social networks are important, no matter where you do business around the world. These interpersonal relationships are called *guanxi* in China, where they are very important due to Confucian values and the unique history of that country. You can discover the extent to which you apply guanxi values in your business and personal relationships by locating this self-assessment in Connect if it is assigned by your instructor.

Energy Company Improves Productivity through Social Networks

Operations staff at a global oil and gas company were not using the best available production methods because they didn't share best practices with their peers in other countries or with the company's technical experts. Instead, employees shared information mainly with local coworkers and technical staff who they already knew well. The company's solution was to transfer some field staff to teams in other regions. These transfers eventually formed and strengthened network relationships across borders, which dramatically improved knowledge sharing and social capital. Within a year, productivity increased by 10 percent and costs due to poor quality fell by two-thirds.[37]

©Susana Gonzalez/Bloomberg/Getty Images

Gaining Power through Social Networks

How do individuals (and teams and organizations) gain social capital from social networks? To answer this question, we need to consider the number, depth, variety, and centrality of connections that people have in their networks.

Strong Ties, Weak Ties, Many Ties The volume of information, favors, and other social capital that people receive from networks usually increases with the number of people connected to them. Some people have an amazing capacity to maintain their connectivity with many people. Emerging social network technologies (Facebook, LinkedIn, etc.) have further amplified this capacity to maintain numerous connections.[38] However, the more people you know, the less time and energy you have to form "strong ties." Strong ties are close-knit relationships, which are evident from how often we interact with people, how intensely we share resources with them, how much we experience psychological closeness to them, and whether we have multiple- or single-purpose relationships with them (e.g., friend, coworker, sports partner). Strong ties are valuable because they offer resources more quickly and usually more plentifully than are available from weak ties (i.e., acquaintances). Strong ties also offer

greater social support and greater cooperation for favors and assistance.[39]

Some minimal connection strength is necessary to remain in any social network, but strong connections aren't necessarily the most valuable ties. Instead, having weak ties (i.e., being merely acquaintances) with people from diverse networks can be more valuable than having strong ties (i.e., having close friendships) with people in similar networks.[40] Why is this so? Strong ties—our close-knit circle of friends—tend to be similar to us and to each other, and similar people tend to have the same information and connections that we already have.[41] Weak ties, on the other hand, are acquaintances who are usually different from us and therefore offer resources we do not possess. Furthermore, by serving as a "bridge" across several unrelated networks, we receive unique resources from each network rather than more of the same resources.

The importance of weak ties is revealed in job hunting and career development.[42] People with diverse networks tend to be more successful job seekers because they have a wider net to catch new job opportunities. In contrast, people who belong to

Having weak ties (acquaintances) with people from diverse networks can be more valuable than having strong ties (close friendships) with people in similar networks.
©David Malan/Photographer's Choice RF/Getty Images

similar overlapping networks tend to receive fewer leads, many of which they already knew about. As careers require more movement across many organizations and industries, you need to establish connections with people across a diverse range of industries, professions, and other spheres of life.

Social Network Centrality Earlier in this chapter, we explained that centrality is an important contingency of power. This contingency also applies to social networks.[43] The more central a person (or team or organization) is located in the network, the more social capital and therefore more power he or she acquires. Centrality is your importance in that network.

Three factors determine your centrality in a social network. One factor is your "betweenness," which literally refers to how much you are located between others in the network. In Exhibit 9.3, Person A has high betweenness centrality because he or she is a gatekeeper who controls the flow of information to and from many other people in the network. Person H has less betweenness, whereas Person F and several other network members in the diagram have no betweenness. The more betweenness you have, the more you control the distribution of information and other resources to people on either side of you.

A second factor in centrality is the number or percentage of connections you have to others in the network (called *degree centrality*). Recall that the more people are connected to you, the more resources (information, favors, etc.) will be available. The number of connections also increases centrality because you are more visible to other members of the network. Although being a member of a network gives you access to resources in that network, having a direct connection to more people within the network makes that resource sharing more fluid.

A third factor in centrality is the "closeness" of the relationship with others in the network. High closeness refers to strong ties. It is depicted by shorter, more direct, and efficient paths or connections with others in the network. For example, Person A has fairly high closeness centrality because he or she has direct paths to most of the network, and many of these paths are short (implying stronger, more intense, efficient, and high-quality communication links). Your centrality increases with your closeness to others in the network because they are affected more quickly and significantly by you.

> Your centrality increases with your closeness to others in the network because they are affected more quickly and significantly by you.

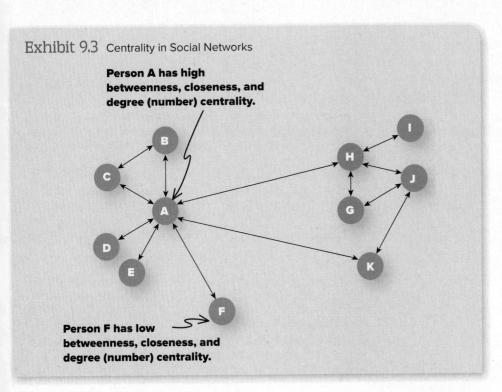

Exhibit 9.3 Centrality in Social Networks

Person A has high betweenness, closeness, and degree (number) centrality.

Person F has low betweenness, closeness, and degree (number) centrality.

One last observation is that Exhibit 9.3 illustrates two clusters of people in the network. The gap between these two clusters is called a **structural hole**.[44] Notice that Person A provides the main bridge across this structural hole (connecting to H and K in the other cluster). This bridging role gives Person A additional power in the network. By bridging this gap, Person A becomes a broker—someone who connects two independent networks and controls information flow between them. Research shows that the more brokering relationships you have, the more likely you are to get early promotions and higher pay.

The Dark Side of Social Networks Social networks are inherent in all organizations, yet they can create a formidable barrier to those who are excluded from those networks.[45] Women are often excluded from informal male social networks because of the natural tendency of people to network with others who are similar, and because women and men tend to have somewhat different interests and social activities. "From my experience, women and men tend to mainly network with their own genders," says Sharon Ritchey, chief operating officer at AXA U.S. She warns that gendered networks can be a liability for women because most senior management positions are still held by men. Consequently, men "are more likely to hear about jobs at the senior levels—and then pass these tips along to their mostly male networks. This obviously works against women, because men tend to hear earlier and more often about upper-level job leads."[46]

Sharon Ritchey recommends overcoming the male network barrier by encouraging women to include more men in their networks. Deloitte Touche Tohmatsu actively helps women in social networks. Several years ago, executives at the accounting and consulting firm discovered that many junior female employees quit before reaching partnership level because they felt isolated from powerful male social networks. Deloitte now supports mentoring, formal women's network groups, and measurement of career progress to ensure that female staff members have the same career development opportunities as their male colleagues.[47]

CONSEQUENCES OF POWER

How does power affect the power holder? The answer depends to some extent on the type of power.[49] When people feel empowered (high self-determination, meaning, competence, and impact), they believe they have power over themselves and freedom from being influenced by others. Empowerment tends to increase motivation, job satisfaction, organizational commitment, and job performance. However, this feeling of being in control and free from others' authority also increases automatic rather than mindful thinking. In particular, people who feel powerful usually are more likely to rely on stereotypes, have difficulty empathizing, and generally have less accurate perceptions compared with people who have less power.[50]

The other type of power is one in which an individual has power *over others*, such as the legitimate, reward, and coercive power that managers have over employees in the workplace. This type of power produces a sense of duty or responsibility for the people over whom the power holder has authority. Consequently, people who have power over others tend to be more mindful of their actions and engage in less stereotyping. Even when people feel empowered, they can shift their focus from self to others, so the power becomes viewed more as one of social responsibility than enjoyable for its own sake.[51]

Introverts Can Be Effective Networkers, Too[48]

Networking requires communication and the confidence to introduce yourself to strangers. These practices come more naturally to extraverts, but networking experts say that introverts also can be good at networking. Here's how:

Networking is about listening, not just talking. Networking is two-way communication, which means that you need to listen to and develop empathy with others in your network. Introverts have a stronger preference than extraverts to listen, so it is an advantage they can use. Good listeners more quickly identify the needs of people they meet and therefore are more likely to convey information of value to others in the network.

Networking is personal, not mass production. People make the mistake that they need to "work the room" by introducing themselves to as many people as possible. But networking is about personal relationships, so it's fine to meet only a handful of people at a particular event. That deeper interaction could produce clearer understanding of the potential relationship and the means to strengthen that relationship.

Network rejection is about misalignment, not personal fault. Some people you meet don't want to continue the conversation. Introverts take these networking failures more personally than do extroverts, who just move on to the next social opportunity. While we always need to reflect and learn from life's events, introverts in particular need to recognize that social interaction rejections are usually misalignments of interests, not evidence of a personal fault.

Networking is a skill, not a personality trait. Introversion is a preference and behavioral tendency, not an innate lack of ability to interact with other people. Some very notable public speakers, politicians, and business leaders are very good at the intense social interaction because they have developed appropriate skills and knowledge. While introverts might not enjoy social interaction as much as do extraverts, they can learn how to effectively meet strangers and form initial social bonds that lead to network relationships.

Networking is (partly) online, not just face-to-face. The Internet has created the best of both worlds for introverts. They can engage in effective networking without the stress or awkwardness of social interaction. At the same time, introverts can't always hide behind an Internet connection. Networking ultimately thrives on plenty of face-to-face interaction, not just emails, text messaging, and social media links. "People remember faces and conversations more than the written word," advises the CEO of one careers company.

Networking can be structured, to some extent. Some experts suggest that networking isn't completely impromptu conversation. This is good news for introverts because they prefer structured social interaction. Before meeting people, introverts can think about specific questions to ask, practice ways to deliver those questions casually (not as a wooden interviewer), and practice answers to common questions that others will ask. And when someone does ask an unexpected question, a short answer can be fine when followed by asking that question or another one back to the other person.

influence any behavior that attempts to alter someone's attitudes or behavior

LO9-4 Describe eight types of influence tactics, three consequences of influencing others, and three contingencies to consider when choosing an influence tactic.

INFLUENCING OTHERS

So far, this chapter has focused on the sources and contingencies of power as well as power derived from social networks. But power is only the *capacity* to influence others. It represents the potential to change someone's attitudes and behavior. **Influence**, on the other hand, refers to any behavior that attempts to alter someone's attitudes or behavior.[52] Influence is power in motion. It applies one or more sources of power to get people to alter their beliefs, feelings, and activities. Consequently, our interest in the remainder of this chapter is on how people use power to influence others.

Influence tactics are woven throughout the social fabric of all organizations. Indeed, influence is central to the definition of leadership. It is an essential process through which people coordinate their effort and act in concert to achieve organizational objectives. Influence operates down, across, and up the corporate hierarchy. Executives ensure that subordinates complete required tasks. Employees influence coworkers to help them with their job assignments.

Types of Influence Tactics

Organizational behavior researchers have devoted considerable attention to the various types of influence tactics found in organizational settings. They do not agree on a definitive list, but the most commonly discussed influence tactics are identified in Exhibit 9.4 and described over the next few pages.[53] The first five are known as "hard" influence tactics because they force behavior change through position power (legitimate, reward, and coercion). The latter three—persuasion, impression management, and exchange—are called "soft" tactics because they rely more on personal sources of power (referent, expert) and appeal to the target person's attitudes and needs.

Silent Authority The silent application of authority occurs when someone complies with a request because of the requester's legitimate power as well as the target person's role expectations.[54] This influence occurs when you comply with your boss's request to complete a particular task. If the task is within your job scope and your boss has the right to make this request, then this influence strategy operates without negotiation, threats, persuasion, or other tactics. Silent authority is the most common form of influence in high power distance cultures.[55]

Assertiveness Assertiveness might be called "vocal authority" because it involves actively applying legitimate and coercive power to influence others. This includes persistently reminding the target of his or her obligations, frequently checking the target's work, confronting the target, and using threats of sanctions to force compliance. Workplace bullying is an extreme form of assertiveness because it involves explicit threats of punishment.

Information Control Earlier in this chapter we explained that people with centrality in social networks have the power to control information. This power translates into influence when the power holder actually distributes information selectively so it

> ## Nothing more enhances authority than silence.[56]
> —Charles de Gaulle, French president and military leader

Exhibit 9.4 Types of Influence Tactics in Organizations

Influence Tactic	Description
Silent authority	Influencing behavior through legitimate power without explicitly referring to that power base.
Assertiveness	Actively applying legitimate and coercive power by applying pressure or threats.
Information control	Explicitly manipulating someone else's access to information for the purpose of changing his or her attitudes and/or behavior.
Coalition formation	Forming a group that attempts to influence others by pooling the resources and power of its members.
Upward appeal	Relying symbolically or in reality on people with higher authority or expertise to support our position.
Persuasion	Using logical arguments, factual evidence, and emotional appeals to convince people of the value of a request.
Impression management	Actively shaping, through self-presentation and other means, the perceptions and attitudes that others have of us. Includes ingratiation, which refers to the influencer's attempt to be more liked by the targeted person or group.
Exchange	Promising benefits or resources in exchange for the target person's compliance.

Dysfunctional Influence through Assertiveness[57]

16% of 96,768 Australian Public Service (APS) employees surveyed say that they had been bullied or harassed at work within the previous 12 months (ranged from 15% to 18% in APS surveys over the previous decade).

91% of 1,543 UK workers surveyed believe their organization does not adequately deal with bullying at work.

20% of 2,951 employees surveyed across 733 fire departments in Japan say they have experienced power harassment—a form of workplace bullying (28% of female and 17.5% of male fire department staff).

29% of 1,738 UK adults surveyed say they have been bullied at work (34% of women versus 23% of men).

27% of 3,372 American full-time employees surveyed say they have been yelled at by their boss in front of coworkers.

©Ingram Publishing

reframes the situation and causes others to change their attitudes and/or behavior. Controlling information might include withholding information that is more critical or favorable, or distributing information to some people but not to others. For example, one study found that CEOs influence their board of directors by selectively feeding and withholding information.[58]

Coalition Formation When people lack sufficient power alone to influence others in the organization, they might form a **coalition** of people who support the proposed change. A coalition is influential in three ways.[59] First, it pools the power and resources of many people, so the coalition potentially has more influence than its members have if they operated alone. Second, the coalition's mere existence can be a source of power by symbolizing the legitimacy of the issue. In other words, a coalition creates a sense that the issue deserves attention because it has broad support. Third, coalitions tap into the power of the social identity process introduced in Chapter 3. A coalition is an informal group that advocates a new set of norms and behaviors. If the coalition has a broad-based membership (i.e., its members come from various parts of the organization), then other employees are more likely to identify with that group and, consequently, accept the ideas the coalition is proposing.

Upward Appeal **Upward appeal** involves calling on higher authority or expertise, or symbolically relying on these sources,

to support the influencer's position. It occurs when someone says, "The boss likely agrees with me on this matter; let's find out!" Upward appeal also occurs when relying on the authority of the firm's policies or values. By reminding others that your request is consistent with the organization's overarching goals, you are implying support from senior executives without formally involving them.

Persuasion **Persuasion** involves the use of facts, logical arguments, and emotional appeals to change another person's beliefs and attitudes, usually for the purpose of changing his or her behavior. This is the most widely used and accepted influence strategy in organizations. It is a quality of effective leaders and, in many societies, a noble skill. The effectiveness of persuasion as an influence tactic depends on characteristics of the persuader, message content, communication channel, and the audience being persuaded (see Exhibit 9.5).[60] People are more persuasive when listeners believe they have expertise and credibility. Credibility is higher when the persuader does not seem to profit from the persuasion attempt, mentions limitations with the position being persuaded, and acknowledges minor positive features of the alternative choices.

The message is more important than the messenger when the issue is important to the audience. Message content is more persuasive when it acknowledges several points of view so the speaker is viewed as more credible and the audience does not feel boxed in by the persuasion attempt. The message also should be limited to a few strong arguments, which are repeated a few times, but not too frequently. The message should use emotional appeals (such as graphically showing the unfortunate consequences of a bad decision), but only in combination with logical arguments and specific recommendations to overcome the threat. Finally, message content is more persuasive when the audience is warned about opposing arguments. This **inoculation effect** causes listeners to generate counterarguments to the anticipated persuasion attempts, which makes the opponent's subsequent persuasion attempts less effective.[61]

Two other considerations when persuading people are the communication channel and characteristics of the audience. Generally, persuasion works best through communication

Persuasion tends to work best through communication channels with high social presence and media-richness, such as in face-to-face conversations.
©Monkey Business Images/Shutterstock

channels with high social presence and media-richness, such as in face-to-face conversations. The human presence of face-to-face communication increases the persuader's credibility, and the richness of this channel provides faster feedback that the

influence strategy is working. With respect to audience characteristics, it is more difficult to persuade people who have high self-esteem and intelligence, as well as a self-concept that is strongly tied to the opposing viewpoint.[62]

Impression Management Silent authority, assertiveness, information control, coalitions, and upward appeals are somewhat (or very!) forceful ways to influence other people. In contrast, a very soft influence tactic is **impression management**—actively shaping the perceptions and attitudes that others have of us.[63] Impression management mostly occurs through self-presentation. We craft our public images to communicate an identity, such as being important, vulnerable, threatening, or pleasant. For the most part, employees routinely engage in pleasant impression management behaviors to satisfy the basic norms of social behavior, such as the way they dress and how they behave toward coworkers and customers.

Impression management is a common strategy for people trying to get ahead in the workplace. In fact, as we noted earlier, career professionals encourage people to develop a personal "brand"; that is, to form and display an accurate impression of their own distinctive, competitive advantage.[64] Furthermore, people who master the art of personal branding rely on impression

Exhibit 9.5 Elements of Persuasion

Persuasion Element	Characteristics of Effective Persuasion
Persuader characteristics	• Expertise • Credibility • No apparent profit motive • Appears somewhat neutral (acknowledges strengths of alternative choices)
Message content	• Multiple viewpoints (not exclusively supporting the preferred option) • Limited to a few strong arguments (not many arguments) • Repeat arguments, but not excessively • Use emotional appeals in combination with logical arguments • Offer specific solutions to overcome the stated problems • Inoculation effect—audience warned of counterarguments that opponents will present
Communication channel	• Channels with high media-richness and social presence are usually more persuasive
Audience characteristics	Persuasion is *less* effective when the audience • has higher self-esteem • has higher intelligence • has a self-concept tied to an opposing position

Impression Management in Job Interviews[68]

Interviewer Question	Impression Management Principle	Do Say . . .	Don't Say . . .
Why are you interested in this job?	Demonstrate that you researched the job and firm, are motivated, and see alignment with your career.	"This job gives me greater opportunity to apply my current skills (name some) and develop others. This firm also has a great reputation for rewarding successful teams."	"I wondered about that, too, but hopefully I'll be able to get some sort of new skills I can use."
Describe a situation in which you had to deal with a professional disagreement or conflict.	Demonstrate that you are a good team player who is diplomatic, honest, and forthright at conflict handling and problem solving.	"My coworker and I once disagreed on (describe situation). We discussed our different methods and came up with a better way that combined the best of each of our methods."	"I avoid disagreements as much as possible. Better to steer clear of them and hope they go away."
Where do you see yourself in five years' time?	Demonstrate that you are goal-oriented and think about your career (not just current work), how it will benefit the company, and how the job opening is part of that future.	"I want to help the company's bottom line by becoming an expert in (name one of the job's competencies), as well as mentor junior staff as I move into leadership roles."	"I want to be a millionaire before I turn 30 by trading stock market derivatives when I'm not doing this job."
Why do you want to leave your current job?	Demonstrate sensible and justifiable factors that would not be a concern in the new job. Avoid dwelling on personalities and bad experiences.	"I very much enjoy my current job and coworkers, but the company was just acquired by a larger firm and there is a good chance that the entire department will be shut down."	"Everybody hates working at that company. Top management is clueless. Also, I don't like my boss. She always asks me to redo my work because of trivial errors in my calculations."
How many times do a clock's hands overlap in a day?	Demonstrate your process of thinking logically through unexpected problems and your can-do attitude toward solving problems.	"Let's see, there are 24 hours in a day and every time on the clock happens twice, so . . ."	"Gosh, I have no idea. I'm not that good at math."

management through distinctive personal characteristics such as black shirts, tinted hair, or unique signatures.

One subcategory of impression management is *ingratiation*, which is any attempt to increase liking by, or perceived similarity to, some targeted person.[65] Ingratiation comes in several flavors. Employees might flatter their boss in front of others, demonstrate that they have similar attitudes as their boss (e.g., agreeing with the boss's proposal), or ask their boss for advice. Ingratiation is one of the more effective influence tactics at boosting a person's career success.[66] However, people who engage in high levels of ingratiation are less (not more) influential and less likely to get promoted.[67] Why the opposite effect? Those who engage in too much ingratiation are viewed as insincere and self-serving. The terms *apple polishing* and *brown-nosing* are applied to those who ingratiate to excess or in ways that suggest selfish motives for the ingratiation.

Exchange Exchange activities involve the promise of benefits or resources in exchange for the target person's compliance with

your request. Negotiation is an integral part of exchange influence activities. For instance, you might negotiate with your boss for a day off in return for working a less desirable shift at a future date. Exchange also includes applying the norm of reciprocity that we described earlier, such as reminding the target of past benefits or favors with the expectation that the target will now make up for that debt. Earlier in this chapter we explained how people gain power through social networks. They also use norms of reciprocity to influence others in the network. Active networkers build up "exchange credits" by helping colleagues in the short term for reciprocal benefits in the long term.

Consequences and Contingencies of Influence Tactics

Faced with a variety of influence strategies, you are probably asking: Which ones are best? To answer this question, we first need to describe how people react when others try to influence them: resistance, compliance, or commitment (see Exhibit 9.6).[69]

SELF-ASSESSMENT 9.2: What Is Your Approach To Influencing Coworkers?
Working with others in organizations is an ongoing process of coordination and cooperation. Part of that dynamic is changing our attitudes and behavior as well as motivating others to change their attitudes and behavior. In other words, everyone engages in influence tactics to get things done. There are many ways to influence other people, some of which work better than others, depending on the situation. You can discover your preferred influence tactics on coworkers and other peers by locating this self-assessment in Connect if it is assigned by your instructor.

Resistance occurs when people or work units oppose the behavior desired by the influencer. At the extreme, they refuse to engage in the behavior. However, there are degrees of resistance, such as when people perform the required duties yet maintain their opposition by performing the tasks poorly or continuing to complain about the imposed work.

Compliance occurs when people are motivated to implement the influencer's request for purely instrumental reasons. Without external sources to motivate the desired behavior, compliance would not occur. Furthermore, compliance usually involves engaging in the behavior with no more effort than is required.

Commitment is the strongest outcome of influence, whereby people identify with the influencer's request and are highly motivated to implement it even when extrinsic sources of motivation are not present.

People usually react more favorably to soft tactics than to hard tactics. Soft influence tactics rely on personal sources of power (expert and referent power), which tend to build commitment to the influencer's request. In contrast, hard tactics rely on position power (legitimate, reward, and coercion), so they tend to produce compliance or, worse, resistance. Hard tactics also tend to undermine trust, which can hurt future relationships.

Apart from the general preference for soft rather than hard tactics, the most appropriate influence strategy depends on a few contingencies.[70] One obvious contingency is the influencer's strongest sources of power. Those with expertise tend to have more influence using persuasion, whereas those with a strong legitimate power base may be more successful applying silent authority. A second contingency is whether the person being influenced is higher, lower, or at the same level in the organization. As an example, employees may face adverse career consequences by being too assertive with their boss. Meanwhile, supervisors who engage in ingratiation and impression management tend to lose the respect of their staff.

Finally, the most appropriate influence tactic depends on personal, organizational, and cultural values.[71] People with a strong power orientation might feel more comfortable using assertiveness, whereas those who value conformity would make greater use of upward appeals. At an organizational level, firms with a competitive culture might encourage more use of information control and coalition formation, whereas companies with a more collegial culture would likely encourage more influence through persuasion. The preferred influence tactics also vary across societal cultures. Research indicates that ingratiation is much more common among managers in the United States than in Hong Kong. Possibly ingratiation is incompatible with the

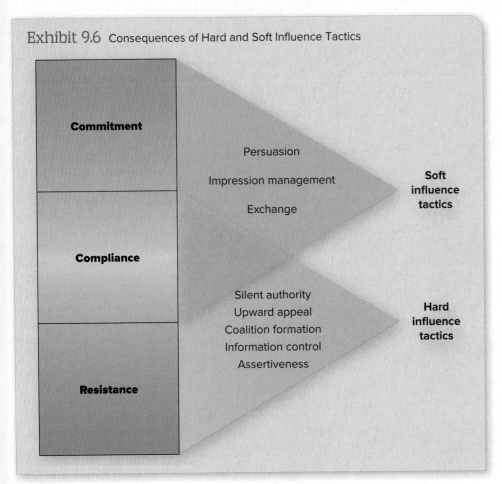

Exhibit 9.6 Consequences of Hard and Soft Influence Tactics

Commitment

Compliance

Resistance

Persuasion
Impression management
Exchange

Soft influence tactics

Silent authority
Upward appeal
Coalition formation
Information control
Assertiveness

Hard influence tactics

more distant roles that managers and employees expect in high power distance cultures.

ORGANIZATIONAL POLITICS

You might have noticed that organizational politics has not been mentioned yet, even though some of the practices or examples described over the past few pages are usually considered political tactics. The phrase was carefully avoided because, for the most part, organizational politics is in the eye of the beholder. You might perceive a coworker's attempt to influence the boss as acceptable behavior for the good of the organization, whereas someone else might perceive the coworker's tactic as brazen organizational politics.

This perceptual issue explains why OB experts increasingly discuss influence tactics as behaviors and organizational politics as perceptions.[72] The influence tactics described earlier are perceived as **organizational politics** when they seem to be self-serving behaviors at the expense of others and possibly contrary to the interests of the entire organization. Of course, some tactics are so blatantly selfish and counterproductive that almost everyone correctly sees them as organizational politics. In other situations, however, a person's behavior might be viewed as political or in the organization's best interest, depending on the observer's point of view.

Employees who experience organizational politics from others have lower job satisfaction, organizational commitment, organizational citizenship, and task performance, as well as higher levels of work-related stress and motivation to leave the organization. "A politically charged work environment can hinder productivity, erode trust, and lead to morale and retention issues," says Renan Silva, a corporate project management office specialist at Serasa Experian, a credit bureau in São Paulo, Brazil.[74] And because political tactics serve individuals rather than organizations, they potentially divert resources away from the organization's effective functioning and may threaten its survival.

OB THEORY TO PRACTICE

Playing Politics with the Vacation Schedule

The vacation roster is a scarce resource, and resource scarcity brings out the worst office politics. One recent poll reported that 13 percent of British employees refused to reveal when they would take their vacations so coworkers wouldn't book the same dates. Another 7 percent said they protected their vacation plans by lying to coworkers about those plans. Five percent were even more Machiavellian; they strategically booked vacation dates that scuttled the plans of a disliked coworker. "I know this is true," says an employee from Newport, Wales, who was not part of the survey. "I had a colleague who knew my holiday habits and would go in on January the 2nd and book every week that he knew I habitually had for holidays because he knew my wife's holidays were fixed and could not be changed. He didn't really need those days; he did it out of spite."[75]

©Ferran Traite Soler/E+/Getty Images

Minimizing Organizational Politics

Researchers have identified several conditions that encourage organizational politics, so we can identify corresponding strategies to keep political activities to a minimum.[76] First, organizational politics are triggered by scarce resources in the workplace. When budgets are slashed, people rely on political tactics to safeguard their resources and maintain the status quo. Although it is not easy to maintain or add resources, sometimes this action is less costly than the consequences of organizational politics.

> Keep your friends close and your enemies closer.[73]
>
> —Attributed to Sun-Tzu, Chinese general, circa 500 B.C.

![Mc Graw Hill Education] **connect®**

SELF-ASSESSMENT 9.3: How Politically Charged is Your School?

Every organization has some degree of organizational politics. Depending on behavioral norms and organizational culture, employees in some companies actively use influence tactics to get their own way for personal gain. In other workplaces, employees who engage in organizational politics are quickly reminded to avoid these tactics, or are eventually asked to work somewhere else. Students can usually sense the level of organizational politics at the college where they are taking courses. You can discover the degree to which you believe the school where you attend classes has a politicized culture by locating this self-assessment in Connect if it is assigned by your instructor.

![Mc Graw Hill Education] **connect®**

SELF-ASSESSMENT 9.4: How Machiavellian Are You?

One of the best-known individual differences in organizational politics is Machiavellianism, named after the 16th-century Italian philosopher who wrote a famous treatise about political behavior (*The Prince*). Machiavellian employees take a perspective of situations and other people that motivates them to apply influence tactics more for personal gain. Although few people want to be viewed as Machiavellian, measures suggest that most of us apply these practices to some extent. You can discover your level of Machiavellianism by locating this self-assessment in Connect if it is assigned by your instructor.

of organizational leaders. To minimize political norms, the organization needs to diagnose and alter systems and role modeling that support self-serving behavior. They should support organizational values that oppose political tactics, such as altruism and focusing on the customer. One of the most important strategies is for leaders to become role models of organizational citizenship rather than symbols of successful organizational politicians.

Personal Characteristics Several personal characteristics affect an individual's motivation to engage in self-serving behavior.[79] This includes a strong need for personal as opposed to socialized power.

Second, political tactics are fueled by ambiguous or complex rules, or the absence of formal rules, because those tactics help people get what they want when decisions lack structural guidelines. Consequently, organizational politics are suppressed when resource allocation decisions are clear and simplified. Third, organizational change tends to bring out more organizational politics, mainly because change creates ambiguity and threatens the employee's power and other valued resources.[77] Consequently, leaders need to apply the organizational change strategies that we describe in Chapter 14, particularly through communication, learning, and involvement. Research has found that employees who are kept informed of what is going on in the organization and who are involved in organizational decisions are less likely to engage in organizational politics.

Fourth, political behavior is more common in work units and organizations where it is tolerated and reinforced. Some companies seem to nurture self-serving behavior through reward systems and the role modeling

Those with a need for personal power seek power for its own sake and try to acquire more power. Some individuals have strong **Machiavellian values**. Machiavellianism is named after Niccolò Machiavelli, the 16th-century Italian philosopher who wrote *The Prince*, a famous treatise about political behavior.

Office Politics By the Numbers[78]

68% of 1,125 Taiwanese office workers polled say they have experienced workplace politics.

54% of 1,100 16–25 year olds polled in the UK say they are not prepared or informed about office politics.

46% of more than 1,000 American office workers polled say that gossiping or spreading rumors is the most common form of office politics where they work.

©SchulteProductions/Getty Images

33% of 1,102 employed Americans polled who don't normally work at a desk say that an important advantage of a non-desk job is not having to deal with office politics.

28% of 2,200 chief financial officers polled say that gossiping or engaging in office politics is the most annoying behavior by coworkers (second highest, following sloppy work).

19% of 7,000 American employees polled believe that office politics are more vicious than national (elected government) politics.

People with high Machiavellian values are comfortable with getting more than they deserve, and they believe that deceit is a natural and acceptable way to achieve this goal. They seldom trust coworkers and tend to use cruder influence tactics to get their own way, such as bypassing their boss or being assertive.[80]

Study Checklist

Connect® Management is available for *M Organizational Behavior.* Additional resources include:

✓ Interactive Applications:
- **Case Analysis:** Apply concepts within the context of a real-world situation.
- **Drag and Drop:** Work through an interactive example to test your knowledge of the concepts.
- **Video Case:** See management in action through interactive videos.

✓ **SmartBook™**—SmartBook is the first and only adaptive reading experience available today. Distinguishing what you know from what you don't, and honing in on concepts you are most likely to forget, SmartBook personalizes content for you in a continuously adapting reading experience. Reading is no longer a passive and linear experience, but an engaging and dynamic one where you are more likely to master and retain important concepts and go to class better prepared.

©Natthawat Jamnapa/123RF

Notes

1. J. J. Gabarro and J. P. Kotter, "Managing Your Boss," *Harvard Business Review* 58, no. 1 (1980): 92–100; B. Tulgan, *It's Okay to Manage Your Boss* (San Francisco: Jossey-Bass, 2010); T. Kucera, "How to Manage Your Manager," *LinkedIn Pulse*, March 5, 2017.

2. J. R. French and B. Raven, "The Bases of Social Power," in *Studies in Social Power*, ed. D. Cartwright (Ann Arbor: University of Michigan Press, 1959), 150–67; A. D. Galinsky et al., "Power and Perspectives Not Taken," *Psychological Science* 17, no. 12 (2006): 1068–74. Also see H. Mintzberg, *Power in and around Organizations* (Englewood Cliffs, NJ: Prentice Hall, 1983), chap. 1; J. Pfeffer, *Managing with Power: Politics and Influence in Organizations* (Boston: Harvard Business School Press, 1992), 17, 30; A. Guinote and T. K. Vescio, "Introduction: Power in Social Psychology," in *The Social Psychology of Power*, ed. A. Guinote and T. K. Vescio (New York: Guilford Press, 2010), 1–18.

3. R. A. Dahl, "The Concept of Power," *Behavioral Science* 2 (1957): 201–18; R. M. Emerson, "Power-Dependence Relations," *American Sociological Review* 27 (1962): 31–41; A. M. Pettigrew, *The Politics of Organizational Decision-Making* (London: Tavistock, 1973).

4. G. A. van Kleef et al., "The Social Dynamics of Breaking the Rules: Antecedents and Consequences of Norm-Violating Behavior," *Current Opinion in Psychology* 6 (2015): 25–31.

5. J. Pfeffer and G. R. Salancik, *The External Control of Organizations* (New York: Harper & Row, 1978), 52–54; K. Cowan, A. K. Paswan, and E. Van Steenburg, "When Inter-Firm Relationship Benefits Mitigate Power Asymmetry," *Industrial Marketing Management* 48 (2015): 140–48.

6. J. R. French and B. Raven, "The Bases of Social Power," in *Studies in Social Power*, ed. D. Cartwright (Ann Arbor: University of Michigan Press, 1959), 150–67; P. M. Podsakoff and C. Schreisheim, "Field Studies of French and Raven's Bases of Power: Critique, Analysis, and Suggestions for Future Research," *Psychological Bulletin* 97 (1985): 387–411; P. P. Carson and K. D. Carson, "Social Power Bases: A Meta-Analytic Examination of Interrelationships and Outcomes," *Journal of Applied Social Psychology* 23 (1993): 1150–69. Most alternative models of power bases parallel French and Raven's list. See P. Heinemann, *Power Bases and Informational Influence Strategies: A Behavioral Study on the Use of Management Accounting Information* (Wiesbaden, Germany: Deutscher Universitäts-Verlag, 2008). Raven subsequently proposed information power as a sixth source of power. We present information power as forms of legitimate and expert power rather than as a distinct sixth power base.

7. Legitimate power and expert power are also consistently the strongest sources of power that coaches have over players in sports. See P. Rylander, "Coaches' Bases of Power: Developing Some Initial Knowledge of Athletes' Compliance with Coaches in Team Sports," *Journal of Applied Sport Psychology* 27, no. 1 (2015): 110–21.

8. C. Barnard, *The Function of the Executive* (Cambridge, MA: Harvard University Press, 1938), 167–70; B. J. Tepper, "What Do Managers Do When Subordinates Just Say, 'No'?: An Analysis of Incidents Involving Refusal to Perform Downward Requests," in *Power and Influence in Organizations*, ed. L. L. Neider and C. A. Schreisheim (Charlotte, NC: IAP/Information Age Publishing, 2006), 1–20.

9. A. I. Shahin and P. L. Wright, "Leadership in the Context of Culture: An Egyptian Perspective," *Leadership & Organization Development Journal* 25, no. 5/6 (2004): 499–511; Y. J. Huo et al., "Leadership and the Management of Conflicts in Diverse Groups: Why Acknowledging versus Neglecting Subgroup Identity Matters," *European Journal of Social Psychology* 35, no. 2 (2005): 237–54.

10. B. Crumley, "Game of Death: France's Shocking TV Experiment," *Time*, March 17, 2010; M. Portillo, "Would You Torture This Man?," *Sunday Telegraph* (London), March 21, 2010, 22. A recent variation of deference to authority occurred on British television. Four strangers were individually encouraged to assist the head of a (fictitious) charity by impersonating a wealthy would-be donor who died before making the donation, then kicking the supposedly dead body, and later throwing the body off a roof. See H. Mount, "Could You Be Talked into Murder?," *Daily Mail* (London), January 14, 2016, 16.

11. B. H. Raven, "Kurt Lewin Address: Influence, Power, Religion, and the Mechanisms of Social Control," *Journal of Social Issues* 55 (1999): 161–86.

12. A. W. Gouldner, "The Norm of Reciprocity: A Preliminary Statement," *American Sociological Review* 25 (1960): 161-78; M. Koslowsky and J. Schwarzwald, "Power Tactics Preference in Organizations: Individual and Situational Factors," in *Power and Interdependence in Organizations*, ed. D. Tjosvold and B. Wisse (New York: Cambridge University Press, 2009), 244-61.

13. A. Einstein, *The Ultimate Quotable Einstein*, ed. A. Calaprice (Princeton, NJ: Princeton University Press, 2011), 161. Originally in a letter to Swiss teacher Jost Winteler on July 8, 1901.

14. G. Yukl and C. M. Falbe, "Importance of Different Power Sources in Downward and Lateral Relations," *Journal of Applied Psychology* 76 (1991): 416-23; B. H. Raven, "Kurt Lewin Address: Influence, Power, Religion, and the Mechanisms of Social Control," *Journal of Social Issues* 55 (1999): 161-86.

15. A. M. Pettigrew, "Information Control as a Power Resource," *Sociology* 6, no. 2 (1972): 187-204; P. L. Dawes, D. Y. Lee, and G. R. Dowling, "Information Control and Influence in Emergent Buying Centers," *Journal of Marketing* 62, no. 3 (1998): 55-68; J. Webster et al., "Beyond Knowledge Sharing: Withholding Knowledge at Work," *Research in Personnel and Human Resources Management* 27 (2008): 1-37; C. E. Connelly et al., "Knowledge Hiding in Organizations," *Journal of Organizational Behavior* 33, no. 1 (2012): 64-88.

16. S. L. Robinson, J. O'Reilly, and W. Wang, "Invisible at Work: An Integrated Model of Workplace Ostracism," *Journal of Management* 39, no. 1 (2013): 203-31.

17. J. M. Peiro and J. L. Melia, "Formal and Informal Interpersonal Power in Organisations: Testing a Bifactorial Model of Power in Role-Sets," *Applied Psychology* 52, no. 1 (2003): 14-35.

18. C. R. Hinings et al., "Structural Conditions of Intraorganizational Power," *Administrative Science Quarterly* 19 (1974): 22-44. Also see C. S. Saunders, "The Strategic Contingency Theory of Power: Multiple Perspectives," *Journal of Management Studies* 27 (1990): 1-21.

19. R. B. Cialdini and N. J. Goldstein, "Social Influence: Compliance and Conformity," *Annual Review of Psychology* 55 (2004): 591-621.

20. C. K. Hofling et al., "An Experimental Study in Nurse-Physician Relationships," *Journal of Nervous and Mental Disease* 143, no. 2 (1966): 171-77.

21. C. Perkel, "It's Not CSI," *Canadian Press*, November 10, 2007; "Dr. Charles Smith: The Man behind the Public Inquiry," *CBC News* (Toronto), August 10, 2010; J. Chipman, *Death in the Family* (Toronto: Doubleday Canada, 2017).

22. K. Miyahara, "Charisma: From Weber to Contemporary Sociology," *Sociological Inquiry* 53, no. 4 (1983): 368-88; J. D. Kudisch and M. L. Poteet, "Expert Power, Referent Power, and Charisma: Toward the Resolution of a Theoretical Debate," *Journal of Business & Psychology* 10 (1995): 177-95; D. Ladkin, "The Enchantment of the Charismatic Leader: Charisma Reconsidered as Aesthetic Encounter," *Leadership* 2, no. 2 (2006): 165-79.

23. D. J. Hickson et al., "A Strategic Contingencies' Theory of Intraorganizational Power," *Administrative Science Quarterly* 16 (1971): 216-27; C. R. Hinings et al., "Structural Conditions of Intraorganizational Power," *Administrative Science Quarterly* 19 (1974): 22-44; R. M. Kanter, "Power Failure in Management Circuits," *Harvard Business Review* (1979): 65-75.

24. A. Bryant, "The Right Job? It's Much Like the Right Spouse," *The New York Times*, May 22, 2011, 2.

25. D. J. Hickson et al., "A Strategic Contingencies' Theory of Intraorganizational Power," *Administrative Science Quarterly* 16 (1971): 219-21; J. D. Hackman, "Power and Centrality in the Allocation of Resources in Colleges and Universities," *Administrative Science Quarterly* 30 (1985): 61-77; D. J. Brass and M. E. Burkhardt, "Potential Power and Power Use: An Investigation of Structure and Behavior," *Academy of Management Journal* 36 (1993): 441-70.

26. A. Caza, "Typology of the Eight Domains of Discretion in Organizations," *Journal of Management Studies* 49, no. 1 (2012): 144-77.

27. B. E. Ashforth, "The Experience of Powerlessness in Organizations," *Organizational Behavior and Human Decision Processes* 43 (1989): 207-42; D. B. Wangrow, D. J. Schepker, and V. L. Barker, "Managerial Discretion: An Empirical Review and Focus on Future Research Directions," *Journal of Management* 41, no. 1 (2015): 99-135.

28. S. Wasserman and K. Faust, *Social Network Analysis: Methods and Applications*, Structural Analysis in the Social Sciences (Cambridge, UK: Cambridge University Press, 1994), chap. 1; D. J. Brass et al., "Taking Stock of Networks and Organizations: A Multilevel Perspective," *Academy of Management Journal* 47, no. 6 (2004): 795-817.

29. M. Grossetti, "Where Do Social Relations Come From?: A Study of Personal Networks in the Toulouse Area of France," *Social Networks* 27, no. 4 (2005): 289-300.

30. R. J. Taormina and J. H. Gao, "A Research Model for Guanxi Behavior: Antecedents, Measures, and Outcomes of Chinese Social Networking," *Social Science Research* 39, no. 6 (2010): 1195-212; J. Barbalet, "Guanxi, Tie Strength, and Network Attributes," *American Behavioral Scientist* 59, no. 8 (2015): 1038-50; X.-A. Zhang, N. Li, and T. B. Harris, "Putting Non-Work Ties to Work: The Case of Guanxi in Supervisor-Subordinate Relationships," *Leadership Quarterly* 26, no. 1 (2015): 37-54. For problems with guanxi, see W. R. Vanhonacker, "When Good Guanxi Turns Bad," *Harvard Business Review* 82, no. 4 (2004): 18-19; F. Yang, "Guanxi Human Resource Management Practices as a Double-Edged Sword: The Moderating Role of Political Skill," *Asia Pacific Journal of Human Resources* 52, no. 4 (2014): 496-510.

31. A. Portes, "Social Capital: Its Origins and Applications in Modern Society," *Annual Review of Sociology* 24 (1998): 1-24; P. S. Adler and S. W. Kwon, "Social Capital: Prospects for a New Concept," *Academy of Management Review* 27, no. 1 (2002): 17-40; R. Lee, "Social Capital and Business and Management: Setting a Research Agenda," *International Journal of Management Reviews* 11, no. 3 (2009): 247-73.

32. R. F. Chisholm, *Developing Network Organizations: Learning from Practice and Theory* (Reading, MA: Addison-Wesley Longman, 1998); W. S. Chow and L. S. Chan, "Social Network, Social Trust and Shared Goals in Organizational Knowledge Sharing," *Information & Management* 45, no. 7 (2008): 458-65.

33. R. S. Burt, *Structural Holes: The Social Structure of Competition* (Cambridge, MA: Harvard University Press, 1992).

34. M. T. Rivera, S. B. Soderstrom, and B. Uzzi, "Dynamics of Dyads in Social Networks: Assortative, Relational, and Proximity Mechanisms," *Annual Review of Sociology* 36 (2010): 91-115.

35. R. Cross and R. J. Thomas, *Driving Results through Social Networks: How Top Organizations Leverage Networks for Performance and Growth* (San Francisco: Jossey-Bass, 2009); R. McDermott and D. Archibald, "Harnessing Your Staff's Informal Networks," *Harvard Business Review* 88, no. 3 (2010): 82-89.

36. M. Kilduff and D. Krackhardt, *Interpersonal Networks in Organizations: Cognition, Personality, Dynamics, and Culture* (New York: Cambridge University Press, 2008).

37. T. Gibbs, S. Heywood, and L. Weiss, "Organizing for an Emerging World," *McKinsey Quarterly* (2012): 1-11.

38. N. B. Ellison, C. Steinfield, and C. Lampe, "The Benefits of Facebook 'Friends': Social Capital and College Students' Use of Online Social Network Sites," *Journal of Computer-Mediated Communication* 12, no. 4 (2007): 1143-68.

39. D. J. Brass et al., "Taking Stock of Networks and Organizations: A Multilevel Perspective," *Academy of Management Journal* 47, no. 6 (2004): 795–817; D. Melamed and B. Simpson, "Strong Ties Promote the Evolution of Cooperation in Dynamic Networks," *Social Networks* 45 (2016): 32–44.

40. M. S. Granovetter, "The Strength of Weak Ties," *American Journal of Sociology* 78 (1973): 1360–80; B. Erickson, "Social Networks," in *The Blackwell Companion to Sociology*, ed. J. R. Blau (Malden, MA: Blackwell, 2004), 314–26.

41. B. Uzzi and S. Dunlap, "How to Build Your Network," *Harvard Business Review* 83, no. 12 (2005): 53–60.

42. S. C. de Janasz and M. L. Forret, "Learning the Art of Networking: A Critical Skill for Enhancing Social Capital and Career Success," *Journal of Management Education* 32, no. 5 (2008): 629–50; Y. Zenou, "A Dynamic Model of Weak and Strong Ties in the Labor Market," *Journal of Labor Economics* 33, no. 4 (2015): 891–932.

43. C. Phelps, R. Heidl, and A. Wadhwa, "Knowledge, Networks, and Knowledge Networks: A Review and Research Agenda," *Journal of Management* 38, no. 4 (2012): 1115–66.

44. R. S. Burt, *Structural Holes: The Social Structure of Competition* (Cambridge, MA: Harvard University Press, 1992); D. J. Brass and D. M. Krackhardt, "Power, Politics, and Social Networks in Organizations," in *Politics in Organizations: Theory and Research Considerations*, ed. G. R. Ferris and D. C. Treadway (New York: Routledge, 2012), 355–75.

45. B. R. Ragins and E. Sundstrom, "Gender and Power in Organizations: A Longitudinal Perspective," *Psychological Bulletin* 105 (1989): 51–88; S. McDonald et al., "Frontiers of Sociological Research on Networks, Work, and Inequality," in *Networks, Work and Inequality*, ed. S. McDonald, Research in the Sociology of Work (Bingley, UK: Emerald Group Publishing Limited, 2013), 1–41.

46. S. Ritchey, "The Biggest Mistake Women Make When Networking," *Fortune*, February 1, 2016.

47. D. M. McCracken, "Winning the Talent War for Women: Sometimes It Takes a Revolution," *Harvard Business Review* (2000): 159–67.

48. Y. Amichai-Hamburger, G. Wainapel, and S. Fox, "'On the Internet No One Knows I'm an Introvert': Extroversion, Neuroticism, and Internet Interaction," *Cyber-Psychology & Behavior* 5, no. 2 (2002): 125–28; K. Brooks, "Networking 101 for Introverts," *Psychology Today* (2010); D. Zack, *Networking for People Who Hate Networking* (San Francisco: Berret-Koehler, 2010).

49. J. Lammers, J. I. Stoker, and D. A. Stapel, "Differentiating Social and Personal Power: Opposite Effects on Stereotyping, but Parallel Effects on Behavioral Approach Tendencies," *Psychological Science* 20, no. 12 (2009): 1543–49.

50. J. Lammers et al., "Power and Morality," *Current Opinion in Psychology* 6 (2015): 15–19.

51. A. D. Galinsky et al., "Acceleration with Steering: The Synergistic Benefits of Combining Power and Perspective-Taking," *Social Psychological and Personality Science* 5, no. 6 (2014): 627–35.

52. K. Atuahene-Gima and H. Li, "Marketing's Influence Tactics in New Product Development: A Study of High Technology Firms in China," *Journal of Product Innovation Management* 17 (2000): 451–70; A. Somech and A. Drach-Zahavy, "Relative Power and Influence Strategy: The Effects of Agent/Target Organizational Power on Superiors' Choices of Influence Strategies," *Journal of Organizational Behavior* 23 (2002): 167–79.

53. D. Kipnis, S. M. Schmidt, and I. Wilkinson, "Intraorganizational Influence Tactics: Explorations in Getting One's Way," *Journal of Applied Psychology* 65 (1980): 440–52; G. Yukl, "Power and the Interpersonal Influence of Leaders," in *Power and Interdependence in Organizations*, ed. D. Tjosvold and B. Wisse (New York: Cambridge University Press, 2009), 207–23.

54. R. B. Cialdini and N. J. Goldstein, "Social Influence: Compliance and Conformity," *Annual Review of Psychology* 55 (2004): 591–621.

55. A. Rao and K. Hashimoto, "Universal and Culturally Specific Aspects of Managerial Influence: A Study of Japanese Managers," *Leadership Quarterly* 8 (1997): 295–312. Silent authority as an influence tactic in non-Western cultures also is discussed in S. F. Pasa, "Leadership Influence in a High Power Distance and Collectivist Culture," *Leadership & Organization Development Journal* 21 (2000): 414–26.

56. C. de Gaulle, *The Edge of the Sword (Le fil de l'epée)*, trans. G. Hopkins (London: Faber, 1960), 59.

57. CareerBuilder, "Office Bullying Plagues Workers across Races, Job Levels and Educational Attainment, According to Careerbuilder's New Study," news release (Chicago: CareerBuilder, September 18, 2014); Trades Union Congress, "Nearly a Third of People Are Bullied at Work, Says TUC," news release (London: Trades Union Congress, November 12, 2015); Family Lives, "Family Lives Extended News Release: Bullying in the Workplace," news release (Hatfield, UK: Family Lives, January 12, 2015); Australian Public Service Commission, *State of the Service Report* (Canberra: Commonwealth of Australia, December 2016); "Workplace Bullying Widespread at Fire Departments, Survey Shows," *Japan Times*, March 29, 2017.

58. S. Maitlis, "Taking It from the Top: How CEOs Influence (and Fail to Influence) Their Boards," *Organization Studies* 25, no. 8 (2004): 1275–311. This type of influence is a form of manipulation. See P. Fleming and A. Spicer, "Power in Management and Organization Science," *The Academy of Management Annals* 8, no. 1 (2014): 237–98.

59. A. T. Cobb, "Toward the Study of Organizational Coalitions: Participant Concerns and Activities in a Simulated Organizational Setting," *Human Relations* 44 (1991): 1057–79; E. A. Mannix, "Organizations as Resource Dilemmas: The Effects of Power Balance on Coalition Formation in Small Groups," *Organizational Behavior and Human Decision Processes* 55 (1993): 1–22; D. J. Terry, M. A. Hogg, and K. M. White, "The Theory of Planned Behavior: Self-Identity, Social Identity and Group Norms," *British Journal of Social Psychology* 38 (1999): 225–44.

60. A. P. Brief, *Attitudes in and around Organizations* (Thousand Oaks, CA: Sage, 1998), 69–84; D. J. O'Keefe, *Persuasion: Theory and Research* (Thousand Oaks, CA: Sage, 2002); R. H. Gass and J. S. Seiter, *Persuasion: Social Influence and Compliance Gaining*, 5th ed. (New York: Routledge, 2014).

61. These and other features of message content in persuasion are detailed in R. Petty and J. Cacioppo, *Attitudes and Persuasion: Classic and Contemporary Approaches* (Dubuque, IA: W. C. Brown, 1981); M. Pfau, E. A. Szabo, and J. Anderson, "The Role and Impact of Affect in the Process of Resistance to Persuasion," *Human Communication Research* 27 (2001): 216–52; D. J. O'Keefe, *Persuasion: Theory and Research* (Thousand Oaks, CA: Sage, 2002), chap. 9; R. Buck et al., "Emotion and Reason in Persuasion: Applying the ARI Model and the CASC Scale," *Journal of Business Research* 57, no. 6 (2004): 647–56; W. D. Crano and R. Prislin, "Attitudes and Persuasion," *Annual Review of Psychology* 57 (2006): 345–74.

62. N. Rhodes and W. Wood, "Self-Esteem and Intelligence Affect Influenceability: The Mediating Role of Message Reception," *Psychological Bulletin* 111, no. 1 (1992): 156–71.

63. M. Bolino, D. Long, and W. Turnley, "Impression Management in Organizations: Critical Questions, Answers, and Areas for Future Research," *Annual Review of Organizational Psychology and Organizational Behavior* 3, no. 1 (2016): 377–406.

64. T. Peters, "The Brand Called You," *Fast Company*, August 1997; J. Sills, "Becoming Your Own Brand," *Psychology Today* 41, no. 1 (2008): 62–63.

65. D. Strutton and L. E. Pelton, "Effects of Ingratiation on Lateral Relationship Quality within Sales Team Settings," *Journal of Business Research* 43 (1998): 1–12; R. Vonk, "Self-Serving Interpretations of Flattery: Why Ingratiation Works," *Journal of Personality and Social Psychology* 82 (2002): 515–26.

66. C. A. Higgins, T. A. Judge, and G. R. Ferris, "Influence Tactics and Work Outcomes: A Meta-Analysis," *Journal of Organizational Behavior* 24 (2003): 90–106.

67. D. Strutton, L. E. Pelton, and J. F. Tanner, "Shall We Gather in the Garden: The Effect of Ingratiatory Behaviors on Buyer Trust in Salespeople," *Industrial Marketing Management* 25 (1996): 151–62; J. O'Neil, "An Investigation of the Sources of Influence of Corporate Public Relations Practitioners," *Public Relations Review* 29 (2003): 159–69.

68. J. Foster, "Here Are Best Answers to Job Interview Questions," *The Herald (Rock Hill, S.C.)*, April 4, 2010; "Common Interview Questions and How to Answer Them," *Advice & Tips* (Sydney: Seek, September 19, 2013), https://www.seek.com.au/career-advice/common-interview-questions-and-how-to-answer-them (accessed July 3, 2017); J. Haden, "27 Most Common Job Interview Questions and Answers," *Inc.*, June 20, 2016; "Ten Tough Interview Questions and Ten Great Answers," *Job Search Advice* (Seattle: CollegeGrad, 2017), https://collegegrad.com/jobsearch/mastering-the-interview/ten-tough-interview-questions-and-ten-great-answers (accessed July 3, 2017); M. Cheary, "Common Interview Questions and Answers," *Interview Techniques* (London: Reed, 2017) (accessed July 3, 2017).

69. C. M. Falbe and G. Yukl, "Consequences for Managers of Using Single Influence Tactics and Combinations of Tactics," *Academy of Management Journal* 35 (1992): 638–52.

70. G. Yukl and J. Tracey, "Consequences of Influence Tactics Used with Subordinates, Peers, and the Boss," *Journal of Applied Psychology* 77, no. 4 (1992): 525–35; B. Oc and M. R. Bashshur, "Followership, Leadership and Social Influence," *Leadership Quarterly* 24, no. 6 (2013): 919–34; M. B. Wadsworth and A. L. Blanchard, "Influence Tactics in Virtual Teams," *Computers in Human Behavior* 44 (2015): 386–93.

71. P. P. Fu et al., "The Impact of Societal Cultural Values and Individual Social Beliefs on the Perceived Effectiveness of Managerial Influence Strategies: A Meso Approach," *Journal of International Business Studies* 35, no. 4 (2004): 284–305; A. N. Smith et al., "Gendered Influence: A Gender Role Perspective on the Use and Effectiveness of Influence Tactics," *Journal of Management* 39, no. 5 (2013): 1156–83; C. C. Lewis and J. Ryan, "Age and Influence Tactics: A Life-Stage Development Theory Perspective," *The International Journal of Human Resource Management* 25, no. 15 (2014): 2146–58.

72. Organizational politics is a badly convoluted construct. Early literature defined it as influence tactics outside the formal role that could be either selfish or altruistic. Unfortunately, that definition fails to recognize the highly subjective nature of the definition and doesn't distinguish political behavior from other influence behavior. See J. Pfeffer, *Power in Organizations* (Boston: Pitman, 1981); H. Mintzberg, *Power in and around Organizations* (Englewood Cliffs, NJ: Prentice Hall, 1983). More recent scholars recognized that behavior is political or not depending on whether it is perceived by others as self-serving. From this definition, organizational politics benefit the politician, not the organization or coworkers. Yet, some scholars are returning to the view that organizational politics can be good or bad, suggesting that political tactics are just influence tactics with a different name. See G. R. Ferris and D. C. Treadway, "Politics in Organizations: History, Construct Specification, and Research Directions," in *Politics in Organizations: Theory and Research Considerations*, ed. G. R. Ferris and D. C. Treadway (New York: Routledge, 2012), 3–26; D. A. Lepisto and M. G. Pratt, "Politics in Perspective: On the Theoretical Challenges and Opportunities in Studying Organizational Politics," in *Politics in Organizations: Theory and Research Considerations*, ed. G. R. Ferris and D. C. Treadway (New York: Routledge, 2012), 67–98.

73. This famous quotation is attributed to both Nicolo Machiavelli and Sun-tzu. None of Machiavelli's five main books (translated) has any statement close to this quotation. Sun-tzu's book *Art of War* (translated) does not have this quotation either, but he makes a similar statement about spies: "Hence it is that with none in the whole army are more intimate relations to be maintained than with spies." See Sun-tzu, *The Art of War*, trans. L. Giles (Mineola, NY: Dover, 2002), 98.

74. K. M. Kacmar and R. A. Baron, "Organizational Politics: The State of the Field, Links to Related Processes, and an Agenda for Future Research," in *Research in Personnel and Human Resources Management*, ed. G. R. Ferris (Greenwich, CT: JAI Press, 1999), 1–39; E. Vigoda, "Stress-Related Aftermaths to Workplace Politics," *Journal of Organizational Behavior* 23, no. 5 (August 2002): 571–91. C. H. Chang, C. C. Rosen, and P. E. Levy, "The Relationship between Perceptions of Organizational Politics and Employee Attitudes, Strain, and Behavior: A Meta-Analytic Examination," *Academy of Management Journal* 52, no. 4 (2009): 779–801. The quotation is from M. Landry, "Navigating the Political Minefield," *PM Network*, March 2013, 38–43.

75. L. Hull, "Covert War in the Workplace . . . over the Holiday Rota," *Mail Online*, August 7, 2013; "Office Wars: Tis the Season to Be Spiteful," *Officebroker Blog*, 2013, www.officebroker.com/blog/.

76. C. Hardy, *Strategies for Retrenchment and Turnaround: The Politics of Survival* (Berlin: Walter de Gruyter, 1990), chap. 14; G. R. Ferris et al., "Perceptions of Organizational Politics: Prediction, Stress-Related Implications, and Outcomes," *Human Relations* 49 (1996): 233–63; M. C. Andrews and K. M. Kacmar, "Discriminating among Organizational Politics, Justice, and Support," *Journal of Organizational Behavior* 22 (2001): 347–66.

77. S. Blazejewski and W. Dorow, "Managing Organizational Politics for Radical Change: The Case of Beiersdorf-Lechia S.A., Poznan," *Journal of World Business* 38 (2003): 204–23.

78. Robert Walters Australia, *Robert Walters Employee Insights Newsletter* (Sydney: Robert Walters, August 2012); CareerBuilder, "More Than One-Third of Workers Discuss Politics at Work," news release (Chicago: CareerBuilder, March 1, 2012); "Wasting Time at Work 2012," salary.com, 2012, www.salary.com/wasting-time-at-work-2012/slide/11/ (accessed May 28, 2014); "Nearly 70% Experience 'Workplace Politics': Poll" (Taiwan: Focus Taiwan News Channel, September 30, 2013), http://focustaiwan.tw/news/asoc/201309300033.aspx (accessed May 28, 2014); CareerBuilder, "New CareerBuilder Study Explores the Perks and Pitfalls of Working in a Desk Job vs. a Non-Desk Job," news release (Chicago: CareerBuilder, May 22, 2014).

79. L. W. Porter, R. W. Allen, and H. L. Angle, "The Politics of Upward Influence in Organizations," *Research in Organizational Behavior* 3 (1981): 120–22; R. J. House, "Power and Personality in Complex Organizations," *Research in Organizational Behavior* 10 (1988): 305–57.

80. R. Christie and F. Geis, *Studies in Machiavellianism* (New York: Academic Press, 1970); S. R. Kessler et al., "Re-Examining Machiavelli: A Three-Dimensional Model of Machiavellianism in the Workplace," *Journal of Applied Social Psychology* 40, no. 8 (2010): 1868–96; E. O'Boyle et al., "A Meta-Analysis of the Dark Triad and Work Behavior: A Social Exchange Perspective," *Journal of Applied Psychology* 97, no. 3 (2012): 557–79.

10 | Conflict and Negotiation in the Workplace

Learning Objectives

After you read this chapter, you should be able to:

LO10-1 Define conflict and debate its positive and negative consequences in the workplace.

LO10-2 Distinguish task from relationship conflict and describe three strategies to minimize relationship conflict during task conflict episodes.

LO10-3 Diagram the conflict process model and describe six structural sources of conflict in organizations.

LO10-4 Outline the five conflict-handling styles and discuss the circumstances in which each would be most appropriate.

LO10-5 Apply the six structural approaches to conflict management and describe the three types of third-party dispute resolution.

LO10-6 Discuss activities in the negotiation preparation, process, and setting that improve negotiation effectiveness.

eam decision making at Amazon.com is not a casual social gathering. "There's an incredible amount of challenging the other person," admits a former senior market researcher at the online retailer. "You want to have absolute certainty about what you are saying." In fact, one of Amazon's principles states that leaders should "respectfully challenge decisions when they disagree, even when doing so is uncomfortable or exhausting." Another Amazon executive explains that "it would certainly be much easier and socially cohesive to just compromise and not debate, but that may lead to the wrong decision."

Some observers and employees say that by encouraging employees to challenge each other, Amazon is unnecessarily escalating emotional conflict that can get personal (called *relationship conflict*). However, others counter that Amazon discourages relationship conflict, pointing out that "*respectfully* challenge" means focusing on the problem, not the person. "We debate politely and respectfully, and you are given constructive feedback to course-correct if you are rude or disrespectful," says a middle management engineer.[1]

The current debate about Amazon's practice of encouraging "respectful" debate highlights the reality that conflict can be good or bad, depending on how it is done. The challenge is to enable beneficial conflict and suppress dysfunctional conflict. We begin this chapter by defining conflict and discussing the age-old question: Is conflict good or bad? Next, we look at the conflict process and examine in detail the main factors that cause or amplify conflict. The five styles of handling conflict are then described, including the contingencies of conflict handling as well as gender and cross-cultural differences. This is followed by discussion of the most important structural approaches to conflict resolution. Next, we look at the role of managers and others in third-party conflict resolution. The final section of this chapter reviews key issues in negotiating conflict resolution.

LO10-1 Define conflict and debate its positive and negative consequences in the workplace.

THE MEANING AND CONSEQUENCES OF CONFLICT

Conflict is a fact of life in organizations. Companies are continuously adapting to their external environment, yet there is no clear road map on what changes are best. Employees disagree on the direction or form of change in individual behavior, work unit activities, and organizational-level adaptations. These conflict episodes occur because of clashing work goals, divergent personal values and experiences, and a variety of other reasons that we discuss in this chapter.

Conflict is a process in which one party perceives that its interests are being opposed or negatively affected by another party.[2] It may occur when one party obstructs another's goals in some way, or just from one party's perception that the other party is going to do so. Conflict is ultimately based on perceptions; it exists whenever one party *believes* that another might obstruct its efforts, regardless of whether the other party actually intends to do so.

Is Conflict Good or Bad?

One of the oldest debates in organizational behavior is whether conflict is good or bad—or, more recently, what forms of conflict are good or bad—for organizations.[3] The dominant view over most of this time has been that conflict is dysfunctional.[4] The "conflict-is-bad" school of thought emphasizes that organizations work best through harmonious relations, and that employee–management conflict undermines organizational effectiveness. Even moderately low levels of disagreement tatter the fabric of workplace relations and sap energy

Conflict is ultimately based on perceptions; it exists whenever one party *believes* that another might obstruct its efforts, regardless of whether the other party actually intends to do so.
©fizkes/Shutterstock

from productive activities. Disagreement with one's supervisor, for example, wastes productive time, violates the hierarchy of command, and questions the efficient assignment of authority (where managers make the decisions and employees follow them).

Although the "conflict-is-bad" perspective is now considered too simplistic, conflict can indeed have negative consequences under some circumstances (see Exhibit 10.1).[5] Conflict has been criticized for reducing employee performance by consuming otherwise productive time. It is often stressful, which consumes personal energy and distracts employees from their work. It also increases job dissatisfaction, resulting in higher turnover and lower customer service.[6]

People who experience conflict also tend to reduce their information sharing and other forms of coordination with each other. Ironically, with less communication, the feuding parties are more likely to escalate their disagreement because each side relies increasingly on distorted perceptions

Benefits of Conflict In the 1920s, when most organizational scholars viewed conflict as inherently dysfunctional, a few experts argued that conflict can have positive outcomes.[7] But it wasn't until the 1970s that conflict management experts began to embrace the notion that some level of conflict can be beneficial.[8] They formed an "optimal conflict" perspective, which states that organizations are most effective when employees experience some level of conflict, but become less effective with high levels of conflict.[9]

What are the benefits of conflict? Conflict energizes people to debate issues and evaluate alternatives more thoroughly. They probe and test each other's way of thinking to better understand the underlying issues that need to be addressed. This discussion and debate tests the logic of arguments and encourages participants to reexamine their basic assumptions about the problem and its possible solution. It prevents individuals and teams from making inferior

> # Conflict is the gadfly of thought. It stirs us to observation and memory. It instigates to invention. It shocks us out of sheeplike passivity, and sets us at noting and contriving.[10]
>
> —John Dewey, educational philosopher/psychologist

and stereotypes of the other party. Conflict fuels organizational politics, such as motivating employees to find ways to undermine the credibility of their opponents. Finally, conflict among team members may undermine team cohesion and performance.

decisions and potentially helps them develop sounder and more creative solutions.[11]

A second potential benefit is that moderate levels of conflict prevent organizations from becoming nonresponsive to their external environment. Differences of opinion encourage employees to engage in active thinking, and this often involves ongoing questioning and vigilance about how the organization can be more closely aligned with its customers, suppliers, and other stakeholders.[12] A third benefit of conflict occurs when team members have a dispute or competition with external sources. This form of conflict represents an external challenge that potentially increases cohesion within the team (see Chapter 7). People are more motivated to work together when faced with an external threat, such as conflict with people outside the team.

Exhibit 10.1 Consequences of Workplace Conflict

Negative Consequences	Positive Consequences
• Lower performance	• Better decision making
• Higher stress, dissatisfaction, and turnover	—Tests logic of arguments
• Less information sharing and coordination	—Questions assumptions
• Increased organizational politics	• More responsive to changing environment
• Wasted resources	• Stronger team cohesion (conflict between the team and outside opponents)
• Weakened team cohesion (conflict among team members)	

LO10-2 Distinguish task from relationship conflict and describe three strategies to minimize relationship conflict during task conflict episodes.

THE EMERGING VIEW: TASK AND RELATIONSHIP CONFLICT

The "optimal conflict" perspective remains popular and may be true in some respects; too much of any conflict is probably dysfunctional. However, the emerging school of thought is that there are various types of conflict with different consequences. The two dominant types are task conflict and relationship conflict.[13]

Task Conflict

Task conflict (also called *constructive conflict*) occurs when people focus their discussion around the issue (i.e., the "task") while showing respect for people with other points of view. We view task conflict as an umbrella term for disagreements about the task or decision, including what task should be performed, how should it be done, and who should perform the various task roles.[14] This type of conflict debates the various alternatives and

questioning the competence of the people who introduce or support that idea. It also occurs when someone uses status to defend a position ("My suggestion is better because I have the most experience!") because status-based arguments inherently undermine the worth of others in the debate. Relationship conflict even occurs when someone is abrasive or assertive to the extent that the behavior demeans others in the conversation. For example, relationship conflict can occur when a manager bangs his or her fist on the desk while making a logical argument; the physical action implies that the speaker has more power and the followers need harsh signals to get their attention.

Relationship conflict is dysfunctional because it threatens self-esteem, self-enhancement, and self-verification processes (see Chapter 3). It usually triggers defense mechanisms and a competitive orientation between the parties. Relationship conflict also reduces mutual trust because it emphasizes interpersonal differences that weaken any bond that exists between the parties.[17] Relationship conflict escalates more easily than task conflict because the adversaries become less motivated to communicate and share information, making it more difficult for them to discover common

> Task conflict keeps the debate focused on the issue and avoids any attention to the competence or power of the participants.

arguments so they can be clarified, redesigned, and tested for logical soundness. The focus is on the assumptions and logical foundation of the ideas presented, not on the characteristics of the people who presented them. In other words, task conflict keeps the debate focused on the issue and avoids any attention to the competence or power of the participants.

Research indicates that task conflict tends to produce the beneficial outcomes described earlier, particularly better decision making.[15] However, there is increasing evidence of an upper limit to the beneficial intensity of any disagreement, above which it would be difficult to remain constructive. In other words, there is likely an optimal level of task conflict.[16]

Relationship Conflict

Whereas task conflict focuses on the issues, **relationship conflict** focuses on characteristics of the people in the dispute. This type of conflict occurs when someone tries to dismiss an idea by

ground and ultimately resolve the conflict. Instead, they rely increasingly on distorted perceptions and stereotypes, which tend to reinforce their perceptions of threat.

Separating Task from Relationship Conflict

From our discussion so far, the logical recommendation is for organizations to encourage task conflict and minimize relationship conflict. This idea sounds good in theory, but separating these two types of conflict isn't easy in practice. Research indicates that we experience some degree of relationship conflict whenever we are engaged in constructive debate.[18] No matter how diplomatically someone questions our ideas and actions, he or she potentially threatens our self-esteem and our public image, which usually triggers our drive to defend. The stronger the level of debate and the more the issue is tied to our self-view, the

People experience some degree of relationship conflict whenever they engage in constructive debate, but relationship conflict can be minimized through team-level emotional intelligence, cohesion, and supportive norms.
©ESB Basic/Shutterstock

more likely that task conflict will evolve into (or mix with) relationship conflict. Fortunately, three conditions potentially minimize the level of relationship conflict during task conflict episodes.[19]

- *Emotional intelligence and emotional stability.* Relationship conflict is less likely to occur, or is less likely to escalate, when team members have high levels of emotional intelligence and its associated personality characteristics: emotional stability.[20] Employees with higher emotional intelligence and stability are better able to regulate their emotions during debate, which reduces the risk of escalating perceptions of interpersonal hostility. They are also more likely to view a coworker's emotional reaction as valuable information about that person's needs and expectations, rather than as a personal attack.

- *Cohesive team.* Relationship conflict is suppressed when the conflict occurs within a highly cohesive team. The longer people work together, get to know each other, and develop mutual trust, the more latitude they give to each other to show emotions without being personally offended. This might explain why task conflict is more effective in top management teams than in teams of more junior staff.[21] Strong cohesion also allows each person to know about and anticipate the behaviors and emotions of his or her teammates. Another benefit is that cohesion produces a stronger social identity with the group, so team members are motivated to avoid escalating relationship conflict during otherwise emotionally turbulent discussions.

- *Supportive team norms.* Various team norms can hold relationship conflict at bay during task-focused debate. When team norms encourage openness, for instance, team members learn to appreciate honest dialogue without personally reacting to any emotional display during the disagreements.[22] Other norms might discourage team members from displaying negative emotions toward coworkers. Team norms also encourage tactics that diffuse relationship conflict when it first appears. For instance, research has found that teams with low relationship conflict use humor to maintain positive group emotions, which offsets negative feelings team members might develop toward some coworkers during debate.

LO10-3 Diagram the conflict process model and describe six structural sources of conflict in organizations.

CONFLICT PROCESS MODEL

Now that we have outlined the history and current perspectives of conflict and its outcomes, let's look at the model of the conflict process, shown in Exhibit 10.2.[23] This model begins with the sources of conflict, which we will describe in the next section. At some point, the sources of conflict lead one or both

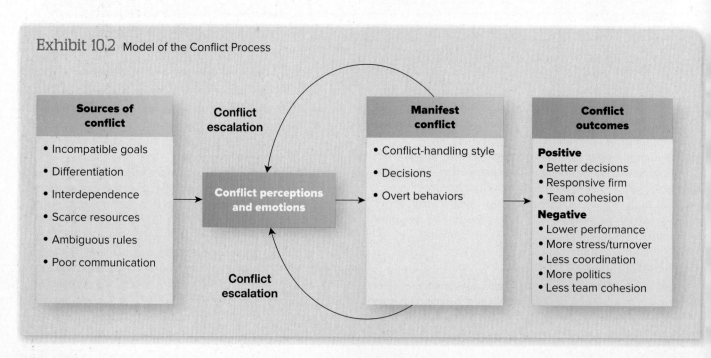

Exhibit 10.2 Model of the Conflict Process

Sources of conflict	Conflict escalation		Manifest conflict	Conflict outcomes
• Incompatible goals • Differentiation • Interdependence • Scarce resources • Ambiguous rules • Poor communication	Conflict perceptions and emotions		• Conflict-handling style • Decisions • Overt behaviors	**Positive** • Better decisions • Responsive firm • Team cohesion **Negative** • Lower performance • More stress/turnover • Less coordination • More politics • Less team cohesion
	Conflict escalation			

parties to perceive that conflict exists. They become aware that one party's statements and actions are incompatible with their own goals or beliefs. These perceptions usually interact with emotions experienced about the conflict.[24]

Conflict perceptions and emotions produce manifest conflict—the decisions and behaviors of one party toward the other. These *conflict episodes* may range from subtle nonverbal behaviors to warlike aggression. Particularly when people experience high levels of conflict-generated emotions, they have difficulty finding the words and expressions that communicate effectively without further irritating the relationship.[25] Conflict is also behaviorally revealed by the style each side uses to resolve the conflict. Some people tend to avoid the conflict whereas others try to defeat those with opposing views. We discuss different conflict handling styles later in this chapter.

Exhibit 10.2 shows arrows looping back from manifest conflict to conflict perceptions and emotions. These arrows illustrate that the conflict process is really a series of episodes that potentially cycle into conflict escalation.[26] It doesn't take much to start this conflict cycle—just an inappropriate comment, a misunderstanding, or an action that lacks diplomacy. These behaviors cause the other party to perceive that conflict exists. Even if the first party did not intend to demonstrate conflict, the second party's response may create that perception.

People experience conflict because their different training, values, beliefs, and experiences (differentiation) produce divergent beliefs about the best way to achieve their common goals.
©Barbara Penoyar/Getty Images

STRUCTURAL SOURCES OF CONFLICT IN ORGANIZATIONS

The conflict model starts with the sources of conflict, so we need to understand these sources to effectively diagnose conflict episodes and subsequently resolve the conflict or occasionally to generate conflict where it is lacking. The six main conditions that cause conflict in organizational settings are incompatible goals, differentiation, interdependence, scarce resources, ambiguous rules, and communication problems.

Incompatible Goals

Goal incompatibility occurs when the goals of one person or department seem to interfere with another person's or department's goals.[27] For example, the production department strives for cost-efficiency by scheduling long production runs whereas the sales team emphasizes customer service by delivering the client's product as quickly as possible. If the company runs out of a particular product, the production team would prefer to have clients wait until the next production run. This infuriates sales representatives, who would rather change production quickly to satisfy consumer demand.

Differentiation

Another source of conflict is differentiation—differences among people and work units regarding their training, values, beliefs, and experiences. Differentiation can be distinguished from goal incompatibility; two people or departments may agree on a common goal (serving customers better) but have different beliefs about how to achieve that goal (e.g., standardize employee behavior versus give employees autonomy in customer interactions). Differentiation produces the classic tension between employees from two companies brought together through a merger.[28] Even when people from both companies want the integrated organization to succeed, they fight over the "right way" to do things because of their unique experiences in the separate companies.

Differentiation is also usually a factor in intergenerational conflict. Younger and older employees have different needs, different expectations, and different workplace practices, which sometimes produce conflicting preferences and actions. Studies suggest that these intergenerational differences occur because people develop social identities around technological

> Every generation needs a new revolution.[30]
> —Attributed to Thomas Jefferson, American Founding Father and third president

developments and other pivotal social events that are unique to their era.[29]

Interdependence

All conflict is caused to some extent by interdependence because conflict exists only when one party perceives that its interests are being opposed or negatively affected by another party. Task interdependence refers to the extent to which employees must share materials, information, or expertise to perform their jobs (see Chapter 7). Conflict is inherently about relationships because people and work units are affected by others only when they have some level of interdependence.

The risk of conflict increases with the level of interdependence.[31] Employees usually have the lowest risk of conflict when working with others in a pooled interdependence relationship. Pooled interdependence occurs where individuals operate independently except for reliance on a common resource or authority. The potential for conflict is higher in sequential interdependence work relationships, such as an assembly line. The highest risk of conflict tends to occur in reciprocal interdependence situations. With reciprocal interdependence, employees have high mutual dependence on each other as well as higher centrality. Consequently, relationships with reciprocal interdependence have the strongest and most immediate risk of interfering with each other's objectives.

Scarce Resources

Resource scarcity generates conflict because each person or unit requiring the same resource necessarily undermines others who also need that resource to fulfill their goals. Most labor strikes, for instance, occur because there aren't enough financial and other resources for employees and company owners to each receive the outcomes they seek, such as higher pay (employees) and higher investment returns (stockholders). Budget deliberations within organizations also produce conflict because there aren't enough funds to satisfy the goals of each work unit. The more resources one group receives, the fewer resources other groups will receive. Fortunately, these interests aren't perfectly opposing in complex negotiations, but limited resources are typically a major source of friction.

Ambiguous Rules

Ambiguous rules—or the complete lack of rules—breed conflict. This occurs because uncertainty increases the risk that one party intends to interfere with the other party's goals. Ambiguity also encourages political tactics and, in some cases, employees enter a free-for-all battle to win decisions in their favor. This explains why conflict is more common during mergers and acquisitions. Employees from both companies have conflicting practices and values, and few rules have developed to minimize the maneuvering for power and resources.[32] When clear rules exist, on the other hand, employees know what to expect from each other and have agreed to abide by those rules.

Ambiguous rules or the complete lack of rules breeds conflict because uncertainty increases the risk that one party intends to interfere with the other party's goals.
©T.Dallas/Shutterstock

Communication Problems

Conflict often occurs due to the lack of opportunity, ability, or motivation to communicate effectively. Let's look at each of these causes. First, when two parties lack the opportunity to communicate, they tend to rely more on stereotypes to understand the other party in the conflict. Unfortunately, stereotypes are sufficiently subjective that emotions can negatively distort the meaning of an opponent's actions, thereby escalating perceptions of conflict. Second, some people lack the necessary skills to communicate in a diplomatic, nonconfrontational manner. When one party communicates its disagreement arrogantly, opponents are more likely to heighten their perception of the conflict. This may lead opponents to reciprocate with a similar response, which further escalates the conflict.[33]

A third problem is that relationship conflict is uncomfortable, so people are less motivated to communicate with others in a disagreement. Unfortunately, less communication can further escalate the conflict because each side has less accurate information about the other side's intentions. To fill in the missing pieces, they rely on distorted images and stereotypes of the other party. Perceptions are further distorted because people in conflict situations tend to engage in more differentiation with those who are unlike themselves (see Chapter 3). This differentiation creates a more positive self-concept and a more negative image of the opponent. We begin to see competitors less favorably so our self-concept remains positive during these conflict episodes.[34]

Flashpoints of Conflict in the Workplace[35]

33% of 617 American and 1,007 UK office employees surveyed say that miscommunication and lack of communication are the most common sources of conflict with other departments (less than 1% difference between results in these two countries).

48% of 1,000 Australian and New Zealand professionals surveyed say they have experienced conflict caused by intergenerational differences (most often due to differing expectations about the company's values and culture).

44% of 2,195 UK employees say the most serious recent conflict incident focused on differences in personality or styles of working.

56% of 427 working Americans surveyed identify personality clashes as a major source of conflict (highest source).

23% of 617 American and 1,007 UK office employees surveyed say that conflicting priorities are the most common sources of conflict with other departments (same percent within each country).

10% of 617 American office employees say they don't experience conflict with any department, group, or team in their organization (12% of 1,007 UK employees say the same).

©donskarpo/Shutterstock

respond to perceived and felt conflict through various conflict-handling strategies. Follett's original list was expanded and refined over the years into the five-category model shown in Exhibit 10.3. This model recognizes that how people respond behaviorally to a conflict situation depends on the relative importance they place on maximizing outcomes for themselves and for the other party.[36]

- *Problem solving*. Problem solving tries to find a solution that is beneficial for both parties. This is known as the **win–win orientation** because people using this style believe the resources at stake are expandable rather than fixed if the parties work together to find a creative solution. Information sharing is an important feature of this style because both parties collaborate to identify common ground and potential solutions that satisfy everyone involved.

- *Forcing*. Forcing tries to win the conflict at the other's expense. People who use this style typically have a **win–lose orientation**—they believe the parties are drawing from a fixed pie, so the more one party receives, the less the other party will receive. Consequently, this style relies on assertiveness and other hard influence tactics (see Chapter 9) to get one's own way.

- *Avoiding*. Avoiding tries to smooth over or evade conflict situations altogether. A common avoidance strategy is to steer clear of the coworkers associated with the conflict. A second avoidance strategy is to minimize discussion of the sensitive topic when interacting with the other person in the conflict. Notice from these examples that avoidance does not necessarily mean that we have a low concern for both one's own and the other party's interests. We might be very concerned about the issue but conclude that avoidance is the best solution, at least in the short term.[37]

LO10-4 Outline the five conflict-handling styles and discuss the circumstances in which each would be most appropriate.

INTERPERSONAL CONFLICT-HANDLING STYLES

The six sources of conflict lead to conflict perceptions and emotions that, in turn, motivate people to respond in some way to the conflict. More than 70 years ago, organizational behavior pioneer Mary Parker Follett observed that people

> People who use the forcing style typically have a win-lose orientation—they believe the parties are drawing from a fixed pie, so the more one party receives, the less the other party will receive.

Exhibit 10.3 Interpersonal Conflict-Handling Styles

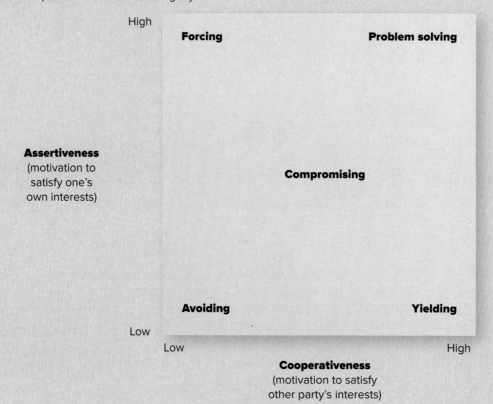

Source: C. K. W. de Dreu, A. Evers, B. Beersma, E. S. Kluwer and A. Nauta, "A Theory-Based Measure of Conflict Management Strategies in the Workplace," *Journal of Organizational Behavior* 22 (2001): 645–68. Reprinted with permission of John Wiley & Sons, Inc.

- *Yielding.* Yielding involves giving in completely to the other side's wishes, or at least cooperating with little or no attention to your own interests. This style involves making unilateral concessions and unconditional promises, as well as offering help with no expectation of reciprocal help.

- *Compromising.* Compromising involves looking for a position in which your losses are offset by equally valued gains. It involves actively searching for a middle ground between the interests of the two parties. Compromising also is associated with matching the other party's concessions and making conditional offers ("If you do X, I'll do Y.").

Choosing the Best Conflict-Handling Style

Chances are that you prefer one or two conflict-handling styles more than the others. You might typically engage in avoiding or yielding because disagreement makes you feel uncomfortable and is contrary to your self-view as someone who likes to get along with everyone. Or perhaps you prefer the compromising and forcing strategies because they reflect your strong need for achievement and to control your environment. People usually gravitate toward one or two conflict-handling styles that match their personality, personal and cultural values, and past experience.[38] However, the best style depends on the situation, so we need to understand and develop the capacity to use any of the five styles for the appropriate occasions.[39] The contingencies, as well as problems with using each conflict-handling style, are outlined in Exhibit 10.4.

Exhibit 10.4 Conflict-Handling Style Contingencies and Problems

Conflict-Handling Style	Preferred Style When . . .	Problems with this Style
Problem solving	• Interests are not perfectly opposing (i.e., not pure win–lose) • Parties have trust, openness, and time to share information • Issues are complex	• Sharing information that the other party might use to his or her advantage
Forcing	• You have a deep conviction about your position (e.g., believe other person's behavior is unethical) • Dispute requires a quick solution • Other party would take advantage of more cooperative strategies	• Highest risk of relationship conflict • May damage long-term relations, reducing future problem solving
Avoiding	• Conflict has become too emotionally charged • Cost of trying to resolve the conflict outweighs the benefits	• Doesn't usually resolve the conflict • May increase other party's frustration
Yielding	• Other party has substantially more power • Issue is much less important to you than to the other party • The value and logic of your position aren't as clear	• Increases other party's expectations in future conflict episodes
Compromising	• Parties have equal power • Time pressure to resolve the conflict • Parties lack trust/openness for problem solving	• Suboptimal solution where mutual gains are possible

Problem solving is widely recognized as the preferred conflict-handling style, whenever possible, because it is the best strategy to guide the parties toward a win–win solution. In addition, the problem-solving style tends to improve long-term relationships, reduce stress, and minimize emotional defensiveness and other indications of relationship conflict.[40] This style works best when there are opportunities for mutual gains, such as when the conflict is complex with multiple elements.

The problem-solving style is not optimal in all situations, however. If the conflict is simple and perfectly opposing (each party wants more of a single fixed pie), then the problem-solving style will waste time and increase frustration. It also takes more time and requires a fairly high degree of trust because there is a risk that the other party will take advantage of the information you have openly shared. The problem-solving style can be stressful and

The problem-solving style of conflict handling is less effective when the conflict is simple and perfectly opposing (each party wants more of a single fixed pie).
©Pandora Studio/Shutterstock

difficult when people experience strong feelings of conflict, likely because these negative emotions undermine trust in the other party.[41]

The conflict-avoidance style is often ineffective because it doesn't resolve the conflict and may increase the other party's frustration. However, avoiding may be the best strategy where conflict has become emotionally charged or where conflict resolution would cost more than its benefits.[42] The forcing style is usually inappropriate because it frequently generates relationship conflict more quickly or intensely than other conflict-handling styles. However, forcing may be necessary when you know you are correct (e.g., the other party's position is unethical or based on obviously flawed logic), the dispute requires a quick solution, or the other party would take advantage of a more cooperative conflict-handling style.

The yielding style may be appropriate when the other party has substantially more power, the issue is not as important to

> # The more arguments you win, the fewer friends you will have.[43]
> —Unknown source, popular adage since late 1800s

you as to the other party, and you aren't confident that your position has superior logical or ethical justification.[44] On the other hand, yielding behaviors may give the other side unrealistically high expectations, thereby motivating them to seek more from you in the future. In the long run, yielding may produce more conflict, rather than resolve it. "Raised voices, red faces, and table thumping is a far less dysfunctional way of challenging each other than withdrawal, passivity and sullen acceptance," explains one conflict management consultant. "It doesn't mean that people agree with you: they just take their misgivings underground and spread them throughout the organization, which has a corrosive effect."[45]

The compromising style may be best when the problem-solving approach offers little hope for mutual gain, both parties have equal power, and both are under time pressure to settle their differences. However, we rarely know whether the parties have perfectly opposing interests, yet the compromise approach assumes this win–lose orientation. Therefore, entering a conflict with the compromising style may cause the parties to overlook better solutions because they have not attempted to share enough information and creatively look for win–win alternatives.

Cultural and Gender Differences in Conflict-Handling Styles

Cultural values and norms influence the conflict-handling style used most often in a society, so they also represent an important contingency when choosing the preferred conflict-handling approach in that culture. For example, people who frequently use the conflict avoidance style might have more problems in cultures where the forcing style is common.[47]

Men and women also rely on different conflict-handling styles to some degree.[48] The clearest difference is that men are more likely than women to use the forcing style, whether as managers or nonmanagement employees. Female managers are more likely than male managers to use the avoiding style, whereas this difference is less pronounced between female and male nonmanagement employees. The male preference for forcing has a logical foundation. Compared to men, women pay more attention to the relationship between the parties, so their preferred style tries to protect the relationship. This is apparent in less use of the forcing and more use of the avoiding styles of conflict handling. Women are also slightly more likely than men to use the compromising and yielding styles.

LO10-5 Apply the six structural approaches to conflict management and describe the three types of third-party dispute resolution.

STRUCTURAL APPROACHES TO CONFLICT MANAGEMENT

Conflict-handling styles describe how we approach the other party in a conflict situation. But conflict management also involves altering the underlying structural causes of potential conflict. The main structural approaches parallel the sources of conflict discussed earlier. These structural approaches include emphasizing superordinate goals, reducing differentiation, improving communication and understanding, reducing task interdependence, increasing resources, and clarifying rules and procedures.

Emphasizing Superordinate Goals

One of the oldest recommendations for resolving conflict is to refocus the parties' attention around superordinate goals and away from the conflicting subordinate goals.[49] **Superordinate goals** are goals that the conflicting employees or departments value and whose attainment requires the joint resources and effort of those parties.[50] These goals are called superordinate because they are higher-order aspirations such as the organization's strategic objectives rather than objectives specific to the individual or work unit. Research indicates that the most effective executive teams frame their

Steering Clear of Workplace Conflict[46]

37% of 616 American managers surveyed say they are uncomfortable giving direct performance feedback/criticism to their employees that they might respond badly to.

25% of 2,195 UK employees say the most common negative behavior resulting from recent conflict episodes was the refusal to work together or cooperate with each other.

46% of 1,554 Australian employees polled say they would rather seek a new job than deal with a workplace conflict.

20% of 926 American employees surveyed say they avoid some coworkers because of their political views (54% of employees say they avoid talking about politics at all with colleagues).

©Alhovik/Shutterstock

One of the oldest recommendations for resolving conflict is to refocus the parties' attention around superordinate goals and away from the conflicting subordinate goals.
©Pixtal/age fotostock

Reducing Differentiation

Differentiation—differences regarding training, values, beliefs, and experiences—was identified earlier as one of the main sources of workplace conflict. Therefore, reducing differentiation is a logical approach to reducing dysfunctional conflict. As people develop common experiences and beliefs, they become more motivated to coordinate activities and resolve their disputes through constructive discussion.[53] One way to reduce differentiation is to rotate key staff to different departments or regions throughout their career. This career development process develops common experiences around the entire company rather than within different areas. Another way to reduce differentiation is to have employees from different parts of the organization work together on important (and hopefully successful) projects. These projects become a common ground for otherwise diverse employee groups. A third strategy is to build and maintain a strong organizational culture. Employees have shared values and assumptions in a company with a strong culture, and Chapter 13 describes specific activities to support a strong culture.

Improving Communication and Mutual Understanding

A third way to resolve dysfunctional conflict is to give the conflicting parties more opportunities to communicate and understand each other. This recommendation applies two principles and practices introduced in Chapter 3: the Johari Window model and meaningful interaction. Although both were previously described as ways to improve self-awareness, they are equally valuable to improve other-awareness.

In the Johari Window process, individuals disclose more about themselves so others have a better understanding of the underlying causes of their behavior. A variation of Johari Window occurs in "lunch and learn" sessions, where employees in one functional area describe work and its challenges to co-workers in other areas. Meaningful interaction potentially improves mutual understanding through the contact hypothesis, which says that we develop a more person-specific and accurate understanding of others by working closely with them.[54]

Although communication and mutual understanding can work well, there are two important warnings. First, these interventions should be applied only where differentiation is sufficiently low or *after* differentiation has been reduced. If perceived differentiation remains high, attempts to manage conflict through dialogue might escalate rather than reduce relationship conflict. The reason is that when forced to interact with people who we believe are quite different and in conflict with us, we tend to select information that reinforces that view.[55]

The second warning is that people in collectivist and high power distance cultures are less comfortable with the practice of resolving differences through direct and open communication.[56] Recall that people in collectivist cultures prefer an avoidance conflict-handling style because it is the most consistent with harmony and face saving. Direct communication is a high-risk

decisions as superordinate goals that rise above each executive's departmental or divisional goals. Similarly, effective leaders reduce conflict through an inspirational vision that unifies employees and makes them less preoccupied with their subordinate goal differences.[51]

Suppose that marketing staff members want a new product released quickly, whereas engineers want more time to test and add new features. Leaders can potentially reduce this interdepartmental conflict by reminding both groups of the company's mission to serve customers, or by pointing out that competitors currently threaten the company's leadership in the industry. By increasing commitment to companywide goals (customer focus, competitiveness), engineering and marketing employees pay less attention to their competing departmental-level goals, which reduces their perceived conflict with each other. Superordinate goals also potentially reduce the problem of differentiation because they establish feelings of a shared social identity (work for the same company).[52]

A buffer reduces potential conflict by reducing the level of interdependence between two or more people or work units.
©auremar/123RF

strategy because it easily threatens the need to save face and maintain harmony.

Reducing Interdependence

Conflict occurs where people are dependent on each other, so another way to reduce dysfunctional conflict is to minimize the level of interdependence between the parties. Three ways to reduce interdependence among employees and work units are to create buffers, use integrators, and combine jobs.

- *Create buffers.* A buffer is any mechanism that loosens the coupling between two or more people or work units. This decoupling reduces the potential for conflict because the buffer reduces the effect of one party on the other. Building up inventories between people in an assembly line would be a buffer, for example, because each employee is less dependent in the short term on the previous person along that line.

- *Use integrators.* Integrators are employees who coordinate the activities of work units toward the completion of a shared task or project. For example, an individual might be responsible for coordinating the efforts of the research, production, advertising, and marketing departments in launching a new product line. Integrators reduce the amount of direct interaction required among diverse work units. Instead, work units communicate with each other indirectly through the integrator. Integrators rarely have direct authority over the departments they integrate, so they must rely on referent power and persuasion to manage conflict and accomplish the work.

- *Combine jobs.* Combining jobs is both a form of job enrichment and a way to reduce task interdependence. Consider a toaster assembly system where one person inserts the heating element, another adds the

sides, and so on. By combining these tasks so that each person assembles an entire toaster, the employees now have a pooled rather than sequential form of task interdependence and the likelihood of dysfunctional conflict is reduced.

Increasing Resources

Resource scarcity is a source of conflict, so increasing the amount of resources available would have the opposite effect. This might not be a feasible strategy for minimizing dysfunctional conflict due to the costs involved. However, these costs need to be compared against the costs of dysfunctional conflict due to the resource scarcity.

Clarifying Rules and Procedures

Conflicts that arise from ambiguous rules can be minimized by establishing rules and procedures. If two departments are fighting over the use of a new laboratory, a schedule might be established that allocates the lab exclusively to each team at certain times of the day or week.

third-party conflict resolution any attempt by a relatively neutral person to help conflicting parties resolve their differences

Exhibit 10.5 Types of Third-Party Intervention

High

| | Mediation | Inquisition |

Level of process control

Arbitration

Low

Low | High

Level of decision control

between the disputing parties. However, the parties make the final decision about how to resolve their differences. Thus, mediators have little or no control over the conflict resolution decision.[58]

Choosing the Best Third-Party Intervention Strategy

Team leaders, executives, and coworkers regularly intervene in workplace disputes. Sometimes they adopt a mediator role; other times they serve as arbitrators. Occasionally, they begin with one approach then switch to another. However, research suggests that managers and other people in positions of authority usually adopt an inquisitional approach whereby they dominate the intervention process as well as make a binding decision.[60]

Managers tend to rely on the inquisition approach because it is consistent with the decision-oriented nature of managerial jobs. This approach also gives them control over the conflict process and outcome and tends to resolve disputes efficiently. However, inquisition is usually the least effective third-party conflict resolution method in organizational settings.[61] One problem is that leaders who take an inquisitional role tend to collect limited information about the problem, so their imposed decision may produce an ineffective solution to the conflict. Another problem is that employees often view inquisitional procedures and outcomes as unfair because they have little control over this approach. In particular, the inquisitional approach potentially violates several practices required to support procedural justice (see Chapter 5).

THIRD-PARTY CONFLICT RESOLUTION

Most of this chapter has focused on people directly involved in a conflict, yet many disputes among employees and departments are resolved with the assistance of a manager. **Third-party conflict resolution** is any attempt by a relatively neutral person to help the parties resolve their differences. There are three main third-party dispute resolution activities: arbitration, inquisition, and mediation. These interventions can be classified by their level of control over the process and control over the decision (see Exhibit 10.5).[57]

- *Arbitration*—Arbitrators have high control over the final decision but low control over the process. Executives engage in this strategy by following previously agreed-upon rules of due process, listening to arguments from the disputing employees, and making a binding decision. Arbitration is applied as the final stage of grievances by unionized employees in many countries, but it also is increasingly applied to nonunion conflicts.

- *Inquisition*—Inquisitors control all discussion about the conflict. Like arbitrators, inquisitors have high decision control because they determine how to resolve the conflict. However, inquisitors also have high process control because they choose which information to examine and how to examine it, and they generally decide how the conflict resolution process will be handled.

- *Mediation*—Mediators have high control over the intervention process. In fact, their main purpose is to manage the process and context of interaction

Managers as Third-Party Conflict Handlers[59]

47% of 411 New Zealand employees surveyed say that they turn to their manager to help resolve a workplace conflict.

37% of 2,195 UK employees surveyed say they handle conflict by taking the matter to their manager and/or HR to resolve.

42% of 1,279 employees surveyed in the U.S. and several other countries say their leader sometimes or never handles workplace conflict effectively.

15% is the average percentage of work time that 2,200 chief financial officers say they spend intervening in employee disputes (compared with 18%, 18%, 13%, and 9%, when the same question was asked to a broader group of senior managers in 2011, 1996, 1991, and 1986, respectively).

©ATIC12/Getty Images

Which third-party intervention is most appropriate in organizations? The answer partly depends on the situation, such as the type of dispute, the relationship between the manager and employees, and cultural values such as power distance.[62] Also, any third-party approach has more favorable results when it applies the procedural justice practices described in Chapter 5.[63] But generally speaking, for everyday disagreements between two employees, the mediation approach is usually best because this gives employees more responsibility for resolving their own disputes. The third-party representative merely establishes an appropriate context for conflict resolution. Although not as efficient as other strategies, mediation potentially offers the highest level of employee satisfaction with the conflict process and outcomes.[64] When employees cannot resolve their differences through mediation, arbitration seems to work best because the predetermined rules of evidence and other processes create a higher sense of procedural fairness.[65] Arbitration also is preferred where the organization's goals should take priority over individual goals.

OB THEORY TO PRACTICE

Third-Party Conflict Resolution without Bosses

Employees at Morning Star Company can't rely on their boss to settle disagreements because there aren't any bosses at the California tomato processing company. Instead, those who can't resolve a conflict invite another coworker to mediate the situation and possibly recommend a solution. If anyone in the disagreement still isn't satisfied, then several colleagues form a panel to review and arbitrate the conflict. Almost all conflicts are resolved by this stage. But in rare instances, the matter can be brought to the attention of Morning Star's president, who either makes—or designates an arbitrator to make—a binding final decision. "When a panel of peers gets convened, people can see that the process is fair and reasonable," explains Morning Star founder Chris Rufer. "Everyone knows they have recourse."[66]

©flairmicro/123RF

RESOLVING CONFLICT THROUGH NEGOTIATION

Negotiation occurs whenever two or more conflicting parties attempt to resolve their divergent goals by redefining the terms of their interdependence. In other words, people negotiate when they think that discussion can produce a more satisfactory arrangement (at least for them) in their exchange of goods or services. This is not an obscure practice reserved for labor and management bosses when hammering out a collective agreement. Everyone negotiates, every day. Most of the time you don't even realize that you are in negotiations.

Negotiation is particularly evident in the workplace because employees work interdependently with each other. They negotiate with their supervisors over next month's work assignments, with customers over the sale and delivery schedules of their product, and with coworkers over when to have lunch. And yes, they occasionally negotiate with each other in labor disputes and collective agreements.

Distributive versus Integrative Approaches to Negotiation

Earlier in this chapter, we noted that people tend to view conflict in two opposing ways. They adopt a win–lose orientation when taking the view that one party necessarily loses when the other party gains. In negotiations, this is called the *distributive* approach because the negotiator believes those involved in the conflict must distribute portions from a fixed pie. The opposing view is a win–win orientation, known as the *integrative* or *mutual gains* approach to negotiations. This approach exists when negotiators believe the resources at stake are expandable rather than fixed if the parties work creatively together to find a solution.

Distributive negotiation is most common when the parties have only one item to resolve, such as product price or starting salary. Integrative negotiation is more common when multiple issues are open for discussion. Multiple issues provide greater opportunity for mutual gains because each issue or element in the negotiation has different value to each party. Consider the example of a buyer who wants to pay a low price for several dozen manufactured items from a seller but doesn't need the entire order at once and needs the payment schedule spread over time due to limited cash flow. The seller values a high price due to rising costs, but also values steady production. Through negotiation, the parties learn that spreading out the delivery schedule benefits both of them, and that the buyer would agree to a higher price if payments could be spread out with the delivery schedule.

Negotiators usually begin with a cautiously integrative approach to negotiations, but they sometimes shift to a distributive

Multiple issues provide greater opportunity for mutual gains (integrative negotiation) because each issue or element in the negotiation has different value to each party.
©Helder Almeida/123RF

approach as it becomes apparent that the parties have similar preferences for a limited number of items. Another factor is the individual's personality and past experience. Some people have a natural tendency to be competitive and think more distributively whereas others more frequently believe that conflicts have an integrative solution.

Preparing to Negotiate

Preparation is essential for successful negotiations. You can't resolve disagreements unless you know what you want, why you want it, and what power you have to get it. You also need to anticipate the other party for each of these factors.

Develop Goals and Understand Needs Successful negotiators consider the goals they want to achieve from the exchange as well as what needs they are trying to fulfill from those goals. The distinction between goals and needs is important because specific needs can be satisfied by different goals. For example, an employee might negotiate for a promotion (a goal), but what the employee really wants is more status and interesting work (underlying needs). Effective negotiators try to understand their own needs and avoid becoming locked into fixed goals. Focusing on needs enables negotiators to actively consider different proposals and opportunities, some of which could fulfill their needs better than their original negotiation goals. Preparation also includes anticipating the other party's goals and their underlying needs, based on available information before negotiation sessions begin.

Effective negotiators recognize that their goals consist of target points along a range: what they will initially request in the negotiations, what they want to achieve in the best possible situation, and what minimum acceptable result they will accept (see Exhibit 10.6).[67] The *initial offer point*—your opening offer to the other side—requires careful consideration because it can influence the negotiation outcome. If the initial offer is set higher—but not outrageously higher—than expected by the other party, it can anchor the negotiation at a higher point along the range by reframing the other party's perception of what is considered a "high" or "low" demand (see Chapter 6).[68] In other words, a high initial offer point can potentially move the outcome closer to your target point.

The *target point* is your realistic goal or expectation for a final agreement. This position must consider alternative strategies to achieve those objectives and test underlying assumptions about the situation.[69] Negotiators who set high, specific target points usually obtain better outcomes than those with low or vague target points. In this respect, a target point needs to possess the same characteristics as effective goal setting (see Chapter 5). Unfortunately, perceptual distortions cause inexperienced negotiators to form overly optimistic expectations, which can only be averted through careful reflection of the facts. The *resistance point* is the point beyond which you will make no further concessions. How do you determine the resistance point—the point beyond which you walk away from the negotiations? The answer

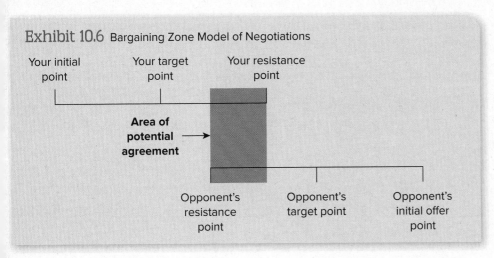

Exhibit 10.6 Bargaining Zone Model of Negotiations

Your initial point | Your target point | Your resistance point

Area of potential agreement

Opponent's resistance point | Opponent's target point | Opponent's initial offer point

requires thoughtful comparison of how your negotiation goals might be achieved through some other means—your BATNA.

Know Your BATNA and Power

BATNA is the acronym for the **best alternative to a negotiated agreement**. BATNA estimates your power in the negotiation because it represents the estimated cost to you of walking away from the relationship. If sources outside the current negotiation are willing to negotiate with you for the product or service you need, then you have a high BATNA because it would cost you very little to walk away from the current negotiation. Having more than one BATNA to a negotiation increases your power. A common problem, however, is that people tend to overestimate their BATNA. They wrongly believe there are plenty of other ways to achieve their objective rather than through this negotiation. Wise advice here is to actively investigate multiple alternatives, not just the option being negotiated.

Your power in the negotiation depends on the sources and contingencies of power discussed in Chapter 9. For example, you have more power to negotiate a better starting salary and job

The best alternative to a negotiated settlement (BATNA) estimates your power in the negotiation because it represents the estimated cost to you of walking away from the relationship.
©Ryan McVay/Stockbyte/Getty Images

conditions if you have valued skills and experience that few other people possess (high expertise with low substitutability), the employer knows that you possess these talents (high visibility), and the company will experience costs or lost opportunities fairly quickly if this position is not filled soon (high centrality). Not surprisingly, BATNA tends to be higher for those with favorable sources and contingencies of power because they would be in demand in the marketplace.

The Negotiation Process

The negotiation process is a complex human interaction that draws on many topics in this book, including perceptions, attitudes, motivation, decision making, and communication. The most important specific negotiation practices are to gather information, manage concessions, manage time, and build the relationship.

Gather Information Information is the cornerstone of effective negotiations.[70] In distributive situations, some types of information reveal the other party's resistance point. Information also can potentially transform distributive negotiations into integrative negotiations by discovering multiple dimensions that were not previously considered. For example, a simple negotiation over salary may reveal that the employee would prefer more performance-based pay and less fixed salary. Thus, mutual gains may be possible because there is now more

---

OB THEORY TO PRACTICE

Gathering Information in Negotiations

▶ Spend most of the negotiation time listening closely to the other party, including arguments, explanations, and issues they try to avoid discussing.

▶ Ask open-ended questions, including probe questions ("Tell me more about that"), to draw out details about the other party's needs and goals.

▶ Observe the opponent's nonverbal communication, such as how eager or reluctant he or she is to discuss specific topics, as subtle indicators of the opponent's motivation and needs.

▶ Summarize the information presented by the other side and ask for confirmation of what you said and clarification on specific points.

▶ Share information slowly to determine whether the other side will reciprocate.

▶ Communicate your inner thoughts and feelings (hopes and concerns) about what the other party has said, thereby encouraging the other party to help dissolve any concerns and affirm the foundations of hope.

than one variable to negotiate. The key practices for gathering information in negotiations are listening, asking, and cautiously volunteering information.

Manage Concessions Most of us think about making concessions when engaging in negotiations.[71] Successful negotiators actually make fewer concessions and each concession is smaller than those of average negotiators, particularly in distributive negotiations where both parties know the bargaining zone.[72] Even so, the process of making concessions is important to all parties. Concessions symbolize each party's motivation to bargain in good faith. Ultimately, concessions are necessary for the parties to move toward the area of agreement.

A key objective of concessions is to discover in the other party and communicate your own relative importance of each issue being negotiated. This occurs by presenting multi-issue concessions rather than just one element at a time.[73] You might offer a client a specific price, delivery date, and guarantee period, for example. The other party's counteroffer signals which of the multiple items are more and which are less important to them. Your subsequent concessions similarly signal how important each issue is to your group.

Concessions need to be clearly labeled as such and should be accompanied by an expectation that the other party will reciprocate. They also should be offered in installments because people experience more positive emotions from a few smaller concessions than from one large concession.[74] Generally, the best strategy is to be moderately tough and give just enough concessions to communicate sincerity and motivation to resolve the conflict.

Manage Time Negotiators tend to make more concessions as the deadline gets closer.[75] This can be a liability if you are under time pressure, or it can be an advantage if the other party alone is under time pressure. Negotiators with more power in the relationship sometimes apply time pressure through an "exploding offer" whereby they give the opponent a very short time to accept their offer.[76] These time-limited offers are frequently found in consumer sales ("on sale today only!") and in some job offers. They produce time pressure, which can motivate the other party to accept the offer and

> A key objective of concessions is to discover in the other party and communicate your own relative importance of each issue being negotiated.

forfeit the opportunity to explore their BATNA. Another time factor is that the more time someone has invested in the negotiation, the more committed he or she becomes to ensuring an agreement is reached. This commitment increases the tendency to make unwarranted concessions so that the negotiations do not fail.

Build the Relationship Building and maintaining trust is important in all negotiations.[77] In purely distributive negotiation situations, trust keeps the parties focused on the issue rather than personalities, motivates them to return to the bargaining table when negotiations stall, and encourages the parties to engage in future negotiations. Trust is also critical in integrative negotiations because it motivates the parties to share information and actively search for mutual gains.

How do you build trust in negotiations? One approach is to discover common backgrounds and interests, such as places you have lived, favorite hobbies and sports teams, and so forth. If there are substantial differences between the parties (age, gender, etc.), consider including team members who closely match the backgrounds of the other party. First impressions are also important. Recall from earlier chapters in this book that people attach emotions to incoming stimuli in a fraction of a second. Therefore, you need to be sensitive to your nonverbal cues, appearance, and initial statements.

Signaling trustworthiness also helps strengthen the relationship. We can do this by demonstrating that we are reliable, will keep our promises, and have shared goals and values with the other party. Trustworthiness also increases by developing a shared understanding of the negotiation process, including its norms and expectations about speed and timing.[78] Finally, relationship building demands emotional intelligence.[79] This includes managing the emotions you display to the other party, particularly avoiding an image of superiority, aggressiveness, or insensitivity. Emotional intelligence also involves managing the other party's emotions. We can use well-placed flattery, humor, and other methods to keep everyone in a good mood and to diffuse dysfunctional tension.[80]

The Negotiation Setting

The effectiveness of negotiating depends to some extent on the environment in which the negotiations occur. Location is an important situational characteristic. It is easier to negotiate on

Negotiators with more power in the relationship sometimes apply time pressure through an "exploding offer," whereby they give the opponent a very short time in which to accept their offer.
©gstockstudio/123RF

your own turf because you are familiar with the negotiating environment and are able to maintain comfortable routines.[81] Also, there is no need to cope with travel-related stress or depend on others for resources during the negotiation. Due to these strategic advantages of home turf, many negotiators agree to neutral territory.

The physical distance between the parties and formality of the setting can influence their orientation toward each other and the disputed issues. So can the seating arrangements. People who sit face-to-face are more likely to develop a win–lose orientation toward the conflict situation. In contrast, some negotiation groups deliberately intersperse participants around the table to convey a win–win orientation. Others arrange the seating so that both parties face a whiteboard, reflecting the notion that both parties face the same problem or issue.

Most negotiators have audiences—anyone with a vested interest in the negotiation outcomes, such as executives, other team members, or the general public. Negotiators tend to act differently when their audience observes the negotiation or has detailed information about the process, compared to situations in which the audience sees only the end results.[82] When the audience has direct surveillance over the proceedings, negotiators tend to be more competitive, less willing to make concessions, and more likely to engage in assertive tactics against the other party. This "hard-line" behavior shows the audience that the negotiator is working for their interests. With their audience watching, negotiators also have more interest in saving face.

Gender and Negotiation

When it comes to negotiation, women tend to have poorer economic outcomes than do men.[83] Women tend to set lower personal target points and are more likely to accept offers just above their resistance points. Men set high target points and push to get a deal as close to their target point as possible. Women also are less likely than men to use alternatives to improve their outcomes. One explanation for these differences is that women give higher priority than men to interpersonal relations in the exchange. This is consistent with why there are gender differences in conflict-handling styles, discussed earlier in this chapter. Giving more concessions and even avoiding the negotiation process altogether (accepting the salary offered when hired) are ways that women try to maintain good relations. This also is consistent with evidence that women have a stronger dislike of negotiation activities.

Differences also exist in how men and women are treated by the other negotiating party. Female negotiators have a significantly higher risk than men of being deceived by the other party and receiving less generous offers than men for the same job or product.[84] Furthermore, women who use effective negotiation tactics—such as making fewer and smaller concessions—are viewed less favorably by the opposing negotiator than when men use these tactics. This reaction likely occurs because some effective negotiation activities violate female stereotypes, so women are viewed as more aggressive than men doing exactly the same thing. The result is that the other negotiator becomes less trustful and engages in harder tactics.

Fortunately, women perform as well as men in negotiations when they receive training and gain experience. Women also negotiate well when the situation signals that negotiation is expected, such as when a job opening states that the salary is negotiable. Another factor that improves negotiation outcomes for women is how well they know the expected bargaining range. For example, women negotiate a better starting salary when they research the salary range for that position.

OB THEORY TO PRACTICE

Reducing the Gender Pay Gap by Teaching Women How to Negotiate

Susanne Smith (not her real name) was shocked to discover that two male coworkers earned almost double her salary. The Boston area web developer worried that confronting her boss about a pay raise would backfire, but she took that chance and was given a 20 percent increase (still well below her male coworkers). The experience made Smith angry with herself for accepting whatever salary was offered when hired whereas her male coworkers had negotiated a higher pay deal. "I was like the bargain-basement candidate that didn't bother to negotiate," she says.

Studies report that, compared to men, women negotiate less, have lower target points, and give more concessions. The City of Boston, the Women's Foundation of Montana, and other groups are addressing this source of gender pay gap by offering free negotiation workshops for women. "We know that women need some concrete skills and tools to take to the negotiation table," explains the head of Boston's Office of Women's Advancement.[85]

©Morsa/Digital Vision/Getty Images

Study Checklist

Connect® Management is available for *M Organizational Behavior.* Additional resources include:

✓ Interactive Applications:
- **Case Analysis:** Apply concepts within the context of a real-world situation.
- **Drag and Drop:** Work through an interactive example to test your knowledge of the concepts.
- **Video Case:** See management in action through interactive videos.

✓ **SmartBook™**—SmartBook is the first and only adaptive reading experience available today. Distinguishing what you know from what you don't, and honing in on concepts you are most likely to forget, SmartBook personalizes content for you in a continuously adapting reading experience. Reading is no longer a passive and linear experience, but an engaging and dynamic one where you are more likely to master and retain important concepts and go to class better prepared.

©Natthawat Jamnapa/123RF

Notes

1. G. Anders, "Inside Amazon's Idea Machine: How Bezos Decodes Customers," *Forbes*, April 23, 2012; J. Kantor and D. Streitfeld, "Amazon's Bruising, Thrilling Workplace," *The New York Times*, August 16, 2015; N. Ciubotariu, "An Amazonian's Response to 'Inside Amazon: Wrestling Big Ideas in a Bruising Workplace,'" *LinkedIn Pulse*, August 16, 2015, www.linkedin.com/pulse/amazonians-response-inside-amazon-wrestling-big-ideas-nick-ciubotariu.

2. J. A. Wall and R. R. Callister, "Conflict and Its Management," *Journal of Management* 21 (1995): 515-58; M. A. Rahim, *Managing Conflict in Organizations*, 4th ed. (New Brunswick, NJ: Transaction, 2011), 15-17; D. Tjosvold, A. S. H. Wong, and N. Y. F. Chen, "Constructively Managing Conflicts in Organizations," *Annual Review of Organizational Psychology and Organizational Behavior* 1, no. 1 (2014): 545-68.

3. For example, see R. R. Blake, H. A. Shepard, and J. S. Mouton, *Managing Intergroup Conflict in Industry* (Houston: Gulf, 1964); K. E. Boulding, "Organization and Conflict," *Conflict Resolution* 1, no. 2 (1957): 122-34; C. Argyris, "The Individual and Organization: Some Problems of Mutual Adjustment," *Administrative Science Quarterly* 2, no. 1 (1957): 1-24; L. Urwick, *The Elements of Administration*, 2nd ed. (London: Pitman, 1947).

4. M. A. Rahim, *Managing Conflict in Organizations,* 4th ed. (New Brunswick, NJ: Transaction, 2011), 15-17.

5. C. K. W. De Dreu and L. R. Weingart, "A Contingency Theory of Task Conflict and Performance in Groups and Organizational Teams," in *International Handbook of Organizational Teamwork and Cooperative Working*, ed. M. A. West, D. Tjosvold, and K. G. Smith (Chichester, UK: Wiley, 2003), 151-66; S. Rispens, "Benefits and Detrimental Effects of Conflict," in *Handbook of Conflict Management Research*, ed. O. B. Ayoko, N. M. Ashkanasy, and K. A. Jehn (Cheltenham, UK: Edward Elgar, 2014), 19-32.

6. F. R. C. de Wit, L. L. Greer, and K. A. Jehn, "The Paradox of Intragroup Conflict: A Meta-Analysis," *Journal of Applied Psychology* 97, no. 2 (2012): 360-90; L. L. Meier et al., "Relationship and Task Conflict at Work: Interactive Short-Term Effects on Angry Mood and Somatic Complaints,"*Journal of Occupational Health Psychology* 18, no. 2 (2013): 144-56.

7. M. P. Follett, "Constructive Conflict," in *Dynamic Administration: The Collected Papers of Mary Parker Follett*, ed. H. C. Metcalf and L. Urwick (Bath, UK: Management Publications Trust, 1941), 30-49.

8. Although the 1970s marked a point when the benefits of conflict became widely acknowledged, a few earlier writers also had expressed this view. See H. Assael, "Constructive Role of Interorganizational Conflict," *Administrative Science Quarterly* 14, no. 4 (1969): 573-82; L. A. Coser, *The Functions of Social Conflict* (New York: Free Press, 1956); J. A. Litterer, "Conflict in Organization: A Re-Examination," *Academy of Management Journal* 9 (1966): 178-86.

9. M. Duarte and G. Davies, "Testing the Conflict-Performance Assumption in Business-to-Business Relationships," *Industrial Marketing Management* 32 (2003): 91-99; M. A. Rahim, "Toward a Theory of Managing Organizational Conflict," *International Journal of Conflict Management* 13, no. 3 (2002): 206-35; J. D. Shaw et al., "A Contingency Model of Conflict and Team Effectiveness," *Journal of Applied Psychology* 96, no. 2 (2011): 391-400.

10. J. Dewey, *Human Nature and Conduct: An Introduction to Social Psychology* (New York: Holt, 1922), 300.

11. P. J. Carnevale, "Creativity in the Outcomes of Conflict," in *The Handbook of Conflict Resolution: Theory and Practice*, ed. M. Deutsch, P. T. Coleman, and E. C. Marcus (San Francisco: Jossey-Bass, 2006), 414-35; P. J. Boyle, D. Hanlon, and J. E. Russo, "The Value of Task Conflict to Group Decisions," *Journal of Behavioral Decision Making* 25, no. 3 (2012): 217-27.

12. K. M. Eisenhardt, J. L. Kahwajy, and L. J. Bourgeois III, "Conflict and Strategic Choice: How Top Management Teams Disagree," *California Management Review* 39 (1997): 42-62; T. Greitemeyer et al., "Information Sampling and Group Decision Making: The Effects of an Advocacy Decision Procedure and Task Experience," *Journal of Experimental Psychology: Applied* 12, no. 1 (2006): 31-42; U. Klocke, "How to Improve Decision Making in Small Groups: Effects of Dissent and Training Interventions," *Small Group Research* 38, no. 3 (2007): 437-68.

13. K. A. Jehn and C. Bendersky, "Intragroup Conflict in Organizations: A Contingency Perspective on the Conflict–Outcome Relationship," *Research in Organizational Behavior* 25 (2003): 187-242; L. H. Pelled, K. M. Eisenhardt, and K. R. Xin, "Exploring the Black Box: An Analysis of Work Group Diversity, Conflict, and Performance," *Administrative Science Quarterly* 44 (1999): 1-28; H. Guetzkow and J. Gyr, "An Analysis of Conflict in Decision-Making Groups," *Human Relations* 7,

no. 3 (1954): 367–82. The notion of two types of conflict dates back to Georg Simmel, who described two types of conflict: one with a personal and subjective goal, the other with an impersonal and objective quality. See L. A. Coser, *The Functions of Social Conflict* (New York: Free Press, 1956), 112. Contemporary scholars use various labels for task and relationship conflict. We have avoided the "cognitive" and "affective" conflict labels because cognitions and emotions are interconnected processes in all human activity. A third type of conflict, process conflict, is excluded due to limited research and doubts about its distinction from task conflict.

14. Conflict experts recently introduced *process conflict* to encompass the latter two parts—how the work should be done and who should perform the various task roles. But until evidence and measurement clarify this distinction and its importance, we will refer to "task conflict" to encompass all forms of task-related disagreement, including task content, process, roles, resources, and other activity-related issues. See K. A. Jehn, "Types of Conflict: The History and Future of Conflict Definitions and Typologies," in *Handbook of Conflict Management Research*, ed. O. B. Ayoko, N. M. Ashkanasy, and K. A. Jehn (Cheltenham, UK: Edward Elgar, 2014), 3–18.

15. F. R. C. de Wit, L. L. Greer, and K. A. Jehn, "The Paradox of Intragroup Conflict: A Meta-Analysis," *Journal of Applied Psychology* 97, no. 2 (2012): 360–90. Earlier meta-analyses reported either nonsignificant or somewhat negative correlations between task conflict and team outcomes. However, the recent meta-analysis and other writers point to several methodological problems with conflict research that explain the mixed findings. For a review, see M. L. Loughry and A. C. Amason, "Why Won't Task Conflict Cooperate? Deciphering Stubborn Results," *International Journal of Conflict Management* 25, no. 4 (2014): 333–58.

16. J. L. Farh, C. Lee, and C. I. C. Farh, "Task Conflict and Team Creativity: A Question of How Much and When," *Journal of Applied Psychology* 95, no. 6 (2010): 1173–80; G. Todorova, J. B. Bear, and L. R. Weingart, "Can Conflict Be Energizing? A Study of Task Conflict, Positive Emotions, and Job Satisfaction," *Journal of Applied Psychology* 99, no. 3 (2014): 451–67.

17. R. S. Lau and A. T. Cobb, "Understanding the Connections between Relationship Conflict and Performance: The Intervening Roles of Trust and Exchange," *Journal of Organizational Behavior* 31, no. 6 (2010): 898–917.

18. C. K. W. De Dreu and L. R. Weingart, "Task versus Relationship Conflict, Team Performance, and Team Member Satisfaction: A Meta-Analysis," *Journal of Applied Psychology* 88 (2003): 587–604; A. C. Mooney, P. J. Holahan, and A. C. Amason, "Don't Take It Personally: Exploring Cognitive Conflict as a Mediator of Affective Conflict," *Journal of Management Studies* 44, no. 5 (2007): 733–58; K. Choi and B. Cho, "Competing Hypotheses Analyses of the Associations between Group Task Conflict and Group Relationship Conflict," *Journal of Organizational Behavior* 32, no. 8 (2011): 1106–26.

19. J. X. Yang and K. W. Mossholder, "Decoupling Task and Relationship Conflict: The Role of Intergroup Emotional Processing," *Journal of Organizational Behavior* 25 (2004): 589–605; B. H. Bradley et al., "Ready to Rumble: How Team Personality Composition and Task Conflict Interact to Improve Performance," *Journal of Applied Psychology* 98, no. 2 (2013): 385–92; B. H. Bradley et al., "Reaping the Benefits of Task Conflict in Teams: The Critical Role of Team Psychological Safety Climate," *Journal of Applied Psychology* 97, no. 1 (2012): 151–58.

20. P. L. Curseu, S. Boros, and L. A. G. Oerlemans, "Task and Relationship Conflict in Short-Term and Long-Term Groups: The Critical Role of Emotion Regulation," *International Journal of Conflict Management* 23, no. 1 (2012): 97–107; A. Schlaerth, N. Ensari, and J. Christian, "A Meta-Analytical Review of the Relationship between Emotional Intelligence and Leaders' Constructive Conflict Management," *Group Processes & Intergroup Relations* 16, no. 1 (2013): 126–36.

21. F. R. C. de Wit, L. L. Greer, and K. A. Jehn, "The Paradox of Intragroup Conflict: A Meta-Analysis," *Journal of Applied Psychology* 97, no. 2 (March 2012): 360–90.

22. A. C. Amason and H. J. Sapienza, "The Effects of Top Management Team Size and Interaction Norms on Cognitive and Affective Conflict," *Journal of Management* 23, no. 4 (1997): 495–516. Supportive team norms likely include open-mindedness, which is known to improve team performance from conflict. See D. Tjosvold, A. S. H. Wong, and N. Y. F. Chen, "Constructively Managing Conflicts in Organizations," *Annual Review of Organizational Psychology and Organizational Behavior* 1, no. 1 (2014): 545–68.

23. L. Pondy, "Organizational Conflict: Concepts and Models," *Administrative Science Quarterly* 2 (1967): 296–320; K. W. Thomas, "Conflict and Negotiation Processes in Organizations," in *Handbook of Industrial and Organizational Psychology*, ed. M. D. Dunnette and L. M. Hough (Palo Alto, CA: Consulting Psychologists Press, 1992), 651–718.

24. H. Barki and J. Hartwick, "Conceptualizing the Construct of Interpersonal Conflict," *International Journal of Conflict Management* 15, no. 3 (2004): 216–44.

25. M. A. Von Glinow, D. L. Shapiro, and J. M. Brett, "Can We Talk, and Should We? Managing Emotional Conflict in Multicultural Teams," *Academy of Management Review* 29, no. 4 (2004): 578–92.

26. J. M. Brett, D. L. Shapiro, and A. L. Lytle, "Breaking the Bonds of Reciprocity in Negotiations," *Academy of Management Journal* 41 (1998): 410–24; G. E. Martin and T. J. Bergman, "The Dynamics of Behavioral Response to Conflict in the Workplace," *Journal of Occupational & Organizational Psychology* 69 (1996): 377–87.

27. R. E. Walton and J. M. Dutton, "The Management of Conflict: A Model and Review," *Administrative Science Quarterly* 14 (1969): 73–84; S. M. Schmidt and T. A. Kochan, "Conflict: Toward Conceptual Clarity," *Administrative Science Quarterly* 17, no. 3 (1972): 359–70.

28. R. M. Sarala, "The Impact of Cultural Differences and Acculturation Factors on Post-Acquisition Conflict," *Scandinavian Journal of Management* 26, no. 1 (2010): 38–56.

29. J. A. McMullin, T. Duerden Comeau, and E. Jovic, "Generational Affinities and Discourses of Difference: A Case Study of Highly Skilled Information Technology Workers," *British Journal of Sociology* 58, no. 2 (2007): 297–316.

30. Although this quotation is widely attributed to Thomas Jefferson, scholars suggest that the third U.S. president and a founding father of the nation did not make this statement. However, Jefferson did write that young people should bring about change. According to one source, the popular quotation is a derivation of Jefferson's statement in a letter to Colonel William S. Smith on November 13, 1787: "God forbid we should ever be 20 years without such a rebellion." T. Jefferson, *Memoir, Correspondence, and Miscellanies, from the Papers of Thomas Jefferson*, 2nd ed. (Boston: Gray and Bowen, 1830), 267. See http://wiki.monticello.org.

31. P. C. Earley and G. B. Northcraft, "Goal Setting, Resource Interdependence, and Conflict Management," in *Managing Conflict: An Interdisciplinary Approach*, ed. M. A. Rahim (New York: Praeger, 1989), 161–70; K. Jehn, "A Multimethod Examination of the Benefits and Detriments of Intragroup Conflict," *Administrative Science Quarterly* 40 (1995): 245–82.

32. A. Risberg, "Employee Experiences of Acquisition Processes," *Journal of World Business* 36 (2001): 58–84.

33. K. A. Jehn and C. Bendersky, "Intragroup Conflict in Organizations: A Contingency Perspective on the Conflict-Outcome Relationship," in *Research in Organizational Behavior: An Annual Series of Analytical Essays and Critical Reviews*, vol. 25, ed. R. M. Kramer and B. M. Staw (Oxford, UK: Elsevier Science Ltd., 2003), 187–242.

34. M. Hewstone, M. Rubin, and H. Willis, "Intergroup Bias," *Annual Review of Psychology* 53 (2002): 575–604; J. Jetten, R. Spears, and T. Postmes, "Intergroup Distinctiveness and Differentiation: A Meta-Analytic Integration," *Journal of Personality and Social Psychology* 86, no. 6 (2004): 862–79.

35. Workplace Options, "Office Taboos? Four out of Ten Americans Talk About Politics and Religion at Work," news release (Raleigh, NC: Workplace Options, August 19, 2013); *UK State of Work Survey: Executive Summary* (Basingstoke, UK: Workfront, November 2014); J. Gifford, *Getting under the Skin of Workplace Conflict: Tracing the Experiences of Employees* (London: Chartered Institute of Personnel and Development, April 2015); *Attracting, Retaining, and Developing Millennial Professionals*, Robert Walters Whitepaper (Sydney: R. Walters, September 2015); *The State of Enterprise Work* (Lehi, UT: Workfront, October 2015).

36. M. P. Follett, "Constructive Conflict," in *Dynamic Administration: The Collected Papers of Mary Parker Follett*, ed. H. C. Metcalf and L. Urwick, (Bath, UK: Management Publications Trust, 1941), 30–49; R. R. Blake, H. A. Shepard, and J. S. Mouton, *Managing Intergroup Conflict in Industry* (Houston: Gulf Publishing, 1964); T. Ruble and K. Thomas, "Support for a Two-Dimensional Model of Conflict Behavior," *Organizational Behavior and Human Performance* 16 (1976): 143–55; C. K. W. de Dreu et al., "A Theory-Based Measure of Conflict Management Strategies in the Workplace," *Journal of Organizational Behavior* 22 (2001): 645–68; D. Tjosvold, A. S. H. Wong, and N. Y. F. Chen, "Constructively Managing Conflicts in Organizations," *Annual Review of Organizational Psychology and Organizational Behavior* 1, no. 1 (2014): 545–68.

37. Q. Wang, E. L. Fink, and D. A. Cai, "The Effect of Conflict Goals on Avoidance Strategies: What Does Not Communicating Communicate?," *Human Communication Research* 38, no. 2 (2012): 222–52.

38. Several studies identify the antecedents of preferred conflict style. For example, see P. J. Moberg, "Linking Conflict Strategy to the Five-Factor Model: Theoretical and Empirical Foundations," *International Journal of Conflict Management* 12, no. 1 (2001): 47–68; H. A. Shih and E. Susanto, "Conflict Management Styles, Emotional Intelligence, and Job Performance in Public Organizations," *International Journal of Conflict Management* 21, no. 2 (2010): 147–68; J. E. Barbuto Jr., K. A. Phipps, and Y. Xu, "Testing Relationships between Personality, Conflict Styles and Effectiveness," *International Journal of Conflict Management* 21, no. 4 (2010): 434–47.

39. D. W. Johnson et al., "Effects of Cooperative, Competitive, and Individualistic Goal Structures on Achievement: A Meta-Analysis," *Psychological Bulletin* 89 (1981): 47–62; G. A. Callanan, C. D. Benzing, and D. F. Perri, "Choice of Conflict-Handling Strategy: A Matter of Context," *Journal of Psychology* 140, no. 3 (2006): 269–88; Z. Ma et al., "The Impact of Group-Oriented Values on Choice of Conflict Management Styles and Outcomes: An Empirical Study in Turkey," *International Journal of Human Resource Management* 23, no. 18 (2012): 3776–93.

40. X. M. Song, J. Xile, and B. Dyer, "Antecedents and Consequences of Marketing Managers' Conflict-Handling Behaviors," *Journal of Marketing* 64 (2000): 50–66; L. A. DeChurch, K. L. Hamilton, and C. Haas, "Effects of Conflict Management Strategies on Perceptions of Intragroup Conflict," *Group Dynamics* 11, no. 1 (2007): 66–78; D. G. Oore, M. P. Leiter, and D. E. LeBlanc, "Individual and Organizational Factors Promoting Successful Responses to Workplace Conflict," *Canadian Psychology* 56, no. 3 (2015): 301–10.

41. G. A. Chung-Yan and C. Moeller, "The Psychosocial Costs of Conflict Management Styles," *International Journal of Conflict Management* 21, no. 4 (2010): 382–99.

42. C. K. W. de Dreu and A. E. M. Van Vianen, "Managing Relationship Conflict and the Effectiveness of Organizational Teams," *Journal of Organizational Behavior* 22 (2001): 309–28; J. B. Bear, L. R. Weingart, and G. Todorova, "Gender and the Emotional Experience of Relationship Conflict: The Differential Effectiveness of Avoidant Conflict Management," *Negotiation and Conflict Management Research* 7, no. 4 (2014): 213–31.

43. Several variations of this quotation have appeared over the past century. The field of marketing has an even older version of this quotation—Win an argument and lose a sale (or customer). Marketing textbooks and trade publications cited it in the 1890s. The "friends" version of this quotation has occasionally been attributed to Edward Wood, 1st Earl of Halifax, but we could not verify this. In any event, the earliest marketing/sales version probably predates Lord Halifax's birth. Dale Carnegie surely popularized the idea behind the notion that winning arguments loses friends. The entire first chapter of Part 3 in his best-selling book *How to Win Friends and Influence People* (1936) is devoted to this topic: "You Can't Win an Argument." The version of the quotation cited here is published in E. Knowles, *Little Oxford Dictionary of Proverbs* (Oxford, UK: Oxford University Press, 2009), 21.

44. A. Ergeneli, S. M. Camgoz, and P. B. Karapinar, "The Relationship between Self-Efficacy and Conflict-Handling Styles in Terms of Relative Authority Positions of the Two Parties," *Social Behavior & Personality: An International Journal* 38, no. 1 (2010): 13–28.

45. J. Simms, "Blood in the Boardroom," *Director* (2009): 48.

46. "Half of Aussie Workers 'Would Rather Quit'," *Sydney Morning Herald*, August 22, 2012; J. Gifford, *Getting under the Skin of Workplace Conflict: Tracing the Experiences of Employees* (London: Chartered Institute of Personnel and Development, April 2015); Interact, "New Interact Report: Many Leaders Shrink from Straight Talk with Employees," news release (Charlotte, NC: Interact, February 2015); American Psychological Association, "1 in 4 Employees Negatively Affected by Political Talk at Work This Election Season, Finds New Survey," news release (Washington, DC: American Psychological Association, September 14, 2016).

47. C. H. Tinsley, "How Negotiators Get to Yes: Predicting the Constellation of Strategies Used across Cultures to Negotiate Conflict," *Journal of Applied Psychology* 86, no. 4 (2001): 583–93; J. L. Holt and C. J. DeVore, "Culture, Gender, Organizational Role, and Styles of Conflict Resolution: A Meta-Analysis," *International Journal of Intercultural Relations* 29, no. 2 (2005): 165–96; Z. Ma, "Conflict Management Styles as Indicators of Behavioral Pattern in Business Negotiation," *International Journal of Conflict Management* 18, no. 3/4 (2007): 260–79.

48. J. L. Holt and C. J. DeVore, "Culture, Gender, Organizational Role, and Styles of Conflict Resolution: A Meta-Analysis," *International Journal of Intercultural Relations* 29, no. 2 (2005): 165–96; M. Davis, S. Capobianco, and L. Kraus, "Gender Differences in Responding to Conflict in the Workplace: Evidence from a

Large Sample of Working Adults," *Sex Roles* 63, no. 7 (2010): 500–14; B. M. Gayle, R. W. Preiss, and M. Allen, "Where Are We Now? A Meta-Analytic Review of Sex Difference Expectations for Conflict Management Strategy Selection," in *Managing Interpersonal Conflict: Advances through Meta-Analysis,* ed. N. A. Burrell et al. (New York: Routledge, 2014), 226–47.

49. K. Lewin, *Resolving Social Conflicts* (New York: Harper, 1948).

50. J. D. Hunger and L. W. Stern, "An Assessment of the Functionality of the Superordinate Goal in Reducing Conflict," *Academy of Management Journal* 19, no. 4 (1976): 591–605; M. Sherif, "Superordinate Goals in the Reduction of Intergroup Conflict," *American Journal of Sociology* 63, no. 4 (1958): 349–56.

51. M. Sherif, "Superordinate Goals in the Reduction of Intergroup Conflict," *American Journal of Sociology* 63, no. 4 (1958): 349–56; K. M. Eisenhardt, J. L. Kahwajy, and L. J. Bourgeois III, "How Management Teams Can Have a Good Fight," *Harvard Business Review* (July/August 1997): 77–85; X. M. Song, J. Xie, and B. Dyer, "Antecedents and Consequences of Marketing Managers' Conflict-Handling Behaviors," *Journal of Marketing* 64 (January 2000): 50–66; O. Doucet, J. Poitras, and D. Chenevert, "The Impacts of Leadership on Workplace Conflicts," *International Journal of Conflict Management* 20, no. 4 (2009): 340–54.

52. R. S. Lau and A. T. Cobb, "Understanding the Connections between Relationship Conflict and Performance: The Intervening Roles of Trust and Exchange," *Journal of Organizational Behavior* 31, no. 6 (2010): 898–917.

53. H. C. Triandis, "The Future of Workforce Diversity in International Organisations: A Commentary," *Applied Psychology: An International Journal* 52, no. 3 (2003): 486–95.

54. T. F. Pettigrew, "Intergroup Contact Theory," *Annual Review of Psychology* 49 (1998): 65–85; S. Brickson, "The Impact of Identity Orientation on Individual and Organizational Outcomes in Demographically Diverse Settings," *Academy of Management Review* 25 (2000): 82–101; J. Dixon and K. Durrheim, "Contact and the Ecology of Racial Division: Some Varieties of Informal Segregation," *British Journal of Social Psychology* 42 (2003): 1–23.

55. H. C. Triandis, "The Future of Workforce Diversity in International Organisations: A Commentary," *Applied Psychology: An International Journal* 52, no. 3 (2003): 486–95.

56. M. A. Von Glinow, D. L. Shapiro, and J. M. Brett, "Can We Talk, and Should We? Managing Emotional Conflict in Multicultural Teams," *Academy of Management Review* 29, no. 4 (2004): 578–92.

57. L. L. Putnam, "Beyond Third Party Role: Disputes and Managerial Intervention," *Employee Responsibilities and Rights Journal* 7 (1994): 23–36; A. R. Elangovan, "The Manager as the Third Party: Deciding How to Intervene in Employee Disputes," in *Negotiation: Readings, Exercises, and Cases,* ed. R. J. Lewicki, J. A. Litterer, and D. Saunders (New York: McGraw-Hill, 1999), 458–69. For a somewhat different taxonomy of managerial conflict intervention, see P. G. Irving and J. P. Meyer, "A Multidimensional Scaling Analysis of Managerial Third-Party Conflict Intervention Strategies," *Canadian Journal of Behavioural Science* 29, no. 1 (1997): 7–18. A recent review describes 10 species of third-party intervention, but these consist of variations of the three types described here. See D. E. Conlon et al., "Third Party Interventions across Cultures: No 'One Best Choice,'" in *Research in Personnel and Human Resources Management* (Greenwich, CT: JAI, 2007), 309–49.

58. J. A. Wall and T. C. Dunne, "Mediation Research: A Current Review," *Negotiation Journal* 28, no. 2 (2012): 217–44; K. Bollen and M. Euwema, "Workplace Mediation: An Underdeveloped Research Area," *Negotiation Journal* 29, no. 3 (2013): 329–53.

59. Accountemps, "'Office Ghouls' Don't Strike Only on Halloween," news release (Menlo Park, CA: Accountemps, October 18, 2006); P. Weaver and S. Mitchell, *Lessons for Leaders from the People Who Matter* (Pittsburgh: Development Dimensions International, February 16, 2012); *Conflict in New Zealand Workplaces Study* (Auckland: FairWay Resolution, August 2014); J. Gifford, *Getting under the Skin of Workplace Conflict: Tracing the Experiences of Employees* (London: Chartered Institute of Personnel and Development, April 2015); Accountemps, "Clash of the Coworkers," news release (Menlo Park, CA: PRNewswire, March 9, 2017).

60. B. H. Sheppard, "Managers as Inquisitors: Lessons from the Law," in *Bargaining inside Organizations,* ed. M. H. Bazerman and R. J. Lewicki (Beverly Hills, CA: Sage, 1983). Even in cultures that support managerial mediation, managers slip easily into inquisition and arbitration approaches where conflict has escalated. See M. K. Kozan, C. Ergin, and K. Varoglu, "Bases of Power and Conflict Intervention Strategy: A Study on Turkish Managers," *International Journal of Conflict Management* 25, no. 1 (2014): 38–60.

61. R. Karambayya and J. M. Brett, "Managers Handling Disputes: Third Party Roles and Perceptions of Fairness," *Academy of Management Journal* 32 (1989): 687–704; R. Cropanzano et al., "Disputant Reactions to Managerial Conflict Resolution Tactics," *Group & Organization Management* 24 (1999): 124–53.

62. A. R. Elangovan, "Managerial Intervention in Organizational Disputes: Testing a Prescriptive Model of Strategy Selection," *International Journal of Conflict Management* 4 (1998): 301–35; P. S. Nugent, "Managing Conflict: Third-Party Interventions for Managers," *Academy of Management Executive* 16, no. 1 (2002): 139–54.

63. K. Bollen, H. Ittner, and M. C. Euwema, "Mediating Hierarchical Labor Conflicts: Procedural Justice Makes a Difference—for Subordinates," *Group Decision and Negotiation* 21, no. 5 (2012): 621–36; R. Nesbit, T. Nabatchi, and L. B. Bingham, "Employees, Supervisors, and Workplace Mediation: Experiences of Justice and Settlement," *Review of Public Personnel Administration* 32, no. 3 (2012): 260–87.

64. J. P. Meyer, J. M. Gemmell, and P. G. Irving, "Evaluating the Management of Interpersonal Conflict in Organizations: A Factor-Analytic Study of Outcome Criteria," *Canadian Journal of Administrative Sciences* 14 (1997): 1–13; L. B. Bingham, "Employment Dispute Resolution: The Case for Mediation," *Conflict Resolution Quarterly* 22, no. 1/2 (2004): 145–74; M. Hyde et al., "Workplace Conflict Resolution and the Health of Employees in the Swedish and Finnish Units of an Industrial Company," *Social Science & Medicine* 63, no. 8 (2006): 2218–27.

65. W. H. Ross and D. E. Conlon, "Hybrid Forms of Third-Party Dispute Resolution: Theoretical Implications of Combining Mediation and Arbitration," *Academy of Management Review* 25, no. 2 (2000): 416–27; W. H. Ross, C. Brantmeier, and T. Ciriacks, "The Impact of Hybrid Dispute-Resolution Procedures on Constituent Fairness Judgments," *Journal of Applied Social Psychology* 32, no. 6 (2002): 1151–88.

66. G. Hamel, "First, Let's Fire All the Managers," *Harvard Business Review* 89, no. 12 (2011): 48–60; D. Kirkpatrick, "Self-Management's Success at Morning Star," *T&D*, October 2013, 25–27; "Colleague Principles," Morning Star Company, 2016, http://morningstarco.com/index.cgi?Page=About%20Us/Colleague%20Principles (accessed May 25, 2016).

67. R. Stagner and H. Rosen, *Psychology of Union-Management Relations* (Belmont, CA: Wadsworth, 1965), 95–96, 108–10; R. E. Walton and R. B. McKersie, *A Behavioral Theory of Labor Negotiations: An Analysis of a Social Interaction System* (New York: McGraw-Hill, 1965), 41–46; L. Thompson, *The Mind and Heart of the Negotiator* (Upper Saddle River, NJ: Prentice Hall, 1998), chap. 2.

68. A. Tversky and D. Kahneman, "Judgment under Uncertainty: Heuristics and Biases," *Science* 185, no. 4157 (1974): 1124–31; J. D. Jasper and S. D. Christman, "A Neuropsychological Dimension for Anchoring Effects," *Journal of Behavioral Decision Making* 18 (2005): 343–69.

69. S. Doctoroff, "Reengineering Negotiations," *Sloan Management Review* 39 (1998): 63–71; D. C. Zetik and A. F. Stuhlmacher, "Goal Setting and Negotiation Performance: A Meta-Analysis," *Group Processes & Intergroup Relations* 5 (2002): 35–52.

70. L. L. Thompson, "Information Exchange in Negotiation," *Journal of Experimental Social Psychology* 27 (1991): 161–79; R. Fells, *Effective Negotiation: From Research to Results*, 2nd ed. (Melbourne: Cambridge University Press, 2012), chap. 6.

71. S. Kwon and L. R. Weingart, "Unilateral Concessions from the Other Party: Concession Behavior, Attributions, and Negotiation Judgments," *Journal of Applied Psychology* 89, no. 2 (2004): 263–78; R. Fells, *Effective Negotiation* (Cambridge, UK: Cambridge University Press, 2012), chap. 8.

72. A. R. Herrman and M. Allen, "Hardline versus Softline Bargaining Strategies: A Meta-Analytic Review," in *Managing Interpersonal Conflict: Advances through Meta-Analysis*, ed. N. A. Burrell et al. (New York: Routledge, 2014), 213–25; J. Hüffmeier et al., "Being Tough or Being Nice? A Meta-Analysis on the Impact of Hard- and Softline Strategies in Distributive Negotiations," *Journal of Management* 40, no. 3 (2014): 866–92.

73. R. J. Lewicki et al., *Negotiation*, 4th ed. (New York: McGraw-Hill/Irwin, 2003), 95; M. Olekalns and P. L. Smith, "Testing the Relationships among Negotiators' Motivational Orientations, Strategy Choices, and Outcomes," *Journal of Experimental Social Psychology* 39, no. 2 (2003): 101–17.

74. D. Malhotra, "The Fine Art of Making Concessions," *Negotiation* (2006): 3–5.

75. A. F. Stuhlmacher, T. L. Gillespie, and M. V. Champagne, "The Impact of Time Pressure in Negotiation: A Meta-Analysis," *International Journal of Conflict Management* 9, no. 2 (1998): 97–116; C. K. W. de Dreu, "Time Pressure and Closing of the Mind in Negotiation," *Organizational Behavior and Human Decision Processes* 91 (2003): 280–95. However, time pressure can be beneficial under some circumstances. See M. Pinfari, "Time to Agree: Is Time Pressure Good for Peace Negotiations?," *Journal of Conflict Resolution* 55, no. 5 (2011): 683–709.

76. As with other forms of time pressure, the exploding offer effects on negotiation outcomes are complex. Those who apply these offers can be worse off in the negotiation under some circumstances. See N. Lau et al., "Exploding Offers Can Blow up in More Than One Way," *Decision Analysis* 11, no. 3 (2014): 171–88; W. Güth and M. G. Kocher, "More Than Thirty Years of Ultimatum Bargaining Experiments: Motives, Variations, and a Survey of the Recent Literature," *Journal of Economic Behavior & Organization* 108 (2014): 396–409.

77. M. Olekalns and P. L. Smith, "Moments in Time: Metacognition, Trust, and Outcomes in Dyadic Negotiations," *Personality and Social Psychology Bulletin* 31, no. 12 (2005): 1696–707.

78. D. W. Choi, "Shared Metacognition in Integrative Negotiation," *International Journal of Conflict Management* 21, no. 3 (2010): 309–33.

79. J. M. Brett et al., "Sticks and Stones: Language, Face, and Online Dispute Resolution," *Academy of Management Journal* 50, no. 1 (2007): 85–99; D. Pietroni et al., "Emotions as Strategic Information: Effects of Other's Emotional Expressions on Fixed-Pie Perception, Demands, and Integrative Behavior in Negotiation," *Journal of Experimental Social Psychology* 44, no. 6 (2008): 1444–54; D. Druckman and M. Olekalns, "Emotions in Negotiation," *Group Decision and Negotiation* 17, no. 1 (2008): 1–11; M. J. Boland and W. H. Ross, "Emotional Intelligence and Dispute Mediation in Escalating and De-Escalating Situations," *Journal of Applied Social Psychology* 40, no. 12 (2010): 3059–105.

80. P. J. Carnevale and A. M. Isen, "The Influence of Positive Affect and Visual Access on the Discovery of Integrative Solutions in Bilateral Negotiation," *Organizational Behavior and Human Decision Processes* 37 (1986): 1–13; L. Thompson, *The Mind and Heart of the Negotiator* (Upper Saddle River, NJ: Prentice Hall, 1998), chap. 2.

81. J. W. Salacuse and J. Z. Rubin, "Your Place or Mine? Site Location and Negotiation," *Negotiation Journal* 6 (1990): 5–10; J. Mayfield et al., "How Location Impacts International Business Negotiations," *Review of Business* 19 (1998): 21–24.

82. R. J. Lewicki et al., *Negotiation*, 4th ed. (New York: McGraw-Hill/Irwin, 2003), 298–322.

83. J. A. Kennedy and L. J. Kray, "A Pawn in Someone Else's Game?: The Cognitive, Motivational, and Paradigmatic Barriers to Women's Excelling in Negotiation," *Research in Organizational Behavior* 35 (2015): 3–28; J. Mazei et al., "A Meta-Analysis on Gender Differences in Negotiation Outcomes and Their Moderators," *Psychological Bulletin* 141, no. 1 (2015): 85–104.

84. I. Ayres and P. Siegelman, "Race and Gender Discrimination in Bargaining for a New Car," *American Economic Review* 83, no 3 (1995): 304–21; L. J. Kray, J. A. Kennedy, and A. B. Van Zant, "Not Competent Enough to Know the Difference? Gender Stereotypes about Women's Ease of Being Misled Predict Negotiator Deception," *Organizational Behavior and Human Decision Processes* 125, no. 2 (2014): 61–72.

85. M. Ferguson, "Workshop Helps Young Workers Negotiate Salaries," *Billings Gazette* (Montana), November 22, 2015, C1; P. Smith, "Mayor Martin Walsh Hosts Free Salary Negotiation Workshops," *Daily Free Press* (Boston University), April 6, 2016; I. Caputo, "When It Comes to Negotiating Salaries, Women Face Traps That Men Don't," *Boston Globe*, April 24, 2016, R30.

11 | Leadership in Organizational Settings

Learning Objectives

After you read this chapter, you should be able to:

LO11-1 Define leadership and shared leadership.

LO11-2 Describe the four elements of transformational leadership and explain why they are important for organizational change.

LO11-3 Compare managerial leadership with transformational leadership, and describe the features of task-oriented, people-oriented, and servant leadership.

LO11-4 Discuss the elements of path–goal leadership theory and leadership substitutes theory.

LO11-5 Describe the two components of the implicit leadership perspective.

LO11-6 Identify eight personal attributes associated with effective leaders and describe authentic leadership.

LO11-7 Discuss cultural and gender similarities and differences in leadership.

A t EllisDon Corporation, leaders aren't just people in management jobs. The Canadian construction services giant believes that leadership extends to every employee in the organization. "Everyone is a leader, everyone is accountable to each other, and everyone is involved in the success of the company as a whole," says EllisDon CEO Geoff Smith. "It's a leadership philosophy throughout our company." EllisDon supports shared leadership by setting objectives and then giving employees a high degree of autonomy to achieve them. "Get good people, give them the authority, give them the support, and then get out of their way so you create leaders around you," Smith advises.[1]

Executives at EllisDon recognize that leadership is a role, not a formal position assigned to specific people. It is also one of the most researched and discussed topics in the field of organizational behavior.[2] Google returns a whopping 533 million web pages where leadership is mentioned. Google Scholar lists 287,000 journal articles and books with leader or leadership in the title. Amazon lists more than 31,000 books in the English language with leadership in the title. The number of books or documents with the words leader or leadership added to the U.S. Library of Congress catalog over the past decade was four times more than two decades earlier and 48 times more than during the first decade of the 1900s.

The topic of leadership receives so much attention because we are captivated by the capacity of some individuals to influence and motivate beyond expectations a large collective of people. This chapter explores leadership from four perspectives: transformational, managerial, implicit, and personal attributes.[3] Although some of these perspectives are currently more popular than others, each helps us to more fully understand the complex issue of leadership. The final section of this chapter looks at cross-cultural and gender issues in organizational leadership. But first, we learn about the meaning of leadership as well as shared leadership.

LO11-1 Define leadership and shared leadership.

WHAT IS LEADERSHIP?

Several years ago, dozens of leadership experts from around the world reached a consensus that leadership is about influencing, motivating, and enabling others to contribute toward the effectiveness and success of the organizations of which they are members.[5] This definition has two key components. First, leaders motivate others through persuasion and other influence tactics. They use their communication skills, rewards, and other resources to energize the collective toward the achievement of challenging objectives. Second, leaders are enablers. They allocate resources, alter work relationships, minimize external disruptions, and establish other work environment changes that make it easier for employees to achieve organizational objectives.

Shared Leadership

Organizational behavior experts have long argued that leadership is not about specific positions in the organizational

The Leadership Report Card[4]

78% of 7,096 business and human resource leaders surveyed across 130 countries say that leadership development is currently important or very important in their organization (86% say so in Germany, China, and India; 72% in the U.S.; 65% in France).

62% of 3,031 American full-time employees surveyed rated their boss's performance as 'A' or 'B'.

38% of 1,019 employees surveyed in India say they could perform their boss's job better than the boss.

36% of 1,000 human resources leaders surveyed in the U.S. and U.K. say that their organization's greatest skill is in "leadership" (lowest out of four skill groups).

26% of 1,019 employees surveyed in India say their boss should not be in a leadership role.

18% of current managers have the high talent needed to effectively manage others (Gallup's estimate from analysis of 2.5 million manager-led teams).

16% of 3,031 American full-time employees surveyed gave low ratings ('D' or 'F') to their boss's performance.

©Inti St Clair/Blend Images

shared leadership the view that leadership is a role, not a position assigned to one person; consequently, people within the team and organization lead each other

transformational leadership a leadership perspective that explains how leaders change teams or organizations by creating, communicating, and modeling a vision for the organization or work unit and inspiring employees to strive for that vision

hierarchy. Formal leaders are responsible for "leading" others, but companies are far more effective when everyone assumes leadership responsibilities in various ways and at various times. This emerging view, called **shared leadership**, is based on the idea that leadership is a role, not a position.[6] It doesn't belong to just one individual in the work unit. Instead,

when Gore employees are asked, "Are you a leader?" in annual surveys, more than 50 percent of them answer yes.[8]

Shared leadership flourishes in organizations where the formal leaders are willing to delegate power and encourage employees to take initiative and risks without fear of failure (i.e., a learning orientation culture). Shared leadership also calls for a collaborative rather than internally competitive culture because employees succeed in shared leadership roles only when their coworkers support them in these roles. Furthermore, shared leadership lacks formal authority, so it operates best when employees learn to influence others through their enthusiasm, logical analysis, and involvement of coworkers in their idea or vision.

> ## "We've abandoned the Great Man model of leadership that long characterized Fiat and have created a culture where everyone is expected to lead."[9]
>
> —Sergio Marchionne, CEO of Fiat Chrysler Automobiles and Ferrari

employees lead each other as the occasion arises. Shared leadership exists when employees champion the introduction of new technologies and products.[7] It also exists when employees engage in organizational citizenship behaviors to assist the performance and well-being of coworkers and the overall team.

Shared leadership typically supplements formal leadership; that is, employees lead along with the formal manager, rather than as a replacement for that manager. However, W. L. Gore & Associates, Semco SA, Valve Corporation, and a few other unique companies rely almost completely on shared leadership because they don't have any formal managers on the organizational chart. In fact,

Shared leadership is based on the idea that leadership is a role, not a position; everyone assumes leadership responsibilities in various ways and at various times.
©Inti St Clair/Blend Images

LO11-2 Describe the four elements of transformational leadership and explain why they are important for organizational change.

TRANSFORMATIONAL LEADERSHIP PERSPECTIVE

Most leadership concepts and practices can be organized into four perspectives: transformational, managerial, implicit, and personal attributes. By far the most popular of these perspectives today—and arguably the most important in the domain of leadership—is transformational leadership. **Transformational leadership** views leaders as change agents. They move the organization or work unit in a new direction that will provide better opportunities and alignment with the external environment.

The four elements of transformational leadership models most frequently identified in the literature are develop and communicate a strategic vision, model the vision, encourage experimentation, and build commitment to the vision (see Exhibit 11.1).[10] Transformational leaders create, communicate, and model a shared vision for the team or organization. They encourage experimentation so employees find a better path to the future. Through these and other activities, transformational leaders also build commitment in followers to strive for that vision.

Exhibit 11.1 Elements of Transformational Leadership

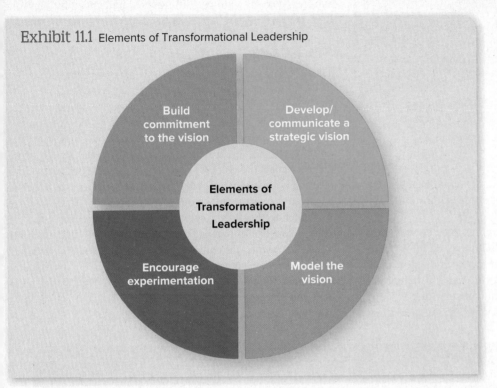

Elements of Transformational Leadership

- Build commitment to the vision
- Develop/ communicate a strategic vision
- Model the vision
- Encourage experimentation

Develop and Communicate a Strategic Vision

The heart of transformational leadership is a strategic *vision*.[11] A vision is a positive image or model of the future that energizes and unifies employees.[12] Sometimes this vision is created by the leader; at other times, it is formed by employees or other stakeholders and then adopted and championed by the formal leader. William Rogers, CEO of British radio station group UKRD, emphasizes that one of the key features of successful leaders is their "clarity of vision, so people can say: 'I know where we're going, what this journey is about, what our noble cause is.' For us, it's not just running a radio group and commercial success—it's about changing people's lives, impacting on communities."[13]

An effective strategic vision has several identifiable features.[15] It refers to an idealized future with a higher purpose. This purpose is associated with personal values that directly or indirectly fulfill the needs of multiple stakeholders. A values-based vision is particularly meaningful and appealing to employees, which energizes them to strive for that ideal. Another reason why a strategic vision motivates employees is because it is a distant goal that is both challenging and abstract. A vision is challenging because it requires substantial transformation, such as new work practices and belief systems.

A strategic vision is necessarily abstract for two reasons. One reason is that the vision hasn't yet been experienced (at least, not in this company or industry), so it isn't possible to detail exactly what the vision looks like. The other reason is that an abstract description enables the vision to remain stable over time, yet is sufficiently flexible to accommodate operational adjustments in a shifting external environment.

Another feature of an effective vision is that it is unifying. It is a superordinate objective that bonds employees together and aligns their personal values with the organization's values. In fact, a successful vision is really a shared vision because employees

Not Quite Leading with Vision[16]

47% of 1,200 Canadian employees surveyed strongly or somewhat agree that senior management in their organization communicates a clear vision.

42% of more than 40,000 employees surveyed in 300 global companies say they know their organization's vision, mission, and values.

61% of 32,000 employees surveyed globally say their company's leaders communicate a clear and compelling vision of the future.

40% of 1,061 American employees surveyed say they don't get (understand) the company's vision or have never seen it.

38% of 168,000 employees surveyed across 30 countries say they either do not believe in their employer's mission/purpose (vision) or don't understand it.

©Barbara Penoyar/Stockbyte/Getty Images

Effective transformational leaders frame the vision and generate desired emotions in followers through the use of symbols, metaphors, and stories.
©Rawpixel.com/Shutterstock

collectively define themselves by this aspirational image of the future as part of their identification with the organization.

Communicate the Vision A strategic vision's effectiveness depends on how leaders convey it to followers and other stakeholders.[17] Effective transformational leaders generate meaning and motivation in followers by relying on symbols, metaphors, stories, and other vehicles that transcend plain language.[18] Metaphors and related communication tools "frame" the vision, meaning that they guide or construct the listener's mental model of the situation. For example, to transform DaVita into the most customer-focused dialysis treatment group (now the largest in the United States), leaders referred to the company as a village and employees (called teammates) are citizens of that village who "cross the bridge," meaning that they make a commitment to the community. "The words we use, while simple in nature, are packed with meaning," explains a DaVita executive.[19]

Borrowing images from other experiences creates a richer understanding of the abstract vision. These communication tools also generate desired emotions, which motivate people to pursue the vision. For instance, when McDonald's faced the daunting challenge of opening the company's first restaurants in Russia (back when it was the USSR), CEO George Cohen frequently reminded his team members that they were establishing "hamburger diplomacy."[20]

Transformational leaders also communicate the vision with humility, sincerity, and a level of passion that reflects their personal belief in the vision and optimism that employees can succeed. They strengthen team orientation and employee self-efficacy by referring to the team's strengths and potential. By focusing on shared experiences and the central role of employees in achievement of the vision, transformational leaders suppress leader–follower differences, deflect attention from themselves, and avoid any image of superiority over the team.[21]

Model the Vision

Transformational leaders not only talk about a vision; they enact it. They "walk the talk" by stepping outside the executive suite and doing things that symbolize the vision.[22] Leaders model the vision through significant events such as visiting customers, moving their offices closer to (or further from) employees, and holding ceremonies to symbolize significant change. However, they also enact the vision by ensuring that routine daily activities—meeting agendas, dress codes, executive schedules—are consistent with the vision and its underlying values.

Modeling the vision legitimizes and demonstrates what the vision looks like in practice. It also builds employee trust in the leader. The greater the consistency between the leader's words and actions, the more employees will believe in and be willing to follow the leader. "Great leaders walk the talk," says Mike Perlis, president and chief executive officer of Forbes Media. "They lead by example. There isn't anything they ask people to do they're not willing to do themselves."[23] Surveys report that "leading by example" is the most important attribute of effective leaders and is one of the most important characteristics of a company's culture.[24]

Encourage Experimentation

Transformational leadership is about change, and central to any change is discovering new behaviors and practices that are better aligned with the desired vision. Transformational leaders support this journey by encouraging employees to question current practices and to experiment with new ways that are potentially more consistent with the vision's future state.[26] In other words, transformational leaders support a learning orientation (see Chapter 6). They want employees to continuously question current practices, actively experiment with new ideas and work processes, and view reasonable mistakes as a natural part of the learning process.[27]

> **When employees are able to see their leadership live by the values that guide them, it helps to establish a sense of organizational trust and credibility.**[25]
>
> —David Ossip, Ceridian chair & CEO

Build Commitment toward the Vision

Transforming a vision into reality requires employee commitment, and transformational leaders build this commitment in several ways.[28] Their words, symbols, and stories build a contagious enthusiasm that energizes people to adopt the vision as their own. Leaders demonstrate a can-do attitude by enacting and behaving consistently with their vision. This persistence and consistency reflect an image of honesty, trust, and integrity. By encouraging experimentation, leaders involve employees in the change process so it is a collective activity. Leaders also build commitment through rewards, recognition, and celebrations as employees pass milestones along the road to the desired vision.

Transformational Leadership and Charisma

Are transformational leaders also charismatic leaders? Although some leadership experts think charisma is an essential part of transformational leadership, evidence suggests that charisma is distinctly different from transformational leadership.[29] Charisma is a personal trait or relational quality that provides referent power over followers, whereas transformational leadership is a set of behaviors that engage followers toward a better future.[30] Furthermore, transformational leadership motivates followers through behaviors that persuade and earn trust, whereas

Transformational leaders are not necessarily charismatic, and charismatic leaders are not necessarily transformational.
©Yuganov Konstantin/Shutterstock

necessarily charismatic, and charismatic leaders are not necessarily transformational.

Evaluating the Transformational Leadership Perspective

Transformational leaders do make a difference.[33] Subordinates are more satisfied and have higher affective organizational commitment under transformational leaders. They also perform their jobs better, engage in more organizational citizenship behaviors, and make better or more creative decisions. Although transformational leadership is valuable, the theory has a few imperfections.[34] One problem is that some transformational leadership models and measures suffer from circular logic.

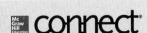
charismatic leadership motivates followers directly through the leader's inherent referent power. For instance, communicating an inspiring vision is a transformational leadership behavior that motivates followers to strive for that vision. This motivational effect exists separate from the leader's charismatic appeal. If the leader is highly charismatic, however, his or her charisma will amplify follower motivation.

Being charismatic is not inherently good or bad, but several research studies have concluded that charismatic leadership can produce negative consequences.[31] One concern is that charismatic leadership tends to produce dependent followers. Transformational leadership has the opposite effect—it builds follower empowerment, which tends to reduce dependence on the leader. Another concern is that leaders who possess the gift of charisma may become intoxicated by this power, which leads to a greater focus on self-interest than on the common good.[32] The main point here is that transformational leaders are not

They define and measure transformational leadership by its effects on employees and then measure that effect as an outcome of transformational leadership. For example, they measure transformational leadership by how much employees are inspired by the leader, then they report (not surprisingly) that transformational leadership is effective because it inspires employees. Instead, transformational leadership needs to be defined and measured purely as a set of behaviors, such as using metaphors to communicate the vision and engaging in behaviors that reflect the stated vision.

A second concern is that some transformational leadership theories combine leader behaviors with the personal characteristics of leaders. For instance, transformational leaders are described as visionary, imaginative, sensitive, and thoughtful, yet these personal characteristics are really predictors of transformational leadership behaviors.[35] A third concern is that transformational leadership is usually described as a universal

managerial leadership a leadership perspective stating that effective leaders help employees improve their performance and well-being toward current objectives and practices

concept; the theory implies that it should be applied in all situations. Only a few studies have investigated whether this transformational leadership is more valuable in some situations than others.[36] Preliminary evidence suggests that the transformational leadership perspective is relevant across cultures. However, there may be specific elements of transformational leadership, such as the way visions are communicated and modeled, that are more appropriate in North America than in other cultures.

LO11-3 Compare managerial leadership with transformational leadership, and describe the features of task-oriented, people-oriented, and servant leadership.

MANAGERIAL LEADERSHIP PERSPECTIVE

Leaders don't spend all (or even most) of their time transforming the organization or work unit. They also engage in **managerial leadership**—daily activities that support and guide the performance and well-being of individual employees and the work unit toward current objectives and practices. Leadership experts recognize that leading (transformational leadership) differs from managing (managerial leadership).[37] Although the distinction between these two perspectives remains somewhat fuzzy, each cluster has a reasonably clear set of activities and strong research foundation.

contrast, leaders "do the right thing," which means that transformational leadership behaviors change the organization or work unit so its objectives are aligned more closely with the external environment.

A second distinction is that managerial leadership is more micro-focused and concrete because it relates to the specific performance and well-being objectives of individual employees and the immediate work unit. Transformational leadership is more macro-focused and abstract. It is directed toward an imprecise strategic vision for an entire organization, department, or team.

Interdependence of Managerial and Transformational Leadership

Although transformational and managerial leadership are discussed as two leadership perspectives, they are more appropriately viewed as *interdependent* perspectives.[40] In other words, transformational leadership and managerial leadership depend on each other. Transformational leadership identifies, communicates, and builds commitment to a better future for the organization or work unit. But these transformational leadership behaviors are not enough for organizational success. That success also requires managerial leadership to translate the abstract vision into more specific operational behaviors and practices, and to continuously improve employee performance and well-being in the pursuit of that future ideal. Managerial leadership also depends on transformational leadership to set the right direction. Otherwise, managers might produce operational excellence toward goals that are misaligned with the organization's long-term survival.

Senior executive positions call for more transformational leadership behavior than do managerial positions further down the hierarchy, likely because transformational leadership requires

> ## Managers are people who do things right and leaders are people who do the right thing.[38]
> —Warren Bennis, leadership scholar (based on earlier writing by Peter Drucker)

One distinction between these two perspectives is that managerial leadership assumes the organization's (or department's) objectives are stable and aligned with the external environment, whereas transformational leadership assumes the organization (or department) is misaligned with its environment and therefore needs to change its direction.[39] An often-cited saying is that managers "do things right," which means that managerial leadership behaviors focus on making employees and work units more effective at established objectives and practices. In

more discretion to enable macro-level change. However, managerial and transformational leadership are not embodied in different people or positions in the organization. Every manager needs to apply both transformational and managerial leadership behaviors to varying degrees. Indeed, even frontline nonmanagement employees who engage in shared leadership may be managerial (helping coworkers through a difficult project) or transformational (championing more customer-friendly norms in the work unit).

Transformational leadership requires managerial leadership to translate the abstract vision into more specific operational behaviors and practices; managerial leadership requires transformational leadership to set the right direction.
©Rawpixel.com/Shutterstock

Task-Oriented and People-Oriented Leadership

Managerial leadership research began in the 1940s when several universities launched intensive investigations to answer the question "What behaviors make leaders effective?" They studied first-line supervisors by asking subordinates to rate their bosses on many behaviors. These independent research teams essentially identified the same two clusters of leadership behavior from literally thousands of items (Exhibit 11.2).[41]

One cluster, called *task-oriented leadership*, includes behaviors that define and structure work roles. Task-oriented leaders assign employees to specific tasks, set goals and deadlines, clarify work duties and procedures, define work procedures, and plan work activities. The other cluster represents *people-oriented leadership*. This cluster includes behaviors such as listening to employees' ideas, creating a pleasant physical work environment, showing interest in staff, appreciating employees for their contributions, and showing consideration of employee needs.

These early managerial leadership studies tried to find out whether effective managers are more task-oriented or more people-oriented. This proved to be a difficult question to answer because each style has its advantages and disadvantages. In fact, recent evidence suggests that effective leaders rely on both styles, but in different circumstances.[42] When leaders apply high levels of people-oriented leadership behavior, their employees tend to have more positive attitudes as well as lower absenteeism, grievances, stress, and turnover. When leaders apply task-oriented leadership behaviors, their employees tend to have higher job performance. Not surprisingly, employees generally prefer people-oriented bosses and they form negative attitudes toward bosses who are mostly task-oriented. However, task-oriented leadership also is appreciated to some degree. For example, college students value task-oriented instructors because those instructors provide clear expectations and well-prepared lectures that abide by the course objectives.[43]

Servant Leadership

Servant leadership is an extension or variation of people-oriented leadership because it defines leadership as serving others. In particular, servant leaders assist others in their need fulfillment, personal development, and growth.[44] Servant leaders ask, "How can I help you?" rather than expecting employees to serve them. Servant leaders have been described as selfless, egalitarian, humble, nurturing, empathetic, and ethical coaches. The main objective of servant leadership is to help followers and other

> **servant leadership** the view that leaders serve followers, rather than vice versa; leaders help employees fulfill their needs and are coaches, stewards, and facilitators of employee development

Exhibit 11.2 Task- and People-Oriented Leadership Styles

Leaders are task-oriented when they . . .	Leaders are people-oriented when they . . .
• Assign work and clarify responsibilities. • Set goals and deadlines. • Evaluate and provide feedback on work quality. • Establish well-defined best work procedures. • Plan future work activities.	• Show interest in others as people. • Listen to employees. • Make the workplace more pleasant. • Show appreciation to employees for their performance contribution. • Are considerate of employee needs.

path–goal leadership theory a leadership theory stating that effective leaders choose the most appropriate leadership style(s), depending on the employee and situation, to influence employee expectations about desired results and their positive outcomes

stakeholders fulfill their needs and potential, particularly "to become healthier, wiser, freer, more autonomous, more likely themselves to become servants."[45] This description captures three key features of servant leadership:[46]

- *Natural desire or "calling" to serve others.* Servant leaders have a deep commitment to help others in their personal growth for that purpose alone. This commitment is not merely an instrument to achieve company objectives. It is a selfless desire to support others that goes beyond the leader's role obligation.

- *Humble, egalitarian, accepting relationship with followers.* Servant leaders do not view leadership as a position of power. Rather, they serve without drawing attention to themselves, without evoking superior status, and without being judgmental about others or defensive of criticisms received.

> Servant leaders selflessly assist others in their need fulfillment, personal development, and growth.

- *Ethical decisions and behavior.* Servant leaders display sensitivity to and enactment of moral values. They are not swayed by deviant social pressures or expectations. Servant leaders maintain moral integrity by relying on personal values to anchor their decisions and behavior. In this respect, servant leadership relies heavily on authentic leadership, which we discuss later in this chapter.

Servant leadership was introduced four decades ago and has had a steady following over the years, particularly among practitioners and religious leaders. Scholarly interest in this topic has bloomed quite recently, but the concept still faces a number of conceptual hurdles.[48] Although servant leadership writers generally agree on the three features described here, many have included other characteristics that lack agreement and might confound the concept with its predictors and outcomes. Still, the notion that leaders should be servants has considerable currency and for many centuries has been embedded in the principles of major religions. One study also found that companies have higher performance (return on assets) when their chief executive officer exhibits servant leadership behaviors.[49]

OB THEORY TO PRACTICE

U.S. Army Values Emphasize Servant Leadership

Servant leadership has recently gained the attention of organizational behavior scholars, but it has been ingrained in military leadership for decades. "If you look at our Army Values, the center of that is selfless service," explains General Daniel Allyn, vice chief of staff of the U.S. Army (front right in photo). "The idea of servant leadership is you put others before yourself. That, to me, is an inherent quality of leadership, and our Warrior Ethos also speaks to it in 'I'll never leave a fallen comrade.' That implies that we're going to do all we can to ensure that we're always looking after the needs of our Soldiers."[47]

Photo by Staff Sgt. George Gutierrez

LO11-4 Discuss the elements of path–goal leadership theory and leadership substitutes theory.

PATH–GOAL AND LEADERSHIP SUBSTITUTES THEORIES

Path–Goal Leadership Theory

The earliest managerial leadership studies not only identified the task-oriented and people-oriented leadership styles; they also concluded that the best leadership style depends on the situation.[50] This "it depends" view is consistent with the contingency anchor of organizational behavior discussed in Chapter 1. The dominant theory that applies this contingency approach to managerial leadership is **path–goal leadership theory**. This theory states that effective leaders choose one or more leadership styles to influence employee expectations (their preferred path) regarding achievement of desired results (their work-related goals), as well as their perceived satisfaction with those results (outcome valences). Leaders clarify the link between employee behaviors and outcomes, influence the valence of those outcomes, provide a work environment to facilitate goal accomplishment, and so forth.[51] Notice from this description that path–goal theory builds on the expectancy theory of motivation (Chapter 5) and its underlying rational decision-making formula (Chapter 6).[52]

Path–Goal Leadership Styles Exhibit 11.3 presents the path-goal theory of leadership. This model specifically highlights four leadership styles and several contingency factors leading to three indicators of leader effectiveness. The four leadership styles are[53]

- *Directive.* Directive leadership is the same as task-oriented leadership, described earlier. This leadership style consists of clarifying behaviors that provide a psychological structure for subordinates. It includes clarifying performance goals, the means to reach those goals, and the standards against which performance will be judged. Directive leadership also includes judicious use of rewards and disciplinary actions.

- *Supportive.* Supportive leadership is the same as people-oriented leadership, described earlier. This style provides psychological support for subordinates. The leader is friendly and approachable; makes the work more pleasant; treats employees with respect; and shows concern for the status, needs, and well-being of employees.

- *Participative.* Participative leadership behaviors encourage and facilitate employee involvement in decisions beyond their normal work activities. The leader consults with his or her staff, asks for their suggestions, and carefully reflects on employee views before making a decision. Participative leadership relates to involving employees in decisions (see Chapter 6).

- *Achievement-oriented.* This leadership style emphasizes behaviors that encourage employees to reach their peak performance. The leader sets challenging goals, expects employees to perform at their highest level, continuously seeks improvement in employee performance, and shows a high degree of confidence that employees will assume responsibility and accomplish challenging goals. Achievement-oriented leadership applies goal-setting theory as well as positive expectations in self-fulfilling prophecy.

Path–Goal Theory Contingencies As a contingency theory, path–goal theory states that each of the four leadership styles will be more effective in some situations than in others. The theory contends that effective leaders are capable of selecting the most appropriate behavioral style (or styles) for each

Path–goal theory states that a combination of directive and supportive leadership is best for employees who are (or perceive themselves to be) inexperienced and unskilled.
©Echo/Getty Images

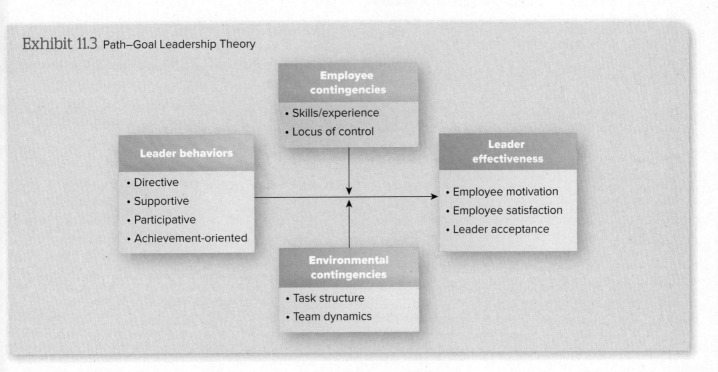

Exhibit 11.3 Path–Goal Leadership Theory

Employee contingencies
- Skills/experience
- Locus of control

Leader behaviors
- Directive
- Supportive
- Participative
- Achievement-oriented

Environmental contingencies
- Task structure
- Team dynamics

Leader effectiveness
- Employee motivation
- Employee satisfaction
- Leader acceptance

situation. Leaders often use two or more styles at the same time, if these styles are appropriate for the circumstances. The model specifies two sets of situational variables: (1) employee characteristics and (2) characteristics of the employee's work environment. Several employee and workplace contingencies have been studied, but the following four have received the most attention:[54]

- *Skill and experience.* A combination of directive and supportive leadership is best for employees who are (or perceive themselves to be) inexperienced and unskilled.[55] Directive leadership involves providing information about how to accomplish the task, whereas supportive leadership offers support to cope with the uncertainties of unfamiliar work situations. This style is detrimental when employees are skilled and experienced because it introduces too much supervisory control.

- *Locus of control.* People with an internal locus of control believe that they have control over their work environment (see Chapter 3). Consequently, these employees prefer participative and achievement-oriented leadership styles and may become frustrated with a directive style. In contrast, people with an external locus of control believe that their performance is due more to luck and fate, so they tend to be more satisfied with directive and supportive leadership.

- *Task structure.* Leaders should adopt the directive style when the task is nonroutine because this style minimizes the role ambiguity that tends to occur in complex work situations (particularly for inexperienced employees).[56] The directive style is ineffective when employees have routine and simple tasks because the manager's guidance serves no purpose and may be viewed as unnecessarily micromanaging. Employees in highly routine and simple jobs may require supportive leadership to help them cope with the tedious nature of the work and lack of control over the pace of work. Participative leadership is preferred for employees performing nonroutine tasks because the lack of rules and procedures gives them more discretion to achieve challenging goals. The participative style is ineffective for employees in routine tasks because they lack discretion over their work.

- *Team dynamics.* Cohesive teams with performance-oriented norms act as a substitute for most leader interventions. High team cohesion substitutes for supportive leadership, whereas performance-oriented team norms substitute for directive and possibly achievement-oriented leadership. Thus, when team cohesion is low, leaders should use a supportive style. Leaders should apply a directive style to counteract team norms that oppose the team's formal objectives. For example, the team leader may need to exert authority if team members have developed a norm to "take it easy" rather than get a project completed on time.

Evaluating Path–Goal Theory Path-goal theory has received more research support than other managerial leadership models. In fact, one study reported that path-goal theory explains more about effective leadership than does the transformational leadership model.[57] This stronger effect is likely because most managers spend more of their time engaging in managerial rather than transformational leadership.[58]

Support for the path-goal model is far from ideal, however. A few contingencies (e.g., task structure) have limited research support. Other contingencies and leadership styles in the path-goal leadership model haven't been investigated at all.[59] Another concern is that as path-goal theory expands, the model may become too complex for practical use. Few people would be able to remember all the contingencies and the appropriate leadership styles for those contingencies.

Another limitation of path-goal theory is its assumption that effective leaders can fluidly adapt their behavior and managerial styles to the immediate situation. In reality, it takes considerable effort to choose and enact different styles to match the situation. Leaders typically prefer one style that is most consistent with their personality and values.[60] They seem to be less flexible as path-goal theory assumes shifting to the other styles. Some experts even suggest that leadership styles are hardwired.[61] Leaders with high agreeableness personality and benevolence values tend to prefer supportive leadership, for example, whereas leaders with high conscientiousness personality and achievement values feel more comfortable with the directive style of leadership.[62] If managerial styles are anchored in personal characteristics, then it may be better to move managers to situations that fit their preferred leadership style than to expect managers to fluidly change style with the situation.

Leadership Substitutes Theory

Path-goal leadership theory recommends using different styles for managing employees in various situations. But **leadership substitutes theory** identifies conditions that either limit the leader's ability to influence subordinates or make a particular leadership style unnecessary.[63] The literature identifies several conditions that possibly substitute for task-oriented or people-oriented leadership (see Exhibit 11.4).

Exhibit 11.4 Possible Leadership Substitutes

Managerial Leadership Style	Possible Substitutes for that Style
Task-oriented	• Performance-based rewards
	• Employee is skilled and experienced
	• Guidance from coworkers
	• Team norms reinforce task objectives
	• Work is intrinsically motivating
	• Employee applies self-leadership
People-oriented	• Supportive coworkers
	• Employee is skilled and experienced
	• Work is intrinsically satisfying
	• Employee uses effective stress coping

Based on ideas in S. Kerr and J. M. Jermier, "Substitutes for Leadership: Their Meaning and Measurement," *Organizational Behavior and Human Performance* 22 (December 1978): 375–403; P. M. Podsakoff and S. B. MacKenzie, "Kerr and Jermier's Substitutes for Leadership Model: Background, Empirical Assessment, and Suggestions for Future Research," *Leadership Quarterly* 8 (1997): 117–32.

Task-oriented leadership may be redundant or have less value when the employee receives performance-based reward systems, the work is intrinsically motivating, and the employee applies self-leadership practices.
©Maridav/Shutterstock

Consistent with path–goal theory, task-oriented leadership is likely less valuable for employees as they gain skill and experience in the job.[64] This leadership style also may be redundant or have less value when performance-based reward systems keep employees directed toward organizational goals, when the work is intrinsically motivating, and when the employee applies self-leadership practices (engages in self-set goals, self-reinforcement, positive self-talk, etc). Teams likely substitute for task-oriented leadership.[65] Team norms that support organizational goals motivate team members to encourage (or pressure) coworkers to perform their tasks and possibly even to apply achievement-oriented performance expectations.[66] Coworkers also engage in organizational citizenship behaviors by instructing less-experienced employees, thereby requiring less task-oriented leadership from the formal manager.

People-oriented leadership may be less valuable for employee well-being when other forms of social support are available (such as supportive team members) and when the employee applies other mechanisms to minimize his or her stress (such as using effective coping strategies and experiencing intrinsically satisfying work). Skilled and experienced employees also have higher self-efficacy, which results in less stressful work and therefore less need for people-oriented leadership interaction from the boss.

The leadership substitutes model has intuitive appeal, but the evidence so far is mixed. Some studies show that a few substitutes do replace the need for task- or people-oriented leadership, but others do not. The difficulties of statistically testing for leadership substitutes may account for some problems, but a few writers contend that the limited support is evidence that leadership plays a critical role regardless of the situation.[67] At this point, we can conclude that leadership substitutes might reduce the need for leaders, but they do not completely replace leaders in these situations.

LO11-5 Describe the two components of the implicit leadership perspective.

IMPLICIT LEADERSHIP PERSPECTIVE

Research on transformational and managerial leadership has found that leaders do "make a difference"; that is, leaders significantly influence the performance of their departments and organizations. However, a third leadership perspective, called **implicit leadership theory**, explains that followers' perceptions also play a role in a leader's effectiveness. The implicit leadership perspective has two components: leader prototypes and the romance of leadership.[68]

Prototypes of Effective Leaders

One aspect of implicit leadership theory states that everyone has *leadership prototypes*—preconceived beliefs about the features

Leadership prototypes are preconceived beliefs about the features and behaviors of effective leaders, which shape the follower's expectations and acceptance of someone as a leader.
©Syda Productions/Shutterstock

> The implicit leadership perspective highlights the fact that leadership is a perception of followers as much as the actual behaviors and formal roles of people calling themselves leaders.

and behaviors of effective leaders.[69] These prototypes, which develop through socialization within the family and society, shape the follower's expectations and acceptance of someone as a leader. These expectations and affirmations influence the employee's willingness to be a follower. Leadership prototypes not only support a person's role as leader; they also influence follower perceptions of the leader's effectiveness. In other words, a leader is often perceived as more effective when he or she looks like and acts consistently with the prototype of a leader.[70]

Why does this prototype comparison process occur? People want to trust their leader before they are willing to serve as followers, yet the leader's actual effectiveness usually isn't known for several months or possibly years. The prototype comparison process is a quick (although faulty) way of estimating the leader's effectiveness.

The Romance of Leadership

Along with relying on implicit prototypes of effective leaders, followers tend to inflate the perceived influence of leaders on the organization's success. This "romance of leadership" effect exists because people in most cultures want to believe that leaders make a difference.

There are two basic reasons why people overestimate the leader's influence on organizational outcomes.[71] First, leadership is a useful way for us to simplify life events. It is easier to explain organizational successes and failures in terms of the leader's ability than by analyzing a complex array of other forces. Second, there is a strong tendency in the United States and other Western cultures to believe that life events are generated more by people than by uncontrollable natural forces.[72] This illusion of control is satisfied by believing that events result from the rational actions of leaders. In other words, employees feel better believing that leaders make a difference, so they actively look for evidence that this is so.

One way that followers inflate their perceptions that leaders make a difference is through fundamental attribution error (see Chapter 3). Research has found that (at least in Western cultures) leaders are given credit or blame for the company's success or failure because employees do not readily see the external forces that also influence these events. Leaders reinforce this belief by taking credit for organizational successes.[73]

The implicit leadership perspective provides valuable advice to improve leadership acceptance. It highlights the fact that leadership is a perception of followers as much as the actual behaviors and formal roles of people calling themselves leaders. Potential leaders must be sensitive to this fact, understand what followers expect, and act accordingly. Individuals who do not naturally fit leadership prototypes need to provide more direct evidence of their effectiveness as leaders.

LO11-6 Identify eight personal attributes associated with effective leaders and describe authentic leadership.

PERSONAL ATTRIBUTES PERSPECTIVE OF LEADERSHIP

Since the beginning of recorded civilization, people have been interested in the personal characteristics that distinguish great leaders from the rest of us.[74] However, a groundbreaking review in the late 1940s concluded that none of the traits studied up to that point could be associated with successful leaders. This conclusion was revised a decade later to suggest that a few traits are associated with effective leaders.[75] These findings caused many scholars to give up their search for the personal characteristics of effective leaders.

Most Important Leadership Attributes

Over the past two decades, leadership experts have returned to the notion that effective leaders possess specific personal attributes. Most scholarly studies long ago were apparently plagued by methodological problems, lack of theoretical foundation, and inconsistent definitions of leadership. More recent studies have largely addressed these problems, with the result that several attributes are now consistently identified with effective leadership or leader emergence. The main leadership attributes (not in any particular order) are personality, self-concept, leadership motivation, drive, integrity, knowledge of the business, cognitive and practical intelligence, and emotional intelligence:[76]

Personality Most of the Big Five personality dimensions (see Chapter 2) are associated with effective leadership.[77] However, the strongest predictors are high levels of extraversion (outgoing, talkative, sociable, and assertive) and conscientiousness (careful, dependable, and self-disciplined). With high extraversion, effective leaders are comfortable having an influential role in social settings. With higher conscientiousness, effective leaders set higher goals for themselves (and others), are organized, and have a strong sense of duty to fulfill work obligations.

wielding power over others (see Chapter 5).[80] Leadership motivation is also necessary because, even in organizations where coworkers support each other, leaders are in contests for positions further up the hierarchy. Effective leaders thrive rather than wither in the face of this competition.[81]

Drive Related to their high conscientiousness, extraversion, and self-evaluation, successful leaders have a moderately high need for achievement (see Chapter 5). This drive represents the inner motivation that leaders possess to pursue their goals and encourage others to move forward with theirs. Drive inspires inquisitiveness, an action orientation, and measured boldness to take the organization or team into uncharted waters.

Integrity Integrity involves having strong moral principles, which supports the tendency to be truthful and to be consistent in words and deeds. Leaders have a high moral capacity to

> **Effective leaders have a strong need for *socialized power*, meaning that they want power to lead others in accomplishing organizational objectives and similar good deeds.**

Self-Concept Successful leaders have a complex, internally consistent, and clear self-concept as a leader (see Chapter 3). This "leader identity" also includes a positive self-evaluation, including high self-esteem, self-efficacy, and internal locus of control.[78] Many people in leadership positions default to daily managerial leadership and define themselves as managers. Effective leaders, on the other hand, view themselves as both transformational and managerial, and are confident with both of these self-views.[79]

Leadership Motivation Effective leaders don't just view themselves as leaders. They also are motivated to lead others. They have a strong need for *socialized power*, meaning that they want power to lead others in accomplishing organizational objectives and similar good deeds. This contrasts with a need for *personalized power*, which is the desire to have power for personal gain or for the thrill one might experience from

judge dilemmas using sound values and to act accordingly. Notice that integrity is ultimately based on the leader's values, which provide an anchor for consistency. Several large-scale studies have reported that employees identify integrity and honesty as the most important characteristics of effective leaders.[82]

Employee Perceptions of Senior Leadership Integrity[83]

75% of more than 1,000 American office workers surveyed identify integrity as one of the most important attributes in a corporate leader (top attribute, followed by fairness).

65% of 828 full-time American employees surveyed say they trust senior leaders (by comparison, 80% trust coworkers).

62% of 181,131 Canadian federal government employees surveyed say senior managers in their department/agency lead by example in ethical behavior (whereas 18% disagree).

©Aquir/Shutterstock

21% of 1,512 American employees surveyed say they don't trust their employer.

52% of 407,789 U.S. federal government employees surveyed say their organization's senior leaders maintain high standards of honesty and integrity.

Knowledge of the Business Effective leaders possess tacit and explicit knowledge of the business environment in which they operate, including subtle indications of emerging trends. Knowledge of the business also includes a good understanding of how their organization works effectively.

Cognitive and Practical Intelligence Leaders have above-average cognitive ability to process enormous amounts of information. Leaders aren't necessarily geniuses; rather, they have a superior ability to analyze a variety of complex alternatives and opportunities. Furthermore, leaders have practical intelligence. This means that they can think through the relevance and application of ideas in real-world settings. Practical intelligence is particularly evident where problems are poorly defined, information is missing, and more than one solution may be plausible.[84]

Emotional Intelligence Effective leaders have a high level of emotional intelligence. They are able to recognize and regulate emotions in themselves and in other people (see Chapter 4).[85] For example, effective leaders can tell when their conversations are having the intended emotional effect on employees. They also are able to recognize and change their own emotional state to suit the situation, such as feeling optimistic and determined in spite of recent business setbacks.

Authentic Leadership

A few paragraphs ago, we said that successful leaders have a complex, internally consistent, and clear self-concept as a leader, and that they have a strong positive self-evaluation. These characteristics lay the foundation for **authentic leadership**, which refers to how well leaders are aware of, feel comfortable with, and act consistently with their values, personality, and self-concept.[86] Authenticity is mainly about knowing yourself and being yourself (see Exhibit 11.5). Leaders learn more about their personality, values, thoughts, and habits by reflecting on various situations and personal experiences. They also improve this self-awareness by receiving feedback from trusted

Authentic leadership begins by knowing yourself better through self-reflection and receptivity to feedback from trusted sources.
©michaeljung/Shutterstock

people inside and outside the organization. Both self-reflection and receptivity to feedback require high levels of emotional intelligence.

As people learn more about themselves, they gain a greater understanding of their inner purpose, which, in turn, generates a long-term passion for achieving something worthwhile for the organization or society. Some leadership experts suggest that this inner purpose emerges from a life story, typically initiated by a transformative event or experience earlier in life.[87]

Authentic leadership is more than self-awareness; it also involves behaving in ways that are consistent with that self-concept rather than pretending to be someone else. It is difficult enough to lead others as your natural self; to lead others while pretending to be someone else is nearly impossible. To be themselves, great leaders regulate their decisions and behavior in several ways. First, they develop their own style and, where appropriate, move into positions where that style is most effective. Although effective leaders adapt their behavior to the situation to some extent, they invariably understand and rely on decision methods and interpersonal styles that feel most comfortable to them.

Second, effective leaders continually think about and consistently apply their stable hierarchy of personal values to those decisions and behaviors. Leaders face many pressures and temptations, such as achieving short-term stock price targets at the cost of long-term profitability. Experts note that authentic leaders demonstrate self-discipline by remaining anchored to their values. Third, leaders maintain consistency around their self-concept by having a strong, positive core self-evaluation. They have high self-esteem and self-efficacy as well as an internal locus of control (Chapter 3).

Exhibit 11.5 Authentic Leadership

Know yourself:	**Be yourself:**
• Engage in self-reflection. • Receive feedback from trusted sources. • Understand your life story.	• Develop your own style. • Apply your values. • Maintain a positive core self-evaluation.

Personal Attributes Perspective Limitations and Practical Implications

Personality, experience, self-concept, and other personal characteristics potentially contribute to a leader's effectiveness. Still, the leadership attributes perspective has a few limitations.[88] First, it assumes that all effective leaders have the same personal characteristics that are equally important in all situations. This is probably a false assumption; leadership is far too complex to have a universal list of traits that apply to every condition. Some attributes might not be important all the time. Second, alternative combinations of attributes may be equally successful; two people with different sets of personal characteristics might be equally good leaders. Third, the personal attributes perspective views leadership as something within a person, yet experts emphasize that leadership is relational. People are effective leaders because of their favorable relationships with followers, not just because they possess specific personal characteristics.[89]

Also remember from our discussion earlier in this chapter that, in the short term, followers tend to define others as effective or ineffective leaders based on their personal characteristics rather than whether the leader actually makes a difference to the organization's success. People who exhibit self-confidence, extraversion, and other traits are called leaders because they fit the widely held prototype of an effective leader. Alternatively, if someone is successful, observers might assign several nonobservable personal characteristics to him or her, such as intelligence, confidence, and drive. In short, the link between personal characteristics and effective leadership is muddied by several perceptual distortions.

One important final point: The personal attributes perspective of leadership does not necessarily imply that leadership is a talent acquired at birth. On the contrary, attributes indicate only leadership *potential*, not leadership performance. People with these characteristics become effective leaders only after they have developed and mastered the necessary leadership behaviors. However, even those with fewer leadership attributes may become very effective leaders by more fully developing their potential.

> **LO11-7** Discuss cultural and gender similarities and differences in leadership.

CROSS-CULTURAL AND GENDER ISSUES IN LEADERSHIP

Along with the four perspectives of leadership presented throughout this chapter, cultural values and practices affect what leaders do. Culture shapes the leader's values and norms, which influence his or her decisions and actions. Cultural values

Cultural values influence the leader's decisions and actions; they also shape the expectations that followers have of their leaders.
©Rawpixel.com/Shutterstock

also shape the expectations that followers have of their leaders. An executive who acts inconsistently with cultural expectations is more likely to be perceived as an ineffective leader. Furthermore, leaders who deviate from those values may experience various forms of influence to get them to conform to the leadership norms and expectations of the society. Thus, differences in leadership practices across cultures are partly explained by implicit leadership theory, which was described earlier in this chapter.

A major global research project over the past two decades has found that some features of leadership are universal and some differ across cultures.[90] One leadership category, called "charismatic visionary," is a universally recognized concept and middle managers around the world believe it is characteristic of effective leaders. Charismatic visionary represents a cluster of concepts including visionary, inspirational, performance orientation, integrity, and decisiveness.[91] In contrast, participative leadership is perceived as characteristic of effective leadership in low power distance cultures but less so in high power distance cultures. In summary, some features of leadership are universal and some differ across cultures.

Gender and Leadership

Studies in work settings have generally found that male and female leaders do not differ in their levels of task-oriented or people-oriented leadership. The main explanation is that real-world jobs require similar behavior from male and female job incumbents.[92] However, women do adopt a participative leadership style more readily than their male counterparts. One possible reason is that, compared to boys, girls are often raised to be more egalitarian and less status-oriented, which is consistent with being participative. There is also some evidence that, compared to men, women have somewhat better interpersonal skills, and this translates into their relatively greater use of the participative leadership style. A third explanation is that employees, on the basis of their own gender stereotypes, expect female leaders to be more participative, so female leaders comply with follower expectations to some extent.

Surveys report that women are rated higher than men on the emerging leadership qualities of coaching, teamwork, and empowering employees.[93] Yet research also suggests that women are evaluated negatively when they try to apply the full range of leadership styles, particularly more directive and autocratic approaches. Thus,

ironically, women may be well suited to contemporary leadership roles, yet they often continue to face limitations of leadership due to followers' gender stereotypes and prototypes of leaders.[94] Overall, both male and female leaders must be sensitive to the fact that followers have expectations about how leaders should act. Leaders who deviate from those expectations may discover that followers evaluate them more harshly.

Study Checklist

Connect® Management is available for *M Organizational Behavior.* Additional resources include:

✓ Interactive Applications:
- **Decision Generator**
- **Drag and Drop:** Work through an interactive example to test your knowledge of the concepts.
- **Video Case:** See management in action through interactive videos

✓ **SmartBook™**—SmartBook is the first and only adaptive reading experience available today. Distinguishing what you know from what you don't, and honing in on concepts you are most likely to forget, SmartBook personalizes content for you in a continuously adapting reading experience. Reading is no longer a passive and linear experience, but an engaging and dynamic one where you are more likely to master and retain important concepts and go to class better prepared.

©Natthawat Jamnapa/123RF

Notes

1. C. McMorrow, *Entrepreneurs Turn Us On: 20 Years of Recognizing Bright Ideas,* EY Entrepreneur of the year—Ontario 2013, Ernst & Young (October 2013); D. Ovsey, "'Get out of the Way,'" *National Post,* February 18, 2014.

2. Most of these statistics were collected in March 2017. Library of Congress data were collected in 2010.

3. Many of these perspectives are summarized in R. N. Kanungo, "Leadership in Organizations: Looking Ahead to the 21st Century," *Canadian Psychology* 39 (1998): 71–82; G. A. Yukl, *Leadership in Organizations,* 8th ed. (Upper Saddle River, NJ: Pearson Education, 2013).

4. *State of the American Manager: Analytics and Advice for Leaders* (Washington, DC: Gallup, March 2015); CareerBuilder, "4 in 10 Indian Employees Believe Their Boss Has Room for Improvement," news release (Noida, India: CareerMuse, August 6, 2015); *Connecting the Dots between Retention and Employee Development,* Saba Global Workforce Survey (Redwood Shores, CA: Saba, November 2015); CareerBuilder, "Bosses in the Western U.S. Receive Higher Praise from Their Employees," news release (Chicago: PR Newswire, May 25, 2016); *Rewriting the Rules for the Digital Age,* 2017 Deloitte Global Human Capital Trends, Deloitte (New York: Deloitte University Press, February 2017).

5. R. House, M. Javidan, and P. Dorfman, "Project GLOBE: An Introduction," *Applied Psychology: An International Review* 50 (2001): 489–505; R. House et al., "Understanding Cultures and Implicit Leadership Theories across the Globe: An Introduction to Project GLOBE," *Journal of World Business* 37 (2002): 3–10.

6. J. A. Raelin, "We the Leaders: In Order to Form a Leaderful Organization," *Journal of Leadership & Organizational Studies* 12, no. 2 (2005): 18–30; C. L. Pearce, J. A. Conger, and E. A. Locke, "Shared Leadership Theory," *Leadership Quarterly* 19, no. 5 (2008): 622–28; E. Engel Small and J. R. Rentsch, "Shared Leadership in Teams: A Matter of Distribution," *Journal of Personnel Psychology* 9, no. 4 (2010): 203–11.

7. C. A. Beatty, "Implementing Advanced Manufacturing Technologies: Rules of the Road," *Sloan Management Review* (1992): 49–60; J. M. Howell, "The Right Stuff: Identifying and Developing Effective Champions of Innovation," *Academy of Management Executive* 19, no. 2 (2005): 108–19; J. M. Howell and C. M. Shea, "Effects of Champion Behavior, Team Potency, and External Communication Activities on Predicting Team Performance," *Group & Organization Management* 31, no. 2 (2006): 180–211.

8. D. Anfuso, "Core Values Shape W. L. Gore's Innovative Culture," *Workforce* 78, no. 3 (1999): 48–53.

9. S. Marchionne, "Fiat's Extreme Makeover," *Harvard Business Review* (2008): 45–48.

10. Most or all of these elements are included in W. Bennis and B. Nanus, *Leaders: The Strategies for Taking Charge* (New York: Harper & Row, 1985); N. M. Tichy and M. A. Devanna, *The Transformational Leader* (New York: Wiley, 1986); B. M. Bass and R. E. Riggio, *Transformational Leadership,* 2nd ed. (Mahwah, NJ: Erlbaum, 2006); J. M. Kouzes and B. Z. Posner, *The Leadership Challenge,* 5th ed. (San Francisco: Jossey-Bass, 2012).

11. Strategic collective vision has been identified as a key factor in leadership since Chester Barnard's seminal book in organizational behavior. See C. Barnard, *The Functions of the Executive* (Cambridge, MA: Harvard University Press, 1938), 86–89.

12. W. Bennis and B. Nanus, *Leaders: The Strategies for Taking Charge* (New York: Harper & Row, 1985), 27–33, 89; R. E. Quinn, *Building the Bridge as You Walk on It: A Guide for Leading Change* (San Francisco: Jossey-Bass, 2004), chap. 11; R. Gill, *Theory and Practice of Leadership* (London: Sage, 2011), chap. 4; D. O'Connell, K. Hickerson, and A. Pillutla, "Organizational Visioning: An Integrative Review," *Group & Organization Management* 36, no. 1 (2011): 103–25.

13. J. Faragher, "Employee Engagement: The Secret of UKRD's Success," *Personnel Today*, May 3, 2013; S. Waite, "Warm Hearts Bring Cheer and Rewards," *Sunday Times* (London), March 3, 2013.

14. N. Augustine, *Augustine's Laws*, 3rd ed. (New York: Viking, 1986), 32.

15. J. M. Strange and M. D. Mumford, "The Origins of Vision: Effects of Reflection, Models, and Analysis," *Leadership Quarterly* 16, no. 1 (2005): 121–48; S. Kantabutra, "Toward a Behavioral Theory of Vision in Organizational Settings," *Leadership & Organization Development Journal* 30, no. 4 (2009): 319–37; S. A. Kirkpatrick, "Lead through Vision and Values," in *Handbook of Principles of Organizational Behavior*, ed. E. A. Locke (Chichester, UK: Wiley, 2010), 367–87; R. Gill, *Theory and Practice of Leadership* (London: Sage, 2011), chap. 4.

16. Canadian Management Centre, *Build a Better Workplace: Employee Engagement Edition* (Toronto: Canadian Management Centre, August 23, 2012); Kelly Services, *The Leadership Disconnect* (Troy, MI: Kelly Services, August 2012); TINYpulse, *7 Vital Trends Disrupting Today's Workplace*, 2013 TINYpulse Employment Engagement Survey (Seattle: TINYpulse, December 2013); Root, "New Study Reveals What U.S. Employees Think about Today's Workplace," news release (Sylvania, OH: Root, March 26, 2013); Towers Watson, *Global Workforce Study: At a Glance*, (London: Towers Watson, August 2014).

17. J. A. Conger and R. N. Kanungo, *Charismatic Leadership in Organizations* (Thousand Oaks, CA: Sage, 1998), 173–83; M. Venus, D. Stam, and D. van Knippenberg, "Leader Emotion as a Catalyst of Effective Leader Communication of Visions, Value-Laden Messages, and Goals," *Organizational Behavior and Human Decision Processes* 122, no. 1 (2013): 53–68; J. Mayfield, M. Mayfield, and W. C. Sharbrough, "Strategic Vision and Values in Top Leaders' Communications: Motivating Language at a Higher Level," *International Journal of Business Communication* 52, no. 1 (2015): 97–121.

18. D. A. Waldman, P. A. Balthazard, and S. J. Peterson, "Leadership and Neuroscience: Can We Revolutionize the Way That Inspirational Leaders Are Identified and Developed?," *Academy of Management Perspectives* 25, no. 1 (2011): 60–74; S. Denning, *The Leader's Guide to Storytelling: Mastering the Art and Discipline of Business Narrative*, rev. ed. (San Francisco: Jossey-Bass, 2011); J. C. Sarros et al., "Leaders and Their Use of Motivating Language," *Leadership & Organization Development Journal* 35, no. 3 (2014): 226–40; A. M. Carton, C. Murphy, and J. R. Clark, "A (Blurry) Vision of the Future: How Leader Rhetoric About Ultimate Goals Influences Performance," *Academy of Management Journal* 57, no. 6 (2014): 1544–70.

19. R. Shook, *Heart & Soul: Five American Companies That Are Making the World a Better Place* (Dallas: BenBella Books, 2010), 155–222.

20. L. Black, "Hamburger Diplomacy," *Report on Business Magazine*, August 1988, 30–36.

21. J. E. Baur et al., "More Than One Way to Articulate a Vision: A Configurations Approach to Leader Charismatic Rhetoric and Influence," *Leadership Quarterly* 27, no. 1 (2016): 156–71.

22. D. E. Berlew, "Leadership and Organizational Excitement," *California Management Review* 17, no. 2 (1974): 21–30; W. Bennis and B. Nanus, *Leaders: The Strategies for Taking Charge* (New York: Harper & Row, 1985), 43–55; T. Simons, "Behavioral Integrity: The Perceived Alignment between Managers' Words and Deeds as a Research Focus," *Organization Science* 13, no. 1 (2002): 18–35.

23. S. Kolesnikov-Jessop, "You're the Conductor: Listen to the Music You Can Create with the Group," *The New York Times*, April 11, 2016.

24. For a discussion of trust in leadership, see C. S. Burke et al., "Trust in Leadership: A Multi-Level Review and Integration," *Leadership Quarterly* 18, no. 6 (2007): 606–32. The surveys on leading by example are reported in J. C. Maxwell, "People Do What People See," *BusinessWeek*, November 19, 2007, 32; Kronos, "Who's the Boss of Workplace Culture?," news release (Chelmsford, MA: Kronos, March 9, 2016). In the earlier survey, "leading by example" was the most important attribute of effective leaders. In the recent survey, HR professionals and managers rated "leading by example" as the top attribute of a company's culture, whereas employees ranked it below pay, coworker respect, and work–life balance.

25. D. Ossip, "Create a Culture of Engagement for Successful Customer Outcomes," *The CEO Forum* 2015, 30–31.

26. B. M. Bass and R. E. Riggio, *Transformational Leadership*, 2nd ed. (Mahwah, NJ: Erlbaum, 2006), 7; J. M. Kouzes and B. Z. Posner, *The Leadership Challenge*, 5th ed. (San Francisco: Jossey-Bass, 2012), chaps. 6 and 7.

27. W. E. Baker and J. M. Sinkula, "The Synergistic Effect of Market Orientation and Learning Orientation on Organizational Performance," *Academy of Marketing Science Journal* 27, no. 4 (1999): 411–27; Z. Emden, A. Yaprak, and S. T. Cavusgil, "Learning from Experience in International Alliances: Antecedents and Firm Performance Implications," *Journal of Business Research* 58, no. 7 (2005): 883–92.

28. J. M. Kouzes and B. Z. Posner, *The Leadership Challenge*, 5th ed. (San Francisco: Jossey-Bass, 2012).

29. R. J. House, "A 1976 Theory of Charismatic Leadership," in *Leadership: The Cutting Edge*, ed. J. G. Hunt and L. L. Larson (Carbondale: Southern Illinois University Press, 1977), 189–207; J. A. Conger, "Charismatic Leadership," in *The Sage Handbook of Leadership*, ed. A. Bryman et al. (London: Sage, 2011), 86–102.

30. J. E. Barbuto Jr., "Taking the Charisma out of Transformational Leadership," *Journal of Social Behavior & Personality* 12 (1997): 689–97; Y. A. Nur, "Charisma and Managerial Leadership: The Gift That Never Was," *Business Horizons* 41 (1998): 19–26; M. D. Mumford and J. R. Van Doorn, "The Leadership of Pragmatism: Reconsidering Franklin in the Age of Charisma," *Leadership Quarterly* 12, no. 3 (2001): 279–309; A. Fanelli, "Bringing Out Charisma: CEO Charisma and External Stakeholders," *Academy of Management Review* 31, no. 4 (2006): 1049–61; M. J. Platow et al., "A Special Gift We Bestow on You for Being Representative of Us: Considering Leader Charisma from a Self-Categorization Perspective," *British Journal of Social Psychology* 45, no. 2 (2006): 303–20.

31. B. Shamir et al., "Correlates of Charismatic Leader Behavior in Military Units: Subordinates' Attitudes, Unit Characteristics, and Superiors' Appraisals of Leader Performance," *Academy of Management Journal* 41, no. 4 (1998): 387–409; R. E. de Vries, R. A. Roe, and T. C. B. Taillieu, "On Charisma and Need for Leadership," *European Journal of Work and Organizational Psychology* 8 (1999): 109–33; R. Khurana, *Searching for a Corporate Savior: The Irrational Quest for Charismatic CEOs* (Princeton, NJ: Princeton University Press, 2002); R. E. de Vries, R. D. Pathak, and A. R. Paquin, "The Paradox of Power Sharing: Participative Charismatic Leaders Have Subordinates with More Instead of Less Need for Leadership," *European Journal of Work and Organizational Psychology* 20, no. 6

(2010): 779–804. The effect of charismatic leadership on follower dependence also was noted earlier by U.S. government leader John Gardner. See J. W. Gardner, *On Leadership* (New York: Free Press, 1990), 34–36.

32. J. Lipman-Blumen, "A Pox on Charisma: Why Connective Leadership and Character Count," in *The Drucker Difference: What the World's Greatest Management Thinker Means to Today's Business Leaders*, ed. C. L. Pearce, J. A. Maciariello, and H. Yamawaki (New York: McGraw-Hill, 2010), 149–74.

33. A. Mackey, "The Effect of CEOs on Firm Performance," *Strategic Management Journal* 29, no. 12 (2008): 1357–67; J. Barling, T. Weber, and E. K. Kelloway, "Effects of Transformational Leadership Training on Attitudinal and Financial Outcomes: A Field Experiment," *Journal of Applied Psychology* 81 (1996): 827–32. However, one study reported that transformational leadership is less effective than authoritarian (command-control with punishment) leadership in resource scarcity environments. See X. Huang et al., "When Authoritarian Leaders Outperform Transformational Leaders: Firm Performance in a Harsh Economic Environment," *Academy of Management Discoveries* 1, no. 2 (2015): 180–200.

34. A. Bryman, "Leadership in Organizations," in *Handbook of Organization Studies*, ed. S. R. Clegg, C. Hardy, and W. R. Nord (Thousand Oaks, CA: Sage, 1996), 276–92; D. van Knippenberg and S. B. Sitkin, "A Critical Assessment of Charismatic–Transformational Leadership Research: Back to the Drawing Board?," *Academy of Management Annals* 7, no. 1 (2013): 1–60.

35. G. Yukl and J. W. Michel, "A Critical Assessment of Research on Effective Leadership Behavior," in *Advances in Authentic and Ethical Leadership*, ed. L. L. Neider and C. A. Schriesheim (Charlotte, NC: Information Age, 2014), 209–30.

36. B. S. Pawar and K. K. Eastman, "The Nature and Implications of Contextual Influences on Transformational Leadership: A Conceptual Examination," *Academy of Management Review* 22 (1997): 80–109; C. P. Egri and S. Herman, "Leadership in the North American Environmental Sector: Values, Leadership Styles, and Contexts of Environmental Leaders and Their Organizations," *Academy of Management Journal* 43, no. 4 (2000): 571–604.

37. A. Zaleznik, "Managers and Leaders: Are They Different?," *Harvard Business Review* 55, no. 3 (1977): 67–78; J. P. Kotter, *A Force for Change: How Leadership Differs from Management* (New York: Free Press, 1990); E. A. Locke, *The Essence of Leadership* (New York: Lexington Books, 1991); G. Yukl and R. Lepsinger, "Why Integrating the Leading and Managing Roles Is Essential for Organizational Effectiveness," *Organizational Dynamics* 34, no. 4 (2005): 361–75; D. V. Simonet and R. P. Tett, "Five Perspectives on the Leadership–Management Relationship: A Competency-Based Evaluation and Integration," *Journal of Leadership & Organizational Studies* 20, no. 2 (2013): 199–213.

38. W. Bennis and B. Nanus, *Leaders: The Strategies for Taking Charge* (New York: Harper & Row, 1985), 20. Peter Drucker also is widely cited as the source of this quotation. The closest passage we could find, however, is in the first two pages of *The Effective Executive* (1966) where Drucker states that effective executives "get the right things done." On the next page, he states that manual workers only need efficiency, "that is, the ability to do things right rather than the ability to get the right things done." See P. F. Drucker, *The Effective Executive* (New York: Harper Business, 1966), 1–2.

39. R. J. House and R. N. Aditya, "The Social Scientific Study of Leadership: Quo Vadis?," *Journal of Management* 23, no. 3 (1997): 409–73.

40. G. Yukl and R. Lepsinger, "Why Integrating the Leading and Managing Roles Is Essential for Organizational Effectiveness," *Organizational Dynamics* 34, no. 4 (2005): 361–75. One recent critique of leadership theories suggests that scholars need to further clarify the distinction, if any exists, between leading and managing. See S. T. Hannah et al., "Debunking the False Dichotomy of Leadership Idealism and Pragmatism: Critical Evaluation and Support of Newer Genre Leadership Theories," *Journal of Organizational Behavior* 35, no. 5 (2014): 598–621.

41. E. A. Fleishman, "The Description of Supervisory Behavior," *Journal of Applied Psychology* 37, no. 1 (1953): 1–6. For discussion on methodological problems with the development of these people-versus-task-oriented leadership constructs, see C. A. Schriesheim, R. J. House, and S. Kerr, "Leader Initiating Structure: A Reconciliation of Discrepant Research Results and Some Empirical Tests," *Organizational Behavior and Human Performance* 15, no. 2 (1976): 297–321; L. Tracy, "Consideration and Initiating Structure: Are They Basic Dimensions of Leader Behavior?," *Social Behavior and Personality* 15, no. 1 (1987): 21–33.

42. A. K. Korman, "Consideration, Initiating Structure, and Organizational Criteria—a Review," *Personnel Psychology* 19 (1966): 349–62; E. A. Fleishman, "Twenty Years of Consideration and Structure," in *Current Developments in the Study of Leadership*, ed. E. A. Fleishman and J. C. Hunt (Carbondale: Southern Illinois University Press, 1973), 1–40; T. A. Judge, R. F. Piccolo, and R. Ilies, "The Forgotten Ones?: The Validity of Consideration and Initiating Structure in Leadership Research," *Journal of Applied Psychology* 89, no. 1 (2004): 36–51; D. S. DeRue et al., "Trait and Behavioral Theories of Leadership: An Integration and Meta-Analytic Test of Their Relative Validity," *Personnel Psychology* 64, no. 1 (2011): 7–52; G. A. Yukl, *Leadership in Organizations*, 8th ed. (Upper Saddle River, NJ: Pearson Education, 2013), 62–75.

43. V. V. Baba, "Serendipity in Leadership: Initiating Structure and Consideration in the Classroom," *Human Relations* 42 (1989): 509–25.

44. S. J. Peterson, B. M. Galvin, and D. Lange, "CEO Servant Leadership: Exploring Executive Characteristics and Firm Performance," *Personnel Psychology* 65, no. 3 (2012): 565–96.

45. R. K. Greenleaf, *Servant Leadership: A Journey into the Nature of Legitimate Power & Greatness* (Mahwah, NJ: Paulist Press, 1977; repr., 2002), 27.

46. S. Sendjaya, J. C. Sarros, and J. C. Santora, "Defining and Measuring Servant Leadership Behaviour in Organizations," *Journal of Management Studies* 45, no. 2 (2008): 402–24; R. C. Liden et al., "Servant Leadership: Development of a Multidimensional Measure and Multi-Level Assessment," *Leadership Quarterly* 19, no. 2 (2008): 161–77; D. van Dierendonck, "Servant Leadership: A Review and Synthesis," *Journal of Management* 37, no. 4 (2011): 1228–61; R. VanMeter et al., "In Search of Clarity on Servant Leadership: Domain Specification and Reconceptualization," *AMS Review* 6, no. 1 (March 29, 2016): 59–78.

47. J. Mattson, "'Sergeant' Means 'Servant': How NCOs Typify the Servant Leader," *NCO Journal*, May 14, 2013. For a more detailed discussion of servant leadership in the military, see D. Campbell, *The Leader's Code: Mission, Character, Service, and Getting the Job Done* (New York: Random House, 2013).

48. R. VanMeter et al., "In Search of Clarity on Servant Leadership: Domain Specification and Reconceptualization," *AMS Review* 6, no. 1 (March 29, 2016): 59–78.

49. S. J. Peterson, B. M. Galvin, and D. Lange, "CEO Servant Leadership: Exploring Executive Characteristics and Firm Performance," *Personnel Psychology* 65, no. 3 (2012): 565–96.

50. S. Kerr et al., "Towards a Contingency Theory of Leadership Based Upon the Consideration and Initiating Structure Literature," *Organizational Behavior and Human Performance* 12 (1974): 62–82; L. L. Larson, J. G. Hunt, and R. N. Osborn, "The Great Hi-Hi Leader Behavior Myth: A Lesson from Occam's Razor," *Academy of Management Journal* 19 (1976): 628–41.

51. R. J. House, "A Path Goal Theory of Leader Effectiveness," *Administrative Science Quarterly* 16, no. 3 (1971): 321–39; M. G. Evans, "Extensions of a Path–Goal Theory of Motivation," *Journal of Applied Psychology* 59 (1974): 172–78; R. J. House and T. R. Mitchell, "Path–Goal Theory of Leadership," *Journal of Contemporary Business* (1974): 81–97; M. G. Evans, "Path Goal Theory of Leadership," in *Leadership*, ed. L. L. Neider and C. A. Schriesheim (Greenwich, CT: Information Age, 2002), 115–38.

52. For a thorough study of how expectancy theory of motivation relates to leadership, see R. G. Isaac, W. J. Zerbe, and D. C. Pitt, "Leadership and Motivation: The Effective Application of Expectancy Theory," *Journal of Managerial Issues* 13 (2001): 212–26.

53. R. J. House, "Path-Goal Theory of Leadership: Lessons, Legacy, and a Reformulated Theory," *The Leadership Quarterly* 7, no. 3 (1996): 323–52.

54. J. Indvik, "Path–Goal Theory of Leadership: A Meta-Analysis," *Academy of Management Proceedings* (1986): 189–92; J. C. Wofford and L. Z. Liska, "Path–Goal Theories of Leadership: A Meta-Analysis," *Journal of Management* 19 (1993): 857–76.

55. J. D. Houghton and S. K. Yoho, "Toward a Contingency Model of Leadership and Psychological Empowerment: When Should Self-Leadership Be Encouraged?," *Journal of Leadership & Organizational Studies* 11, no. 4 (2005): 65–83.

56. R. T. Keller, "A Test of the Path–Goal Theory of Leadership with Need for Clarity as a Moderator in Research and Development Organizations," *Journal of Applied Psychology* 74 (1989): 208–12.

57. R. P. Vecchio, J. E. Justin, and C. L. Pearce, "The Utility of Transactional and Transformational Leadership for Predicting Performance and Satisfaction within a Path–Goal Theory Framework," *Journal of Occupational and Organizational Psychology* 81 (2008): 71–82.

58. B. Carroll and L. Levy, "Defaulting to Management: Leadership Defined by What It Is Not," *Organization* 15, no. 1 (2008): 75–96; I. Holmberg and M. Tyrstrup, "Well Then—What Now? An Everyday Approach to Managerial Leadership," *Leadership* 6, no. 4 (2010): 353–72.

59. C. A. Schriesheim and L. L. Neider, "Path–Goal Leadership Theory: The Long and Winding Road," *Leadership Quarterly* 7 (1996): 317–21.

60. The earliest contingency theory of leadership in the 1960s introduced the notion that managers have preferred styles and limited flexibility to use other styles. That theory had various flaws (so is not described here) but deserves recognition for proposing that it is better to move managers to situations that fit their leadership style than to expect managers to fluidly change style with the situation. See F. E. Fiedler, "Engineer the Job to Fit the Manager," *Harvard Business Review* 43, no. 5 (1965): 115–22; F. E. Fiedler, *A Theory of Leadership Effectiveness* (New York: McGraw-Hill, 1967); F. E. Fiedler and M. M. Chemers, *Leadership and Effective Management* (Glenview, IL: Scott, Foresman, 1974).

61. N. Nicholson, *Executive Instinct* (New York: Crown, 2000).

62. T. A. Judge, R. F. Piccolo, and R. Ilies, "The Forgotten Ones?: The Validity of Consideration and Initiating Structure in Leadership Research," *Journal of Applied Psychology* 89, no. 1 (2004): 36–51; T. A. Judge, R. F. Piccolo, and T. Kosalka, "The Bright and Dark Sides of Leader Traits: A Review and Theoretical Extension of the Leader Trait Paradigm," *Leadership Quarterly* 20 (2009): 855–75.

63. S. Kerr and J. M. Jermier, "Substitutes for Leadership: Their Meaning and Measurement," *Organizational Behavior and Human Performance* 22 (December 1978): 375–403.

64. This observation also has been made by C. A. Schriesheim, "Substitutes-for-Leadership Theory: Development and Basic Concepts," *Leadership Quarterly* 8 (1997): 103–08.

65. D. F. Elloy and A. Randolph, "The Effect of Superleader Behavior on Autonomous Work Groups in a Government Operated Railway Service," *Public Personnel Management* 26 (1997): 257–72; C. C. Manz and H. Sims Jr., *The New SuperLeadership: Leading Others to Lead Themselves* (San Francisco: Berrett-Koehler, 2001).

66. M. L. Loughry, "Coworkers Are Watching: Performance Implications of Peer Monitoring," *Academy of Management Proceedings* (2002): O1–O6.

67. P. M. Podsakoff and S. B. MacKenzie, "Kerr and Jermier's Substitutes for Leadership Model: Background, Empirical Assessment, and Suggestions for Future Research," *Leadership Quarterly* 8 (1997): 117–32; S. D. Dionne et al., "Neutralizing Substitutes for Leadership Theory: Leadership Effects and Common-Source Bias," *Journal of Applied Psychology* 87, no. 3 (2002): 454–64; J. R. Villa et al., "Problems with Detecting Moderators in Leadership Research Using Moderated Multiple Regression," *Leadership Quarterly* 14, no. 1 (2003): 3–23; S. D. Dionne et al., "Substitutes for Leadership, or Not," *Leadership Quarterly* 16, no. 1 (2005): 169–93.

68. J. R. Meindl, "On Leadership: An Alternative to the Conventional Wisdom," *Research in Organizational Behavior* 12 (1990): 159–203; L. R. Offermann, J. K. Kennedy, and P. W. Wirtz, "Implicit Leadership Theories: Content, Structure, and Generalizability," *Leadership Quarterly* 5, no. 1 (1994): 43–58; R. J. Hall and R. G. Lord, "Multi-Level Information Processing Explanations of Followers' Leadership Perceptions," *Leadership Quarterly* 6 (1995): 265–87; O. Epitropaki and R. Martin, "Implicit Leadership Theories in Applied Settings: Factor Structure, Generalizability, and Stability over Time," *Journal of Applied Psychology* 89, no. 2 (2004): 293–310. For a broader discussion of the social construction of leadership, see G. T. Fairhurst and D. Grant, "The Social Construction of Leadership: A Sailing Guide," *Management Communication Quarterly* 24, no. 2 (2010): 171–210.

69. R. G. Lord et al., "Contextual Constraints on Prototype Generation and Their Multilevel Consequences for Leadership Perceptions," *Leadership Quarterly* 12, no. 3 (2001): 311–38; K. A. Scott and D. J. Brown, "Female First, Leader Second? Gender Bias in the Encoding of Leadership Behavior," *Organizational Behavior and Human Decision Processes* 101 (2006): 230–42; S. J. Shondrick, J. E. Dinh, and R. G. Lord, "Developments in Implicit Leadership Theory and Cognitive Science: Applications to Improving Measurement and Understanding Alternatives to Hierarchical Leadership," *Leadership Quarterly* 21, no. 6 (2010): 959–78.

70. S. F. Cronshaw and R. G. Lord, "Effects of Categorization, Attribution, and Encoding Processes on Leadership Perceptions," *Journal of Applied Psychology* 72 (1987): 97–106; J. L. Nye and D. R. Forsyth, "The Effects of Prototype-Based Biases on Leadership Appraisals: A Test of Leadership Categorization Theory," *Small Group Research* 22 (1991): 360–79.

71. R. Meindl, "On Leadership: An Alternative to the Conventional Wisdom," *Research in Organizational Behavior* 12 (1990): 163; B. Schyns, J. R. Meindl, and M. A. Croon, "The Romance of Leadership Scale: Cross-Cultural Testing and Refinement," *Leadership* 3, no. 1 (2007): 29–46; J. Felfe and L. E. Petersen, "Romance of Leadership and Management Decision Making," *European Journal of Work and Organizational Psychology* 16, no. 1 (2007): 1–24.

72. J. Pfeffer, "The Ambiguity of Leadership," *Academy of Management Review* 2 (1977): 102–12.

73. R. Weber et al., "The Illusion of Leadership: Misattribution of Cause in Coordination Games," *Organization Science* 12, no. 5 (2001): 582–98; N. Ensari and S. E. Murphy, "Cross-Cultural Variations in Leadership Perceptions and Attribution of Charisma to the Leader," *Organizational Behavior and Human Decision Processes* 92 (2003): 52–66; M. L. A. Hayward, V. P. Rindova, and T. G. Pollock, "Believing One's Own Press: The Causes and Consequences of CEO Celebrity," *Strategic Management Journal* 25, no. 7 (2004): 637–53.

74. The history of the trait perspective of leadership, as well as current research on this topic, is nicely summarized in S. J. Zaccaro, C. Kemp, and P. Bader, "Leader Traits and Attributes," in *The Nature of Leadership*, ed. J. Antonakis, A. T. Cianciolo, and R. J. Sternberg (Thousand Oaks, CA: Sage, 2004), 101–24.

75. R. M. Stogdill, *Handbook of Leadership* (New York: Free Press, 1974), chap. 5.

76. This list is based on S. A. Kirkpatrick and E. A. Locke, "Leadership: Do Traits Matter?," *Academy of Management Executive* 5 (1991): 48–60; S. J. Zaccaro, C. Kemp, and P. Bader, "Leader Traits and Attributes," in *The Nature of Leadership*, ed. J. Antonakis, A. T. Cianciolo, and R. J. Sternberg (Thousand Oaks, CA: Sage, 2004), 101–24; G. A. Yukl, *Leadership in Organizations*, 8th ed. (Upper Saddle River, NJ: Pearson Education, 2013), chap. 6.

77. T. A. Judge et al., "Personality and Leadership: A Qualitative and Quantitative Review," *Journal of Applied Psychology* 87, no. 4 (2002): 765–80; D. S. Derue et al., "Trait and Behavioral Theories of Leadership: An Integration and Meta-Analytic Test of Their Relative Validity," *Personnel Psychology* 64, no. 1 (2011): 7–52; A. Deinert et al., "Transformational Leadership Sub-Dimensions and Their Link to Leaders' Personality and Performance," *Leadership Quarterly* 26, no. 6 (2015): 1095–120; A. D. Parr, S. T. Lanza, and P. Bernthal, "Personality Profiles of Effective Leadership Performance in Assessment Centers," *Human Performance* 29, no. 2 (2016): 143–57.

78. D. V. Day, M. M. Harrison, and S. M. Halpin, *An Integrative Approach to Leader Development: Connecting Adult Development, Identity, and Expertise* (New York: Routledge, 2009); D. S. DeRue and S. J. Ashford, "Who Will Lead and Who Will Follow? A Social Process of Leadership Identity Construction in Organizations," *Academy of Management Review* 35, no. 4 (2010): 627–47; H. Ibarra et al., "Leadership and Identity: An Examination of Three Theories and New Research Directions," in *The Oxford Handbook of Leadership and Organizations*, ed. D. V. Day (New York: Oxford University Press, 2014), 285–301; L. Guillén, M. Mayo, and K. Korotov, "Is Leadership a Part of Me? A Leader Identity Approach to Understanding the Motivation to Lead," *Leadership Quarterly* 26, no. 5 (2015): 802–20.

79. B. Carroll and L. Levy, "Defaulting to Management: Leadership Defined by What It Is Not," *Organization* 15, no. 1 (2008): 75–96.

80. One recent study suggests that leaders retain their power by undermining followers' power. See C. Case and J. Maner, "Divide and Conquer: When and Why Leaders Undermine the Cohesive Fabric of Their Group," *Journal of Personality and Social Psychology* 107, no. 6 (2014): 1033–50.

81. J. B. Miner, "Twenty Years of Research on Role Motivation Theory of Managerial Effectiveness," *Personnel Psychology* 31 (1978): 739–60; C. J. Vinkenburg et al., "Arena: A Critical Conceptual Framework of Top Management Selection," *Group & Organization Management* 39, no. 1 (2014): 33–68; B. L. Connelly et al., "Tournament Theory: Thirty Years of Contests and Competitions," *Journal of Management* 40, no. 1 (2014): 16–47; Y. Baruch and Y. Vardi, "A Fresh Look at the Dark Side of Contemporary Careers: Toward a Realistic Discourse," *British Journal of Management* 27, no. 2 (2016): 355–72.

82. For surveys on the importance of leader integrity, see J. M. Kouzes and B. Z. Posner, *The Leadership Challenge*, 5th ed. (San Francisco: Jossey-Bass, 2012), chap. 2; Robert Half, "What Is the Most Important Leadership Attribute?," news release (Menlo Park, CA: PR Newswire, September 22, 2016); S. Giles, "The Most Important Leadership Competencies, According to Leaders around the World," *Harvard Business Review Digital Articles*, March 2016, 2–6.

83. Treasury Board of Canada, *2014 Public Service Employee Survey: Summary Report* (Ottawa: Treasury Board of Canada, February 2015); "New Globoforce Survey Shows Recognition Creates More Human-Focused Workplaces," news release (Southborough, MA and Dublin, Ireland: Business Wire, March 24, 2016); U.S. Office of Personnel Management, *Federal Employee Viewpoint Survey* (Washington, DC: Office of Personnel Management, September 2016); Robert Half, "What Is the Most Important Leadership Attribute?," news release (Menlo Park, CA: PR Newswire, September 22, 2016); *Work and Well-Being Survey*, Center for Organizational Excellence (Washington, DC: American Psychological Association, May 30, 2017).

84. J. Hedlund et al., "Identifying and Assessing Tacit Knowledge: Understanding the Practical Intelligence of Military Leaders," *Leadership Quarterly* 14, no. 2 (2003): 117–40; R. J. Sternberg, "A Systems Model of Leadership: WICS," *American Psychologist* 62, no. 1 (2007): 34–42.

85. J. M. George, "Emotions and Leadership: The Role of Emotional Intelligence," *Human Relations* 53 (2000): 1027–55; D. Goleman, R. Boyatzis, and A. McKee, *Primal Leaders* (Boston: Harvard Business School Press, 2002); R. G. Lord and R. J. Hall, "Identity, Deep Structure and the Development of Leadership Skill," *Leadership Quarterly* 16, no. 4 (2005): 591–615; C. Skinner and P. Spurgeon, "Valuing Empathy and Emotional Intelligence in Health Leadership: A Study of Empathy, Leadership Behaviour and Outcome Effectiveness," *Health Services Management Research* 18, no. 1 (2005): 1–12.

86. B. George, *Authentic Leadership* (San Francisco: Jossey-Bass, 2004); W. L. Gardner et al., "'Can You See the Real Me?' A Self-Based Model of Authentic Leader and Follower Development," *Leadership Quarterly* 16 (2005): 343–72; B. George, *True North* (San Francisco: Jossey-Bass, 2007), chap. 4; M. E. Palanski and F. J. Yammarino, "Integrity and Leadership: Clearing the Conceptual Confusion," *European Management Journal* 25, no. 3 (2007): 171–84; F. O. Walumbwa et al., "Authentic Leadership: Development and Validation of a Theory-Based Measure," *Journal of Management* 34, no. 1 (2008): 89–126.

87. W. G. Bennis and R. J. Thomas, "Crucibles of Leadership," *Harvard Business Review* 80, no. 9 (2002): 39–45; R. J. Thomas, *Crucibles of Leadership: How to Learn from Experience to Become a Great Leader* (Boston: Harvard Business Press, 2008).

88. R. Jacobs, "Using Human Resource Functions to Enhance Emotional Intelligence," in *The Emotionally Intelligent Workplace*, ed. C. Cherniss and D. Goleman (San Francisco: Jossey-Bass, 2001), 161–63; J. A. Conger and D. A. Ready, "Rethinking Leadership Competencies," *Leader to Leader* (2004): 41–47.

89. R. G. Lord and D. J. Brown, *Leadership Processes and Self-Identity: A Follower-Centered Approach to Leadership* (Mahwah, NJ: Erlbaum, 2004); R. Bolden and J. Gosling, "Leadership Competencies: Time to Change the Tune?," *Leadership* 2, no. 2 (2006): 147–63.

90. Six of the Project GLOBE clusters are described in a special issue of the *Journal of World Business* 37 (2000). For an overview of Project GLOBE, see R. House, M. Javidan, and P. Dorfman, "Project GLOBE: An Introduction," *Applied Psychology: An International Review* 50 (2001): 489–505; R. House et al., "Understanding Cultures and Implicit Leadership Theories across the Globe: An Introduction to Project GLOBE," *Journal of World Business* 37 (2002): 3–10.

91. J. C. Jesuino, "Latin Europe Cluster: From South to North," *Journal of World Business* 37 (2002): 88. Another GLOBE study, of Iranian managers, also reported that "charismatic visionary" stands out as a primary leadership dimension. See A. Dastmalchian, M. Javidan, and K. Alam, "Effective Leadership and Culture in Iran: An Empirical Study," *Applied Psychology: An International Review* 50 (2001): 532–58.

92. G. N. Powell, "One More Time: Do Female and Male Managers Differ?," *Academy of Management Executive* 4 (1990): 68–75; M. L. van Engen and T. M. Willemsen, "Sex and Leadership Styles: A Meta-Analysis of Research Published in the 1990s," *Psychological Reports* 94, no. 1 (2004): 3–18.

93. A. H. Eagly, M. C. Johannesen-Schmidt, and M. L. van Engen, "Transformational, Transactional, and Laissez-Faire Leadership Styles: A Meta-Analysis Comparing Women and Men," *Psychological Bulletin* 129 (2003): 569–91; S. Paustian-Underdahl, L. Walker, and D. Woehr, "Gender and Perceptions of Leadership Effectiveness: A Meta-Analysis of Contextual Moderators," *Journal of Applied Psychology* 99, no. 6 (2014): 1129–45.

94. A. H. Eagly, S. J. Karau, and M. G. Makhijani, "Gender and the Effectiveness of Leaders: A Meta-Analysis," *Psychological Bulletin* 117 (1995): 125–45; M. E. Heilman et al., "Penalties for Success: Reactions to Women Who Succeed at Male Gender-Typed Tasks," *Journal of Applied Psychology* 89, no. 3 (2004): 416–27; A. H. Eagly, "Achieving Relational Authenticity in Leadership: Does Gender Matter?," *Leadership Quarterly* 16, no. 3 (2005): 459–74; A. J. Anderson et al., "The Effectiveness of Three Strategies to Reduce the Influence of Bias in Evaluations of Female Leaders," *Journal of Applied Social Psychology* 45, no. 9 (2015): 522–39.

PART 4

12 | Designing Organizational Structures

Learning Objectives

After you read this chapter, you should be able to:

LO12-1 Describe three types of coordination in organizational structures.

LO12-2 Discuss the role and effects of span of control, centralization, and formalization, and relate these elements to organic and mechanistic organizational structures.

LO12-3 Identify and evaluate five types of departmentalization.

LO12-4 Explain how the external environment, organizational size, technology, and strategy are relevant when designing an organizational structure.

organizational structure
the division of labor as well as the patterns of coordination, communication, workflow, and formal power that direct organizational activities

amsung Electronics is one of the world's largest technology companies, yet the South Korean maker of smartphones, tablets, televisions, and home appliances wants to be as nimble as a high-tech startup. The magic ingredient for this transformation is a new organizational structure. "Samsung will stay away from top-down structures and build bottom-up structures, while the company will put more focus on improving efficiency by introducing programs to self-motivate employees," the company explains.

This transformation, called "Start-up Samsung," will be challenging because the conglomerate's existing organizational structure is almost the opposite of what most startups look like. As with most large Korean firms, Samsung has had a tall, rigid hierarchy with power centralized at the top of the organization and seven well-defined status titles below the executive level. Samsung employees tended to follow orders without question, communicated with other departments mainly through their manager, routinely wrote detailed reports to management, and attended endless meetings.

Samsung's new organizational structure has a flatter hierarchy with only four career levels. Employees are expected to speak up about new ideas and to use the company's internal communications portal to coordinate informally and spontaneously with co-workers elsewhere in the company. Formal reports and meetings with management are now discouraged. "Samsung's top management plans to kill unnecessary internal meetings and require executives to end the rigidity of internal reporting systems," says Samsung's statement about the changes.[1]

Samsung Electronics is relying on its new organizational structure to keep the South Korean technology giant nimble and competitive. **Organizational structure** refers to the division of labor as well as the patterns of coordination, communication, workflow, and formal power that direct organizational activities. It formally dictates what activities receive the most attention as well as financial, power, and information resources. At Samsung, for example, power and resources previously concentrated around the top of the hierarchy, whereas the company now wants to delegate some of that authority and accountability to frontline employees and lower levels of management.

The topic of organizational structure typically conjures up images of an organizational chart. Organizational structure includes these reporting relationships, but it also includes other features that relate to work standards and rules, team dynamics, power relationships, information flow, and job design. The organization's structure is an important instrument in an executive's toolkit for organizational change because it establishes new communication patterns and aligns employee behavior with the corporate vision.

Indeed, one recent global survey of 7,000 business and human resources leaders in 130 countries reported that organizational design was their firm's most important trend or priority to improve human capital (leadership and corporate culture were second and third most important, respectively).[2]

This chapter begins by introducing the two fundamental processes in organizational structure: division of labor and coordination. This is followed by a detailed investigation of the four main elements of organizational structure: span of control, centralization, formalization, and departmentalization. The latter part of this chapter examines the contingencies of organizational design, including external environment, organizational size, technology, and strategy.

LO12-1 Describe three types of coordination in organizational structures.

DIVISION OF LABOR AND COORDINATION

All organizational structures include two fundamental requirements: the division of labor into distinct tasks and the coordination of that labor so employees are able to accomplish common goals.[3] Organizations are groups of people who work interdependently toward some purpose. To effectively accomplish this common purpose, most work is divided into manageable chunks, particularly when there are many different tasks required to complete the work. Organizations also introduce various coordinating mechanisms to ensure that everyone is working effectively toward the same objectives.

Division of Labor

Division of labor refers to the subdivision of work into separate jobs assigned to different people. Subdivided work leads to job

All organizational structures include two fundamental requirements: the division of labor into distinct tasks and the coordination of that labor.
©Vetta/Getty Images

specialization because each job now includes a narrow subset of the tasks necessary to complete the product or service. Samsung divides its employees into thousands of specific jobs to more effectively design, manufacture, and market new products. As companies get larger, this horizontal division of labor is usually accompanied by vertical division of labor. Some people are assigned the task of supervising employees, others are responsible for managing those supervisors, and so on.

Why do companies divide the work into several jobs? As we described in Chapter 5, job specialization increases work efficiency.[4] Job incumbents can master their tasks more quickly when work cycles are shorter. Less time is wasted changing from one task to another. Training costs are lower because employees require fewer physical and mental skills to accomplish the assigned work. Finally, job specialization makes it easier to match people with specific aptitudes or skills to the jobs for which they are best suited. It is almost impossible for one person working alone to design, manufacture, and sell a new smartphone; instead, this enterprise requires hundreds of people with diverse knowledge and skills.

Coordination of Work Activities

When people divide work among themselves, they require coordinating mechanisms to ensure that everyone works in concert. In fact, the extent to which work can be effectively divided among several people and work units depends on how well the divided work can be coordinated. When an organization divides work beyond its capacity to coordinate that work, individual effort is wasted due to misalignment, duplication, and mistiming of tasks. Coordination also tends to become more expensive and difficult as the division of labor increases. Therefore, companies specialize jobs only to the point where it isn't too costly or challenging to coordinate the people in those jobs.[5]

Every organization—from the two-person corner convenience store to the largest corporate entity—uses one or more of the following coordinating mechanisms:[6] informal communication, formal hierarchy, and standardization (see Exhibit 12.1). These forms of coordination align the work of staff within the same department as well as across work units. The coordinating mechanisms are also critical when several organizations work together, such as in joint ventures and humanitarian aid programs.[7]

Coordination through Informal Communication All organizations rely on informal communication as a coordinating mechanism. This process includes sharing information on mutual tasks as well as forming common mental models so that employees synchronize work activities using the same mental road map.[8] Informal communication is vital in nonroutine and ambiguous situations because employees need to exchange a large volume of information through face-to-face communication and other media-rich channels. Samsung's new structure encourages more informal communication because much of the work among engineers relates to novel ideas, which are nonroutine and ambiguous.

Although coordination through informal communication is easiest in small firms, information technologies have further enabled this coordinating mechanism at Samsung and in other large organizations.[9] Companies employing thousands of people also support informal communication by keeping each production site small. Magna International follows this principle by keeping most of its plants to no more than 200 employees. The global auto-parts manufacturer has found that employees have difficulty remembering each other's names in plants that are any larger, a situation that makes informal communication more difficult as a coordinating mechanism.[10]

Larger organizations also encourage coordination through informal communication by assigning *liaison roles* to employees,

Exhibit 12.1 Coordinating Mechanisms in Organizations

Form of Coordination	Description	Subtypes/Strategies
Informal communication	Sharing information on mutual tasks; forming common mental models to synchronize work activities	Direct communication Liaison roles Integrator roles Temporary teams
Formal hierarchy	Assigning legitimate power to individuals, who then use this power to direct work processes and allocate resources	Direct supervision Formal communication channels
Standardization	Creating routine patterns of behavior or output	Standardized skills Standardized processes Standardized output

Sources: Based on information in J. Galbraith, *Designing Complex Organizations* (Reading, MA: Addison-Wesley, 1973), 8–19; H. Mintzberg, *The Structuring of Organizations* (Englewood Cliffs, NJ: Prentice Hall, 1979), chap. 1; D. A. Nadler and M. L. Tushman, *Competing by Design: The Power of Organizational Architecture* (New York: Oxford University Press, 1997), chap. 6.

Organizations encourage coordination through informal communication by forming temporary cross-functional teams in which employees are given considerable authority and autonomy.
©Pressmaster/Shutterstock

who are expected to communicate and share information with coworkers in other work units. Where coordination is required among several work units, companies create *integrator roles*. These people are responsible for coordinating a work process by encouraging employees in each work unit to share information and informally coordinate work activities. Integrators do not have authority over the people involved in that process, so they must rely on persuasion and commitment. Brand managers for luxury perfumes have integrator roles because they ensure that the work of fragrance developers, bottle designers, advertising creatives, production, and other groups are aligned with the brand's image and meaning.[11]

Another way that organizations—particularly large businesses—encourage coordination through informal communication is by forming temporary cross-functional teams in which employees are given considerable authority and autonomy. This process is now common in vehicle design, which Toyota pioneered more than three decades ago. As design engineers work on product specifications, team members from production engineering, manufacturing, marketing, purchasing, and other departments provide immediate feedback as well as begin their contribution to the process. Without the informal coordination available through teams, the preliminary car design would pass from one department to the next—a much slower process.[12]

Coordination through Formal Hierarchy
Informal communication is the most flexible form of coordination, but it can become chaotic as the number of employees increases.

Consequently, as organizations grow, they rely increasingly on a second coordinating mechanism: formal hierarchy.[13] Hierarchy assigns legitimate power to individuals, who then use this power to direct work processes and allocate resources. In other words, work is coordinated through direct supervision—the chain of command. For instance, Walmart stores have managers and assistant managers who are responsible for ensuring that employees are properly trained, perform their respective tasks, and coordinate effectively with other staff.

A century ago, management scholars applauded the formal hierarchy as the best coordinating mechanism for large organizations. They argued that organizations are most effective when managers exercise their authority and employees receive orders from only one supervisor. The chain of command—in which information flows across work units only through supervisors and managers—was viewed as the backbone of organizational strength.

Although still important, formal hierarchy is much less popular today. One problem, which Samsung is trying to minimize with its new structure, is that hierarchical organizations are not as agile for coordination in complex and novel situations. Formal communication through the chain of command is rarely as fast or accurate as informal direct communication among employees. Another concern with formal hierarchy is that managers are able to closely supervise only a limited number of employees. As the business grows, the number of supervisors and layers of management must increase, resulting in a costly bureaucracy. A third problem is that today's workforce demands more autonomy over work and more involvement in company decisions. Coordination through formal hierarchy tends to limit employee autonomy and involvement, which increases employee complaints of being "micromanaged."

Coordination through Micromanagement[14]

44% of 434 American human resource professionals polled identify micromanaging as a major complaint or concern that younger employees have about older managers.

59% of 450 American employees surveyed say they have worked for a micromanager.

31% of 97,000 employees surveyed in 30 countries describe their company's leadership as oppressive or authoritative.
©Steve Hamblin/Corbis

18% of 300 American human resource managers say that micromanaging employees has the most negative effect on employee morale (second only to lack of open, honest communication).

25% of 500 American employees surveyed say they currently work for a "micromanager."

span of control the
number of people directly
reporting to the next level
above in the hierarchy

Coordination through Standardization Standardization, the third means of coordination, involves creating routine patterns of behavior or output. This coordinating mechanism takes three distinct forms:

- *Standardized processes.* Quality and consistency of a product or service often can be improved by standardizing work activities through job descriptions and procedures.[15] For example, flowcharts represent coordination through standardized processes. This coordinating mechanism works best when the task is routine (such as mass production) or simple (such as stocking shelves), but it is less effective in nonroutine and complex work such as product design (which occurs among employees at Samsung's creativity center).

- *Standardized outputs.* This form of standardization involves ensuring that individuals and work units have clearly defined goals and output measures (e.g., customer satisfaction, production efficiency). For instance, to coordinate the work of salespeople, companies assign sales targets rather than specific behaviors.

- *Standardized skills.* When work activities are too complex to standardize through processes or goals, companies often coordinate work effort by extensively training employees or hiring people who have learned precise role behaviors from educational programs. Samsung and other technology companies rely on coordination through standardized skills. They carefully hire people for their skills in software engineering and other disciplines so they can perform tasks without continuous supervision, precise job descriptions, or exacting work process guidelines. Training is also a form of standardization through skills. Many companies have in-house training programs where employees learn how to perform tasks consistent with company expectations.

Division of labor and coordination of work represent the two fundamental ingredients of all organizations. But how work is divided, which coordinating mechanisms are emphasized, who makes decisions, and other issues are related to the four elements of organizational structure that we discuss over the next two sections of this chapter.

LO12-2 Discuss the role and effects of span of control, centralization, and formalization, and relate these elements to organic and mechanistic organizational structures.

ELEMENTS OF ORGANIZATIONAL STRUCTURE

Organizational structure has four elements that apply to every organization. This section introduces three of them: span of control, centralization, and formalization. The fourth element—departmentalization—is presented in the next section.

Span of Control

Span of control (also called *span of management*) refers to the number of people directly reporting to the next level above in the hierarchy. A narrow span of control exists when very few people report directly to a manager, whereas a wide span exists when a manager has many direct reports.[16] A century ago, French engineer and management scholar Henri Fayol strongly recommended a relatively narrow span of control, typically no more than 20 employees per supervisor and 6 supervisors per manager. Fayol championed formal hierarchy as the primary coordinating mechanism, so he believed that supervisors should closely monitor and coach employees. His views were similar to those of Napoleon, who declared that senior military leaders should have no more than five officers directly reporting to them. These prescriptions were based on the belief that managers simply could not monitor and control any more subordinates closely enough.[17]

Today, we know better. The best-performing manufacturing plants currently have an average of 38 production employees per supervisor (see Exhibit 12.2).[18] What's the secret here? Did Fayol, Napoleon, and others miscalculate the optimal span of control? The answer is that those sympathetic to hierarchical control believed that employees should perform the physical tasks, whereas supervisors and other management personnel should make the decisions and monitor employees to make sure they performed their tasks. In contrast, the best-performing manufacturing operations today rely on self-directed teams, so direct supervision (formal hierarchy) is supplemented with other coordinating mechanisms. Self-directed teams coordinate mainly through informal communication and various forms of standardization (i.e., training and processes), so formal hierarchy plays more of a supporting role.

Managers often can accommodate a wider span of control because staff members are self-managing and coordinate mainly through standardized skills. For example, more than two dozen employees, ranging from project specialists to sales support staff, report directly to Amy Geiger, director of sales operations at Sunrise Identity. "Amy is a big proponent of letting her employees be self-led," says one of Geiger's direct reports at the Bellevue, Washington, marketing and merchandising agency. "She is against micromanaging and wants her employees to grow from their own learned experiences."[20]

A second factor influencing the best span of control is whether employees perform routine tasks. A wider span of control is possible when employees perform routine jobs because they require less direction or advice from supervisors. A narrow span of control is necessary when employees perform novel or complex tasks because these employees tend to require more supervisory decisions and coaching. This principle is illustrated in a survey of property and casualty insurers. The average span of control in commercial-policy processing departments is around 15 employees per supervisor, whereas the span of control is 6.1 in claims service and 5.5 in commercial underwriting. Staff members in the latter two departments perform more

Exhibit 12.2 Recommended, Actual, Estimated, and Enforced Spans of Control[19]

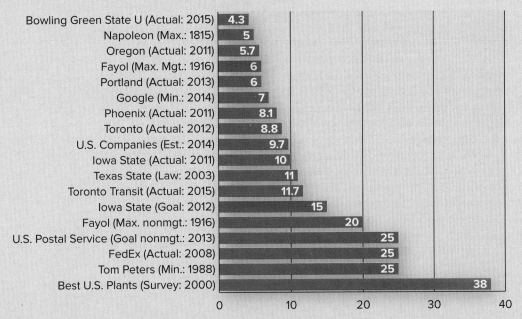

Bowling Green State U (Actual: 2015)	4.3
Napoleon (Max.: 1815)	5
Oregon (Actual: 2011)	5.7
Fayol (Max. Mgt.: 1916)	6
Portland (Actual: 2013)	6
Google (Min.: 2014)	7
Phoenix (Actual: 2011)	8.1
Toronto (Actual: 2012)	8.8
U.S. Companies (Est.: 2014)	9.7
Iowa State (Actual: 2011)	10
Texas State (Law: 2003)	11
Toronto Transit (Actual: 2015)	11.7
Iowa State (Goal: 2012)	15
Fayol (Max. nonmgt.: 1916)	20
U.S. Postal Service (Goal nonmgt.: 2013)	25
FedEx (Actual: 2008)	25
Tom Peters (Min.: 1988)	25
Best U.S. Plants (Survey: 2000)	38

Note: Data represent the average number of direct reports per manager. "Max." is the maximum spans of control recommended by Napoleon Bonaparte and Henri Fayol. "Min." is the minimum span of control applied to teams by Google and recommended by Tom Peters. "Est." is the estimated average span of control across all major U.S. companies, according to consulting firm Deloitte. "Goal" refers to the span of control targets that the U.S. Postal Service and State of Iowa are trying to achieve. (USPS currently exceeds its goal.) The State of Texas number is the span of control mandated by law. The Best U.S. Plants number is the average span of control in American manufacturing facilities identified by *Industry Week* magazine as the most effective. "Actual" refers to the spans of control reported in the cities of Phoenix, Portland, and Toronto; the public service of the U.S. states of Oregon and Iowa; Bowling Green State University; the Toronto Transit Commission; and FedEx Corporation in the years indicated. The City of Toronto number excludes firefighters and parks, which have unusually high spans of control. When these units are included, Toronto's span of control is 16.29.

technical work, so they have more novel and complex tasks, which requires more active supervision. Commercial-policy processing, on the other hand, is like production work. Tasks are routine and have few exceptions, so managers have less coordinating to do with each employee.[21]

A third influence on span of control is the degree of interdependence among employees within the department or team.[22] Generally, a narrow span of control is necessary for highly interdependent jobs because employees tend to experience more conflict with each other, which requires more of a manager's time to resolve. Also, employees are less clear on their personal work performance in highly interdependent tasks, so supervisors spend more time providing coaching and feedback.

Tall versus Flat Structures Span of control is interconnected with organizational size (number of employees) and the number of layers in the organizational hierarchy. Consider two companies with the same number of employees. If Company A

As companies grow, they usually build taller structures to enable some degree of direct supervision as a coordinating mechanism.
©Ilya Terentyev/Getty Images

has a wider span of control (more direct reports per manager) than Company B, then Company A necessarily has fewer layers of management (i.e., a flatter structure). The reason for this relationship is that a company with a wider span of control has more employees per supervisor, more supervisors for each middle manager, and so on. This larger number of direct reports, compared to a company with a narrower span of control, is possible only by removing layers of management.

The interconnection of span of control, organizational size (number of employees), and number of management layers has important implications for companies. As organizations grow, they typically employ more people, which means they must widen the span of control, build a taller hierarchy, or both. Most companies end up building taller structures because they rely on direct supervision to some extent as a coordinating mechanism and there are limits to how many people each manager can coordinate.

Unfortunately, building a taller hierarchy (more layers of management) creates

centralization the degree to which formal decision authority is held by a small group of people, typically those at the top of the organizational hierarchy

problems. One concern is that executives in tall structures tend to receive lower-quality and less timely information. People tend to filter, distort, and simplify information before it is passed to higher levels in the hierarchy because they are motivated to frame the information in a positive light or to summarize it more efficiently. In contrast, in flat hierarchies, information is manipulated less and is usually transmitted much more quickly than in tall hierarchies.

A second problem is that taller structures have higher overhead costs. With more managers per employee, tall hierarchies necessarily have more people administering the company, thereby reducing the percentage of staff who are actually making the product or providing the service. A third issue with tall hierarchies is that employees usually feel less empowered and engaged in their work. Hierarchies are power structures, so more levels of hierarchy tend to draw power away from people at the bottom of that hierarchy. Indeed, the size of the hierarchy itself tends to focus power around managers rather than employees.[23]

These problems with tall hierarchies have prompted companies to reduce management layers. For example, McDonald's Corp. and BCE (Canada's largest telecommunications company) recently sliced out three layers of management. McDonald's CEO Steve Easterbrook says that the delayering "has meant the visibility and the flow of ideas and the transparency was just much, much quicker for all of us as we're making our business decisions." Conagra Foods also recently restructured into a flatter organization. CEO Sean Connolly says the packaged food company now has "fewer layers, broader spans of control and the workforce, we believe, is right-sized for speed, empowerment, agility, all the things we need to do."[25]

There are potential negative consequences of flattening the hierarchy, however.[26] Critics warn that all companies need managers to translate corporate strategy into coherent daily operations. Delayering widens the span of control, leaving managers with less time to effectively coach employees, resolve conflicts, and make operational decisions within the work unit. Fewer layers also reduce the company's ability to develop managerial skills because there are fewer positions and steps to develop management talent. Promotions are also riskier because they involve a larger jump in responsibility in flatter, compared to taller, hierarchies.

Centralization and Decentralization

Centralization means that formal decision-making authority is held by a small group of people, typically those at the top of the organizational hierarchy. Most organizations begin with centralized structures because the founder makes most of the decisions and tries to direct the business toward his or her vision. As organizations grow, however, they diversify and their environments

> ❝ Any new idea condemned to struggle upward through multiple levels of rigidly hierarchical, risk-averse management is an idea that won't see daylight . . . until it's too late.[24] ❞
>
> —Sergio Marchionne, CEO of Fiat Chrysler Automobiles and Ferrari

become more complex. Senior executives aren't able to process all the decisions that significantly influence the business. Consequently, larger organizations typically *decentralize*; that is, they disperse decision authority and power throughout the organization.

The optimal level of centralization or decentralization depends on several contingencies that we will examine later in this chapter. However, different degrees of decentralization can occur simultaneously in different parts of an organization. For instance, 7-Eleven centralizes decisions about information technology and supplier purchasing to improve buying power, increase cost-efficiencies, and minimize complexity across the organization. Yet it decentralizes local inventory decisions to store managers because they have the best information about their customers and can respond quickly to local market needs. "We could never predict a busload of football players on a Friday night, but the store manager can," explains a 7-Eleven executive.[28]

Formalization

Formalization is the degree to which organizations standardize behavior through rules, procedures, formal training, and related mechanisms.[29] In other words, companies become more formalized as they increasingly rely on various forms of standardization to coordinate work. McDonald's restaurants and most other efficient fast-food chains typically have a high degree of formalization because they rely on standardization of work processes as a coordinating mechanism. Employees have precisely defined roles, right down to how much mustard should be dispensed, how many pickles should be applied, and how long each hamburger should be cooked.

Older companies tend to become more formalized because work activities become routinized, making them easier to document into standardized practices. Larger companies also tend to have more formalization because direct supervision and informal communication among employees do not operate as easily when large numbers of people are involved. External influences, such as government safety legislation and strict accounting rules, also encourage formalization.

Formalization may increase efficiency and compliance, but it also can create problems.[30] Rules and procedures reduce organizational flexibility, so employees follow prescribed behaviors even when the situation clearly calls for a customized response. High levels of formalization tend to undermine organizational

> ❝ Companies become more formalized as they increasingly rely on various forms of standardization to coordinate work. ❞

learning and creativity. Some work rules become so convoluted that organizational efficiency would decline if they were actually followed as prescribed. Formalization is also a source of job dissatisfaction and work stress. Finally, rules and procedures have been known to take on a life of their own in some organizations. They become the focus of attention rather than the organization's ultimate objectives of producing a product or service and serving its dominant stakeholders.

Mechanistic versus Organic Structures

We discussed span of control, centralization, and formalization together because they cluster around two broader organizational forms: mechanistic and organic structures (see Exhibit 12.3).[31] A **mechanistic structure** is characterized by a narrow span of control and a high degree of formalization and centralization. Mechanistic structures have many rules and procedures, limited decision making at lower levels, tall hierarchies of people in specialized roles, and vertical rather than horizontal communication flows. Tasks are rigidly defined and are altered only when sanctioned by higher authorities. Although now changing its structure, Samsung has traditionally had a mechanistic structure, which is apparent by the Korean firm's centralized decision making, clearly defined job descriptions, and work activities heavily guided by established rules and procedures.

formalization the degree to which organizations standardize behavior through rules, procedures, formal training, and related mechanisms

mechanistic structure an organizational structure with a narrow span of control and a high degree of formalization and centralization

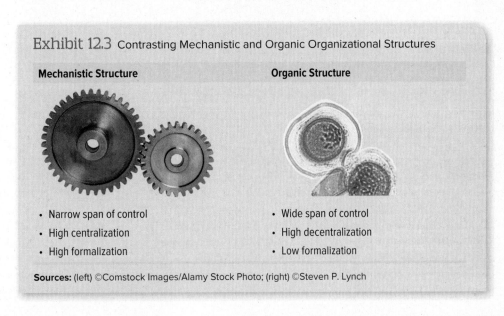

Exhibit 12.3 Contrasting Mechanistic and Organic Organizational Structures

Mechanistic Structure
- Narrow span of control
- High centralization
- High formalization

Organic Structure
- Wide span of control
- High decentralization
- Low formalization

Sources: (left) ©Comstock Images/Alamy Stock Photo; (right) ©Steven P. Lynch

Companies with an **organic structure** have the opposite characteristics. They operate with a wide span of control, decentralized decision making, and little formalization. Tasks are fluid, adjusting to new situations and organizational needs. In extremely organic organizations, decision making is decentralized down to teams and individuals, and employees have enough autonomy to adapt their job duties to fit the situation.

As a general rule, mechanistic structures operate better in stable environments because they rely on efficiency and routine behaviors. Organic structures work better in rapidly changing (i.e., dynamic) environments because they are more flexible and responsive to the changes. Organic structures are also more compatible with organizational learning and high-performance workplaces because they emphasize information sharing and an empowered workforce rather than hierarchy and status.[32] However, the effectiveness of organic structures depends on how well employees have developed their roles and expertise.[33] Without these conditions, employees are unable to coordinate effectively with each other, resulting in errors and gross inefficiencies.

strategy for coordinating organizational activities because it influences organizational behavior in the following ways:[34]

- Departmentalization establishes the chain of command—the system of common supervision among positions and units within the organization. It frames the membership of formal work teams and typically determines which positions and units must share resources. Thus, departmentalization establishes interdependencies among employees and subunits.

- Departmentalization focuses people around common mental models or ways of thinking, such as serving clients, developing products, or supporting a particular skill set. This focus is typically anchored around the common budgets and measures of performance assigned to employees within each departmental unit.

- Departmentalization encourages specific people and work units to coordinate through informal communication. With common supervision and resources, members within each configuration typically work near each other, so they can use frequent and informal interaction to get the work done.

There are almost as many organizational charts as there are businesses, but the five most common pure types of departmentalization are simple, functional, divisional, team-based, and matrix.

Simple Structure

Most companies begin with a *simple structure*.[35] They employ only a few people and typically offer only one distinct product or service. There is minimal hierarchy—usually just employees reporting to the owners. Employees perform broadly defined roles because there are insufficient economies of scale to assign them to specialized jobs. The simple structure is highly flexible and minimizes the walls that form between employees in other structures. However, the simple structure usually depends on the owner's direct supervision to coordinate work activities, so it is very difficult to operate as the company grows and becomes more complex.

LO12-3 Identify and evaluate five types of departmentalization.

FORMS OF DEPARTMENTALIZATION

Span of control, centralization, and formalization are important elements of organizational structure, but most people think about organizational charts when the discussion of organizational structure arises. The organizational chart represents the fourth element in the structuring of organizations, called *departmentalization*. Departmentalization specifies how employees and their activities are grouped together. It is a fundamental

Functional Structure

As organizations grow, they typically shift from a simple structure to a functional structure. Even after they adopt more complex organizational structures that we discuss later, they will have a functional structure at some level of the hierarchy. A **functional structure** organizes employees around specific knowledge or other resources (see Exhibit 12.4). Employees with marketing expertise are grouped into a marketing unit, those with production skills are located in manufacturing, engineers are found in product development, and so on. Organizations with functional structures are typically centralized to coordinate their activities effectively.

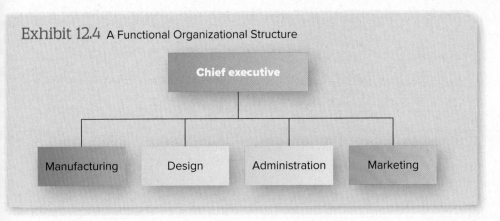

Exhibit 12.4 A Functional Organizational Structure

```
                    Chief executive
        ┌──────────┬──────────────┬──────────┐
   Manufacturing   Design   Administration   Marketing
```

Evaluating the Functional Structure The functional structure creates specialized pools of talent that typically serve everyone in the organization. Pooling talent into one group improves economies of scale compared to dispersing functional specialists over different parts of the organization. The functional structure also increases employee identity with the specialization or profession. Direct supervision is easier in a functional structure because managers oversee people with common issues and expertise.[36]

The functional structure also has limitations.[37] Grouping employees around their skills tends to focus attention on those skills and related professional needs rather than on the company's products, services, or client needs. Unless people are transferred from one function to the next, they might not develop a broader understanding of the business. Compared with other structures, the functional structure usually produces more dysfunctional conflict and poorer coordination in serving clients or developing products. These problems occur because employees need to work with coworkers in other departments to complete organizational tasks, yet they have different subgoals and mental models about how to perform the work effectively. Together, these problems require substantial

By grouping employees around their skills, the functional structure focuses attention on those skills rather than on the company's products, services, or client needs.
©tkemot/Shutterstock

divisional structure an organizational structure in which employees are organized around geographic areas, outputs (products or services), or clients

formal controls and coordination when people are organized around functions.

Divisional Structure

The **divisional structure** (sometimes called the *multidivisional* or *M-form* structure) groups employees around geographic areas, outputs (products or services), or clients. Exhibit 12.5 illustrates these three variations of divisional structure.[38] The *geographic divisional structure* organizes employees around distinct regions of the country or world. Exhibit 12.5(a) illustrates a simplified version of the geographic divisional structure adopted by Kone, the Finland-based global elevator and escalator company. The *product/service divisional structure* organizes employees around distinct outputs. Exhibit 12.5(b) illustrates the four product divisions at Danone, the France-based global food company. The *client divisional structure* organizes employees around specific customer groups. Exhibit 12.5(c) illustrates a customer-focused divisional structure adopted by the U.S. Internal Revenue Service.[39]

Which form of divisional structure should large organizations adopt? The answer depends mainly on the primary source of environmental diversity or uncertainty.[40] Suppose an organization has one type of product sold to people across the country. If customers have different needs across regions, or if state governments impose different regulations on the product, then a geographic structure would be best so the company can be more vigilant about this diversity. On the other hand, if the company sells several types of products across the country and customer preferences and government regulations are similar everywhere, then a product structure would likely work best.

Kone, the global elevator and escalator company, is organized mainly around geographic regions, likely because regulations and sales channels vary much more by region than by product. McDonald's is organized into four geographic divisions (high growth, established, franchised) and is further organized by specific countries or zones within each of these divisions. This geographic organization makes sense because even though it makes the same Big Mac throughout the world, McDonald's has more fish products in Hong Kong and more vegetarian products in India, in line with traditional diets in those countries. Danone has dozens of country managers to anticipate and respond to cultural differences. However, the French dairy products maker places product groups (waters, dairy, medical, early life) at the top of its organizational structure, possibly because marketing and manufacturing activities vary much more across product divisions than across regions.

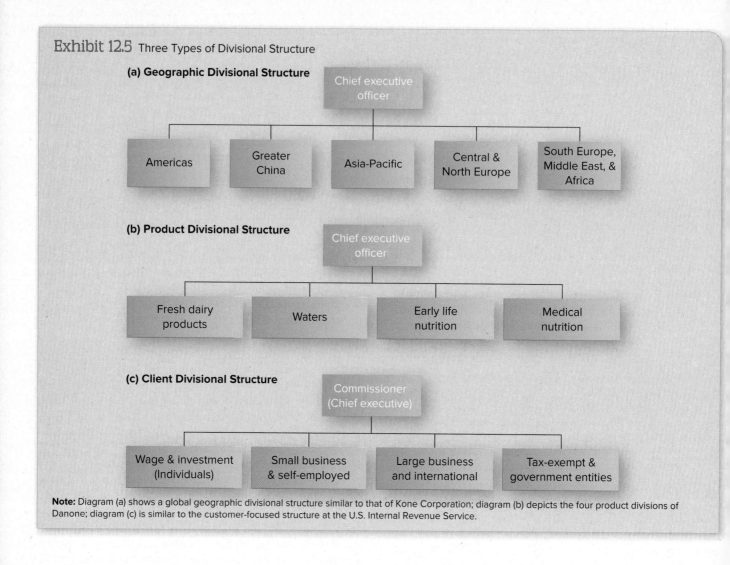

Exhibit 12.5 Three Types of Divisional Structure

(a) Geographic Divisional Structure

Chief executive officer
- Americas
- Greater China
- Asia-Pacific
- Central & North Europe
- South Europe, Middle East, & Africa

(b) Product Divisional Structure

Chief executive officer
- Fresh dairy products
- Waters
- Early life nutrition
- Medical nutrition

(c) Client Divisional Structure

Commissioner (Chief executive)
- Wage & investment (Individuals)
- Small business & self-employed
- Large business and international
- Tax-exempt & government entities

Note: Diagram (a) shows a global geographic divisional structure similar to that of Kone Corporation; diagram (b) depicts the four product divisions of Danone; diagram (c) is similar to the customer-focused structure at the U.S. Internal Revenue Service.

Many companies are moving away from structures that organize people around geographic clusters.[41] One reason is that clients can purchase products online and communicate with businesses from almost anywhere in the world, so local representation is becoming less important. Reduced geographic variation is another reason for the shift away from geographic structures; freer trade has reduced government intervention, and consumer preferences for many products and services are becoming more similar (converging) around the world. The third reason is that large companies increasingly have global business customers who demand one global point of purchase, not one in every country or region.

Evaluating the Divisional Structure The divisional organizational structure is a building-block structure; it accommodates growth relatively easily. As the company develops new products, services, or clients, it can sprout new divisions. The divisional structure is also outcome-focused. It directs employee attention to customers and products, rather than to their own specialized knowledge.[42]

Whether an organization should adopt a geographic, product, or client-focused structure depends mainly on the primary source of environmental diversity or uncertainty.
©David Pearson/REX/Shutterstock

These advantages are offset by a number of limitations. First, the divisional structure tends to duplicate resources, such as production equipment and engineering or information technology expertise. Also, unless the division is quite large, resources are not used as efficiently as they are in functional structures where resources are pooled across the entire organization. The divisional structure also creates silos of knowledge. Expertise is spread across several autonomous business units, and this reduces the ability and perhaps motivation of the people in one division to share their knowledge with counterparts in other divisions. In contrast, a functional structure organizes experts together, thereby supporting knowledge sharing.

Finally, the preferred divisional structure depends on the company's primary source of environmental diversity or uncertainty. This principle seems to be applied easily enough at McDonald's and the U.S. Internal Revenue Service, but many global organizations experience diversity and uncertainty in terms of geography, product, *and* clients. Consequently, some organizations revise their structures back and forth or create complex structures that attempt to give all three dimensions equal status. This waffling generates further complications because organizational structure decisions shift power and status among executives. If the company switches from a geographic to a product structure, people who lead the geographic fiefdoms suddenly get demoted under the product chiefs. In short, leaders of global organizations struggle to find the best divisional structure, often resulting in the departure of some executives and frustration among those who remain.

Team-Based Structure

A **team-based organizational structure** is built around self-directed teams that complete an entire piece of work, such as manufacturing a product or developing an electronic game. This type of structure is usually organic. There is a wide span of control because teams operate with minimal supervision. There is no formal leader in its most extreme variation, just someone selected by other team members to help coordinate the work and liaise with top management.

Team structures are highly decentralized because almost all day-to-day decisions are made by team members rather than someone further up the organizational hierarchy. Many team-based structures also have low formalization because teams are given relatively few rules about how to organize their work. Instead, executives assign quality and quantity output targets, and often productivity improvement goals, to each team. Teams are then encouraged to use available resources and their own initiative to achieve those objectives.

Team-based structures are usually found within the manufacturing or service operations of larger divisional structures. Several GE Aircraft Engines plants are organized as team-based structures, but these plants operate within GE's larger divisional structure. However, a small number of firms apply the team-based structure from top to bottom, including W. L. Gore & Associates, Semco SA, Morning Star Company, and Valve Corporation, where almost all employees work in teams.

Evaluating the Team-Based Structure

The team-based structure has gained popularity because it is more flexible and responsive in turbulent environments.[43] It tends to reduce costs because teams have less reliance on formal hierarchy (direct supervision). A cross-functional team structure improves communication and cooperation across traditional boundaries. With greater autonomy, this structure also allows quicker and more informed decision making.[44] For this reason, some hospitals have shifted from functional departments to cross-functional teams. Teams composed of nurses, radiologists, anesthetists, a pharmacology representative, possibly social workers, a rehabilitation therapist, and other specialists communicate and coordinate more efficiently, thereby reducing delays and errors.[45]

Some hospitals have shifted from functional departments to cross-functional teams to improve communication and cooperation across traditional specialist boundaries.
©Fuse/Getty Images

> One limitation of the divisional structure is that, unless the division is quite large, resources are not used as efficiently as they are in functional structures where resources are pooled across the entire organization.

matrix structure an organizational structure that overlays two structures (such as a geographic divisional and a product divisional structure) in order to leverage the benefits of both

The team-based structure also has several limitations. It can be costly to maintain due to the need for ongoing interpersonal skills training. Teamwork potentially takes more time to coordinate than formal hierarchy during the early stages of team development. Employees may experience more stress due to increased ambiguity in their roles. Team leaders also experience more stress due to increased conflict, loss of functional power, and unclear career progression ladders. In addition, team structures suffer from duplication of resources and potential competition (and lack of resource sharing) across teams.[46]

Matrix Structure

ABB Group, one of the world's largest power and automation technology engineering firms, has four product divisions, such as power grids and process automation. It employs more than 140,000 people across 100 countries, so the global giant also has several regional groups (Americas, AMEA, and Europe). What organizational structure would work best for ABB? For example, should the head of power grids in North America report to the worldwide head of power products in Zurich, Switzerland, or to the head of the Americas operations?

For ABB, the answer is to have a **matrix structure**, which overlays two structures (in this case, a product divisional and geographic divisional structure) to leverage the benefits of both.[47] Exhibit 12.6 shows a product–geographic matrix structure, which is a simplified version of ABB's structure. The dots represent the individuals who have two bosses. For example, the head of power grids in Europe reports to ABB's worldwide president of power grids as well as to ABB's president of European regional operations.

A common mistake is to assume that everyone in this type of matrix organizational structure reports to two bosses. In reality, only managers at one level in the organization (typically country-specific product managers) have two bosses. For example, as mentioned, ABB's executive responsible for power grids in Europe reports to both the product and regional leaders. However, employees below that country product leader report to only one manager in the European operations.

The product–geographic matrix structure is the most common matrix design among global companies. For instance, Shiseido, Procter & Gamble, and Shell have variations of this matrix structure because these firms recognize that regional groups and product/services groups are equally important. Other variations of matrix structures also exist in global businesses. H&M, the Swedish fast-fashion retail group, has a matrix organizational structure that intersects its brands-based divisions (H&M, H&M Home, Cheap Monday, Monki, Cos, etc.) with almost a dozen functional groups (logistics, production, accounting, human resources, etc).[48]

Exhibit 12.6 Matrix Organizational Structure at ABB Group

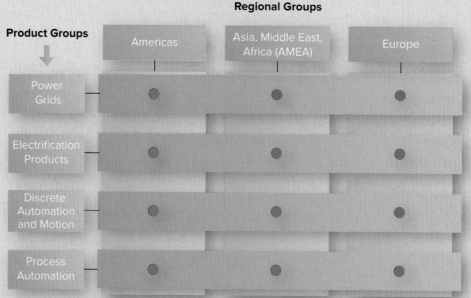

● Product leader in that region

Note: This diagram is for illustrative purposes only. It represents a simplified version of ABB's most recent structure. The complete top-level structure also has three nonmatrixed functional groups (finance, legal, HR) reporting to the CEO. In addition, this diagram assumes ABB has a pure matrix structure, in which both product and regional chiefs have equal power. ABB says it continues to have a matrix structure, but its recent reorganization seems to give more direct line authority to product groups rather than regional groups.

Global organizations tend to have complex designs that combine different types of structures, so a "pure" matrix design is relatively uncommon. A pure matrix gives equal power to leaders of both groups (products and regions, for example), whereas in reality companies often give more power to one set of groups while the other set of groups has mostly "dotted line" or advisory authority. So, although ABB's head of power grids has two bosses, the global president of power grids might have more final say or line authority than the regional leader on most issues.

Some companies also deviate from the pure matrix structure by applying it only to some regions. One such example is Cummins Inc., which is mainly organized around product divisions but has a matrix structure in China, India, and Russia. These markets are large, have high potential, and tend to be less visible to headquarters, so the country leaders are given as much authority as the product leaders within those regions. "I think in China there's still enough lack of transparency, there's still enough uniqueness to the market that having some kind of coordination across business units gets the greatest synergies," explains Michael Barbalas, a board member of the American Chamber of Commerce in China.[49]

A second type of matrix structure, which can be applied to small or large companies, overlays a functional structure with a project structure.[50] BioWare adopted this project–functional matrix structure soon after the electronic games company was born two decades ago. Most BioWare employees have two managers. One manager leads the specific project to which employees are assigned, such as *Star Wars*, *Mass Effect*, and *Dragon Age*; the other manager is head of the employee's functional specialization, such as art, programming, audio, quality assurance, and design.[51] Employees are assigned permanently to their functional unit but physically work with the temporary project team. When the project nears completion, the functional boss reassigns employees in his or her functional specialization to another project.

Evaluating the Matrix Structure The project–functional matrix structure usually makes very good use of resources and expertise, making it ideal for project-based organizations with fluctuating workloads. When properly managed, it improves communication efficiency, project flexibility, and innovation, compared to purely functional or divisional designs. It focuses employees on serving clients or creating products, yet keeps people organized around their specialization. The result is that knowledge sharing improves and human resources are used more efficiently.

Matrix structures for global organizations are also a logical choice when, as in the case of ABB Group, two different dimensions (regions and products) are equally important. Structures determine executive power and what should receive priority; the matrix structure works best when the business environment is complex and two different dimensions deserve equal attention and integration. Executives who have worked in a global matrix also say they have more freedom, likely because their two bosses are more advisory and less oriented toward command-and-control leadership.[52]

The many advantages of the matrix structure are offset by well-known problems.[54] One concern is that it increases conflict among managers who equally share power. Employees working at the matrix level have two bosses and, consequently, two sets of priorities that aren't always aligned with each other. Project leaders might squabble with functional leaders regarding the assignment of specific employees to projects as well as regarding the employee's technical competence. However, successful companies manage this conflict by developing and promoting leaders who can work effectively in matrix structures. "Of course there's potential for friction," says an executive at IBM India. "In fact, one of the prerequisites to attaining a leadership position at IBM is the ability to function in a matrix structure."[55]

Ambiguous accountability is another challenge with matrix structures. In a functional or divisional structure, one manager is responsible for everything, even the most unexpected issues. But in a matrix structure, the unusual problems don't get resolved because neither manager takes ownership of them.[56] Due to this ambiguous accountability, matrix structures have been blamed for corporate ethical misconduct, such as embezzlement at Hana Financial Group in Korea and massive bribery at Siemens AG in Germany. The combination of dysfunctional conflict and ambiguous accountability in matrix structures also explains why some employees experience more stress and why some managers are less satisfied with their work arrangements.

LO12-4 Explain how the external environment, organizational size, technology, and strategy are relevant when designing an organizational structure.

CONTINGENCIES OF ORGANIZATIONAL DESIGN

Most organizational behavior theories and concepts have contingencies: Ideas that work well in one situation might not work as well in another situation. This contingency approach is certainly relevant when choosing the most appropriate organizational structure.[57] In this section, we introduce four contingencies of organizational design: external environment, size, technology, and strategy.

External Environment

The best structure for an organization depends on its external environment. The external environment includes anything outside the organization, including most stakeholders (e.g., clients, suppliers, government), resources (e.g., raw materials, human resources, information, finances), and competitors. Four characteristics of external environments influence the type of organizational structure best suited to a particular situation: dynamism, complexity, diversity, and hostility.[58]

Dynamic versus Stable Environments Dynamic environments have a high rate of change, leading to novel situations and a lack of identifiable patterns. Organic structures, particularly those in which employees are experienced and coordinate well in teams, are better suited to dynamic environments, so the organization can adapt more quickly to changes.[59] In contrast, stable environments are characterized by regular cycles of activity and steady changes in supply and demand for inputs and outputs. Events are more predictable, enabling the firm to apply rules and procedures. Mechanistic structures are more efficient when the environment is predictable, so they tend to be more profitable than organic structures under these conditions.

Complex versus Simple Environments Complex environments have many elements, whereas simple environments have few things to monitor. As an example, a major university library operates in a more complex environment than a small-town public library. The university library's clients require several types of services—book borrowing, online full-text databases, research centers, course reserve collections, and so on. A small-town public library has fewer of these demands placed on it. The more complex the environment, the more decentralized the

Mechanistic structures are better suited to stable environments, which have regular cycles of activity and predictable changes in supply and demand for inputs and outputs.
©Monty Rakusen/Cultura/Getty Images

organization should become. Decentralization is a logical choice for complex environments because decisions are pushed down to people and subunits who possess the information needed to make informed choices.

Diverse versus Integrated Environments Organizations located in diverse environments have a greater variety of products or services, clients, and regions. In contrast, an integrated environment has only one client, product, and geographic area. The more diversified the environment, the more the firm needs to use a divisional structure aligned with that diversity. If it sells a single product around the world, a geographic divisional structure would align best with the firm's geographic diversity, for example. Diverse environments also call for decentralization. By pushing decision making further down the hierarchy, the company can adapt better and more quickly to diverse clients, government requirements, and other circumstances related to that diversity.

Hostile versus Munificent Environments Firms located in hostile environments face resource scarcity and more competition in the marketplace. These conditions are typically dynamic

OB THEORY TO PRACTICE

Choosing the Best Organizational Structure for the Environment

- Organic structures are better suited for dynamic environments; mechanistic structures are usually more effective for stable environments.

- Organizations should be more decentralized as environments become more complex.

- Diverse environments call for a divisional structure aligned with the highest form of diversity.

- Organic structures are better suited for hostile environments; mechanistic structures are usually more effective in munificent environments

as well because they reduce the predictability of access to resources and demand for outputs. Organic structures tend to be best in hostile environments. However, when the environment is extremely unfavorable—such as a severe shortage of supplies or tumbling market share—organizations tend to temporarily centralize so that decisions can be made more quickly and executives feel more comfortable being in control.[60] Ironically, centralization may result in lower-quality decisions during organizational crises because top management has less information, particularly when the environment is complex.

Organizational Size

Larger organizations have different structures than do smaller organizations, for good reason.[61] As the number of employees increases, job specialization increases due to a greater division of labor. The greater division of labor requires more elaborate coordinating mechanisms. Thus, larger firms make greater use of standardization (particularly work processes and outcomes) to coordinate work activities. These coordinating mechanisms create an administrative hierarchy and greater formalization. Historically, larger organizations make less use of informal communication as a coordinating mechanism. However, emerging information technologies and increased emphasis on empowerment have caused informal communication to regain its importance in large firms.[62]

Larger organizations also tend to be more decentralized than are smaller organizations. Executives have neither sufficient time nor expertise to process all the decisions that significantly influence the business as it grows. Therefore, decision-making authority is pushed down to lower levels, where employees are able to make decisions on issues within their narrower range of responsibility.

Technology

Technology is another factor to consider when designing the best organizational structure for the situation.[63] *Technology* refers to the mechanisms or processes an organization relies on to make its products or services. In other words, technology isn't just the equipment used to make something; it also includes how the production process is physically arranged and how the production work is divided among employees.

The two main technological contingencies are task variability and task analyzability, both of which we described as job characteristics in Chapter 5. *Task variability* refers to how predictable the job duties are from one day to the next. In jobs with high variability, employees perform several types of tasks, but they don't know which of those tasks are required from one day to the next. Low variability occurs when the work is highly routine and predictable. *Task analyzability* refers to how much the job can be performed using known procedures and rules. In jobs with high task analyzability, employees have well-defined guidelines to direct them through the work process. In jobs with low task analyzability, employees tackle unique situations with few (if any) guidelines to help them determine the best course of action.

An organic, rather than a mechanistic, structure should be introduced where employees perform tasks with high variability and low analyzability, such as in a research setting. The reason is that employees face unique situations with little opportunity for repetition. In contrast, a mechanistic structure is preferred where the technology has low variability and high analyzability, such as an assembly line. Assembly work is routine, is highly predictable, and has well-established procedures—an ideal situation for a mechanistic structure to operate efficiently.

Organizational Strategy

Organizational strategy refers to the way the organization positions itself in its environment in relation to its stakeholders,

Organizations tend to be more decentralized as they grow because executives have neither sufficient time nor expertise to process all the decisions that significantly influence a large business.
©Matej Kastelic/Shutterstock

given the organization's resources, capabilities, and mission.[64] In other words, strategy represents the decisions and actions applied to achieve the organization's goals. Although size, technology, and environment influence the optimal organizational structure, these contingencies do not necessarily determine structure. Instead, corporate leaders formulate and implement strategies that shape both the characteristics of these contingencies as well as the organization's resulting structure.

This concept is summed up with the simple phrase "structure follows strategy."[65] Organizational leaders decide how large to grow and which technologies to use. They take steps to define and manipulate their environments, rather than let the organization's fate be entirely determined by external influences (see the open systems perspective in Chapter 1). Furthermore, organizational structures don't evolve as a natural response to environmental conditions; they result from conscious human decisions. Thus, organizational strategy influences both the contingencies of structure and the structure itself.

If a company's strategy is to compete through innovation, a more organic structure would be preferred because it is easier for employees to share knowledge and be creative. If a company chooses a low-cost strategy, a mechanistic structure is preferred because it maximizes production and service efficiency.[66] Overall, it is now apparent that organizational structure is influenced by size, technology, and environment, but the organization's strategy may reshape these elements and loosen their connection to organizational structure.

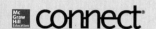

SELF-ASSESSMENT 12.2: Does Your Job Require An Organic or Mechanistic Structure?

Different jobs require different types of organizational structures. For some jobs, employees work better in an organic structure. In other jobs, a mechanistic structure helps incumbents perform their work better. Think of the job you currently have or recently held, or even your "job" as a student. You can discover which structure is better for your job by locating this self-assessment in Connect if it is assigned by your instructor.

Study Checklist

Connect® Management is available for *M Organizational Behavior.* Additional resources include:

✓ Interactive Applications:
- **Decision Generator**
- **Drag and Drop:** Work through an interactive example to test your knowledge of the concepts.
- **Video Case:** See management in action through interactive videos.

✓ **SmartBook™**—SmartBook is the first and only adaptive reading experience available today. Distinguishing what you know from what you don't, and honing in on concepts you are most likely to forget, SmartBook personalizes content for you in a continuously adapting reading experience. Reading is no longer a passive and linear experience, but an engaging and dynamic one where you are more likely to master and retain important concepts and go to class better prepared.

©Natthawat Jamnapa/123RF

Notes

1. "Samsung Emulates Silicon Valley by Letting Staff Take on Pet Projects," *Today* (Singapore), November 20, 2015, 55; Y.-C. Kim, "Samsung to Overhaul Rigid Business Structure," *Korea Times*, March 24, 2016; "Korean Companies Seek to Drop Job Titles," *Korea Herald*, April 6, 2016; "Samsung to Streamline Job Titles," *The Nation* (Bangkok), February 11, 2017; "Samsung to Demolish Rigid, Top-Down Corporate Culture," *Korea Times*, February 11, 2017.

2. S. Ranson, R. Hinings, and R. Greenwood, "The Structuring of Organizational Structure," *Administrative Science Quarterly* 25 (1980): 1–14; J. E. Johanson, "Intraorganizational Influence," *Management Communication Quarterly* 13 (2000): 393–435; K. Walsh, "Interpreting the Impact of Culture on Structure," *Journal of Applied Behavioral Science* 40, no. 3 (2004): 302–22. The recent survey is reported in J. Bersin et al., "The New Organization: Different by Design," in *Global Human Capital Trends 2016* (Westlake, TX: Deloitte University Press, 2016), 1–14.

3. H. Mintzberg, *The Structuring of Organizations* (Englewood Cliffs, NJ: Prentice Hall, 1979), 2–3.

4. E. E. Lawler III, *Motivation in Work Organizations* (Monterey, CA: Brooks/Cole, 1973); M. A. Campion, "Ability Requirement Implications of Job Design: An Interdisciplinary Perspective," *Personnel Psychology* 42 (1989): 1–24.

5. G. S. Becker and K. M. Murphy, "The Division of Labor, Coordination Costs, and Knowledge," *Quarterly Journal of Economics* 107, no. 4 (1992): 1137–60; L. Borghans and B. Weel, "The Division of Labour, Worker Organisation, and Technological Change," *The Economic Journal* 116, no. 509 (2006): F45–F72.

6. H. Mintzberg, *The Structuring of Organizations* (Englewood Cliffs, NJ: Prentice Hall, 1979), chap. 1; D. A. Nadler and M. L. Tushman, *Competing by Design: The Power of Organizational Architecture* (New York: Oxford University Press, 1997), chap. 6; J. R. Galbraith, *Designing Organizations: An Executive Guide to Strategy, Structure, and Process* (San Francisco: Jossey-Bass, 2002), chap. 4.

7. J. Stephenson Jr., "Making Humanitarian Relief Networks More Effective: Operational Coordination, Trust and Sense Making," *Disasters* 29, no. 4 (2005): 337.

8. A. Willem, M. Buelens, and H. Scarbrough, "The Role of Inter-Unit Coordination Mechanisms in Knowledge Sharing: A Case Study of a British MNC," *Journal of Information Science* 32, no. 6 (2006): 539-61; R. R. Gulati, "Silo Busting," *Harvard Business Review* 85, no. 5 (2007): 98-108.

9. L. Borghans and B. Weel, "The Division of Labour, Worker Organisation, and Technological Change," *The Economic Journal* 116, no. 509 (2006): F45-F72.

10. T. Van Alphen, "Magna in Overdrive," *Toronto Star*, July 24, 2006.

11. J. R. Galbraith, *Designing Organizations: An Executive Guide to Strategy, Structure, and Process* (San Francisco, CA: Jossey-Bass, 2002), 66-72; D. Aaker, *Spanning Silos: The New CMO Imperative* (Cambridge, MA: Harvard Business Press, 2008), 95-96; A. Pike, *Brands and Branding Geographies* (Cheltenham, UK: Edward Elgar, 2011), 133.

12. S. M. Sapuan, M. R. Osman, and Y. Nukman, "State of the Art of the Concurrent Engineering Technique in the Automotive Industry," *Journal of Engineering Design* 17, no. 2 (2006): 143-57; D. M. Anderson, *Design for Manufacturing: How to Use Concurrent Engineering to Rapidly Develop Low-Cost, High-Quality Products for Lean Management* (Boca Raton, FL: CRC Press/Taylor & Francis, 2014), chap. 2.

13. A. H. Van De Ven, A. L. Delbecq, and R. J. Koenig Jr., "Determinants of Coordination Modes within Organizations," *American Sociological Review* 41, no. 2 (1976): 322-38.

14. T. Gould, "How Employees Really Feel about Their Bosses," *HR Morning*, July 2, 2011; Kelly Services, *Effective Employers: The Evolving Workforce*, Kelly Global Workforce Index (Troy, MI: Kelly Services, November 2011); Society for Human Resource Management, *SHRM Poll: Intergenerational Conflict in the Workplace* (Alexandria, VA: Society for Human Resource Management, April 29, 2011); Accountemps, "Something to Talk about," news release (Toronto: Accountemps, October 22, 2013); Accountemps, "Survey: More Than Half of Employees Have Worked for a Micromanager," news release (Menlo Park, CA: PR Newswire, July 1, 2014).

15. Y. M. Hsieh and A. T. Hsieh, "Enhancement of Service Quality with Job Standardisation," *Service Industries Journal* 21 (2001): 147-66.

16. B. Davison, "Management Span of Control: How Wide Is Too Wide?," *Journal of Business Strategy* 24, no. 4 (2003): 22-29; N. A. Theobald and S. Nicholson-Crotty, "The Many Faces of Span of Control: Organizational Structure across Multiple Goals," *Administration Society* 36, no. 6 (2005): 648-60; R. M. Meyer, "Span of Management: Concept Analysis," *Journal of Advanced Nursing* 63, no. 1 (2008): 104-12.

17. D. D. Van Fleet and A. G. Bedeian, "A History of the Span of Management," *Academy of Management Review* 2 (1977): 356-72; H. Fayol, *General and Industrial Management*, trans. C. Storrs (London: Pitman, 1949); D. A. Wren, A. G. Bedeian, and J. D. Breeze, "The Foundations of Henri Fayol's Administrative Theory," *Management Decision* 40, no. 9 (2002): 906-18.

18. D. Drickhamer, "Lessons from the Leading Edge," *IndustryWeek*, February 21, 2000, 23-26.

19. D. Thompson, "More on the Span of Control Issue," *Statesman Journal Blog* (Oregon), May 16, 2011; Iowa State Legislative Services Agency, *Span of Control*, Fiscal Note, Iowa State (Des Moines: Iowa Legislature, March 10, 2011); Western Management Consultants, *Service Efficiency Study Program Management Span of Control Review Report to the City Manager* (Toronto: City of Toronto, October 31, 2012); U.S. Postal Service, *Supervisor Workhours and Span of Control: Management Advisory* (Washington, DC: U.S. Postal Service, April 4, 2013); N. Fish and S. Novick, *FY 2013-14 Budget Subcommittee #1 Final Report* (Portland, Oregon: City of Portland, April 8, 2013); E. Schmidt and J. Rosenberg, *How Google Works* (New York: Grand Central, 2014), 42-44; S. Stoll, *Accenture Update: Progress Report through August 31, 2015* (Bowling Green, OH: Bowling Green State University, September 18, 2015); WMC Consultants, *Toronto Transit Commission Organizational Review Report* (Toronto: Toronto Transit Commission, July 2015); *The New Organization: Different by Design*, Global Human Capital Trends 2016 (New York: Deloitte University Press, 2016).

20. T. B. Filipski, "Best Bosses of 2015," *PPB Magazine*, September 24, 2015.

21. J. Greenwald, "Ward Compares the Best with the Rest," *Business Insurance*, August 26, 2002, 16. One recent article also emphasized that claims managers require a narrow span of control. See M. T. Murdock, "Getting Claim Costs under Control: Improve Your Loss Ratio Using These Proven Fundamentals," *Claims Journal*, March 1, 2016.

22. J. H. Gittell, "Supervisory Span, Relational Coordination and Flight Departure Performance: A Reassessment of Postbureaucracy Theory," *Organization Science* 12, no. 4 (2001): 468-83.

23. T. D. Wall, J. L. Cordery, and C. W. Clegg, "Empowerment, Performance, and Operational Uncertainty: A Theoretical Integration," *Applied Psychology: An International Review* 51 (2002): 146-69.

24. S. Marchionne, "Navigating the New Automotive Epoch," *Vital Speeches of the Day* (2010): 134-37.

25. C. Pellegrini, "BCE's George Cope Named Canada's Outstanding CEO of the Year," *Financial Post Magazine*, November 10, 2015; Conagra Foods, "Conagra Brands Investor Day," news release (Chicago: CQ FD Disclosure, October 18, 2016); McDonald's Corp., "McDonald's Corp at Sanford C Bernstein Strategic Decision Conference," news release (Oak Brook, IL: Bloomberg, May 31, 2017).

26. Q. N. Huy, "In Praise of Middle Managers," *Harvard Business Review* 79 (2001): 72-79; C. R. Littler, R. Wiesner, and R. Dunford, "The Dynamics of Delayering: Changing Management Structures in Three Countries," *Journal of Management Studies* 40, no. 2 (2003): 225-56; H. J. Leavitt, *Top Down: Why Hierarchies Are Here to Stay and How to Manage Them More Effectively* (Cambridge: Harvard Business School Press, 2005); L. McCann, J. Morris, and J. Hassard, "Normalized Intensity: The New Labour Process of Middle Management," *Journal of Management Studies* 45, no. 2 (2008): 343-71; "Why Middle Managers May Be the Most Important People in Your Company," *Knowledge @ Wharton*, May 25, 2011.

27. H. Furness, "BBC to Cut 1,000 Jobs in Management Cull," *The Telegraph* (London), July 2, 2015; "A Simpler and Leaner BBC," news release (London: BBC, July 2, 2015); "Speech by Tony Hall to the Media & Telecoms Conference," news release (London: BBC, March 8, 2016).

28. The variations of decentralization within a company are discussed in G. Masada, "To Centralize or Decentralize?," *Optimize*, May 2005, 58–61. The 7-Eleven example is described in J. G. Kelley, "Slurpees and Sausages: 7-Eleven Holds School," *Richmond* (VA) *Times-Dispatch*, March 12, 2004, C1; S. Marling, "The 24-Hour Supply Chain," *InformationWeek*, January 26, 2004, 43.

29. H. Mintzberg, *The Structuring of Organizations* (Englewood Cliffs, NJ: Prentice Hall, 1979), chap. 5.

30. W. Dessein and T. Santos, "Adaptive Organizations," *Journal of Political Economy* 114, no. 5 (2006): 956–95; A. A. M. Nasurdin et al., "Organizational Structure and Organizational Climate as Potential Predictors of Job Stress: Evidence from Malaysia," *International Journal of Commerce and Management* 16, no. 2 (2006): 116–29; C. J. Chen and J. W. Huang, "How Organizational Climate and Structure Affect Knowledge Management—The Social Interaction Perspective," *International Journal of Information Management* 27, no. 2 (2007): 104–18.

31. T. Burns and G. Stalker, *The Management of Innovation* (London: Tavistock, 1961).

32. J. Tata, S. Prasad, and R. Thom, "The Influence of Organizational Structure on the Effectiveness of TQM Programs," *Journal of Managerial Issues* 11, no. 4 (1999): 440–53; A. Lam, "Tacit Knowledge, Organizational Learning and Societal Institutions: An Integrated Framework," *Organization Studies* 21 (2000): 487–513.

33. W. D. Sine, H. Mitsuhashi, and D. A. Kirsch, "Revisiting Burns and Stalker: Formal Structure and New Venture Performance in Emerging Economic Sectors," *Academy of Management Journal* 49, no. 1 (2006): 121–32.

34. H. Mintzberg, *The Structuring of Organizations* (Englewood Cliffs, NJ: Prentice Hall, 1979), 106.

35. H. Mintzberg, *The Structuring of Organizations* (Englewood Cliffs, NJ: Prentice Hall, 1979), chap. 17; R. M. Burton, B. Obel, and G. DeSanctis, *Organizational Design: A Step-by-Step Approach*, 2nd ed. (Cambridge, UK: Cambridge University Press, 2011), 61–63.

36. J. R. Galbraith, *Designing Organizations: An Executive Guide to Strategy, Structure, and Process* (San Francisco: Jossey-Bass, 2002), 23–25; R. M. Burton, B. Obel, and G. DeSanctis, *Organizational Design: A Step-by-Step Approach*, 2nd ed. (Cambridge, UK: Cambridge University Press, 2011), 63–65.

37. E. E. Lawler III, *Rewarding Excellence: Pay Strategies for the New Economy* (San Francisco: Jossey-Bass, 2000), 31–34.

38. The evolutionary development of the divisional structure is described in J. R. Galbraith, "The Evolution of Enterprise Organization Designs," *Journal of Organization Design* 1, no. 2 (2012): 1–13.

39. These structures were identified from corporate websites and annual reports. The organizations typically rely on a mixture of structures (typically functional units along with the divisional units shown here), so the charts shown have been adapted and simplified for learning purposes.

40. M. Goold and A. Campbell, "Do You Have a Well-Designed Organization?," *Harvard Business Review* 80 (2002): 117–24. Others have added factors such as economies of scale and what resources need to be controlled the most. See G. Kesler and A. Kates, *Leading Organization Design: How to Make Organization Design Decisions to Drive the Results You Want* (San Francisco: Jossey-Bass, 2011), chap. 3.

41. J. R. Galbraith, "Structuring Global Organizations," in *Tomorrow's Organization*, ed. S. A. Mohrman et al. (San Francisco: Jossey-Bass, 1998), 103–29; C. Homburg, J. P. Workman Jr., and O. Jensen, "Fundamental Changes in Marketing Organization: The Movement toward a Customer-Focused Organizational Structure," *Academy of Marketing Science Journal* 28 (2000): 459–78; T. H. Davenport, J. G. Harris, and A. K. Kohli, "How Do They Know Their Customers So Well?," *Sloan Management Review* 42 (2001): 63–73; J. R. Galbraith, "Organizing to Deliver Solutions," *Organizational Dynamics* 31 (2002): 194–207.

42. R. M. Burton, B. Obel, and G. DeSanctis, *Organizational Design: A Step-by-Step Approach,* 2nd ed. (Cambridge, UK: Cambridge University Press, 2011), 65–68.

43. J. R. Galbraith, E. E. Lawler III, and Associates, *Organizing for the Future: The New Logic for Managing Complex Organizations* (San Francisco: Jossey-Bass, 1993); R. Bettis and M. Hitt, "The New Competitive Landscape," *Strategic Management Journal* 16 (1995): 7–19.

44. P. C. Ensign, "Interdependence, Coordination, and Structure in Complex Organizations: Implications for Organization Design," *Mid-Atlantic Journal of Business* 34 (1998): 5–22.

45. M. M. Fanning, "A Circular Organization Chart Promotes a Hospital-Wide Focus on Teams," *Hospital & Health Services Administration* 42 (1997): 243–54; L. Y. Chan and B. E. Lynn, "Operating in Turbulent Times: How Ontario's Hospitals Are Meeting the Current Funding Crisis," *Health Care Management Review* 23 (1998): 7–18.

46. R. Cross, "Looking before You Leap: Assessing the Jump to Teams in Knowledge-Based Work," *Business Horizons* 43, no. 5 (2000): 29–36; M. Fenton-O'Creevy, "Employee Involvement and the Middle Manager: Saboteur or Scapegoat?," *Human Resource Management Journal* 11 (2001): 24–40; C. Douglas and W. L. Gardner, "Transition to Self-Directed Work Teams: Implications of Transition Time and Self-Monitoring for Managers' Use of Influence Tactics," *Journal of Organizational Behavior* 25 (2004): 47–65; G. Garda, K. Lindstrom, and M. Dallnera, "Towards a Learning Organization: The Introduction of a Client-Centered Team-Based Organization in Administrative Surveying Work," *Applied Ergonomics* 34 (2003): 97–105.

47. S. M. Davis and P. R. Lawrence, *Matrix* (Reading, MA: Addison-Wesley, 1977); J. R. Galbraith, *Designing Matrix Organizations That Actually Work* (San Francisco: Jossey-Bass, 2009); G. Kesler and A. Kates, *Leading Organization Design: How to Make Organization Design Decisions to Drive the Results You Want* (San Francisco: Jossey-Bass, 2011), chap. 7.

48. H&M's matrix structure is illustrated and described in *Corporate Governance Report 2016* (Stockholm: H & M Hennes & Mauritz AB, March 2017). Shiseido's recently introduced matrix structure is described in *Our Global Management Organization Is Fully Operational*, Annual Report 2015 (Tokyo: Shiseido, May 2016).

49. Deloitte U.S. Chinese Services Group, *Balancing Flexibility and Control: Optimizing Your Organizational Structure in China*, Board Brief China (New York: Deloitte, 2008).

50. R. C. Ford and W. A. Randolph, "Cross-Functional Structures: A Review and Integration of Matrix Organization and Project Management," *Journal of Management* 18 (1992): 267–94.

51. R. Muzyka and G. Zeschuk, "Managing Multiple Projects," *Game Developer*, March 2003, 34–42.

52. J. X. J. Qiu and L. Donaldson, "Stopford and Wells Were Right! MNC Matrix Structures *Do* Fit a 'High-High' Strategy," *Management International Review (MIR)* 52, no. 5 (2012): 671–89; D. Ganguly and M. Mitra, "Survive the Matrix," *Economic Times* (Mumbai, India), March 29, 2013.

53. D. Ciampa and M. Watkins, "Rx for New CEOs," *Chief Executive*, January 2008.

54. G. Calabrese, "Communication and Co-operation in Product Development: A Case Study of a European Car Producer," *R&D Management* 27 (1997): 239–52; T. Sy and L. S. D'Annunzio, "Challenges and Strategies of Matrix Organizations: Top-Level and Mid-Level Managers' Perspectives," *Human Resource Planning* 28, no. 1 (2005): 39–48; J. Wolf and W. G. Egelhoff, "An Empirical Evaluation of Conflict in MNC Matrix Structure Firms," *International Business Review* 22, no. 3 (2013): 591–601.

55. D. Ganguly, "Matrix Evolutions," *Economic Times* (Mumbai, India), February 18, 2012.

56. D. A. Nadler and M. L. Tushman, *Competing by Design: The Power of Organizational Architecture* (New York: Oxford University Press, 1997), chap. 6; M. Goold and A. Campbell, "Structured Networks: Towards the Well-Designed Matrix," *Long Range Planning* 36, no. 5 (2003): 427–39.

57. L. Donaldson, *The Contingency Theory of Organizations* (Thousand Oaks, CA: Sage, 2001); J. Birkinshaw, R. Nobel, and J. Ridderstråle, "Knowledge as a Contingency Variable: Do the Characteristics of Knowledge Predict Organizational Structure?," *Organization Science* 13, no. 3 (2002): 274–89.

58. P. R. Lawrence and J. W. Lorsch, *Organization and Environment* (Homewood, IL: Irwin, 1967); H. Mintzberg, *The Structuring of Organizations* (Englewood Cliffs, NJ: Prentice Hall, 1979), chap. 15.

59. T. Burns and G. Stalker, *The Management of Innovation* (London: Tavistock, 1961); P. R. Lawrence and J. W. Lorsch, *Organization and Environment* (Homewood, IL: Irwin, 1967).

60. H. Mintzberg, *The Structuring of Organizations* (Englewood Cliffs, NJ: Prentice Hall, 1979), 282.

61. D. S. Pugh and C. R. Hinings, *Organizational Structure: Extensions and Replications* (Farnborough, UK: Lexington Books, 1976); H. Mintzberg, *The Structuring of Organizations* (Englewood Cliffs, NJ: Prentice Hall, 1979), chap. 13.

62. J. R. Galbraith, *Designing Matrix Organizations That Actually Work* (San Francisco: Jossey-Bass, 2009), 52–55; G. Hertel, S. Geister, and U. Konradt, "Managing Virtual Teams: A Review of Current Empirical Research," *Human Resource Management Review* 15 (2005): 69–95.

63. C. Perrow, "A Framework for the Comparative Analysis of Organizations," *American Sociological Review* 32 (1967): 194–208; D. Gerwin, "The Comparative Analysis of Structure and Technology: A Critical Appraisal," *Academy of Management Review* 4, no. 1 (1979): 41–51; C. C. Miller et al., "Understanding Technology-Structure Relationships: Theory Development and Meta-Analytic Theory Testing," *Academy of Management Journal* 34, no. 2 (1991): 370–99.

64. R. H. Kilmann, *Beyond the Quick Fix* (San Francisco: Jossey-Bass, 1984), 38.

65. A. D. Chandler, *Strategy and Structure* (Cambridge, MA: MIT Press, 1962).

66. D. Miller, "Configurations of Strategy and Structure," *Strategic Management Journal* 7 (1986): 233–49.

13 | Organizational Culture

LO13-1 Describe the elements of organizational culture and discuss the importance of organizational subcultures.

LO13-2 Describe four categories of artifacts through which corporate culture is deciphered.

LO13-3 Discuss the importance of organizational culture and the conditions under which organizational culture strength improves organizational performance.

LO13-4 Compare and contrast four strategies for merging organizational cultures.

LO13-5 Describe five strategies for changing and strengthening an organization's culture, including the application of attraction–selection–attrition theory.

LO13-6 Describe the organizational socialization process and identify strategies to improve that process.

organizational culture
the values and assumptions
shared within an organization

The phrase "organizational culture" was rarely uttered before 1982.[1] Today, the concept is on the minds of most executives and is almost daily the subject of popular-press articles. Whenever a company is in deep trouble or very successful, its organizational culture is usually implicated as a key part of the explanation. The following recent newspaper and magazine headlines illustrate this point.[2]

- "Amazon and Whole Foods Are Headed for a Culture Clash." This article from *Fortune* magazine warns that employees at Whole Foods will experience conflict and stress because its culture contrasts sharply from the culture at Amazon, which recently acquired the food retailer.

- "Uber Pays a $26 Billion Price for Its Toxic Corporate Culture." The respected author of this article in the *Sydney Morning Herald* explains that Uber's organizational culture caused the numerous scandals (sexual harassment, alleged software theft, bullying) that have plagued the "ride-sharing" company and led to the departure of its founder and more than 70 executives.

- "Lax Corporate Culture Set Up Takata's Fall." This piece in the *Nikkei Asian Review* outlines how air bag manufacturer Takata's corporate culture created a "breeding ground" for misconduct (falsifying safety data) and lax quality standards, which led to its recent bankruptcy.

> The thing I have learned at IBM is that culture is everything.[6]
>
> —Louis V. Gerstner, Jr., former CEO of IBM and RJR Nabisco

Organizational culture consists of the values and assumptions shared within an organization.[3] It defines what is important and unimportant in the company and, consequently, directs everyone in the organization toward the "right way" of doing things. You might think of organizational culture as the company's DNA—invisible to the naked eye, yet a powerful template that shapes what happens in the workplace.

This chapter begins by identifying the elements of organizational culture and then describing how culture is deciphered through artifacts. Next, we examine the relationship between organizational culture and organizational effectiveness, including the effects of cultural strength, fit, and adaptability. Our attention then turns to the challenges of and solutions to merging organizational cultures. The latter part of this chapter examines ways to change and strengthen organizational culture and looks more closely at the related topic of organizational socialization.

which are discussed in the next section of this chapter. *Values* are stable, evaluative beliefs that guide our preferences for outcomes or courses of action in a variety of situations (see Chapters 1 and 2).[4] They are conscious perceptions about what is good or bad, right or wrong. In the context of organizational culture, values are discussed as *shared values*, which are values that people within the organization or work unit have in common and place near the top of their hierarchy of values.[5]

Organizational culture also consists of *shared assumptions*—a deeper element that some experts believe is the essence of corporate culture. Shared assumptions are nonconscious, taken-for-granted perceptions or ideal prototypes of behavior that are considered the correct way to think and act toward problems and opportunities. Shared assumptions are so deeply ingrained that you probably wouldn't discover them by surveying employees. Only by observing employees, analyzing their decisions, and debriefing them on their actions would these assumptions rise to the surface.

Espoused versus Enacted Values

Most corporate websites have "Careers" web pages for job candidates, and many of these sites proudly list the company's core values. Do these values really represent the organization's culture? Some do, but these pages more likely describe *espoused values*—the values that corporate leaders hope will eventually become the organization's culture, or at least the values they want others to believe guide the organization's decisions and actions.[7] Espoused values are usually socially desirable, so they present a positive public image. Even if top management acts

---

LO13-1 Describe the elements of organizational culture and discuss the importance of organizational subcultures.

ELEMENTS OF ORGANIZATIONAL CULTURE

Organizational culture consists of shared values and assumptions. Exhibit 13.1 illustrates how these shared values and assumptions relate to each other and are associated with artifacts,

Exhibit 13.1 Organizational Culture Assumptions, Values, and Artifacts

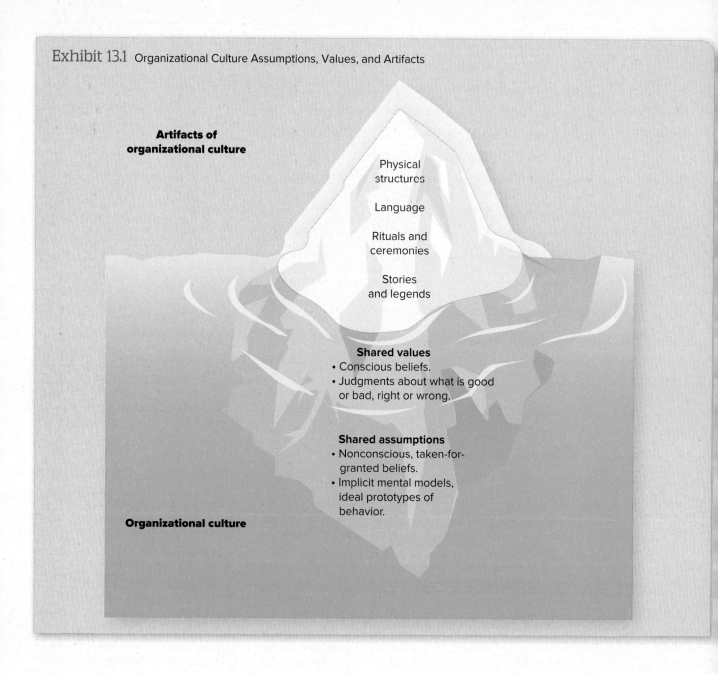

Artifacts of
organizational culture

Physical
structures

Language

Rituals and
ceremonies

Stories
and legends

Shared values
- Conscious beliefs.
- Judgments about what is good
  or bad, right or wrong.

Shared assumptions
- Nonconscious, taken-for-
  granted beliefs.
- Implicit mental models,
  ideal prototypes of
  behavior.

Organizational culture

consistently with the espoused values, lower-level employees might not do so. Employees bring diverse personal values to the organization, some of which might conflict with the organization's espoused values.

An organization's culture is defined by its *enacted values*, not its espoused values. Values are *enacted* when they actually guide and influence decisions and behavior. They are values put into practice. Enacted values are apparent when watching executives and other employees in action, including their decisions, where they focus their attention and resources, how they behave toward stakeholders, and the outcomes of those decisions and behavior.

Content of Organizational Culture

Organizations differ considerably in their cultural content, that is, the relative ordering of shared values.[9] Consider Netflix and

PPL Corporation. Netflix seems to prioritize individual performance with undertones of internal competitiveness. For instance, the online streaming media provider points out that "We're a team, not a family"; that "Netflix leaders hire, develop, and cut smartly"; and that "adequate performance gets a generous severance package." In contrast, electrical utility PPL seems to prioritize fulfillment of stakeholder needs, such as employee safety, customer service, and community support. It emphasizes mutual respect rather than competitive performance. PPL's six values include ensuring safety/health, delivering customer service, valuing each other and appreciating differences, getting the job done right, doing the right thing, and investing in communities.[10]

How many corporate cultures are there? Several models and measures classify organizational culture into a handful of easy-to-remember categories. One of these, shown in Exhibit 13.2,

Corporate Culture Alignments and Misalignments[8]

90% of nearly 2,000 CEOs and CFOs surveyed say organizational culture is important at their company.

82% of more than 7,000 business leaders across 130 countries say that an organization's culture is a potential competitive advantage.

58% of 812 managers (majority in human resources) in the UK say their organization's espoused values generally reflect the actual values practiced by management.

51% of 2,219 executives and employees surveyed across several countries think their organization's culture is in need of a major overhaul.

15% of nearly 2,000 CEOs and CFOs surveyed say their own corporate culture is exactly where it needs to be.

12% of more than 7,000 business leaders across 130 countries say their company is driving the "right" corporate culture.

©Flying Colours Ltd/Getty Images

Unfortunately, the models oversimplify the diversity of cultural values in organizations. There are dozens of individual values, and many more combinations of values, so the number of organizational cultures that these models describe likely falls considerably short of the full set.

The diversity of corporate cultures is evident in a recent study of espoused values at the top 500 American companies.[12] The study distilled these values down to nine categories. Integrity appeared most often, followed by teamwork, innovation, respect, quality, safety, community, communication, and hard work. But each of these categories includes a large number of specific values. The "respect" category, for instance, includes the specific values of diversity, inclusion, development, empowerment, and dignity. Because there are dozens of espoused values, there would be an equally long list of enacted values.

Another concern is that organizational culture models and measures typically ignore the shared assumptions aspect of culture. This oversight likely occurs because measuring shared assumptions is even more difficult than measuring shared values. A third concern is that many organizational culture models incorrectly assume that organizations have a fairly clear, unified culture that is easily decipherable.[13] In reality, an organization's culture is typically blurry and fragmented. As we discuss next, organizations consist of diverse subcultures in which clusters of employees across the organization have different experiences and backgrounds that influence their preferred values. Furthermore, an organization's culture is founded on the values of its employees. Employees have diverse hierarchies of values, so an organization's culture necessarily has noticeable variability.

identifies seven corporate cultures. Another popular model identifies four organizational cultures organized in a two-by-two table representing internal versus external focus and flexibility versus control. Other models organize cultures around a circle with 8 or 12 categories. These circumplex models suggest that some cultures are opposite to others, such as an avoidance culture versus a self-actualization culture, or a power culture versus a collegial culture.[11]

These organizational culture models and surveys are popular with corporate leaders faced with the messy business of diagnosing their company's culture and identifying what kind of culture they want to develop.

Exhibit 13.2 Organizational Culture Profile Dimensions and Characteristics

Organizational Culture Dimension	Characteristics of the Dimension
Innovation	Experimenting, opportunity seeking, risk taking, few rules, low cautiousness
Stability	Predictability, security, rule-oriented
Respect for people	Fairness, tolerance
Outcome orientation	Action-oriented, high expectations, results-oriented
Attention to detail	Precise, analytic
Team orientation	Collaboration, people-oriented
Aggressiveness	Competitive, low emphasis on social responsibility

Source: Based on information in C. A. O'Reilly III, J. Chatman, and D. F. Caldwell, "People and Organizational Culture: A Profile Comparison Approach to Assessing Person–Organization Fit," *Academy of Management Journal* 34, no. 3 (1991): 487–518.

artifacts the observable symbols and signs of an organization's culture

Thus, many of the popular organizational culture models and measures oversimplify the variety of organizational cultures and falsely presume that organizations can easily be identified within these categories.

Organizational Subcultures

When discussing organizational culture, we are really referring to the *dominant culture*, that is, the values and assumptions shared most consistently and widely by the organization's members. The dominant culture is usually supported by senior management, but not always. Cultural values and assumptions also can persist in spite of senior management's desire for another culture. Furthermore, organizations are composed of *subcultures* located throughout their various divisions, geographic regions, and occupational groups.[14] Some subcultures enhance the dominant culture by espousing parallel assumptions and values. Others differ from but do not conflict with the dominant culture. Still others are called *countercultures* because they embrace values or assumptions that directly oppose the organization's dominant culture. It is also possible that some organizations (including some universities, according to one study) consist of subcultures with no decipherable dominant culture at all.[15]

Some subcultures enhance the dominant culture, whereas others are called *countercultures* because their values or assumptions oppose the organization's dominant culture.
©Mediaphotos/iStock/Getty Images Plus

Subcultures, particularly countercultures, potentially create conflict and dissension among employees, but they also serve two important functions.[16] First, they maintain the organization's standards of performance and ethical behavior. Employees who hold countercultural values are an important source of surveillance and critical review of the dominant order. They encourage constructive conflict and more creative thinking about how the organization should interact with its environment. Subcultures potentially support ethical conduct by preventing employees from blindly following one set of values. Subculture members continually question the "obvious" decisions and actions of the majority, thereby making everyone more mindful of the consequences of their actions.

Subcultures serve a second valuable function: they are spawning grounds for emerging values that keep the firm aligned with the evolving needs and expectations of customers, suppliers, communities, and other stakeholders. Companies eventually need to replace their existing dominant values with ones that are more appropriate for the changing environment. Those emerging cultural values and assumptions usually exist in subcultures long before they are ideal for the organization. If subcultures are suppressed, the organization may take longer to discover, develop, and adopt the emerging desired culture.

LO13-2 Describe four categories of artifacts through which corporate culture is deciphered.

DECIPHERING ORGANIZATIONAL CULTURE THROUGH ARTIFACTS

Shared values and assumptions are not easily measured through surveys and might not be accurately reflected in the organization's values statements. Instead, as Exhibit 13.1 illustrated earlier, an organization's culture needs to be deciphered through a detailed investigation of artifacts. **Artifacts** are the observable symbols and signs of an organization's culture, such as the way visitors are greeted, the organization's physical layout, and how employees are rewarded.[17] A few experts suggest that artifacts are the essence of organizational culture, whereas most others (including the authors of this book) view artifacts as symbols or indicators of culture. In other words, culture is cognitive (values and assumptions inside people's heads) whereas artifacts are observable manifestations of

An organization's culture needs to be deciphered through a detailed investigation of artifacts, such as workplace behavior, everyday conversations, documents, and physical settings.
©View Pictures/REX/Shutterstock

that culture. Either way, artifacts are important because they represent and reinforce an organization's culture.

Artifacts provide valuable evidence about a company's culture.[18] An organization's ambiguous (fragmented) culture is best understood by observing workplace behavior, listening to everyday conversations among staff and with customers, studying written documents and emails, viewing physical structures and settings, and interviewing staff about corporate stories. In other words, to truly understand an organization's culture, we need to sample information from a variety of organizational artifacts.

The Mayo Clinic conducted such an assessment a few years ago. An anthropologist was hired to decipher the medical organization's culture at its headquarters in Minnesota and to identify ways of transferring that culture to its two newer sites in Florida and Arizona. For six weeks, the anthropologist shadowed employees, posed as a patient in waiting rooms, did countless interviews, and accompanied physicians on patient visits. The final report outlined Mayo's dominant culture and how its satellite operations varied from that culture.[19] Over the next few pages, we review four broad categories of artifacts: organizational stories and legends, language, rituals and ceremonies, and physical structures and symbols.

Organizational Stories and Legends

Stories and legends about the company's founders and past events permeate strong organizational cultures. Some tales recount heroic deeds, whereas others ridicule incidents that deviated from the firm's core values. Organizational stories and legends serve as powerful social prescriptions of the way things should (or should not) be done. They add human realism to corporate expectations, individual performance standards, and the criteria for getting fired. Stories also produce emotions in listeners, and these emotions tend to improve listeners' memory of the lesson within the story.[20] Stories communicate corporate culture most effectively when they describe real people, are assumed to be true, and are known by employees throughout the organization. Stories are also prescriptive—they advise people what to do or not to do.[21]

Organizational Language

The language of the workplace speaks volumes about the company's culture. How employees talk to each other, describe customers, express anger, and greet stakeholders are all verbal symbols of shared values and assumptions. An organization's culture particularly stands out when employees habitually use customized phrases and labels.

Employees at DaVita HealthCare Partners, Inc., refer to their company as the "village" and its chief executive is the "mayor." Employees (called teammates) at the Denver-based provider of kidney care and dialysis services become "citizens" of the village as they "cross the bridge," meaning that they embrace the company's culture. These aren't contrived slogans. The language symbolizes DaVita's deeply held cultural beliefs that employee

> ## What we say—and how we say it—can deeply affect a company's culture.[22]
>
> —Tom Kelley and David Kelley, partner (Tom) and founder (David) of IDEO

well-being and performance depend on the human connection of workplace community that, in turn, translates into superior service to DaVita's patients.[23]

Language also captures less complimentary cultural values. At Goldman Sachs, "elephant trades" are apparently large investment transactions with huge profit potential, so the investment firm allegedly encourages its salespeople to go "elephant hunting" (seeking out these large trades from clients). A former Goldman Sachs manager reported that some employees at the investment firm also routinely described their clients as "muppets." "My muppet client didn't put me in comp on the trade we just printed," said one salesperson, meaning that the client was a fool because he didn't compare prices, so the salesperson overcharged him. The "muppet" label seems to reveal a culture with a derogatory view of clients. When this language use became public, Goldman Sachs scanned its internal emails for the "muppet" label and warned employees not to use the term.[24]

Rituals and Ceremonies

Rituals are the programmed routines of daily organizational life that dramatize an organization's culture.[25] They include how visitors are greeted, how often senior executives visit subordinates, how people communicate with each other, how much time employees take for lunch, and so on. These rituals are repetitive, predictable events that have symbolic meaning of underlying cultural values and assumptions. For instance, BMW's fast-paced culture is quite literally apparent in the way employees walk around the German automaker's offices. "When you move through the corridors and hallways of other companies' buildings, people kind of crawl, they walk slowly," observes a BMW executive. "But BMW people tend to move faster."[26] **Ceremonies** are more formal artifacts than rituals. Ceremonies are planned activities conducted specifically for the benefit of an audience. This would include publicly rewarding (or punishing) employees or celebrating the launch of a new product or newly won contract.

Physical Structures and Symbols

The size, shape, location, and age of buildings both reflect and influence an organization's culture. Buildings might support a company's emphasis on teamwork, environmental friendliness, hierarchy, or any other set of values.[27] Even if the building doesn't make much of a statement, there is a treasure-trove of physical artifacts inside. Desks, chairs, office space, and wall hangings (or lack of them) are just a few of the items that might convey cultural meaning.[28] Each physical artifact alone might not say much, but put enough of them together and an image begins to form of how they symbolize the organization's culture.

For example, one prominent workspace design and manufacturing company recently identified the workspace features typically found at companies with several different cultures. Exhibit 13.3

> ## We shape our buildings; thereafter, they shape us.[29]
> —Winston Churchill, former Prime Minister of the United Kingdom

Exhibit 13.3 Workspace Design and Organizational Culture

Collaborative and creative cultures

- More team space
- Informal space
- Low/medium enclosure
- Flexible environment
- Organic layout

Controlling and competitive cultures

- More individual space
- More formal than informal space
- High/medium enclosure
- More fixed environment
- More structured, symmetrical layout

Photos: (Left) ©Robert Daly/Getty Images; (Right) ©Hero Images/Getty Images

Source: Based on information in *How to Create a Successful Organizational Culture: Build It—Literally* (Holland, MI: Haworth Inc., June 2015).

summarizes the physical space design of collaborative and creative cultures compared to cultures that emphasize efficiency (control) and competition. Collaborative and creative cultures value more teamwork and flexibility, so space design is informal and enables spontaneous group discussion. Controlling and competitive cultures tend to have more structural office arrangements and provide more space for individual work than teamwork.

> **LO13-3** Discuss the importance of organizational culture and the conditions under which organizational culture strength improves organizational performance.

IS ORGANIZATIONAL CULTURE IMPORTANT?

Does organizational culture improve organizational effectiveness? Launi Skinner thinks so. "You can have the best strategy in the world, but culture will kill strategy," warns the CEO of First West Credit Union in Vancouver, Canada, and former senior executive at Starbucks in the United States. Bill Emerson, Vice Chair of Rock Holdings Inc. (parent company of Quicken Loans), agrees. When asked why the Detroit-based finance company has grown so quickly, Emerson replied: "The No. 1 thing is culture. It allows us to move very quickly and react very quickly in making business decisions."[30]

Launi Skinner, Bill Emerson, and many other leaders believe that an organization's success partly depends on its culture. Several popular-press management books similarly assert that the most successful companies have strong cultures. In fact, one popular management book, *Built to Last*, suggests that successful companies are "cultlike" (although not actually cults, the authors are careful to point out).[32] Does OB research support this view that companies are more effective when they have a strong culture? Yes, potentially, but the evidence indicates that the relationship depends on a few conditions.[33]

Meaning and Potential Benefits of a Strong Culture

Before discussing these contingencies, let's examine the meaning of a "strong" organizational culture and its potential benefits. The strength of an organization's culture refers to how widely and deeply employees hold the company's dominant values and assumptions. In a strong organizational culture, most employees across all subunits understand and embrace the dominant values. These values and assumptions are also institutionalized through well-established artifacts, which further entrench the culture. In addition, strong cultures tend to be long-lasting; some can be traced back to the values and assumptions established by the company's founder. In contrast, companies have weak cultures when the dominant values are held mainly by a few people at the top of the organization, the culture is difficult to interpret from artifacts, and the cultural values and assumptions are unstable over time or highly varied across the organization.

Under specific conditions, companies are more effective when they have strong cultures because of the three important functions listed in Exhibit 13.4 and described below:

- *Control system.* Organizational culture is a deeply embedded form of social control that influences employee decisions and behavior.[34] Culture is pervasive and operates nonconsciously. Think of it as an automatic pilot, nonconsciously directing employees so their behavior is consistent with organizational expectations. For this reason, some writers describe organizational culture as a compass that points everyone in the same direction.

- *Social glue.* Organizational culture is the social glue that bonds people together and makes them feel part of the organizational experience.[35] Employees are motivated to internalize the organization's dominant culture because it fulfills their need for social identity. This social glue attracts new staff and retains top performers. It also becomes the common thread that holds employees together in global organizations.

- *Sense making.* Organizational culture helps employees to make sense of what goes on and why things happen in the company.[36] Corporate culture also makes it easier for them to understand what is expected of them. For instance, research has found that sales employees in companies with stronger organizational cultures have clearer role perceptions and less role-related stress.[37]

Contingencies of Organizational Culture and Effectiveness

Studies have found only a moderately positive relationship between culture strength and organizational effectiveness. The reason for this weak link is that strong cultures improve organizational effectiveness only under specific conditions (see Exhibit 13.4). The three main contingencies are (1) whether the culture content is aligned with the environment; (2) whether the culture is moderately strong, not cultlike; and (3) whether the culture incorporates an adaptive culture.

Exhibit 13.4 Potential Benefits and Contingencies of Culture Strength

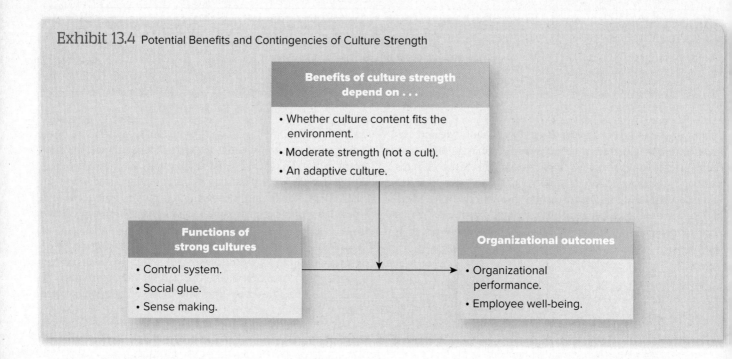

Benefits of culture strength depend on . . .
- Whether culture content fits the environment.
- Moderate strength (not a cult).
- An adaptive culture.

Functions of strong cultures
- Control system.
- Social glue.
- Sense making.

Organizational outcomes
- Organizational performance.
- Employee well-being.

> The values of the company are really the bedrock—
> the glue which holds the firm together.[38]
>
> —Nandan Nilekani, co-founder and former CEO of Infosys

Culture Content Is Aligned with the External Environment The benefits of a strong culture depend on whether its content—the culture's dominant values and assumptions—is aligned with the external environment. Companies require an employee-centric culture in environments where business success depends mainly on employee talent, whereas an efficiency-focused culture may be more critical for companies in environments with strong competition and standardized products. If the dominant values are congruent with the environment, then employees are more likely to engage in decisions and behaviors that improve the organization's interaction with that environment. But when the dominant values are misaligned with the environment, a strong culture encourages decisions and behaviors that can undermine the organization's connection with its stakeholders.

For example, Coles became a successful competitor in the Australian retail food industry after it was acquired by Wesfarmers, which injected a strong culture around performance and customer service. Wesfarmers is a highly successful Australian conglomerate, but it doesn't nurture the same culture in all of its businesses (food, hardware, clothing, office supplies, fertilizers, mining, etc.). Instead, Wesfarmers' executive team encourages each company to maintain a strong culture around the values that matter most for that industry and its stakeholders. "It would be a huge mistake if we tried to impose one culture over all these businesses," explains Richard Goyder, who recently stepped down as Wesfarmers CEO. "Bunnings (Australia's largest home improvement retailer) and Coles have to be customer-centric, whereas our coal business has to be absolutely focused on safety."[39]

Culture Strength Is Not the Level of a Cult A second contingency is the degree of culture strength. Various experts suggest that companies with very strong cultures (i.e., corporate "cults") may be less effective than companies with moderately strong cultures.[40] One reason why corporate cults may undermine organizational effectiveness is that they lock people into mental models, which can blind them to new opportunities and unique problems. The effect of these very strong cultures is that people overlook or incorrectly define subtle misalignments between the organization's activities and the changing environment.

The other reason why very strong cultures may be dysfunctional is that they suppress dissenting subcultures. The challenge for organizational leaders is to maintain not only a strong culture but one that allows subcultural diversity. Subcultures

Corporate cults tend to undermine organizational effectiveness by locking people into mental models, which can blind them from seeing new opportunities and unique problems.
©Mediaphotos/iStock/Getty Images Plus

encourage task-oriented conflict, which improves creative thinking and offers some level of ethical vigilance over the dominant culture. In the long run, a subculture's nascent values could become important dominant values as the environment changes. Corporate cults suppress subcultures, thereby undermining these benefits.

Culture Is an Adaptive Culture A third condition influencing the effect of cultural strength on organizational effectiveness is whether the culture content includes an **adaptive culture**.[41] In an adaptive culture, employees are receptive to change, including the ongoing alignment of the organization to its environment and continuous improvement of internal processes. Thus, employees in adaptive cultures see things from an open systems perspective and take responsibility for the organization's performance and alignment with the external environment.

In an adaptive culture, receptivity to change extends to internal processes and roles. Employees believe that satisfying stakeholder needs requires continuous improvement of internal work processes. They also recognize the importance of remaining flexible in their own work roles. The phrase "That's not my job" is found in nonadaptive cultures. Finally, an adaptive culture has a strong *learning orientation* because being receptive to change necessarily means that the company also supports action-oriented discovery. With a learning orientation, employees welcome new learning opportunities, actively experiment with new ideas and practices, view reasonable mistakes as a natural part of the learning process, and continuously question past practices (see Chapter 6).[43]

Organizational Culture and Business Ethics

An organization's culture influences the ethical conduct of its employees. This makes sense because good behavior is driven by ethical values, and ethical values become embedded in an organization's dominant culture. For example, AIA Group, Hong Kong's largest life insurance company (by number of policies), has a strong culture focused on "doing the right thing, in the right way, with the right people, and the results will come." This means that employees are expected to think through the ramifications of their actions (right thing) and ensure they always work with integrity and teamwork (right way).[44]

The opposite is equally true. There are numerous instances where an organization's culture has been the apparent cause of unethical conduct. For example, critics suggest that Uber's "toxic culture" explains many of the ride-sharing company's public embarrassments, including allegations of sexual harassment, bullying, privacy violations, anti-competitive activities, and theft of proprietary technology.[45] Uber has 14 espoused

Uber's recent problems illustrate the principle that leaders create an ethical organization by actively working on the enacted culture that steers employee behavior.
©Vincenzo Mancuso/Shutterstock

> **"You have to create a culture that not only accepts change but seeks out how to change.**[42]
>
> —Dan Akerson, former GM CEO

bicultural audit a process of diagnosing cultural relations between companies and determining the extent to which cultural clashes will likely occur

values, including "always be hustlin'" and "step on toes," which emphasize aggressive tactics and seem to give permission to skirt legal boundaries. Uber faces lawsuits and government investigations and has experienced increasing difficulty hiring new talent, particularly women. Dozens of Uber staff have been fired, particularly after an independent report reviewed the internal behavior problems. The point here is that culture and ethics go hand-in-hand. To create a more ethical organization, leaders need to work on the enacted culture that steers employee behavior.

LO13-4 Compare and contrast four strategies for merging organizational cultures.

MERGING ORGANIZATIONAL CULTURES

Mergers and acquisitions often fail financially when the merging organizations have incompatible cultures.[46] Unless the acquired firm is left to operate independently, companies with clashing cultures tend to undermine employee performance and customer service. Consequently, several studies estimate that only between 30 and 50 percent of corporate acquisitions add value.[47]

Bicultural Audit

Organizational leaders can minimize cultural collisions in corporate mergers and fulfill their duty of due diligence by conducting a bicultural audit.[49] A **bicultural audit** diagnoses cultural relations between the companies and determines the extent to which cultural clashes will likely occur. The process begins by identifying cultural differences between the merging companies. This might occur by surveying employees or through an extended series of meetings where executives and staff of both firms discuss how they think through important decisions in their business. From the survey data or meetings, the parties determine which differences between the two firms will result in conflict and which cultural values provide common ground on which to build a cultural foundation in the merged organization. The final stage involves identifying strategies and preparing action plans to bridge the two organizations' cultures.

Strategies for Merging Different Organizational Cultures

In some cases, the bicultural audit results in a decision to end merger talks because the two cultures are too different to merge effectively. However, even with substantially different cultures, two companies may form a workable union if they apply the appropriate merger strategy. The four main strategies for merging different corporate cultures are assimilation, deculturation, integration, and separation (see Exhibit 13.5).[50]

Assimilation Assimilation occurs when employees at the acquired company willingly embrace the cultural values of the acquiring organization. Typically, this strategy works best when the acquired company has a weak culture that is either similar to the acquiring company's culture or is dysfunctional, whereas the acquiring company's culture is strong and aligned with the external environment. The cultural assimilation strategy seldom produces cultural clashes because the acquiring firm's culture is highly respected and the acquired firm's culture is fairly easily altered. The assimilation strategy occurred when Southwest Airlines acquired AirTran Airways. The two firms already had

Corporate Culture Risks in Mergers and Acquisitions[48]

76% of 803 executives surveyed who were recently involved in M&A activity say alignment of cultures is important to the overall success of post-merger integration.

58% of 200 senior executives surveyed worldwide who are involved in mergers/acquisitions say they could have improved upon cultural fit in their most recent deal.

51% of 200 senior executives surveyed worldwide who are involved in mergers/acquisitions say that cultural factors are overestimated for the success of a merger/acquisition deal.

54% of 553 M&A executives say that cultural and HR matters are the most consistently challenging issues in merger/acquisitions (top-ranked issue).

52% of 803 executives surveyed who were recently involved in M&A activity say they aligned the merged companies' cultures by interviewing employees at both firms during the integration process.

Photos: ©Volodymyr Krasyuk/Shutterstock; ©Mike Flippo/Shutterstock

Exhibit 13.5 Strategies for Merging Different Organizational Cultures

Merger Strategy	Description	Works Best When . . .
Assimilation	Acquired company embraces acquiring firm's culture.	Acquired firm has a weak culture and acquiring firm's culture is strong and successful.
Deculturation	Acquiring firm imposes its culture on unwilling acquired firm.	Rarely works—may be necessary only when acquired firm's culture is dysfunctional but its employees aren't yet aware of the problems.
Integration	Merging companies combine the two or more cultures into a new composite culture.	Existing cultures at both firms are relatively weak or have overlapping values and can be improved.
Separation	Merging companies remain distinct entities with minimal exchange of culture or organizational practices.	Firms operate successfully in different businesses requiring different cultures.

Sources: Based on ideas in A. R. Malekzadeh and A. Nahavandi, "Making Mergers Work by Managing Cultures," *Journal of Business Strategy* 11 (May/June 1990): 55–57; K. W. Smith, "A Brand-New Culture for the Merged Firm," *Mergers and Acquisitions* 35 (June 2000): 45–50.

> Integration works best when the cultures of both merging companies could be improved, which motivates employees to adopt the best cultural elements of the separate entities.

similar cultures, but Southwest's legendary "Southwest way" culture also made the acquisition relatively free of culture clashes. "It's helpful that Southwest has a great cultural reputation," says a Southwest executive about the AirTran Airways acquisition.[51]

Deculturation Assimilation is rare. Employees usually resist organizational change, particularly when they are asked to throw away personal and cultural values. Under these conditions, some acquiring companies apply a *deculturation* strategy by imposing their culture and business practices on the acquired organization. The acquiring firm strips away reward systems and other artifacts that support the old culture. People who cannot adopt the acquiring company's culture often lose their jobs. Deculturation may be necessary when the acquired firm's culture doesn't work, even when employees in the acquired company aren't convinced of this. However, this strategy is difficult to apply effectively because the acquired firm's employees resist the cultural intrusions from the buying firm, thereby delaying or undermining the merger process.

Integration A third strategy is to combine the cultures of the two firms into one new composite culture that preserves the best features of the previous cultures. Integration is slow and potentially risky because there are many forces preserving the existing cultures. Still, this strategy should be considered when the

companies have relatively weak cultures or when their cultures include several overlapping values. Integration works best when the cultures of both merging companies could be improved, which motivates employees to adopt the best cultural elements of the separate entities. Incorporating the best cultural elements of the original companies symbolizes that employees from both firms have meaningful values for the combined organization. "Find one thing in the organization that was good and use it as a cornerstone for a new culture," advises Bob Every, a respected Australian business leader who orchestrated several mergers and acquisitions. "People don't want to work for an organization for years and then be told its rubbish."[52]

Separation A separation strategy occurs when the merging companies agree to remain distinct entities with minimal exchange of culture or organizational practices. This strategy is most appropriate when the two merging companies are in unrelated industries because the most appropriate cultural values tend to differ by industry. Separation is also the preferred approach for the corporate cultures of diversified conglomerates. The cultural separation strategy is rare, however. Executives in acquiring firms usually have difficulty keeping their hands off the acquired firm. According to one estimate, only 15 percent of mergers leave the acquired company as a stand-alone unit.[53]

Alaska's Acquisition of Virgin America: Cultural Separation or Integration?

Alaska Airlines' decision to acquire Virgin America brought audible gasps from customers and investment analysts alike. Both airlines are successful and their routes are complementary, but many observers question the cultural fit of a combined airline. "I think of [Virgin America] as a young, hip airline. Alaska is more of a friendly aunt," says one business traveller.

At first, Alaska Air Group CEO Brad Tilden asserted that both airlines have similar cultures focused on employees, customers, and safety. But after a few months, Tilden admitted he was struggling to decide whether the cultures are sufficiently different that they should be kept separate. Creating a single airline with the best cultural elements of both (integration strategy) would be more cost-efficient, but maintaining Alaska and Virgin as distinct operations (separation strategy) might avoid an internal culture clash and retain valued Virgin staff and customers.

The company eventually chose the separation strategy for the first few years, but the Virgin brand will eventually disappear. "Alaska Airlines and Virgin America are different airlines, but we believe different works," Tilden announced when the merger was completed. He also plans to bring some of Virgin's "hip culture" to Alaska.

©Andy Cross/Denver Post/Getty Images

"Culture has been a real challenge in many mergers, so we're working to do things differently," says Ben Minicucci, the Alaska Air executive who became Virgin America CEO after the merger. "We are being very thoughtful about culture and are working to create an environment that reflects who we are and where we've been, that also enables us to work together, be bold, and succeed in a rapidly evolving industry."[54]

> If you don't spend time to create a culture in your organization, one will create itself. And the one that creates itself is probably not going to be good.[56]
>
> —Bill Emerson, Vice Chair of Rock Holdings Inc. (parent company of Quicken Loans)

LO13-5 Describe five strategies for changing and strengthening an organization's culture, including the application of attraction–selection–attrition theory.

CHANGING AND STRENGTHENING ORGANIZATIONAL CULTURE

Is it possible to change an organization's culture? Yes, but doing so isn't easy, the change rarely occurs quickly, and often the culture ends up changing (or replacing) corporate leaders. A few experts argue that an organization's culture "cannot be managed," so attempting to change the company's values and assumptions is a waste of time.[55] This may be an extreme view, but organizational culture experts generally agree that changing an organization's culture is a monumental challenge. At the same time, the external environment changes over time, so organizations need to shift their culture to maintain alignment with the emerging environment.

Over the next few pages, we will highlight five strategies that have had some success at altering and strengthening corporate cultures. These strategies, illustrated in Exhibit 13.6, are not exhaustive, but each seems to work well under the right circumstances.

Model Desired Culture through the Actions of Founders and Leaders

Whether deliberately or haphazardly, the company's founder usually forms an organization's culture.[57] The founder's personality, values, habits, and critical events all play a role in establishing the firm's core values and assumptions. The founder is

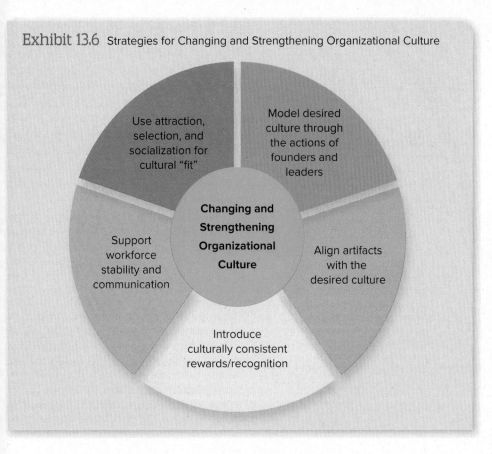

Exhibit 13.6 Strategies for Changing and Strengthening Organizational Culture

- Use attraction, selection, and socialization for cultural "fit"
- Model desired culture through the actions of founders and leaders
- Support workforce stability and communication
- **Changing and Strengthening Organizational Culture**
- Align artifacts with the desired culture
- Introduce culturally consistent rewards/recognition

is reinforced or discouraged. Corporate cultures also can be strengthened through the artifacts of stories and behaviors. According to Max De Pree, former CEO of furniture manufacturer Herman Miller Inc., every organization needs "tribal storytellers" to keep the organization's history and culture alive.[60] Leaders play a role by creating memorable events that symbolize the cultural values they want to develop or maintain.

Introduce Culturally Consistent Rewards and Recognition

Reward systems and informal recognition practices are artifacts, but they deserve separate discussion because of their powerful effect on strengthening or reshaping an organization's culture.[61] For example, to change Home Depot's freewheeling culture, Robert Nardelli introduced precise measures of corporate performance and drilled managers with weekly performance objectives related to those metrics. A two-hour weekly conference call became a ritual in which Home Depot's top executives were held accountable for the previous week's goals. These actions reinforced a more disciplined (and centralized) performance-oriented culture.[62]

often an inspiring visionary who provides a compelling role model for others to follow. In later years, organizational culture is reinforced through stories and legends about the founder that symbolize the core values.

Although founders usually establish an organization's culture, subsequent leaders need to actively guide, reinforce, and sometimes alter that culture.[58] The process of leading cultural change is associated with both transformational leadership and authentic leadership (see Chapter 11). In each of those models, leaders base their words and actions on personal values, and those values potentially become a reflection of the organization's values. For instance, one recent study found that the preferred conflict-handling style of leaders influences the work unit's or organization's cultural expectations on how employees address conflict situations. Another study reported that work units or companies with strong servant leadership were more likely to have a culture that valued providing service to others.[59]

Align Artifacts with the Desired Culture

Artifacts represent more than just the visible indicators of a company's culture. They are also mechanisms that keep the culture in place or shift the culture to a new set of values and assumptions. As we discuss in the next chapter on organizational change, systems and structures are important instruments to support the desired state of affairs. These systems and structures are artifacts, such as the workplace layout, reporting structure, office rituals, type of information distributed, and language that

Artifacts don't just symbolize a company's culture; they also keep the culture in place or shift the culture to a new set of values and assumptions.
©Jetta Productions/Blend Images/Getty Images

Corporate Culture Fit during the Hiring Process[64]

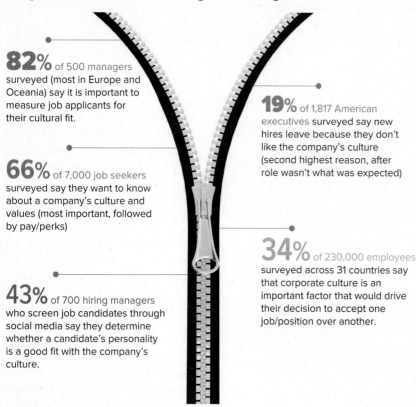

82% of 500 managers surveyed (most in Europe and Oceania) say it is important to measure job applicants for their cultural fit.

66% of 7,000 job seekers surveyed say they want to know about a company's culture and values (most important, followed by pay/perks)

43% of 700 hiring managers who screen job candidates through social media say they determine whether a candidate's personality is a good fit with the company's culture.

19% of 1,817 American executives surveyed say new hires leave because they don't like the company's culture (second highest reason, after role wasn't what was expected)

34% of 230,000 employees surveyed across 31 countries say that corporate culture is an important factor that would drive their decision to accept one job/position over another.

©alxpin/E+/Getty Images

Support Workforce Stability and Communication

An organization's culture is embedded in the minds of its employees. Organizational stories are rarely written down; rituals and ceremonies do not usually exist in procedure manuals; organizational metaphors are not found in corporate directories. Thus, a strong culture depends on a stable workforce. Workforce stability is also important because it takes time for employees to fully understand the organization's culture and how to enact it in their daily work lives. The organization's culture can literally disintegrate during periods of high turnover and precipitous downsizing because the corporate memory leaves with these employees. A strong organizational culture also depends on a workplace where employees regularly interact with each other. This ongoing communication enables employees to develop shared language, stories, and other artifacts.

Use Attraction, Selection, and Socialization for Cultural Fit

A valuable way to strengthen and possibly change an organization's culture is to recruit and select job applicants whose values are compatible with the culture. This process of recruiting, selecting, and retaining applicants whose values are congruent with the organization's culture is explained by **attraction–selection–attrition (ASA) theory**.[63] ASA theory states that organizations have a natural tendency to attract, select, and retain people with values and personality characteristics that are consistent with the organization's character, resulting in a more homogeneous organization and a stronger culture.

- *Attraction.* Job applicants engage in self-selection by avoiding prospective employers whose values seem incompatible with their own values.[65] They look for subtle artifacts during interviews and through public information that communicate the company's culture. Some organizations encourage this self-selection by actively describing their cultures. At Bankwest, for instance, job seekers can complete an online quiz that estimates their fit with the Australian financial institution's collegial, developmental, customer-focused culture.[66]

- *Selection.* How well the person "fits in" with the company's culture is often a factor in deciding which job applicants to hire.[67] Zappos carefully selects applicants whose personal values are aligned with the company's values. The applicant is first assessed for technical skills and experience at the online shoe and clothing retailer, then the applicant receives "a separate set of interviews purely for culture fit," says CEO Tony Hsieh. Unusual methods are sometimes applied to determine how well an applicant's values are compatible with Zappos' culture. For example, to determine an applicant's humility (one of Zappos' core values), staff ask the Zappos-hired driver how well he or she was treated by the applicant during the drive to the company's headquarters in Las Vegas.

- *Attrition.* People seek environments that are sufficiently congruent with their personal values and are motivated to leave environments that are a poor fit. This occurs because person–organization values congruence supports their social identity and minimizes internal role conflict. Even if employees aren't forced out, many quit when values incongruence is sufficiently high.[68] Several companies (Zappos, G Adventures, etc.) will even pay newcomers to quit within the first few weeks of employment if the newcomers conclude that their personal values conflict with the company's culture.

> People seek environments that are sufficiently congruent with their personal values and are motivated to leave environments that are a poor fit.

ORGANIZATIONAL SOCIALIZATION

Organizational socialization is another process that companies rely on to maintain a strong corporate culture and, more generally, help people to adjust to new employment. **Organizational socialization** is the process by which individuals learn the values, expected behaviors, and social knowledge necessary to assume their roles in the organization.[69] This process can potentially change employee values to become more aligned with the company's culture. However, changing an employee's personal values is much more difficult than is often assumed because values are fairly stable beyond early adulthood. More likely, effective socialization gives newcomers a clearer understanding about the company's values and how they are translated into specific on-the-job behaviors.[70]

Along with supporting the organization's culture, socialization helps newcomers adjust to coworkers, work procedures, and other corporate realities. Research indicates that when employees are effectively socialized into the organization, they tend to perform better, have higher job satisfaction, and remain longer with the organization.[71]

Learning and Adjustment Process

Organizational socialization is a process of both learning and adjustment. It is a learning process because newcomers try to make sense of the company's physical workplace, social dynamics, and strategic and cultural environment. They learn about the organization's performance expectations, power dynamics, corporate culture, company history, and jargon. They also need to form successful and satisfying relationships with other people from whom they can learn the ropes.[72] In other words, effective socialization supports newcomers' *organizational comprehension*. It accelerates development of an accurate cognitive map of the physical, social, strategic, and cultural dynamics of the organization. Ideally, this learning should be distributed over time to minimize information overload.

Organizational socialization is also an adjustment process because individuals need to adapt to their new work environment. They develop new work roles that reconfigure their social identity, adopt new team norms, and practice new behaviors.[73] The adjustment process is fairly rapid for many people, usually occurring within a few months. However, newcomers with diverse work experience seem to adjust better than those with limited previous experience, possibly because they have a larger toolkit of knowledge and skills to make the adjustment possible.[74]

Stages of Organizational Socialization

Organizational socialization is a continuous process, beginning before you submit a job application and continuing throughout your career within the company. However, it is most intense during movement across organizational boundaries, such as when you first join a company or get transferred to an international assignment. Each of these transitions is a process that can be divided into three stages. Our focus here is on the socialization of new employees, so the three stages are called preemployment socialization, encounter, and role management (see Exhibit 13.7). These stages parallel the individual's transition from outsider to newcomer and then to insider.[75]

attraction–selection–attrition (ASA) theory a theory that states that organizations have a natural tendency to attract, select, and retain people with values and personality characteristics that are consistent with the organization's character, resulting in a more homogeneous organization and a stronger culture

organizational socialization the process by which individuals learn the values, expected behaviors, and social knowledge necessary to assume their roles in the organization

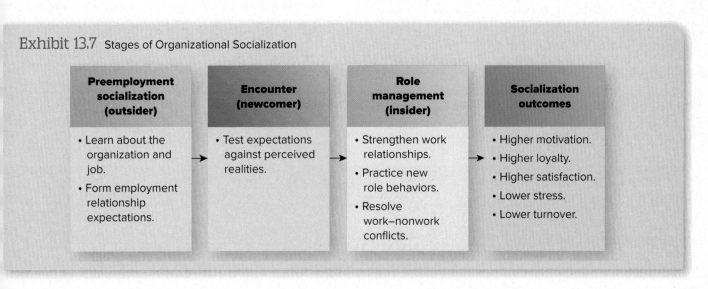

Exhibit 13.7 Stages of Organizational Socialization

Preemployment socialization (outsider)	Encounter (newcomer)	Role management (insider)	Socialization outcomes
• Learn about the organization and job. • Form employment relationship expectations.	• Test expectations against perceived realities.	• Strengthen work relationships. • Practice new role behaviors. • Resolve work–nonwork conflicts.	• Higher motivation. • Higher loyalty. • Higher satisfaction. • Lower stress. • Lower turnover.

Stage 1: Preemployment Socialization Think back to the months and weeks before you began working in a new job (or attending a new school). You actively searched for information about the company, formed expectations about working there, and felt some anticipation about fitting into that environment. The preemployment socialization stage encompasses all the learning and adjustment that occurs before the first day of work. In fact, a large part of the socialization adjustment process occurs during this stage.[76]

The main problem with preemployment socialization is that outsiders rely on indirect information about what it is like to work in the organization. This information is often distorted by inherent conflicts that arise during the mating dance between employer and applicant.[77] One conflict occurs between the employer's need to attract qualified applicants and the applicant's need for complete information to make accurate employment decisions. Many firms describe only positive aspects of the job and company, causing applicants to accept job offers with incomplete or false expectations.

Another conflict that prevents accurate exchange of information occurs when applicants avoid asking important questions about the company because they want to convey a favorable image to their prospective employer. For instance, applicants usually don't like to ask about starting salaries and promotion opportunities because it makes them seem greedy or aggressive. Yet, unless the employer provides this information, applicants might fill in the missing details with false assumptions that produce inaccurate expectations.

Two other types of conflict tend to distort preemployment information for employers. Applicants engage in impression management when seeking employment, motivating them to hide negative information, act out of character, and occasionally embellish information about their past accomplishments. At the same time, employers are sometimes reluctant to ask some types of questions or use potentially valuable selection devices because they might scare off applicants. Unfortunately, employers form inaccurate expectations about job candidates because they receive exaggerated résumés and are often reluctant to ask for more delicate information from those applicants.

Stage 2: Encounter The first day on the job typically marks the beginning of the encounter stage of organizational socialization. This is the stage in which newcomers test how well their preemployment expectations fit reality. Many companies fail that test, resulting in **reality shock**—the stress that results when employees perceive discrepancies between their preemployment expectations and on-the-job reality.[78] Reality shock doesn't

The main problem with preemployment socialization is that outsiders rely on indirect information about what it is like to work in the organization.
©Rawpixel.com/Shutterstock

necessarily occur on the first day; it might develop over several weeks or even months as newcomers form a better understanding of their new work environment.

Reality shock is common in many organizations.[79] Newcomers sometimes face *unmet expectations* whereby the employer doesn't deliver on its promises, such as failing to provide challenging projects or the resources to get the work done. However, new hires also experience reality shock due to *unrealistic expectations*, which are distorted work expectations formed from the information exchange conflicts described earlier. Whatever the cause, reality shock impedes the learning and adjustment process because the newcomer's energy is directed toward managing the resulting stress.[80]

Stage 3: Role Management Role management, the third stage of organizational socialization, really begins during preemployment socialization, but it is most active as employees make the transition from newcomers to insiders. They strengthen relationships with coworkers and supervisors, practice new role behaviors, and adopt attitudes and values consistent with their new positions and the organization. Role management also involves resolving the conflicts between work and nonwork activities, including resolving discrepancies between their personal values and those emphasized by the organizational culture.

Improving the Socialization Process

Companies have a tendency to exaggerate positive features of the job and neglect to mention the undesirable elements. Their motivation is to attract as many job applicants as possible, which they

> **Newcomers sometimes face *unmet expectations* whereby the employer doesn't deliver on its promises, such as failing to provide challenging projects or the resources to get the work done.**

assume will improve the selection choices. Unfortunately, this flypaper approach often ends badly. Those hired soon discover that the actual workplace is not as favorable as the employer's marketing hype (i.e., unmet expectations), resulting in reality shock. In contrast, a **realistic job preview (RJP)** offers a balance of positive and negative information about the job and work context.[81] This balanced description of the company and work helps job applicants decide for themselves whether their skills, needs, and values are compatible with the job and organization.

RJPs scare away some applicants, but they also tend to reduce turnover and increase job performance.[82] This occurs because RJPs help applicants develop more accurate preemployment expectations, which, in turn, minimize reality shock. RJPs represent a type of vaccination by preparing employees for the more challenging and troublesome aspects of the work context. There is also some evidence that RJPs increase affective organizational commitment. One explanation is that companies providing candid information are easier to trust. Another explanation is that RJPs show respect and concern for the employee's expectations and welfare.[83]

Socialization Agents Ask new employees what most helped them adjust to their jobs and chances are they will mention helpful coworkers, bosses, or maybe even friends who work elsewhere in the organization. The fact is, socialization agents play a central

role in this process.[85] Supervisors tend to provide technical information, performance feedback, and information about job duties. They also improve the socialization process by giving newcomers reasonably challenging first assignments, buffering them from excessive demands, helping them form social ties with coworkers, and generating positive emotions around their new work experience.[86]

Coworkers are important socialization agents because they are easily accessible, can answer questions when problems arise, and serve as role models for appropriate behavior. New employees tend to receive this information and support when coworkers welcome them into the work team. Coworkers also aid the socialization process by being flexible and tolerant in their interactions with new hires.

Newcomer socialization is most successful when companies help to strengthen social bonds between the new hires and current employees. Cisco Systems is a role model in this regard. For example, one newcomer at the California-based Internet technology company recently described how during the first two weeks teammates helped her learn about the work context, took her out to restaurants, actively sought her ideas in team meetings, and held a game night so everyone could have fun socializing after work.[87]

> **realistic job preview (RJP)** a method of improving organizational socialization in which job applicants are given a balance of positive and negative information about the job and work context

---

OB THEORY TO PRACTICE

Connected Socialization at trivago

trivago, the world's largest hotel search company, puts considerable resources into its talent (employee) socialization process. Before their first day of work, new hires are assigned a buddy to answer their questions. The entire first week of employment is dedicated to socialization and other aspects of onboarding at the company's headquarters in Düsseldorf, Germany.

Throughout the week, new employees attend information sessions (as shown in this photo) and enjoy several events that help them learn more about the company and form strong bonds with each other. "The whole mission during this week is to get to know trivago, integrate into our culture here, and get to know as many people as possible," explains Samantha Strube, trivago's talent integration team leader.[84]

©trivago

Study Checklist

Connect® Management is available for *M Organizational Behavior.* Additional resources include:

✓ Interactive Applications:
- **Decision Generator**
- **Sequencing**
- **Video Case:** See management in action through interactive videos.

✓ **SmartBook™**—SmartBook is the first and only adaptive reading experience available today. Distinguishing what you know from what you don't, and honing in on concepts you are most likely to forget, SmartBook personalizes content for you in a continuously adapting reading experience. Reading is no longer a passive and linear experience, but an engaging and dynamic one where you are more likely to master and retain important concepts and go to class better prepared.

Notes

1. The terms *organizational culture* and *corporate culture* were popularized in 1982 in T. E. Deal and A. A. Kennedy, *Corporate Cultures* (Reading, MA: Addison-Wesley, 1982); T. J. Peters and R. H. Waterman, *In Search of Excellence: Lessons from America's Best-Run Companies* (New York: Warner, 1982). However, this phrase did appear more than a decade earlier in N. Margulies, "Organizational Culture and Psychological Growth," *The Journal of Applied Behavioral Science* 5, no. 4 (1969): 491–508; S. Silverzweig and R. F. Allen, "Changing the Corporate Culture," *Sloan Management Review* 17, no. 3 (1976): 33–34.

2. "Lax Corporate Culture Set up Takata's Fall," *Nikkei Asian Review*, July 3, 2017; R. Wartzman, "Amazon and Whole Foods Are Headed for a Culture Clash," *Fortune*, June 27, 2017; E. Knight, "Uber Pays a $26 Billion Price for Its Toxic Corporate Culture," *Sydney Morning Herald* (Australia), July 1, 2017.

3. A. Williams, P. Dobson, and M. Walters, *Changing Culture: New Organizational Approaches* (London: Institute of Personnel Management, 1989); E. H. Schein, "What Is Culture?," in *Reframing Organizational Culture*, ed. P. J. Frost et al. (Newbury Park, CA: Sage, 1991), 243–53.

4. B. M. Meglino and E. C. Ravlin, "Individual Values in Organizations: Concepts, Controversies, and Research," *Journal of Management* 24, no. 3 (1998): 351–89; B. R. Agle and C. B. Caldwell, "Understanding Research on Values in Business," *Business and Society* 38, no. 3 (1999): 326–87; S. Hitlin and J. A. Pilavin, "Values: Reviving a Dormant Concept," *Annual Review of Sociology* 30 (2004): 359–93.

5. N. M. Ashkanasy, "The Case for Culture," in *Debating Organization*, ed. R. Westwood and S. Clegg (Malden, MA: Blackwell, 2003), 300–10.

6. M. Lagace, "Gerstner: Changing Culture at IBM," *HBS Working Knowledge*, September 12, 2002.

7. B. Kabanoff and J. Daly, "Espoused Values in Organisations," *Australian Journal of Management* 27, Special issue (2002): 89–104.

8. D. Aguirre, R. von Post, and M. Alpern, *Culture's Role in Enabling Organizational Change* (New York: strategy&, November 9, 2013); Columbia Business School and Duke University School of Business, "CEOs and CFOs Share How Corporate Culture Matters," news release (New York: Columbia Business School, November 19, 2015); D. Lucy et al., *The Management Agenda 2016* (West Sussex, UK: Roffey Park, February 2016); Deloitte University Press, *The New Organization: Different by Design*, Global Human Capital Trends 2016 (New York: Deloitte University Press, 2016).

9. C. Ostroff, A. J. Kinicki, and R. S. Muhammad, "Organizational Culture and Climate," in *Handbook of Psychology*, 2nd ed., ed. I. B. Weiner (New York: Wiley, 2012), 643–76.

10. R. Hastings and P. McCord, *Netflix Culture: Freedom and Responsibility* (Los Gatos, CA: Netflix, August 2009); T. Stenovec, "One Reason for Netflix's Success—It Treats Employees Like Grownups," *Huffington Post*, February 28, 2015; V. Giang, "The Woman Who Created Netflix's Enviable Company Culture," *Fast Company*, February 2, 2016; *PPL Corporation: Vision & Values* (Allentown, PA: PPL Corporation, February 13, 2016). Netflix recently updated its organizational culture statement, but the underlying values are similar to the 2009 document. See R. Hastings, "Culture at Netflix" (Los Gatos, CA: Netflix, June 21, 2017), https://jobs.netflix.com/culture (accessed July 11, 2017).

11. C. A. O'Reilly III, J. Chatman, and D. F. Caldwell, "People and Organizational Culture: A Profile Comparison Approach to Assessing Person-Organization Fit," *Academy of Management Journal* 34 (1991): 487–516; J. J. van Muijen, "Organizational Culture," in *A Handbook of Work and Organizational Psychology: Organizational Psychology*, ed. P. J. D. Drenth, H. Thierry, and C. J. de Wolff (East Sussex, UK: Psychology Press, 1998), 113–32; P. A. Balthazard, R. A. Cooke, and R. E. Potter, "Dysfunctional Culture, Dysfunctional Organization: Capturing the Behavioral Norms That Form Organizational Culture and Drive Performance," *Journal of Managerial Psychology* 21, no. 8 (2006): 709–32; C. Helfrich et al., "Assessing an Organizational Culture Instrument Based on the Competing Values Framework: Exploratory and Confirmatory Factor Analyses," *Implementation Science* 2, no. 1 (2007): 13. For reviews of organizational culture survey instruments, see T. Scott et al., "The Quantitative Measurement of Organizational Culture in Health Care: A Review of the Available Instruments," *Health Services Research* 38, no. 3 (2003): 923–45; D. E. Leidner and T. Kayworth, "A Review of Culture in Information Systems Research: Toward a Theory of Information Technology Culture Conflict," *MIS Quarterly* 30, no. 2 (2006): 357–99; S. Scott-Findlay and C. A. Estabrooks, "Mapping the Organizational Culture Research in Nursing: A Literature Review," *Journal of Advanced Nursing* 56, no. 5 (2006): 498–513.

12. L. Guiso, P. Sapienza, and L. Zingales, "The Value of Corporate Culture," *Journal of Financial Economics* 117, no. 1 (2015): 60–76.

13. J. Martin, P. J. Frost, and O. A. O'Neill, "Organizational Culture: Beyond Struggles for Intellectual Dominance," in *Handbook of Organization Studies*, ed. S. Clegg et al. (London: Sage, 2006), 725–53; N. E. Fenton and S. Inglis, "A Critical Perspective on Organizational Values," *Nonprofit Management and Leadership* 17, no. 3 (2007): 335–47; K. Haukelid, "Theories of (Safety) Culture Revisited—An Anthropological Approach," *Safety Science* 46, no. 3 (2008): 413–26.

14. G. Hofstede, "Identifying Organizational Subcultures: An Empirical Approach," *Journal of Management Studies* 35, no. 1 (1990): 1–12; J. Martin and C. Siehl, "Organizational Culture and Counterculture: An Uneasy Symbiosis," *Organizational Dynamics* (1983): 52–64; E. Ogbonna and L. C. Harris, "Organisational Culture in the Age of the Internet: An Exploratory Study," *New Technology, Work and Employment* 21, no. 2 (2006): 162–75.

15. H. Silver, "Does a University Have a Culture?," *Studies in Higher Education* 28, no. 2 (2003): 157–69.

16. A. Sinclair, "Approaches to Organizational Culture and Ethics," *Journal of Business Ethics* 12 (1993); T. E. Deal and A. A. Kennedy, *The New Corporate Cultures* (Cambridge, MA: Perseus Books, 1999), chap. 10; A. Boisnier and J. Chatman, "The Role of Subcultures in Agile Organizations," in *Leading and Managing People in Dynamic Organizations*, ed. R. Petersen and E. Mannix (Mahwah, NJ: Erlbaum, 2003), 87–112; C. Morrill, M. N. Zald, and H. Rao, "Covert Political Conflict in Organizations: Challenges from Below," *Annual Review of Sociology* 29, no. 1 (2003): 391–415.

17. J. S. Ott, *The Organizational Culture Perspective* (Pacific Grove, CA: Brooks/Cole, 1989), chap. 2; J. S. Pederson and J. S. Sorensen, *Organizational Cultures in Theory and Practice* (Aldershot, UK: Gower, 1989), 27–29; M. O. Jones, *Studying Organizational Symbolism: What, How, Why?* (Thousand Oaks, CA: Sage, 1996).

18. A. Furnham and B. Gunter, "Corporate Culture: Definition, Diagnosis, and Change," *International Review of Industrial and Organizational Psychology* 8 (1993): 233–61; E. H. Schein, "Organizational Culture," *American Psychologist* (1990): 109–19; E. H. Schein, *The Corporate Culture Survival Guide* (San Francisco: Jossey-Bass, 1999), chap. 4.

19. M. Doehrman, "Anthropologists—Deep in the Corporate Bush," *Daily Record* (Kansas City, MO), July 19, 2005, 1.

20. T. E. Deal and A. A. Kennedy, *Corporate Cultures* (Reading, MA: Addison-Wesley, 1982), chap. 5; C. J. Boudens, "The Story of Work: A Narrative Analysis of Workplace Emotion," *Organization Studies* 26, no. 9 (2005): 1285–306; S. Denning, *The Leader's Guide to Storytelling* (San Francisco: Jossey-Bass, 2005).

21. J. C. Meyer, "Tell Me a Story: Eliciting Organizational Values from Narratives," *Communication Quarterly* 43 (1995): 210–24; W. Swap et al., "Using Mentoring and Storytelling to Transfer Knowledge in the Workplace," *Journal of Management Information Systems* 18 (2001): 95–114; A. L. Wilkins, "Organizational Stories as Symbols Which Control the Organization," in *Organizational Symbolism*, ed. L. R. Pondy et al. (Greenwich, CT: JAI Press, 1984), 81–92; R. Zemke, "Storytelling: Back to a Basic," *Training* 27, no. 3 (1990): 44–50.

22. T. Kelley and D. Kelley, *Creative Confidence: Unleashing the Creative Potential within Us All* (New York: Random House, 2013), 198.

23. J. Mossman, "Employee-Friendly Workplace Culture a Key to Company Success," *Denver Post*, April 21, 2013; Darden MBA, "'Community First, Company Second': Javier Rodriguez, DaVita Kidney Care" (YouTube, November 18, 2015), http://www.youtube.com/watch?v=sdTYtXSEIFQ (accessed June 15, 2016); Stanford Graduate School of Business, "DaVita CEO Kent Thiry on Building a Signature Company Culture" (YouTube, November 23, 2015), http://www.youtube.com/watch?v=9CN85CFllME (accessed June 15, 2016).

24. G. Smith, *Why I Left Goldman Sachs: A Wall Street Story* (New York: Grand Central Publishing, 2012); R. Blackden, "Goldman Sachs in Hunt for 'Muppet' Email," *The Telegraph*, March 22, 2012; B. Tuttle, "16 Amazing Facts About the Muppets That'll Make You Laugh, Cry & Sing Along," *Money*, September 22, 2015. Goldman Sachs apparently found the word "muppets" in 0.3 percent of all emails over the previous year or two, but almost all of those messages referred to a staff outing to watch the latest Muppet film. Even so, the word "muppet" is apparently widely used today by investors (when being gullible about investment advice) and others in the investment community.

25. A. C. T. Smith and B. Stewart, "Organizational Rituals: Features, Functions and Mechanisms," *International Journal of Management Reviews* 13 (2011): 113–33.

26. "The Ultimate Chairman," *Business Times Singapore*, September 3, 2005.

27. G. Turner and J. Myerson, *New Workspace New Culture: Office Design as a Catalyst for Change* (Aldershot, UK: Gower, 1998).

28. K. D. Elsbach and B. A. Bechky, "It's More Than a Desk: Working Smarter through Leveraged Office Design," *California Management Review* 49, no. 2 (2007): 80–101.

29. Churchill apparently made this statement on October 28, 1943, in the British House of Commons, when London, damaged by bombings in World War II, was about to be rebuilt.

30. B. O'Connor, "CEO Credits Quicken Loans' Culture for Firm's Success," *Detroit News*, May 1, 2013, C2; "First West Credit Union CEO Places Focus on Leadership Brand," *CEO Series* (Vancouver: Simon Fraser University, October 29, 2013), http://beedie.sfu.ca/blog/2013/10/7405/ (accessed June 16, 2016).

31. T. E. Deal and A. A. Kennedy, *The New Corporate Cultures* (Reading, MA: Perseus Books, 1999), 22.

32. R. Barrett, *Building a Values-Driven Organization: A Whole System Approach to Cultural Transformation* (Burlington, MA: Butterworth-Heinemann, 2006); J. C. Collins and J. I. Porras, *Built to Last: Successful Habits of Visionary Companies* (London: Century, 1994); J. M. Kouzes and B. Z. Posner, *The Leadership Challenge*, 4th ed. (San Francisco: Jossey-Bass, 2007), chap. 3; T. E. Deal and A. A. Kennedy, *The New Corporate Cultures* (Cambridge, MA: Perseus Books, 1999).

33. C. Siehl and J. Martin, "Organizational Culture: A Key to Financial Performance?," in *Organizational Climate and Culture*, ed. B. Schneider (San Francisco: Jossey-Bass, 1990), 241–81; G. G. Gordon and N. Di-Tomaso, "Predicting Corporate Performance from Organizational Culture," *Journal of Management Studies* 29 (1992): 783–98; J. P. Kotter and J. L. Heskett, *Corporate Culture and Performance* (New York: Free Press, 1992); C. P. M. Wilderom, U. Glunk, and R. Maslowski, "Organizational Culture as a Predictor of Organizational Performance," in *Handbook of Organizational Culture and Climate*, ed. N. M. Ashkanasy, C. P. M. Wilderom, and M. F. Peterson (Thousand Oaks, CA: Sage, 2000), 193–210; A. Carmeli and A. Tishler, "The Relationships between Intangible Organizational Elements and Organizational Performance," *Strategic Management Journal* 25 (2004): 1257–78; S. Teerikangas and P. Very, "The Culture–Performance Relationship in M&A: From Yes/No to How," *British Journal of Management* 17, no. S1 (2006): S31–S48.

34. Y. Wiener, "Forms of Value Systems: A Focus on Organizational Effectiveness and Cultural Change and Maintenance," *Academy of Management Review* 13, no. 4 (1988): 534–45; J. A. Chatman and S. E. Cha, "Leading by Leveraging Culture," *California Management Review* 45 (2003): 20–34; M. Alvesson, *Understanding Organizational Culture*, 2nd ed. (London: Sage, 2013).

35. B. Ashforth and F. Mael, "Social Identity Theory and the Organization," *Academy of Management Review* 14 (1989): 20–39; M. Alvesson, *Understanding Organizational Culture*, 2nd ed. (London: Sage, 2013).

36. M. R. Louis, "Surprise and Sensemaking: What Newcomers Experience in Entering Unfamiliar Organizational Settings," *Administrative Science Quarterly* 25 (1980): 226–51; S. G. Harris, "Organizational Culture and Individual Sensemaking: A Schema-Based Perspective," *Organization Science* 5 (1994): 309–21.

37. J. W. Barnes et al., "The Role of Culture Strength in Shaping Sales Force Outcomes," *Journal of Personal Selling & Sales Management* 26, no. 3 (2006): 255–70.

38. Heidrick & Struggles, *Leadership Challenges Emerge as Asia Pacific Companies Go Global* (Melbourne: August 2008).

39. D. Frith, "Follow the Leader," *Business Review Weekly*, April 19, 2012, 18.

40. C. A. O'Reilly III and J. A. Chatman, "Culture as Social Control: Corporations, Cults, and Commitment," *Research in Organizational Behavior* 18 (1996): 157–200; B. Spector and H. Lane, "Exploring the Distinctions between a High Performance Culture and a Cult," *Strategy & Leadership* 35, no. 3 (2007): 18–24.

41. J. P. Kotter and J. L. Heskett, *Corporate Culture and Performance* (New York: Free Press, 1992), chap. 4; B. M. Bass and R. E. Riggio, *Transformational Leadership*, 2nd ed. (New York: Routledge, 2006), chap. 7; D. P. Costanza et al., "The Effect of Adaptive Organizational Culture on Long-Term Survival," *Journal of Business and Psychology* (2015): 1–21.

42. T. Krisher and D. A. Durbin, "General Motors CEO Akerson Leads Comeback from Bankruptcy by Ruffling Company's Bureaucracy," *Associated Press Newswires*, December 17, 2011.

43. W. E. Baker and J. M. Sinkula, "The Synergistic Effect of Market Orientation and Learning Orientation on Organizational Performance," *Academy of Marketing Science Journal* 27, no. 4 (1999): 411–27; Z. Emden, A. Yaprak, and S. T. Cavusgil, "Learning from Experience in International Alliances: Antecedents and Firm Performance Implications," *Journal of Business Research* 58, no. 7 (2005): 883–92.

44. *AIA Code of Conduct* (Hong Kong: AIA Group Limited, April 30, 2015); K. Whitehead, "Case Study: AIA, Hong Kong," *People Management Asia*, January 21, 2016, 10–11.

45. E. Dwoskin and T. C. Frankel, "Uber's Big Problem: Attracting Talent," *Washington Post*, June 18, 2017, G04; J. C. Wong, "Uber's 'Hustle-Oriented' Culture Becomes a Black Mark on Employees' Résumés," *Guardian*, March 7, 2017; E. Knight, "Uber Pays a $26 Billion Price for Its Toxic Corporate Culture," *Sydney Morning Herald* (Australia), July 1, 2017; S. Levin, "Uber's Scandals, Blunders and PR Disasters: The Full List," *Guardian*, June 18, 2017; B. Edelman, "Uber Can't Be Fixed—It's Time for Regulators to Shut It Down," *Harvard Business Review* (June 21, 2017); G. Bensinger and J. S. Lublin, "Uber Fires More Than 20 People in Harassment Investigation," *The Wall Street Journal*, June 7, 2017.

46. M. L. Marks, "Adding Cultural Fit to Your Diligence Checklist," *Mergers & Acquisitions* 34, no. 3 (1999): 14–20; E. H. Schein, *The Corporate Culture Survival Guide* (San Francisco: Jossey-Bass, 1999), chap. 8; S. Teerikangas and P. Very, "The Culture-Performance Relationship in M&A: From Yes/No to How," *British Journal of Management* 17, no. S1 (2006): S31–S48; G. K. Stahl and A. Voigt, "Do Cultural Differences Matter in Mergers and Acquisitions? A Tentative Model and Examination," *Organization Science* 19, no. 1 (2008): 160–76.

47. J. P. Daly et al., "The Effects of Initial Differences in Firms' Espoused Values on Their Postmerger Performance," *Journal of Applied Behavioral Science* 40, no. 3 (2004): 323–43; C. Cook and D. Spitzer, *World Class Transactions* (London: KPMG, 2001); J. Krug, *Mergers and Acquisitions: Turmoil in Top Management Teams* (Williston, VT: Business Expert Press, 2009).

48. *The Right Combination: Managing Integration for Deal Success* (London: EY, May 2014); *Integration Report 2015: Putting the Pieces Together* (New York: Deloitte M&A Institute, March 2015); KPMG, *U.S. Executives on M&A: Full Speed Ahead in 2016* (New York: Fortune Knowledge Group, January 2016).

49. C. A. Schorg, C. A. Raiborn, and M. F. Massoud, "Using a 'Cultural Audit' to Pick M&A Winners," *Journal of Corporate Accounting & Finance* (2004): 47–55; W. Locke, "Higher Education Mergers: Integrating Organisational Cultures and Developing Appropriate Management Styles," *Higher Education Quarterly* 61, no. 1 (2007): 83–102.

50. A. R. Malekazedeh and A. Nahavandi, "Making Mergers Work by Managing Cultures," *Journal of Business Strategy* (1990): 55–57; K. W. Smith, "A Brand-New Culture for the Merged Firm," *Mergers and Acquisitions* 35 (2000): 45–50.

51. M. Joyce, "AirTran Employees Getting New Culture," *Dallas Business Journal*, July 8, 2011.

52. A. Hyland, "Howzat? Wesfarmers and Boral Chairman Bob Every on Career and Overcoming Adversity," *Australian Financial Review*, July 6, 2015.

53. Hewitt Associates, "Mergers and Acquisitions May Be Driven by Business Strategy—but Often Stumble over People and Culture Issues" (Lincolnshire, IL: PR Newswire, 1998).

54. M. Krupnick, "Virgin America Fans Ask if Alaska Airlines Takeover Will Mean Loss of Cool," *New York Times*, April 11, 2016; S. Mayerowitz, "Alaska Airlines CEO Says He Might Keep Virgin America Brand," Associated Press, June 15, 2016; Alaska Air Group, "Alaska Air Group Closes Acquisition of Virgin America, Becomes the 5th Largest U.S. Airline," news release (San Francisco: Alaska Air Group, December 14, 2016); H. Martin, "Virgin America Will Disappear into Alaska Airlines in 2019," *Los Angeles Times*, March 22, 2017.

55. J. Martin, "Can Organizational Culture Be Managed?," in *Organizational Culture*, ed. P. J. Frost et al. (Beverly Hills, CA: Sage, 1985), 95–98.

56. B. O'Connor, "CEO Credits Quicken Loans' Culture for Firm's Success," *Detroit News*, May 1, 2013, C2.

57. E. H. Schein, "The Role of the Founder in Creating Organizational Culture," *Organizational Dynamics* 12, no. 1 (1983): 13–28; A. S. Tsui et al., "Unpacking the Relationship between CEO Leadership Behavior and Organizational Culture," *Leadership Quarterly* 17 (2006): 113–37; Y. Berson, S. Oreg, and T. Dvir, "CEO Values, Organizational Culture and Firm Outcomes," *Journal of Organizational Behavior* 29, no. 5 (2008): 615–33; B. Schneider, M. G. Ehrhart, and W. H. Macey, "Organizational Climate and Culture," *Annual Review of Psychology* 64, no. 1 (2013): 361–88.

58. Y. Berson, S. Oreg, and T. Dvir, "CEO Values, Organizational Culture and Firm Outcomes," *Journal of Organizational Behavior* 29, no. 5 (2008): 615–33; A. S. Klein, J. Wallis, and R. A. Cooke, "The Impact of Leadership Styles on Organizational Culture and Firm Effectiveness: An Empirical Study," *Journal of Management & Organization* 19 (2013): 241–54; D. V. Day, M. A. Griffin, and K. R. Louw, "The Climate and Culture of Leadership in Organizations," in *The Oxford Handbook of Organizational Climate and Culture*, ed. B. Schneider and K. M. Barbera (New York: Oxford University Press, 2014), 101–17.

59. M. J. Gelfand et al., "Conflict Cultures in Organizations: How Leaders Shape Conflict Cultures and Their Organizational-Level Consequences," *Journal of Applied Psychology* 97, no. 6 (2012): 1131–47; R. C. Liden et al., "Servant Leadership and Serving Culture: Influence on Individual and Unit Performance," *Academy of Management Journal* 57, no. 5 (2014): 1434–52.

60. M. De Pree, *Leadership Is an Art* (East Lansing: Michigan State University Press, 1987).

61. J. Kerr and J. W. Slocum Jr., "Managing Corporate Culture through Reward Systems," *Academy of Management Executive* 1 (1987): 99–107; J. M. Higgins et al., "Using Cultural Artifacts to Change and Perpetuate Strategy," *Journal of Change Management* 6, no. 4 (2006): 397–415; H. Hofstetter and I. Harpaz, "Declared versus Actual Organizational Culture as Indicated by an Organization's Performance Appraisal," *International Journal of Human Resource Management* (2011): 1–22.

62. R. Charan, "Home Depot's Blueprint for Culture Change," *Harvard Business Review* (2006): 61–70.

63. B. Schneider, "The People Make the Place," *Personnel Psychology* 40, no. 3 (1987): 437–53; B. Schneider et al., "Personality and Organizations: A Test of the Homogeneity of Personality Hypothesis," *Journal of Applied Psychology* 83, no. 3 (1998): 462–70; T. R. Giberson, C. J. Resick, and M. W. Dickson, "Embedding Leader Characteristics: An Examination of Homogeneity of Personality and Values in Organizations," *Journal of Applied Psychology* 90, no. 5 (2005): 1002–10.

64. Cubiks International, *Cubiks International Survey on Job and Cultural Fit* (Guildford, UK: Cubiks International, July 2013); Kelly Services, *Engaging Active and Passive Job Seekers*, Kelly Global Workforce Index (Troy, MI: Kelly Services, May 2014); *2016 Global Talent Trends: Data on How Candidates Want to Be Recruited*, LinkedIn (Sunnyvale, CA: LinkedIn, June 28, 2016); CareerBuilder, "Number of Employers Using Social Media to Screen Candidates Has Increased 500 Percent

over the Last Decade," news release (Chicago: CareerBuilder, April 28, 2016); Korn Ferry, "Korn Ferry Futurestep Survey: 90 Percent of Executives Say New Hire Retention an Issue," news release (Los Angeles: Korn Ferry, March 21, 2017).

65. T. A. Judge and D. M. Cable, "Applicant Personality, Organizational Culture, and Organization Attraction," *Personnel Psychology* 50, no. 2 (1997): 359–94; D. S. Chapman et al., "Applicant Attraction to Organizations and Job Choice: A Meta-Analytic Review of the Correlates of Recruiting Outcomes," *Journal of Applied Psychology* 90, no. 5 (2005): 928–44; A. L. Kristof-Brown, R. D. Zimmerman, and E. C. Johnson, "Consequences of Individuals' Fit at Work: A Meta-Analysis of Person–Job, Person–Organization, Person–Group, and Person–Supervisor Fit," *Personnel Psychology* 58, no. 2 (2005): 281–342; C. Hu, H. C. Su, and C. I. B. Chen, "The Effect of Person–Organization Fit Feedback via Recruitment Web Sites on Applicant Attraction," *Computers in Human Behavior* 23, no. 5 (2007): 2509–23.

66. Bankwest, "Is This Your Happy Place?," *Bankwest Careers* (Perth, 2016), http://www.bankwest.com.au/about-us/bankwest-careers-overview/is-this-your-happy-place (accessed June 17, 2016).

67. A. Kristof-Brown, "Perceived Applicant Fit: Distinguishing between Recruiters' Perceptions of Person–Job and Person–Organization Fit," *Personnel Psychology* 53, no. 3 (2000): 643–71; A. E. M. Van Vianen, "Person–Organization Fit: The Match between Newcomers' and Recruiters' Preferences for Organizational Cultures," *Personnel Psychology* 53 (2000): 113–49.

68. D. M. Cable and J. R. Edwards, "Complementary and Supplementary Fit: A Theoretical and Empirical Integration," *Journal of Applied Psychology* 89, no. 5 (2004): 822–34.

69. J. Van Maanen, "Breaking In: Socialization to Work," in *Handbook of Work, Organization, and Society*, ed. R. Dubin (Chicago: Rand McNally, 1976).

70. S. L. McShane, G. O'Neill, and T. Travaglione, "Managing Employee Values in Values-Driven Organizations: Contradiction, Façade, and Illusions" (paper presented at the 21st Annual ANZAM Conference, Sydney, Australia, December 2007); S. L. McShane, G. O'Neill, and T. Travaglione, "Rethinking the Values-Driven Organization Process: From Values Engineering to Behavioral Domain Training" (paper presented at the Academy of Management 2008 Annual Meeting, Anaheim, CA, 2008).

71. D. G. Allen, "Do Organizational Socialization Tactics Influence Newcomer Embeddedness and Turnover?," *Journal of Management* 32, no. 2 (2006): 237–56; A. M. Saks, K. L. Uggerslev, and N. E. Fassina, "Socialization Tactics and Newcomer Adjustment: A Meta-Analytic Review and Test of a Model," *Journal of Vocational Behavior* 70, no. 3 (2007): 413–46.

72. G. T. Chao et al., "Organizational Socialization: Its Content and Consequences," *Journal of Applied Psychology* 79 (1994): 450–63; H. D. Cooper-Thomas and N. Anderson, "Organizational Socialization: A Field Study into Socialization Success and Rate," *International Journal of Selection and Assessment* 13, no. 2 (2005): 116–28.

73. N. Nicholson, "A Theory of Work Role Transitions," *Administrative Science Quarterly* 29 (1984): 172–91; A. Elfering et al., "First Years in Job: A Three-Wave Analysis of Work Experiences," *Journal of Vocational Behavior* 70, no. 1 (2007): 97–115; B. E. Ashforth, D. M. Sluss, and A. M. Saks, "Socialization Tactics, Proactive Behavior, and Newcomer Learning: Integrating Socialization Models," *Journal of Vocational Behavior* 70, no. 3 (2007): 447–62; T. N. Bauer, "Newcomer Adjustment during Organizational Socialization: A Meta-Analytic Review of Antecedents, Outcomes, and Methods," *Journal of Applied Psychology* 92, no. 3 (2007): 707–21.

74. J. M. Beyer and D. R. Hannah, "Building on the Past: Enacting Established Personal Identities in a New Work Setting," *Organization Science* 13 (2002): 636–52; H. D. C. Thomas and N. Anderson, "Newcomer Adjustment: The Relationship between Organizational Socialization Tactics, Information Acquisition and Attitudes," *Journal of Occupational and Organizational Psychology* 75 (2002): 423–37.

75. L. W. Porter, E. E. Lawler III, and J. R. Hackman, *Behavior in Organizations* (New York: McGraw-Hill, 1975), 163–67; J. Van Maanen, "Breaking In: Socialization to Work," in *Handbook of Work, Organization, and Society,* ed. R. Dubin (Chicago: Rand McNally, 1976), 67–130; D. C. Feldman, "The Multiple Socialization of Organization Members," *Academy of Management Review* 6 (1981): 309–18.

76. B. E. Ashforth and A. M. Saks, "Socialization Tactics: Longitudinal Effects on Newcomer Adjustment," *Academy of Management Journal* 39 (1996): 149–78; J. D. Kammeyer-Mueller and C. R. Wanberg, "Unwrapping the Organizational Entry Process: Disentangling Multiple Antecedents and Their Pathways to Adjustment," *Journal of Applied Psychology* 88, no. 5 (2003): 779–94.

77. L. W. Porter, E. E. Lawler III, and J. R. Hackman, *Behavior in Organizations* (New York: McGraw-Hill, 1975), chap. 5.

78. M. R. Louis, "Surprise and Sensemaking: What Newcomers Experience in Entering Unfamiliar Organizational Settings," *Administrative Science Quarterly* 25 (1980): 226–51.

79. S. L. Robinson and D. M. Rousseau, "Violating the Psychological Contract: Not the Exception but the Norm," *Journal of Organizational Behavior* 15 (1994): 245–59.

80. D. L. Nelson, "Organizational Socialization: A Stress Perspective," *Journal of Occupational Behavior* 8 (1987): 311–24; A. Elfering et al., "First Years in Job: A Three-Wave Analysis of Work Experiences," *Journal of Vocational Behavior* 70, no. 1 (2007): 97–115.

81. J. P. Wanous, *Organizational Entry* (Reading, MA: Addison-Wesley, 1992); J. A. Breaugh and M. Starke, "Research on Employee Recruitment: So Many Studies, So Many Remaining Questions," *Journal of Management* 26, no. 3 (2000): 405–34.

82. J. M. Phillips, "Effects of Realistic Job Previews on Multiple Organizational Outcomes: A Meta-Analysis," *Academy of Management Journal* 41 (1998): 673–90.

83. Y. Ganzach et al., "Social Exchange and Organizational Commitment: Decision-Making Training for Job Choice as an Alternative to the Realistic Job Preview," *Personnel Psychology* 55 (2002): 613–37.

84. "Onboarding at trivago" (Düsseldorf, Germany: YouTube, April 9, 2015), http://www.youtube.com/watch?v=qqO02NLKCEI (accessed June 17, 2016).

85. C. Ostroff and S. W. J. Koslowski, "Organizational Socialization as a Learning Process: The Role of Information Acquisition," *Personnel Psychology* 45 (1992): 849–74; H. D. Cooper-Thomas and N. Anderson, "Organizational Socialization: A Field Study into Socialization Success and Rate," *International Journal of Selection and Assessment* 13, no. 2 (2005): 116–28; S. Nifadkar and T. Bauer, "Breach of Belongingness: Newcomer Relationship Conflict, Information, and Task-Related Outcomes during Organizational Socialization," *Journal of Applied Psychology* 101, no. 1 (2016): 1–13.

86. S. Nifadkar, A. S. Tsui, and B. E. Ashforth, "The Way You Make Me Feel and Behave: Supervisor-Triggered Newcomer Affect and Approach-Avoidance Behavior," *Academy of Management Journal* 55, no. 5 (2012): 1146–68.

87. K. Pike, "My First 30 Days at Cisco," *Life at Cisco*, Cisco Systems, Inc., March 29, 2016, http://blogs.cisco.com/lifeatcisco/my-first-30-day-at-cisco.

14 | Organizational Change

Learning Objectives

After you read this chapter, you should be able to:

LO14-1 Describe the elements of Lewin's force field analysis model.

LO14-2 Discuss the reasons why people resist organizational change and how change agents should view this resistance.

LO14-3 Outline six strategies for minimizing resistance to change, and debate ways to effectively create an urgency to change.

LO14-4 Discuss how leadership, coalitions, social networks, and pilot projects assist organizational change.

LO14-5 Describe and compare action research and appreciative inquiry as formal approaches to organizational change.

LO14-6 Discuss two cross-cultural and three ethical issues in organizational change.

General Motors (GM) has in-sourced almost all of its information technology (IT) work, hired 10,000 IT employees to replace contractors, built new IT innovation centers, and reduced 23 data centers owned by suppliers to just two centers owned by GM. GM's chief information officer, Randy Mott, and his executive team faced many logistical challenges throughout the transformation.

GM's information technology executives also were challenged by resistance from line managers, many of whom were concerned that GM's IT staff wouldn't provide the same quality of service that the external contractors had provided. "This supplier is doing a great job for me, so don't mess it up," some managers warned. Line managers' fear of the unknown and perceived negative outcomes about the IT changes led to "some really frank discussions," Mott acknowledges. "In the early days we were fighting the fact that the IT organization's credibility for building and creating and supporting things was not high."[1]

The transformation of General Motors' information technology strategy and operations illustrates a few of the challenges in organizational change. Although GM's information technology change process seems to have proceeded smoothly, most organizational change is messy, requiring considerable leadership effort and vigilance. As we will describe throughout this chapter, the challenge of change is not just in deciding which way to go; the challenge is in the execution of this strategy. When leaders discover the need for change and identify some ideas about the preferred route to a better future, the change process involves navigating around the numerous obstacles and gaining organizationwide support for that change.

This chapter unfolds as follows. We begin by introducing Lewin's model of change and its component parts. This discussion includes sources of resistance to change, ways to minimize this resistance, and ways to stabilize desired behaviors. Next, the chapter examines two approaches to organizational change—action research and appreciative inquiry. The final section of this chapter considers both cross-cultural and ethical issues in organizational change.

LEWIN'S FORCE FIELD ANALYSIS MODEL

Change is the norm, not the exception, in successful organizations. One of the fundamental messages throughout this book is that organizations operate as open systems. As such, they need to continually evolve with ongoing changes in their external environment, such as consumer needs, global competition, technology, community expectations, government (de)regulation, and environmental standards. Successful organizations monitor their environments and take appropriate steps to maintain a compatible fit with new external conditions. Rather than resist change, employees in successful companies embrace change as an integral part of organizational life.

It is easy to see environmental forces pushing companies to change the way they operate. What is more difficult to see is the complex interplay of these forces on the internal dynamics of organizations. Social psychologist Kurt Lewin developed a

Ready for Organizational Change?[2]

84% of C-suite (CEO, COO, CFO, etc.) leaders feel confident that their industry is prepared for future workplace changes.

82% of 1,487 American employees/managers involved in a corporate transformation say their CEO communicates a compelling change story to the organization.

46% of 1,487 American employees/managers involved in a corporate transformation say that the CEO's visible engagement/commitment to the change has been most effective at engaging employees in the process.

43% of 1,000 American employees feel confident that their industry is prepared for future workplace changes.

26% of 1,713 American executives involved in a corporate transformation say the change initiative has been very or completely successful.

©sarahdesign/Shutterstock

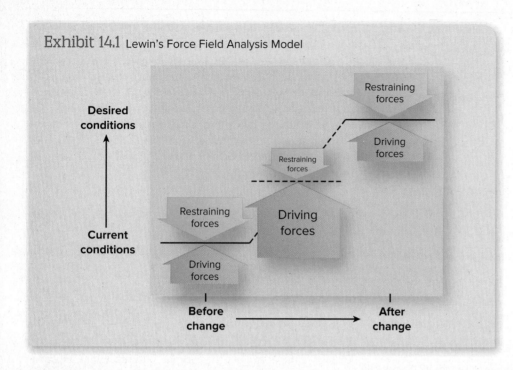

Exhibit 14.1 Lewin's Force Field Analysis Model

and restraining forces are roughly in equilibrium—that is, they are of approximately equal strength in opposite directions.

Lewin's force field model emphasizes that effective change occurs by **unfreezing** the current situation, moving to a desired condition, and then **refreezing** the system so it remains in the desired state. Unfreezing involves producing disequilibrium between the driving and restraining forces. As we will describe later, this may occur by increasing the driving forces, reducing the restraining forces, or doing a combination of both. Refreezing occurs when the organization's systems and structures are aligned with the desired behaviors. They must support and reinforce

> I've always believed that when the rate of change inside an institution becomes slower than the rate of change outside, the end is in sight. The only question is when.[3]
>
> —Jack Welch, former General Electric CEO

model to describe this process using the metaphor of a force field (see Exhibit 14.1).[4] Although it was developed more than 50 years ago, recent reviews affirm that Lewin's **force field analysis** model remains one of the most widely respected ways of viewing the change process.[5]

One side of the force field model represents the *driving forces* that push organizations toward a new state of affairs. These might include new competitors or technologies, evolving client expectations, or a host of other environmental changes. Corporate leaders also produce driving forces even when external forces for change aren't apparent. For instance, some experts call for "divine discontent" as a key feature of successful organizations, meaning that leaders continually urge employees to strive for higher standards or better practices. Even when the company outshines the competition, employees believe they can do better. "We have a habit of divine discontent with our performance," says creative agency Ogilvy & Mather about its corporate culture. "It is an antidote to smugness."[6]

The other side of Lewin's model represents the *restraining forces* that maintain the status quo. These restraining forces are commonly called "resistance to change" because they appear to block the change process. Stability occurs when the driving

the new role patterns and prevent the organization from slipping back into the old way of doing things. Over the next few pages, we use Lewin's model to understand why change is blocked and how the process can evolve more smoothly.

LO14-2 Discuss the reasons why people resist organizational change and how change agents should view this resistance.

UNDERSTANDING RESISTANCE TO CHANGE

United Airlines struggled to resolve operational and customer service problems after its merger with Continental Airlines. United executives say the poor results were partly due to the challenges of combining complex reservation and operational systems. But they also were frustrated by subtle forms of employee resistance to change. Some Continental employees opposed United Airlines' operational practices, while some

Resistance to change takes many forms, ranging from overt work stoppages to subtle attempts to continue the old ways.
©Jacob Wackerhausen/iStock/Getty Images Plus; ©McGraw-Hill Education/ Mark Dierker, photographer

interpret that disagreement as relationship conflict (see Chapter 10). They describe the people opposing change as unreasonable, dysfunctional, and irrational reactionaries to a beneficial initiative. This perspective shapes the change agent's response to resistance. Perversely, the change agent's conflict-oriented response to resistance tends to escalate the conflict, which often generates even stronger resistance to the change initiative.

A more productive approach is to view resistance to change as task conflict. From the task conflict perspective, resistance is a signal either that the change agent has not sufficiently prepared employees for change or that the change initiative should be altered or improved.[11] Employees might not feel a sufficiently strong urgency to change, or they might feel the change strategy is ill-conceived. Even if they recognize the need for change and agree with the strategy, employees might resist because they lack confidence to change or believe the change will make them worse off than the current situation. Resistance takes many forms, and change agents need to decipher those different types of resistance to understand their underlying causes.[12]

Resistance is also a form of voice, so discussion potentially improves procedural justice through voice (see Chapter 5) as well as decision making (see Chapter 6). By redirecting initial forms of resistance into constructive conversations, change agents can generate a feeling of fairness among employees. Furthermore, resistance is motivated behavior; it potentially engages people to think about the change strategy and process. Change agents can harness that motivational force to ultimately strengthen commitment to the change initiative.

United Airlines employees failed to adopt Continental's customer service standards. "You know, the cultural change takes time," explained the former United Airlines CEO who orchestrated the merger. "And people resist change. People are sort of set in their ways."[7]

Executives at United Airlines experienced considerable *resistance to change* following the merger with Continental Airlines. Resistance to change takes many forms, ranging from overt work stoppages to subtle attempts to continue the old ways.[8] A study of bank employees reported that subtle resistance is much more common than overt resistance. Some employees in that study avoided the desired changes by moving into different jobs. Others continued to perform tasks the old way as long as management didn't notice. Even when employees complied with the planned changes, they showed resistance by performing the new task while letting customers know that they disapproved of these changes forced on them![9]

Most change agents are understandably frustrated by passive or active resistance to their planned change. However, resistance is a common and natural human response. Even when people support change, they typically assume that it is others—not themselves—who need to do the changing. Resistance is a form of conflict, but change agents unfortunately sometimes

> Faced with the choice between changing one's mind and proving that there is no need to do so, almost everyone gets busy on the proof.[10]
>
> —John Kenneth Galbraith, economics scholar, U.S. ambassador, author

Why Employees Resist Change

Change management experts have developed a long list of reasons why people resist change.[13] Some people inherently oppose change because of their personality and values.[14] Aside from these dispositional factors, employees typically oppose organizational change because they lack sufficient motivation, ability, role clarity, or situational support to change their attitudes, decisions, and behavior.[15] In other words, an employee's readiness for change depends on all four elements of the MARS model. These

MARS elements are the foundations of the six most commonly cited reasons why people resist change: (1) negative valence of change, (2) fear of the unknown, (3) not-invented-here syndrome, (4) breaking routines, (5) incongruent team dynamics, and (6) incongruent organizational systems and structures.

Negative Valence of Change Employees usually resist change when they believe the post-change situation will have more negative than positive outcomes.[16] In other words, they apply (although imperfectly) the rational choice decision-making model (Chapter 6) to estimate whether the change will make them better or worse off (i.e., positive or negative valence). This cost–benefit analysis mainly considers how the change will affect them personally. However, resistance also increases when employees believe the change will do more harm than good to the team, organization, or society.[17]

Fear of the Unknown Organizational change usually has a degree of uncertainty, and employees tend to assume the worst when they are unsure whether the change will have good or bad outcomes. Uncertainty also is associated with lack of personal control, which is another source of negative emotions.[18] Consequently, the uncertainty of organizational change is usually considered less desirable than the relative certainty of the status quo. This condition pushes the cost–benefit calculation of the change even further into negative territory.

Not-Invented-Here Syndrome Employees sometimes oppose or even discreetly undermine organizational change initiatives that originate elsewhere. This "not-invented-here" syndrome is most apparent among employees who are usually responsible for the knowledge or initiative.[19] For example, information technology staff are more likely to resist implementing new technology championed by marketing or finance employees. If the IT staff

> When you are leading for growth, you know you are going to disrupt comfortable routines and ask for new behavior, new priorities, new skills. Even when we want to change, and do change, we tend to relax and the rubber band snaps us back into our comfort zones.[21]
>
> —Ray Davis,
> Executive Chair of Umpqua Bank

support the change, they are implicitly acknowledging another group's superiority within IT's own area of expertise. To protect their self-worth, some employees deliberately inflate problems with changes that they did not initiate, just to "prove" that those ideas were not superior to their own. As one consultant warned: "Unless they're scared enough to listen, they'll never forgive you for being right and for knowing something they don't."[20]

Breaking Routines People are creatures of habit. They typically resist initiatives that require them to break those automated routines and to learn new role patterns. And unless the new patterns of behavior are strongly supported and reinforced, employees tend to revert to their past routines and habits.

Incongruent Team Dynamics Teams develop and enforce conformity to a set of norms that guide behavior (see Chapter 7). However, conformity to existing team norms may discourage employees from accepting organizational change. For instance, organizational initiatives to improve customer service may be thwarted by team norms that discourage the extra effort expected to serve customers at this higher standard.

Employees usually resist change when they believe the post-change situation will have more negative than positive outcomes.
©Ingram Publishing

Facing the Challenge of Resistance to Change[22]

65%
of 2,219 executives and employees surveyed globally say they suffer from change fatigue (feeling worn out from changing too much or too often).

48%
of 2,219 executives and employees surveyed globally say their company doesn't have the necessary capabilities to ensure that change is sustained over time.

28%
of 1,512 employed Americans who recently experienced organizational change say they doubt that the change will work as intended or achieve its objectives (43% say they are confident the change will have the desired effects.)

37%
of 814 recruitment professionals surveyed in the U.S., U.K., China, and five other countries say the main barrier to innovation in their organization is a corporate culture that resists change (top reason).

21%
of 1,007 Australian employees surveyed say they would prefer things to remain the same (when asked to choose this option or one of several types of change initiatives to improve workplace productivity).

©Brand X Pictures/Stockbyte/Getty Images

Incongruent Organizational Systems Rewards, information systems, patterns of authority, career paths, selection criteria, and other systems and structures are both friends and foes of organizational change. When properly aligned, they reinforce desired behaviors. When misaligned, they pull people back into their old attitudes and behavior. Even enthusiastic employees lose momentum after failing to overcome the structural confines of the past.

LO14-3 Outline six strategies for minimizing resistance to change, and debate ways to effectively create an urgency to change.

UNFREEZING, CHANGING, AND REFREEZING

According to Lewin's force field analysis model, effective change occurs by unfreezing the current situation, moving to a desired condition, and then refreezing the system so it remains in this desired state. Unfreezing occurs when the driving forces are stronger than the restraining forces. This happens by making the driving forces stronger, weakening or removing the restraining forces, or doing both.

The first option is to increase the driving forces, which motivates employees to change through fear or threats (real or contrived). This strategy rarely works, however, because the action of increasing the driving forces alone is usually met with an equal and opposing increase in the restraining forces. A useful metaphor is pushing against the coils of a mattress. The harder corporate leaders push for change, the stronger the restraining forces push back. This antagonism threatens the change effort by producing tension and conflict within the organization.

The second option is to weaken or remove the restraining forces. The problem with this change strategy is that it provides no motivation for change. To some extent, weakening the restraining forces is like clearing a pathway for change. An unobstructed road makes it easier to travel to the destination but does not motivate anyone to go there. The preferred option, therefore, is to both increase the driving forces and reduce or remove the restraining forces. Increasing the driving forces creates an urgency for change, while reducing the restraining forces lessens motivation to oppose the change and removes obstacles such as lack of ability and situational constraints.

Creating an Urgency for Change

A few months after he became CEO of Nokia Corporation, Stephen Elop sent employees a scorching email, warning them about the urgency for change. "I have learned that we

Unfreezing occurs by making the driving forces stronger, weakening or removing the restraining forces, or doing both.
©Lightspring/Shutterstock

Some companies increase the urgency for change by putting executives and employees in direct contact with customers.
©Kzenon/Shutterstock

employees don't understand why they need to change and leaders are surprised when their change initiatives do not have much effect.

Some companies increase the urgency for change by putting executives and employees in direct contact with customers. Dissatisfied customers and other stakeholders represent a compelling driving force for change because the organization's survival typically depends on having customers who are satisfied with the product or service. Personal interaction with customers also provides a human element that further energizes employees to change current behavior patterns.[25]

Creating an Urgency for Change without External Forces Exposing employees to external forces can strengthen the urgency for change, but leaders often need to begin the change process before problems come knocking at the company's door. The challenge is greatest when companies are successful in their markets. Studies have found that when the organization is performing well, decision makers become less vigilant about external threats and are more resistant to change. "The biggest risk is that complacency can also come with that success," warns Richard Goyder, who recently stepped down as CEO of Wesfarmers, Australia's largest conglomerate. "That complacency may result in risk-aversion, or it may simply show up as a lack of urgency, as people take the foot off the accelerator and just assume that success will come as it always has."[26]

Creating an urgency for change when the organization is the market leader requires a lot of persuasive influence that helps employees visualize future competitive threats and environmental shifts. Experts warn, however, that employees may see this strategy as manipulative, which produces cynicism about change and undermines trust in the change agent.[27] Fortunately, the urgency for change doesn't need to originate from problems or threats to the company; this motivation also can develop through the leader's vision of a more appealing future. A vision depicting a better future for the organization effectively makes the current situation less appealing. When the vision connects to employees' values and needs, it can be a motivating force for change even when external problems are insignificant.

are standing on a burning platform," wrote Elop. "And, we have more than one explosion—we have multiple points of scorching heat that are fueling a blazing fire around us." Elop specifically described strong competition from Apple and Google, Nokia's tumbling brand preference, and its falling credit rating.[23]

Nokia has since sold its mobile phone division, but this incident illustrates how executives recognize the need for a strong urgency for change.[24] Developing an urgency for change typically occurs by informing or reminding employees about competitors and changing consumer trends, impending government regulations, and other forms of turbulence in the external environment. These are the main driving forces in Lewin's model. They push people out of their comfort zones, energizing them to face the risks that change creates. In many organizations, however, leaders buffer employees from the external environment to such an extent that these driving forces are hardly felt by anyone below the top executive level. The result is that

Reducing the Restraining Forces

Earlier, we used the mattress metaphor to explain that increasing the driving forces alone will not bring about change because employees often push back harder to offset the opposing forces. Instead, change agents need to address each of the sources of resistance. Six of the main strategies for minimizing resistance to change are outlined in Exhibit 14.2. Communication, learning, employee involvement, and stress management should be the first priorities for leading change.[28] However, negotiation and coercion may be required where some people will clearly lose something from the change and in cases where the speed of change is critical.

Communication Communication is the highest priority and first strategy required for any organizational change. Communication improves the change process in at least two ways.[29] One benefit is that communication generates the urgency for change that we described previously. Leaders motivate employees to support the change by candidly telling them about the external threats and opportunities that make change so important. The second benefit of communication is that it minimizes resistance to change by illuminating the future and thereby reducing fear of the unknown. The more leaders communicate details about the vision as well as milestones already achieved, the more easily employees can understand their own roles in that future. "The most practical piece of advice I can offer others is to recognize the critical importance of open communication in times of change," says Chris Catliff, CEO of Blueshore Financial in Vancouver, Canada. "Be consistent, repetitive, and authentic. Tell them [employees and others] why you are changing and what you hope to gain from the change.[30]

Learning Learning is an important process in most organizational change initiatives because employees need new knowledge and skills to fit the organization's evolving requirements. Learning not only helps employees perform better following the change; it also increases their readiness for change by strengthening their belief about working successfully in the new situation (called *change self-efficacy*). And when employees develop stronger change self-efficacy, they develop a stronger acceptance of and commitment to the change.[32]

Exhibit 14.2 Strategies for Minimizing Resistance to Change

Strategy	Example	When Applied	Problems
Communication	Customer complaint letters are shown to employees.	When employees don't feel an urgency for change, don't know how the change will affect them, or resist change due to a fear of the unknown.	Time-consuming and potentially costly.
Learning	Employees learn how to work in teams as company adopts a team-based structure.	When employees need to break old routines and adopt new role patterns.	Time-consuming, potentially costly, and some employees might not be able to learn the new skills.
Employee involvement	Company forms a task force to recommend new customer service practices.	When the change effort needs more employee commitment, some employees need to protect their self-worth, and/or employee ideas would improve decisions about the change strategy.	Very time-consuming. Might lead to conflict and poor decisions if employees' interests are incompatible with organizational needs.
Stress management	Employees attend sessions to discuss their worries about the change.	When communication, training, and involvement do not sufficiently ease employee worries.	Time-consuming and potentially expensive. Some methods may not reduce stress for all employees.
Negotiation	Employees agree to replace strict job categories with multiskilled job clusters in return for increased job security.	When employees will clearly lose something of value from the change and would not otherwise support the new conditions. Also necessary when the company must change quickly.	May be expensive, particularly if other employees want to negotiate their support. Also tends to produce compliance but not commitment to the change.
Coercion	Company president tells managers to "get on board" the change or leave.	When other strategies are ineffective and the company needs to change quickly.	Can lead to subtler forms of resistance, as well as long-term antagonism with the change agent.

Sources: Adapted from P. R. Lawrence, "How to Deal with Resistance to Change," *Harvard Business Review* (May/June 1954): 49–57; J. P. Kotter and L. A. Schlesinger, "Choosing Strategies for Change," *Harvard Business Review* 57 (1979): 106–14.

At What Stage in the Change Process Do Companies Begin Communicating with Employees about the Change?[31]

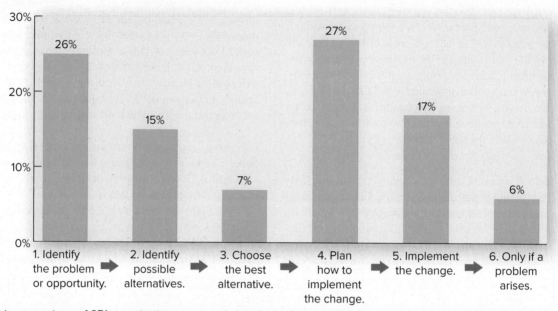

Figures indicate percentage of 651 organizations surveyed globally (half in Asia-Pacific region) that "activate the internal communication function" (i.e., begin involving staff responsible for communicating with employees) at each stage of the change process. Half (50 percent) do not begin communicating the change with employees until after the change strategy has been selected.

Employee Involvement Employee involvement is almost essential in the change process, although a low level of involvement may be necessary when the change must occur quickly or employee interests are highly incompatible with the organization's needs. The potential benefits of employee involvement, which were discussed in Chapter 6, are relevant to organizational change. Employees who participate in decisions about a change tend to feel more personal responsibility for its successful implementation, rather than being disinterested agents of someone else's decisions.[33] This sense of ownership also minimizes the not-invented-here syndrome and fear of the unknown. Furthermore, the work environment is so complex that determining the best direction of the change effort requires ideas and knowledge of many people.

Stress Management Organizational change is a stressful experience for many people because it threatens self-esteem and creates uncertainty about the future.[34] Communication, learning,

and employee involvement can reduce some of the stressors.[35] However, research indicates that companies also need to introduce stress management practices to help employees cope with changes.[36] In particular, stress management minimizes resistance by removing some of the negative valence and fear of the unknown about the change process. Stress also saps energy, so minimizing stress potentially increases employee motivation to support the change process.

Negotiation As long as people resist change, organizational change strategies will require a variety of influence tactics. Negotiation is a form of influence that involves the promise of benefits or resources in exchange for the target person's compliance with the influencer's request. This strategy potentially gains support from those who would otherwise lose out from the change. However, this support usually goes no further than compliance with the change effort. Negotiation rarely produces commitment to change, so it might not be effective in the long term.

> Employees who participate in decisions about a change tend to feel more personal responsibility for its successful implementation, rather than being disinterested agents of someone else's decisions.

Coercion If all else fails, leaders rely on coercion as part of the change process. Coercion includes a range of assertive influence behaviors (see Chapter 9), such as persistently reminding people of their obligations, frequently monitoring behavior to ensure compliance, confronting people who do not change, and using threats of punishment (including dismissal) to force compliance.

Firing people or urging them to leave is the least desirable way to change organizations. However, these forms of coercion are sometimes necessary when speed is essential and other tactics are ineffective. In particular, it may be necessary to remove several members of an executive team who are unwilling or unable to change their existing mental models of the ideal organization. This is also a radical form of organizational "unlearning" (see Chapter 1) because when executives leave, they remove knowledge of the organization's past routines that have become dysfunctional.[37] Even so, coercion is a risky strategy because survivors (employees who do not leave) may have less trust in corporate leaders and engage in more political tactics to protect their own job security.

Refreezing the Desired Conditions

Unfreezing and changing behavior won't produce lasting change. People are creatures of habit, so they easily slip back into familiar patterns. Therefore, leaders need to refreeze the new behaviors by realigning organizational systems and team

dynamics with the desired changes.[39] The desired patterns of behavior can be "nailed down" by changing the physical structure and situational conditions. Organizational rewards are also powerful systems that refreeze behaviors.[40] If the change process is supposed to encourage efficiency, then rewards should be realigned to motivate and reinforce efficient behavior.

Information systems play a complementary role in the change process, particularly as conduits for feedback.[41] Feedback mechanisms help employees learn how well they are moving toward the desired objectives, and they provide a permanent architecture to support the new behavior patterns in the long term. The adage "What gets measured, gets done" applies here. Employees concentrate on the new priorities when they receive a continuous flow of feedback about how well they are achieving those goals.

> **LO14-4** Discuss how leadership, coalitions, social networks, and pilot projects assist organizational change.

LEADERSHIP, COALITIONS, AND PILOT PROJECTS

Kurt Lewin's force field analysis model is a useful template to explain the dynamics of organizational change. But it overlooks four other ingredients in effective change processes: leadership, coalitions and social networks, and pilot projects.

Transformational Leadership and Change

Effective change requires one or more change champions who apply the elements of transformational leadership that were discussed in Chapter 11. They develop a vision of the organization's desired future state, communicate that vision in ways that are meaningful to others, make decisions and act in ways that are consistent with that vision, and encourage employees to experiment with ways to align work activities more closely with the vision.[42]

A key element of leading change is a strategic vision.[43] A leader's vision provides a sense of direction and establishes the critical success factors against which the real changes are evaluated. Furthermore, a vision provides an emotional foundation for the change because it links the individual's values and self-concept to the desired change.[44] A strategic vision also minimizes employee fear of the unknown and provides a better understanding of what behaviors employees must learn for the desired future.

Coalitions, Social Networks, and Change

One of the great truths of organizational change is that change agents cannot lead the initiative alone. They need the assistance of several people with a similar degree of commitment to the

---

OB THEORY TO PRACTICE

Zenefits Urges Employees to "Make Space" for Those Who Support a Compliance Culture

Zenefits provides cloud-based employee benefits software and earns revenue as a broker of health insurance sold through that software. However, the start-up firm developed a campus frat-house reputation and gave only casual attention to rules and regulations. It was this disregard for regulations that sailed Zenefits into turbulent waters and forced the departure of the company's founder.

On his first day as Zenefits' new (temporary) CEO, veteran Internet leader David Sacks created an urgency for change by emphasizing that in the insurance business "compliance is like oxygen. Without it, we die." He also relied on more coercive change leadership strategies to ensure that future employees support the company's transformation. Several dozen employees were fired or laid off due to possible compliance violations. A voluntary separation package was offered to any employee who didn't want to give his or her full support to the company's future.

"The next few months are going to be an exciting time at Zenefits and we want everyone participating in that," Sacks wrote in an email to staff four months after becoming CEO. "But if you can't get excited about that, then frankly we need you to make space for someone who will. Because Zenefits is at a point where will matters as much as skill, and we need everyone committed and contributing to the push ahead."[38]

A leader's vision provides a sense of direction and establishes the critical success factors against which the real changes are evaluated.
©Rawpixel.com/Shutterstock

change.[45] Indeed, some research suggests that this group—often called a *guiding coalition*—may be the most important factor in the success of public-sector organizational change programs.[46]

Membership in the guiding coalition extends beyond the executive team. Ideally, it includes a diagonal swath of employees representing different functions and most levels of the organization. The guiding coalition is sometimes formed from a special task force that initially investigates the opportunities for change. Members of the guiding coalition also should be influence leaders; that is, they should be highly respected by peers in their area of the organization.

Social Networks and Viral Change The change process can be strengthened through social networks, which are structures of people connected to each other through one or more forms of interdependence (see Chapter 9). They have an important role in communication and influence, both of which are key ingredients for organizational change. To some extent, coalition members support the change process by feeding into these networks. But social networks contribute to organizational change whether or not the change agent has a formal coalition.

Social networks are not easily controlled, yet some change agents have tapped into social networks to build a groundswell

---

OB THEORY TO PRACTICE

Trailblazing Viral Change at RSA Insurance

RSA Insurance Group recently launched a flexible benefits package that required employees to pick their preferred benefits options. But instead of just emailing reminders, the human resources group relied on a viral change process that more effectively motivated employees to choose their options.

HR carefully described the flexible benefits plan to 500 "trailblazers"—early adopters of the company's new internal social network (Yammer) who had a large following of coworkers. Trailblazers were soon posting their views about the preferred flexible benefits offered. These posts were read by thousands of employees, many of whom would have ignored the email memos from HR.

"We used people in the network to communicate what their favorite elements of the proposition were," explains RSA's director of internal communications. Trailblazers are role models whose ideas receive considerable interest from other employees, so they are far more effective at changing employee behavior (signing up for preferred benefits) than HR accomplishes through impersonal emails.[49]

©franckreporter/Getty Images

of support for a change initiative. This *viral change* process adopts principles found in word-of-mouth and viral marketing.[47] Viral and word-of-mouth marketing occur when information seeded to a few people is transmitted to others through their friendship connections. Within organizations, social networks represent the channels through which news and opinions about change initiatives are transmitted. Participants in that network have relatively high trust, so their information and views are more persuasive than from more formal channels. Social networks also provide opportunities for behavior observation—employees observe each other's behavior and often adopt that behavior themselves. As key people in the network change their behavior, that behavior is copied by others in the network.[48]

Pilot Projects and Diffusion of Change

Many companies introduce change through a pilot project, which involves applying change to one work unit or section of the organization. This cautious approach tests the effectiveness of the change as well as the strategies to gain employee support for the change, yet is more flexible and less risky than company-wide initiatives.[50] Pilot projects also make it easier to select organizational groups that are most ready for change, thus increasing the change initiative's likelihood of success.

How do we diffuse the pilot project's change to other parts of the organization? The answer is guided by the MARS model of individual behavior and performance (see Chapter 2). First, employees are more likely to adopt the practices of a pilot project when they are motivated to do so.[51] This occurs when the pilot project is successful and people in the pilot project receive recognition and rewards for changing their previous work practices. Diffusion also occurs more successfully when managers support and reinforce the desired behaviors. More generally, change agents need to minimize the sources of resistance to change that we discussed earlier in this chapter.

Second, employees must have the ability—the required skills and knowledge—to adopt the practices introduced in the pilot project. According to innovation diffusion studies, people adopt ideas more readily when they have an opportunity to interact with and learn from those who have already applied the new practices.[52]

Third, pilot projects get diffused when employees have clear role perceptions—that is, when they understand how the practices in a pilot project apply to them even though they are in a completely different functional area. The challenge here is for change agents to provide guidance that is not too specific (not too narrowly defined around the pilot project environment) because it might not seem relevant to other areas of the organization. At the same time, the pilot project intervention should not be described too broadly or abstractly to other employees because this makes the information too vague. Finally, employees require supportive situational factors, including the resources and time necessary to adopt the practices demonstrated in the pilot project.

LO14-5 Describe and compare action research and appreciative inquiry as formal approaches to organizational change.

TWO APPROACHES TO ORGANIZATIONAL CHANGE

So far, this chapter has examined the dynamics of change that occur every day in organizations. However, organizational change agents and consultants also apply various structured approaches to organizational change. This section introduces two of the leading approaches: action research and appreciative inquiry.

The philosophy of action research is that meaningful change is a combination of action orientation (changing attitudes and behavior) and research orientation (testing theory).
©Monty Rakusen/Getty Images

Action Research Approach

Along with introducing the force field model, Kurt Lewin recommended an **action research** approach to the change process. The philosophy of action research is that meaningful change is a combination of action orientation (changing attitudes and behavior) and research orientation (testing theory).[53] On one hand, the change process needs to be action-oriented because the ultimate goal is to change the workplace. An action orientation involves diagnosing current problems and applying interventions that resolve those problems. On the other hand, the change process is a research study because change agents apply a conceptual framework (such as team dynamics or organizational culture) to a real situation. As with any good research, the change process involves collecting data to diagnose problems more effectively and to systematically evaluate how well the theory works in practice.[54]

Within this dual framework of action and research, the action research approach adopts an open systems view. It recognizes that organizations have many interdependent parts, so change agents need to anticipate both the intended and the unintended consequences of their interventions. Action research is also a highly participative process because open systems change requires both the knowledge and the commitment of members within that system. Indeed, employees are essentially co-researchers as well as participants in the intervention. Overall, action research is a data-based, problem-oriented process that diagnoses the need for change, introduces the intervention, and then evaluates and stabilizes the desired changes. The main phases of action research are illustrated in Exhibit 14.3:[55]

1. *Form client–consultant relationship.* Action research usually assumes that the change agent originates outside the system (such as a consultant), so the process begins by forming the client–consultant relationship. Consultants need to determine the client's readiness for change, including whether people are motivated to participate in the process, are open to meaningful change, and possess the abilities to complete the process.

2. *Diagnose the need for change.* Action research is a problem-oriented activity that carefully diagnoses the problem to determine the appropriate direction for the change effort. Organizational diagnosis relies on systematic analysis of the situation. It involves gathering and analyzing data about an ongoing system, including interviews and surveys of employees and other stakeholders. Organizational diagnosis also involves employees so they improve, understand, and support the appropriate change method, the schedule for the actions involved, and the expected standards of successful change.

3. *Introduce intervention.* This stage in the action research model applies one or more actions to correct the problem. It may include any of the prescriptions mentioned in this book, such as building more effective teams, managing conflict, building a better organizational structure, or changing the corporate culture. An important issue is how quickly the changes should occur.[56] Some experts recommend *incremental change*, in which the organization fine-tunes the system and takes small steps toward a desired state. Others claim that *rapid change* is often required, in which the system is overhauled decisively and quickly.

4. *Evaluate and stabilize change.* Action research recommends evaluating the effectiveness of the intervention against the standards established in the diagnostic stage. Unfortunately, even when these standards are clearly stated, the effectiveness of an intervention might not be apparent for several years or might be difficult to separate from other factors. If the activity has the desired effect, the change agent and participants need to stabilize the new conditions. This refers to the refreezing process that was described earlier in this chapter. Rewards, information systems, team norms, and other conditions are redesigned so they support the new values and behaviors.

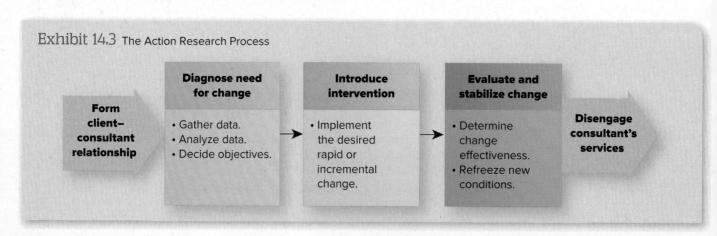

Exhibit 14.3 The Action Research Process

Form client–consultant relationship → **Diagnose need for change**
- Gather data.
- Analyze data.
- Decide objectives.

→ **Introduce intervention**
- Implement the desired rapid or incremental change.

→ **Evaluate and stabilize change**
- Determine change effectiveness.
- Refreeze new conditions.

→ **Disengage consultant's services**

The action research approach has dominated organizational change thinking since it was introduced in the 1940s. However, some experts are concerned that the problem-oriented nature of action research—in which something is wrong that must be fixed—focuses on the negative dynamics of the group or system rather than its positive opportunities and potential. This concern with action research has led to the development of a more positive approach to organizational change, called *appreciative inquiry*.[57]

> Action research recommends evaluating the effectiveness of the intervention against the standards established in the diagnostic stage.

Appreciative Inquiry Approach

Appreciative inquiry tries to break out of the problem-solving mentality of traditional change management practices by reframing relationships around the positive and the possible. It searches for organizational (or team) strengths and capabilities and then applies that knowledge for further success and well-being. Appreciative inquiry is therefore deeply grounded in the emerging philosophy of **positive organizational behavior**, which suggests that focusing on an individual's positive qualities rather than on what is wrong with the person will improve organizational success and personal well-being. In other words, this approach emphasizes building on strengths rather than trying to directly correct problems.[58]

Appreciative inquiry improves open dialogue by redirecting the group's attention away from its own issues. This is especially useful when participants are aware of their problems or already suffer from negativity in their relationships. The positive orientation of appreciative inquiry enables groups to overcome these negative tensions and build a more hopeful perspective of their future by focusing on what is possible.[59] This positive approach to change also suggests that change agents should adapt an optimistic view of possibilities, such as seeing a glass half full rather than half empty. Therefore, appreciative inquiry actively frames reality in a way that provides constructive value for future development.

Appreciative inquiry's positive focus is illustrated by the intervention conducted a few years ago at Heidelberg USA. The American arm of the world's largest printing press manufacturer (Heidelberger Druckmaschinen AG) experienced morale-busting product setbacks as well as downsizing due to the weak economy. To rebuild employee morale and engagement, Heidelberg held a two-day appreciative inquiry summit involving one-third of its staff. Organized into diverse groups from across the organization, participants envisioned what Heidelberg would ideally look like in the future. From these sessions emerged a new vision and greater autonomy for employees to serve customers. "Appreciative inquiry can energize an organization even in tough times because it begins the conversation with possibilities instead of problems," says a senior executive at Heidelberg USA.[60]

Along with adapting a positive approach to change, appreciative inquiry recognizes that the questions we ask and the language we use construct different realities. The questions we ask determine the information we receive, which in turn affects which change intervention we choose. Furthermore, appreciative inquiry takes the view that change occurs as soon as we interact with others and seek information from them. The moment we ask questions of others, we are changing those people. Finally, appreciative inquiry embraces the power of strategic vision in the change process. It recognizes that people are motivated and guided by an abstract vision of the future that is aligned with their personal values. We noted the importance of visions earlier in this chapter (change agents) and in our discussion of transformational leadership (Chapter 11).

Appreciative inquiry tries to break out of the problem-solving mentality of traditional change management practices by reframing relationships around the positive and the possible.
©Colin Anderson/Blend Images LLC

action research a problem-focused change process that combines action orientation (changing attitudes and behavior) and research orientation (testing theory through data collection and analysis)

appreciative inquiry an organizational change strategy that directs the group's attention away from its own problems and focuses participants on the group's potential and positive elements

positive organizational behavior a perspective of organizational behavior that focuses on building positive qualities and traits within individuals or institutions as opposed to focusing on what is wrong with them

Exhibit 14.4 The Four-D Model of Appreciative Inquiry

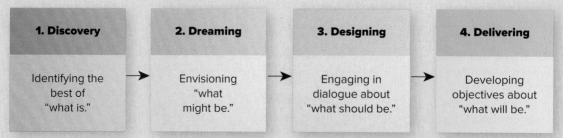

1. Discovery	2. Dreaming	3. Designing	4. Delivering
Identifying the best of "what is."	Envisioning "what might be."	Engaging in dialogue about "what should be."	Developing objectives about "what will be."

Sources: Based on F. J. Barrett and D. L. Cooperrider, "Generative Metaphor Intervention: A New Approach for Working with Systems Divided by Conflict and Caught in Defensive Perception," *Journal of Applied Behavioral Science* 26 (1990): 229; D. Whitney and C. Schau, "Appreciative Inquiry: An Innovative Process for Organization Change," *Employment Relations Today* 25 (Spring 1998): 11–21; D. L. Cooperrider and D. K. Whitney, *Appreciative Inquiry: A Positive Revolution in Change* (San Francisco: Berrett-Koehler, 2005), chap. 3.

The Four-D Model of Appreciative Inquiry Appreciative inquiry follows the "Four-D" process shown in Exhibit 14.4. The model's name refers to its four stages, which begins with *discovery*—identifying the positive elements of the observed events or organization.[61] This might involve documenting positive customer experiences elsewhere in the organization. Or it might include interviewing members of another organization to discover its fundamental strengths. As participants discuss their findings, they shift into the *dreaming* stage by envisioning what might be possible in an ideal organization. By pointing out a hypothetical ideal organization or situation, participants feel safer revealing their hopes and aspirations than they would if they were discussing their own organization or predicament.

As participants make their private thoughts public to the group, the process shifts into the third stage, called *designing*. Designing involves dialogue in which participants listen with selfless receptivity to each other's models and assumptions and eventually form a collective model for thinking within the team. In effect, they create a common image of what should be. As this model takes shape, group members shift the focus back to their own situation. In the final stage of appreciative inquiry, called *delivering* (also known as *destiny*), participants establish specific objectives and direction for their own organization on the basis of their model of what will be.

Appreciative inquiry has been successfully implemented in organizations across a range of industries, including Heidelberg USA, Toronto Western Hospital, British Broadcasting Corporation, and Hunter Douglas. However, it is not always the best approach to organizational change. Appreciative inquiry depends on participants' ability to let go of the problem-oriented approach, including the "blame game" of determining who may have been responsible for past failures. It also requires leaders who are willing to accept appreciative inquiry's less structured process.[62] Overall, appreciative inquiry can be an effective approach to organizational change, but we are still discovering its potential and limitations.

OB THEORY TO PRACTICE

Appreciative Inquiry Guides Leadership at Toronto Western Hospital

Toronto Western Hospital (TWH) held an appreciative inquiry (AI) retreat at which staff discussed the Canadian hospital's past successes and crafted a vision for its future. TWH's executive team believed the AI philosophy should guide daily leadership behavior, so they developed and taught a positive leadership program, which has since been completed by more than 150 leaders at the hospital.

Kathy Sabo, executive lead at TWH when the positive leadership program was launched, says the program teaches hospital leaders to "embed [AI] in our daily work differently than we do now—not just focused on a particular initiative but how do we enact it daily." The program has improved TWH's balanced scorecard results, patient satisfaction, and staff engagement. "We've seen really positive outcomes in how people apply the [AI] theory, how they behave as leaders, how that has impacted their staff," observes Sabo, who recently retired.[63]

©Digital Vision/Alamy Stock Photo

CROSS-CULTURAL AND ETHICAL ISSUES IN ORGANIZATIONAL CHANGE

Throughout this chapter, we have emphasized that change is inevitable and often continuous because organizations need to remain aligned with the dynamic external environment. Yet, we also need to be aware of cross-cultural and ethical issues with any change process. Many organizational change practices are built around Western cultural assumptions and values, which may differ from and sometimes conflict with assumptions and values in other cultures.[64] One possible cross-cultural limitation is that Western organizational change models, such as Lewin's force field analysis, often assume change has a beginning and an ending in a logical linear sequence (that is, a straight line from point A to point B). Yet change is viewed more as a cyclical phenomenon in some cultures, such as the earth's revolution around the sun or a pendulum swinging back and forth. Other cultures have more of an interconnected view of change, whereby one change leads to another (often unplanned) change, which leads to another change, and so on until the change objective is ultimately achieved in a more circuitous way.

Another cross-cultural issue with some organizational change interventions is the assumption that effective organizational change is necessarily punctuated by tension and overt conflict. Indeed, some change interventions encourage such conflict. But this direct confrontation view is incompatible with cultures that emphasize harmony and equilibrium. These cross-cultural differences suggest that a more contingency-oriented perspective is required for organizational change to work effectively in this era of globalization.

Some organizational change practices also face ethical issues.[65] One ethical concern is the risk of violating individual privacy rights. The action research model is built on the idea of collecting information from organizational members, yet this assumes that employees will provide personal information and reveal emotions they would not normally divulge.[66] A second ethical concern is that some change activities potentially increase management's power by inducing compliance and conformity in organizational members. For instance, action research is a systemwide activity that requires employee participation rather than allowing individuals to get involved voluntarily. A third concern is that some organizational change interventions undermine the individual's self-esteem. The unfreezing process requires that participants disconfirm their existing beliefs, sometimes including their own competence at certain tasks or interpersonal relations.

Organizational change is usually more difficult than it initially seems. Yet the dilemma is that most organizations operate in hyperfast environments that demand continuous and rapid adaptation. Organizations survive and gain competitive advantage by mastering the complex dynamics of moving people through the continuous process of change as quickly as the external environment is changing.

ORGANIZATIONAL BEHAVIOR: THE JOURNEY CONTINUES

More than a century ago, industrialist Andrew Carnegie said: "Take away my people, but leave my factories, and soon grass will grow on the factory floors. Take away my factories, but leave my people, and soon we will have a new and better factory."[67] Carnegie's statement reflects the message woven throughout this textbook: Organizations are not buildings or machinery or financial assets; rather, they are the people in them. Organizations are human entities—full of life, sometimes fragile, and always exciting.

Andrew Carnegie
©Bettmann/Getty Images

Study Checklist

Connect® Management is available for *M Organizational Behavior*. Additional resources include:

✓ Interactive Applications:
- **Case Analysis:** Apply concepts within the context of a real-world situation.
- **Drag and Drop:** Work through an interactive example to test your knowledge of the concepts.
- **Video Case:** See management in action through interactive videos.

✓ **SmartBook**™—SmartBook is the first and only adaptive reading experience available today. Distinguishing what you know from what you don't, and honing in on concepts you are most likely to forget, SmartBook personalizes content for you in a continuously adapting reading experience. Reading is no longer a passive and linear experience, but an engaging and dynamic one where you are more likely to master and retain important concepts and go to class better prepared.

©Natthawat Jamnapa/123RF

Notes

1. A. Bongard, "GM CIO Mott Is Confident IT Transformation Making Progress," *automotiveIT International*, June 4, 2014; R. Preston, "General Motors' IT Transformation: Building Downturn-Resistant Profitability," *Forbes*, April 14, 2016.

2. D. Jacquemont, D. Maor, and A. Reich, *How to Beat the Transformation Odds* (New York: McKinsey & Company, April 2015); D. Maor, A. Reich, and L. Yocarini, *The People Power of Transformations* (New York: McKinsey & Company, February 2017); Addison Group, "Addison Group Survey Finds Nearly Half of Staff Level Employees Don't Feel Confident Their Industry," news release (Chicago: Addison Group, June 5, 2017).

3. J. Welch, *Jack: Straight from the Heart* (New York: Warner Business Books, 2001), 432.

4. K. Lewin, *Field Theory in Social Science* (New York: Harper & Row, 1951).

5. D. Coghlan and T. Brannick, "Kurt Lewin: The 'Practical Theorist' for the 21st Century," *Irish Journal of Management* 24, no. 2 (2003): 31–37; B. Burnes, "Kurt Lewin and the Planned Approach to Change: A Re-appraisal," *Journal of Management Studies* 41, no. 6 (2004): 977–1002.

6. Ogilvy & Mather, "Corporate Culture" (New York, 2017), http://www.ogilvy.com/About/Our-History/Corporate-Culture.aspx (accessed March 27, 2017).

7. J. Mouawad, "Largest Airline Has Bigger Troubles," *International Herald Tribune*, November 30, 2012, 14; M. Mecham, "Not Yet United," *Overhaul & Maintenance*, April 2012, 46; M. Brownell, "Here's Why United Was Just Named America's Worst Airline," *Daily Finance*, June 18, 2013; D. Bennett, "United's Quest to Be Less Awful," *Bloomberg Businessweek*, January 14, 2016.

8. Some experts suggest that resistance to change should be restated in a more positive way by its opposite: readiness for change. See M. Choi and W. E. A. Ruona, "Individual Readiness for Organizational Change and Its Implications for Human Resource and Organization Development," *Human Resource Development Review* 10, no. 1 (2011): 46–73.

9. S. Chreim, "Postscript to Change: Survivors' Retrospective Views of Organizational Changes," *Personnel Review* 35, no. 3 (2006): 315–35.

10. J. K. Galbraith, *Economics, Peace, and Laughter* (Boston: Houghton Mifflin, 1971), 50.

11. E. B. Dent and S. G. Goldberg, "Challenging 'Resistance to Change,'" *Journal of Applied Behavioral Science* 35 (1999): 25–41; D. B. Fedor, S. Caldwell, and D. M. Herold, "The Effects of Organizational Changes on Employee Commitment: A Multilevel Investigation," *Personnel Psychology* 59, no. 1 (2006): 1–29.

12. B. J. Tepper et al., "Subordinates' Resistance and Managers' Evaluations of Subordinates' Performance," *Journal of Management* 32, no. 2 (2006): 185–209; J. D. Ford, L. W. Ford, and A. D'Amelio, "Resistance to Change: The Rest of the Story," *Academy of Management Review* 33, no. 2 (2008): 362–77.

13. D. A. Nadler, "The Effective Management of Organizational Change," in *Handbook of Organizational Behavior*, ed. J. W. Lorsch (Englewood Cliffs, NJ: Prentice Hall, 1987), 358–69; R. Maurer, *Beyond the Wall of Resistance: Unconventional Strategies to Build Support for Change* (Austin, TX: Bard Books, 1996); P. Strebel, "Why Do Employees Resist Change?," *Harvard Business Review* (1996): 86–92; D. A. Nadler, *Champions of Change* (San Francisco: Jossey-Bass, 1998).

14. S. Oreg et al., "Dispositional Resistance to Change: Measurement Equivalence and the Link to Personal Values across 17 Nations," *Journal of Applied Psychology* 93, no. 4 (2008): 935–44.

15. R. R. Sharma, *Change Management: Concepts and Applications* (New Delhi: Tata McGraw-Hill, 2007), chap. 4; I. Cinite, L. E. Duxbury, and C. Higgins, "Measurement of Perceived Organizational Readiness for Change in the Public Sector," *British Journal of Management* 20, no. 2 (2009): 265–77; A. A. Armenakis and S. G. Harris, "Reflections: Our Journey in Organizational Change Research and Practice," *Journal of Change Management* 9, no. 2 (2009): 127–42; S. Jaros, "Commitment to Organizational Change: A Critical Review," *Journal of Change Management* 10, no. 1 (2010): 79–108.

16. D. T. Holt et al., "Readiness for Organizational Change: The Systematic Development of a Scale," *Journal of Applied Behavioral Science* 43, no. 2 (2007): 232–55; G. Bohner and N. Dickel, "Attitudes and Attitude Change," *Annual Review of Psychology* 62, no. 1 (2011): 391–417; A. M. García-Cabrera and F. García-Barba Hernández, "Differentiating the Three Components of Resistance to Change: The Moderating Effect of Organization-Based Self-Esteem on the Employee Involvement-Resistance Relation," *Human Resource Development Quarterly* 25, no. 4 (2014): 441–69.

17. R. de la Sablonnière et al., "Profound Organizational Change, Psychological Distress and Burnout Symptoms: The Mediator Role of Collective Relative Deprivation," *Group Processes & Intergroup Relations* 15, no. 6 (2012): 776–90.

18. S. Oreg, M. Vakola, and A. Armenakis, "Change Recipients' Reactions to Organizational Change: A 60-Year Review of Quantitative Studies," *Journal of Applied Behavioral Science* 47, no. 4 (2011): 461–524.

19. D. Grosse Kathoefer and J. Leker, "Knowledge Transfer in Academia: An Exploratory Study on the Not-Invented-Here Syndrome," *Journal of Technology Transfer* 37, no. 5 (2012): 658–75; A. L. A. Burcharth, M. P. Knudsen, and H. A. Søndergaard, "Neither Invented nor Shared Here: The Impact and Management of Attitudes for the Adoption of Open Innovation Practices," *Technovation* 34, no. 3 (2014): 149–61.

20. V. Newman, "The Psychology of Managing for Innovation," *KM Review* 9, no. 6 (2007): 10–15.

21. R. Davis, *Leading for Growth: How Umpqua Bank Got Cool and Created a Culture of Greatness* (San Francisco: Jossey-Bass, 2007), 40.

22. Futurestep, *The Innovation Imperative* (Los Angeles: June 2013); D. Aguirre and M. Alpern, "10 Principles of Leading Change Management," *strategy+business*, Summer 2014; *Australian Future of Work Poll* (Melbourne: Centre for Workplace Leadership, March 2014); Center for Organizational Excellence, *Work and Well-Being Survey* (Washington, D.C.: American Psychological Association, May 30, 2017).

23. C. Lawton and J. Lublin, "Nokia Names Microsoft's Stephen Elop as New CEO, Kallasvuo Ousted," *The Wall Street Journal*, September 11, 2010; C. Ziegler, "Nokia CEO Stephen Elop Rallies Troops in Brutally Honest 'Burning Platform' Memo? (Update: It's Real!)," *Engadget*, February 8, 2011.

24. J. P. Kotter, *A Sense of Urgency* (Boston: Harvard Business School Press, 2008); S. H. Appelbaum et al., "Back to the Future: Revisiting Kotter's 1996 Change Model," *Journal of Management Development* 31, no. 8 (2012): 764–82.

25. L. D. Goodstein and H. R. Butz, "Customer Value: The Linchpin of Organizational Change," *Organizational Dynamics* 27 (1998): 21–35.

26. D. Miller, *The Icarus Paradox: How Exceptional Companies Bring about Their Own Downfall* (New York: HarperBusiness, 1990); S. Finkelstein, *Why Smart Executives Fail* (New York: Viking, 2003); A.C. Amason and A.C. Mooney, "The Icarus Paradox Revisited: How Strong Performance Sows the Seeds of Dysfunction in Future Strategic Decision-Making," *Strategic Organization* 6, no. 4 (2008): 407–34. Richard Goyder's quotation is from "Sustaining High Performance (Richard Goyder: Wesfarmers)," *CEO Forum*, September 2006.

27. T. F. Cawsey and G. Deszca, *Toolkit for Organizational Change* (Los Angeles: Sage, 2007), 104.

28. J. P. Kotter and L. A. Schlesinger, "Choosing Strategies for Change," *Harvard Business Review* (1979): 106–14.

29. J. P. Kotter and D. S. Cohen, *The Heart of Change* (Boston: Harvard Business School Press, 2002), 83–98; J. Allen et al., "Uncertainty during Organizational Change: Managing Perceptions through Communication," *Journal of Change Management* 7, no. 2 (2007): 187–210; A. E. Rafferty, N. L. Jimmieson, and A. A. Armenakis, "Change Readiness: A Multilevel Review," *Journal of Management* 39, no. 1 (2013): 110–35; M. van den Heuvel et al., "Adapting to Change: The Value of Change Information and Meaning-Making," *Journal of Vocational Behavior* 83, no. 1 (2013): 11–21.

30. Jostle, "Culture Hero Series: Chris Catliff, Blueshore Financial," *The Jostle Blog*, October 30, 2013, http://blog.jostle.me/blog/culture-hero-series-chris-catliff-north-shore-credit-union.

31. Towers Watson, *2013–2014 Change and Communication ROI: The 10th Anniversary Report* (New York: Towers Watson, December 2013). These statistics are interpolated from data on high- and low-effectiveness companies provided in the most recent survey (2013–2014) as well as from total sample results provided in corresponding earlier surveys. High and low effectiveness company results were very similar for most categories.

32. D. M. Herold and S. D. Caldwell, "Beyond Change Management: A Multilevel Investigation of Contextual and Personal Influences on Employees' Commitment to Change," *Journal of Applied Psychology* 92, no. 4 (2007): 942–51; D. T. Holt and J. M. Vardaman, "Toward a Comprehensive Understanding of Readiness for Change: The Case for an Expanded Conceptualization," *Journal of Change Management* 13, no. 1 (2013): 9–18.

33. K. T. Dirks, L. L. Cummings, and J. L. Pierce, "Psychological Ownership in Organizations: Conditions under Which Individuals Promote and Resist Change," *Research in Organizational Change and Development* 9 (1996): 1–23; E. A. Lofquist, "Doomed to Fail: A Case Study of Change Implementation Collapse in the Norwegian Civil Aviation Industry," *Journal of Change Management* 11, no. 2 (2011): 223–43; L. K. Lewis and T. L. Russ, "Soliciting and Using Input during Organizational Change Initiatives: What Are Practitioners Doing," *Management Communication Quarterly* 26, no. 2 (2012): 267–94.

34. S. G. Bamberger et al., "Impact of Organisational Change on Mental Health: A Systematic Review," *Occupational and Environmental Medicine* 69, no. 8 (2012): 592–98.

35. N. T. Tan, "Maximising Human Resource Potential in the Midst of Organisational Change," *Singapore Management Review* 27, no. 2 (2005): 25–35; A. E. Rafferty and S. L. D. Restubog, "The Impact of Change Process and Context on Change Reactions and Turnover during a Merger," *Journal of Management* 36, no. 5 (2010): 1309–38.

36. M. McHugh, "The Stress Factor: Another Item for the Change Management Agenda?," *Journal of Organizational Change Management* 10 (1997): 345–62; D. Buchanan, T. Claydon, and M. Doyle, "Organisation Development and Change: The Legacy of the Nineties," *Human Resource Management Journal* 9 (1999): 20–37.

37. D. Nicolini and M. B. Meznar, "The Social Construction of Organizational Learning: Conceptual and Practical Issues in the Field," *Human Relations* 48 (1995): 727–46.

38. W. Alden, "Startup Zenefits under Scrutiny for Flouting Insurance Laws," *BuzzFeed*, November 25, 2015; C. Suddath and E. Newcomer, "The HR Startup Has an HR Problem," *Bloomberg Businessweek*, May 9–15, 2016, 62; D. Sacks, "The New Zenefits—Becoming the Compliance Company," *Zenefits Blog*, Zenefits, 2016, http://www.zenefits.com/blog/new-zenefits-becoming-compliance-company/; K. Kokalitcheva, "Zenefits' Investigation Leaves Some Questions Unanswered," *Fortune*, May 9, 2016; A. Hesseldahl, "Zenefits Is Firing 106 People and Offering Buyouts to More as It Restructures," *recode*, June 14, 2016.

39. E. E. Lawler III, "Pay Can Be a Change Agent," *Compensation & Benefits Management* 16 (2000): 23–26; D. S. Cohen and J. P. Kotter, *The Heart of Change Field Guide* (Boston: Harvard Business School Press, 2005), 161–77; M. A. Roberto and L. C. Levesque, "The Art of Making Change Initiatives Stick," *MIT Sloan Management Review* 46, no. 4 (2005): 53–60.

40. E. E. Lawler III, "Pay Can Be a Change Agent," *Compensation & Benefits Management* 16 (2000): 23–26.

41. L. D. Goodstein and H. R. Butz, "Customer Value: The Linchpin of Organizational Change," *Organizational Dynamics* 27 (1998): 21–35; R. H. Miles, "Leading Corporate Transformation: Are You up to the Task?," in *The Leader's Change Handbook,* ed. J. A. Conger, G. M. Spreitzer, and E. E. Lawler III (San Francisco: Jossey-Bass, 1999), 221–67.

42. R. E. Quinn, *Building the Bridge as You Walk on It: A Guide for Leading Change* (San Francisco: Jossey-Bass, 2004), chap. 11; D. M. Herold et al., "The Effects of Transformational and Change Leadership on Employees' Commitment to a Change: A Multilevel Study," *Journal of Applied Psychology* 93, no. 2 (2008): 346–57.

43. M. S. Cole, S. G. Harris, and J. B. Bernerth, "Exploring the Implications of Vision, Appropriateness, and Execution of Organizational Change," *Leadership & Organization Development Journal* 27, no. 5 (2006): 352–67; S. Kirkpatrick, "Leading through Vision and Values," in *Handbook of Principles of Organizational Behavior: Indispensable Knowledge for Evidence-Based Management*, ed. E. Locke (Hoboken: Wiley, 2010), 367–87; V. Lundy and P. P. Morin, "Project Leadership Influences Resistance to Change: The Case of the Canadian Public Service," *Project Management Journal* 44, no. 4 (2013): 45–64.

44. J. P. Kotter and D. S. Cohen, *The Heart of Change* (Boston: Harvard Business School Press, 2002), 61–82; D. S. Cohen and J. P. Kotter, *The Heart of Change Field Guide* (Boston: Harvard Business School Press, 2005).

45. J. P. Kotter, "Leading Change: Why Transformation Efforts Fail," *Harvard Business Review* (1995): 59–67.

46. J. B. Cunningham and S. K. James, "Implementing Change in Public Sector Organizations," *Management Decision* 47, no. 2 (2009): 330.

47. A. De Bruyn and G. L. Lilien, "A Multi-Stage Model of Word-of-Mouth Influence through Viral Marketing," *International Journal of Research in Marketing* 25, no. 3 (2008): 151–63; J. Y. C. Ho and M. Dempsey, "Viral Marketing: Motivations to Forward Online Content," *Journal of Business Research* 63, no. 9/10 (2010): 1000–06; M. Williams and F. Buttle, "The Eight Pillars of WOM Management: Lessons from a Multiple Case Study," *Australasian Marketing Journal* 19, no. 2 (2011): 85–92.

48. L. Herrero, *Homo Imitans* (Beaconsfield Bucks, UK: meetingminds, 2011).

49. V. Arnstein, "RSA Group Engages Staff with Social Media Network," *Employee Benefits*, September 1, 2015; S. Shah, "Why RSA Insurance Picked BT Global Services over Atos Origin to Host Microsoft Collaboration Products in the Cloud," *Computing*, October 21, 2015.

50. M. Beer, R. A. Eisenstat, and B. Spector, *The Critical Path to Corporate Renewal* (Boston: Harvard Business School Press, 1990).

51. M. Beer, R. A. Eisenstat, and B. Spector, *The Critical Path to Corporate Renewal* (Boston: Harvard Business School Press, 1990), chap. 5; R. E. Walton, "Successful Strategies for Diffusing Work Innovations," *Journal of Contemporary Business* (1977): 1–22; R. E. Walton, *Innovating to Compete: Lessons for Diffusing and Managing Change in the Workplace* (San Francisco: Jossey-Bass, 1987).

52. E. M. Rogers, *Diffusion of Innovations*, 4th ed. (New York: Free Press, 1995).

53. P. Reason and H. Bradbury, *Handbook of Action Research* (London: Sage, 2001); D. Coghlan and T. Brannick, "Kurt Lewin: The 'Practical Theorist' for the 21st Century," *Irish Journal of Management* 24, no. 2 (2003): 31–37; C. Huxham and S. Vangen, "Researching Organizational Practice through Action Research: Case Studies and Design Choices," *Organizational Research Methods* 6 (2003): 383–403.

54. V. J. Marsick and M. A. Gephart, "Action Research: Building the Capacity for Learning and Change," *Human Resource Planning* 26 (2003): 14–18.

55. L. Dickens and K. Watkins, "Action Research: Rethinking Lewin," *Management Learning* 30 (1999): 127–40; J. Heron and P. Reason, "The Practice of Co-operative Inquiry: Research 'with' Rather Than 'on' People," in *Handbook of Action Research*, ed. P. Reason and H. Bradbury (Thousand Oaks, CA: Sage, 2001), 179–88.

56. D. A. Nadler, "Organizational Frame Bending: Types of Change in the Complex Organization," in *Corporate Transformation: Revitalizing Organizations for a Competitive World*, ed. R. H. Kilmann, T. J. Covin, and Associates (San Francisco: Jossey-Bass, 1988), 66–83; K. E. Weick and R. E. Quinn, "Organizational Change and Development," *Annual Review of Psychology* 50 (1999): 361–86.

57. T. M. Egan and C. M. Lancaster, "Comparing Appreciative Inquiry to Action Research: OD Practitioner Perspectives," *Organization Development Journal* 23, no. 2 (2005): 29–49.

58. N. Turner, J. Barling, and A. Zacharatos, "Positive Psychology at Work," in *Handbook of Positive Psychology*, ed. C. R. Snyder and S. Lopez (Oxford, UK: Oxford University Press, 2002), 715–30; K. Cameron, J. E. Dutton, and R. E. Quinn, eds., *Positive Organizational Scholarship: Foundation of a New Discipline* (San Francisco: Berrett-Koehler, 2003); S. L. Gable and J. Haidt, "What (and Why) Is Positive Psychology?," *Review of General Psychology* 9, no. 2 (2005): 103–10; M. E. P. Seligman et al., "Positive Psychology Progress: Empirical Validation of Interventions," *American Psychologist* 60, no. 5 (2005): 410–21.

59. D. K. Whitney and D. L. Cooperrider, "The Appreciative Inquiry Summit: Overview and Applications," *Employment Relations Today* 25 (1998): 17–28; J. M. Watkins and B. J. Mohr, *Appreciative Inquiry: Change at the Speed of Imagination* (San Francisco: Jossey-Bass, 2001).

60. D. Meinert, "Positive Momentum," *HR Magazine* 58, no. 6 (2013): 68–74.

61. F. J. Barrett and D. L. Cooperrider, "Generative Metaphor Intervention: A New Approach for Working with Systems Divided by Conflict and Caught in Defensive Perception," *Journal of Applied Behavioral Science* 26 (1990): 219–39; D. K. Whitney and D. L. Cooperrider, "The Appreciative Inquiry Summit: Overview and Applications," *Employment Relations Today* 25 (1998): 17–28; J. M. Watkins and B. J. Mohr, *Appreciative Inquiry: Change at the Speed of Imagination* (San Francisco: Jossey-Bass, 2001), 15–21.

62. T. F. Yaeger, P. F. Sorensen, and U. Bengtsson, "Assessment of the State of Appreciative Inquiry: Past, Present, and Future," *Research in Organizational Change and Development* 15 (2004): 297-319; G. R. Bushe and A. F. Kassam, "When Is Appreciative Inquiry Transformational? A Meta-Case Analysis," *Journal of Applied Behavioral Science* 41, no. 2 (2005): 161-81.

63. Z. Pedersen, "Using Appreciative Inquiry to Focus on Positives, Transform Workplace Culture," *Canadian HR Reporter*, August 13, 2012, 10-12; Z. Pedersen, *Appreciative Inquiry and Changing Workplace Culture* (Toronto: YouTube, 2012); M. K. McCarthy, M. J. McNally, and K. Sabo, "Toronto Western Hospital Positive Leadership Program: Creating a Culture of Excellence," in *National Health Leadership Conference* (Niagara Falls, Ontario: Canadian College of Health Leaders, 2013).

64. T. C. Head and P. F. Sorenson, "Cultural Values and Organizational Development: A Seven-Country Study," *Leadership and Organization Development Journal* 14 (1993): 3-7; R. J. Marshak, "Lewin Meets Confucius: A Review of the OD Model of Change," *Journal of Applied Behavioral Science* 29 (1993): 395-415; C. M. Lau, "A Culture-Based Perspective of Organization Development Implementation," *Research in Organizational Change and Development* 9 (1996): 49-79; C. M. Lau and H. Y. Ngo, "Organization Development and Firm Performance: A Comparison of Multinational and Local Firms," *Journal of International Business Studies* 32, no. 1 (2001): 95-114.

65. M. McKendall, "The Tyranny of Change: Organizational Development Revisited," *Journal of Business Ethics* 12 (1993): 93-104; C. M. D. Deaner, "A Model of Organization Development Ethics," *Public Administration Quarterly* 17 (1994): 435-46.

66. G. A. Walter, "Organization Development and Individual Rights," *Journal of Applied Behavioral Science* 20 (1984): 423-39.

67. The source of this often-cited quotation was not found. It does not appear, even in other variations, in the books that Andrew Carnegie wrote (such as *Gospel of Wealth*, 1900; *Empire of Business*, 1902; and *Autobiography*, 1920). However, Carnegie may have stated these words (or similar ones) elsewhere. He gave many speeches and wrote numerous articles, parts of which have been reported by other authors.

Organization Index

Name Index

Glossary/Subject Index

M

Machiavellian values *The beliefs that deceit is a natural and acceptable way to influence others and that getting more than one deserves is acceptable,* 227–228

Management
  direct communication with, 203–204
  evidence-based, 11
  human relations school, 4–5
  participative, 152

Management by walking around (MBWA) *A communication practice in which executives get out of their offices and learn from others in the organization through face-to-face dialogue,* 203

Management fads, 11

Managerial leadership *A leadership perspective stating that effective leaders help employees improve their performance and well-being toward current objectives and practices*
  people-oriented, 263262
  servant leadership, 263–264
  task-oriented, 262
  transformational, 263
  MARS model of individual behavior
  ability, 30
  employee resistance to change, 323–325
  formulas, 29
  motivation, 29–30
  and pilot projects, 331
  role perceptions, 30–31
  situational factors, 32
  and values, 41–42
  variables, 29

Maslow's needs hierarchy theory *A motivation theory of needs arranged in a hierarchy, hereby people are motivated to fulfill a higher need as a lower one becomes gratified,* 110, 111–112

Matrix structure *An Organizational structure that overlays two structures (such as a geographic divisional and a product divisional structure) in order to leverage the benefits of both,* 290–292
  at ABB Group, 290
  deviations, 291
  Maximization, 144
  Meaningful interaction
    contact hypothesizes, 70
    empathy, 70
    reducing dependence on stereotypes, 70
  Measurable goals, 119

Mechanistic structure *An organizational structure with a narrow span of control and a high degree of formalization and centralization,* 285

Media, 188
  lean, 196

Media richness *A medium's data-carrying capacity—that is, the volume and variety of information that can be transmuted during a specific time,* 195–196
  exceptions to
    ability to communicate, 196
    communication proficiency, 196–197
    social presence effect, 197
  hierarchy, 196
  versus lean media, 196
Mediation, 245
Medium, 189
Member interaction in teams, 174
Member similarity, in teams, 174
Mental models, 140
  in communication, 189
  team, 170
Mergers. *see* Corporate mergers
Meta-decision, 139
M-form structure, 287
Millennials, 9, 10
  and social media, 191–192

Mindfulness *A person's receptive and impartial attention to and awareness of the present situation as well as to one's own thoughts and emotions in that moment,* 44

Moods, 80
  and decision making, 144
Moral intensity, 44

Moral sensitivity *A person's ability to recognize the presence of an ethical issue and determine its relative importance,* 44

Morphological analysis, 152

Motivation *The forces within a person that affect his or her direction, intensity, and persistence of voluntary behavior*
  and employee drives and needs, 108–114
  expediency theory, 114–115
  four-drive theory, 109–110
  and inequity, 122–123
  and job design, 125
  in path-goal leadership theory, 264–265
  of teams, 163
Multidisciplinary anchor, 11–12
Multidivisional structure, 287
Multisource feedback, 120
Mutual gains approach to negotiation, 246

Myers-Briggs Type Indicator *An instrument designed to measure the elements of Jungian personality theory, particularly preferences regarding perceiving and judging information,* 38

N

Nature *vs.* nurture, 35

Need for achievement (nACH) *A learned need in which people want to accomplish reasonably challenging goals and desire unambiguous feedback and recognition for their success,* 113

Need for affiliation (nAff) *A learned need in which people seek approval from others, conform to their wishes and expectations, and avoid conflict and confrontation,* 113

Need for power (nPow) *A learned need in which people want to control their environment, including people and material resources to benefit either themselves (personalized power) or others (socialized power),* 113

Need principle, 121

Needs *Goal-directed forces that people experience*
  versus individual difference, 109–110
  primary, 108, 111
Negative reinforcement, 117
Neglect, 89

Negotiation *The process whereby two or more conflicting parties attempt to resolve their divergent goals by redefining the terms of their interdependence*
  bargaining zone model, 247
  best alternative to negotiated agreement, 248
  distributive v. integrative approach, 246–247
  gender differences, 250
  preparation for, 247
  process of
    build relationship, 249
    gather information, 248–249
    manage concessions, 249
    manage time, 249
  to reduce resistance to change, 328
  setting for, 249–250
Networking, 220

Neuroticism *A personality dimension describing people who tend to be anxious, insecure, self-conscious, depressed, and temperamental,* 38

Noise, 188, 197–199

Nominal group technique *A variation of brainwriting consisting of three stages in which participants (1) silently and independently document their ideas, (2) collectively describe these ideas to the other team members without critique, and then silently and independently evaluate the ideas presented,* 179

Nonprogrammed decisions, 139
Nonsubstitutbility, 216
Nonverbal communication, 189
  across cultures, 200
  compared to verbal, 192
  and emotional contagion, 192–194
Nonverbal cues, 200
Norming
  in team development, 170, 171

Norm of reciprocity *A felt obligation and social expectation of helping or otherwise giving something of value to someone who has already helped or given something of value to you,* 214

Norms *The informal rules and shared expectations that groups establish to regulate the behavior of their members*
  of divine discontent, 141
  emotional display, 85
  and social acceptance, 195
  of teams, 173–174, 236
Not-invented-here syndrome, 324
Nurture, 35

O

Openness to change, 41

Openness to experience *A personality dimension describing people who are imaginative, creative, unconventional, curious, nonconforming, autonomous, and aesthetically perceptive,* 37–38, 150

Open systems *A perspective that organizations depend on the external environment for resources, affect that environment through their output, and consist of internal subsystems that transform inputs into outputs*
  effective transformation process, 14
  external environment, 13
  organizational subsystems, 13
  organization- environment fit, 13–14
  Opportunity, 139
    identifying, 141
    selecting, 144

Organic structure *An organizational structure with a wide span of control, little formalization, and decentralized decision making,* 286

Organizational behavior modification, 116–117

Organizational behavior modification model (OB Mod) *A theory that explains employee behavior in terms of the antecedent conditions and consequences of that behavior,* 116

Organizational behavior *The study of what people think, feel, and do in and around organizations*
 anchors of knowledge
  contingencies, 11–12
  multidisciplinary, 11
  multiple levels of analysis, 12
  systematic research, 10–12
 Carnegie's view, 335
 coordination, 14
 field of, 3–4
 historical foundations, 4–5
 influence of departmentalization, 286
 integrative model, 20–21
 positive, 67–68, 117
 reasons for studying
  accurate personal theories, 5
  bottom-line value, 6
  career success, 5
  influence events, 5–6
  predict workplace events, 5
  value for everyone, 6
 and self-concept, 60
 and self-verification, 58
 Organizational change.
  see Change

Organizational citizenship behaviors *Various forms of cooperation and helpfulness to others that support the organization's social and psychological context,* 32

 Organizational commitment
  affective, 91
  continuous, 91–93
 Organizational comprehension, 92–93
 Organizational constraints, 94–95

Organizational culture *The values and assumptions shared within an organization*
 artifacts of, 302–305
 benefits of strong culture, 305
 categories of value, 301
 changing and strengthening, 310–312
 collaborative and creative, 305
 contingencies, 305–307
 controlling and competitive, 305
 as control system, 305
 with corporate mergers
  bicultural audit, 308
  strategies, 308–310
 and countercultures, 302
 diversity of, 301
 dominant culture, 302
 elements of, 299–302
 employee-centric, 306
 examples, 299
 models of, 300–301
 for sense making, 305
 social glue, 305
 strong, 305, 306
 subcultures, 302

 and subcultures, 302
 and unethical conduct, 307–308
 and workspace design, 304

Organizational effectiveness *A broad concept represented by several perspectives, including the organization's fit with the external environment, internal subsystem's configuration for high performance emphasis on organizational learning, and ability to satisfy the needs of key stakeholders,* 14–16, 18–20
 achievement of objectives, 12
 high-performance work practices perspective, 16–18
 integrative model of behavior, 20–21
 open systems perspective, 12–14
 Organizational events, 5–6
 Organizational justice
  distributive, 121
  equality principle, 121
  equity principle, 121
  equity theory, 121–123
  need principle, 121
  procedural, 121

Organizational learning *A perspective that holds that organizational effectiveness depends on the organization's capacity to acquire, share, use, and store valuable knowledge*
 acquiring knowledge, 15
 and organizational memory, 16
 sharing knowledge, 15–16
 storing knowledge, 16
 and unlearning, 16
 using knowledge, 16
 Organizational memory, 16
 Organizational politics
  effect on employees, 226
  minimizing, 226–228
  and personal characteristics, 227–228
 Organizational size, 293

Organizational socialization *The process by which individuals learn the values, expected behaviors, an social knowledge necessary to amuse their roles in the organization*

 changing employee values, 313
 improving, 314–315
 learning and adjustment process, 313
 and organizational comprehension, 313
 socialization agents, 315
 stages of, 313–314
 at trivago, 315

Organizational strategy *The way the organization positions itself in its Environment in relation to its stakeholders, given the organization's resources, capabilities, and mission,* 293–294

Organizational structure *The division of labor as well as the patterns of coordination, communication, workflow, and formal power that direct organizational activities*
 centralization, 284–285
 coordination of work activities, 280–282
 decentralization, 285
 departmentalization, 286–292
 and division of labor, 279–280
 external environment
  complex or simple, 292
  diverse *vs.* integrated, 292
  dynamic or stable, 292
  hostile *vs.* munificent, 292–293
 formalization, 285
 mechanistic or organic, 285–286
 and organizational size, 293
 and organizational strategy, 293–294
 Samsung Electronics, 279
 span of control, 282–284
 tall *vs.* flat, 283–284
 and technology, 293
 Organizational values, 40
 Organization for Economic Cooperation and Development
  high-performing work practices, 17

Organizations *Groups of people who work independently toward some purpose,* 3
 adapt to environment, 13
 collective entities, 4
 collective sense of purpose, 4
 consequences of diversity, 9–10
 coping strategies, 215
 developments facing
  emerging employment relationships, 7–8
  globalization, 7
  technological change, 6–7
  telecommuting, 8–9
 environmental fit, 13
 external environment, 292–293
 founders and leaders, 310–311
 incongruent systems, 325
 increasing diversity, 9
 influence environment, 13–14
 joining and staying with, 33
 most admired companies, 3
 move to more favorable environment, 14
 Outcome valences, 115
 Outputs
  standardized, 282
 Overconfidence in team decision making, 178–179

P

Participative leadership, 265
Participative management, 152

Path-goal leadership theory *A leadership theory stating that effective leaders choose the most appropriate*

leadership style(s), depending on the employee and situation, to influence employee expectations about desired results and their positive outcomes
 contingencies, 265–266
 employee and workspace contingencies, 266
 evaluating, 266
 and expectancy theory, 264–265
 limitations, 266
 styles, 265
 People-oriented leadership, 263, 267

Perception *The process of receiving information about and making sense of the world around us*
 developing global mindset, 71
 improving
  awareness of biases, 69
  improving self-awareness, 69
  meaningful interaction, 70
 mental models, 62–63
 processes and problems
  attribution theory, 65–66
  false-consensus effect, 68
  halo effect, 68
  primacy effect, 68
  recency effect, 69
  self-fulfilling prophecy, 67–68
  stereotyping, 63–65
 selective attention, 61
 of world around us, 61–63
 Perceptual biases
  attribution process, 65–66
  awareness of, 69
  false-consensus effect, 58
  halo effect, 58
  primacy effect, 58
  recency effect, 69
  self-fulfilling prophecy, 67–68
  stereotyping, 63–65
 Perceptual defense, 140
 Perceptual grouping, 62
 Perceptual process model, 61
 Performance
  and job satisfaction, 88–89
 Performance-oriented culture, 311
 Performance-to-outcome expectancy, 114
 Performing
  in team development, 170, 171
 Persistence, 29, 150
 Personal attributes perspective of leadership
  authentic leadership, 270
  cognitive practical intelligence, 270
  drive, 269
  emotional intelligence, 270
  integrity, 270
  knowledge of business, 270
  limitations, 271
  motivation, 2697
  personality, 269
  practical applications, 271
  self-concept, 269
 Personal identity, 59

Introduction to the Field of Organizational Behavior

CHAPTER SUMMARY

LO1-1 Define organizational behavior and organizations, and discuss the importance of this field of inquiry.

Organizational behavior is the study of what people think, feel, and do in and around organizations. Organizations are groups of people who work interdependently toward some purpose. OB theories help us (a) comprehend and predict work events, (b) adopt more accurate personal theories, and (c) influence organizational events. OB knowledge is for everyone, not just managers. OB theories and practices are highly beneficial for an organization's survival and success.

LO1-2 Debate the organizational opportunities and challenges of technological change, globalization, emerging employment relationships, and workforce diversity.

Technological change has improved efficiency, interactivity, and well-being, but it also has been a disruptive force in organizations. Information technology has altered communication patterns and power dynamics at work, and has affected our nonwork time, attention span, and techno-stress. Globalization, which refers to various forms of connectivity with people in other parts of the world, has become more intense than ever before because of information technology and transportation systems. It has brought more complexity and new ways of working to the workplace, requiring additional knowledge and skills. It may be an influence on work intensification, reduced job security, and lessening of the work–life balance.

An emerging employment relationship trend is the blurring of work and nonwork time and the associated call for more work–life balance (minimizing conflict between work and nonwork demands). Another employment trend is telecommuting, whereby employees work from home one or more workdays per month rather than commute to the office. Telecommuting potentially benefits employees and employers, but there are also disadvantages and its effectiveness depends on the employee, job, and organization. An organization's workforce has both surface-level diversity (observable demographic and other overt differences in people) and deep-level diversity (differences in personalities, beliefs, values, and attitudes). Diversity may improve creativity and decision making, and provide better awareness and response to diverse communities. However, diversity also poses challenges, such as dysfunctional conflict and slower team development.

LO1-3 Discuss the anchors on which organizational behavior knowledge is based.

The multidisciplinary anchor states that the field should develop from knowledge in other disciplines (e.g., psychology, sociology, economics), not just from its own isolated research base. The systematic research anchor states that OB knowledge should be based on systematic research, consistent with evidence-based management. The contingency anchor states that OB theories generally need to consider that there will be different consequences in different situations. The multiple levels of analysis anchor states that OB topics may be viewed from the individual, team, and organization levels of analysis.

LO1-4 Compare and contrast the four perspectives of organizational effectiveness.

The open systems perspective views organizations as complex organisms that "live" within an external environment, depend on it for resources, then use organizational subsystems to transform those resources into outputs, which are returned to the environment. Organizations receive feedback to maintain a good "fit" with that environment. Fit occurs by adapting to the environment, influencing the environment, or moving to a more favorable environment. Effective transformation processes are efficient, adaptable, and innovative. The

KEY TERMS

corporate social responsibility (CSR) organizational activities intended to benefit society and the environment beyond the firm's immediate financial interests or legal obligations

deep-level diversity differences in the psychological characteristics of employees, including personalities, beliefs, values, and attitudes

ethics the study of moral principles or values that determine whether actions are right or wrong and outcomes are good or bad

evidence-based management the practice of making decisions and taking actions based on research evidence

globalization economic, social, and cultural connectivity with people in other parts of the world

high-performance work practices (HPWPs) a perspective that holds that effective organizations incorporate several workplace practices that leverage the potential of human capital

human capital the stock of knowledge, skills, and abilities among employees that provide economic value to the organization

intellectual capital a company's stock of knowledge, including human capital, structural capital, and relationship capital

learning orientation beliefs and norms that support the acquisition, sharing, and use of knowledge as well as work conditions that nurture these learning processes

open systems a perspective that holds that organizations depend on the external environment for resources, affect that environment through their output, and consist of internal subsystems that transform inputs to outputs

organizational behavior (OB) the study of what people think, feel, and do in and around organizations

organizational effectiveness a broad concept represented by several perspectives, including the organization's fit with the external environment, internal subsystems' configuration for high performance, emphasis on organizational learning, and ability to satisfy the needs of key stakeholders

organizational learning a perspective that holds that organizational effectiveness depends on the organization's capacity to acquire, share, use, and store valuable knowledge

organizations groups of people who work interdependently toward some purpose

relationship capital the value derived from an organization's relationships with customers, suppliers, and others

stakeholders individuals, groups, and other entities that affect, or are affected by, the organization's objectives and actions

structural capital knowledge embedded in an organization's systems and structures

surface-level diversity the observable demographic or physiological differences in people, such as their race, ethnicity, gender, age, and physical disabilities

telecommuting an arrangement whereby, supported by information technology, employees work from home one or more work days per month rather than commute to the office

values relatively stable, evaluative beliefs that guide a person's preferences for outcomes or courses of action in a variety of situations

work–life balance the degree to which a person minimizes conflict between work and nonwork demands

organizational learning perspective states that organizations are effective when they find ways to acquire, share, use, and store knowledge. Intellectual capital consists of human capital, structural capital, and relationship capital. Knowledge is retained in the organizational memory; companies also selectively unlearn.

The high-performance work practices (HPWP) perspective identifies a bundle of systems and structures to leverage workforce potential. The most widely identified HPWPs are employee involvement, job autonomy, employee competency development, and performance- and skill-based rewards. HPWPs improve organizational effectiveness by building human capital, increasing adaptability, and strengthening employee motivation and attitudes. The stakeholder perspective states that organizations are more effective when they understand, manage, and satisfy stakeholder needs and expectations. Leaders manage the interests of diverse stakeholders by relying on their personal and organizational values for guidance. Ethics and corporate social responsibility (CSR) are natural variations of values-based organizations. CSR consists of organizational activities intended to benefit society and the environment beyond the firm's immediate financial interests or legal obligations.

CHAPTER SUMMARY

LO2-1 Describe the four factors that directly influence individual behavior and performance.

Four variables—motivation, ability, role perceptions, and situational factors—which are represented by the acronym MARS, directly influence individual behavior and performance. Motivation represents the forces within a person that affect his or her direction, intensity, and persistence of voluntary behavior; ability includes both the natural aptitudes and the learned capabilities required to successfully complete a task; role perceptions are the extent to which people understand the job duties (roles) assigned to them or expected of them; and situational factors include conditions beyond the employee's immediate control that constrain or facilitate behavior and performance.

LO2-2 Summarize the five types of individual behavior in organizations.

There are five main types of workplace behavior. Task performance refers to goal-directed behaviors under the individual's control that support organizational objectives. It includes proficiency, adaptivity, and proactivity. Organizational citizenship behaviors consist of various forms of cooperation and helpfulness to others that support the organization's social and psychological context. Counterproductive work behaviors are voluntary behaviors that have the potential to directly or indirectly harm the organization. Joining and staying with the organization refers to agreeing to become an organizational member and remaining with the organization. Maintaining work attendance includes minimizing absenteeism when capable of working and avoiding scheduled work when not fit (i.e., low presenteeism).

LO2-3 Describe personality and discuss how the "Big Five" personality dimensions and four MBTI types relate to individual behavior in organizations.

Personality refers to the relatively enduring pattern of thoughts, emotions, and behaviors that characterize a person, along with the psychological processes behind those characteristics. Personality is formed through hereditary (nature) as well as socialization (nurture). The "Big Five" personality dimensions include conscientiousness, agreeableness, neuroticism, openness to experience, and extroversion. Conscientiousness and extraversion are the best overall predictors of job performance in most job groups. Extraversion and openness to experience are the best predictors of adaptive and proactive performance. Emotional stability (low neuroticism) is also associated with better adaptivity. Conscientiousness and agreeableness are the two best personality predictors of organizational citizenship and (negatively) with counterproductive work behaviors.

Based on Jungian personality theory, the Myers-Briggs Type Indicator (MBTI) identifies competing orientations for getting energy (extraversion versus introversion), perceiving information (sensing versus intuiting), processing information and making decisions (thinking versus feeling), and orienting to the external world (judging versus perceiving). The MBTI improves self-awareness for career development and mutual understanding but is more popular than valid.

LO2-4 Summarize Schwartz's model of individual values and discuss the conditions where values influence behavior.

Values are stable, evaluative beliefs that guide our preferences for outcomes or courses of action in a variety of situations. Compared to personality traits, values are evaluative (rather than descriptive), more likely to conflict, and formed more from socialization than heredity. Schwartz's model organizes 57 values into a circumplex of 10 dimensions along two bipolar

Key Terms

ability the natural aptitudes and learned capabilities required to successfully complete a task

achievement-nurturing orientation cross-cultural value describing the degree to which people in a culture emphasize competitive versus cooperative relations with other people

agreeableness a personality dimension describing people who are trusting, helpful, good-natured, considerate, tolerant, selfless, generous, and flexible

collectivism a cross-cultural value describing the degree to which people in a culture emphasize duty to groups to which they belong and to group harmony

conscientiousness a personality dimension describing people who are organized, dependable, goal-focused, thorough, disciplined, methodical, and industrious

counterproductive work behaviors (CWBs) voluntary behaviors that have the potential to directly or indirectly harm the organization

extraversion a personality dimension describing people who are outgoing, talkative, sociable, and assertive

five-factor (Big Five) model (FFM) the five broad dimensions representing most personality traits: conscientiousness, emotional stability, openness to experience, agreeableness, and extraversion

individualism a cross-cultural value describing the degree to which people in a culture emphasize independence and personal uniqueness

mindfulness a person's receptive and impartial attention to and awareness of the present situation as well as to one's own thoughts and emotions in that moment

moral intensity the degree to which an issue demands the application of ethical principles

moral sensitivity a person's ability to recognize the presence of an ethical issue and determine its relative importance

motivation the forces within a person that affect his or her direction, intensity, and persistence of voluntary behavior

Myers-Briggs Type Indicator (MBTI) an instrument designed to measure the elements of Jungian personality theory, particularly preferences regarding perceiving and judging information

neuroticism a personality dimension describing people who tend to be anxious, insecure, self-conscious, depressed, and temperamental

openness to experience a personality dimension describing people who are imaginative, creative, unconventional, curious, nonconforming, autonomous, and aesthetically perceptive

organizational citizenship behaviors (OCBs) various forms of cooperation and helpfulness to others that support the organization's social and psychological context

personality the relatively enduring pattern of thoughts, emotions, and behaviors that characterize a person, along with the psychological processes behind those characteristics

power distance a cross-cultural value describing the degree to which people in a culture accept unequal distribution of power in a society

role perceptions the degree to which a person understands the job duties assigned to or expected of him or her

task performance the individual's voluntary goal-directed behaviors that contribute to organizational objectives

uncertainty avoidance a cross-cultural value describing the degree to which people in a culture tolerate ambiguity (low uncertainty avoidance) or feel threatened by ambiguity and uncertainty (high uncertainty avoidance)

dimensions: openness to change to conservation and self-enhancement to self-transcendence. Values influence behavior in three ways: (1) shaping the attractiveness of choices, (2) framing perceptions of reality, and (3) aligning behavior with self-concept and self-presentation. However, the effect of values on behavior also depends on whether the situation supports or prevents that behavior and on how actively we think about them and understand their relevance to the situation. Values congruence refers to how similar a person's values hierarchy is to the values hierarchy of another source (organization, team, etc.).

LO2-5 Describe three ethical principles and discuss three factors that influence ethical behavior.

Ethics refers to the study of moral principles or values that determine whether actions are right or wrong and outcomes are good or bad. Three ethical principles are utilitarianism (greatest good for the greatest number), individual rights (upholding natural rights), and distributive justice (same or proportional benefits and burdens). Ethical behavior is influenced by the degree to which an issue demands the application of ethical principles (moral intensity), the individual's ability to recognize the presence and relative importance of an ethical issue (moral sensitivity), and situational forces. Ethical conduct at work is supported by codes of ethical conduct, mechanisms for communicating ethical violations, the organization's culture, and the leader's behavior.

LO2-6 Describe five values commonly studied across cultures.

Five values often studied across cultures are individualism (valuing independence and personal uniqueness); collectivism (valuing duty to in-groups and group harmony); power distance (valuing unequal distribution of power); uncertainty avoidance (tolerating or feeling threatened by ambiguity and uncertainty); and achievement-nurturing orientation (valuing competition versus cooperation).

chapter three

Perceiving Ourselves and Others in Organizations

CHAPTER SUMMARY

LO3-1 Describe the elements of self-concept and explain how each affects an individual's behavior and well-being.

Self-concept includes an individual's self-beliefs and self-evaluations. It has three structural characteristics—complexity, consistency, and clarity—all of which influence employee well-being, behavior, and performance. People are inherently motivated to promote and protect their self-concept (self-enhancement) and to verify and maintain their existing self-concept (self-verification). Self-evaluation consists of self-esteem, self-efficacy, and locus of control. Self-concept also consists of both personal identity and social identity. Social identity theory explains how people define themselves by the groups to which they belong or have an emotional attachment.

LO3-2 Outline the perceptual process and discuss the effects of categorical thinking and mental models in that process.

Perception involves selecting, organizing, and interpreting information to make sense of the world around us. Perceptual organization applies categorical thinking—the mostly nonconscious process of organizing people and objects into preconceived categories that are stored in our long-term memory. Mental models—knowledge structures that we develop to describe, explain, and predict the world around us—also help us make sense of incoming stimuli.

LO3-3 Discuss how stereotyping, attribution, self-fulfilling prophecy, and the halo, false-consensus, primacy, and recency effects influence the perceptual process.

Stereotyping occurs when people assign traits to others based on their membership in a social category. This assignment economizes mental effort, fills in missing information, and enhances our self-concept, but it also lays the foundation for stereotype threat as well as systemic and intentional discrimination. The attribution process involves deciding whether an observed behavior or event is caused mainly by the person (internal factors) or the environment (external factors). Attributions are decided by the perceived consistency, distinctiveness, and consensus of the behavior. This process is subject to self-serving bias and fundamental attribution error. A self-fulfilling prophecy occurs when our expectations about another person cause that person to act in a way that is consistent with those expectations. This effect is stronger when employees first join the work unit, when several people hold these expectations, and when the employee has a history of low achievement. Four other perceptual errors commonly noted in organizations are the halo effect, false-consensus effect, primacy effect, and recency effect.

LO3-4 Discuss three ways to improve perceptions, with specific application to organizational situations.

One way to minimize perceptual biases is to become more aware of their existence. Awareness of these biases makes people more mindful of their thoughts and actions, but this training sometimes reinforces rather than reduces reliance on stereotypes and tends to be ineffective for people with deeply held prejudices. A second strategy is to become more aware of biases in our own decisions and behavior. Self-awareness increases through formal tests such as the Implicit Association Test (IAT) and by applying the Johari Window, which is a process in which others provide feedback to you about your behavior, and you offer disclosure to them about yourself. The third strategy is meaningful interaction, which applies the contact hypothesis that people who interact will be less prejudiced or perceptually biased

KEY TERMS

attribution process the perceptual process of deciding whether an observed behavior or event is caused largely by internal or external factors

categorical thinking organizing people and objects into preconceived categories that are stored in our long-term memory

confirmation bias the process of screening out information that is contrary to our values and assumptions, and to more readily accept confirming information

contact hypothesis a theory stating that the more we interact with someone, the less prejudiced or perceptually biased we will be against that person

empathy a person's understanding of and sensitivity to the feelings, thoughts, and situations of others

false-consensus effect a perceptual error in which we overestimate the extent to which others have beliefs and characteristics similar to our own

fundamental attribution error the tendency to see the person rather than the situation as the main cause of that person's behavior

global mindset an individual's ability to perceive, appreciate, and empathize with people from other cultures, and to process complex cross-cultural information

halo effect a perceptual error whereby our general impression of a person, usually based on one prominent characteristic, colors our perception of other characteristics of that person

Johari Window a model of mutual understanding that encourages disclosure and feedback to increase our own open area and reduce the blind, hidden, and unknown areas

locus of control a person's general belief about the amount of control he or she has over personal life events

mental models knowledge structures that we develop to describe, explain, and predict the world around us

perception the process of receiving information about and making sense of the world around us

positive organizational behavior a perspective of organizational behavior that focuses on building positive qualities and traits within individuals or institutions as opposed to focusing on what is wrong with them

primacy effect a perceptual error in which we quickly form an opinion of people based on the first information we receive about them

recency effect a perceptual error in which the most recent information dominates our perception of others

selective attention the process of attending to some information received by our senses and ignoring other information

self-concept an individual's self-beliefs and self-evaluations

self-efficacy a person's belief that he or she has the ability, motivation, correct role perceptions, and favorable situation to complete a task successfully

self-enhancement a person's inherent motivation to have a positive self-concept (and to have others perceive him or her favorably), such as being competent, attractive, lucky, ethical, and important

self-fulfilling prophecy the perceptual process in which our expectations about another person cause that person to act more consistently with those expectations

self-serving bias the tendency to attribute our favorable outcomes to internal factors and our failures to external factors

self-verification a person's inherent motivation to confirm and maintain his or her existing self-concept

social identity theory a theory stating that people define themselves by the groups to which they belong or have an emotional attachment

stereotype threat an individual's concern about confirming a negative stereotype about his or her group

stereotyping the process of assigning traits to people based on their membership in a social category

toward one another. Meaningful interaction is strongest when people work closely and frequently with relatively equal status on a shared meaningful task that requires cooperation and reliance on one another. Meaningful interaction helps improve empathy, which is a person's understanding and sensitivity to the feelings, thoughts, and situations of others.

LO3-5 Outline the main features of a global mindset and justify its usefulness to employees and organizations.

A global mindset refers to an individual's ability to perceive, know about, and process information across cultures. This includes (1) an awareness of, openness to, and respect for other views and practices in the world; (2) the capacity to empathize and act effectively across cultures; (3) an ability to process complex information about novel environments; and (4) the ability to comprehend and reconcile intercultural matters with multiple levels of thinking. A global mindset enables people to develop better cross-cultural relationships, to digest huge volumes of cross-cultural information, and to identify and respond more quickly to emerging global opportunities. Employees develop a global mindset through self-awareness, opportunities to compare their own mental models with people from other cultures, formal cross-cultural training, and immersion in other cultures.

chapter four

Workplace Emotions, Attitudes, and Stress

REVIEW CARD

CHAPTER SUMMARY

LO4-1 Explain how emotions and cognition (conscious reasoning) influence attitudes and behavior.

Emotions are physiological, behavioral, and psychological episodes experienced toward an object, person, or event that create a state of readiness. Emotions differ from attitudes, which represent a cluster of beliefs, feelings, and behavioral intentions toward a person, object, or event. Beliefs are a person's established perceptions about the attitude object. Feelings are positive or negative evaluations of the attitude object. Behavioral intentions represent a motivation to engage in a particular behavior toward the target.

Attitudes have traditionally been described as a purely rational process in which beliefs predict feelings, which predict behavioral intentions, which predict behavior. We now know that emotions have an influence on behavior that is equal to or greater than that of cognition. This dual process is apparent when we internally experience a conflict between what logically seems good or bad and what we emotionally feel is good or bad in a situation. Emotions also affect behavior directly. Behavior sometimes influences our subsequent attitudes through cognitive dissonance.

LO4-2 Discuss the dynamics of emotional labor and the role of emotional intelligence in the workplace.

Emotional labor consists of the effort, planning, and control needed to express organizationally desired emotions during interpersonal transactions. It is more common in jobs requiring a variety of emotions and more intense emotions, as well as in jobs in which interactions with clients are frequent and long in duration. Cultures also differ on the norms of displaying or concealing a person's true emotions. Emotional dissonance is the psychological tension experienced when the emotions people are required to display are quite different from the emotions they actually experience at that moment. Deep acting can minimize this dissonance, as can the practice of hiring people with a natural tendency to display desired emotions.

Emotional intelligence is the ability to perceive and express emotion, assimilate emotion in thought, understand and reason with emotion, and regulate emotion in oneself and others. This concept includes four components arranged in a hierarchy: awareness of one's own emotions, management of one's own emotions, awareness of others' emotions, and management of others' emotions. Emotional intelligence can be learned to some extent, particularly through personal coaching.

LO4-3 Summarize the consequences of job dissatisfaction, as well as strategies to increase organizational (affective) commitment.

Job satisfaction represents a person's evaluation of his or her job and work context. Four types of job dissatisfaction consequences are quitting or otherwise getting away from the dissatisfying situation (exit), attempting to change the dissatisfying situation (voice), patiently waiting for the problem to sort itself out (loyalty), and reducing work effort and performance (neglect). Job satisfaction has a moderate relationship with job performance and with customer satisfaction. Affective organizational commitment (loyalty) is the employee's emotional attachment to, identification with, and involvement in a particular organization. This form contrasts with continuance commitment, which is a calculative bond with the organization. Companies build loyalty through justice and support, shared values, trust, organizational comprehension, and employee involvement.

KEY TERMS

affective organizational commitment an individual's emotional attachment to, involvement in, and identification with an organization

attitudes the cluster of beliefs, assessed feelings, and behavioral intentions toward a person, object, or event (called an attitude object)

cognitive dissonance an emotional experience caused by a perception that our beliefs, feelings, and behavior are incongruent with one another

continuance commitment an individual's calculative attachment to an organization

emotional dissonance the psychological tension experienced when the emotions people are required to display are quite different from the emotions they actually experience at that moment

emotional intelligence (EI) a set of abilities to perceive and express emotion, assimilate emotion in thought, understand and reason with emotion, and regulate emotion in oneself and others

emotional labor the effort, planning, and control needed to express organizationally desired emotions during interpersonal transactions

emotions physiological, behavioral, and psychological episodes experienced toward an object, person, or event that create a state of readiness

exit–voice–loyalty–neglect (EVLN) model the four ways, as indicated in the name, that employees respond to job dissatisfaction

general adaptation syndrome a model of the stress experience, consisting of three stages: alarm reaction, resistance, and exhaustion

job satisfaction a person's evaluation of his or her job and work context

service profit chain model a theory explaining how employees' job satisfaction influences company profitability indirectly through service quality, customer loyalty, and related factors

stress an adaptive response to a situation that is perceived as challenging or threatening to the person's well-being

LO4-4 Describe the stress experience and review four major stressors.

Stress is an adaptive response to a situation that is perceived as challenging or threatening to a person's well-being. The stress experience, called the general adaptation syndrome, involves moving through three stages: alarm, resistance, and exhaustion. Stressors are the causes of stress and include any environmental conditions that place a physical or emotional demand on a person. Four of the most common workplace stressors are organizational constraints, interpersonal conflict, work overload, and low task control.

LO4-5 Identify five ways to manage workplace stress.

Many interventions are available to manage work-related stress, including removing the stressor, withdrawing from the stressor, changing stress perceptions, controlling stress consequences, and receiving social support.

CHAPTER SUMMARY

LO5-1 Define employee engagement.

Employee engagement is defined as an individual's emotional and cognitive (rational) motivation, particularly a focused, intense, persistent, and purposive effort toward work-related goals. It is emotional involvement in, commitment to, and satisfaction with the work, as well as a high level of absorption in the work and sense of self-efficacy about performing the work.

LO5-2 Explain how drives and emotions influence employee motivation, and discuss the employee motivation implications of four-drive theory, Maslow's needs hierarchy, intrinsic and extrinsic motivation, and learned needs theory.

Motivation consists of the forces within a person that affect his or her direction, intensity, and persistence of voluntary behavior in the workplace. Drives (also called primary needs) are neural states that energize individuals to correct deficiencies or maintain an internal equilibrium. They generate emotions, which put us in a state of readiness to act. Needs—goal-directed forces that people experience—are shaped by the individual's self-concept (including personality and values), social norms, and past experience.

Four-drive theory states that everyone has four innate drives: acquire, bond, comprehend, and defend. These drives activate emotions that people regulate through social norms, past experience, and personal values. The main recommendation from four-drive theory is to ensure that individual jobs and workplaces provide a balanced opportunity to fulfill the four drives. Maslow's needs hierarchy theory groups needs into a hierarchy of five levels and states that the lowest needs are initially most important, but higher needs become more important as the lower ones are satisfied. Although very popular, the theory lacks research support, mainly because it wrongly assumes that everyone has the same hierarchy. The emerging evidence suggests that needs hierarchies vary from one person to the next, according to their personal values.

Intrinsic motivation refers to motivation controlled by the individual and experienced from the activity itself, whereas extrinsic motivation occurs when people are motivated to receive something that is beyond their personal control for instrumental reasons. Intrinsic motivation is anchored in the innate drives for competence and autonomy. Some research suggests that extrinsic motivators may reduce existing intrinsic motivation to some extent and under some conditions, but the effect is often minimal. McClelland's learned needs theory argues that needs can be strengthened through learning. The three needs studied in this respect have been need for achievement, need for power, and need for affiliation.

LO5-3 Discuss the expectancy theory model, including its practical implications.

Expectancy theory states that work effort is determined by the perception that effort will result in a particular level of performance (E-to-P expectancy), the perception that a specific behavior or performance level will lead to specific outcomes (P-to-O expectancy), and the valences that the person feels for those outcomes. The E-to-P expectancy increases by improving the employee's ability and confidence to perform the job. The P-to-O expectancy increases by measuring performance accurately, distributing higher rewards to better performers, and showing employees that rewards are performance-based. Outcome valences increase by finding out what employees want and using these resources as rewards.

KEY TERMS

distributive justice perceived fairness in the individual's ratio of outcomes to contributions relative to a comparison of other's ratio of outcomes to contributions

drives hardwired characteristics of the brain that correct deficiencies or maintain an internal equilibrium by producing emotions to energize individuals

employee engagement individual emotional and cognitive motivation, particularly a focused, intense, persistent, and purposive effort toward work-related goals

equity theory a theory explaining how people develop perceptions of fairness in the distribution and exchange of resources

expectancy theory a motivation theory based on the idea that work effort is directed toward behaviors that people believe will lead to desired outcomes

four-drive theory a motivation theory based on the innate drives to acquire, bond, learn, and defend that incorporates both emotions and rationality

goal setting the process of motivating employees and clarifying their role perceptions by establishing performance objectives

job characteristics model a job design model that relates the motivational properties of jobs to specific personal and organizational consequences of those properties

job design the process of assigning tasks to a job, including the interdependency of those tasks with other jobs

job enlargement the practice of adding more tasks to an existing job

job enrichment the practice of giving employees more responsibility for scheduling, coordinating, and planning their own work

job specialization the result of a division of labor, in which work is subdivided into separate jobs assigned to different people

Maslow's needs hierarchy theory a motivation theory of needs arranged in a hierarchy, whereby people are motivated to fulfill a higher need as a lower one becomes gratified

motivation the forces within a person that affect his or her direction, intensity, and persistence of voluntary behavior

need for achievement (nAch) a learned need in which people want to accomplish reasonably challenging goals and desire unambiguous feedback and recognition for their success

need for affiliation (nAff) a learned need in which people seek approval from others, conform to their wishes and expectations, and avoid conflict and confrontation

need for power (nPow) a learned need in which people want to control their environment, including people and material resources, to benefit either themselves (personalized power) or others (socialized power)

needs goal-directed forces that people experience

organizational behavior modification (OB Mod) a theory that explains employee behavior in terms of the antecedent conditions and consequences of that behavior

procedural justice perceived fairness of the procedures used to decide the distribution of resources

scientific management the practice of systematically partitioning work into its smallest elements and standardizing tasks to achieve maximum efficiency

self-reinforcement reinforcement that occurs when an employee has control over a reinforcer but doesn't "take" it until completing a self-set goal

skill variety the extent to which employees must use different skills and talents to perform tasks within their jobs

social cognitive theory a theory that explains how learning and motivation occur by observing and modeling others as well as by anticipating the consequences of our behavior

strengths-based coaching a positive organizational behavior approach to coaching and feedback that focuses on building and leveraging the employee's strengths rather than trying to correct his or her weaknesses

task identity the degree to which a job requires completion of a whole or an identifiable piece of work

task interdependence the extent to which team members must share materials, information, or expertise in order to perform their jobs

task significance the degree to which a job has a substantial impact on the organization and/or larger society

LO5-4 Outline organizational behavior modification (OB Mod) and social cognitive theory, and explain their relevance to employee motivation.

Organizational behavior modification takes the behaviorist view that the environment teaches people to alter their behavior so that they maximize positive consequences and minimize adverse consequences. Antecedents are environmental stimuli that provoke (not necessarily cause) behavior. Consequences are events following behavior that influence its future occurrence. Consequences include positive reinforcement, punishment, negative reinforcement, and extinction. The schedules of reinforcement also influence behavior.

Social cognitive theory states that much learning and motivation occur by observing and modeling others, as well as by anticipating the consequences of our behavior. It suggests that people typically infer (rather than only directly experience) cause-and-effect relationships, anticipate the consequences of their actions, develop self-efficacy in performing behavior, exercise personal control over their behavior, and reflect on their direct experiences. The theory emphasizes self-regulation of individual behavior, including self-reinforcement, which is the tendency of people to reward and punish themselves as a consequence of their actions.

LO5-5 Describe the characteristics of effective goal setting and feedback.

Goal setting is the process of motivating employees and clarifying their role perceptions by establishing performance objectives. Goals are more effective when they are SMARTER (specific, measurable, achievable, relevant, time-framed, exciting, and reviewed). Effective feedback is specific, relevant, timely, credible, and sufficiently frequent. Strengths-based coaching (also known as *appreciative coaching*) maximizes employee potential by focusing on their strengths rather than weaknesses. Employees usually prefer nonsocial feedback sources to learn about their progress toward goal accomplishment.

LO5-6 Summarize equity theory and describe ways to improve procedural justice.

Organizational justice consists of distributive justice (perceived fairness in the outcomes we receive relative to our contributions and the outcomes and contributions of others) and procedural justice (fairness of the procedures used to decide the distribution of resources). Equity theory has four elements: outcome/input ratio, comparison other, equity evaluation, and consequences of inequity. The theory also explains what people are motivated to do when they feel inequitably treated. Companies need to consider not only equity in the distribution of resources but also fairness in the process of making resource allocation decisions.

LO5-7 List the advantages and disadvantages of job specialization and explain how to improve employee motivation through job design.

Job design is the process of assigning tasks to a job, including the interdependency of those tasks with other jobs. Job specialization subdivides work into separate jobs for different people. This increases work efficiency because employees master the tasks quickly, spend less time changing tasks, require less training, and can be matched more closely with the jobs best suited to their skills. However, job specialization may reduce work motivation; create mental health problems; lower product or service quality; and increase costs through discontentment, absenteeism, and turnover.

The job characteristics model is a template for job redesign that specifies core job dimensions, psychological states, and individual differences. The five core job dimensions are skill variety, task identity, task significance, autonomy, and job feedback. Jobs also vary in their required social interaction (task interdependence), predictability of work activities (task variability), and procedural clarity (task analyzability). Contemporary job design strategies try to motivate employees through job rotation, job enlargement, and job enrichment. Organizations introduce job rotation to reduce job boredom, develop a more flexible workforce, and reduce the incidence of repetitive strain injuries. Job enlargement involves increasing the number of tasks within the job. Two ways to enrich jobs are clustering tasks into natural groups and establishing client relationships.

chapter SIX

Decision Making and Creativity

CHAPTER SUMMARY

LO6-1 Describe the elements of rational choice decision making.

Decision making is a conscious process of making choices among one or more alternatives with the intention of moving toward some desired state of affairs. Rational choice decision making identifies the best choice by calculating the expected valence of numerous outcomes and the probability of those outcomes. It also follows the logical process of identifying problems and opportunities, choosing the best decision style, developing alternative solutions, choosing the best solution, implementing the selected alternative, and evaluating decision outcomes.

LO6-2 Explain why people differ from rational choice decision making when identifying problems/opportunities, evaluating/choosing alternatives, and evaluating decision outcomes.

Solution-focused problem identification, decisive leadership, stakeholder framing, perceptual defense, and mental models affect our ability to objectively identify problems and opportunities. We can minimize these challenges by being aware of the human limitations and discussing the situation with colleagues.

Evaluating and choosing alternatives is often challenging because organizational goals are ambiguous or in conflict, human information processing is incomplete and subjective, and people tend to satisfice rather than maximize. Decision makers also short-circuit the evaluation process when faced with an opportunity rather than a problem. People generally make better choices by systematically evaluating alternatives. Scenario planning can help make future decisions without the pressure and emotions that occur during real emergencies.

Confirmation bias and escalation of commitment make it difficult to evaluate decision outcomes accurately. Escalation is mainly caused by the self-justification effect, self-enhancement effect, prospect theory effect, and sunk costs effect. These problems are minimized by separating decision choosers from decision evaluators, establishing a preset level at which the decision is abandoned or reevaluated, relying on more systematic and clear feedback about the project's success, and involving several people in decision making.

LO6-3 Discuss the roles of emotions and intuition in decision making.

Emotions shape our preferences for alternatives and the process we follow to evaluate alternatives. We also listen in on our emotions for guidance when making decisions. This latter activity relates to intuition—the ability to know when a problem or opportunity exists and to select the best course of action without conscious reasoning. Intuition is both an emotional experience and a rapid, nonconscious, analytic process that involves pattern matching and action scripts.

LO6-4 Describe employee characteristics, workplace conditions, and specific activities that support creativity.

Creativity is the development of original ideas that make a socially recognized contribution. The four creativity stages are preparation, incubation, illumination, and verification. Incubation assists divergent thinking, which involves reframing the problem in a unique way and generating different approaches to the issue.

Four of the main features of creative people are intelligence, persistence, expertise, and independent imagination. Creativity also is strengthened for everyone when the work environment supports a learning orientation, the job has high intrinsic motivation, the

KEY TERMS

anchoring and adjustment heuristic a natural tendency for people to be influenced by an initial anchor point such that they do not sufficiently move away from that point as new information is provided

availability heuristic a natural tendency to assign higher probabilities to objects or events that are easier to recall from memory, even though ease of recall is also affected by nonprobability factors (e.g., emotional response, recent events)

bounded rationality the view that people are bounded in their decision-making capabilities, including access to limited information, limited information processing, and tendency toward satisficing rather than maximizing when making choices

cognitive dissonance an emotional experience caused by a perception that our beliefs, feelings, and behavior are incongruent with one another

confirmation bias the process of screening out information that is contrary to our values and assumptions, and to more readily accept confirming information

creativity the development of original ideas that make a socially recognized contribution

decision making the conscious process of making choices among alternatives with the intention of moving toward some desired state of affairs

design thinking a human-centered, solution-focused creative process that applies both intuition and analytical thinking to clarify problems and generate innovative solutions

divergent thinking reframing a problem in a unique way and generating different approaches to the issue

employee involvement the degree to which employees influence how their work is organized and carried out

escalation of commitment the tendency to repeat an apparently bad decision or allocate more resources to a failing course of action

implicit favorite a preferred alternative that the decision maker uses repeatedly as a comparison with other choices

intuition the ability to know when a problem or opportunity exists and to select the best course of action without conscious reasoning

learning orientation beliefs and norms that support the acquisition, sharing, and use of knowledge as well as work conditions that nurture these learning processes

mental models knowledge structures that we develop to describe, explain, and predict the world around us

prospect theory effect a natural tendency to feel more dissatisfaction from losing a particular amount than satisfaction from gaining an equal amount

representativeness heuristic a natural tendency to evaluate probabilities of events or objects by the degree to which they resemble (are representative of) other events or objects rather than on objective probability information

satisficing selecting an alternative that is satisfactory or "good enough," rather than the alternative with the highest value (maximization)

scenario planning a systematic process of thinking about alternative futures and what the organization should do to anticipate and react to those environments

self-enhancement a person's inherent motivation to have a positive self-concept (and to have others perceive him or her favorably), such as being competent, attractive, lucky, ethical, and important

organization provides a reasonable level of job security, and project leaders provide appropriate goals, time pressure, and resources. Four types of activities that encourage creativity are redefining the problem, associative play, cross-pollination, and design thinking. Design thinking is a human-centered, solution-focused creative process that applies both intuition and analytical thinking to clarify problems and generate innovative solutions.

LO6-5 Describe the benefits of employee involvement and identify four contingencies that affect the optimal level of employee involvement.

Employee involvement refers to the degree that employees influence how their work is organized and carried out. The level of participation may range from an employee providing specific information to management without knowing the problem or issue, to complete involvement in all phases of the decision process. Employee involvement may lead to higher decision quality and commitment, but several contingencies need to be considered, including the decision structure, source of decision knowledge, decision commitment, and risk of conflict.

CHAPTER SUMMARY

LO7-1 Explain why employees join informal groups, and discuss the benefits and limitations of teams.

Teams are groups of two or more people who interact and influence one another, are mutually accountable for achieving common goals associated with organizational objectives, and perceive themselves as a social entity within an organization. All teams are groups because they consist of people with a unifying relationship; not all groups are teams because some groups do not exist to serve organizational objectives.

People join informal groups (and are motivated to be on formal teams) for four reasons: (1) They have an innate drive to bond, (2) group membership is an inherent ingredient in a person's self-concept, (3) some personal goals are accomplished better in groups, and (4) individuals are comforted in stressful situations by the mere presence of other people. Teams have become popular because they tend to make better decisions, support the knowledge management process, and provide superior customer service. Teams are not always as effective as individuals working alone. Process losses and social loafing drag down team performance.

LO7-2 Outline the team effectiveness model and discuss how task characteristics, team size, and team composition influence team effectiveness.

Team effectiveness includes the team's ability to achieve its objectives, fulfill the needs of its members, and maintain its survival. The model of team effectiveness considers the team and organizational environment, team design, and team processes. Three team design elements are task characteristics, team size, and team composition. Teams tend to be better suited for situations in which the work is complex yet tasks are well-structured and have high task interdependence. Teams should be large enough to perform the work yet small enough for efficient coordination and meaningful involvement. Effective teams are composed of people with the competencies and motivation to perform tasks in a team environment. Team member diversity has advantages and disadvantages for team performance.

LO7-3 Discuss how the four team processes—team development, norms, cohesion, and trust—influence team effectiveness.

Teams develop through the stages of forming, storming, norming, performing, and eventually adjourning. Within these stages are two distinct team development processes: developing team identity and developing team mental models and coordinating routines. Team development can be accelerated through team building—any formal activity intended to improve the development and functioning of a work team. Teams develop norms to regulate and guide member behavior. These norms may be influenced by initial experiences, critical events, and the values and experiences that team members bring to the group.

Team cohesion—the degree of attraction people feel toward the team and their motivation to remain members—increases with member similarity, smaller team size, higher degree of interaction, somewhat difficult entry, team success, and external challenges. Cohesion increases team performance when the team has high interdependence and its norms are congruent with organizational goals. Trust refers to positive expectations one person has toward another person in situations involving risk. People trust others on the basis of three foundations: calculus, knowledge, and identification.

KEY TERMS

brainstorming a freewheeling, face-to-face meeting where team members aren't allowed to criticize but are encouraged to speak freely, generate as many ideas as possible, and build on the ideas of others

brainwriting a variation of brainstorming whereby participants write (rather than speak about) and share their ideas

Brooks's law the principle that adding more people to a late software project only makes it later

electronic brainstorming a form of brainstorming that relies on networked computers for submitting and sharing creative ideas

evaluation apprehension a decision-making problem that occurs when individuals are reluctant to mention ideas that seem silly because they believe (often correctly) that other team members are silently evaluating them

nominal group technique a variation of brainwriting consisting of three stages in which participants (1) silently and independently document their ideas, (2) collectively describe these ideas to the other team members without critique, and then (3) silently and independently evaluate the ideas presented

norms the informal rules and shared expectations that groups establish to regulate the behavior of their members

process losses resources (including time and energy) expended toward team development and maintenance rather than the task

production blocking a time constraint in team decision making due to the procedural requirement that only one person may speak at a time

role a set of behaviors that people are expected to perform because they hold certain positions in a team and organization

self-directed teams (SDTs) cross-functional work groups that are organized around work processes, complete an entire piece of work requiring several interdependent tasks, and have substantial autonomy over the execution of those tasks

social loafing the problem that occurs when people exert less effort (and usually perform at a lower level) when working in teams than when working alone

task interdependence the extent to which team members must share materials, information, or expertise in order to perform their jobs

team building a process that consists of formal activities intended to improve the development and functioning of a work team

team cohesion the degree of attraction people feel toward the team and their motivation to remain members

team efficacy the collective belief among team members in the team's capability to successfully complete a task

teams groups of two or more people who interact with and influence each other, are mutually accountable for achieving common goals associated with organizational objectives, and perceive themselves as a social entity within an organization

virtual (remote) teams teams whose members operate across space, time, and organizational boundaries and are linked through information technologies to achieve organizational tasks

LO7-4 **Discuss the characteristics and factors required for the success of self-directed teams and virtual (remote) teams.**

Self-directed teams (SDTs) complete an entire piece of work requiring several interdependent tasks, and they have substantial autonomy over the execution of their tasks. Members of virtual teams operate across space, time, and organizational boundaries and are linked through information technologies to achieve organizational tasks. Virtual (remote) teams are more effective when the team members have certain competencies, the team has the freedom to choose the preferred communication channels, and the members meet face-to-face fairly early in the team development process.

LO7-5 **Identify four constraints on team decision making and discuss the advantages and disadvantages of four structures aimed at improving team decision making.**

Team decisions are impeded by time constraints, evaluation apprehension, conformity to peer pressure, and overconfidence. Teams minimize these issues with critical thinking norms, diverse team membership, optimal team size, and procedures that prevent the leader and others from dominating. Four structures also potentially improve decision making in team settings: brainstorming, brainwriting, electronic brainstorming, and nominal group technique.

CHAPTER SUMMARY

LO8-1 Explain why communication is important in organizations, and discuss four influences on effective communication encoding and decoding.

Communication refers to the process by which information is transmitted and *understood* between two or more people. Communication supports work coordination, organizational learning, decision making, the changing of others' behavior, and employee well-being. The communication process involves forming, encoding, and transmitting the intended message to a receiver, who then decodes the message and provides feedback to the sender. Effective communication occurs when the sender's thoughts are transmitted to and understood by the intended receiver. The effectiveness of this process depends on whether the sender and receiver have similar codebooks, the sender's proficiency at encoding that message to the audience, the sender's and receiver's motivation and ability to transmit messages through that particular communication channel, and their common mental models of the communication context.

LO8-2 Compare and contrast the advantages of and problems with electronic mail, other verbal communication media, and nonverbal communication.

The two main types of communication channels are verbal and nonverbal. Various forms of Internet-based communication are widely used in organizations, with email being the most popular. Although efficient and a useful filing cabinet, email (and most other forms of written digital communication) is relatively poor at communicating emotions; it tends to reduce politeness and respect; it is an inefficient medium for communicating in ambiguous, complex, and novel situations; and it contributes to information overload. Social media, which are Internet- or mobile-based channels that allow users to generate and interactively share information, are slowly replacing or supplementing email in organizations. Social media are more conversational and reciprocally interactive than traditional channels. They are "social" by encouraging collaboration and the formation of virtual communities. Nonverbal communication includes facial gestures, voice intonation, physical distance, and even silence. Unlike verbal communication, nonverbal communication is less rule-bound and is mostly automatic and nonconscious. Some nonverbal communication is automatic through a process called emotional contagion.

LO8-3 Discuss the relevance of synchronicity, social presence, social acceptance, and media richness when choosing the preferred communication channel.

The most appropriate communication medium depends on several factors. Synchronicity refers to the channel's capacity for the sender and receiver to communicate at the same time (synchronous) or at different times (asynchronous). Synchronous channels are better when the issue is urgent or the topic is complex. Asynchronous channels are better when it is costly for both parties to communicate at the same time or when the receiver should have time to reflect before responding. A channel has high social presence when it creates psychological closeness to the other party and awareness of their humanness. This is valuable when the parties need to empathize or influence each other. Social acceptance refers to how well the communication medium is approved and supported by others. This acceptance depends on organization or societal norms, each party's preferences and skills with the channel, and the symbolic meaning of a channel. Media richness refers to a channel's data-carrying capacity. Nonroutine and ambiguous situations require rich media. However, technology-based lean media may be possible where users can multicommunicate, have high proficiency with that technology, and don't have social distractions.

KEY TERMS

communication the process by which information is transmitted and *understood* between two or more people

emotional contagion the nonconscious process of "catching" or sharing another person's emotions by mimicking that person's facial expressions and other nonverbal behavior

grapevine an unstructured and informal communication network founded on social relationships rather than organizational charts or job descriptions

information overload a condition in which the volume of information received exceeds the person's capacity to process it

management by walking around (MBWA) a communication practice in which executives get out of their offices and learn from others in the organization through face-to-face dialogue

media richness a medium's data-carrying capacity—that is, the volume and variety of information that can be transmitted during a specific time

persuasion the use of facts, logical arguments, and emotional appeals to change another person's beliefs and attitudes, usually for the purpose of changing the person's behavior

social presence the extent to which a communication channel creates psychological closeness to others, awareness of their humanness, and appreciation of the interpersonal relationship

synchronicity the extent to which the channel requires or allows both sender and receiver to be actively involved in the conversation at the same time (synchronous) or at different times (asynchronous)

LO8-4 Discuss various barriers (noise) to effective communication, including cross-cultural and gender-based differences in communication.

Several barriers create noise in the communication process. People misinterpret messages because of misaligned codebooks due to different languages, jargon, and the use of ambiguous phrases. Filtering messages and information overload are two other communication barriers. These problems are often amplified in cross-cultural settings, where these problems occur, along with differences in the meaning of nonverbal cues, silence, and conversational overlaps. There are also some communication differences between men and women, such as the tendency for men to exert status and engage in report talk in conversations, whereas women use more rapport talk and are more sensitive to nonverbal cues.

LO8-5 Explain how to get your message across more effectively, and summarize the elements of active listening.

To get a message across, the sender must learn to empathize with the receiver, repeat the message, choose an appropriate time for the conversation, and be descriptive rather than evaluative. Listening includes sensing, evaluating, and responding. Active listeners support these processes by postponing evaluation, avoiding interruptions, maintaining interest, empathizing, organizing information, showing interest, and clarifying the message.

LO8-6 Summarize effective communication strategies in organizational hierarchies, and review the role and relevance of the organizational grapevine.

Some companies try to encourage communication across the organization through workspace design as well as through Internet-based communication channels. Some executives also meet directly with employees by engaging in management by walking around (MBWA) and by holding town-hall meetings.

In any organization, employees rely on the grapevine, particularly during times of uncertainty. The grapevine is an unstructured and informal network founded on social relationships rather than organizational charts or job descriptions. Although early research identified several unique features of the grapevine, some of these features may be changing as the Internet plays an increasing role in grapevine communication.

CHAPTER SUMMARY

LO9-1 Describe the dependence model of power and the five sources of power in organizations.

Power is the capacity to influence others. It exists when one party perceives that he or she is dependent on the other for something of value. However, the dependent person also must have countervailing power—some power over the dominant party—to maintain the relationship, and the parties must have some level of trust.

There are five power bases. Legitimate power is an agreement among organizational members that people in certain roles can request certain behaviors of others. This power has restrictions, represented by the target person's zone of indifference. It also includes the norm of reciprocity (a feeling of obligation to help someone who has helped you), as well as control over the flow of information to others. Reward power is derived from the ability to control the allocation of rewards valued by others and to remove negative sanctions. Coercive power is the ability to apply punishment. Expert power is the capacity to influence others by possessing knowledge or skills that they value. An important form of expert power is the (perceived) ability to manage uncertainties in the business environment. People have referent power when others identify with them, like them, or otherwise respect them.

LO9-2 Discuss the four contingencies of power.

Four contingencies determine whether these power bases translate into real power. Individuals and work units are more powerful when they are nonsubstitutable. Employees, work units, and organizations reduce substitutability by controlling tasks, knowledge, and labor and by differentiating themselves from competitors. A second contingency is centrality. People have more power when they have high centrality, which means that many people are quickly affected by their actions. The third contingency, visibility, refers to the idea that power increases to the extent that a person's or work unit's competencies are known to others. Discretion, the fourth contingency of power, refers to the freedom to exercise judgment. Power increases when people have the freedom to use their power.

LO9-3 Explain how people and work units gain power through social networks.

Social networks are social structures of individuals or social units (e.g., departments, organizations) that connect to one another through one or more forms of interdependence. People receive power in social networks through social capital, which is the goodwill and resulting resources shared among members in a social network. Three main resources from social networks are information, visibility, and referent power.

Employees gain social capital through their relationship in the social network. Social capital tends to increase with the number of network ties. Strong ties (close-knit relationships) also can increase social capital because these connections offer more resources more quickly. However, having weak ties with people from diverse networks can be more valuable than having strong ties with people in similar networks. Weak ties provide more resources that we do not already possess. Another influence on social capital is the person's centrality in the network. Network centrality is determined in several ways, including the extent to which you are located between others in the network (betweenness), how many direct ties you have (degree), and the closeness of these ties. People also gain power by bridging structural holes—linking two or more clusters of people in a network.

KEY TERMS

centrality a contingency of power pertaining to the degree and nature of interdependence between the power holder and others

charisma a personal characteristic or special "gift" that serves as a form of interpersonal attraction and referent power over others

coalition a group that attempts to influence people outside the group by pooling the resources and power of its members

countervailing power the capacity of a person, team, or organization to keep a more powerful person or group in the exchange relationship

impression management actively shaping through self-presentation and other means the perceptions and attitudes that others have of us

influence any behavior that attempts to alter someone's attitudes or behavior

inoculation effect a persuasive communication strategy of warning listeners that others will try to influence them in the future and that they should be wary of the opponent's arguments

legitimate power an agreement among organizational members that people in certain roles can request certain behaviors of others

Machiavellian values the beliefs that deceit is a natural and acceptable way to influence others and that getting more than one deserves is acceptable

norm of reciprocity a felt obligation and social expectation of helping or otherwise giving something of value to someone who has already helped or given something of value to you

organizational politics behaviors that others perceive as self-serving tactics at the expense of other people and possibly the organization

persuasion the use of facts, logical arguments, and emotional appeals to change another person's beliefs and attitudes, usually for the purpose of changing the person's behavior

power the capacity of a person, team, or organization to influence others

referent power the capacity to influence others on the basis of an identification with and respect for the power holder

social capital the knowledge and other resources available to people or social units (teams, organizations) from a durable network that connects them to others

social networks social structures of individuals or social units that are connected to each other through one or more forms of interdependence

structural hole an area between two or more dense social network areas that lacks network ties

upward appeal a type of influence in which someone with higher authority or expertise is called on in reality or symbolically to support the influencer's position

LO9-4 Describe eight types of influence tactics, three consequences of influencing others, and three contingencies to consider when choosing an influence tactic.

Influence refers to any behavior that attempts to alter someone's attitudes or behavior. The most widely studied influence tactics are silent authority, assertiveness, information control, coalition formation, upward appeal, impression management, persuasion, and exchange. "Soft" influence tactics such as friendly persuasion and subtle ingratiation are more acceptable than "hard" tactics such as upward appeal and assertiveness. However, the most appropriate influence tactic also depends on the influencer's power base; whether the person being influenced is higher, lower, or at the same level in the organization; and personal, organizational, and cultural values regarding influence behavior.

LO9-5 Identify the organizational conditions and personal characteristics associated with organizational politics, as well as ways to minimize organizational politics.

Organizational politics refer to influence tactics that others perceive to be self-serving behaviors, sometimes contrary to the interests of the organization. It is more common when ambiguous decisions allocate scarce resources and when the organization tolerates or rewards political behavior. Individuals with a high need for personal power and strong Machiavellian values have a higher propensity to use political tactics. Organizational politics can be minimized by providing clear rules for resource allocation, establishing a free flow of information, using education and involvement during organizational change, supporting team norms and a corporate culture that discourages political behavior, and having leaders who role model organizational citizenship rather than political savvy.

Conflict and Negotiation in the Workplace

CHAPTER SUMMARY

LO10-1 Define conflict and debate its positive and negative consequences in the workplace.

Conflict is the process in which one party perceives that its interests are being opposed or negatively affected by another party. The earliest view of conflict was that it was dysfunctional for organizations. Even today, we recognize that conflict sometimes or to some degree consumes productive time, increases stress and job dissatisfaction, discourages coordination and resource sharing, undermines customer service, fuels organizational politics, and undermines team cohesion. But conflict also can be beneficial. It is known to motivate more active thinking about problems and possible solutions, encourage more active monitoring of the organization in its environment, and improve team cohesion (where the conflict source is external).

LO10-2 Distinguish task from relationship conflict and describe three strategies to minimize relationship conflict during task conflict episodes.

Task conflict occurs when people focus their discussion around the issue while showing respect for people with other points of view. Relationship conflict exists when people view each other, rather than the issue, as the source of conflict. It is apparent when people attack each other's credibility and display aggression toward the other party. It is difficult to separate task from relationship conflict. However, three strategies or conditions that minimize relationship conflict during constructive debate are (1) emotional intelligence and emotional stability of the participants, (2) team cohesion, and (3) supportive team norms.

LO10-3 Diagram the conflict process model and describe six structural sources of conflict in organizations.

The conflict process model begins with the six structural sources of conflict: incompatible goals, differentiation (different values and beliefs), interdependence, scarce resources, ambiguous rules, and communication problems. These sources lead one or more parties to perceive a conflict and to experience conflict emotions. This produces manifest conflict, such as behaviors toward the other side. The conflict process often escalates through a series of episodes.

LO10-4 Outline the five conflict-handling styles and discuss the circumstances in which each would be most appropriate.

There are five known conflict-handling styles: problem solving, forcing, avoiding, yielding, and compromising. People who use problem solving have a win–win orientation. Other styles, particularly forcing, assume a win–lose orientation. In general, people gravitate toward one or two preferred conflict-handling styles that match their personality, personal and cultural values, and past experience.

The best style depends on the situation. Problem solving is best when interests are not perfectly opposing, the parties trust each other, and the issues are complex. Forcing works best when you strongly believe in your position, the dispute requires quick action, and the other party would take advantage of a cooperative style. Avoidance is preferred when the conflict has become emotional or the cost of resolution is higher than its benefits. Yielding works well when the other party has substantially more power, the issue is less important to you, and you are not confident in the logical soundness of your position. Compromising is preferred when the parties have equal power, they are under time pressure, and they lack trust.

KEY TERMS

best alternative to a negotiated settlement (BATNA) the best outcome you might achieve through some other course of action if you abandon the current negotiation

conflict the process in which one party perceives that its interests are being opposed or negatively affected by another party

negotiation the process whereby two or more conflicting parties attempt to resolve their divergent goals by redefining the terms of their interdependence

relationship conflict a type of conflict in which people focus on characteristics of other individuals, rather than on the issues, as the source of conflict

superordinate goals goals that the conflicting parties value and whose attainment requires the joint resources and effort of those parties

task conflict a type of conflict in which people focus their discussion around the issue while showing respect for people who have other points of view

third-party conflict resolution any attempt by a relatively neutral person to help conflicting parties resolve their differences

win–lose orientation the belief that conflicting parties are drawing from a fixed pie, so the more one party receives, the less the other party will receive

win–win orientation the belief that conflicting parties will find a mutually beneficial solution to their disagreement

LO10-5 Apply the six structural approaches to conflict management and describe the three types of third-party dispute resolution.

Structural approaches to conflict management include emphasizing superordinate goals, reducing differentiation, improving communication and understanding, reducing interdependence, increasing resources, and clarifying rules and procedures.

Third-party conflict resolution is any attempt by a relatively neutral person to help the parties resolve their differences. The three main forms of third-party dispute resolution are mediation, arbitration, and inquisition. Managers tend to use an inquisition approach, though mediation and arbitration often are more appropriate, depending on the situation.

LO10-6 Discuss activities in the negotiation preparation, process, and setting that improve negotiation effectiveness.

Negotiation occurs whenever two or more conflicting parties attempt to resolve their divergent goals by redefining the terms of their interdependence. Effective negotiators engage in several preparation activities. These include determining their initial, target, and resistance positions; understanding their needs behind these goals; and knowing their alternatives to the negotiation (BATNA). They set higher initial offer and target positions, which anchor the negotiation at a higher level.

During the negotiation process, effective negotiators devote more attention to gathering than giving information. They try to determine the other party's underlying needs rather than just their stated positions. They make fewer and smaller concessions but use concessions strategically to discover the other party's priorities and to maintain trust. They try to avoid time traps (negotiating under deadlines set by the other side), and they engage in practices to maintain a positive relationship with the other party. Characteristics of the setting—including location, physical setting, and audience characteristics—are also important in successful negotiations.

Leadership in Organizational Settings

CHAPTER SUMMARY

LO11-1 Define leadership and shared leadership.

Leadership is defined as the ability to influence, motivate, and enable others to contribute to the effectiveness and success of the organizations of which they are members. Leaders use influence to motivate followers and arrange the work environment so they do the job more effectively. Shared leadership views leadership as a role rather than a formal position, so employees throughout the organization act informally as leaders as the occasion arises. These situations include serving as champions for specific ideas or changes, as well as filling leadership roles where it is needed.

LO11-2 Describe the four elements of transformational leadership and explain why they are important for organizational change.

Transformational leadership begins with a strategic vision, which is a positive representation of a future state that energizes and unifies employees. A vision is values-based, a distant goal, abstract, and meaningful to employees. Transformational leaders effectively communicate the vision by framing it around values; showing sincerity and passion toward the vision; and using symbols, metaphors, and other vehicles that create richer meaning for the vision. Transformational leaders model the vision (walk the talk) and encourage employees to experiment with new behaviors and practices that are potentially more consistent with the visionary future state. They also build employee commitment to the vision through the preceding activities, as well as by celebrating milestones to the vision. Transformational leaders are not necessarily charismatic, and charismatic leaders do not necessarily apply transformational leadership behaviors.

LO11-3 Compare managerial leadership with transformational leadership, and describe the features of task-oriented, people-oriented, and servant leadership.

Managerial leadership includes the daily activities that support and guide the performance and well-being of individual employees and the work unit to achieve current objectives and practices. Transformational and managerial leadership are dependent on each other, but they differ in their assumptions of stability versus change and their micro versus macro focus.

Task-oriented behaviors include assigning employees to specific tasks, clarifying their work duties and procedures, ensuring they follow company rules, and pushing them to reach their performance capacity. People-oriented behaviors include showing mutual trust and respect for subordinates, demonstrating a genuine concern for their needs, and having a desire to look out for their welfare.

Servant leadership defines leadership as serving others to support their need fulfillment and personal development and growth. Servant leaders have a natural desire or "calling" to serve others. They maintain a relationship with others that is humble, egalitarian, and accepting. Servant leaders also anchor their decisions and actions in ethical principles and practices.

KEY TERMS

authentic leadership the view that effective leaders need to be aware of, feel comfortable with, and act consistently with their values, personality, and self-concept

implicit leadership theory a theory stating that people evaluate a leader's effectiveness in terms of how well that person fits preconceived beliefs about the features and behaviors of effective leaders (leadership prototypes) and that people tend to inflate the influence of leaders on organizational events

leadership influencing, motivating, and enabling others to contribute toward the effectiveness and success of the organizations of which they are members

leadership substitutes theory a theory identifying conditions that either limit a leader's ability to influence subordinates or make a particular leadership style unnecessary

managerial leadership a leadership perspective stating that effective leaders help employees improve their performance and well-being toward current objectives and practices

path–goal leadership theory a leadership theory stating that effective leaders choose the most appropriate leadership style(s), depending on the employee and situation, to influence employee expectations about desired results and their positive outcomes

servant leadership the view that leaders serve followers, rather than vice versa; leaders help employees fulfill their needs and are coaches, stewards, and facilitators of employee development

shared leadership the view that leadership is a role, not a position assigned to one person; consequently, people within the team and organization lead each other

transformational leadership a leadership perspective that explains how leaders change teams or organizations by creating, communicating, and modeling a vision for the organization or work unit and inspiring employees to strive for that vision

LO11-4 Discuss the elements of path–goal leadership theory and leadership substitutes theory.

The path–goal theory of leadership takes the view that effective managerial leadership involves diagnosing the situation and using the most appropriate style for it. The core model identifies four leadership styles—directive, supportive, participative, and achievement-oriented—and several contingencies related to the characteristics of the employee and of the situation. Leadership substitutes theory identifies contingencies that either limit the leader's ability to influence subordinates or make a particular leadership style unnecessary.

LO11-5 Describe the two components of the implicit leadership perspective.

According to the implicit leadership perspective, people have leadership prototypes, which they use to evaluate the leader's effectiveness. Furthermore, people form a romance of leadership; they want to believe that leaders make a difference, so they engage in fundamental attribution error and other perceptual distortions to support this belief in the leader's impact.

LO11-6 Identify eight personal attributes associated with effective leaders and describe authentic leadership.

The personal attributes perspective identifies the characteristics of effective leaders. Recent writing suggests that leaders have specific personality characteristics, positive self-concept, leadership motivation, drive, integrity, knowledge of the business, cognitive and practical intelligence, and emotional intelligence. Authentic leadership refers to how well leaders are aware of, feel comfortable with, and act consistently with their self-concept. This concept consists mainly of two parts: self-awareness and engaging in behavior that is consistent with one's self-concept.

LO11-7 Discuss cultural and gender similarities and differences in leadership.

Cultural values influence the leader's personal values, which in turn influence his or her leadership practices. Women generally do not differ from men in the degree of people-oriented or task-oriented leadership. However, female leaders more often adopt a participative style. Research also suggests that people evaluate female leaders on the basis of gender stereotypes, which may result in higher or lower ratings.

CHAPTER SUMMARY

LO12-1 Describe three types of coordination in organizational structures.

Organizational structure is the division of labor as well as the patterns of coordination, communication, workflow, and formal power that direct organizational activities. All organizational structures divide labor into distinct tasks and coordinate that labor to accomplish common goals. The primary means of coordination are informal communication, formal hierarchy, and standardization.

LO12-2 Discuss the role and effects of span of control, centralization, and formalization, and relate these elements to organic and mechanistic organizational structures.

The four basic elements of organizational structure are span of control, centralization, formalization, and departmentalization. The optimal span of control—the number of people directly reporting to the next level in the hierarchy—depends on what coordinating mechanisms are present other than formal hierarchy, whether employees perform routine tasks, and how much interdependence there is among employees within the department.

Centralization occurs when formal decision authority is held by a small group of people, typically senior executives. Many companies decentralize as they become larger and more complex, but some sections of the company may remain centralized while other sections decentralize. Formalization is the degree to which organizations standardize behavior through rules, procedures, formal training, and related mechanisms. Companies become more formalized as they get older and larger. Formalization tends to reduce organizational flexibility, organizational learning, creativity, and job satisfaction.

Span of control, centralization, and formalization cluster into mechanistic and organic structures. Mechanistic structures are characterized by a narrow span of control and a high degree of formalization and centralization. Companies with an organic structure have the opposite characteristics.

LO12-3 Identify and evaluate five types of departmentalization.

Departmentalization specifies how employees and their activities are grouped together. It establishes the chain of command, focuses people around common mental models, and encourages coordination through informal communication among people and subunits. A simple structure employs few people, has minimal hierarchy, and typically offers one distinct product or service. A functional structure organizes employees around specific knowledge or other resources. This structure fosters greater specialization and improves direct supervision, but it weakens the focus on serving clients or developing products.

A divisional structure groups employees around geographic areas, clients, or outputs. This structure accommodates growth and focuses employee attention on products or customers rather than tasks. However, this structure also duplicates resources and creates silos of knowledge. Team-based structures are very flat, with low formalization, and organize self-directed teams around work processes rather than functional specialties. The matrix structure combines two structures to leverage the benefits of both types. However, this approach requires more coordination than functional or pure divisional structures, may dilute accountability, and increases conflict.

KEY TERMS

centralization the degree to which formal decision authority is held by a small group of people, typically those at the top of the organizational hierarchy

divisional structure an organizational structure in which employees are organized around geographic areas, outputs (products or services), or clients

formalization the degree to which organizations standardize behavior through rules, procedures, formal training, and related mechanisms

functional structure an organizational structure in which employees are organized around specific knowledge or other resources

matrix structure an organizational structure that overlays two structures (such as a geographic divisional and a product divisional structure) in order to leverage the benefits of both

mechanistic structure an organizational structure with a narrow span of control and a high degree of formalization and centralization

organic structure an organizational structure with a wide span of control, little formalization, and decentralized decision making

organizational strategy the way the organization positions itself in its environment in relation to its stakeholders, given the organization's resources, capabilities, and mission

organizational structure the division of labor as well as the patterns of coordination, communication, workflow, and formal power that direct organizational activities

span of control the number of people directly reporting to the next level above in the hierarchy

team-based organizational structure an organizational structure built around self-directed teams that complete an entire piece of work

LO12-4 Explain how the external environment, organizational size, technology, and strategy are relevant when designing an organizational structure.

The best organizational structure depends on whether the environment is dynamic or stable, complex or simple, diverse or integrated, and hostile or munificent. Another contingency is the organization's size. Larger organizations need to become more decentralized and more formalized. The work unit's technology—including variability of work and analyzability of problems—influences whether it should adopt an organic or mechanistic structure. These contingencies influence but do not necessarily determine structure. Instead, corporate leaders formulate and implement strategies that shape both the characteristics of these contingencies and the organization's resulting structure.

CHAPTER SUMMARY

LO13-1 Describe the elements of organizational culture and discuss the importance of organizational subcultures.

Organizational culture consists of the values and assumptions shared within an organization. Shared assumptions are nonconscious, taken-for-granted perceptions or beliefs that have worked so well in the past that they are considered the correct way to think and act toward problems and opportunities. Values are stable, evaluative beliefs that guide our preferences for outcomes or courses of action in a variety of situations.

Organizations differ in their cultural content, that is, the relative ordering of values. There are several classifications of organizational culture, but they tend to oversimplify the wide variety of cultures and completely ignore the underlying assumptions of culture. Organizations have subcultures as well as the dominant culture. Subcultures maintain the organization's standards of performance and ethical behavior. They are also the source of emerging values that replace misaligned core values.

LO13-2 Describe four categories of artifacts through which corporate culture is deciphered.

Artifacts are the observable symbols and signs of an organization's culture. Four broad categories of artifacts include organizational stories and legends, rituals and ceremonies, language, and physical structures and symbols. Understanding an organization's culture requires the assessment of many artifacts because they are subtle and often ambiguous.

LO13-3 Discuss the importance of organizational culture and the conditions under which organizational culture strength improves organizational performance.

Organizational culture has three main functions: a form of social control, the "social glue" that bonds people together, and a way to help employees make sense of the workplace. Companies with strong cultures generally perform better than those with weak cultures, but only when the cultural content is appropriate for the organization's environment. Also, the culture should not be so strong that it drives out dissenting values, which may form emerging values for the future. Organizations should have adaptive cultures in which employees support ongoing change in the organization and their own roles.

LO13-4 Compare and contrast four strategies for merging organizational cultures.

Organizational culture clashes are common in mergers and acquisitions. This problem can be minimized by performing a bicultural audit to diagnose the compatibility of the organizational cultures. The four main strategies for merging different corporate cultures are integration, deculturation, assimilation, and separation.

KEY TERMS

adaptive culture an organizational culture in which employees are receptive to change, including the ongoing alignment of the organization to its environment and continuous improvement of internal processes

artifacts the observable symbols and signs of an organization's culture

attraction–selection–attrition (ASA) theory a theory that states that organizations have a natural tendency to attract, select, and retain people with values and personality characteristics that are consistent with the organization's character, resulting in a more homogeneous organization and a stronger culture

bicultural audit a process of diagnosing cultural relations between companies and determining the extent to which cultural clashes will likely occur

ceremonies planned displays of organizational culture, conducted specifically for the benefit of an audience

organizational culture the values and assumptions shared within an organization

organizational socialization the process by which individuals learn the values, expected behaviors, and social knowledge necessary to assume their roles in the organization

realistic job preview (RJP) a method of improving organizational socialization in which job applicants are given a balance of positive and negative information about the job and work context

reality shock the stress that results when employees perceive discrepancies between their preemployment expectations and on-the-job reality

rituals the programmed routines of daily organizational life that dramatize the organization's culture

LO13-5 Describe five strategies for changing and strengthening an organization's culture, including the application of attraction–selection–attrition theory.

An organization's culture begins with its founders and leaders because they use personal values to transform the organization. The founder's activities are later retold as organizational stories. Companies also introduce artifacts as mechanisms to maintain or change the culture. A related strategy is to introduce rewards and recognition practices that are consistent with the desired cultural values. A fourth method to change and strengthen an organization's culture is to support workforce stability and communication. Stability is necessary because culture exists in employees. Communication activities improve sharing of the culture. Finally, companies strengthen and change their culture by attracting and selecting applicants with personal values that fit the company's culture, by encouraging those with misaligned values to leave the company, and by engaging in organizational socialization—the process by which individuals learn the values, expected behaviors, and social knowledge necessary to assume their roles in the organization.

LO13-6 Describe the organizational socialization process and identify strategies to improve that process.

Organizational socialization is the process by which individuals learn the values, expected behaviors, and social knowledge necessary to assume their roles in the organization. It is a process of both learning and adjustment. Employees typically pass through three socialization stages: preemployment, encounter, and role management. To manage the socialization process, organizations should introduce realistic job previews (RJPs) and recognize the value of socialization agents in the process. These RJPs give job applicants a realistic balance of positive and negative information about the job and work context. Socialization agents provide information and social support during the socialization process.

CHAPTER SUMMARY

LO14-1 Describe the elements of Lewin's force field analysis model.

Lewin's force field analysis model states that all systems have driving and restraining forces. Change occurs through the process of unfreezing, changing, and refreezing. Unfreezing produces disequilibrium between the driving and restraining forces. Refreezing realigns the organization's systems and structures with the desired behaviors.

LO14-2 Discuss the reasons why people resist organizational change and how change agents should view this resistance.

Restraining forces are manifested as employee resistance to change. The main reasons people resist change are the negative valence of change, fear of the unknown, not-invented-here syndrome, breaking routines, incongruent team dynamics, and incongruent organizational systems. Resistance to change should be viewed as a resource, not an inherent obstacle to change. Change agents need to view resistance as task conflict rather than relationship conflict. Resistance is a signal that the change agent has not sufficiently strengthened employee readiness for change. It is also a form of voice, so discussion potentially improves procedural justice.

LO14-3 Outline six strategies for minimizing resistance to change, and debate ways to effectively create an urgency to change.

Organizational change requires employees to have an urgency for change. This typically occurs by informing them about driving forces in the external environment. Urgency to change also develops by putting employees in direct contact with customers. Leaders often need to create an urgency to change before the external pressures are felt, and this can occur through a vision of a more appealing future.

Resistance to change may be minimized by keeping employees informed about what to expect from the change effort (communicating); teaching employees valuable skills for the desired future (learning); involving them in the change process; helping employees cope with the stress of change; negotiating trade-offs with those who will clearly lose from the change effort; and using coercion (sparingly and as a last resort).

LO14-4 Discuss how leadership, coalitions, social networks, and pilot projects assist organizational change.

Every successful change requires transformational leaders with a clear, well-articulated vision of the desired future state. They also need the assistance of several people (a guiding coalition) who are located throughout the organization. In addition, change occurs more informally through social networks. Viral change operates through social networks using influencers.

Many organizational change initiatives begin with a pilot project. The success of the pilot project is then diffused to other parts of the organization. This occurs by motivating employees to adopt the pilot project's methods, training people to know how to adopt these practices, helping clarify how the pilot can be applied to different areas, and providing time and resources to support this diffusion.

KEY TERMS

action research a problem-focused change process that combines action orientation (changing attitudes and behavior) and research orientation (testing theory through data collection and analysis)

appreciative inquiry an organizational change strategy that directs the group's attention away from its own problems and focuses participants on the group's potential and positive elements

force field analysis Kurt Lewin's model of systemwide change that helps change agents diagnose the forces that drive and restrain proposed organizational change

positive organizational behavior a perspective of organizational behavior that focuses on building positive qualities and traits within individuals or institutions as opposed to focusing on what is wrong with them

refreezing the latter part of the change process, in which systems and structures are introduced that reinforce and maintain the desired behaviors

unfreezing the first part of the change process, in which the change agent produces disequilibrium between the driving and restraining forces

LO14-5 Describe and compare action research and appreciative inquiry as formal approaches to organizational change.

Action research is a highly participative, open systems approach to change management that combines an action orientation (changing attitudes and behavior) with research orientation (testing theory). It is a data-based, problem-oriented process that diagnoses the need for change, introduces the intervention, and then evaluates and stabilizes the desired changes.

Appreciative inquiry embraces the positive organizational behavior principle by focusing participants on the positive and possible. This approach to change also applies the constructionist, simultaneity, poetic, and anticipatory principles. The four stages of appreciative inquiry include discovery, dreaming, designing, and delivering.

LO14-6 Discuss two cross-cultural and three ethical issues in organizational change.

One significant concern is that organizational change theories developed with a Western cultural orientation potentially conflict with cultural values in some other countries. Also, organizational change practices can raise one or more ethical concerns, including increasing management's power over employees, threatening individual privacy rights, and undermining individual self-esteem.